COLLECTED PAPERS OF MARTIN KAY

CSLI Studies in Computational Linguistics

This series covers all areas of computational linguistics and language technology, with a special emphasis on work which has direct relevance to practical applications, makes formal advances, and incorporates insights into natural language processing from other fields, especially linguistics and psychology. Books in this series describe groundbreaking research or provide an accessible and up-to-date overview of an area for nonspecialists. Also included are works documenting freely available resources for language processing, such as software, grammars, dictionaries, and corpora.

Series edited by Ann Copestake

CSLI Studies in Computational Linguistics

COLLECTED PAPERS OF
MARTIN KAY
A Half Century of
Computational Linguistics

with the editorial
assistance of
Dan Flickinger &
Stephan Oepen

CSLI
PUBLICATIONS
STANFORD

Copyright © 2010
CSLI Publications
Center for the Study of Language and Information
Leland Stanford Junior University
Printed in the United States
14 13 12 11 10   1 2 3 4 5

Library of Congress Cataloging-in-Publication Data

Kay, Martin
  Collected papers of Martin Kay : a half century of computational linguistics /
  Martin Kay ; with the editorial assistance of Dan Flickinger and Stephan Oepen.
      p. cm.
  Includes bibliographical references and index.

  ISBN 978-1-57586-571-3 (alk. paper)

  1. Computational linguistics.   I. Flickinger, Daniel P. II. Oepen, Stephan. III. Title.

  P98.K39 2010
  410′.285–dc22

                                                                2010033559
                            CIP

∞ The acid-free paper used in this book meets the minimum requirements of the American
National Standard for Information Sciences—Permanence of Paper for Printed Library
Materials, ANSI Z39.48-1984.

CSLI was founded in 1983 by researchers from Stanford University, SRI International, and Xerox
PARC to further the research and development of integrated theories of language, information, and
computation. CSLI headquarters and CSLI Publications are located on the campus of Stanford
University.

CSLI Publications reports new developments in the study of language,
information, and computation. Please visit our web site at
http://cslipublications.stanford.edu/
for comments on this and other titles, as well as for changes
and corrections by the author and publisher.

Contents

Foreword

The field of research now known as computational linguistics began in the middle of the twentieth century, soon after the invention of modern computing. Almost from the start, Martin Kay has been helping to shape and advance this field. His publications over the past fifty years have broadened and deepened the study of how computational modeling can help illuminate our understanding of human language. While many scholars in the field know of his foundational contributions to their own research areas, perhaps fewer are familiar with the full scope of his work to date. This volume brings together the great majority of his publications for the first fifty years of his research, to help to show how the field has emerged and to contribute to its further development.

The choice of publications included in this volume resulted from a series of relaxed conversations in Martin's sunny California garden, where the three of us discussed the relative merits of every paper he ever published for which we were still able to obtain a copy. Our criteria included judgments about historical significance, impact on current research, and illumination of the way forward, with Martin naturally serving as the final arbiter on papers where consensus was elusive. The extant papers which did not make it into this volume are nonetheless still available in electronic form, on the CSLI Publications website.

Organization of the volume is chronological by the original publication date of each paper, starting with "A Parsing Procedure" from 1962. We were unable to obtain copies of five earlier papers which Martin published as technical reports with the Cambridge Language Research Unit in 1959 and 1960, though we include these titles in the full list of his publications to date at the end of this volume. A cumulative reference list is also provided at the end of the volume, giving full bibliographic details for the citations identified at the end of each chapter.

While editing this volume with him, we have appreciated the opportunity to acquaint ourselves with Martin's first fifty years of published research (as well as with his selection of French wines), and we hope that the book will improve accessibility to the astonishing wealth and frequent delights of his contributions to computational linguistics. We are grateful to the Center for the Study of Language and Information and the Linguistics Department at Stanford University, to the Palo Alto Research Center, and to the University of Oslo, for supporting the production of this volume.

Dan Flickinger and Stephan Oepen   *(on the occasion of Martin Kay's 75th birthday)*

Acknowledgements

Kay, Martin. 1962. "A Parsing Procedure." In *Symposium on Modern Techniques of Language Translation*, 328–329.

Kay, Martin. 1963. "Rules of Interpretation — An Approach to the Problem of Computation in the Semantics of Natural Language." In Cicely M. Popplewell, ed. *Proceedings of IFIP Congress* 62, 318–321. Munich, Germany. Amsterdam, The Netherlands: North-Holland Publishing Company.

Kay, Martin. 1964. "The Logic of Cognate Recognition in Historical Linguistics." The RAND Corporation, Report RM-4224-PR.

Kay, Martin and Theodore Ziehe. 1965. "Natural Language in Computer Form." The RAND Corporation, Report RM-4390-PR.

Kay, Martin. 1966. "The Tabular Parser: A Parsing Program for Phrase Structure and Dependency." The RAND Corporation, Report RM-4933-PR.

Kay, Martin. 1967. "Experiments with a Powerful Parser." In *Proceedings of the Second International Congress sur le Traitement Automatique des Langues ('Automatic Language Processing')*, 1–20. Grenoble, France.

Kay, Martin. 1968. "From Semantics to Syntax." In Manfred Bierwisch and Karl Erich Heidolf, eds., *Progress in Linguistics*, 114–126. The Hague: Mouton.

Kay, Martin. 1969. "Computational Linguistics at RAND." The RAND Corporation, Report P-4023.

Kay, Martin. 1969. "The Computer System to Aid the Linguistic Field Worker." The RAND Corporation, Report P-4095.

Kay, Martin. 1969. "Computational Competence and Linguistic Performance." The RAND Corporation, Report P-4093.

Kay, Martin. 1970. "Performance Grammars." The RAND Corporation, Report P-4391.

Bisbey, Richard and Martin Kay. 1972. "The MIND Translation System: A Study in Man-Machine Collaboration." The RAND Corporation, Report P-4786.

Kay, Martin. 1973. "The MIND System." In Randall Rustin, ed., *Natural Language Processing*, 155–188. New York: Algorithmics Press.

Kay, Martin. 1973. "Automatic Translation of Natural Languages." In *Daedalus, Journal of the American Academy of Arts and Sciences* 102:3, 217–230.

Kay, Martin. 1973. "Morphological analysis." In *Proceedings of the 5th Conference on Computational Linguistics*, 205–223. Pisa, Italy.

Kay, Martin. 1975. "Syntactic Processing and the Functional Sentence Perspective." In *Theoretical Issues in Natural Language Processing (TINLAP-1)*, 12–15. Cambridge, Massachusetts.

Kay, Martin. 1978. "Overview of Computer Aids in Translation." In *Proceedings of FBIS Seminar on Computer Support to Translation,* 23–29. Washington D.C.: Foreign Broadcast Information Service.

Kay, Martin. 1978. "The Proper Place of Men and Machines in Translation." In *The Foreign Broadcast Information Service Seminar on Machine Translation.* Washington D.C.

Kay, Martin. 1979. "Functional Grammar." In Christina Chiarello et al., eds., *The Fifth Annual Meeting of the Berkeley Linguistics Society,* 142–158. Berkeley, California: Berkeley Linguistics Society.

Kay, Martin. 1980. "Algorithm Schemata and Data Structures in Syntactic Processing." Xerox CSL 80-12.

Kay, Martin. 1983. "When Meta-rules are not Meta-rules." In Karen Sparck Jones and Yorick Wilks, eds., *Automatic Natural Language Parsing,* 94–116. Chichester/New York: Ellis Horwood/Wiley.

Kay, Martin. 1984. "Functional Unification Grammar: A Formalism for Machine Translation." In *International Conference on Computational Linguistics (COLING 84),* 75–78. Stanford, California: Association for Computational Linguistics.

Kay, Martin. 1985. "Parsing in Functional Unification Grammar." In David R. Dowty, Lauri Karttunen, and Arnold M. Zwicky, eds., *Natural Language Parsing,* 251–278. Cambridge, UK: Cambridge University Press.

Karttunen, Lauri and Martin Kay. 1985. "Parsing in Free Word Order Languages." In David R. Dowty, Lauri Karttunen, and Arnold M. Zwicky, eds., *Natural Language Parsing,* 279–306. Cambridge, UK: Cambridge University Press.

Karttunen, Lauri and Martin Kay. 1985. "Structure Sharing with Binary Trees." In *Proceedings of the 23rd Annual Meeting of the Association for Computational Linguistics,* 133–136. Chicago, Illinois.

Kay, Martin. 1985. "Unification in Grammar." In Veronica Dahl and Patrick Saint-Dizier, eds., *Natural Language Understanding and Logic Programming,* 233-240. Amsterdam: North Holland.

Kay, Martin. 1986. "Machine Translation will not work." In *ACL Proceedings, 24th Annual Meeting,* 268–268.

Kay, Martin, 1987. "The Linguistic Connection." In *Proceedings of the 1987 Workshop on Theoretical Issues in Natural Language Processing,* 51–57. Las Cruces, New Mexico.

Kay, Martin. 1987. "Nonconcatenative Finite-State Morphology." *Proceedings of the Third Conference of the European Chapter of the Association for Computational Linguistics,* 2–10. Copenhagen, Denmark.

Kay, Martin. 1989. "Head-Driven Parsing." In *International Parsing Workshop,* 52–62. Pittsburgh.

Kay, Martin. 1989. "Machines and People in Translation." In Makoto Nagao, ed., *Machine Translation Summit,* 26–27. Tokyo: Ohmsha.

Johnson, Mark and Martin Kay. 1990. "Semantic Abstraction and Anaphora." In H. Karlgren, ed., *Proceedings of the 13th International Conference on Computational Linguistics,* 17–27. Helsinki, Finland.

Kay, Martin. 1990. "Computational Linguistics." In Allen Kent and James G. Williams, eds., *The Encyclopedia of Computer Science and Technology,* volume 21, supplement 6.

Kay, Martin. 1992. "Ongoing directions in Computational Linguistics." *Proceedings of COLING.*

Kay, Martin. 1992. "Unification." In Michael Rosner and Roderick Johnson, eds., *Computational Linguistics and Formal Semantics,* 1–29. Cambridge University Press.

Kay, Martin. 1992. "Foreword." In W. J. Hutchins and H. L. Somers, eds., *An introduction to machine translation.*

Röscheisen, Martin and Martin Kay. 1993. "Text-Translation Alignment." In *Computational Linguistics (Special issue on using large corpora)* 19:1, 121–142.

Kaplan, Ronald M. and Martin Kay. 1994. "Regular Models of Phonological Rule Systems." In *Computational Linguistics (Special Issue on Computational Phonology)* 20:3.

Johnson, Mark and Martin Kay. 1994. "Parsing and Empty Nodes." In *Computational Linguistics* 20:2, 289–300.

Kay, Martin. 1994. "Machine Translation. The Disappointing Past and Present." In Ronald A. Cole, Joseph Mariani, Hans Uszkoreit, Annie Zaenen, and Victor Zue, eds., *Survey of the State of the Art in Human Language Technology,* 232–234.

Kay, Martin. 1996. "Chart Generation." *Proceedings of the ACL,* 200–204.

Kay, Martin. 1997. "It's Still the Proper Place." In *Machine Translation,* 12:1-2, 35–38.

Kay, Martin. 1999. "Chart Translation." In *Proceedings of Machine Translation Summit VII "MT in the Great Translation Era",* 9–14. Singapore.

Kay, Martin. 2000. "David G. Hays." In W. John Hutchins, ed., *Early Years in Machine Translation: Memoirs and Biographies of Pioneers,* 165–170. Amsterdam/Philadelphia: John Benjamins Publishing Company.

Kay, Martin. 2000. "Preface." In Jean Vronis, ed., *Parallel text processing: alignment and use of translation corpora,* xv-xx. Dordrecht: Kluwer.

Kay, Martin. 2000. "Guides and oracles for linear-time parsing." In *Proceedings of the 6th International Workshop on Parsing Technologies (IWPT 03),* 6–9.

Kay, Martin. 2003. "Introduction." In Ruslan Mitkov, ed., *Handbook of Computational Linguistics,* xvii-xx. Oxford, UK: Oxford University Press.

Kay, Martin. 2004. "Substring Alignment Using Suffix Trees." *Proceedings of CICLing,* 275–282.

Kay, Martin. 2006. "Translation, Meaning, and Reference." In Miriam Butt, Mary Dalrymple, and Tracy Holloway King, eds., *Intelligent Linguistic Architectures. Variations on Themes by Ronald M. Kaplan.* Stanford: CSLI Publications.

Kay, Martin. 2004. "Antonio Zampolli." In *Proceedings of Fourth International Conference on Language Resources and Evaluation,* xli-xliii. Lisbon, Portugal.

Kay, Martin. 2005. "A Life of Language." In *Computational Linguistics* 31:4, 425–438.

1

Introduction

The last paper in this collection, entitled "A Life of Language", is the edited transcript of an autobiographical talk I gave at the annual meeting of the Association for Computational Linguistics in 2005 when it honored me with a lifetime achievement award.

In that paper, I lament the eclipse of Computational Linguistics by Natural Language Processing and particularly the usurpation of the former term by those that ply the latter trade. The remaining papers that my friends have so kindly collected here are mainly about Computational Linguistics, an activity whose origins are in engineering but whose aspirations are decidedly scientific. Natural Language Processing pursues the original engineering aims, unencumbered by scientific aspirations or pretensions.

The best that can be hoped for the papers in this volume is that they will come to be viewed as chronicling some of the first faltering steps towards a linguistics that is informed in interesting ways by computer science. But, if the view that this was an ill-conceived aim prevails and Computational Linguistics is swallowed up by Natural Language Processing, then they may even be seen as having been an impediment to progress. When the papers were written, I thought of them as contributing to a Computational Linguistics that eventually might provide the scientific basis for Natural Language Processing. I believe that, in some ways, this effort has already been very successful. Current engineering efforts, based on a rejection of any serious scientific underpinning are, I believe, fatally flawed. I devote a considerable part of this introductory essay to expanding on that claim.

I take it that scientists try to understand their subject mainly for its own sake, though they are gratified when some of what they do proves useful. Engineers seek only the understanding needed to reach practical ends. Computational Linguists, like other linguists, want to know how children learn languages, how different languages are related, how languages change over time, and how language affects society, and society language. Above all, they want to know how it is that one person, by making noises in the presence of another, can create complex structures in the latter's head that have a design very close to the one the speaker intended. In other words, they want to plumb the mysteries of language as a tool for communication.

If some linguists like to qualify their subject as "computational", it is not because, unlike their more humanistic colleagues, they have acquired some facility in writing programs or because they routinely search large bodies of text for illustrative examples.

What really distinguishes computational linguists is less that they use computers than that they look to computer science for insight into their problems. If communication is indeed about building structures by remote control in the heads of others, then it is all about *process*, and computer science is the science of process, conceived in its most fundamental and abstract way. In the words of Abney (2010): "Language is a computational system, and there is a depth of understanding [of it] that is simply unachievable without a thorough knowledge of computation."

Language as a Digital System

The very fundamental relationship that their subject has with computation is something that linguists have been reluctant to acknowledge. This is doubtless in part because, while it fills an apparently mundane function in everyday life, language also provides structure to civilizations, shape to religions, and material to artists. While largely profane, there is always a touch of the sacred about it. But, at least since the latter part of the nineteenth century, linguists began to remark on what we would now call the *digital* nature of language. Baudouin de Courtenay's notion of the *phoneme* was a notable step in this direction (see "The Kazan school of Polish linguistics and its place in the international development of phonology" in Jakobson (1971)). According to this view, speech consists of a sequence of segments each of which corresponds to one of a finite set of psychological entities, called *phonemes*, which are characteristic of the particular language.

We live in an analog world where one thing shades smoothly into the next. An utterance is an indefinitely variable pattern of sound. Apart from occasional brief periods of silence, there are few places where it breaks naturally into parts, and few categories into which physics or physiology naturally places any such parts.

But, at a deeper level, language is made up of *signs*, each of which has two components. One, which de Saussure (1915) called the *signifiant*, lives in the analog world that is available to our senses, and the other part, which is hidden from view in the digital world, he called the *signifié*. Phonologists, including de Courtenay himself, have had trouble defining the phoneme in a way that they found entirely satisfactory. But, while the basic idea has shown some erosion around the edges, it remains basically extremely robust.

By virtue of their hidden parts—their *signifiés*—the phonemes do indeed break the sounds used in a given language into parts, and they provide a finite set of categories into which they fall. Linguists in the structuralist tradition devised a technique, relying on *minimal pairs*, for this purpose. Suppose, for example, that one member of an English speaking community reads a list of words, and another member writes them down. Suppose, furthermore, that the list contains both "bet" and "bait". If the second person consistently distinguishes these correctly, it must presumably be on the basis of the vowels that they contain, since they are otherwise identical. This shows that the vowel sounds correspond to different phonemes. The pair "cot" and "caught", on the other hand, will be perceived as different by the speakers of some North American dialects, and the same by others, thus showing that these speakers have different phonemic inventories.

Purely monolingual speakers of English, hearing the words "dessus" and "dessous" spoken by a Frenchman, may hear some difference in the sound of their second vowels but nevertheless may well assume that the same word has been pronounced twice. This is because the difference does not correspond to a distinction between English phonemes. If asked to repeat the words, the English speaker might well say the same thing twice because he has categorized them identically. To a French speaker, however, the absolute difference between the vowels corresponds to an absolute difference between the words. The first means "above" and the second means "below".

Asked to repeat an utterance by a speaker of another dialect, a person may produce a very different sequence of sounds which both people will generally acknowledge as representing the same sequence of words. This is because the speaker's message, which consists of a sequence of items chosen from a finite inventory, is converted into a stream of sound which is then converted back into a discrete sequence of items from the same inventory by the hearer. The speaker converts from a digital to an analog representation which is then converted back to a digital form by the hearer. While the analog sounds may differ considerably, the sequence of digital words are essentially identical.

The digital nature of natural language, as well as other coding systems, is manifested in all its parts. In English, every noun and noun phrase is either singular or plural. The difference correlates strongly with whether one or more than one entity is being referred to. The same is true of German. However, a "pair of glasses" is used in situations where a German speaker would use "eine Brille", a singular noun phrase. A pair of glasses contains two pieces of glass, but they are assembled into a single object, which could therefore be said to have both singular and plural aspects, But the vocabulary of the language is a digital system that does not allow for a word that is somehow intermediate between one category and another.

The immense power of language to facilitate communication on a limitless diversity of subjects comes directly from its fundamentally digital nature. The inventory of phonemes is small enough to be internalized completely by every speaker of a language. The inventory of words is large and open ended so that speakers cannot learn it all, but words are made up of phonemes so that speakers can learn new words, and recognize them accurately in the speech of others. Similarities and differences among the components of a digital system are not important, but only whether a pair of symbols are the same or different. Likewise, no notion of similarity is required between a *signifiant* and its *signifié* and there is no restriction on what the language can be used to talk about. This is what de Saussure referred to as *"L'arbitraire du sign"*—the arbitrary nature of the sign. *L'arbitraire du sign* totally separates symbols from their referents, thus conferring on languages complete flexibility in what they can express, and a corresponding opacity as a result of which nothing about the content of an utterance or a text can be discovered by someone who does not know the set of arbitrary correspondences that is the code.

Natural Language Processing and the New Science

Natural Language Processing is about making computers translate texts, answer questions, find documents, and the like, well enough for practical purposes. These are nontrivial operations and one would naturally suppose that the engineering they require would need a firm basis in science. For the most part, however, linguistic engineers show no greater interest than any other citizen in how children learn languages, how languages are related, and change over time, and how language and society might affect one another. Generally they are not particularly interested in how a person can build structures in the head of another and how communication works. They have looked at the works of the linguists and have found them wanting.

For one thing, much of what linguists do apparently has little relevance for the engineer. The parts that might be relevant—phonetics and phonology, syntax and semantics—are pursued in a manner that does not meet commonly accepted scientific standards. The attempt to build out of linguistics a science that fully supports the notion of repeatable experiments has simply failed. As Abney points out, the data against which the predictions of a linguistic theory are tested consists of intuitive judgements by native speakers, and chief among these, as often as not, is the investigator.

Natural Language Processing has therefore constructed for itself a new science of language, concentrating on those aspects of the subject that seem to be required to serve very specific engineering needs, and anchored in the best scientific practices. Ideally, the new science would be based entirely on naturally occurring text and utterances. But the opacity that comes with *l'arbitraire du signe* makes this impossible because the message that the text conveys remains a psychological reality, hidden from public view.

Annotated Corpora and Zipf's Law

The next best thing is to work with texts that have been annotated so as to reveal something of the message. A tagger, for example, which assigns parts of speech to the words in a text, can be obtained by applying supervised machine learning techniques to sufficiently large texts that have been annotated in the required manner by native speakers. In the same way, a program can be developed that associates with ambiguous words in a text, the sense that is in play in a particular context. In each case, the idea is to provide to a machine learning system, a larger number of examples of correct solutions to the problem, from which it will infer the generalizations necessary to treat boundless numbers of other, as yet unseen, examples.

Abney would have us believe that, through procedures like these, Natural Language Processing will give rise to a new Computational Linguistics, and thus, a new linguistics. He is encouraged in this view by his observations of how research based on machine learning proceeds. The parameters that define a model are set; a new model is "trained" based on a corpus of annotated data; and the performance of the new model is assessed, in some purely objective way, against data that was not used in the training. The cycle then repeats in the classic scientific manner, adjusting the parameters to produce a new model, but keeping the training data the same so that the results obtained in each cycle will be comparable.

But there is something wrong with this picture. Indeed there is very little right about it. A more ample view of the scientific method would have much to say about hypotheses and how they are tested, modified, and tested again. In the linguistic version, however, the setting of parameters has slipped in to replace the hypotheses in the classical picture.

This is for the good and sufficient reason that there are no hypotheses here. The nearest we get to a hypothesis is a claim that a small increment in this or that parameter will cause a positive change in the evaluation. This is science tied so closely to engineering as to be no longer worthy of the name.

More interesting and consequential hypotheses would surely concern the nature of the experiment more fundamentally. Consider the case of part-of-speech tagging. What are these parts of speech anyway and where do they come from? At worst, they reflect a nineteenth-century attempt to make English grammar look less impoverished when compared with that of Latin. At best, they come from an uncomfortable combination of contributions from various more or less compatible modern grammatical theories, together with some pragmatic decisions intended to make the annotators' task easier. What is the part of speech of "ago"? Many people will say that it is an adverb on the grounds that any word that does not obviously have any other part of speech is thereby shown to be an adverb. In practice, the matter is usually settled by a handbook with which the annotators must become familiar and which has the purpose of maintaining a measure of consistency rather than any real scientific basis. So, the annotators' task is not well defined; no objective assessment can be made of how well it is done, short of repeating it several times and basing the assessment on the vote of the majority; indeed there is no clear idea of what it would be like for the result to be accurate or inaccurate.

The situation with word-sense disambiguation is worse. As with part-of-speech tagging, the task is meaningful only in the context of an underlying theory. But that is a commodity that is in even shorter supply here. Prince Charles is not a child any more, and yet he is the child of Queen Elizabeth. Is this enough to demonstrate that "child" has two meanings? Suppose that, in the presence of a group of people, some quite young and some less so, I say "These are not my children", then which sense am I invoking? I take it that, in this context, the sentence means something like "Of these people, I am not the father of those who are not yet adults". So I seem to be invoking both senses, which is presumably something that normally occurs only in very special situations, such as jokes and poetry. But the sentence would, I believe, strike no one as linguistically remarkable.

The number of senses that a dictionary ascribes to the word "have" seems to be more or less proportional to the size of the dictionary. But the number of examples that are collected under a given sense seems to depend on how easily the casual reader is expected to be able to grasp them. For example, different senses are generally proposed for having a cold, a color, an idea, and a price. But presumably all of these could be subsumed under a definition somewhat like the following:

> If A is the *carrier*, or *matrix*, by virtue of which B exists, then A *has* B. For example, for there to be a cold, a color, an idea, or a price, there must be someone or something that *has* it, and by virtue of which this instance of it exists.

There are very few situations that meet these conditions for which it is inappropriate to use the verb "have", but the definition is not as readily digestible as some. Fortunately, despite the size of its entry, "have" is a word that nobody ever looks up.

The devotion of the early structuralist linguists to behaviorism is due in large measure to the horror with which they contemplated a semantics that connected language with the world. To attempt this would be to start down the slippery slope that could only end with linguistics responsible for the whole of science. But behaviorism was too confining and Chomsky, in particular, correctly saw it as an impediment to his program. But nothing coherent was ever put in its place. My own introduction to language as an object of study was in a group devoted to the proposition that the most serious problems of ambiguity could be solved by the appropriate use of classifications of words like the one enshrined in Roget's Thesaurus of English Words and Phrases. Perhaps no work in history has distilled so much collective intuition in such a wholly unscientific way to such remarkably good utilitarian effect. Roget's scientific career is now over, since his thesaurus has been superseded by Wordnet. Wordnet is a remarkable achievement, with an altogether finer classification, especially of nouns, than Roget ever achieved, and with a greater number of relations among words, including hyponyms, hypernyms, and even meronyms. But, for all its undoubted utility, it remains, at best, a compendium of intuitions.

Whatever theoretical basis there might be for *sense* in activities based on annotation, it is devoutly to be hoped that it will change little and rarely because it is manifested in the most prolix form imaginable, namely as a set of atomic examples—the annotations—with no generalizations whatsoever. But we have hardly scratched the surface of the problem.

The distribution of linguistic phenomena—phonemes, words, affixes, grammatical rules—are known to be subject to Zipf's law, according to which a small number of them are extremely frequent and a large number of them are very infrequent. Many are seen only once in a corpus of whatever size. For the researcher seeking insight in running text, Zipf's law is a law of sharply diminishing returns because the marginal value of each succeeding observation falls continuously, and very steeply at first. The interval that separates occurrences of useful annotations grows rapidly as one moves through the text.

Features

Like many researchers with scientific pretensions, linguists have seen their first job to be that of finding a classification scheme in which to organize linguistic phenomena. In particular, they have been concerned to find sets of orthogonal dimensions for the scheme that will simplify the later statement of various kinds of generalization. So, for example, there are three principal dimensions on which German nouns and noun phrases are organized—number, gender, and case. There are two numbers, three genders, and four cases.[1] No determiner, adjective, or noun makes all the 24 distinctions that would be theoretically possible with this scheme, but complete noun phrases do.

We refer to dimensions like number, gender, and case, as *attributes*, and to the particular values that occupy a dimension as *values*.

The three-dimensional classification makes it possible to state useful generalizations, such as: the subject of a sentence is in the nominative; diminutives are neuter; the only place where nominative and accusative are distinguished is in the nominative singular of the masculine case. Simple noun phrases consist of a determiner followed by some

---

[1]We ignore the weak/strong distinction in adjectives

number of adjectives, and a noun, all of which must *agree* on all three dimensions. In other words, they can be described by the following pairs of rules

$$N_{n,g,c} \rightarrow A_{n,g,c}N_{n,g,c}$$
$$NP_{n,g,c} \rightarrow Det_{n,g,c}N_{n,g,c}$$

where n, g, and c are variables that can take values in the three dimensions. Using only the standard machinery of context-free grammar, we should have been forced to write 48 rules. In the context of machine learning, the grammar would presumably be probabilistic and the probabilities of each of the 48 rules would be trained independently of the others because there would be no way of taking advantage of the generalizations. Presumably, the same problem would arise in training a part-of-speech tagger for German.

Machine Translation

Of the relatively little space in this volume that is devoted to Natural Language Processing, most concerns the subject that introduced me to the subject in the first place, namely machine translation. This constitutes a particularly interesting case for the new paradigm for a number of reasons. First, it is a task that is for which there is a very large and rapidly growing demand. Second, it is a task that is normally performed by highly trained specialists who are in short supply. Third, examples of the kind needed for machine learning occur naturally, thus enhancing their scientific respectability and, at the same time, greatly reducing their cost, which is presumably generally defrayed by the translator's original customer. Fourth, at least some of the phenomena involved in translation are not subject to Zipf's law.

The prospect sounds encouraging. Nevertheless, most of what I have had to say about machine translation has consisted of dire predictions for its future and charges of irresponsible naiveté on the part of many who predict, especially when talking to sponsors, dramatic advances just around the corner. My grounds for this pessimism are set out at length in several places in this volume. I summarize them briefly here only to show how they relate to the new pseudo-science.

The stereotypical layman has an ambivalent attitude to translation. He sees it as plausible that translating Shakespeare should be challenging, but is at pains to understand why replacing words by corresponding words in another language, with an occasional trick here and there, should not have the desired result in ordinary cases. That it cannot be all that difficult is borne out by the fact that clicking on "translate this page", on the few occasions when he has tried it, has sometimes produced something comprehensible.

Translating the World Wide Web

Text retrieved from the World Wide Web constitutes an entirely unique linguistic genre. One of the most striking of its properties is that the customers of the web have learnt to approach it with great hopes but few expectations. Access to the web generally has no incremental cost to the user who therefore does not feel entitled to any particular level of service from it. If his question is not answered or his curiosity satisfied, he goes away disappointed, but returns next time with undiminished optimism. It is the same with the translations. He is not looking for polish or style. He is looking for something of which he can make a little sense and that contains some suggestions concerning the answers to his questions. It should therefore come as no surprise that companies that specialize in searching the web are the ones that have made the most extravagant claims about advances in machine translation and that it is in the context of this application that we are invited to assess their progress.

The stereotypical layman is not entirely naive. He took a few years of Spanish in school and remembers translation exercises designed to test one's ability to remember the Spanish words listed against particular English words in the vocabulary section of each lesson and in the back of the book. An important part of the translation exercises always involved replacing words with their counterparts in these lists. But the aim of the translation exercise is precisely to demonstrate that the students have learnt the lists, and not to do what translators do.

Pedagogical Translation

The schoolroom exercise strongly encourages a view according to which a long translation is the concatenation of shorter translations, which are concatenations of still smaller translations, and so on, down to the level of the word. Some minor rearrangement is sometimes done at the lowest levels because adjectives often follow the nouns they modify in Spanish and pronouns have to be in special places relative to the verb, but the broad picture remains intact. The trouble is that departures from this model are severe and occur much more frequently than is generally acknowledged, even by people who work with translations a lot.

Nonliteral Translation

Here is an English sentence from the first section of the proceedings of the European Parliament routinely used for training statistical machine translation systems:

> The Cunha report on multiannual guidance programmes comes before Parliament on Thursday and contains a proposal in paragraph 6 that a form of quota penalties should be introduced for countries which fail to meet their fleet reduction targets annually.

I do not know what the original language was, but here is the French version:

> Le paragraphe - 6 du rapport Cunha sur les programmes d'orientation pluriannuels , qui sera soumis au Parlement ce jeudi , propose d'introduire des sanctions applicables aux pays qui ne respectent pas les objectifs annuels de réduction de leur flotte.

The following is a translation of this into English, which is fairly close to word-for-word:

> Paragraph 6 of the Cunha report on multinational orientation programs, which will be submitted to the Parliament this Thursday proposes introducing sanctions applicable to countries that do not respect the annual reduction targets of their fleets.

The official English version says that *the Cunha report contains something in paragraph 6*. But the French says that *paragraph 6 of the Cunha proposes something*. The official English talks about *countries which fail to meet their fleet reduction targets annually*, but the French talks of *countries that do not respect the annual reduction targets of their fleets*.

Ours is not to question why the translator chose this strategy in this case. The point is that it represents a kind of strategy that is employed quite frequently, and it requires inference based on what is actually being said and not simply manipulation of words. To take but one example, it requires the inference that, if something is in paragraph 6 of a report, then it is in the report.

Equivalence of Source and Target

My pessimism about machine translation is based on the conviction—universally shared by professional translators and serious students of the field—that a source text typically contains only part of the information required to translate it competently into another language, the rest coming from the translator's interpretation of the text. In other words, it involves processing signs, including both their *significants* and their *signifiés*, and not just symbols—not just *significants*. We should expect any task of which this is true to be automatically placed beyond the reach of the new machine-learning paradigm, which has access only to texts. But, if the connection between the *significants* that make up one text and those that make up the other are mediated through their *signifiés*, then the pair contains significant amounts of information about these normally hidden parts. Indeed, if a translation means substantially the same as the original on which it is based, then their *signifiés* are essentially the same. Studying such pairs of texts using appropriate statistical techniques should therefore reveal much about linguistic signs that is normally hidden. Indeed, it may be only such techniques as these that can provide objective, scientific information on the part of the linguistic sign that is normally hidden.

The trouble, as I have often argued, is that a translation does not, and cannot mean substantially the same as the original, unless we define "meaning" in such a way as to make the claim circular. The higher the quality of the translation, the more clear this becomes. Suppose that a text to be translated into French contains the sentence "It is important that there should be as little as possible in the paper". The translator must add substantive information because, in French, it is impossible to leave open the question of whether the word "paper" should be taken as referring to the physical substance, a newspaper, or a scientific paper. The translator must choose among the words "papier", "journal", and "article" or "document". The appearance shortly before of the sentence "Acid is the archivist's main enemy." almost certainly resolves the question in favor of "papier". If, instead, the earlier sentence were "Deliberate fabrication is the journalist's main enemy.", the correct translation should probably be "journal", and "Deliberate fabrication is the scientific editor's main enemy." would bias the decision in favor of "article" or "document".

Let us pursue the example one step further. Suppose the preceding sentences were "Acid is the archivist's main enemy. There is a lot of misleading material around seeming to show that this is not the case." Now, the weight swings back in favor of "article" or "document". These examples are, of course, contrived. In reality, the matter would have just one correct outcome, and there would be not the slightest doubt in the translator's mind about what it should be. But there is no reason to suppose that that outcome would be determined by, or even reflected in, a few words in the immediate vicinity of the ambiguous item. The information that needs to be added when translating the English word "paper" into French comes from inferences based on what the text is saying and what the translator knows about various kinds of paper and various roles they can fill in our lives and our culture.

Some texts are more difficult to understand than others and, to this extent, they are more difficult to translate. Obscurity is rarely the author's aim, except in key places in mystery novels, so that the information required to resolve ambiguities in a text is at hand more often than not. But there is almost nothing in the knowledge a writer might expect of his reader that might not be called upon to resolve some ambiguity, and thereby to play a critical role in enabling the translator to supply crucial information. I take this to imply either that, by processing sufficient quantities of translation, a machine could acquire knowledge equivalent in every way to human experience, or that human translators will always have a great advantage over machines.

Few would probably contest this conclusion, but also, few would see it as very consequential. Even the most ambitious and demanding researchers or consumers of translation, do not expect perfection. I suspect, however, that knowledge of the world, and people and culture is crucially involved in the great majority of the translations that are made, and that fully automatic, high quality, machine translation will therefore remain an unfulfilled dream for a very long time. Be that as it may, no one can seriously expect that these needs can be supplied by language models based on 5-grams of words. But this place—the *language models*—is the only one that the new paradigm for Natural Language Processing provides for them to reside.

Zipf's Law and Language Models

The advertised role of the language model is to place target words and phrases that translate material in the source text, in an acceptable order. There is an interplay between this and the translation model that supplied the translations because the aim is to maximize the probability of this final result. A less probable set of word and phrase translations may therefore win out over a more probable one, if it allows for a sufficiently more probable ordering.

The probability of a sequence of target words is estimated on the basis of the probabilities of the word n-grams that it contains. These probabilities, in turn, are estimated on the basis of large amounts of text, preferably of the same kind as the material to be translated. No translations are required for this text, so that the language model can be trained on very large amounts of text and, indeed, it is generally believed that the effectiveness of a language model continues to improve indefinitely, the larger the amount of text on which it is based becomes.

However, it is clear that the larger the amount of training material involved, the less reasonable it is to refer to an n-gram model as a *language* model because, as such, it is clearly subject to Zipf's law which, as we have seen, is a law of diminishing returns. The interval separating genuinely new additions to the linguistically interesting items of information grows very rapidly, especially in the early stages. But a large language model is, nevertheless, better than a small one, not because of the significantly greater amount of information about the language that it contains, but of its very much greater coverage of knowledge of the world and the domains covered by the texts on which it was trained. Not surprisingly, it has often been remarked that statistical machine translation systems are extremely sensitive to changes in the subject matter of the texts to which they are applied.

Zipf explained the observations underlying his law on the basis of a principle of least effort. A speaker will continue use familiar linguistic devices so long as they continue to serve his purposes, turning to more exotic ones only when forced to do so. This gives rise to a situation in which the most frequently occurring devices are the most generally useful ones. This, in its turn, makes it possible to learn fairly quickly enough of a language to fill a wide variety of needs. But our claim is that it is these needs, rather than the linguistic resources needed to fill them, that a so-called language model captures.

The trouble with the *n*-gram model, whether it is viewed as a repository of linguistic information or as a model of the world, is clearly that it is laughably inadequate in either role. As a genuine model of language, it is based on the idea that the most significant relations contracted by a word are with those that are nearest to it in the string and, if linguists have learnt anything during the last hundred years, it is that this is not the case. As a model of the world, it is clearly even less appropriate, and presumably no one would actually propose that it fill this role. However, the argument I have just sketched shows that this is the function it is being relied upon to fulfill.

Reference Translations

One of the places where the scientific respectability of machine translation by machine learning is at its most hollow is where the quality of the translations produced is evaluated. This is a matter that causes some embarrassment even among the most enthusiastic proponents of this approach. Since the cycle of setting parameters, training models, making translations and evaluating results repeats very frequently, and involves very large amounts of material, the possibility of having the quality of the translations produced assessed by human judges is simply not open. Furthermore, human judgments would doubtless be regarded as subjective and therefore unscientific. The alternative that is in fact used is to automatically compare the translations produced by the system with versions, called *reference* translations, produced by professional human translators. Ideally, several human translations are used for this purpose but, as we suggested earlier, there is generally no economically viable alternative to using translations that have been produced for independent reasons and there is rarely more than one of these available.

Everyone acknowledges the principal failing in this strategy, namely that most sentences allow a variety of translations into almost any other language. If the translation contains a word that is not in the reference, this counts as an error, regardless of whether it might have occurred in another reference. The problem is compounded by the fact that it frequently happens that the reference translation is, in a purely technical sense, wrong.

Faulty Training Material

Much training of statistical machine translation systems is, as we remarked above, based on the transcripts of debates in the European Parliament, and the first text in the standard set of these contains the English sentence "I should like to observe a minute's silence". The French version is "je souhaiterais . . . que nous observions une minute de silence" which translates more literally into English as "I would like us to observe a minute's silence". Pragmatically, these amount to the same thing in the given context, but wishing to do something, and wishing for a body to which one belongs to do something, are not generally the same.

A few lines later, the English transcript contains the sentence "Would it be appropriate for you, Madam President, to write a letter . . . ". The corresponding French version is "Ne pensez-vous pas , Madame la Présidente , qu'il conviendrait d'écrire une lettre ...". Once again, the pragmatic effect is the same, even though the French says nothing about who should write the letter.

Departures from what might seem to be, in the purely technical sense, correct often occur when the translator judges that the more obvious approach might give a result that would be infelicitous in some way. Consider the following sentence from a technical manual:

> To switch the power on, press the ON/OFF pushbutton. This will automatically start the measurement of relative humidity (RH).

It was translated into French as follows:

> La mesure de l'humidité relative (mesure-HR) est automatiquement sélectionnée à la mise en marche.

A nearly word for word version of this in English would be:

> Measurement of relative humidity (RH) is automatically selected when starting.

Sentences are frequently reorganized to some degree, and sometimes quite massively in this way in the hope of preserving smoothness and the intended interpretation. Their effect on machine learning can only be deleterious because most of what is learnt from such an example could be applied correctly almost nowhere else.

In spite of everything that we have said, machine translation can often produce a translation of a web page that is useful for some purposes and it is probably good enough to help intelligence analysts at the CIA determine whether the writer of an email is likely to be a terrorist. In short, it is probably useful in many situations where it is sufficient to get the gist of the original. Sometimes, it might provide a useful first draft for a mediocre translator, though it would probably still provide only frustration to a real professional. In any case, it is still very much in its infancy and, if it continues to progress at its present rate, it may be expected to fill a wider range of needs and to fill them better.

I predict that machine translation, together with other branches of Natural Language Processing, will indeed continue to progress, though at a more modest rate, and that it will do so only to the extent that its developers abandon their insistence that everything be based on machine learning. In particular, they will do well to acknowledge the value of some of the advances that have been made in Computational and Theoretical Linguistics, some of which are reflected in the papers in this volume.

Computational Linguistics

Locality—Charts and Finite-state Automata

So, what are these advances, how genuine are they, and how do they relate to the papers in this volume? Some of the most important concern the notions of locality in language that we have already referred to. They come in three flavors, according to the distance over which they operate. The most difficult to understand covers the longest distances. One thing that it concerns is commonality of reference among pronouns and other linguistic elements. A related matter is information structure—the proper maintenance of the distinction between referents that are being introduced to the discussion for the first time and those that are there already. These matters are hardly touched on in this volume.

The second domain of locality is the sentence, that is, syntax. This is where the most striking successes of computational linguistics have taken place. One of the most robust intuitions in linguistics, going back to Pāṇini, concerns the recursive properties of sentences. A sentence is a sequence of one or more phrases, and a phrase is either a word or a sequence of phrases. This intuition is captured in its most direct form by context-free grammars.

Transformational grammar, introduced by Harris (1952), Harris (1957) and widely popularized by Chomsky (1957), went beyond phrase structure in an attempt to capture another robust intuition, namely that sentences naturally fall together into families—actives and passives, assertions and questions, positives and negatives. A restriction on one member of a family, such as that the subject of the main verb must be animate, is generally reflected in the other members of the family. Harris designated one member of each family as a *kernel* sentence. The set of kernel sentences were described by a context-free grammar. The remaining members of the family were derived from the kernel member by transformational rules. In Chomsky's version, all the members of the family, referred to as *surface structures*, were derived by transformational rules from a single *deep* structure which, however, was an abstraction that was not itself required to be a member of the family.

The rules of a context free grammar are not fundamentally procedural. They are generally treated as procedural for pedagogical purposes, but they can equally well be understood as purely declarative patterns sanctioning nodes in syntactic tree structures. Transformational rules, by contrast, are essentially procedural and, while these rules are no longer part of more recent theories in this tradition, explicit procedures remain at the center of the theory.

Transformational rules are like small computer programs specifying, in a step-by-step manner, how parts of a tree structure are to be rearranged, deleted, or replaced. This may seem to add weight to my claim that linguistics and computer science are natural bedfellows. On the contrary, it in fact demonstrates a naiveté with respect to the characterization of processes which has several serious problems. First, the claim that an utterance is associated with a particular abstract structure, such as a phrase-structure, is obviously a great deal easier to substantiate than that it resulted from a particular set of manipulations of structures, occurring in a specific sequence. Second, it biases the whole theory strongly towards that of the speaker and away from the hearer. Just as there is no way of writing a program that reverses the effect of a given program, so there is no way of reversing the effect of a transformational rule, still less of an entire sequence of rules. Third, it is very difficult to determine whether the process has, in fact, been specified correctly. Fourth, it is generally not possible to tell whether one description of the process is equivalent to another. Fifth, it is impossible to distinguish what is important in the specification from what is incidental.

The attempt to create a reversible version of transformational grammar met with little success. In large measure, this was because very few transformational grammarians were computational linguists. Many of the leaders of the field were convinced that the time had not yet come when it would be possible to build interesting computational models of linguistic processes. Despite all the claims about its scientific rigor, transformational grammar and it derivatives remained ill-formalized and difficult to track.

My own early attempts to provide a reversible transformational grammar are chronicled in "Experiments with a Powerful Parser," which attempted to mimic transformational grammar with what are, in effect general rewriting rules. I knew nothing about recursively enumerable sets or the ugly fate that awaited any who ventured near them. But the paper does describe the second step in the direction of general chart parsers. The first step had been taken by John Cocke with what we now know as the Cocke-Kasami-Younger algorithm. The third and fourth steps were the introduction of the agenda and a retreat from general rewriting rules to phrase-structure rules.

I wrote about general, agenda-driven chart parsing in "Algorithm Schemata and Data Structures for Syntactic Processing". I introduced the term *algorithm schema* for the situation where the steps in a computation could take place in various different orders determined mainly by when the data required for a given step became available. I argued that an algorithm resulted from imposing a particular order on the steps, but when the steps corresponded to tasks on an agenda which could be reordered arbitrarily to comply with extraneous demands, one had an algorithm schema. In other words, an algorithm schema corresponded to a family of equivalent algorithms and, to that extent, was more abstract than any of them.

Generally, the algorithms generated from a particular schema differ not in their computational complexity, but in the expected efficiency of the overall process. They make it possible to largely decouple a person's strategy for exploring a large search space from the algorithm that will be applied to the items found in it. I take efficiency, in this sense, to be a measure of psychological plausibility and therefore an important component of computational linguistics. It is, of course, also an important component of statistical language processing, which generally involves pursuing only a small number of the most probable search directions.

Algorithm schemata constitute a move in the direction of specifying processes in a more abstract way. I am sympathetic to the argument that chart parsing is a bad place to look for psychologically plausible models of language processing, at least when it is assumed that all the tasks that are put on the agenda are all destined to be carried out sooner or later. But when this is not the case, a number of psychological strategies for analyzing sentences can be captured and experimented with simply by varying the agenda-management policy. I argued earlier that Computational Linguistics has much to contribute to linguistics and, although the suggestions in this paper have had little effect on the field so far, they seem to me to provide important support to the argument.

Further support for the importance of agenda-driven chart parsing comes from the observation that it can be readily adapted to other problems in language processing. Two of these are discussed in the papers "Chart Generation" and "Chart Translation". The first of these introduces an important generalization of chart parsing based on the fact that the input to the process need not be a string, but any structure in which there are points of articulation analogous to the points in a string where substrings come together. The input to a generator often takes the form of a directed graph as, for example, with Minimal Recursion Semantics (Copestake, Flickinger, Pollard and Sag 2005) which is based, to some degree on "From Semantics to Syntax" in this volume.

The proposal that a chart should form the principal data structure in a machine-translation system has in fact been taken up recently by some members of the Natural Language Processing community, notably Lopez (2008). A major advantage of charts, according to Lopez, is that they make it possible to separate the search space from the search logic, as we suggested above.

The third domain of locality is that of the word. It may be arguable that, in the morphology of some languages, notably the Bantu languages of East Africa, the full recursive power of phrase-structure formalisms is required. But it is almost always correct, revealing, and practically helpful, to treat the words of a language as a regular set of morpheme sequences and also of phoneme sequences. It may nevertheless be thought inadequate as a theory of morphology because it still lacks sufficient strong generative power, but this objection does not hold for phonology.

Together with Ron Kaplan (Kaplan and Kay 1994), I proposed a model of phonology, equivalent to the one proposed in *The Sound Pattern of English* (Chomsky and Halle 1968) but, crucially, based on the weaker formalism. This is another example of the symbiotic relationship between linguistics and computer science.

Unification

As we have already remarked, context-free grammars can often be made smaller and more perspicuous by providing them with some mechanism for capturing attributes and associated values and for specifying that certain relations—such as equality—should exist among them.

"The Tabular Parser" (1966) is an early attempt to extend context-free grammar so as to capture generalizations, and thus to make it smaller and more perspicuous. The idea was that there should be a main grammar and also a set of auxiliary grammars. Any rule could be annotated with the name of another grammar one of whose rules would also have to apply to any phrase built by this rule. German agreement within the simple noun phrase could be captured by three auxiliary grammars, one each for number, gender, and case. Some of these grammars could also be called upon elsewhere, such as in subject-verb agreement.

The idea of recursive phrase structure is at the base of all theories of syntax. Augmented Transition Network Grammars (ATNs) (Woods 1970) extended the basic idea in two ways. First, the string of categories on the right-hand side of a phrase-structure rule was replaced by a regular expression, thus making it possible to eliminate some uninformative structure. This extension remains today in Lexical Functional Grammar (Bresnan and Kaplan 1982). More importantly, Woods introduced the notion of *registers* whose contents could be manipulated in the course of matching rules against sentences. The motivation for this goes back to transformational grammar where sentences had deep as well as surface structures. In ATNs, as in context-free grammar, surface structure is simply a record of which rules apply where in the course of deriving a sentence. The deep structure is built as a result of manipulations of the contents of registers in the course of applying those rules. Eventually, one designated register, associated with the root of the surface-structure tree, contains the surface structure.

ATNs were explicitly computational devices, developed to direct the operation of a parser in the analysis of sentences. From a computational point of view, they suffered from the obverse of the problem that transformational grammar had. Transformational grammar could not be "reversed" in any straightforward manner to direct the operation of a parser, and ATNs could not be "reversed" to direct the operation of a generator. It therefore became a matter of interest to reduce the power of one or the other of them so that it could fill both roles. Modifying ATNs required limiting the kinds of operations that could be performed on registers. The key turned out to be to treat them as logical, rather then programming, variables so that any value assigned to them remained unchanged except in the case where the value was a structure containing other variables. These could acquire values later, but the same restriction also prevented these values from later changes. These ideas crystalized in the notion of attribute-value unification which is at the core of a number of grammatical formalisms.

My own attempt to design a grammatical formalism based on unification resulted in "Functional Grammar" (this volume) which I did not pursue, mainly because it still seemed to favor generation over analysis. However several other formalisms which, collectively, came to be known as *unification grammar* acquired a considerable following. Notable among them are Lexical Functional Grammar and Head-Driven Phrase Structure Grammar.

Of this development, Abney (*op cit.*) writes:

> Arguably the most productive interaction [between computational and other linguists] has been the body of work on unification-based formalisms, including Lexical-Functional Grammar (LFG) and Head-driven Phrase Structure Grammar (HPSG). The principal researchers have included both linguists and computational linguists. Unification-based formalisms were a major focus of research during the 1980s, and features and unification have become part of the standard curriculum in computational linguistics.
>
> Even so, the unification-based work may be the exception that proves the rule.

However, he completely misunderstands the effects that these developments had on linguistics and Computational Linguistics. He says:

> ...the fundamental goal of the enterprise is to keep the interaction between linguists and computational linguists at a minimum. The fundamental goal is to allow computationally-naive linguists to do their jobs, and linguistically-naive computer scientists to do their jobs, and to achieve language processing by the union of their efforts.

In short, rather than providing a conduit for linguistics to influence computational linguistics, or vice versa, the most successful interaction between the fields has had as its aim a hardening of the lines, a strict division of labor between the fields

Parallel reasoning would presumably support the claim that programming languages effectively drive a wedge between computer architects and engineers on the one hand, and the programmers who exploit them. That the architects and engineers do not talk in terms of recursion, and objects, and type inference does not make them naive about programming any more than programmers are shown to be naive about computer engineering because they do not talk in terms of busses, and gates and frame buffers. The field contains several sub-specialties whose members do, however, come together when they need to talk about processes and remote procedure calls, and concurrency. Abney's argument is backwards. Computational Linguists are indeed linguists and among their most important and successful contributions have been the various varieties of unification grammar. Some specialize in the design of grammars and some in the design of parsers, but they come together on matters like long-distance dependency, extraposition, and the handling of conjunctions.

Coda

Despite the gloomy view that I have taken of Computational Linguistics, there is in fact much in the present situation from which one may take heart. Increasingly, practitioners of Natural Language Processing are showing an awareness that words are not always separated by spaces; some languages have a lot more morphology than English; sentences in languages like English need verbs; there is more to textual coherence than n-grams. There is even a sense that linguists may have had something like the right take on some of these problems. The trouble is that no member of the Natural Language Processing community can risk the opprobrium that would come with suggesting an approach to any problem that was not based on machine learning.

The list of advantages of machine learning is long and impressive, including at least the following:

1. Systems with different parameter settings or trained on new data can be created cheaply and fast.
2. Prohibitive amounts of human labor are eliminated.
3. Subjective judgments are reduced.
4. Researchers do not need to know the languages of the systems they build.

On the other hand, there are many things that are known already and do not need to be learned again. For example, the knowledge required to map the forms of an English noun or verb onto a canonical form, or *lemma*, taking into account the various spelling changes that this entails, is well known to many people. There are many other languages for which it is more complex but, once it is done, it does not have to be done again and the chance that a better result could be produced by machine learning is small.

The number of context-free rules that one can extract from a tree bank even of a morphologically impoverished language like English is daunting. No person would wish to write such a set of rules, and no one in their right mind would even try. The right way to write rules is with a powerful grammatical formalism that takes advantage of features arranged on various more or less orthogonal dimensions. With such tools, the task of writing a grammar becomes tractable, teachable, and effective. The grammar may not cover all the constructions that the language allows, but it will certainly cover more than any that could be learnt automatically, either now or in the near future. Its rules will doubtless need to be annotated with probabilities for it to function well in an engineering environment.

Linguists are coming to see that some of the conclusions they reach can be made more solid if they are based on considerable quantities of naturally occurring data, analyzed with the help of good statistical techniques. It is greatly to be hoped that computer scientists will soon come to see, not only that there is much that humans know about the languages they speak, but that some of what they know can be learnt only by appealing to them, because only they have the key.

Publications referenced

Abney 2010; Copestake, Flickinger, Pollard, and Sag 2005; Bresnan and Kaplan 1982; Chomsky 1957; Chomsky and Halle 1968; de Saussure 1915; Harris 1952; Harris 1957; Jakobson 1971; Kaplan and Kay 1994; Lopez 2008; Woods 1970.

2

A Parsing Procedure

A large family of strategies can be devised for a parsing procedure, in such a way that all immediate constituent structures allowed by a given grammar are developed quickly and easily. The one presented here has been chosen, because it enables the notion of *presupposition* to be fully exploited as a means of referring to the grammar. This works as follows: For each immediate-constituent rule of the form $A \to B\ C$, one of the elements on the right-hand side is chosen as presupposing the other. For example, we may say "C presupposes a preceding B to form A" and write

$$C\ |\ -\ B\ |\ A.$$

Alternatively, we may write

$$B\ |\ +\ C\ |\ A.$$

The plus and minus signs indicate whether the presupposed item comes to the left or the right. The choice of the presupposed item in a rule is made with a view to minimizing the greatest number of items presupposed by any one item.

The parsing procedure has the following salient characteristics:

1. A constitute consists of two and only two constituents.
2. All partial structures ending at a given word in the sentence are developed before the following word is examined.

In describing the procedure, we shall allow ourselves to say that a constitute A precedes another constitute B only if the first word of B immediately follows the last word of A.

The first word of the sentence is read into the machine, and its n grammar codes entered in the first n spaces on the main data list. The entries are annotated to show that they are constitutes beginning with the first word of the sentence. A counter is associated with each word read into the machine, indicating the point in the list where the first grammar code for that word is stored. These counters, together with the word numbers in the data list, enable the items which precede a given word to be located very readily.

Also associated with each word is a *prediction list* . The prediction list for the first word of a sentence is always empty; and the list for the second word is completed as soon as the first word has been read into the machine. If the first word, or, in general any new item, presupposes a following item, a note of the relevant grammatical details is made on the prediction list of the following word. We are now ready to read the second word. Its m grammar codes become the next m entries in the data list. A new pointer is set and predictions are made as before. Parsing proper now begins. Each grammar code for the new word is considered in turn to see if it fills any of the predictions in the list for that word, and if it presupposes any of the items which precede it in the sentence. If either of these conditions is met, a new constitute is formed and an appropriate entry made in the next available space in the data list. The new entry is marked with the word number of the first word which it includes, and also with references to the two entries in the list which represent its constituents, all having the new word as last member.

These are now taken in turn as potential right-hand constituents of new constitutes. The process continues in this manner until all the items currently on the data list have been considered together with all the items which precede them, as candidates for a new constituent. Only then is a new word brought into the store.

Consider the sentence: "We are parsing sentences". A very simplified grammar will enable us to develop two structures.

VERB	+ NOUN	PREDICATE
VERB	− NOUN	SENTENCE
PRES. PARTICIPLE	− AUXILIARY	VERB
PREDICATE	− NOUN	SENTENCE
ADJECTIVE	+ NOUN	NOUN

At the end of the procedure, the data list might appear as follows as in Table 1.

TABLE 1

NO.	WORD	GRAMMAR CODE	WORD NUMBER	FIRST CONSTIT.	SECOND CONSTIT.
1	WE	NOUN	1	0	0
2	ARE	AUXILIARY	2	0	0
3		VERB	2	0	0
4		SENTENCE	1	1	3
5	PARSING	PRES.PART.	3	0	0
6		ADJECTIVE	3	0	0
7		NOUN	3	0	0
8		VERB	2	2	5
9		PREDICATE	2	3	7
10		SENTENCE	1	1	8
11		SENTENCE	1	1	9
12	SENTENCES	NOUN	4	0	0
13		NOUN	3	6	12
14		PREDICATE	2	8	12
15		PREDICATE	2	3	13
16		SENTENCE	1	1	14
17		SENTENCE	1	1	15

The results happen to be the last two entries on the list. The complete trees can be traced out using the last two colums.

Discussion

R. M. NEEDHAM (UK): Since it is easy to devise many procedures, and individual ones present little novelty, how does one choose a good one?

M. KAY (UK). I wish I could give a good general answer to this question. Whatever reasons one may find are unlikely to be more than superficial. However the following points may be of interest.

1. Presupposition is only useful in a few procedures.
2. It is often difficult to identify the end of a sentence, since the period is not used only for this purpose. A procedure, such as the one described, which identifies everything up to a given point in the sentence may be useful, in that it can be discontinued only when a suitable result occurs together with appropriate punctuation. In other words, the length of the sentence need not be known initially.
3. It might be useful to discover alternative sentence structures in order of their increasing depth, as defined by Yngve. However, this can readily be computed in the process of working down the tree.

All these procedures involve nested cycles of instructions and it is worth considering if any one is particularly suited for use on a given machine.

3

Rules of Interpretation: An Approach to the Problem of Computation in the Semantics of Natural Language

3.1 Traditional Grammar and Descriptive Linguistics

It is commonly held that a complete description of any language must have two parts, grammar and vocabulary. The study of vocabulary is concerned with describing the primitive symbols used in the language and their relations to features of the external world. Grammar accounts for the ways in which these symbols are combined to form more complex structures. The aspects of language normally thought of as belonging to grammar, fall under three heads:

i) Features of language, whether they be primitive symbols like words, or more complex structures like phrases and sentences, whose primary function seems to be that of expressing *relations* among other elements. On this basis, for example, a distinction is frequently made between *full words*, which represent features of the external world, and *function words*, which serve to indicate relations between them.

ii) Linguistic elements, readily distinguishable by some peculiarity of form or usage, which make up closed, and usually fairly small sets. The phonemes of a language form such a set and so do inflectional endings, articles, prepositions, auxiliary verbs and the like.

iii) Features which the usage of a particular language requires in certain situations and which are not, therefore, at the discretion of the speaker to include or leave out as he pleases. We may think of them as a sort of tax which the language levies on its users. It is, for example, difficult for speakers of English to talk about objects without mentioning whether one or more is in question, even though this information may have no direct relevance to the speaker's message. Similarly, an indication must be given, according to a standard formula, of the time of occurrence of an event relative to some frame of reference. The Chinese are exempt from both of these levies though they are subject to others. Often the required feature is of an entirely formal kind as in the case of gender in most of the Indo-European languages.

For any given language it is normally found that these three categories overlap heavily.

It is ascribed to the credit of *structural* or *descriptive* linguistics, that a much simpler scheme has been put in the place of the above. Many of the vague and ill-defined terms have either been defined more sharply or shown to be redundant. In short, a scientific discipline capable of holding up its head with the purest of natural science, now stands in the place of what was previously at best poetic. This paper puts forward a different view, maintaining that the linguists have vigorously thrown away at least one baby with the bath-water. A comparison of the old and new approaches shows that what we used to call *grammar* was, in reality, concerned with two very different types of phenomenon, one of which has become the proper study of descriptive linguistics, while the other came near to being banished into complete obscurity. At least one of the babies which went with the bath-water, though it may not have seemed very robust, deserved better than this Spartan treatment. I shall characterize those features of language which interest the descriptive linguist, as *rules of formation*, and distinguish them sharply from the outcast baby which is the subject of this paper and which I shall call *rules of interpretation*.[1]

3.2 Rules of Formation

The rules of formation of a language include all that it is necessary to know to distinguish an expression belonging to the language from one belonging to another language or to no language at all. They contain a budget of primitive symbols and specify what sequences of these symbols are acceptable as expressions in the language. They may also go further to distinguish certain classes of expressions, such as sentences, but this is not necessary. The classic definition of rules of formation, due to Chomsky, is as follows:

> "The fundamental aim of the linguistic analysis of a language L is to separate the *grammatical* sequences which are the sentences of L, from the *ungrammatical* sequences which are not sentences of L, and to study the structure of the grammatical sequences. The grammar of L will thus be a device that generates all the grammatical sequences of L and none of the ungrammatical ones." (Chomsky 1957).

For the purpose of our discussion, we may leave aside the question of whether a device which will generate the grammatical sequences of L is formally equivalent to a device which will recognize the grammatical sequences of L; in either case it is true that only rules of formation are involved. Both devices would require an inventory of rules of formation for the language, but that is not to say that they would require the same rules, because the rules of a language will, in general, not be unique. Rules of formation also have the following interesting property. Given a text in an unknown language, it is possible to start compiling a list of rules of formation. As more text is considered, the list will become more like the one required for the total language, and the probability that each rule is applicable to the total language will become steadily greater. Thus, deriving a set of rules of formation for a text is a problem of the classic black-box type. The rules of formation characterize a language as a formal system of a certain kind without regard to its function as a symbolic system. It is true that linguists use the fact that language is also a symbolic system in arriving at some of their conclusions, but the final statement involves only rules of formation.

---

[1]These terms are not intended to recall the work of Carnap with which they are only remotely and fortuitously connected.

3.3 Rules of Interpretation

Consider now the case of an intelligent young Martian making his first trip to the Earth. He has prepared himself by memorizing a grammar of the English language written by the foremost American linguists, and also a compendious vocabulary. He knows what all the words in the vocabulary denote, and he can construct and analyse the syntactic structure of any English sentence. To his dismay, when he eventually arrives on Earth he finds that he is barely able to communicate. He can buy simple things in shops by pronouncing the one-word name of the thing he wants, but he is at a loss when the effect cannot be achieved with a single word. Why is this? Has he not learned the grammar so that he can produce faultless sentences? Unfortunately, all the books he studied were silent on the question of the meanings of phrases and sentences, so that he is quite unable to predict the consequences of uttering any expression, even though he knows it to be well-formed and that the meanings of the words are appropriate to the message he wishes to convey. He knows the words "red" and "brick" and what they mean, and the grammar tells him that the phrases "red brick" and "brick red" are both acceptable in English, but people respond to them in different ways. He may have observed that people occasionally say "Please pass the salt", but he does not know why they choose that expression instead of "Please salt the pass", nor under what circumstances it would be appropriate to say the latter. A rule which is used to derive the meaning of a phrase or sentence from the meanings of its constituents is a rule of interpretation. When we say that in English the word "red" may occur before "brick" to form the phrase "red brick", we are making a remark about the rules of formation of English; when we say that the word "red" may be used to qualify the word "brick", we are making a remark about the rules of interpretation of English. The particular rule which is invoked to interpret a phrase like "red brick" seems at first to be very simple. A red brick is clearly that which is at once red and a brick. The phrase is applicable to those features of the world to which the words "red" and "brick" are individually applicable and the required result is given by a logical product. However, this implies that the relation of qualification is symmetrical and that "red brick" has the same meaning as "brick red".

A great many difficulties attend the study of rules of interpretation in natural language. It might seem that a useful first step would be to compile a list of some commonly used and easily identified rules. However, even so simple and informal an activity as this may be impossible, and would almost certainly produce more difficulties than it resolved. Consider the simple phrase "snow man". Clearly a snow man is a man made of snow. The qualified word names an object made of the substance which the qualifier names. This is a common situation and many examples can be adduced. An ice man, on the other hand, is not a man made of ice, but a man who delivers ice. The difference between "snow man" and "ice man" is greater than the differences between the meanings of the individual words would lead one to expect, and this may be accounted for by invoking two different rules of interpretation. However, there are at least two other equally plausible ways in which the difference could be accounted for. The first involves admitting "snow man" or "ice man" or both, as idioms, that is, as lexical primitives to the internal constitutions of which rules of interpretation do not apply. Another possibility is to say that one of the meanings of "ice" is "who delivers ice" and one of the meanings of "snow" is "made of snow". In this case, a single rule of interpretation suffices to account for both phrases.

There is another strong objection to attempting to list rules of interpretation intuitively. The result of such an enterprise will be a list of phrases or phrase types against each of which one or more paraphrases will be entered. It will thus resemble, on the one hand, a traveller's phrase book and on the other, an ill-disciplined assortment of grammatical transformations. In any case, it can do little but complicate the early stages of the investigation. The rules applicable to a given phrase are sufficiently opaque in themselves to make it unwise to undertake their simultaneous study in pairs of partially parallel phrases.

3.4 A Model for Qualification

The approach advocated here involves setting up a minimal calculus using, in the first instance, only one type of relation; that of *qualification*. This calculus is used as the basis for a model of the system of rules of interpretation of a language. By causing the model to transform words into phrases and *vice versa*, and by making an intuitive judgment of the similarity in meaning between the words and the corresponding phrases, we hope to arrive at some estimate of the types of relations involved and their roles in the total economy of the system.

We shall use lower-case letters $(a, b, c, \ldots)$ as variables. The constants of the system are those English words which may function as nouns or adjectives. The expression ab is used to stand for "a qualifies b". We shall write $ab = c$ when ab has the same meaning as c. We now set the following restrictions on the relation of qualification for the purpose of this model:

i) The reflexive law: $aa = a$

ii) The anti-symmetric law: $(ab = ba) \Rightarrow (a = b)$

iii) The transitive law does not apply: $(ab) \cdot (bc) \nRightarrow ac$

iv) The several modifiers of a single item are unordered: $a(bc) = b(ac)$.

Given the two formulae

(1) $ab = c$

and

(2) $dc = e$

we may substitute ab for c in (2) and write

(3) $d(ab) = e$.

Now consider a simple example. The following formulae are given initially:

(4) young human = child

(5) male child = boy

(6) male human = man.

Substituting for "child" in (5), we obtain

(7) male (young human) = boy

which, by (iv), we may rewrite as

(8) young (male human) = boy.

Lastly, from (6) we may substitute "man" for "male human" in (8) and obtain

(9) young man = boy.

A great many examples can be constructed in this way, some producing results that are intuitively acceptable and others producing nonsense. At this stage, our only object is to separate those cases where a particular relation holds, from those where it does not, in the hope that formal criteria will emerge for distinguishing them. If there are sufficient cases where the rule does apply, we may then go on to construct new rules to account for the residue and so on.

The main difficulty here, as in all language study, is that the volume of data to be examined is exceedingly large, and unless a systematic discovery procedure can be devised (using mechanical aids wherever possible) the study of rules of interpretation is likely to remain at the trivial level of our example. In this case, we must not be surprised if the notion that descriptive linguistics provides the only really serious approach to the study of language, continues to gain ground. Let us therefore turn our attention to the possibility of constructing a mechanical model which will enable us to examine the consequences of a rule like the one we have suggested, when applied to large bodies of data. The model will be a very simple one.

3.5   Computation Methods

The relation of qualification as we have defined it, together with a great many others of the same general kind, can conveniently be embodied in a computer program similar to that developed by Feigenbaum (1961) for simulating verbal-learning behaviour. Data are presented to the program in the form of equations or definitions, e.g. "child = young human" or "A child is a young human". Each word or phrase is associated with a node in a *net* which is *grown* in a piecemeal fashion to accommodate incoming data (Fig. 1). The program is able to complete parts of the net which are not supplied by the data. The method is entirely straightforward. In Fig. 1, the downward path from the node corresponding to "human being" to "boy" is by way of the lines marked "young" and "male", in that order. According to our hypothesis, qualifiers are unordered and it should therefore be possible to take the "male" path first. This would take us as far as "man". We may now construct a path from here to "boy" and mark it "young". As the net grows larger, the proportion of paths constructed by the program may be expected to increase, and it is on the basis of these paths that the efficacy of the rules will be judged.

There is not space here to discuss numbers of different rules of interpretation which might be found to be applicable in, say, English. At this stage it is more important to establish that they are as crucial a part of language as are rules of formation. The descriptive linguist, in so far as his interest in the language remains purely academic, is free to define the object of his study in such a way that rules of interpretation are excluded, but the development of machine translation is entirely dependent on their being well understood. A net of the kind described here, but also incorporating other rules, is in fact directly usable as a dictionary for a machine translation program.

A net generated from a simple rule of interpretation such as the one we described, or from a number of such rules, turns out to have a number of features in common with the lattices of the Cambridge Language Research Unit. The lines in the diagram can, for example, be interpreted as inclusion relations in the straightforward sense that

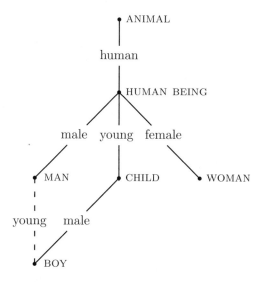

FIGURE 1 Part of a qualification net

more specific terms fall under more general terms. If a word in a text is replaced by one occurring above it in the net, the sentence in which it occurs will differ in meaning from the original sentence only in being less specific. However, the lattice model was rejected because of the very small number of relations which could be defined in it, and in particular because of the impossibility of defining any but commutative relations. One of the great advantages of the lattice model is that it provides a convenient measure of semantic similarity, namely lattice distance. This feature is preserved in the net.

3.6 Machine Translation

The theoretical implications of this kind of work will take a long time to emerge, and, as we have remarked, there are a great many questions which cannot be approached at this stage. However, the implications of a device like the semantic net may be much more immediate in machine translation. Every translator knows that the situation in which a word is best translated by a phrase or a phrase by a word, or a group of words is the rule rather than the exception. The most sophisticated approach to the problem of meaning which has so far gained any currency in machine translation is embodied in the list; a one-to-one mapping of the words of one language onto the words of another. If a phrase is to be reproduced by a word, or *vice versa*, the dictionary maker must have predicted it; he must have foreseen that the particular group of words might occur together and that they could best be rendered by a single word. The net provides a way in which a machine program could make substitutions of this kind without the dictionary-maker having foreseen the particular usage. Words and phrases of two or more languages can be stored at the nodes of the net. A node is created only when one of the languages has a single word to fill that position, but there is no requirement that each language should be represented at each node. The strategy of the translation process might then be somewhat as follows. The phrase structure of each input sentence is determined. The grammar which is used for this analysis also furnishes for each phrase an indication of the rule or rules of interpretation appropriate to it. The rules are then applied to the phrases and nodes in the net located for as many of them as possible. Here the strategy of the translation process was described in the last section. If, as is unlikely, a node is found to correspond to a complete sentence, and if the target language is represented at this node, then the sentence can be rendered by the single word. Otherwise, the immediate constituents of the sentence are examined until a word or phrase is found to represent every constituent. It may be that the level of the word is reached in some places without an equivalent having been found in the target language. In this case it is necessary to work up the semantic net still further to construct a phrase which can be used to represent the word; that is to say, a path leading downwards from a node where the target language is represented to the source language word.

Machine translation research, however far it may still be from its final objective, has done a great service in revealing an important gap in language study. It is generally agreed that a sophisticated technique for syntactic analysis is one of the first requirements and it is admitted, however reluctantly, that the problem of meaning will have to be faced one day. What is missing is the bridge which links these two. I am claiming that the investigation of rules of interpretation is a matter of the greatest urgency, for providing as they do this link between syntax and semantics, grammar and vocabulary, they may be expected to have consequences for the study of rules of formation. In general, the phrase-structure grammar of a language is not uniquely defined. The decision as to which is the best grammar must be made, at least in part, on the basis of the rules which are required to interpret the phrases which it identifies. Therefore, the study of the rules of interpretation of a language cannot be made to wait until the syntax is complete, for this may make the formulation of the rules impossibly difficult. It is rather the case that the study of rules of formation and rules of interpretation should be conducted in parallel at every step.

Discussion

M. A. WOODBURY (USA). Please explain your discussion of "red brick house" and "brick red house".

M. KAY (USA). Actually I discussed "brick red" and "red brick" without the word "house" following. It must be assumed that the formal structure of the phrase under consideration is known at this stage. We may take it that, in both the phrases you cite, the two adjectives form single units or constitutes. The rules of interpretation must therefore be applied to this unit first, and then to the combination of this unit and the following noun.

J. BEČVÁR (CSSR). There are difficulties with the commutativity of adjectives, e.g. "French German dictionary" and "German French dictionary".

Abstracts

This paper distinguishes sharply between rules of formation, hitherto the principal interest of descriptive linguists, and rules of interpretation which belong partly to semantics and partly to syntax. A model is proposed in which the learning of a new word is viewed as a process whereby the grammatical function, as well as a semantic index for the word, are entered against it in an inventory stored inside the learner. The semantic index of a phrase is then constructed, as required, from the semantic indices of the constituents.

A computer program is outlined which will use rules of interpretation to associate words and phrases with positions in a net which will be grown piecemeal to accommodate incoming data. The computer will be able to assemble and select from its data in different ways. Eventually, it is hoped that the net may be usable as a dictionary for mechanical translation; a dictionary which will be able to provide a phrase in the target language to represent a word in the source language, and *vice versa*, without the phrase being stored explicitly in the machine and without the necessity for the dictionary maker to have foreseen the particular use.

Cet article établit une nette distinction entre les règles de génération, qui jusqu'ici représentent l'intérêt de base de la linguistique descriptive, et les règles d'interprétation qui appartiennent d'une part à la sémantique et d'autre part à la syntaxe. Il propose un modèle dans lequel on considère l'enseignement d'un mot nouveau comme un processus selon lequel on enregistre aux côtés du mot dans une mémoire-apprenti, le rôle grammatical ainsi qu'un indice sémantique correspondant à ce mot. L'indice sémantique d'un syntagme se déduit alors selon les règles des indices sémantiques des constituants du syntagme.

On esquisse un programme pour l'ordinateur utilisant les règles d'interprétation pour associer aux mots et aux syntagmes des positions définies dans une matrice qui sera construite pièce à pièce en vue de l'adapter aux nouvelles données éventuelles. L'ordinateur pourra assembler et choisir parmi ses données de diverses manières. On peut éventuellement espérer que cette matrice pourra servir de dictionnaire à la traduction automatique, dictionnaire qui pourra fournir dans la langue cible le syntagme correspondant au mot de la langue source et inversement, sans que le syntagne soit enregistré de façon explicite dans la machine et sans que l'usage particulier de ce mot ait été necessairement prévu au moment de la constitution du dictionnaire.

Diese Arbeit unterscheidet scharf zwischen den *Regeln des Satzbaus* – bisher das Hauptinteresse der beschreibenden Sprachwissenschaftler – und den *Regeln der Interpretation*, die teils der Semantik, teils der Syntax entstammen. Es wird ein Modell vorgeschlagen, in dem das Erlernen eines neuen Wortes als ein Vorgang angesehen wird, durch den die grammatische Funktion ebenso wie ein semantischer Index dieses Wortes dem Wort in einem Verzeichnis gegenübergestellt wird, das im Lernenden gespeichert ist. Der semantische Index eines Satzes wird dann nach Bedarf aus den semantischen Indizes seiner Bestandteile konstruiert.

Ein Rechenmaschinenprogramm wird umrissen, das Regeln der Interpretation dazu benützt, Wörtern und Sätzen Positionen in einem *Netz* zuzuordnen, das stückweise *aufgebaut* wird und so ankommende Daten unterbringt. Der Rechner kann dann diese Daten in verschiedener Weise sammeln und aussondern. Man hofft, dass dieses Netz als Wörterbuch dienen kann, das eine Phrase in der Zielsprache fur ein Wort der Ausgangssprache liefert und umgekehrt, ohne die betreffende Phrase explizit in der Maschine speichern und deren spezielle Verwendung in dem Wörterbuch voraussehen zu müssen.

Este trabajo distingue con precisión entre las reglas de formatión, de aquí el interés principal de los lingüistas descriptivos, y reglas de interpretación que pertenecen en parte a la semántica y en parte a la sintaxis. Se propone un modelo en el cual la enseñanza de una nueva palabra es considerada como un proceso en el que entra la función gramatical y el índice semántico en un inventario situado en una memoria interna del instructor. El índice semántico de una frase se construye entonces, según se necesita, a partir de los índices semánticos de los componentes de la frase.

Se describe un programa que usa reglas de interpretación para asociar palabras y frases con posiciones de una red, la cual crecerá gradualmente para incluir los datos que llegan. La calculadora será capaz de conjuntar y seleccionar significados a partir de los datos de formas diferentes. Eventualmente se espera que la red pueda ser usada como un diccionario para traducción mecánica, un diccionario capaz de suministrar una frase correcta para representar una palabra en el lenguaje fuente y viceversa sin que la frase esté alma cenada de forma explícita en la máquina, y sin que el confeccionador del diccionario tenga que haber previsto el uso particular.

Acknowledgements

I am deeply indebted to D. G. Hays of the RAND Corporation and M. Hollis of the University of California for their invaluable help in developing the ideas in this paper.

Publications referenced

Chomsky 1957; Feigenbaum 1961.

4

The Logic of Cognate Recognition in Historical Linguistics

Preface

This report presents an exercise in the application of combinatory methods to linguistic analysis. There are many areas of linguistics in which such methods could be profitably applied. Historical linguistics, and in particular the comparative method, is an interesting place to start for several reasons. First, it is an area in which well-defined analytic procedures are of particular importance. Not only are there no more speakers of the languages concerned, but in most cases, there are no texts either. Secondly, the comparative method is an easy case, but one in which it is possible to demonstrate basic methods which are useful in many situations. Thirdly, there is an interesting parallel to be drawn between the comparison of words which is made in the comparative method and the comparison of sentences made in the study of translation. The object of both enterprises is to specify transformations of one set of strings into another.

This work was begun as part of a seminar project under Professor S. Lamb at the University of California, Berkeley. A program was written for the IBM 7090 computer which successfully applied the method to small samples of data. This embodied some novel techniques for manipulating truth-functional expressions developed by the author in collaboration with Martin Hollis.

Summary

The "comparative method" is one of the principal tools of historical linguistics, but it is not the well-defined technique that the name suggests. This paper presents a formalization in terms of elementary propositional logic of one of the most crucial steps in the comparative method, namely, that in which modern derivatives of prehistoric phonemes are recognized. The basic assumption on which the theory rests is that the words of a hypothetical prehistoric language should be constructed in such a way as to minimize the total number of phonemes in the language and of the statements that need to be made to account for the forms of the modern words.

The theory is sufficiently specific to provide an algorithm for a computer program. However, the amount of computation rises sharply with any increase in the amount of data to be considered, and with present techniques it is prohibitive even for trivially small data sets. Nevertheless, the theory provides a basis on which more efficient heuristic procedures might be built.

Widespread parallelism between form and meaning, denotation, or grammatical function

31

among the vocabularies of different languages is usually explained on the hypothesis of genetic relationship. The hypothesis is established if the evolution of the languages from a common parent can be traced through written records. But this is not the common case. Most often, the hypothesis can at best be supported by internal evidence. The purpose of the comparative method is to marshal this evidence.

The comparative method seeks to fit similarities in sets of forms (words or morphemes) into a single scheme whose coherence will be the measure of kinship among the languages. For each associated set of forms which are judged to be related, an artificial form is constructed which fills the role of their common ancestor within the model. The letters in these reconstructed forms stand for the phonemes of the extinct language. The aim is to make the reconstructions in such a way that the history of each form does not have to be written separately. Instead, a history is written for each phoneme in the original language, and from these the history of the forms can be inferred. The history of a phoneme within the model consists of a set of rules specifying its development from one of the phonemes of the original language. There must be a complete set of rules determining for each phoneme in the reconstructions what its descendant will be in any given language and in any given environment.

The explanatory value of a set of reconstructions is assessed on the basis of the linguistic plausibility of the reconstructed forms and on the range of application of the rules for deriving modern from supposed ancient forms. It is the rules that must carry the major part of the burden. The system as a whole can only be said to be coherent if a small set of simple rules accounts for a relatively large amount of data. The principal aim of this essay is to make this notion of coherence precise.

The term "comparative method" suggests a recipe which, conscientiously followed, will lead inexorably to the required result. This is misleading. The method is usually taught by displaying, in a carefully chosen order, words from various Indo-European languages, together with the reconstructions that have been made from them. A sufficiently sympathetic student is readily convinced that the reconstructions, in some sense, "follow" from the extant forms. If they do follow, then it would be right that the logical moves should be set out in detail, at least for some cases. In this essay, a theoretical framework is presented within which a method of assessing potentially related sets of forms is completely specified. This should not be thought of as an alternative to the comparative method, but as a formalization of a crucial part of it.

There is much to be gained, both in theory and practice, from formalizing what has hitherto been at best implicit. It is the object of linguistics, no less than of any other science, to exhibit facts as particular cases of more general truths. The more general the truths, the less directly their connection with the brute facts appeals to the intuition. But when a clear line is drawn between theory and practice, logic and data, formal theory and empirical observations, the enterprise can proceed securely, intuitional misgivings notwithstanding. Furthermore, when the logical structure of a theory is spread out and divested of its empirical trappings, its relationship to other apparently unrelated theories may be seen.

The more remote the connection between the languages, the more difficult it is to apply the comparative method. Yet, it is precisely in these cases that the most interesting results are expected. If a pair of languages is judged unrelated, it may be because the pattern of similarities on which a successful set of reconstructions might be based has simply gone unnoticed. Furthermore, if different reconstructions are offered, there is at present no standard of comparison. This is an unsatisfactory state of affairs in a scientific undertaking, and it arises, at least in part, because the subject has no clear theoretical frame of reference.

In his paper, "The Principal Step in Comparative Grammar", Hoenigswald (1950) undertakes to provide a rigorous exposition of the comparative method. His argument is briefly as follows. Data for the comparative method come in the form of phoneme correspondences, e.g.,

Sanskrit:	t	t	t	d	d	dh	p	p	p	b	b	bh
Germanic:	t	d	p	d	t	d	p	b	f	b	p	b

The problem is to group these into sets which are reflexes (i.e., descendants) of the same Indo-European phoneme. Where two phonemes in one language correspond to one phoneme in the other, there is support for the view that they have a common origin. Further support comes from examination of the environments in which corresponding phonemes occur. If a pair of sets never occurs in the same environment, the possibility of regarding them as reflexes of a single phoneme is open, and rules for making the correct derivations can easily be constructed. Thus, the principal step in the comparative method is essentially that of phonemicizing.

We contest the claim of rigor for Hoenigswald's treatment, and, more important, we contest the centrality of what is treated in the comparative method. If linguistic plausibility is a criterion, then phonemicization is a reasonable, and possibly a necessary, technique. However, it cannot be claimed that the process of phonemicizing has the rigor which the comparative method lacks.

That Hoenigswald is not concerned with the principal step in comparative grammar is betrayed in the following quotation:

> "We also assume that the task of weeding out material which is not directly inherited has somehow been accomplished." (Hoenigswald 1950)

As we have pointed out, the problem of deciding what is inherited is distinguishable from that of actually making reconstructions only in the special cases where results can be confirmed from historical records. To pronounce a set of forms related is precisely to provide plausible reconstructions which fall within the scope of generally applicable rules.

4.1 Correspondences and Decompositions

We shall confine the following discussion to cases where only two modern languages are to be considered. This eases the exposition and also the preliminary experiments in implementing the theory. However, little generality is lost, for to extend the method to any number of languages requires only trivial modifications to the definitions of correspondence and decomposition.

We begin by defining some terms. The most basic entities with which we operate will be called *symbols* . Usually these are thought of as representing phonemes. However, much comparative work is done with texts of some antiquity where the phonemic interpretation of letters may be open to doubt. Since our theory makes no appeal to the linguistic status of these entities, we prefer to leave open the possibility of interpreting them differently for different types of data.

We shall speak of strings of symbols, or simply *strings* . It is convenient to admit the possibility of strings with only one member.. Thus, we may say that a word is a string even though the word may consist of only one symbol.

A *correspondence* is an ordered pair of strings. We shall be interested in correspondences where the first member is taken from one extant language and the second from another. We shall represent correspondences by writing the two strings separated by a stroke, e.g., 'abcd/xyz'.

If in the correspondence A/B, A and B are strings of at least k symbols, they can each be divided into k substrings in at least one way. New correspondences can then be set up by associating the ith substring of A with the ith substring of B. The new set of correspondences constitutes a *decomposition* of the original correspondence. In general, there are many ways of decomposing a correspondence into k shorter correspondences. Setting k equal to 2, we have the following decompositions of 'abcd/xyz':

(i)	a/x	bcd/yz
(ii)	a/xy	bcd/z
(iii)	ab/x	cd/yz
(iv)	ab/xy	cd/z
(v)	abc/x	d/yz
(vi)	abc/xy	d/z

With k equal to 3, the decompositions are

(vii)	a/x	b/y	cd/z
(viii)	a/x	bc/y	d/z
(ix)	ab/x	c/y	d/z

Together with the original correspondence, which, by convention, we include as a decomposition, this exhausts all the decompositions of this correspondence.

Two sorts of correspondence are of primary interest in a model of the comparative method. The first is provided by the original set of vocabulary items. The second consists of pairs of strings, both of which are descendants of the same phoneme. Given definitions of correspondence and decomposition possibly more general than those proposed above, then wherever a correspondence of the first type represents a cognate set of forms, it will be possible to decompose it in exactly one way into correspondences of the second type.

Consider now the correspondence 'that/dass', consisting of a pair of vocabulary items from English and German. It can be decomposed in twenty different ways, but only one of these has a correspondence for each Indo-European phoneme, namely:

$$th/d \quad a/a \quad t/ss$$

The main problem still outstanding is to discover a satisfactory criterion for distinguishing this from the nineteen other decompositions.

4.2   Representation by Truth Functions

We have said that the value of a set of reconstructions must be judged in large measure by the scope of the rules required to derive the extant from the constructed forms. In other words, we shall seek the solution in which all the required derivations can be made with the smallest set of rules. In the model we have proposed, a rule is represented by a correspondence. We shall therefore seek the smallest collection of correspondences from which at least one decomposition of each correspondence in the original list can be constructed.

In order to see how the required sets of correspondences and decompositions can be found, we shall reformulate the problem in terms of propositional calculus. Let $c^{(1)}$, $c^{(2)}$, $c^{(3)}$ ... $c^{(n)}$ be the correspondences which represent the original vocabulary list. Let $c_1^{(k)}$, $c_2^{(k)}$, $c_3^{(k)}$ ... be the decompositions of $c^{(k)}$. We now associate with each decomposition $c_i^{(k)}$ a proposition $p_i^{(k)}$ which is *true* if $c_i^{(k)}$ is the decomposition of $c^{(k)}$ that has a correspondence for each phoneme in the ancestral form from which $c^{(k)}$ is supposed to be derived. According to our hypothesis, there is exactly one decomposition of each initial correspondence whose associated proposition is true. Therefore, if $c^{(k)}$ has m decompositions, we can assert

$$(1) \qquad p_i^{(k)} \vee p_2^{(k)} \vee ...p_m^{(k)}.$$

A similar compound proposition is true for each initial correspondence. We can therefore assert

$$(2) \qquad (p_1^{(1)} \vee p_2^{(1)} \vee ...p_m^{(1)}) \ ... \ (p_1^{(n)} \vee p_2^{(n)} \vee ...p_r^{(n)}).$$

This expression can be read somewhat as follows: "Either the first or the second or the third or ... or the last decomposition of the first correspondence from the vocabulary list represents a correct reconstruction *and* either the first or the second or the third or ... or the last decomposition of the second correspondence ..." and so on until "either the first or the second or the third or ... or the last decomposition of the last correspondence from the vocabulary list represents a correct reconstruction." This is already a more complicated formulation than ordinary language is suited to handle. It is partly for this reason, and partly to gain power in doing calculations, that we have turned to the propositional calculus.

Since it will be necessary to write still more complicated expressions, we can profit from a shorthand device permitting us to rewrite (1) in the form

$$(3) \qquad \sum_i p_i^{(k)}.$$

This represents the disjunct of all the $p_i^{(k)}$ obtained by giving i values between 1 and the maximum value it can take. It also suggests a more compact rendering in ordinary language, namely: "One at least of the decompositions of the kth correspondence from the vocabulary list represents a correct reconstruction." A similar shorthand device can be used for conjuncts; rewrite (2) in the form

$$(4) \qquad \prod_k (\sum_i p_i^{(k)})$$

Here, k is caused to range over all possible values, and for each of these values, i takes on all possible values. A suitable English translation is the following: "For each initial correspondence, there is at least one decomposition which represents its correct reconstruction."

We must now consider in more detail the conditions under which a proposition of the form $p_i^{(k)}$ will be true. The decomposition $c_i^{(k)}$ associated with this proposition is made up of a number, say s, of correspondences. These we write as follows:

$$c_{i,1}^{(k)}, c_{i,2}^{(k)}, c_{i,3}^{(k)} ... c_{i,s}^{(k)}$$

With these we also associate propositions

$$p_{i,1}^{(k)}, p_{i,2}^{(k)}, p_{i,3}^{(k)} ... p_{i,s}^{(k)}$$

A proposition $p_{i,j}^{(k)}$ is true whenever the associated correspondence represents a phoneme in the language being reconstructed. Now, the decomposition $c_i^{(k)}$ represents a correct reconstruction if and only if all correspondences which make it up represent phonemes in the ancestral language. In other words, $p_i^{(k)}$ is true just in case all the propositions $p_{i,j}^{(k)}$ are true. We can therefore write

$$p_i^{(k)} \iff p_{i,1}^{(k)}, p_{i,2}^{(k)}, p_{i,3}^{(k)} ... p_{i,s}^{(k)}$$

or, more concisely,

(5) $$p_i^{(k)} \iff \prod_j p_{i,j}^{(k)})$$

Translating into ordinary language, we have: "A given decomposition represents a correct reconstruction if and only if each of its correspondences represents a phoneme of the proto-language."

By virtue of (5), we can write $\prod_j p_{i,j}^{(k)}$ in place of $p_i^{(k)}$ in any proposition and obtain a new proposition with the same truth value. Accordingly, we can rewrite (4) as

(6) $$\prod_k (\sum (\prod_j p_{i,j}^{(k)}))$$

In English: "There is at least one decomposition of every correspondence on the vocabulary list in which every correspondence represents a phoneme of the language being reconstructed."

We now have a proposition (6) expressed entirely in terms of elementary propositions about the correspondences into which the pairs of items on the vocabulary list can be decomposed. This proposition is true if a set of reconstructions can be made. Furthermore, if a set of reconstructions can be made, then for each correspondence that represents a reconstructed phoneme, exactly one elementary proposition is true; the remainder are false. In other words, there is a conjunct of elementary propositions representing reconstructed phonemes which is true and which entails the proposition (6). Our problem therefore reduces to that of discovering the smallest set of propositions of the form $p_{i,j}^{(k)}$ whose conjunction entails (6).

It is a theorem of propositional logic that any truth-functional expression can be reduced to disjunctive form, that is, to a form in which all the conjuncts of elementary propositions which contain no unnecessary members and which entail the whole expression are spelled out. Given this expression, we have only to select the shortest term to obtain the solution of the problem. Fortunately, it is an entirely straightforward matter, at least in principle, to convert the expression to disjunctive form, and the necessary steps may be found in any introductory textbook on formal logic. Their discussion would be out of place in this essay.

4.3   The Theory and the Practice

As the careful reader will have noticed, we have been guilty of some sharp practice in one respect. We have interpreted the correspondences which make up decompositions now as potential proto-phonemes, now as rules of derivation. However, nothing is lost, for each rule is associated with only one proto-phoneme and we have nowhere assumed that we were finding phonemes of the proto-language, but only correspondences which are the reflexes of these phonemes. Starting from a pair of parallel vocabulary lists, we have provided an algorithm for arriving at the point from which Hoenigswald begins. The list of correspondences which he takes as initial data may be regarded as a set of rules of derivation. The problem he sets himself is to decide which rules apply to the same phoneme, and what name that phoneme should have. As he suggests, this can be done by phonemicizing. The problem here is the same as the problem posed for the comparative method as a whole: the terminology suggests to the initiated, no less than to the laity, that what is afoot is the application of an entirely specified theory with well-defined criteria of success and failure. This is not the case. Therefore, before the next stage in the comparative method can be undertaken, a rigorous treatment of phonemics is required. This is beyond the scope of the present paper.

In criticizing Hoenigswald, we took the view that the principal step in the comparative method could not assume a solution to the problem of determining cognates. It is incumbent upon us therefore to show how a pair of forms can be pronounced non-cognate within the proposed theory. A pair of forms is non-cognate if the rules needed to derive it from a form in the proto-language are not applicable elsewhere. Now, consider a pair which decomposes into at least two correspondences, neither of which is of use in deriving other forms. Clearly these two correspondences cannot figure in the solution with the smallest number of rules, for they may be replaced by the decomposition consisting of a single correspondence to give a shorter solution. Therefore, a word is pronounced unrelated to its fellow in the other language if the original correspondence involving the two words appears undecomposed in the final solution.

It frequently occurs that an ancient phoneme is without issue in some of the daughter languages. Other languages in the family show consistent correspondences which bear witness to its existence. The theory, as it stands, could not be expected to give a satisfactory account of this situation. The theoretical solution to the problem is fairly straightforward, although it results in a possibly unacceptable increase in the amount of computation required to implement the theory. Before the decompositions are made, a "zero" phoneme is introduced at the beginning and end of each word and between each pair of phonemes. The shortest solution should then be one in which "zero" was set in correspondence with "zero", but also with other phonemes where an ancient symbol had no reflex in one of the languages.

The situation in which an old symbol disappears in a modern language is indistinguishable, from the point of view of this theory, from that in which a symbol has been introduced into a modern language. Wherever it can be said that a modern language has no reflex of a phoneme of the ancestral language, it can equally well be said that there was no such phoneme and that what appear to be its reflexes in other languages are the results of spontaneous generation. Therefore, if a correspondence of the form A/0 (or 0/A) appears in a solution obtained according to our theory, and '0' is the 'zero' element, we have the choice of reconstructing a zero or a non-zero phoneme in the ancient language.

A similar situation arises when forms in a language with prefixes or suffixes are compared with forms from which these have been lost (cf. O.N. 'kaldr', Got. 'kalds' and O.E. 'ceald'). This can, of course, be dealt with by adding a 'zero' element to the beginning and end of every form. However, there is much to be said for distinguishing these from the 'zero's introduced above. If this is done, affixes will not only be accounted for, but will appear in solutions *as affixes*.

In its present form, the theory takes no account of metathesis. In the terms we have been using, metathesis is said to have occurred when the reconstruction can only be obtained by permuting the symbols of one of the forms in some specified way before making the decompositions. In principle, therefore, metathesis might be coped with by starting not from a simple list of pairs of forms, but from a list in which the forms of one language were paired with all permutations of their equivalents in the other.

It is clear that, by suitably adjusting one or two key definitions, the theoretical framework can be made as general as we wish. The constant feature is the underlying hypothesis that of all the possible reconstruction schemes open, the correct one is that which has the least number of rules of derivation.

It can be reasonably objected that even the simple definitions proposed above are unnecessarily general. Realism requires that the strings which are identified as descendants of phonemes be short – two or three symbols at most. It would be sufficient, therefore, to consider only those decompositions which are made up of short correspondences. An exception would have to be made for the decomposition which consists only of the original correspondence, for only if this is included can sets be identified as non-cognate. The computer program that has been written for the preliminary testing of this theory in fact makes decompositions into correspondences of strings of only two symbols or less. It would be improper, however, to regard this as a change in the basic theoretical structure, for it is simply a concession to expedience. From the theoretical point of view, there is no reason to set one limit on the length of correspondences rather than another; we therefore set none.

4.4   Implementing the Theory

The following list of four words from English and German is as small a set of data as the method can be applied to and produce nontrivial results:

English	German
on	an
nut	Nuß
that	daß
bath	Bad

The reader who is unfamiliar with the propositional calculus or its derivatives may be surprised to learn that it would be altogether out of the question to apply the method even to so small a corpus as this without machine aid. The process of reducing a truth-functional expression to disjunctive form is conceptually trivial, but the amount of computation involved rapidly becomes prohibitive as the number of variables increases. The belligerently incredulous are urged to try the example for themselves.

The possibility of applying the method mechanically is open, but barely so. The author estimates that it would take some four or five hours of computer time to analyze a list of a hundred pairs of forms. Where the connection between a pair of languages is remote, this may well be worthwhile, for the amount of human labor that is put into such problems is often prodigious, and it is inefficiently spread over a long period. Furthermore, as we have pointed out, the failure of present methods to produce a satisfactory result does not demonstrate that one can not in principle be found.

There would certainly be much to be gained by adding certain simple heuristics to the basic method. The word *heuristic* is used in contradistinction to *algorithm* to refer to a procedure which does not guarantee to produce the required results, but produces results which have a high probability of being correct. For example, the more decompositions that a correspondence occurs in, the higher the probability that a correspondence represents a proto-phoneme. Therefore, it is a sound heuristic to use a strategy which finds solutions involving high-frequency correspondences early and which does not continue to find all possible solutions. A statistical analysis would show at what point it would be prudent to discontinue the process.

The strategy used in the computer program finds solutions at approximately evenly spaced time intervals. Furthermore, the time required to find a solution is not the critical quantity, but rather the total number of solutions that can be found in a given set of data. This strategy is therefore ideally suited to refinement by heuristic techniques.

Acknowledgements
This research is sponsored by the United States Air Force under Project RAND – Contract No. AF 49 (638)-700 monitored by the Directorate of Development Plans, Deputy Chief of Staff, Research and Development, Hq USAF. Views or conclusions contained in this Memorandum should not be interpreted as representing the official opinion or policy of the United States Air Force.

Publications referenced
Hoenigswald 1950.

5

Natural Language in Computer Form

WITH THEODORE ZIEHE

Preface

The shortage of text on magnetic tape, for both research on language and for operation of information-retrieval systems, has caused great difficulty in the past. But now, as a by-product of a pilot machine-translation project, the Air Force is producing a large amount of text, and print readers and automatic type-setting systems are almost ready to furnish more text than current facilities can accommodate.

Text on tape is an unstandardized commodity. Many schemes have been suggested for encoding and formatting information about source, type style, and other important features of text. As part of its continuing work in linguistics, The RAND Corporation – in collaboration with groups at the University of California, Berkeley, and the Faculté des Sciences, Grenoble – has developed a scheme that goes somewhat further in scope and flexibility than its predecessors. Several large collections of text are being put into the format described here. The computer programs being written at RAND to manipulate the format are available to others who may wish to avoid duplicating all or part of the work preliminary to linguistic research, literary scholarship, or information retrieval when computer support is required.

This Memorandum is intended for prospective users of the scheme and for designers of language processing systems. It assumes little or no previous knowledge of computation or linguistics, and omits many details of programs – some of which remain to be worked out.

Summary

This Memorandum describes a scheme for recording text in computer-usable form in such a way that all meaningful typographical distinctions are represented in a standard way. Provision is made for texts in different languages and different alphabets and for subsidiary material such as parallel translations and comments of interest to users and librarians. The basic set of encoding conventions is indefinitely extensible to accommodate new kinds of material.

Very large bodies of data require special facilities, and these have been provided by embedding the text encoding scheme in a general file maintenance system. This provides for a comprehensive set of labels for different-sized units of text and makes it easy to retrieve any given unit. It also provides means of correcting and revising material in the file.

It is expected that files of computer-usable text will be built up in a variety of ways and, in particular, that the keypunching of text for this express purpose will become steadily less important. Computer programs are described which simplify conversion of text from these various sources into the standard format. The final section discusses the problem of printing text which has been recorded in the standard format and describes a flexible program for doing this.

Introduction

The use of computers in linguistic and literary study is rapidly becoming more widespread and the natural aversion of humanists in general to mechanical methods is decreasing as the proper place of machines in their pursuits becomes clearer. The amount of material that the student of language or literature must consider in the course of a single study is typically large and usually must be worked over many times.

The fortunate scholar can delegate much of this drudgery to students and research assistants; the yet more fortunate can hand it over to a machine. A linguist needing examples for a grammar, a lexicographer citations for a dictionary, a lawyer references for a brief, a preacher quotations for a sermon, can find them in concordances and indexes prepared by machine or may have them expressly sought by a computer. Words and phrases, rhymes and assonances, dactyls and spondees, aorists and pluperfects, can be docketed, counted, and compared, with never a comma missed. One manuscript can be compared with another and the differences classified; the works of several authors can be surveyed and evidence for the attribution of disputed works collected; bibliographies can be created, maintained and searched; sentences can be generated and parsed; all this and more can be done by machine if programs are available and if the texts are in a form that the machine can read. But there's the rub.

Programming is long and exacting work requiring much skill and experience. This is particularly true of the programming of non-numerical tasks, for programmers are rarely well trained in the appropriate techniques and the many aids and devices which are taken for granted in more traditional numerical computation are largely absent here. However, this situation is improving rapidly as a result of new programming languages and techniques that are being developed. Powerful and flexible programs for carrying out the kinds of operation needed by linguists and literary scholars will shortly be available in the libraries of major computing centers, just as those required by statisticians and physicists are now. A scientist is rightly dissatisfied if he must devote a significant proportion of his time to preparing computer programs. A humanist should be all the more so, since programming is clearly and properly alien to his background.

Collections of powerful linguistic programs are indeed necessary, but they can be of real value only if a satisfactory solution can be found to the problem of obtaining texts in a form the machine can read. This problem is in many ways more vexing than that of programming and is the subject of this manual. Hitherto, it has always been necessary to type out any text to be processed by a computer on a special machine which produces a coded copy of it on punched cards or on paper tape. This is particularly burdensome since the gains in speed and accuracy which come with the use of computers can all too easily be offset if large bodies of text have to be typed out by the researcher or an assistant, proofread, corrected, and modified.

There are several developments which may be expected to ease the heavy burden of typing and keypunching. The first machines capable of reading an ordinary printed page quickly and accurately are now available. There is great demand for them and they will rapidly become better, cheaper, and more widely used. Also, it is becoming clear that the business of producing books and periodicals will benefit greatly from mechanization. Some publishers are already preparing texts in machine form as the first step in their production process. Corrections, line adjustment, pagination, and the final typesetting are then carried out mechanically. The tapes or cards used in the final step of this process can be appropriated by research workers as input to computers.

As text coded on tapes and cards becomes more plentiful, libraries of such materials will doubtless be established, as they have been for microfilm, phonograph records, and the like. Each year, the chance will be greater that the text required by a particular scholar will already have been put into machine form.

This brings us face to face with the central concern of this manual – the question of standards for natural-language text in machine-readable form. As we have seen, computers can be expected to become part of the everyday equipment of linguists and literary scholars only if there is widespread cooperation among all concerned. Mechanical data processing can serve linguistic and literary studies as it ought only if programs and machine-readable text become as public as books, phonograph records, and films. However, to make a commodity public, it is not always sufficient to put it on the open market. A phonograph record which had to be played at 54 r.p.m. would not be really public; neither would an otherwise perfectly normal English newspaper if the letters on each line were arranged from right to left instead of from left to right. It is therefore important that there be general agreement upon the form in which information is to be published.

Standard forms are already fairly well established for the grosser aspects of machine-readable material. The size and shape of punched cards are standard, and most manufacturers of computers, at least in the United States, use the same size of magnetic tape and the same kind of associated recording equipment. Most punched paper tape conforms to one of four standards, of which one is slowly gaining the ascendancy. Machines are, however, available which can be used to read paper tape of all four kinds.

On the other hand, there are not yet any standards for transcribing texts in ordinary language onto any of these media. How shall chapters, sections, and paragraphs be set off from one another? How are titles, subtitles, captions, and footnotes to be represented? What is to be done with scientific and mathematical formulae? How shall the distinctions among italics, boldface, and underlining be preserved? What of accented letters and unusual alphabets? These are, of course, questions which arise whenever we transcribe anything but the simplest kind of text on an ordinary typewriter, for an ordinary typewriter can make only a limited set of marks. But where the computer is concerned, we are denied the typist's ultimate resort of inserting exotic characters by hand. Furthermore, the conventions used for the computer must be carefully chosen and meticulously followed because the computer does not have the human facility for making inferences from context or for overlooking minor inconsistencies of convention. Good conventions are difficult to establish, and this is, in itself, good reason for having a standard, well designed set which all may use.

But how can standard conventions for recording text be established when the physical form of the media used varies from place to place and from time to time? Some people use cards and some paper tape; some feed cards or tape directly into the computer whenever they wish to process it, whereas most first transfer material to magnetic tape or disk, which can be processed more rapidly by a large computer and is more easily stored. A limited amount of information can be punched on a single card, whereas there is much greater freedom with tape. This disparity is indeed troublesome, but less so than at first appears. If large libraries of machine-readable text are to be built up, the principal storage medium used must clearly be cheap, flexible, widely used, durable, compact, and of essentially unlimited capacity. Among the media available at present, magnetic tape best meets these criteria. Furthermore, as we shall see, the fact that text must be recorded on cards or paper tape before transfer to magnetic tape is an advantage rather than a drawback of this medium.

Consider the case of a man who is working on the New Testament and wishes to use a computer to perform certain operations on the Greek text. A general set of text-encoding conventions must clearly provide for texts which use the Greek alphabet, even though machines which have these symbols on their keyboards are rare. Normally, a transliteration scheme must be used at the keyboard and a computer program used to convert this into the standard format. The person who does the typing or keypunching can choose the transliteration which he finds easiest to use, and he need not concern himself with inserting marks to warn the machine that certain characters are to be interpreted in special ways. In any case, a program must be used to transfer the text from the medium on which it is originally punched onto magnetic tape, and this program can be made to do all the necessary conversions. The program can be provided with a table telling it that the text is in Greek and giving the transliteration scheme; it must also be told how chapter and verse divisions are being marked and various other clerical details of this kind. The important point is that the standard format need not be an additional burden to the typist or keypuncher. On the other hand, the designer of the standard format need not be constrained by a concern for the typist. A truly general set of coding conventions is unlikely to be easy to read and write, and it is therefore well that it should never need to be handled in its full complexity by anything but a computer program.

Printing text is, in many ways, similar to typing it. When a computer prints a text, or the results of some operations on a text, it must not be required to follow a single invariable set of rules. Here again, a program intervenes to prepare results in the form most suited to the user's needs, using his own conventions, transliterations, and page layout. Magnetic tape is just sufficiently remote from the everyday concerns of the user to provide him with the generality and flexibility he needs without troubling him with all the details. These details are, of course, given in full in this manual, but the reader should bear in mind that they need concern him only in the initial phases of a project. Once he has decided which of the facilities provided in the system he needs and has set up the necessary input and printing programs, he is free to work in his own way. In Sec. 4 and 5 we give examples of the kinds of typing and printing conventions that can be used and explain in greater detail how conversions are made between these and the standard form.

If a library of machine-readable text were set up for the benefit of a number of users or if one person had a particularly large amount of information to process, then the question of how to keep track of it all would soon arise. It would be necessary to divide the lines of text into units analogous to chapters, books, and collections of related books. Each of these divisions would have to be appropriately labeled so that it could be referred to easily and found when required; so that material could be changed, corrected, or modified; and so that other material could be put in the file before or after it. With such a system would come the need to store a new kind of information which would not be true text but rather information about the text – names of sections, acquisition dates, names of people who have modified or corrected a certain piece of text, indexing information, and so forth. All these things are provided for in the scheme described in this manual, in the form of a simple but powerful set of overall conventions called the *catalog format* ; this is described in Sec. 3.

The reader who is not familiar with computers or programming will find that parts of this manual will not be clear to him on first reading. These parts concern material with which the linguist or literary scholar will need to concern himself only if he intends to become his own programmer – a course which we cannot recommend. This is a manual rather than a textbook and therefore contains much information for reference only. A programmer who sets to work to write basic reading and writing programs, updating and maintenance systems for libraries of text in the format proposed will, of course, have to work back and forth through these details time and time again. Much of this basic programming work has been done for a few computers,[1] and the programs are generally available.

5.1 Codes

A printed page contains letters of whatever sizes, colors, and shapes the typographer's art puts at the service of author, designer, and editor. A magnetic tape – as furnished, for example, by IBM – contains nothing but a very long sequence of binary digits (bits), ones and zeros, blocked in units of 6. The purpose of the somewhat complex codes described in the present section is to simplify the representation of textual matter in binary form. One should not attempt to keep in mind at every moment the configuration of 1's and 0's that represent, say, a Greek alpha or a mathematician's integral sign. Nor would it be convenient to specify a 10-, 11-, or 12-bit pattern for each of the thousand or more characters that must somehow be represented.

5.1.1 Hollerith Characters

If we use six bits as the basic unit, there will be exactly 64 distinguishable patterns, and one of 64 *characters* can be recorded in each unit. Since it is inconvenient to write out 6-bit patterns in discussing machine operation, the customary scheme is to use *octal* digits to stand for 3-bit patterns. Table 1 shows the correspondence. Thus, the name of "000000" is "00" the name of "000001" is "01" and so on. The name of "111111" is

---

[1] IBM 7040, 7044, and 7090.

"77". A reader who is not familiar with binary and octal numbers can best regard the 64 names assigned in this way as perfectly arbitrary.

TABLE 1 Binary patterns and octal digits

Binary	Octal	Binary	Octal
000	0	100	4
001	1	101	5
010	2	110	6
011	3	111	7

The 64 characters can be copied from magnetic tape into the storage device of an electronic computer, and copied from storage onto tape. Only 48 of them can normally be printed on paper for a human reader; for many years, printers controlled by punched cards were designed to print 48 different marks, and the tradition has continued. The 48 standard marks include the letters of the Roman alphabet, the ten decimal digits, a few marks of punctuation, arithmetic signs, and a blank. The other 16 characters that can be recorded on magnetic tape but are not normally printed are designated here by their numbers. Table 2 associates the binary patterns, the octal equivalents, and the 48 "Hollerith" characters that we have been discussing.

TABLE 2 Binary patterns and octal digits

B	O	H	B	O	H	B	O	H	B	O	H
000 000	00	0	010 000	20	+	100 000	40	-	110 000	60*	
000 001	01	1	010 001	21	A	100 001	41	J	110 001	61	/
000 010	02	2	010 010	22	B	100 010	42	K	110 010	62	S
000 011	03	3	010 011	23	C	100 011	43	L	110 011	63	T
000 100	04	4	010 100	24	D	100 100	44	M	110 100	64	U
000 101	05	5	010 101	25	E	100 101	45	N	110 101	65	V
000 110	06	6	010 110	26	F	100 110	46	O	110 110	66	W
000 111	07	7	010 111	27	G	100 111	47	P	110 111	67	X
001 000	10	8	011 000	30	H	101 000	50	Q	111 000	70	Y
001 001	11	9	011 001	31	I	101 001	51	R	111 001	71	Z
001 010	12		011 010	32		101 010	52		111 010	72	
001 011	13	=	011 011	33	.	101 011	53	$	111 011	73	,
001 100	14	'	011 100	34	)	101 100	54	*	111 100	74	(
001 101	15		011 101	35		101 101	55		111 101	75	
001 110	16		011 110	36		101 110	56		111 110	76	
001 111	17		011 111	37		101 111	57		111 111	77	

*Octal 60 corresponds to the Hollerith blank.

Tradition is strong, but modern necessities are stronger. The 48 Hollerith characters are no longer the only ones that can be printed. Other sets of 48, sets of 120, and even sets of 240 are now obtainable. In fact, direct output to machines with all the flexibility of Linotype or Monotype machines is possible. This very powerful printing capability provides added incentive to develop a flexible encoding scheme. We return to questions of output below.

Since the design of most computing machines compels us to work with 64 primitive characters, we have two feasible alternatives for the recording of ordinary texts in which a much larger character set is used. We may represent each distinct printer's mark with a sequence of two or more recordable characters or we may adopt the functional equivalent of the case shift on a typewriter. When the shift lock on the typewriter is depressed, the effect of striking a key is altered. Each key is associated with two marks; one mark is obtained when the machine is in its lower-case shift, the other when it is in upper case. The number of shifts can be increased beyond two, and their use can be extended, for example, to the differentiation of Greek and Roman letters.

5.1.2 The Roman Alphabet

The 64 recordable characters are distributed, by standard machines, into a set of 48 that can be printed and a set of 16 that cannot. We take 15 of the nonprintable characters as *alphabet flags* . The flag for the Roman alphabet is (octal) 35 = (binary) 011101. After an occurrence of this flag, all following characters on a tape are taken to represent letters of the Roman alphabet until another alphabet flag occurs to signal a shift into a different alphabet.

The Roman alphabet is intended for use in transcribing English text, as well as French, German, Portuguese, Rumanian, and others. The 26 letters of the English alphabet are therefore supplemented by ten diacritics. Most punctuation is excluded from the Roman alphabet, to be kept in another (a "punctuation" alphabet) , but one mark, the apostrophe, has been retained.

Five characters are used to identify special fonts of type. These identifiers can also be thought of as shift indicators. They can be used singly or in combination to modify the characters in the current alphabet. The absence of any font identifier is understood to mean lower case, standard font. An identifier is reserved for upper case, another for italics or script, a third for bold face, one for larger type than ordinary, and one for smaller type. Strung together, they can identify words or phrases in several font combinations; e.g., bold-face italics, all caps small size, large-size italics. Three characters are used to identify sequences of marks that are printed as superscripts or subscripts with respect to the ordinary line or with letter spacing in the European manner. Still another character is used to identify the end of any one or combination of the shifts described here.

To complete the set of 48 recordable characters, the Roman alphabet includes a space and an unassigned character.

As examples of use of shift indicators within the Roman alphabet, consider the following encoding; the first line is from source text, the second is Hollerith representation of the characters on magnetic tape:

> We seek the coöperation of all men of good will.
> `1W9E SEEK THE CO=OPERATION OF ALL MEN OF GOOD WILL`
> C'était à l'époque de NAPOLÉON que le héro est né.
> `IC9'(ETAIT )A L'(EPOQUE DE 1NAPOL(EON9 QUE LE H(ERO EST N(E`
> Smith[a] and Jones[b] have disagreed violently.
> `1S9MITH6A9 AND 1J9ONES6B9 HAVE 2DISAGREED9 VIOLENTLY`

In these examples, terminal periods have been omitted from the Hollerith representations. Punctuation belongs in another alphabet and would require flags, use of which is demonstrated in Sec. 2.4. Table 3 recapitulates the coding of the Roman alphabet.

TABLE 3 Code: Roman Alphabet

Letters									Diacritics			Shifts		
T	O	H	T	O	H	T	O	H	T	O	H	T	O	H
A	21	A	J	41	J	S	62	S	ó	74	(	Upper case	01	1
B	22	B	K	42	K	T	63	T	ò	34	)	Italics or script	02	2
C	23	C	L	43	L	U	64	U	ö	13	=	Bold face	03	3
D	24	D	M	44	M	V	65	V	ǫ	73	,	Larger size	04	4
E	25	E	N	45	N	W	66	W	ô	20	+	Smaller size	05	5
F	26	F	O	46	O	X	67	X	õ	53	$	Superscript	06	6
G	27	G	P	47	P	Y	70	Y	ŏ	54	*	Subscript	07	7
H	30	H	Q	50	Q	Z	71	Z	å	33	.	Letter spacing	10	8
I	31	I	R	51	R	'	14	'	ō	40	-	Shift terminator	11	9
									ø	61	/	Blank	60	

NOTE: Column headings: T = text, O = octal, H = Hollerith. In German text, ß is encoded as 73-62, i.e., S with cedilla. In the presentation of diacritics in this table, the letter o is used only to provide a base; the diacritic is encoded independently of the letter it accompanies, as on a typewriter with dead keys.

5.1.3   The Cyrillic Alphabet

The Cyrillic alphabet, used for transcription of Russian text, includes 32 letters. Since no diacritics are needed, there is no difficulty about fitting this alphabet into a set of 48 recordable characters. In addition to the Cyrillic letters, there are represented an apostrophe, a blank, the shift indicators used in the Roman alphabet, and the terminator needed to identify the end of any shift or combination of shifts. Five characters are left unassigned. The code is given in Table 4.

TABLE 4 Code: Cyrillic Alphabet

T	O	H	X	T	O	H	X	T	O	H	X	T	O	H	X
А	14	'	A	И	31	I	J	Т	50	Q	T	Ы	67	X	Y
Б	21	A	B	К	34	)	K	У	51	R	U	Ь	70	Y	'
В	22	B	V	Л	41	J	L	Ф	53	$	F	Э	71	Z	,
Г	23	C	G	М	42	K	M	Ш	54	*	X	Ю	73	,	(
Д	24	D	D	Н	43	L	N	Ц	62	S	C	Я	74	(	=
Е	25	E	E	О	44	M	O	Х	63	T	H	'	13	=	)
Ж	26	F	*	П	45	N	P	Щ	64	U	W				

NOTE: Column headings: T = text, O = octal, H = Hollerith, X = transliteration. Shifts and blank are treated as in the Roman alphabet (see Table 3). No Cyrillic diacritics are provided.

In the following example, the first line is from source text, the second is Hollerith representation of the characters on magnetic tape, and the third is Hollerith-character transliteration of the tape records. Again, alphabet flags are not shown.

ПУХОК ПРОТОНОВ ИЕ́ ЕЛЕКРОСТАТИХЕСКОГО ГЕНЕРАТОРА
1N9RTM) NOMQMLMB HG ZJE)QOMPQ'QHTEP)MCM CELEO'QMO'
1P9UHOK PROTONOV IZ ,LEKTROSTATIHESKOGO GENERATORA

5.1.4 Three Special Alphabets

The Greek alphabet has been coded primarily to permit transcription of mathematical texts and others in which Greek letters are used to denote special concepts. Thus, although an alphabet flag has been assigned and Hollerith characters specified for recording the Greek letters on tape, the characters printed are not uniformly satisfactory as a translation. See Table 5 for this code.

TABLE 5 Code: Greek Alphabet

Letters												Diacritics			
T	O	H	X	T	O	H	X	T	O	H	X	T	O	H	X
A	21	A	A	I	31	I	I	P	50	Q	R	ó	74	(	(
B	22	B	B	K	41	J	K	Σ	51	R	S	ò	34	)	)
Γ	23	C	G	Λ	42	K	L	T	62	S	T	ỏ	14	'	'
Δ	24	D	D	M	43	L	M	Υ	63	T	U	ọ	53	$	H
E	25	E	E	N	44	M	N	Φ	64	U	F	ô	20	+	+
Z	26	F	Z	Ξ	45	N	C	X	65	V	X	ö	13	=	=
H	27	G	Y	O	46	O	O	Ψ	66	W	Q				
Θ	30	H	V	Π	47	P	P	Ω	67	X	W				

NOTE: Column headings: T = text, O = octal, H = Hollerith, X = transliteration. Shifts and blanks are treated as in the Roman alphabet (see Table 3).

The variety of special marks used in commercial and scientific text is so large that it is necessary to define a full set of Hollerith characters for them. The arabic numerals, signs for dollars and cents, arithmetic symbols, and so on, have been given code characters (see Table 6), with 17 more characters available.

TABLE 6 Code: Symbols

Numerals			Arithmetic Symbols			Shifts		
T	O	H	T	O	H	T	O	H
0	00	0	$	53	$	Italic or script	62	S
1	01	1	*	54	*	Bold face	63	T
2	02	2	¢	23	C	Larger size	64	U
3	03	3	&	21	A	Smaller size	65	V
4	04	4	=	13	=	Superscript	66	W
5	05	5	+	20	+	Subscript	67	X
6	06	6	-	40	-	Character spacing	70	Y
7	07	7	x	44	M	Shift terminator	71	Z
8	10	8	÷	24	D			
9	11	9	.	33	.			
			,	73	,			
			%	47	P			
			Space	60				

NOTE: Column headings: T = text, O = octal, H = Hollerith. The period and comma in this alphabet are used as a decimal point and a digit position marker respectively and not as ordinary punctuation.

The following example illustrates the use of the symbol alphabet. Alphabet flags are shown as underlined octal integers.

They paid $17,000 for them, 85% of $20 thousand.

<u>35</u>1T9HEY PAID <u>55</u>$17,000 <u>35</u>FOR THEM<u>15</u>, <u>55</u>85% <u>35</u>OF <u>55</u>$20 <u>35</u>THOUSAND<u>15</u>.

Here the underscored numbers are alphabet flags: 35 for Roman; 55 for symbols; 15 for punctuation.

Some builders of text files will use the Greek and symbol alphabets to transcribe precisely the symbolic material in their sources. Others will prefer to shorten their labors by using cover symbols to replace complex expressions. They may feel, nevertheless, that it is important to differentiate classes of complex expressions according to their ranges of syntactic functions. In transcribing Russian text at RAND, we adopted this procedure and defined an alphabet of cover symbols. Table 7 describes this alphabet, and an editor's manual (Edmundson 1961) describes use of it. Others who use cover symbols will presumably need to establish categories appropriate to their own purposes.

5.1.5 Punctuation and Boundaries

An alphabet of punctuation marks is included in the present system to allow unambiguous representation on tape of the many marks that occur in text. Table 8 lists the marks for which characters have been assigned; 17 additional marks can be added to the alphabet at will.

TABLE 7 Code: Cover Symbols

Text	Octal	Hollerith
Fractions, dates, Roman numerals	05	5
Degrees	0501	51
Degrees of latitude or longitude	050101	511
Hours & minutes (when written with subscripts or superscripts)	050102	512
Percentages	0502	52
Numerals preceded by ordinal sign ("$N^{\underline{o}}$", "#" , etc.)	0503	53
Numerals followed by single letters	050301	531
Bibliography – reference numbers	0504	54
Cardinal numbers ending with "1" except "11"	0505	55
Cardinal numbers ending w/ "2" "3", "4", except "12", "13", "14"	0506	56
Cardinal numbers ending w/ "0" or "5" through "9", & "11" through "19"	0507	57
Ordinary technical expressions	06	6
Chemical expressions	0601	61
Table (when part of sentence)	0603	63
Reference asterisk	0604	64
Relational symbols used alone	0605	65
Ordinary relations	07	7
Chemical relations	0701	71
Ratios	0702	72
Half relations	0705	75
Chemical half relations	0706	76
Plural indicator	64	U
Space	60	

NOTE: These symbols were designed for recording articles from some Russian scientific journals. This accounts for the classification of numerals by last digit. A symbol code followed by the plural marker indicates a sequence of symbols of that type. This alphabet is indefinitely extensible as other applications arise.

TABLE 8 Code: Punctuation

	Text	Octal	Hollerith
(	Open parenthesis	74	(
)	Close parenthesis	34	)
"	Open quotation mark (double)	21	A
"	Close quotation mark (double)	22	B
'	Open quotation mark (single)	23	C
'	Close quotation mark (single)	24	D
[	Open brackets	25	E
]	Close brackets	26	F
⟨⟨	Open double angles	27	G
⟩⟩	Close double angles	30	H
.	Period	33	.
:	Colon	31	I
;	Semicolon	41	J
,	Comma	73	,
-	Hyphen	40	-
–	Dash	47	P
?	Question mark	42	K
¿	Open-question mark (Spanish)	43	L
!	Exclamation mark	44	M
¡	Open exclamation (Spanish)	45	N
...	Ellipsis	46	O
/	Slash	61	/
	Space	60	

NOTE: Shift codes are the same as in the Roman alphabet (see Table 3), except that no upper-case shift is provided.

Two linguistic boundaries are given special status for the benefit of editors who choose to mark sentences and paragraphs in their text files. These two boundaries are represented by two characters in a boundary alphabet (Table 9) which is otherwise free for uses yet to be defined.

TABLE 9 Code: Boundaries

Text	Octal	Hollerith
Beginning of paragraph	47	P
Beginning of sentence	62	S
Space	60	

5.1.6 Flags, Shifts, and Fillers

Some of the 64 characters that can be recorded on tape are used to represent printed marks; the others are either flags or shifts. The flag characters are not said to belong to any alphabet; the shift characters belong to every alphabet, although they have no obvious use in the alphabet of cover symbols. This difference reflects the fact that shifts are part of the linguistic description of a text, whereas flags are only a computational device.

Flags are defined because our tape machines record and recognize 6-bit patterns. Only flag characters have independent definitions; the meaning of a flag is always the same, regardless of context. Each flag signifies that the following nonflag, or *text*, characters are to be interpreted by reference to a certain alphabet. Table 10 shows the flag codes and the alphabets that they designate.

TABLE 10 Code: Alphabet Flags

Alphabet	Octal
Roman	35
Cyrillic	36
Greek	37
Symbols	55
Cover symbols	56
Punctuation	15
Boundaries	16
—	—
Filler	77

The shifts that we define are *graphemes* . It is true that their use could be avoided if we had a sufficiently large set of recordable characters, but using them has advantages beyond mere reduction of the size of the character set. For example, consultation of a dictionary is more convenient if the same word, printed in normal type in one place and in bold face elsewhere, is spelled with the same characters in both places. Isolation of a *bold face* grapheme gives us this advantage without losing the information about type style.

The shift graphemes could have been defined in several ways. Thus, the *range* of a shift could extend (i) over a single letter, (ii) over all letters up to the following blank, (iii) over all letters up to the next shift, or the next shift in a given class, (iv) over all letters up to a terminator specific to the given shift, or (v) over all letters up to a generalized terminator. In our choice of the fifth plan, three criteria of simplicity were relevant: size of alphabet, length of text, and complexity of rules. Plans (i) and (ii) would save one character, the terminator, but lengthen the text; and plan (ii) would not permit encoding of, for example, "unhappiness". Plan (iii) would require introduction of a *normal* shift, perhaps several, in place of the terminator. Plan (iv) would call for more terminators; it would tend to shorten text, as when a word is italicized within a bold-face line, but such occurrences are rare.

It is important to understand that shifts can be used in combination. For example, we have already noted that bold-face italic can be represented by two shift indicators preceding a string of characters, but it is also possible to use a string of identical shifts to represent an extreme degree of an attribute. Thus,

X6Y6Z

represents x^{y^z} , and

X6Y7Z

represents an occurrence of x with a superscript composed of y with subscripted z. Of course, if the occurrence of z were back on the principal line, the encoded representation would be

`X6Y9Z`

In similar fashion,

`LOOK`

encodes a word in normal-size type,

`4LOOK`

encodes a word in large type,

`44LOOK`

encodes a word in still larger type, and so on. Naturally, the editor of a text will not attempt to distinguish more sizes than are essential to retain the meaning.

Of the 64 characters recordable on tape, only one remains to be explained; it serves as a filler. The 6-bit patterns on magnetic tape are recorded and read in groups of 6. Naturally, it is not always possible to code a segment of text so that the number of significant characters is divisible by 6, nor would it be advisable to use blanks, which might have an unintended significance. Hence octal 77, with no Hollerith equivalent, is set aside to serve as a filler. To illustrate use of the filler: If a segment of text should require 63 characters for recording on tape, there would be 10 groups of 6 characters each, then one group of 3 characters plus 3 fillers.

5.2   Organized Files of Text

The user of a file of text on tape will sometimes take the largest available quantity and handle all of it uniformly, collecting, without regard to source, all the instances of a phenomenon that interests him. For other purposes, he will need to discriminate in some way; he may choose to examine only introductory paragraphs in scientific articles or only articles on a certain subject or only dialogue in plays and novels or only titles. To serve him well, text files must be organized and labeled. In Sec. 2 we described the tape representation of unorganized units of text, e.g., printed lines; here we go on to the representation of organizational features – conventions for assembly of many lines of text in a Chinese box arrangement that we call *catalog format* .

Instead of proposing special formats only for text, we apply conventions that are equally appropriate for dictionaries, grammars, and other sorts of material. We thus save the cost of writing many primitive computer programs to synthesize and analyze statements about form; independent of the substance of the catalog, such programs deal *only* with form. If it were necessary to write new programs for files of different materials, we would be tempted to simplify the organization of each file. Since the catalog formats can be used for every file, we feel free to elaborate the organization of each file as far as profitable.

5.2.1   Maps

A catalog is a collection of *data*. Each datum can be large or small, but the datum is the smallest manipulable unit for the programs that operate on catalogs as catalogs; the content of the data is the substance of the catalog. In a text file, most data contain representations of text in the code given in Sec. 2; these data are called *text entries* and each can usually be assumed to contain a line of text. The organization of the file is accomplished by data called *labels* , each marking a significant group of entries. These labels are nested at four levels: A collection of entries is called a *section* and labeled; a labeled collection of sections is a *division* ; a *corpus* label is applied to a collection of divisions; a *text file* is a sequence of corpora and has no label. Any entry or labeled group of entries can be annotated in *description* data.

The catalog-management system uses diagrams like the one in Fig. 1 to specify the form of a catalog. The diagram is a *tree* at its origin is the label for a corpus (CL = corpus label).

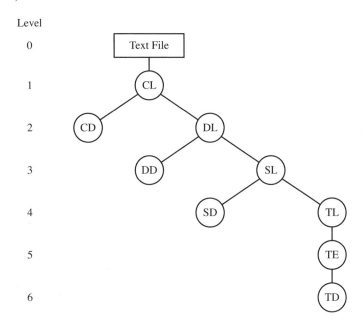

Level

FIGURE 1 Map of a text file in catalog format (see text for explanation of symbols)

Under this node, on the second level, are two *data-class names* , CD = corpus description and DL = division label. In these remarkable *maps* , a single data-class name stands for an unlimited number of data of the named class, just as if one airport on a map of the world could stand for all the world's airports. This simplification, which enables us to draw one map for all catalogs of text before even the first is constructed, is feasible because the catalog-management system imposes enough conventions to guarantee that every datum can be found when the map is followed.

To complete our inspection of Fig. 1, let us use the map as a guide to the preparation of a magnetic tape. We can record only one thing at a time as the tape unrolls; we use the map to decide what datum to take at each step. Starting at the top, we record a corpus label. Next we go to level 2 and begin at the left with a corpus description; if several data of this class are to be recorded, we take them one after another. When all description data for the corpus are on the tape, we move to the next node on the same level, which in this map is a division label. We record the first division label for the corpus; perhaps we intend to record several divisions, each with a label, but we must take everything in the first division, that is, data of all classes named under the DL node in the map, before recording a label for the second division. Thus the map requires that when we have recorded the first division label we move at once to level 3 and record division descriptions (DD). Since there are no nodes under DD, we take as many data of this class as we require and then proceed across level 3 to node SL. Recording the first section label, we move down to level 4 and record our first text label (TL), down to level 5 for a text entry (TE), and down to level 6 for a text description (TD).

Now we are at the bottom of the map. The next datum to be recorded is another text description for the same entry, if any; otherwise, another text entry with its text descriptions under the same text label; otherwise, the next text label within the section. When the last text label in a section has been recorded, followed by its text entries and their descriptions, another section label goes on the tape. What follows the second and each subsequent section label is just like the material following the first, with, of course, no restriction on the number of text labels in any section. When everything pertaining to the last section in a division has been recorded, a new division is begun with its label, description data, and so on. When everything pertaining to the last division is on the tape, a new corpus is begun. The end of the last corpus is the end of the catalog.

In Fig. 2 we present an expanded map with one node for each datum, and a diagram descriptive of material entered on a corresponding hypothetical tape. The figure is to be read like a diagram of syntactic dependencies; each node governs those on the level just below and connected to it, and each node is associated with a segment of the tape diagram by a dotted line.

The main outlines of the map for text files are obvious. A corpus is an enormous block of text; for example, all the Russian text prepared for machine processing at RAND is recorded as two corpora. A division in this corpus corresponds to an issue of a journal, to a book, or to some similar publication unit. Each section is an article or chapter. Descriptions are optional and contain whatever information a particular user feels to be necessary. The description of a corpus can tell in what language it is written, what center produced it, and any other information which would be useful at this size level. The description of a division can specify a scientific discipline, give bibliographic information, and the like. The description of a section can include, for example, the page numbers of the original publication. Text labels are used to differentiate titles, subtitles, authors, summaries, footnotes, body, and the like. They also identify page and line in a way that makes checking the source convenient. Text descriptions, on the other hand, are used for annotation of a freer kind. The map shows that several entry data can follow a text label; this device permits recording of inter-linear texts, in which the first entry under a label contains an original-language line, the second a translation, and so on. Since text descriptions are connected to text entries, not to text labels, the original-language line can be described in one datum, the translation in another.

The catalog-management system permits null data. Although the map shows a text-description datum under each text entry, this facility would not be equally convenient for all users of the format. It would be wasteful to require every user to insert descriptions, wanted or not, for the sake of those whose text must be described. A null datum occupies no space on tape; it need not be mentioned during preparation of a tape file, and it does not appear when the file is consulted. Thanks to this technique, programs

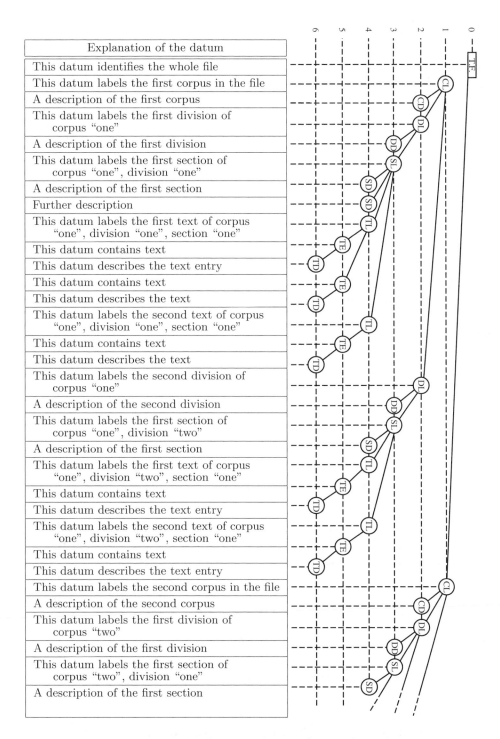

Explanation of the datum
This datum identifies the whole file
This datum labels the first corpus in the file
A description of the first corpus
This datum labels the first division of corpus "one"
A description of the first division
This datum labels the first section of corpus "one", division "one"
A description of the first section
Further description
This datum labels the first text of corpus "one", division "one", section "one"
This datum contains text
This datum describes the text entry
This datum contains text
This datum describes the text
This datum labels the second text of corpus "one", division "one", section "one"
This datum contains text
This datum describes the text
This datum labels the second division of corpus "one"
A description of the second division
This datum labels the first section of corpus "one", division "two"
A description of the first section
This datum labels the first text of corpus "one", division "two", section "one"
This datum contains text
This datum describes the text entry
This datum labels the second text of corpus "one", division "two", section "one"
This datum contains text
This datum describes the text entry
This datum labels the second corpus in the file
A description of the second corpus
This datum labels the first division of corpus "two"
A description of the first division
This datum labels the first section of corpus "two", division "one"
A description of the first section

FIGURE 2 The tree structure of a sample catalog

for manipulation of text need not be altered when descriptions are added or deleted; descriptions can be added to any file without alteration of the map (which is the same for every text file) or conversion of programs; and a library containing some text with descriptions and some without can be scanned from end to end without special attention to this variation.

Data of any class can be left null. For example, it would be possible to record data for several divisions within a single corpus without recording any division labels; the results might be bad, but the boundaries between divisions would be discernible nevertheless.

5.2.2   The Data of a Text File

Form and content are clearly distinguished by the catalog-management system. In Sec. 3.3 we describe the way the system uses data to control form; here we examine the several classes of data in which the substance and organization of a text file are recorded. They are the classes named in the map, Fig. 1.

Each *text entry* is a string of characters, encoded in accordance with the rules of Sec. 2. Since each entry is independent of all others, each must begin with a flag character.

Description data of all types are encoded as text; Sec. 2 applies to them also. It is thus possible to write descriptions with all the elegance of the printer's art, while at the same time a single complex of programs will suffice for the decoding of all data in a text file.

The labels are written with Hollerith characters in restricted formats. Let us take them class by class.

Corpus labels

Each datum in this class consists of 72 characters. The first 24 constitute a corpus name; the remainder are for notes. As many of these characters as desired can be left blank (not null!). If descriptions are for scholarly use, notes within labels are for use by programmers and librarians. Here the manager of a text file can indicate what corrections have been made to a corpus, what special procedures have been applied, and the like.

Division labels

The length of the datum is again 72 characters, but only two are allowed for the name of the division, all the rest being given over to notes. The purpose of the restriction on name length is to encourage a brevity that will be gratifying to all who must write division names repeatedly in instructions for correction, scanning, or analysis of text. The notes can be used for an expanded version of the name, or for librarians' records.

Section labels

The same format is used as for the division labels, and with the same argument.

Text labels

It is intended that a text label be written for each line of original printed text. Since a file will contain a great many text labels, the length of each is limited to six characters. The first character is a type symbol, the remainder an entry name. The type symbols, listed in Table 11, are redundant in a certain sense; they could presumably be reconstructed from the spaces and shift symbols contained within the entry. Since the program for the reconstruction job would be complex, and since users may often want to exclude titles, authors' names, etc., from a search, the redundant symbols have been inserted.

The entry name included in the text label is large in order to permit organization below the level of the section. For example, the five characters can be used for page number and line number, or for scene and line number, or in whatever manner is natural to the text being recorded.

TABLE 11 Text Type Symbols

T	-	Title	A	-	Author
S	-	Summary	E	-	Editor's Note
M	-	Major Section Heading	I	-	Intermediate Section Heading
N	-	Minor Section Heading	B	-	Body
F	-	Footnote	L	-	Bibliography ("Literature")
D	-	Stage Direction	P	-	Speaker (Drama)

5.2.3 Control of Form

The structure of every catalog is described within the catalog itself by means of control terms. We need only sketch these terms and their functions here, since the catalog-management system deserves separate treatment. Indeed, what we have to say about them is of interest mainly to programmers rather than to linguists or others who want to record text in the system. The programs described in Sec. 4 make use of control data in reading catalog tapes and construct them when data are recorded, but in many applications it will not be necessary to do more than take the programs as written and put them to work.

A catalog is recorded on one or more reels of magnetic tape. We estimate that a 2400-foot reel of tape recorded at IBM's highest density will store about 1.5 million running words of text without descriptions, but some large text files will require more than one reel. As we have said, information is recorded on tape as a sequence of 6-bit characters, and these characters are read and recorded six at a time. A *physical record* is a sequence of 36-bit spans preceded and followed by blank tape. Since the space left blank between physical records is long enough for the storage of nearly 600 characters, it is good economy to make records long. On the other hand, a complete physical record must be read or recorded without pause; hence programmers must always set aside enough space in machine memory to contain a record, and memory space is a precious commodity. Our compromise is to limit physical records to 2400 characters, including control data, but this figure is arbitrary and limits may be set to meet needs of users.

The first physical record of each catalog is a *control record* , and the last is an *end-of-file* mark. The end-of-file mark may be followed by another control word beginning a new catalog unrelated in any systematic way to the first. On the other hand, it may contain other information recorded in an altogether different format. The point is that the catalog structures are confined within the boundaries set by end-of-file marks.

Two control data are stored in the control record at the beginning of each tape. The first is a management datum, the second a map datum.

The management datum

This datum consists of exactly four 36-bit spans, used as follows:

1. Record size limit. The number of 36-bit spans ("words") allowed in one physical record on this tape, written as a binary number.
2. Date. The date of writing of the catalog, recorded in Hollerith, with two characters each for month, day, and year.
3. Reel number. The sequence number of the reel of tape within the text file, recorded as a binary number.
4. Repeated data. The number of content data repeated (from preceding reels) at the start of this one.

The fourth item is needed because a user may wish to use a single reel out of a multi-reel text file. When he does, he must identify the first new datum on the selected reel as standing at a certain node in the map of the catalog. To enable him to do so, the necessary data are repeated from reel to reel, but the number repeated is not constant. Item (4) shows where the new material on the reel begins.

The map datum

The symbols in the map of the catalog are listed here in a definite order. A symbol is recorded before those below it in the map, and those below it before those to the right. Thirty-six bits are used to describe each data-class:

1. Data-class name. Three Hollerith characters, or 18 bits.
2. Code. The set of rules to be used in encoding or decoding a datum of this class is identified by one Hollerith character. B = Binary, R = Regular (or RAND; the code of Sec. 2 above), or others to be defined.
3. Empty. Three bits not presently used.
4. Level. The level number of this data class in the map, recorded in binary. 9 bits.

Since the map is given at the beginning of each tape reel, it is possible to use any reel out of a file without special arrangements.

We now turn to the assembly of data into physical records. Each datum is required to fit the Procrustean bed of machine memory, with its 36-bit cells. We describe the control terms added to records as prefixes and suffixes; when they are taken into account, the physical record also fills a whole number of cells.

The *datum control prefix* occupies 54 bits, as follows:

1. Empty. The first 3 bits contain binary zeroes.
2. Datum length. The number of 36-bit cells filled by this datum is given as a 15-bit binary number.
3. Empty. The next 9 bits contain binary zeroes.
4. Data-class name. The class of this datum is identified by its line number in the map at the beginning of the tape reel, given as a 9-bit binary number.
5. Preceding implicit level (PIL). This is defined as follows: (i) The PIL of all data on level 1 is 0; (ii) The PIL of the *first* datum dominated by a null datum is the PIL of the dominating null datum; (iii) The PIL of every other datum is the level of the datum that dominates it. This is given as a 9-bit binary number.

6. Own level. The map level of this datum, given as a 9-bit binary number.

These control terms allow generalized catalog programs to find boundaries of all levels in a catalog tape, no matter how many data in whatever combinations are null. The length of the datum is used in determining where the next prefix begins.

The *datum control suffix* occupies 18 bits, as follows:

1. End of catalog. A single bit, 1 if this is the last datum in the catalog and zero otherwise.
2. End of tape. A single bit to mark the end of a reel.
3. End of physical record. A single bit.
4. Datum length. Same as item (2) of the datum control prefix.

The end markers have an obvious use in programs that read catalogs. The datum length is given in both prefix and suffix in order to facilitate reading from end of tape to beginning as well as in the normal direction.

The data, with their prefixes and suffixes, are put together, with a record control prefix and suffix to complete a physical record.

The *record control prefix* occupies 90 bits, as follows:

1. IOBS tag. Three bits, 101, to allow use of the IOBS level of the IBM Input-Output Control System.
2. Record length. The number of machine memory cells occupied by the record, less one, recorded as a 15-bit binary number.
3. IOBS tag. Three bits, 010.
4. Empty. Nine bits, all zeroes.
5. IOBS tag. The letter M, Hollerith, six bits.
6. FORTRAN tag. Three binary zeroes.
7. Record length. The number of machine memory cells occupied by the record, less two, recorded as a 15-bit binary number.
8. Empty. Seventeen binary zeroes followed by a binary 1.
9. Start of catalog. A single bit, 1 if this is the first physical record after the first control record of a catalog and zero otherwise.
10. Start of tape. A single bit to mark the start of a reel.
11. Start of physical record. Always a binary one.
12. Empty. Fifteen bits, all zeroes.

Items (1) through (5), occupying one memory cell, supply the IOBS program with information it requires. Items (6) through (8) do the same for the FORTRAN input program. Neither of these programs is used by the catalog-management system, but provision for their use is relatively inexpensive and possibly advantageous to some future user of the text. Items (9) through (11) serve as end marks for the catalog system when it reads tape from end to beginning. The record control suffix is eighteen bits, all zero.

Figure 3 shows how the data, with their prefixes and suffixes, fit together to form a physical record. In every record there are four 36-bit cells ahead of the first datum, two between every pair of adjacent data, and one at the end. This layout is followed for every record, including the control record at the beginning of a tape. Only the end-of-file mark is different.

5.3 Writing Text Catalogs

We have observed that the standard catalog format will rarely, if ever, be the first machine-readable form given to a text. Recording on magnetic tape will be from punched sources, usually cards or paper tape. It is therefore inevitable that at least part of any computer program used for putting text into the standard catalog format be written especially for the kind of punched source used. Scholars working with texts in different languages and for different purposes will require their own computer routines, though these need differ from the standard routines only in small details. Routines for converting teletypesetter tape and the tapes used in printing books will differ more markedly from standard. Very special routines are required to convert Monotype tape for use as computer input; there are almost as many conventions for recording text on Monotype tape as there are for all the other media together. In this section, we shall see how computer programs can be designed to convert punched text from a wide variety of sources into the catalog format, the necessary changes being confined to a very restricted part of the program.

A program to put punched text into catalog format must be able to do two things: It must be able to substitute for the character codes of the original machine-readable text the proper sequences of flags, shifts, and character codes in the standard catalog format; and it must be able to recognize the boundaries of entries, sections, divisions and corpora of text and to label them correctly.

An investigator who punches all of his own text on cards or tape can arrange to incorporate the labels he needs at the appropriate places in the text. But if the original coded material (e.g., teletypesetter tape) was not prepared with computer usage in mind, labels will have to be punched separately and merged with the text by the routine which sets up the catalog. The routine must therefore be able to accept input from at least two sources at once. If the new text is to be inserted into, or added at the end of, an existing catalog, then the existing catalog must be read by the routine, making a possible three inputs at the same time.

New text, existing catalogs, and labels constitute the three principal *input channels* of the program to be described. There are also two auxiliary input channels: one to provide a set of *pointers* which establish the relationship between new text entries arriving on one input channel and a set of catalog labels arriving on another; and the other to provide corpus, division, section, and text descriptions. We shall describe how these various input channels are used in the following pages.

The text writer program must be prepared to accept data in different formats from each of its different input channels. Existing catalogs will, of course, always be in the same format. Labels and pointers will be prepared by a given investigator and can readily be made to fit a standard format. Descriptions will usually also be prepared by the investigator and there should be a standard method of punching them. However, descriptions are so similar to ordinary text entries that text-entry flexibility probably should be extended to them. The text writing program has, therefore, a central con-

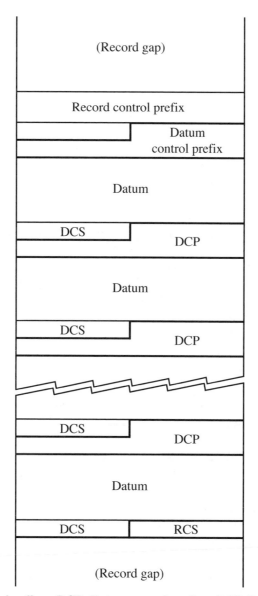

DCS: Datum control suffix   DCP: Datum control prefix   RCS: Record control suffix
Record gap: Blank space between consecutive physical records

FIGURE 3 Layout of a physical record on tape

trolling section which writes the catalog. Data are passed to this controlling section by four more or less standard peripheral sections which read and convert existing catalogs, labels, pointers, and descriptions, and a fifth peripheral section responsible for reading and converting new text. This last section of the program, called the *keypunched text reader* (KTR), is the only part which has to be changed to accommodate different kinds of text.

5.3.1 A KTR for Punched Cards

The simplest application of the text writer program is one in which a text, specially keypunched on cards or paper tape to be put into catalog format, is to be converted and put on magnetic tape. In such an application, the key-punching conventions can be designed to be as convenient as possible. All necessary labels and descriptions can be punched along with the main body of the text so that only one of the input channels of the text writer program will be required.

Let us assume that punched cards are to be used as the input medium. Punched cards have the property that each of the 60 columns represents one character; there are no back-space or underline codes which could result in the number of columns and character positions getting out of step. This makes it convenient to distinguish certain kinds of information by the positions on the card where they are punched. In this case, we shall set aside the first five columns of each card for a simple serial number so that, should the cards be dropped or mixed up in some other way, they can be reordered mechanically. Five columns suffice for 100,000 different numbers which is more than we are ever likely to need. However, if the cards are numbered in tens (00010, 00020, 00030 ...) it will always be possible to insert other cards in case some are accidentally omitted in the first punching or in case a correction results in two cards where there was originally one. The KTR section of the text writing program will check that these serial numbers appear in nondecreasing sequence. Since it will not check that the sequence is strictly ascending, the sure footed and those with small amounts of text to punch may leave these five columns blank. In any case, sequence numbers can be inserted automatically either before or after the other columns of the cards have been punched.

Column 6 of each card will be left blank for the moment except on the very last card of the deck which will be marked with an "E" for "end." This column may later be used for correcting and updating the text once it has been put on tape.

Column 7 will show the kind of information the card carries. Corpus, division, and section labels will be represented by the letters "U", "V", and "W", respectively; their descriptions will be represented by "X", "Y", and "Z". Since text labels are short and occur frequently, it would be inconvenient and wasteful of cards to punch each one on a separate card. We shall therefore arrange to punch text labels on the same cards as the entries themselves. However, there are instances where two or more text entries are covered by the same text label and we must be sure that the entries are properly distinguished on the cards. With this in mind, we shall put a "1" in column 7 for the first entry under a given label, a "2" for the second, a "3" for the third, and so on. If the KTR finds two cards with the same text label and the same number in column 7, it will assume that the second continues the entry begun in the first; if the labels are the same but the number in column 7 is one higher than on the previous card, it will assume that a new entry under the same label has begun. The ability to put more than one entry under the same label will normally be used only for interlinear text and therefore it will create no hardship to limit to nine the number of such entries in this format.

Each entry of text may be accompanied by a description. The description of the first text entry under a given text label will carry the code "A" in column 7, that of the second "B" and so on. In this particular input format, each text-description card is assumed to be a separate entry. With these conventions, there is nothing to prevent a description being provided for a text entry which does not exist. This is less eccentric than it sounds because, if we were to use the same card arrangement for making corrections to the file, it might be necessary to insert or change a description while leaving unaltered the entry described.

The remaining 73 columns will depend on the kind of information carried on the card. A corpus-label card, coded "U" in column 7, will have the 24-character corpus name in columns 8 through 31 and the corpus notes in columns 32 through 79. The first card (00010) shown in the example (Fig. 4) is a corpus-label card; the name of the corpus is "MOLIERE'S PLAYS" and the notes remind the user that this text was put on tape on 10/2/64 and that the tape was corrected on 10/17/64. Card 00020 in the example is a corpus-description card. A corpus-description card has an "X" in column 7, columns 8 through 13 are left blank, and the description itself begins in column 14 and may run to the end of the card; it is punched using the same character-encoding conventions as for the body of the text. Columns 8 through 13 are left blank in order to make description cards as nearly as possible like ordinary entry cards, which will have a label in this space.

A division name is composed of only two characters, and these are punched in columns 8 and 9, immediately following the "V" in column 7. The remaining columns of the card are available for notes. In Figure 4 (card 00030), the beginning of one division, called "P1", is shown. There are no notes associated with it. Section labels are similar to division labels – two characters of section name in columns 8 and 9 followed by notes. Text entries and their associated descriptions are provided with six-character text labels which are punched in columns 8 through 13. The first character of a text-entry label declares the type of the entry (see Sec, 3, Table 11) and the other five characters are an arbitrary name.

There are text entries of six types shown in Figure 4. Card 00050 carries a title and has a "T1" as the first character of its label, i.e., in column 8. Card 00060 gives the act in the play which is regarded as a "major section heading" (coded "M" in column 8). Scene headings (as card 00070) are marked "I" for "intermediate section heading." Each speaker is announced in an entry with column 8 tag "P" , and "D" is used for the stage directions. The remaining text entries constitute the body of the text and are marked with a "B" in column 8. There is, of course, no obligation to punch the title at all, or it may be put more out of the way as description. If it is included in the ordinary text entries, it will always be treated as text by the computer. If it is included as descriptive material, it can more easily be passed over when the text is processed. However, this is largely a matter of taste. Figure 5 summarizes this card layout.

```
00010 UMOLIERE'S PLAYS.        10/2/64 CORRECTED 10/17/64
00020 X      3OXFORD 3EDITION.
00030 VP1
00040 WA1
00050 1TB000104LE BOURGEOIS GENTILHOMME4.
00060 1MB000204ACT ONE4.
00070 1IB000304SCENE ONE4.
00080 1DB000403L'OUVERTURE SE FAIT PAR UN GRAND ASSEMBLAGE
00090 1DB0005D'INSTRUMENTS+ ET DANS LE MILIEU DU TH5E7ATRE ON
00100 1DB0006VOIT UN 5EL6EVE DU 3MA7ITRE DE MUSIQUE, QUI COMPOSE
00110 1DB0007SUR UNE TABLE UN AIR QUE LE 3BOURGEOIS A DEMAND5E
00120 1DB0008POUR UNE S5ER5ENADE.
00130 1PBC00904MA7ITRE DE MUSIQUE4.
00140 1DB0010PARLANT 6A SES MUSICIENS.
00150 1BB001103VENEZ, ENTREZ DANS CETTE SALLE, ET VOUS REPOSEZ L6A EN
00160 1BB0012ATTENDANT QU'IL VIENNE.
00170 1PB001304MA7ITRE 6A DANSER4.
00180 1DB0014PARLANT AUX DANSEURS.
00190 1BB001503ET VOUS AUSSI, DE CE C7OT5E.
00200 1PB001604MA7ITRE DE MUSIQUE4.
00210 1DB00176A L5EL6EVE.
00220 1BB001803EST-CE FAITS
```

FIGURE 4 Example of Punched-card Text Format

In the example given in Fig. 4, we have assumed a corpus consisting of Moliere's plays. Each division might be a different play and each section a different act or scene. Nothing of importance turns on these decisions, which are on a par with the decision as to whether an act should always start at the head of a new page in the book.

So much for the card layout. We must now take up the question of how the text itself is to be encoded. Of all the characters available in the various alphabets (see Sec. 2) of this catalog system, only a few can be expected to occur in any given text, and even fewer with any frequency. Furthermore, not all the frequently occurring characters can be expected to belong to the same code alphabet. For example, characters from the punctuation and, possibly, the boundary alphabets will occur fairly frequently in English texts, whereas the diacritics of the Roman alphabet will be fairly rare. The most desirable solution would be to allow the keypuncher freedom to assign each of the 48 Hollerith characters to a symbol which occurs frequently in the text he happens to be working on. These assignments would be taken to hold except when some special device was used to indicate a departure from them. If 47 of the Hollerith characters were assigned to frequent symbols, then the 48th could be used as this special device; otherwise one of the 16 codes which have no corresponding Hollerith character could be used for this purpose.

In the example in Fig. 4, the text was in French so five of the diacritics are needed. The cedilla occurs only with "c" and the two can therefore be combined for keypunching purposes. The diaresis is not frequent in French, but it is tidy to include it with the other accents and there is room for it among the 48 characters available. In many texts, the beginnings of sentences will not be marked; however, they are marked here if only

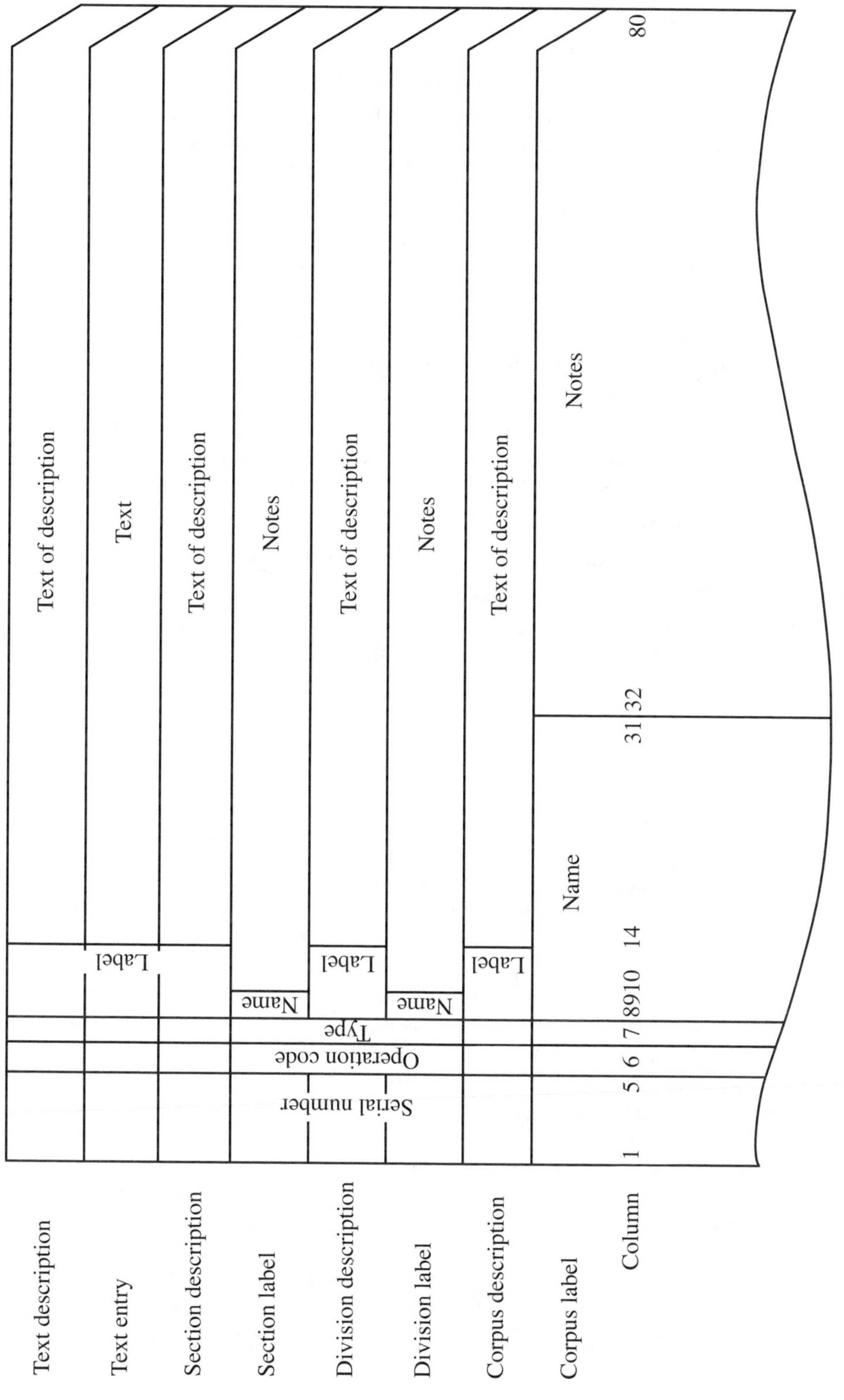

FIGURE 5 A punched-card input layout

to make the example more instructive. Capital letters are used for proper names and at the beginnings of sentences, and a simple way of showing capitalization is required. Also, there are occasional stretches of text, such as headings of speeches, which are all in capitals. Where a word begins with a capital, there is no real necessity to use both an up and a down shift; one character placed before the affected letter should be sufficient. On the other hand, the use of this character before each of the letters of a capitalized word would be cumbersome. The solution is to have two methods of indicating capitalization. One Hollerith character, "3" in our example, is used for "short" capitalization; it affects only the immediately following letter and, therefore, requires no down shift. Another character, 11411, is used for "long" capitalization; its effect continues until cancelled. It is not necessary to commit a third character for cancelling long capitalization; the same character, "4" can be used again in this function without ambiguity.

Table 12, which shows KTR Table 1, gives most of the assignments of text characters to Hollerith characters for keypunching the French in the example, the remainder are given in Table 13, which shows KTR Table 2. The characters found in the original text are given in the column headed "T", and the characters punched into the cards are given in the column headed "P". The remaining two columns must now be explained.

TABLE 12 Table One of a Punched-Card KTR

T	P	N	I	T	P	N	I	T	P	N	I
a	A	1	RA	A	3A	1	R1RAR9	.	.	1	P.
b	B	1	RB	B	3B	1	R1RBR9	,	,	1	P,
c	C	1	RC	C	3C	1	R1RCR9	;	+	1	PJ
d	D	1	RD	D	3D	1	R1RDR9	:	=	1	PI
e	E	1	RE	E	3E	1	R1RER9	!	/	1	PM
f	F	1	RF	F	3F	1	R1RFR9	?	$	1	PK
g	G	1	RG	G	3G	1	R1RGR9	-	-	1	P-
h	H	1	RH	H	3H	1	R1RHR9	'	'	1	R'
i	I	1	RI	I	3I	1	R1RIR9	(	(	1	P(
j	J	1	RJ	J	3J	1	R1RJR9	)	)	1	P)
k	K	1	RK	K	3K	1	R1RKR9	Open "	1	1	PA
l	L	1	RL	L	3L	1	R1RLR9	Close "	2	1	PB
m	M	1	RM	M	3M	1	R1RMR9	Space		1	R
n	N	1	RN	N	3N	1	R1RNR9	Long cap.	4	2	R1
o	Ø	1	RØ	Ø	3Ø	1	R1RØR9	'	5	1	R(
p	P	1	RP	P	3P	1	R1RPR9	'	6	1	R)
q	Q	1	RQ	Q	3Q	1	R1RQR9	^	7	1	R+
r	R	1	RR	R	3R	1	R1RRR9	¨	8	1	R=
s	S	1	RS	S	3S	1	R1RSR9	ç	9	1	R,RC
t	T	1	RT	T	3T	1	R1RTR9	Rm. Alph.	*R	R	
u	U	1	RU	U	3U	1	R1RUR9	Cy. Alph.	*C	C	
v	V	1	RV	V	3V	1	R1RVR9	Gk. Alph.	*G	G	
w	W	1	RW	W	3W	1	R1RWR9	Sy. Alph.	*A	A	
x	X	1	RX	X	3X	1	R1RXR9	Cs. Alph.	*D	D	
y	Y	1	RY	Y	3Y	1	R1RYR9	Pu. Alph.	*P	P	
z	Z	1	RZ	Z	3Z	1	R1RZR9	By. Alph.	*B	B	
Sentence	0	1	BS								

TABLE 13 Table Two of a Punched-Card KTR

T	P	N	I	T	P	N	I	T	P	N	I
A	A	2	RA	N	N	2	RN	'	5	2	R(
B	B	2	RB	Ø	Ø	2	RØ	'	6	2	R)
C	C	2	RC	P	P	2	RP	^	7	2	R+
D	D	2	RD	Q	Q	2	RQ	..	8	2	R=
E	E	2	RE	R	R	2	RR	ç	9	2	R,RC
F	F	2	RF	S	S	2	RS	Space		2	R
G	G	2	RG	T	T	2	RT	Sentence	0	2	BSR1
H	H	2	RH	U	U	2	RU	End cap.	4	1	R9
I	I	2	RI	V	V	2	RV				
J	J	2	RJ	W	W	2	RW				
K	K	2	RK	X	X	2	RX				
L	L	2	RL	Y	Y	2	RY				
M	M	2	RM	Z	Z	2	RZ				

We have made some liberal assumptions about the KTR routine we are describing. If the keypuncher is to be left free to assign interpretations to the Hollerith characters as he will, he must also have some means of conveying to the KTR routine what assignments he has, in fact, made. He can do this in only one way; namely, by punching some other cards which the KTR routine will read before it encounters the text and which contain the necessary correspondences. The columns headed "P" , "N" , and "I" contain all the information that need be punched into these cards. Consider the first entry in Table 12. Column P tells us that an "a" in text is to be punched as "A" . Column N says that the next character in the text is also to be interpreted by reference to this table (which will be KTR Table 1 from the computer's point of view.) The "RA" in column I indicates exactly what must be put on tape; namely, the character represented by a Hollerith "A" in the Roman alphabet (see Table 3 for Roman alphabet). The "ç" is to be punched as "9" and, once again, the following character in text is to be interpreted by reference to this same table. The representation on tape is shown as "R,RC", that is, the Roman alphabet flag, if necessary, the character in the Roman alphabet represented by a Hollerith "," followed by the character in the Roman alphabet represented by a Hollerith "C".

Take, now, the case of a capitalized word or sequence of words. Such a sequence is preceded by a "4" on the punched card, which is the code adopted for long capitalization. This is a very special kind of code because it influences the interpretation of an indefinitely long sequence of codes which follow it. Thus, the punched "4" signals a complete change in the table used for interpreting the succeeding punched characters. Thus, in Table 12, opposite "Long cap." in column T, we find a "4" in column P and a "2" in column N. This "2" means that KTR Table 2 is to be used for interpreting punched characters from this point until further notice. KTR Table 2 is similar to KTR Table 1 except that it allows rather few codes. For example, we have taken the view, however arbitrarily, that all punctuation is lower case; it therefore does not appear in KTR Table 2. The code for "beginning of sentence" is in the boundary alphabet (see Table 9), and we are allowing for the possibility of a beginning of sentence in a capitalized sequence. In order to do this, we must first record the beginning-of-sentence code with the appropriate alphabet flag, and then return to upper-case shift in the Roman alphabet. This accounts for the sequence of four characters in column I. Finally, the character punched as "4" has an entirely different interpretation in this table. It now means "shift into *lower* case." Accordingly, it causes the shift terminator, "9" in the Roman alphabet, to be recorded on tape, and indicates that KTR Table 1 is once again to be used for interpreting succeeding punched characters.

It will now be clear that in both KTR tables the characters in column I come in pairs; the first of each pair specifies an alphabet flag and the second a character in that alphabet. If nothing appears in this column, then nothing will be recorded on tape; if an alphabet flag appears with no character following it, a blank will be recorded on tape. Thus we are able to specify all the characters in all the code alphabets and to distinguish the blank from total absence of a character while using only the 48 symbols that can be keypunched. It need not be supposed that, because we show an alphabet flag before each substantive character in column I, these will all be written on tape. The program will ensure that only necessary alphabet flags and shifts are actually recorded.

One important facility of this KTR still remains to be explained. What is to be done if, from time to time, a character must be punched which, although it can be represented perfectly easily in the tape format, is not provided in the tables constructed for the job on hand? For this purpose, the punch codes "*R", "*C", "*G", etc., have been provided. "*G", for example, causes the Greek alphabet built into the system to be used directly; the Greek letters are represented by the Hollerith codes given for them in Table 5. If it was required to punch a tilde, which is in the Roman alphabet in the system but not in the alphabet we have been using for the French example, it would be sufficient to punch "*R$" (see Table 3). The codes "*G", or "*R", etc., must be repeated before every character to which they apply.

The KTR routine we have been discussing is one which will be implemented on the IBM 7044 computer. It is designed to allow great flexibility, but, as always, this comes at a certain cost. A simpler routine would confine its user to a more rigid set of coding conventions, but would avoid the necessity of setting up detailed tables.

On the other hand, it is undoubtedly a great deal simpler to construct tables of the kind we have described than to write, or have written, a special KTR routine for each particular job. Clearly other routines of equal or greater flexibility could, and doubtless will, be written for punched-card as well as other input media.

5.3.2 Punched Paper Tape

In the KTR which has been described, two methods have been used for distinguishing different kinds of information, card layout and character codes. To a considerable extent, it is possible to barter these against one another. If a serial number is to be useful for sorting punched cards into order when they get into disarray, it must be always in the same columns, but all the other information could have been punched anywhere on the cards and distinguished by character codes. "$E" might have been used to separate entries, "$S" sections, and so forth. The first six characters following an entry separator might be understood to be a text label. Conventions of this kind are usually best avoided with punched cards because distinctions based on position on the card are particularly easy for both humans and computers to make, and because the character set is already severely enough restricted without pre-empting other character combinations unnecessarily.

The method of distinguishing types of information by position is also simple to use with paper tape. In this case, positions are referred to not by column number but by counting character positions from the last line-feed. A character position is not necessarily the same thing as a row of holes on the tape itself, and in this respect, paper tape is different from punched cards. Character positions get out of step with paper-tape codes in a way they never can with card columns. This arises in three ways: (i) When a wrong character is punched in paper tape, it is converted by the typist into a "delete code" which is ignored by all machines which process the tape, including the computer. (ii) When the shift key is depressed or released, a code is punched into the tape which, however, does not account for a character position. (iii) Paper-tape machines are sometimes equipped with a back-space key which causes a code to be punched. This gives it the capability of returning to character positions for which codes have already been issued and either issuing new codes by overtyping the old symbol or modifying what is there by underlining or adding diacritics.

The result of all this is that a given line of type can be produced in a variety of ways, each resulting in a different sequence of codes on the paper tape. A word can be underlined by first typing the whole word, then back-spacing over it and typing in the underline. The underline can be typed first and then the word. Each letter can be typed and underlined before going on to the next. The number of variations is endless, but the final result is the same. It is impossible to tell by inspecting the typescript if the typist spent some time between a certain pair of characters depressing and releasing the shift key; yet the paper tape records all these moves. A well designed KTR – or any other computer program – will reconstruct on the evidence of the punched codes the line of type on the hard copy. This it can do by "imagining" where the carriage of the typewriter would be placed as a result of each move. This reconstructed line would then serve as input to the KTR proper and could be treated in every way like the punched card. With this device, it is possible to make corrections by simply back-spacing over the offending characters and typing corrections on top. Underlining and the insertion of diacritics can be done in any way that suits the typist short of actually man-handling the carriage, a recourse which, since it is essentially hidden from the computer, can only confuse it.

We have mentioned that punched paper tape takes various forms and comes from various sources; in particular, it is produced as a by-product of certain printing processes. A tape of this kind requires a special KTR to handle the special codes and conventions used for different fonts, type styles, etc. But there are also other problems which arise. An investigator who gets access to these tapes typically finds himself confronted with a large cardboard box into which the tape has been allowed to fall after running through the printing machine; but for the investigator, the box and its contents would have been thrown away. A KTR is written, and each length of tape is put on magnetic tape as, say, a separate section in a text catalog. Since the original order of the tapes is

not known, they are taken in any order and the sections are given arbitrary names –
sequence numbers will do. Now the tape is printed using a standard text-catalog printing
program. We assume that the investigator has a hard-copy version of the text at hand.
Using this, he can prepare a new set of labels for the sections which will be in ascending
numerical (or alphabetical) order when the text is properly ordered. He now has the text
writer program read the text catalog from one of its channels and the new labels from
another. The original labels are replaced by the new ones. A standard sort program can
now be used to put the sections of text in order using the new labels as keys. This may
be the final form of the text catalog, or it may be necessary to re-label a second time if
the investigator requires a particular set of labels which will not be in ascending order
in the final catalog. This is one of the many uses to which a multi-channel text writing
program can be put; others include merging catalogs, revising and correcting catalogs,
extracting examples of particular kinds of occurrence from a text and writing them as
a separate catalog and adding descriptions. Separate manuals will describe the details
of how these operations can be performed with particular programs.

5.4 Printing

Text in the standard format must be printed from time to time to be proofread and corrected, to verify the intermediate results of a process, or to display final results; it must
be printed if only to provide the investigator or librarian with an exact record of what
he has on the tapes. As with the other processes we have mentioned, printing requires
a computer program, and the particular programs used will vary considerably with the
purposes to be achieved by printing. Either the emphasis is on showing character-for-
character what is on the magnetic tape, or it is on producing a presentable copy for
publication or circulation among colleagues.

It may not be immediately apparent why there should be these two points of view on
printing. Surely, if real distinctions are made in a text which are worthy of preservation
on magnetic tape, they must be made again when the text is reproduced; otherwise they
are otiose. However, texts, or selections from texts, are printed for differing purposes
and in different styles. If a list of the different words in a text is prepared, possibly with
frequencies or other incidental information, the distinction between words with initial
capital and those entirely in lower case is unlikely to be interesting; what is required is a
standard style: all capitals, all lower case, or all with initial capital. As with capitals, so
with italics, bold face, and other distinctions of type font. Consider also the case where
citations are being printed to exemplify certain words or phrases, say one sentence for
each citation. Here, upper and lower case should probably be preserved, but, for ease of
reading, it may be convenient to capitalize or underline the cited forms.

Another reason for considering different printing conventions comes from the equipment generally available for printing. It is indeed the case that the output of a computer
can be made indistinguishable from that of a high-class printing shop. It is not, as many
believe, necessary for computer results to look like cold, squarely mechanical telegrams
from a remote electronic god. Very few will be able to pay the price of special equipment
capable of printing a very large budget of symbols in a large variety of sizes and type
faces, and even those who can will find it uneconomical for anything but the final results

of a major enterprise. All intermediate, and most final, results will continue for many years to be produced with more modest machinery.

The most common computer printing devices are capable of printing the same 48 Hollerith characters that appear on the keyboard of the card punch. A relatively simple modification to some of these, notably the IBM 1403 printer, enables them to print somewhat enlarged character sets; 120 or even 240 are possible on this machine at some cost in running speed. It is usually a trivial matter to replace the 48 standard characters on an ordinary machine by any other set of 48, and the characters of the enlarged sets can be chosen freely. However, neither of these expedients comes near to providing the flexibility that we have allowed in the text encoding scheme. It was, of course, worth allowing this flexibility against a possible eventual use of more powerful printing machines and, what is more important, against sophisticated machine processes which can take advantage of all the distinctions in the original text.

The problem, then, is similar to that encountered in keypunching text on a machine with only a small set of characters. Sometimes the difficulty can be overcome by dropping certain distinctions, as for example when a vocabulary list is printed all in capitals and without punctuation or diacritics. This can be useful for many purposes. But cases also commonly arise where everything on the tape must be represented on the printed copy. An obvious one is proofreading. If a correction is made on the hard copy produced for proofreading, this correction must be keypunched and presented to a program which will modify the tape. Clearly, the hard copy must contain everything the keypuncher must know in order correctly to reconstruct the catalog entry. In other words, the copy must be such that it would be possible to keypunch the text from it and arrive at exactly the same text catalog on tape as was produced from the original.

5.4.1 A Standard Printing Scheme

Many of the devices used for keypunching can conveniently be taken over to the printing process. The characters which occur most frequently in the text are each assigned one of the symbols on the printing device. The correspondence set up in this way is assumed to hold except when overridden by a special signal. A special signal takes the form of an alphabet flag or shift character which modifies the interpretation of all following symbols up to another special symbol. The special symbols can be distinguished from other symbols more clearly in printing than in keypunching if two lines of print are made to stand for one in the original text. The substantive text characters appear on alternate lines so that the spaces above them are always blank. An alphabet flag or shift is represented by a character on the upper line with a space on the line immediately below. Suppose that the following line has been encoded in the standard format and written on tape:

The Greek μήτηρ comes from the same root as the Russian матр.

This might be printed on a machine equipped with only the 48 Hollerith characters as:

```
 1 9    1 9     G     G                                  1 9     C1 9   C
   T HE   G REEK  M(YTYR  COMES FROM THE SAME ROOT AS THE  R USSIAN    M AT'
```

Using a machine with a large character set including, say, upper and lower case Roman letters and accents, it might appear as:

```
         G     G                                                       C    C
    The Greek mўtyr comes from the same root as the Russian Mat'
```

The first two words, "The Greek," are in the Roman alphabet, and no special symbol is needed to show how they are supposed to be interpreted. Most letters appear in lower case, and it is therefore understood that the upper case letters printed by the 48-character device should be taken as representing lower case except when preceded by the shift character "1" on the upper line. Upper and lower case shift characters are not printed by the device with the larger character set because it is able to show these distinctions directly. The Greek word μήτηρ appears in transliteration in both cases because we are assuming that neither printer is equipped with Greek characters. The fact that it is a transliteration, and from what alphabet, is shown by the two G's on the upper line which serve as a pair of brackets round the transliterated sequence. The same device is used for the Russian word матг.

This example would have been different if the original had read:

```
                    ′
    The Greek mētēr comes from the same root as the Russian mat'
```

With the 48-character printer, this would appear as

```
    1 9   1 9                                                      1 9
     T HE  G REEK M-(ET-ER COMES FROM THE SAME ROOT AS THE  R USSIAN MAT'
```

Here the transliterations are part of the original; no alphabet flags are needed because nothing but Roman letters and diacritics are used. The output of the second printer would be

```
    The Greek mē'tēr comes from the same root as the Russian mat'
```

In this example, we are making the realistic assumption that the device will be capable of printing only one diacritic over a letter; others must precede or follow.

The conventions required for printing a Russian or a Greek text would clearly be different. The best solution would be to use a printer with Russian or Greek characters and to transliterate symbols from other alphabets when they occurred. When this cannot be done, a more usual printer can be used with a different set of standard conventions about how characters are to be interpreted in the absence of alphabet flags. The Roman characters would normally be understood to be transliterations except when explicit "R" appeared on the upper line.

In most cases, a single investigator will work only with one kind of text so that, once he has established his conventions for keypunching and printing, he will not need to change them again. However, in a large center where there are many different kinds of text, or where several individuals are using the services of the same key-punch operators or proofreaders, some care must be taken to see that the various sets of conventions do not become confused. In these circumstances it is desirable that a printing routine be capable of printing as part of each batch of output, what conventions it is using. In other words, it should be able to read from cards or some other input medium tables similar to those used to specify key-punching conventions (Tables 12 and 13), to use these in preparing the printed output, and to print them on that output so that the intepretation will always be clear.

5.4.2 Page Layout

We have consistently taken the line that repetitive operations should, wherever possible, be carried out by standard computer routines whose internal workings need not concern the individual user. Printing is an obvious example of such an operation and, accordingly, we have sketched some features of a general printing program. This is the program used on the IBM 7044 computer at RAND. The principal routines involved can be used as subroutines in any program which produces printed output and not only to prepare a copy of a connected text. They are therefore provided with facilities for arranging information on the page in the way the user requires, for furnishing page headings and numbers and the like.

The printing routines prepare output in units called *rows*. A row may comprise several lines of print, though the number will usually not be very large. In general, a row is divided into columns whose number and width on the printed page is specified by the program using the routines, that is, by the user. In many instances, for example when a straightforward text is being printed, a row will consist of a single line of print and there will be a single column which fills the entire page. If each line is identified with a label, then there would be a small column for the label number, and a large column occupying the rest of the page for the text itself.

The number and width of columns may vary from row to row. Each variant is specified by a *format statement* which is nothing more than a sequence of numbers giving the widths of succeeding columns. Before the preparation of a row of print begins, the printing routines must be supplied with the format statement to be used for that row. Data are then supplied piecemeal, each with an indication of the colurm into which it is to be put and the tables to be used for transliterating it. It is thus possible to print, say, Greek, in one column according to one set of conventions and English in another according to another set.

The data in a given column may be accumulated in various ways. Suppose that a bilingual dictionary is being printed; we may assume that it has been compiled by examining some quantity of parallel text. Let one language be Russian and the other English. There will be two fairly wide columns to accommodate Russian and English words and phrases. The transliteration tables will be different for each of these. Two more columns will accommodate some grammatical information about the words and phrases; this will be a code of a few letters giving the part of speech. Finally, there will be a column for recording the number of times each Russian-English pair has been found in the text. An entry in the dictionary will have information in all of these columns and will be one row of print. The data for the various columns may be supplied by the user's program in any order and we may return to a column to which information has already been supplied as often as we wish. Russian words will begin at the left-most margin of their column and extend as far to the right as necessary; the rest of the column will be left blank. From time to time, a phrase will occur which is too long to fit in the column. It must therefore be broken at the last space which can be fitted on the line and the remainder used to begin a new line. This will continue until the whole phrase is accommodated. Entries in the English column will be handled in the same way. A given Russian word or phrase may have more than one English correspondent, and these must be set off from one another. To provide for this, the printing routines allow the program which uses them to specify, when providing data for a column, that it *must* begin on a new line. The user is, of course, also free to supply a line of blanks to separate items.

A Russian or English word or phrase may, let us suppose, have several part-of-speech codes and these are to appear under one another in a column. In this case, the printer must be instructed to go to a new line, not after the last space it can accommodate on the current line, but at every space. This is one of the options provided by the routines. The column giving the number of times a Russian-English pair has been found in text must also have no more than one item on a line. However, in this case the items are all numbers and we shall want to follow the convention of justifying them to the right so that digits with the same place value fall under one another. Therefore, when these data are sent to the printing routines, it is with an instruction to place them, one on a line, at the right of the field.

There are other instructions which may accompany data to the printer. In the examples we have considered, a long item is split up into as many lines as are needed to accommodate it in the field it is directed to. Sometimes, however, we may wish to print an item only if it will fit on the current line and otherwise to preserve it for a subsequent row or discard it entirely. When a simple copy of a text is being produced, for instance, we may wish to fit as many words on a line as will fit and keep the rest for subsequent lines. This is exactly what would happen if the entire text were printed as a single row with the instruction to go to a new line whenever all the characters up to the next space cannot be fitted on the current one. However, there are practical limits to the size of a single row which come from the fact that it occupies space in the working area of the computer while it is being assembled. It will rarely be practical to print rows representing a whole page of print for this reason. The facility of interrupting the flow of information to the printer when the end of a line has been reached is therefore provided.

Each time a row is printed, the paper advances a certain number of lines. This number is, in fact, the greatest number of lines filled in any column in the row. Unoccupied lines in the other columns are left blank and the next row begins with the next completely free line on the paper. Having printed a row, the user, or his program, may need to know how much space remains on the current page in order that he may decide whether to go to the next before printing the following row, and for this reason he is supplied with a running count of the place he has reached on the page.

When he goes to the next page, he will often want to start by printing a heading. Headings are like other rows of print except that they typically use their own format statement and the information they contain is largely the same from one use to the next. The page count will be different on each occasion, and a title or subtitle may change from time to time, but changes will be relatively rare. It may also happen in the body of a page that the information in a certain column will remain unchanged for a number of rows. To meet this situation, the printing routines can be so arranged that the information printed with a given format statement will always be as on the previous occasion except in those columns where it has been explicitly changed. Thus, in the case of a page heading, the column where the page number is printed will be changed each time the format statement is used whereas the remaining information will normally not be changed.

The printing routines we have described were designed for great flexibility both in the kinds of text they can handle and the printing devices they can serve. However, we do not suppose that every possible need will be filled by these routines so that no others will ever have to be written. In any case, these, like all the other routines we have discussed, will have to be recoded for different makes and models of computers. We hope that these routines will serve most needs, particularly in the printing of intermediate results not intended for publication.

Acknowledgements

This research is sponsored by the United States Air Force under Project RAND – Contract No. AF 49(638)-700 monitored by the Directorate of Development Plans, Deputy Chief of Staff. Research and Development Hq USAF. Views or conclusions contained in this Memorandum should not be interpreted as representing the official opinion or policy of the United States Air Force.

This Memorandum is the first product of a close collaborative effort among the Linguistic Project of The RAND Corporation, the Centre d'Etudes pour la Traduction Automatique of the Centre National de la Recherche Scientifique in Grenoble, and the Machine Translation Project at the University of California, Berkeley. The ideas expounded here came from many people in all three of these centers; only errors and misrepresentations should be ascribed uniquely to us. We are particularly indebted to Professor B. Vauquois and G. Veillon of Grenoble and to C. D. Johnson of Berkeley. D. G. Hays at The RAND Corporation has given us invaluable criticism and encouragement throughout the preparation of the manuscript.

Publications referenced

Edmundson et al. 1961.

6

The Tabular Parser: A Parsing Program for Phrase Structure and Dependency

Preface

Parsing, the process of making explicit the grammatical structure of sentences, is central to almost any process involving the analysis of texts in any language, natural or artificial. Its importance in machine translation, information retrieval, computer-program compiling and command and control systems is generally acknowledged.

A parsing strategy rests on the answers to three questions: (i) what grammatical theory should be used; (ii) what conventions and notations would be most convenient for presenting the information on a particular language required by the chosen theory to a computer; and (iii) what algorithms would be most suitable. This Memorandum concentrates on question (ii). Starting from the observation that phrase-structure and dependency are kindred theories, it presents a notation in which large amounts of the information required by both can be stated simply and concisely. The program uses this information to perform the phrase-structure and dependency parsing of sentences concurrently.

The program consists of a main routine written in FORTRAN IV and a number of subroutines written in the IBM 7040/44 machine language (MAP). It will be made available on request to qualified workers in the field.

Summary

A parsing program for IBM 7040/44 computers is described that finds all phrase and dependency structures assigned to the sentence by a given grammar. The grammar is prepared for the machine in the form of a set of rule tables, which constitute a rich, terse and perspicuous grammatical notation.

6.1 Dependency Phrase Grammar

A phrase-structure rule is one that takes the form

$$A \rightarrow B_1 \ldots B_n$$

where A and B_i are phrase classes or parts of speech. If one of the right-hand members is distinguished as *governor* of the phrase, the rule becomes what we shall call a *dependency phrase rule* . We may write

$$A \rightarrow B_1 \ldots B_n \ (k)$$

where $1 \leq k \leq n$, to show that B_k is the governor of the phrase.

Clearly, a grammar consisting of dependency phrase rules, a *dependency phrase grammar*, generates exactly the same strings as the phrase-structure grammar that differs from it only in failing to appoint a governor in each phrase. However, the descriptions it assigns to sentences can be interpreted indifferently as phrase or dependency structures. In either case, the descriptions contain more than the customary amount of information. In the phrase structure there is a specially marked member of every phrase; in the dependency structure a partial ordering is imposed on the dependents of every governor. An example of this is shown in Fig. 1. The asterisks serve to mark the governors in the phrase-structure diagram; thus "C" governs the phrase "B C" and this phrase governs the whole string "A B C D". In the dependency diagram, "A", "B" and "D" are all shown as dependents of "C", but "B" is in the same phrase and is therefore marked "1", whereas "A" and "D" occur in a phrase of the next higher level and are therefore marked "2". Abundant examples of this kind of correspondence will be displayed in the following pages.

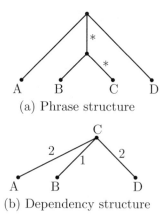

(a) Phrase structure

(b) Dependency structure

FIGURE 1   Equivalent phrase and dependency structures

A family of phrase structures can be set in correspondence with the dependency description of a given sentence, and a family of dependency structures corresponds to any given phrase structure.[1] Also, for any given phrase-structure grammar, there is at least one dependency grammar that generates the same language and that consists entirely of rules of the form

$$A \rightarrow B_1 \ B_2$$

Since, in this paper, we are concerned with the recognition rather than the generation of sentence structures, we shall reverse the normal roles of these rules and write

$$B_1 \ B_2 \rightarrow A$$

Such a *binary phrase-structure grammar* assigns trees with binary branching as sentence descriptions, and inasmuch as a *binary dependency phrase grammar* also assigns phrase descriptions, it is subject to the same restriction. However, the dependency de-

---

[1]See Galfman, H. 1965. "Dependency Systems and Phrase Structure Systems." *Information and Control* 8:3, 304–337.

scriptions that it assigns are not restricted in this way. In fact, as we shall see, all dependency grammars that do not admit violations of projectivity[2] can be couched in a very natural way in terms of binary dependency phrase grammars.

Figures 2 and 3 show pairs of corresponding binary phrase-structure and dependency diagrams. In Fig. 2, the shape of the dependency tree is held constant, and different corresponding phrase structures are exhibited. As the phrase structures change, so do the orderings imposed upon the dependency structures, and since only binary phrases are involved, this ordering is invariably simple. In Fig. 3, the phrase structure is held constant, and different corresponding dependency trees are shown. Each node in a phrase-structure diagram commemorates the application of a dependency phrase rule. The asterisks record which member of the rule was marked as governor.

The following procedure will recover the diagrams on the right of the figures from those on the left, and may be applied to any phrase structure with marked governors to obtain the corresponding dependency tree.

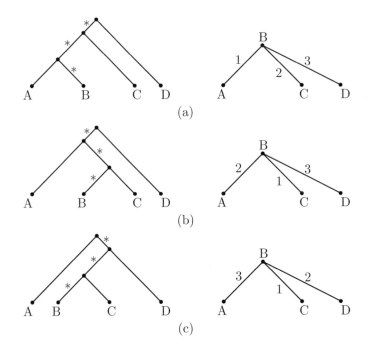

(a)

(b)

(c)

FIGURE 2 Phrase-structure equivalents for similar dependency structures

Wherever the node corresponding to a word is joined to the immediate superior by a line marked with an asterisk, write the word against the superior node, erase the inferior node and the connecting line, and transfer any dependents of the inferior to a superior node. The superior node now has a word written against it, though it may now be connected to other nodes beneath it. Continue this process until no marked lines remain. The new diagram contains a node for each node not at the bottom of a

---

[2]For this term, see D.G. Hays. 1964. "Dependency Theory: A Formalism and Some Observations." *Language* 40:4, 511–524.

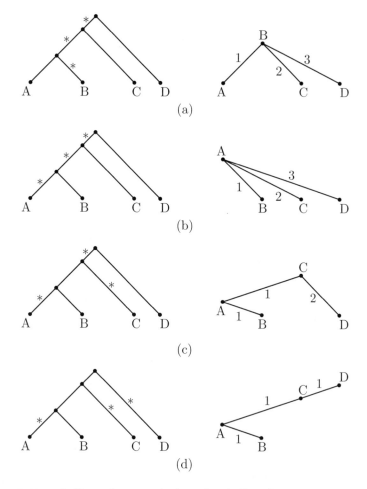

FIGURE 3 Dependency equivalents for similar phrase structures

marked line in the old diagram. Each word standing at the foot of a chain of marked lines has been transferred to the node at the head of that chain and the remaining nodes on the chain effaced. Figure 4 shows the steps in this procedure as applied to the phrase-structure diagram in Fig. 2(a). One way to assign an order to the dependencies on the new diagram is to trace out the path from each dependent to its governor in the old diagram, counting the number of unmarked links traversed. Assign this number to the corresponding line in the new diagram.

6.2 Rule Tables

We shall now describe a condensed form of expression for large phrase-structure or dependency phrase grammars.

Consider a language in which subject and predicate agree in number, and adjective and noun agree in number and gender. And suppose that words may be ambiguous with respect to number and gender. Part of a phrase-structure grammar that applies to this situation is shown in Table 1. Words and phrases are represented by two- or three-letter mnemonic codes in which the first letter refers to one of the major parts of speech (adjective, noun, verb), the second its number (singular, plural) and the third its gender (masculine, feminine, neuter).

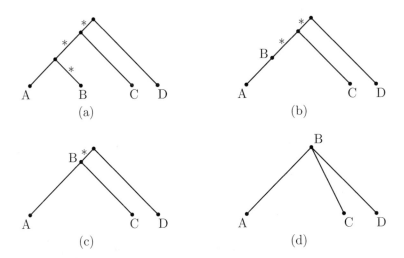

FIGURE 4 Translation from marked phrase-structure to dependency

These codes are adequate only if it is assumed that ambiguous words may receive more than one code. If each word were allowed only one code, so that there would have to be a different one for each range of ambiguities occurring in the lexicon, then even this part of the grammar would become very large.

TABLE 1 Phrase-structure rules for number and gender agreement

ASM	NSM	→	NSM	NSM	VS	→	S
ASF	NSF	→	NSF	NSF	VS	→	S
ASN	NSN	→	NSN	NSN	VS	→	S
APM	NPM	→	NPM	NPM	VP	→	S
APF	NPF	→	NPF	NPF	VP	→	S
APN	NPN	→	NPN	NPN	VP	→	S

The simplification to be suggested will make the formal grammar rules more like our original informal statement. Codes in which each letter has a meaning of its own are easy to remember and work with because they make it possible to isolate important grammatical features and to state generalizations. Grammatical work on computers has always been based on some such scheme,[3] and it has been suggested recently that it may be a matter of theoretical importance to find appropriate ways of factoring out grammatical properties (Chomsky 1965).

We said a noun phrase may be formed from an adjective and a noun provided these agree in number and gender. This statement necessarily involves the part of speech,

---

[3]See *inter alia* Harper et al. 1960; Coppinger and von Susich 1961; Parker-Rhodes et al. 1960.

number, and gender of the phrase, which correspond to the three places in the mnemonic codes for adjectives and nouns. Accordingly, the grammar must have three distinct tables of rules. The first, the *main table*, will contain the rule

$$A \ N \rightarrow N \text{ (Number agreement, gender agreement)}$$

Number agreement is verified by reference to the *number table*, which contains the following rules:

$$S \ S \rightarrow S$$
$$P \ P \rightarrow P$$

A gender table contains the rules:

$$M \ M \rightarrow M$$
$$F \ F \rightarrow F$$
$$N \ N \rightarrow N$$

To specify the use of these tables exactly, it is necessary that the grammar contain an indication of which letters in the mnemonic codes they refer to. This information could be introduced, together with the rules that make up the table, as part of the table's definition, or alternatively, it could be given each time the table was referred to. The second alternative will be used here. Thus, the main table might contain the rule

$$A \ N \rightarrow N \text{ (Number [2,2,2], Gender [3,3,3])}$$

This says that an adjective and a noun may combine to form a noun phrase provided there is a rule in the number table that applies to the second position of their codes and a rule in the gender table that applies to the third position. The third member of each triple gives the position of the resultant code.

It may sometimes be convenient to represent a category, say number, by one letter position in the codes for one part of speech and by another letter position for a different part of speech. For this reason, the positions have been given as triple rather than single numbers. The first two numbers give the potential positions in the codes for the first and second members of the phrase, and the third the position in the code for the resulting phrase where the new character is to be placed. Table 2 gives the revised grammar for the original example.

TABLE 2 Rule tables for number and gender agreement

Start at main table [1,1,1]
Main table
A N → N (Number [2,2,2], Gender [2,2,2])
N V → S (Number [2,2,2])
Number table
S S → S
P P → P
Gender table
M M → M
F F → F
N N → N

Tables of rules allow a further simplification of this grammar to be introduced immediately. The notion of agreement, whether of number, gender or whatever, is one notion and need be expressed only once. The number and gender tables are similar in that they allow combinations of like symbols and prohibit all others. Therefore, if the same letters are used for number and gender, the two can be conflated. Let "A" stand for singular when it occurs in the second position, masculine when it occurs in the third. Let "B" stand for plural in the second position, feminine in the third. "C" will stand for neuter and occur only in the third position. Then the complete set of new grammar codes is as follows:

NAA	Noun, singular, masculine
NAB	Noun, singular, feminine
NAC	Noun, singular, neuter
NBA	Noun, plural, masculine
NBB	Noun, plural, feminine
NBC	Noun, plural, neuter
AAA	Adjective, singular, masculine
AAB	Adjective, singular, feminine
AAC	Adjective, singular, neuter
ABA	Adjective, plural, masculine
ABB	Adjective, plural, feminine
ABC	Adjective, plural, neuter
VA	Verb, singular
VB	Verb, plural

Given this encoding, the tables shown in Table 3 are equivalent to the original grammar.

TABLE 3 Condensed rule tables

Start at main table [1,1,1]
Main table
A N → N (Agreement [2,2,2], Agreement [3,3,3])
N V → S (Agreement [2,2,2])
Agreement table
A A → A
B B → B
C C → C

In connection with the original statement of the grammar (Table 1), we remarked that it was wise to assign more than one grammar code to ambiguous words lest the number of grammar rules pass all reasonable bounds. However, if the grammar is to be used for parsing, that is, for assigning structures to sentences, this may become inconvenient as a general policy. Suppose that, in the language under study, there is number agreement between adjectives and the nouns they modify, but that many adjectives and nouns have the same form in the singular and the plural. In other words, there is widespread ambiguity in the category of number. Consider then what happens when an ambiguous adjective occurs with an ambiguous noun as in the German *meine Schwester*.[4] Both

---

[4]This is one of the situations in which a case is made for transformational grammar; see N. Chomsky. 1957. *Syntactic Structures*, 38ff. Mouton.

words have two grammar codes so that there are four pairs to be considered. Two of these pairs, singular plus singular and plural plus plural, are admissible so that the resulting phrase also has two grammar codes. Now suppose that the adjective and noun in question are the object of a verb with which there is no number agreement, as in German *Er kennt meine Schwester*. The parsing procedure must nevertheless examine both the grammar codes of the adjective-noun phrase in order to discover that both give the same result. If, on the other hand, the adjective and noun had been given one grammar code each, a code which declared their ambiguity, then only one comparison would be required for the construction of each phrase.

The use of rule tables allows some ambiguities to be accommodated without increasing the number of rules unreasonably. However, the possibility of assigning multiple grammar codes should still be kept open, for not all ambiguities are as systematic as the one we have considered. To account for ambiguities of number, the grammar in the example can be extended by introducing the symbol "P" to represent both "singular or plural" and "masculine or feminine". Since ambiguity of gender is not being considered, "P" will never occur in the third position. "P" combines with a preceding or following "A" and contributes an "A" to the resulting phrase. It combines likewise with "B" yielding "B" in the code for the phrase. In these cases, the ambiguity is resolved by the unambiguous partner when the phrase is formed. But "P" also combines with a preceding or following "P" yielding a "P" in the code for the phrase, and in this case, the ambiguity is unresolved.

Consider now the situation in which there are also adjectives and nouns that show all possible patterns of gender ambiguity. The "P" already introduced will serve for "masculine or feminine" and "Q", "R", and "X" can be used for "masculine or neuter", "feminine or neuter", and "masculine, feminine or neuter" respectively. Thus a singular or plural, feminine or neuter adjective will be represented by "APR". The revised grammar tables are shown in Table 4.

If a language with six cases contains adjectives and nouns showing all possible patterns of ambiguity, an agreement table with 3376 entries will be required. While it is unlikely that all these patterns would occur in an actual language, it is clear that ambiguity leads to an altogether unsatisfactory rise in the size of the tables. However, more widespread exploitation of devices already introduced makes it possible to check agreement, and other relations, with respect to large categories and without the grammar becoming hopelessly top-heavy.

Suppose the language we are concerned with has six cases and we wish to provide for a word's having any pattern of ambiguity. Suppose also that there is number and gender ambiguity of the kind already discussed and that the general three-way ambiguity table (Table 4) has been included in the grammar to take care of this. The cases are divided arbitrarily into two groups (nominative, genitive, dative and accusative, instrumental, prepositional) and the same letters used for coding the members of each group as are used for number and gender. Thus "A" may stand for "nominative" in one position and "accusative" in another, "B" for "genitive" here and "instrumental" there, and "C" for "dative" and "prepositional".

TABLE 4 Rule tables for all patterns of number and gender ambiguity

Start at main table [1,1,1]
Main table
A N → N (Agreement [2,2,2], Agreement [3,3,3])
N V → S (Agreement [2,2,2])
Agreement table
A A → A
A P → A
A Q → A
A X → A
P A → A
P Q → A
Q A → A
Q P → A
X A → A
B B → B
B P → B
B R → B
B X → B
P B → B
P R → B
R B → B
R P → B
X B → B
C C → C
C Q → C
C R → C
C X → C
Q C → C
Q R → C
R C → C
R Q → C
X C → C
P P → P
P X → P
X P → P
Q Q → Q
Q X → Q
X Q → Q
R R → R
R X → R
X R → R
X X → X

"P" will stand for "nominative and genitive" as well as "accusative and instrumental", and similarly for "Q", "R", and "A". One further character, say "O", will be needed, to show that no term in this category applies. The code for a word or phrase provides two character positions to represent case, one for each of the two groups of three. Let us assume that the code for a noun has an "N" in the first position, characters for number and gender in the second and third positions and characters for case in positions four and five. The following are examples of grammar codes constructed on this plan:

NAAAO	—	Noun, singular, masculine, nominative
NAAOA	—	Noun, singular, masculine, accusative
NAAAA	—	Noun, singular, masculine, nominative or accusative
NAABO	—	Noun, singular, masculine, genitive
NAAPO	—	Noun, singular, masculine, nominative or genitive
NBBQR	—	Noun, plural, feminine, nominative, dative,
		instrumental or prepositional

In principle, the list could be continued to contain as many as 1323 entries. Furthermore, notice that ambiguity is provided for only within each separate category. This means that a noun that is either nominative singular or accusative plural must still be provided with separate codes. However, the following techniques can readily extended to this and other like situations.

Consider the grammar below containing the last agreement table (Table 4):

Start at main table [1,1,1]

Main table

A N →   N (Agreement [2,2,2], Agreement [3,3,3])

         (Agreement [4,4,4], Agreement [5,5,5]) or

         (Zero [0,0,4], Agreement [5,5,5]) or

         (Agreement [4,4,4], Zero [0,0,5])

N V →   S (Agreement [2,2,2])

Zero table

O O →   O

Two new conventions have been introduced here. The first allows us to join table references with the word "or" and to group them in parentheses. This in fact adds no power to the mechanism already described, but it provides economy of notation and in the amount of work a computer must do to apply the rules. If a rule sanctioning the formation of a new phrase can be found in the tables immediately referred to, then those referred to after the "or" are ignored. But if the necessary rules cannot be found immediately, the tables referred to after the "or" are tried instead.

This produces the results required for our example. Agreement of an adjective and a noun is first sought in both the fourth and the fifth positions of the codes. This can be successful only if both words are ambiguous with respect to case and the ambiguity is such that they have at least one case from each of the two groups represented by positions four and five of the code. If this is not true for a given pair, or if agreement is not found in one of the positions, then the table called "zero" (see below) is applied to position four and the agreement table to position five. If this also fails, then agreement is sought in position four and the zero table applied to position five.

The second new convention is exemplified in the use of the zero table. The references to this from the main table appear to call for an examination of the zeroth position of the grammar codes of a pair of potential phrase members. But since the numbering scheme we have adopted for character positions does not allow for a zero, we use the zeroth character in a grammar code as a sort of variable that will match any specific character found in a rule. In other words, when invited to refer the zeroth character of a code to a grammar table, the machine will disregard that code entirely and consider only whether a rule can be found to match the specified character from the other code. If the zeroth character is specified for both potential phrase members, this means that all the rules in the table referred to automatically apply to the pair. This is the case with the zero table in the example. The effect of this table is to place a zero in a particular position in the code for the new phrase without regard to anything in the codes of the members.

There is an obvious use for a zero in the third position of a table reference also. This simply means that the application of the table, no matter what rule it gives, contributes nothing to the code for the new phrase. It is thus possible to use the agreement tables to check on the compatibility of a pair of items but not to keep any record of the result except where it is relevant.

Clearly, rule tables are as suitable to dependency phrase as to phrase-structure grammars: To the rules in the main table one need only add an indication of which member of the new phrase is to be governor. Indeed, this information may be supplied by any of the tables used in recognizing a phrase, and we shall see later that this capability can be usefully exploited.

6.3 Functions and Dependency Phrase Rule Tables

One way to characterize the notion of parsing is to say that it is a process whereby the grammatical *functions* of the parts of a sentence are derived from the grammatical *categories* of the words in it.[5] When we parse a sentence like *The man hit the ball*, we group the words into phrases and the phrases into larger phrases and, in the process, we discover which of the possible grammatical categories of any ambiguous word or phrase is operative in this particular string. In this case, we discover, for example, that *hit* must be interpreted as a finite verb if this string is to make sense as a sentence. On the other hand, *man*, which might serve as a verb in other contexts, must be taken to be a noun here. This information emerges only when a complete parsing of the entire sentence has been made. For example, this string can be embedded in another sentence to give *The man hit the ball was the boy's father* but this can be successfully parsed only if *hit* is taken as a past participle modifying *man*.[6]

One of the necessary results of parsing is therefore disambiguation with respect to grammatical categories. The only ambiguities that remain result from ambiguities in the sentence as a whole. But another and surely more important result of parsing is the assignment of functions to words and phrases. *The man hit the ball* is recognized as a sentence because it consists of a transitive verb preceded and followed by nouns with all required agreements satisfied. But what we really want to know is not that it is a sentence – we might almost be prepared to trust a speaker or writer to confine himself to sentences, and to mistrust ourselves before him if this seemed not to be the case – what we really want to know is where the subject and object are and what is modifying what. In other words, we want to know not only where the boundaries of the phrases

---

[5] A particularly clear exposition of these notions is to be found in N. Chomsky. 1965. *Aspects of the Theory of Syntax*, 68ff., MIT Press.

[6] For this unexpected example I am indebted to the ingenuity of J.J. Robinson and the meticulousness of the IBM 7044 computer.

are but also what function is served by the members of each.

Grammatical functions – subject, object, modifier, complement – fit more naturally into dependency than phrase-structure theory. They appear as labels on the lines of the dependency tree. Figure 5 gives the phrase-structure and dependency diagrams that result from parsing the French sentence *Les petits ruisseaux font les grandes rivières* ("Little streams make big rivers") using the rule tables given in Table 5.

In this latest grammar, the entries in the main table have four parts. First comes the phrase-structure rule showing what parts of speech may combine and what parts of speech the resulting phrases have. Second is the list of references to other tables giving the conditions for the phrase. The third position is occupied by either a "1" or a "2", indicating whether the first or second member of the phrase is the governor, and finally comes the function, a letter showing what relationship obtains between the governor and dependent of the phrase.

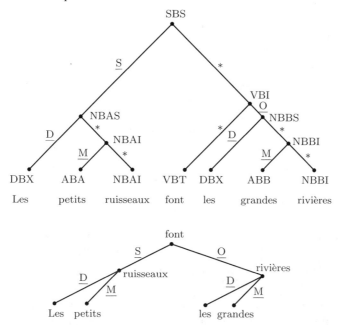

FIGURE 5 Structures with functions marked

One new convention has been added in the rule tables in Table 5. It concerns the order in which the members of a phrase mentioned in the left-hand sides of grammar rules and in the references to tables. The left-hand sides of rules in all but the main table refer not to the first and second members of the phrase respectively, but to the governor and dependent as established by the main table. The *saturation table* is used to ensure that only transitive verbs are given objects and only undetermined nouns are given determiners. With the last convention only one table is needed to handle these situations.

Start at main table [1,1,1]

Main table

A N →   N (Agreement [2,2,2], Agreement [3,3,3]),2,M

D N →   N (Agreement [2,2,2], Agreement [3,3,3]),
           Saturation[4,0,4],2,D

N V →   S (Agreement [2,2,2]), Saturation[3,0,3],2,S

V N →   V Saturation[3,0,3],1,O

Agreement table

A A →   A

A X →   A

X A →   A

B B →   B

B X →   B

X B →   B

X X →   X

Saturation table

I O →   S

T O →   I

D O →   T

The word "saturation" has been coined to refer to a large class of logically similar situations, which, like agreement, are widespread in grammar and can be treated in a natural and compact way with the help of rule tables. A doubly transitive verb may have three nouns or noun phrases appended to it – a direct object, an indirect object and a subject. A transitive verb may have a subject and an object appended, and an intransitive verb only a subject. When a noun phrase is appended to a doubly transitive verb, the resulting phrase is like an ordinary transitive verb; a noun phrase added to a transitive verb results in an intransitive verb phrase; and a noun phrase added to an intransitive verb causes the resulting phrase to be saturated. The codes in the saturation table are initials for the words "double", "transitive", "intransitive", and "saturated". The term "O" occurs in the table because the second potential phrase member is irrelevant here. Noun phrases may also be saturated, as for example, a proper name, or a noun that has collected a full complement of determiners. An ordinary noun, at least in our simple example, is "intransitive" since it may take one determiner. A more sophisticated grammar would doubtless recognize predeterminers, and various other classes of adjectives and noun phrases might therefore be classified as transitive, doubly transitive, possibly triply transitive, and so on.

6.4 The Punched Card Format

The grammar, as it is punched into for use by the computer, consists of two parts, a *directory* and the rule tables themselves. The directory identifies the main table and contains all references to rule tables; a reference from one table to another must be made through the directory. Typically, the first entry in the directory will have the form

ENTER   MAIN,1,1,1

This specifies that the table called "MAIN" is to be referred to first and that the first characters of the grammar codes of the potential phrase members are to be considered.

If a rule is found that applies to the pair, the new symbol for the whole phrase will go in the first character position of the new grammar code. This symbol may, in fact, never see the light of day because the pair of codes may be found unacceptable in some later table. There is nothing special about the word "MAIN". Any sequence of between one and five letters and numbers, provided there is at least one letter, may be the name of any table, including the first one referred to. The table is distinguished only by being the first one in the directory.

An ENTER card may be followed by another ENTER card referring to different columns or to a different table or it may be followed by a card reading "ACCEPT", "ELSE", or "GOTO". Suppose that a given pair of potential phrase members is being considered and a certain rule table is entered from a certain place in the directory. Four things may happen: (i) A rule is found in the table that applies to the pair, and that rule contains a reference to another place in the directory. Usually, that place will be occupied by an ENTER card, and the table it refers to will be the next to be used. In any case, a new part of the directory has become the center of interest. (ii) A rule is found that applies, but the rule makes no explicit reference to the directory. In this case, attention passes to the place immediately following the ENTER that led to that table. If this happens to be an ELSE, the following line is taken. (iii) No rule is found that applies, and the line in the directory immediately following the one leading to that table is not an ELSE. In this case the pair is rejected as a phrase.[7] (iv) No applicable rule is found, and the directory line following the ENTER for the table is an ELSE. A reference to a new location in the directory is punched beginning in column 16 following the word "ELSE", and attention now passes to this location. Notice that "ELSE" has no effect except when an attempt to find an applicable rule in the table referred to by the ENTER line *immediately* preceding it fails. The various possibilities are summarized in Fig. 6.

We have seen the parser may be sent to parts of the directory as a result of applying a rule table to certain characters in a pair of codes. If what is found at a new place in the directory is another ENTER, the events proceed as before. If an ACCEPT is encountered, this means that the current pair of items has passed all tests and the new phrase is accepted. The word "GOTO" (which may not contain any spaces) simply directs attention to a new place in the directory, the name of which is punched beginning in column 16 of the GOTO card.

Consider now the following rule:

$$\text{X Y} \rightarrow \text{Z,, 2, F}$$

This accepts an "X" and a "Y" and delivers a "Z". It says the member from whose code "Y" is taken is to be governor and the function served by the dependent is "F". The next directory entry to be used is the one in line after the current one since no other is explicitly named in the rule. The rule is of the kind we should expect to find in the main table of the grammar, but if it occurred in any other table, what would it mean? Suppose, for example, that when this rule is encountered, the main table has already declared the function to be "G". In this case, the decision made in the main

---

[7]A minor exception to this will be mentioned shortly.

I	II	III	IV
Match found	Matching rule refers to directory entry A (for some A)	Directory entry A = "ACCEPT"	Accept new phrase
		Directory entry A = "ENTER X" (for some X)	Apply table X
		Directory entry A = "ELSE X" (for some X)	Apply column III to entry after A
		Directory line A = "GOTO X" (for some X)	Apply column III to entry X
	Matching rule does not refer to directory	Directory line L+1 = "ACCEPT"	Accept new phrase
		Directory line L+1 = "ENTER X" (for some X)	Apply table X
		Directory line L+1 = "ELSE X" (for some X)	Apply column III to line L+2
		Directory line L+1 = "GOTO X" (for some X)	Apply column III to entry X
No match found	Directory line L+1 = "ELSE X" (for some X)		Apply table X
	Otherwise		Reject phrase

FIGURE 6 Action of the parser on entering a table from directory line 1

table would simply be overridden; the function will now be "F" unless this is overridden yet again by a later rule. Suppose also that the rule in the main table specified the second potential phrase member as governor, so that "X" and "Y" in the present rule refer to the second and first potential members respectively. Once again, the decision of the main table is overridden because this rule says that the item it mentions second is to be governor, and that is the item that came first in the original string. The explanation is as follows. The program assumes, on entry to the main table, that the first of the pair of items up for consideration will be governor. This assumption holds good until a rule is encountered with a "2" after the second comma, and the effect of this is to reverse the current decision on governorship. From this point of view, the main table is seen to operate in exactly the same way as all the rest.

6.5 The Computer Program

Before a grammar can be set to parse a text, it must be translated into a form convenient for the internal operation of the computer but sufficiently lacking in perspicuity from the human standpoint to make the translation step worthwhile. A translation step is made particularly desirable by the fact that the way in which a particular part of the grammar is represented in the machine may depend on a great many other apparently unrelated parts. The name of an entry in the directory, for example, is replaced by the serial number of the entry in the directory as a whole. But if this serial number itself were written, references from all over the grammar would have to be changed every time an entry was added or deleted. To take a more striking example, the names of rule tables are replaced first by a number uniquely identifying their place within the grammar as a whole, and these in turn are later replaced by the addresses of actual cells in the machine.

It will be obvious to a programmer that the kind of translation we are talking about is precisely the kind involved in assembling any computer program, and indeed it may be obvious that, in this case, the translation can be carried out by the standard Macro Assembly Program (MAP).[8] For the non-programmer, some explanation of what MAP is may be interesting, though it is by no means essential for his use of the program.

The directory and grammar tables are not a computer program but the information that a program must have in order to parse text in a specific language. The actual program is the same regardless of the language, the directory entries, or the rules. But the facilities used in the preparation of programs also turn out to be useful for translating the grammar into its internal form. Instructions for the machines (the IBM 7040 and 7044) on which this parsing program is intended to run are usually punched on cards in a format similar to the one we have described – one of a standard set of words punched beginning in column 8, with more specific items of information beginning in column 16 and each item separated from the next by a comma. The part that begins in column 8 is called an *operation* and for each operation, the items that follow may be interpreted in different ways.

The programmer has the option of defining new operations called *macros* in terms of old ones. The details of how he does this are immaterial. Suffice it to say that once the definitions have been introduced by punching them on cards in the approved manner, they can be used just like the original operations from then on. For the purpose of translating grammars in the form we have described, seven macros – "ACCEPT", "ELSE", "ENTER", "GOTO", "RULE", "TABEND" and "TABLE" – have been defined. Each time a grammar is presented to the computer for translation, it must be preceded by a deck of cards containing the definitions of these macros.

One of the advantages of using the standard Macro Assembly Program is that it makes the grammarian eligible for one of the programmer's fringe benefits, namely a *binary deck* containing the results of the translation process. This opaque but compact version of the grammar can be used in place of the original deck in any run of the parsing program that does not require changes in the rules, and the translation process can thus be bypassed. The original form must, of course, be used whenever changes are introduced.

In addition to the grammar, in translated or untranslated form, five other binary decks, which constitute the parsing program proper, must be included in every run. One of these is called SYNTAX and is the only one worthy of comment here – the others contain routines for reading data, printing results, and other pedestrian tasks. SYNTAX contains the routine responsible for maintaining the list of words and phrases that represents what the program knows of the sentence and its structure at any stage in the parsing process. It determines what pairs of words and phrases are potential phrases, ensures that each of these pairs is submitted for adjudication by the grammar exactly once, and adds new phrases to the end of the list.

The strategy followed by the SYNTAX routine is that of John Cocke.[9] It is a morsel

---

[8]See IBM Systems Reference Library, Form C28-6335-1, "IBM 7040/44 Operation System (16132K), Macro Assembly Program (MAP) Language."

[9]See D.G. Hays, 1962, "Automatic Language-Data Processing," in Harold Borko (ed.), *Computer*

strategy,[10] and is to this extent different from a number of other popular methods, notably that of the Harvard Syntactic Analyzer.[11] A morsel strategy is characterized by the large measure of independence of its own structure from the structures it discovers. It cannot be said to be working on one structure for a sentence rather than another at any particular stage. The attempt to form a new phrase out of already established elements is undertaken not because the phrase would be useful in developing this or that structure but because it may prove useful sooner or later, and this is the most convenient time to verify and record it. Clearly, if this policy can be followed consistently and exhaustively, the structures will emerge, as it were, of their own accord.

To describe John Cocke's algorithm, it will be useful to refer to the *string length* of a phrase as the number of words – ultimate constituents of the sentence – that it covers or contains. Thus, a four-word sentence is accepted by a grammar only if a phrase of type "sentence" can be found that covers all four words; such a sentence is a phrase with a string length of four. If the grammar is restricted to binary rules, a phrase with a string length of four can be formed from an ordered pair of phrases with string lengths of one and three, two and two, or three and one. To make this consistent, we interpret a phrase with a string length of one in the obvious way, namely as a single word.

The algorithm finds all phrases with a given string length, say i, before going on to those with length $i+1$. Since phrases are simply added to the end of a list as they identified, this means that all phrases with a given string length come together in a group. The first group consists of the individual words and is given as input to the program; the remainder are established by the algorithm in consultation with the grammar.

A phrase whose string length is the number of words in the whole sentence will be in the last group when the procedure is finished, and therefore it is here that we start looking for complete structures for the sentence. Phrases with smaller string lengths, though they all cover the same number of words, may cover different parts of the original string. The policy is to seek those that cover the leftmost end of the sentence before moving to the right. Thus, within the group of phrases with a given string length, those that cover the first word in the sentence are listed first. Phrases in which the first word covered is the second word in the sentence come next, and so on. Recall that a phrase is said to cover a word not only when the word is a direct member of the phrase, but when it is embedded however deeply in the structure embraced by the phrase.

Even within the narrow class of phrases that have the same string length and cover the same stretch of the sentence, the order of search must be specified. A phrase with a string length of i can only be formed from an adjacent pair of phrases whose string lengths add up to i; the string length of the first member may be anything between 1 and i-l provided that that of the second member is chosen to correspond. In this program, phrases with given string length and coverage are sought in order of increasing length

Applications in the Behavioral Sciences, Prentice Hall, Englewood Cliffs, New Jersey; also J.J. Robinson, 1964, *Automatic Parsing and Fact Retrieval: A Comment on Grammar, Paraphrase, and Meaning*, The RAND Corporation, RM-4005-PR.

[10]This term is due to D.G. Hays; see his "Exhaustive Parsing Procedures," in *Information Processing 62*, Proceedings of the IFIP Congress 1962, North-Holland Publishing Company, 1963.

[11]S. Kuno and A.G. Oettinger, 1962, *Multiple-Path Syntactic Analyzer*, Harvard University Computation Laboratory.

of their first members. The list of phrases is therefore seen to be divided into groups by string length, subgroups by coverage and still smaller units by length of first member. Furthermore, potential phrase members can be widely separated on the list so that the algorithm must be prepared to keep track of each group and subgroup.

In general, there will be more phrases of string length 1 on the list than there are words in the sentence. This is because words typically have more than one grammar code, and each one is accommodated separately. But this only says that phrases of length 1 are like the rest in that there may be more than one of them with the same coverage. To complete the specification of the search strategy, we need only say that for each string length, coverage and length of first member, all possible grammar codes for the first potential member are taken in turn and paired with all grammar codes of the second potential member. A new phrase is formed whenever the grammar allows.

We summarize in Table 6 what has been said about the parsing logic by giving a complete if simple version of the algorithm in ALGOL.[12] The running program differs from this only in a number of minor details, which while they make for efficiency, would obscure the exposition.

6.6 Input and Output

The computer program contains no facilities for a dictionary in which to cull grammar codes for the words in a text (although it would be a simple matter to provide it if required). Consequently, each word in a text offered for parsing must come with its grammar codes appended. The words, which may not be more than eighteen characters long, are punched, one on card, beginning in column 1. A grammar code of not more than eighteen characters is punched on the same card beginning in column 19. If a word has more than one grammar code, the second and subsequent ones are punched each on a separate card, beginning in column 19, columns 1 through 18 being left blank. These cards follow the one bearing the word itself, and there may be any number of them.

Sentences are separated by a card in which the field normally reserved for grammar codes – columns 19 through 36 – is left blank. The remainder of the card will normally be blank also, but the user has the option of punching a code in columns 7 through 12 that affects the form in which the output is printed. The codes "000001" and "000002" respectively, call the first and the second of two output formats shortly to be described. The code "000003" calls both formats, and if no codes are supplied, both formats are also used. These codes affect the output for the sentence they follow and all subsequent sentences up to the next one followed by a code.

The first of the two formats in which results are printed contains complete information on the structures that have been discovered in a form slanted toward phrase-structure rather than dependency. The second is less rich in information but displays the structures as dependency trees.

---

[12]The official definition of ALGOL (from ALGOrithmic Language) is to be found in P. Naur (ed.), "Report on the Algorithmic Language ALGOL 60" *Conmunications of the ACM*, Vol. 3, No. 5, 1960. For more readable expositions, see Daniel D. McCracken, *A Guide to ALGOL Programming*, John Wiley and Sons, Inc., 1962, and E.W. Dijkstra, *A Primer of ALGOL 60 Programming*, Academic Press, New York, 1962.

Table 6 The Parsing Logic in ALGOL

Integer procedure SYNTAX (list, pointer, left, right, words length); value
words, length; integer array list, pointer, left, right; integer words, length;
begin comment This procedure parses a sentence of 'words' words involving
a total of 'length' grammar codes that are assumed to be available to the
procedure GRAM in the form of an array corresponding one-for-one with
'list'. If the ith grammar code belongs to the ith word, then list$[i] = j$, and
throughout the operation of the procedure, if the jth word is the leftmost
covered by the ith item on the list, then list$[i] = j$. left$[i] =$ right$[i] = 0$
if the ith item is a word. If the ith item is a phrase whose members are
the jth and k^{th} items then left$[i] = j$ and right$[i] = k$. GRAM compares
potential phrases with the grammar and, when a phrase is accepted,
makes the appropriate new entries in the list of grammar codes and in
'list', 'left', and 'right'. It increments 'length', the current total number of
grammar codes, to show when a new phrase has been added. 'pointer'
divides 'list' into groups by string length. 'list[pointer$[i]$]' through
'list[pointer$[j + 1] - 1$]' have string length 1. The iteration variables are
as follows:

  i current string length of potential phrases
  j current first word covered by potential phrase
  k current string length of first potential phrase member
  m list entry of current first potential phrase member
  n list entry of current second potential phrase member

integer i, j, k, m, n
pointer$[1] := 1$
for $i := 2$ step 1 until words do
begin pointer$[i] :=$ length+1;
    for $j := 1$ step 1 until words+1 $- i$ do
    for $k := 1$ step 1 until $i - 1$ do
    begin for $m :=$ pointer$[k]$ step 1 until pointer$[k + 1] - 1$ do
        if list$[m] > j$ then goto S2 else if list$[m] = j$ then
        begin for $n :=$ pointer$[j - k]$ step 1 until
            pointer$[i - k + 1] - 1$ do
            if list$[n] > j + k$ then goto S1 else if list$[n] = j + k$ then
            GRAM$(m, n$,length,list,left,right),
        S1:
        end;
    S2:
    end
end;
SYNTAX := length;
end SYNTAX

The results for a sentence begin at the top of a page with a heading of the form
"SENTENCE NUMBER n". This is followed by a line giving the number of times the
grammar was consulted and the total time spent in parsing.

The output under format one consists essentially of a display of the main working
list of the Cocke routine. It is divided into sections, each headed by a line of the form

"STRINGS OF LENGTH i", where i is an integer between 1 and the number of words in the sentence. These sections correspond to the groups into which the internal list is divided (see Sec. 5). If there are no phrases of a given string length, that section is omitted.

The lines bearing the main information are numbered serially for each sentence, and the serial number appears at the left of the page. (See the excerpt below.) Following this are two columns giving the serial numbers in the sentence of the first and last words in the phrase. Therefore, within the group of phrases with string length i, if the first of these numbers is j, the second must be $i + j - 1$. The grammar code of the phrase is listed fourth followed by the word itself. The rest of the page is used for information on the structure of the phrase.

Since an individual word has no internal structure from the syntactic point of view, the only information given about a word is what has just been described. With every other kind of phrase there appears one, and possibly more sets of four columns – a serial number, a function (as described in Sec. 3), and two integers giving the serial numbers in the main list of members of the phrase. The governor is shown before the dependent.

Consider the following extract of output under format one:

STRINGS OF LENGTH 3

21.	2	4	VAAX	ARE	1.	M	8	6
					2.	O	3	9

The twenty-first phrase on the list has a string length of 3 and extends over words 2, 3, and 4. It can easily be identified in the output because its first word is "are". The grammar code of the phrase is "VAAX". Strictly speaking, we have here not one but two phrases. But since they have the same grammar code and coverage, we are justified in treating them as one for purposes that affect the parsing process. Clearly, for every phrase into which one may enter, there is a trivially different phrase formed with the other, and therefore conflating the two not only leads to a saving in computer storage and processing time but also greatly enhances the readability of the results. The two phrases can, in fact, be distinguished by referring to the last four columns, which tell us in this case that one is formed from phrases whose serial numbers on the list are 8 and 6 and that the one with serial number 6 is the dependent with function "M". The second consists of phrase 3 governing phrase 9 with function "O".

Suppose that, later on the same sheet, we find

STRINGS OF LENGTH 5

41.	2	6	VAABC	ARE	1.	C	1	13
					2.	C	21	14
					3.	X	21	15

Here are three phrases collected together as one for procedural purposes. But once again, this is not strictly accurate, for two of the three have item 21 as a member, and this is itself a collection of two phrases. Each of the items containing item 21 is, in reality, at least two phrases. Item 41 is therefore seen to cover a minimum of five phrases.

This simple device of collecting phrases that are equivalent from the point of view of the larger structures they can enter into often leads to spectacular reductions in the space and time required to parse a sentence.

Under format two, an actual dependency diagram is exhibited. Instead of exploiting the condensing device just discussed, each structure is developed individually. Consequently, ambiguous sentences or a permissive grammar can lead to a great amount of output when this format is used. Structures for the whole sentence, if any, are printed first. If there are any phrases that have not been incorporated in any structures for the whole sentence, the longest of these is printed next. If undisplayed phrases still remain, the longest is taken next, and the process continues in this way until every phrase has been printed at least once. A phrase will, of course, be displayed once for each different structure in which it appears, and each time it is printed, all the phrases it covers are necessarily printed also. A phrase is only printed independently if there is no more inclusive phrase in which to show it.

The dependency tree corresponding to the phrase structure stored in the machine is obtained using the algorithm explained in Sec. 1. The words are listed down the page with the governor of the whole sentence or phrase against the left-hand margin. A dotted line extends upward from a word if it has preceding, and downwards if it has following dependents, and short branches from this line lead to the dependents themselves. The function served by a dependent is shown at the junction of the vertical line and the horizontal branch. The following is an example:

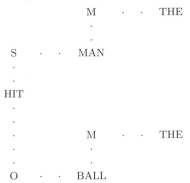

"Man" and "ball" are the subiect and object respectively of "hit" and each has "the" as a modifier.

On the right of the page, opposite each word (not shown here), there appears a number in parentheses giving the serial number in the format-one display of the largest phrase governed by the word in the current structure. This cross reference is useful because, as we have remarked, this display, though perspicuous, in many ways does not give a complete record of the parsing.

Also on the right of the page (and not shown here) are a pair of grammar codes for each word. The first of these is the code of the largest phrase governed by the word in the current structure, sometimes called the *resultant* code of the word. The second is the code assigned to the word initially and used in this construction.

Acknowledgements

This research is sponsored by the United States Air Force under Project RAND – Contract No. AF 49(638)-1700 – monitored by the Directorate of Operational Requirements and Development Plans, Deputy Chief of Staff, Research and Development, Hq USAF. Views or conclusions contained in this Memorandum should not be interpreted as representing the official opinion or policy of the United States Air Force.

7

Experiments with a Powerful Parser

This paper describes a sophisticated syntactic-analysis program for the IBM 7040/44 computer and discusses some of the problems which it brings to light. Basically the program is a nondeterministic device which applies unrestricted rewriting rules to a family of symbol strings and delivers as output all the strings that can be derived from members of the initial family by means of the rules provided. A subsidiary mechanism deals with the relation of *dominance* in the sense common in linguistics. This makes it possible for rules to refer to complete or partial syntactic structures, or *P-markers* , so that the program can be used at least to some extent for transformational analysis.

A program of this kind, which is intended for analysing natural languages, must be capable of operating on a family of strings as a single unit because of the grammatical ambiguity of words. Take, for example, the famous sentence *Time flies like an arrow.* These five words are not, themselves, the primary data on which a parsing program can be expected to operate. Instead, each word is replaced by one or more symbols representing the grammatical categories to which it belongs. The assignments for this example might be somewhat as follows:

Word	Grammatical category
Time	Noun, verb, adjective
flies	Plural noun, 3rd person verb
like	Singular noun, preposition, verb
an	Indefinite article
arrow	Singular noun, adjective

Taking one category symbol for each word, it is possible to form 30 different strings, preserving the order of the original sentence. These 30 strings constitute the family on which the program would operate if set to analyze this sentence.

The program is said to perform as a *non-deterministic* device because whenever two mutually incompatible rules are applicable to the same string neither is given any priority; both are applied, and the resulting strings developed independently. Given the string "A B C" and the rules

$$A\ B\ \Rightarrow\ X\ Y$$
$$B\ C\ \Rightarrow\ Z$$

the program will therefore produce two new strings:

$$X \ Y \ C$$
$$A \ Z$$

The program contains no mechanism for guarding against sequences of rules which do not terminate. If the grammar contains the following rules

$$A \ B \Rightarrow B \ A$$
$$B \ A \Rightarrow A \ B$$

and the string to be parsed contains either "A B" or "B A", then the program will continue substituting these sub-strings for one another until the space available for intermediate results is exhausted. This may not seem to present any particularly severe problem because a pair of rules such as these would never appear in any properly constructed grammar. But, as we shall shortly see, entirely plausible grammars can be constructed for which this problem does arise.

7.1 The Form of Rules

In order to get a general idea of the capabilities of the program, it will be useful first to consider the notation used for presenting rules to it and the way this is interpreted by the machine. In what follows, we shall assume that the reader is familiar with the terminology and usual conventions of phrase-structure and transformational grammar. An example of the simplest kind of rewrite rule is

VPRSG = PRES SG VERB

The "equals" sign is used in place of the more familiar arrow to separate the left and right-hand sides of the rule. The symbols on which the rules operate are words consisting of between one and six alphabetic characters. The above rule will replace the symbol "VPRSG" by a string of three symbols "PRES SG VERB" whenever it occurs. The following rule will invert the order of the symbols "VERB" and "ING"

VERB ING = ING VERB

The simplest way to represent a context free phase structure rule is as in the following example:

NP AUX VP = S

Notice that the normal order of the left and right-hand sides of the rule is reversed because the recognition process consists in rewriting strings as single symbols; the rules must therefore take the form of reductions rather than productions.

The program will accept phrase structure rules in the form we have shown, but, in applying them, it will not keep a record of the total sentence structure to which they contribute. In other words, it will cause a new string to be constructed, but will not relate this string in any way to the string which was rewritten. One way to cause this relationship to be preserved is to write the rule in the following form:

NP.1 AUX.2 VP.3 = S(1 2 3)

The number following the symbols on the left-hand side of the rule function very much like the numbers frequently associated with structural indices in transformational rules. When the left-hand side of the rule is found to match a particular sub-string, the number associated with a given symbol in the rule becomes a pointer to, or a temporary name for, that symbol. With this interpretation, the left-hand side of the above rule can be read somewhat as follows "Find an NP and call it 1; Find an AUX following this and call it 2; Find a VP following this and call it 3."

The numbers in parentheses after a symbol on the right-hand side of a rule are pointers to items identified by the left-hand side, and which the new symbol must dominate. In the example, the symbol "S" is to dominate all the symbols mentioned on the left-hand side.

A pointer may refer to a single symbol, as we have shown, or to a string of symbols. The following rule is equivalent to the one just described:

$$NP.1 \ AUX.1 \ VP.1 = S(1)$$

Furthermore, the string to which a pointer refers need not be continuous. Consider the following example

$$NP.1 \ AUX \ VP.1 = S(1)$$

This will cause any string "NP AUX VP" to be re-written as "S", but the "S" will dominate only "NP" and "VP". There will be no evidence of the intervening "AUX" in the final P-marker which will contain the following phrase:

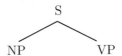

Consider now the following pairs of rules:

$$A.1 \ B.2 \ C.1 \ D.2 = P(1) \ Q(2)$$
$$P.1 \ Q.1 = S(1)$$

If these rules are applied to the string "A B C D" the following P-marker will be formed:

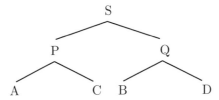

Notice that the first rule in the pair not only re-orders the symbols in the P-marker but forms two phrases simultaneously.

A different way of using pointer numbers on the right-hand side can be illustrated by comparing the effects of the following two rules:

$$N.1 \ SG.1 \ V.2 \ SG.3 = NOUN(1) \ V(2) \ SG(3)$$
$$N.1 \ SG.1 \ V.2 \ SG.2 = NOUN(1) \ 2$$

What is required, we assume, is a context sensitive phrase structure rule which will rewrite "N SG" as "NOUN" in the environment before "V SG". The first rule achieves this effect but also introduces a new "V" dominating the old one, and a new "SG". The second rule does what it really wanted: It constructs a phrase labeled "NOUN" as required, and leaves the symbols referred to by pointer number 2 unchanged.

The context sensitive rule just considered is presumably intended to insure that singular verbs have only singular subjects. A second rule in which "SG" is replaced by "PL" would be required for plural verbs. But, since agreements of this kind may well have to be specified in other parts of the grammar, the situation might better be described by the following three rules:

$$\text{SG.1 = NUM(1)}$$
$$\text{PL.1 = NUM(1)}$$
$$\text{N.1 NUM.2 V.3 2 = NOUN(1 2) 3 2}$$

The first two rules introduce a node labeled "NUM" into the structure above the singular and plural morphemes. The third rule checks for agreement and forms the subject noun phrase. Pointer number 2 is associated with the symbol "NUM" in the second place on the left-hand side, and occurs by itself in the fourth place. This means that the fourth symbol matched by the rule must be "NUM", and also that it must dominate exactly the same sub-tree as the second. In the example we are assuming that "NUM" governs a single node which will be labeled either "SG" or "PL" and the rule will ensure that whichever of these is dominated by the first occurrence of "NUM" will also be dominated by the second occurrence. Notice that noun and verb phrases could be formed simultaneously by the following rule:

$$\text{N.1 NUM.2 V.3 2 = NOUN(1 2) VERB(3 2)}$$

The symbols "ANY" and "NULL" are treated in a special way by this program and should not occur in strings to be analyzed. The use of the symbol "NULL" is illustrated in the rule:

$$\text{PPH = NULL}$$

This will cause the symbol "PPH" to be deleted from any string in which it occurs. The program is non-deterministic in its treatment of rules of this kind, as elsewhere, so that it will consider analyses in which the symbol is deleted, as well as any which can be made by retaining it. The symbol "NULL" is used only on the right-hand sides of rules.

The symbol "ANY" is used only on the left-hand sides of rules and has the property that the word implies, namely that it will match any symbol in a string. The use of this special symbol is illustrated in the following rule:

$$\text{VERB.1 ANY.1 NP.1 = VP(1)}$$

This will form a verb phrase from a verb and a noun phrase, with one intervening word or phrase, whose grammatical category is irrelevant.

Elements on the left-hand sides of rules can be specified as optional by writing a dollar sign to the left or right of the symbol as in the following rules:

$$\text{DET.1 ADJ\$.1 NOUN.1 = NP(1)}$$
$$\text{VERB.1 \$ANY.1 NP.1 = VP(1)}$$

The first of these forms a noun phrase from a determiner and a noun, with or without an intervening adjective. The second is a new version of a rule already considered. A verb phrase is formed from a verb and a noun phrase, with or without an intervening word or phrase of some other type.

Elements can also be specified as repeatable by writing an asterisk against the symbol, as in the following example:

$$\texttt{VERB.1 *NP.1 = VP(1)}$$

This says that a verb phrase may consist of a verb followed by one or more noun phrases. It is often convenient to be able to specify that a given element may occur zero or more times. This is done in the obvious way by combining the dollar sign and the asterisk as in the following rule:

$$\texttt{\$DET.1 *\$ADJ.1 N.1 *PP\$.1 = NP(1)}$$

According to this, a noun may constitute a noun phrase by itself. However the noun may be proceeded by a determiner and any number of adjectives, and followed by a prepositional phrase, and all of these will be embraced by the new noun phrase that is formed. Notice that the asterisk and the dollar sign can be placed before or after the symbol they refer to. The combination is often useful with symbol "ANY" in rules of the following kinds

$$\texttt{N.1 NUM.2 *\$ANY.3 V.4 2 = NOUN(1 2) 3 VERB(4 2)}$$

This is similar to an earlier example. It combines the number morpheme with a subject noun and with a verb, provided that the two agree, and allows for any number of other symbols to intervene. The symbol "ANY" with an asterisk and a dollar sign corresponds in this system to the so-called *variables* in the familiar notation of transformational grammar.

Consider now the following rule:

$$\texttt{SCONJ.1 NP(S).1 = NP(1)}$$

This will form a noun phrase from a subordinating conjunction followed by a noun phrase, provided that this dominates only the symbol "S". Any symbol on the left-hand side of the rule may be followed by an expression in parentheses specifying the string of characters that this symbol must directly dominate. This expression is constructed exactly like the left-hand sides of rules. In particular, it may contain symbols followed by expressions in parentheses. The following rule will serve as an illustration of this, and of another new feature:

$$\texttt{NP(\$DET.1 \$*ANY.1 ADJ(PRPRT.2) \$*ANY.3 N.4 \$PP.5 =}$$
$$\texttt{1 3 4 WH DEF 4 BE ADJ((2)) 5}$$

This rule calls for a noun phrase consisting of a noun, a preceding adjective which dominates a present participle and, optionally, a number of other elements. This noun phrase is replaced by the determiner from the original noun phrase, if there is one, the elements preceding the noun except for the present participle, the noun itself, the symbol "WH", the symbol "DEF", another copy of the noun, the symbol "BE", the symbol "ADJ" dominating exactly those elements originally dominated by "PRPRT" and, finally, any following prepositional phrases the original noun phrase may have contained. The number "2" in double parentheses following "ADJ" on the right-hand side of this rule specifies that this symbol is to dominate, not the present participle itself, but the elements, if any, that it dominates. This device turns out to have wide utility.

Double parentheses can also be used following a symbol on the left-hand side of a rule, but with a different interpretation. We have seen how single parentheses are used to specify the string immediately dominated by a given symbol. Double parentheses enclose a string which must be a *proper analysis* of the sub-tree dominated by the given symbol. A string is said to be a proper analysis of a sub-tree if each terminal symbol of the subtree is dominated by some member of the string. As usual, a symbol is taken to dominate itself. As an example of this, consider the following rule:

```
ART.1 S((ART N.2 ANY*)).1 2 = DET(1) 2
```

This rule applies to a string consisting of an article, a sentence, and a noun. The sentence must be analysable, at some level, as an article followed by a noun, followed by at least one other word or phrase. The noun in the embedded sentence, and the sub-tree it dominates, must be exactly matched by the noun corresponding to the last element on the left-hand side of the rule. The initial article and the embedded sentence will be collected as a phrase under the symbol "DET" and the final noun will be left unchanged.

The principal facilities available for writing rules have now been exemplified. Another kind of rule is also available which has a left-hand side like those already described but no equal sign or right-hand side. However it will be in the best interests of clarity to defer an explanation of how these rules are interpreted.

The user of the program may write rules in exactly the form we have described or may add information to control the order in which the rules are applied. This additional information takes the form of an expression written before the rule and separated from it by a comma. This expression, in its turn, takes one of the following forms:

$$n_1,$$
$$n_1/n_2,$$
$$n_1/n_2/n_3,$$
$$n_1//n_3,$$

n_1 is an integer which orders this rule relative to the others. Since the same integer can be assigned to more than one rule, the ordering is partial. Rules to which no number is explicitly assigned are given the number 0 by the program. n_2 and n_3, when present, are interpreted as follows: Every symbol in the sub-string matched by the left-hand side of the rule must have been produced by a rule with number i, where $n_2 \geq i \geq n_3$. For these purposes the symbols in the original family of strings offered for analysis are treated as though they had been produced by a rule with number 0.

7.2 Phrase-Structure Grammar

It will be clear from what has been said already that this program is an exceedingly powerful device capable of operating on strings and trees in a wide variety of ways. It would clearly be entirely adequate for analyzing sentences with a context-free phrase structure grammar. But this problem has been solved before, and much more simply. We have seen how the notation can be used to write context-sensitive rules, and we should therefore expect the program to be able to analyze sentences with a context-sensitive grammar. However in the design of parsing algorithms, as elsewhere, context-sensitive grammars turn out to be surprisingly more complicated than context-free grammars.

The problem that context-sensitive grammars pose for this program can be shown with a simple example.[1] Consider the following grammar:

$$S \Rightarrow \begin{cases} \text{A B C} & (1) \\ \text{D E (S)} & (2) \end{cases}$$

$$B \Rightarrow \begin{cases} \text{D/A\_\_} & (3) \\ \text{F/\_\_E} & (4) \end{cases}$$

$$D \Rightarrow \begin{cases} \text{G/A\_\_} & (5) \\ \text{B/\_\_E} & (6) \end{cases}$$

This grammar, though trivial, is well behaved in all important ways. The language generated, though regular and unambiguous, is infinite.

Furthermore, every rule is useful for some derivation. Since the language generated is unambiguous, the grammar is necessarily *cycle-free* ; in other words, it produces no derivation in which the same line occurs more than once. Suppose, however, that the grammar is used for analysis and is presented with the string "A D E" – not a sentence of the language. The attempt to analyze this string using rules of the grammar results in a rewriting operation that begins as follows and continues indefinitely:

A D E
A B E   (by rule 3)
A D E   (by rule 6)
A B E   (by rule 3)
etc.

It would clearly be possible, in principle, to equip the program with a procedure for detecting cycles of this sort, but the time required by such a procedure, and the complexity that it would introduce into the program as a whole, are sufficient to rule it out of all practical consideration. It might be argued that the strings which have to be analyzed in practical situations come from real texts and can be assumed to be sentences. The problem of distinguishing sentences from nonsentences is of academic interest. But, in natural languages, the assignment of words to grammatical categories is notoriously ambiguous and for this problem to arise it is enough for suitably ambiguous words to come together in the sentence. A sentence which would be accepted by the above grammar, but which would also give rise to cycles in the analysis, might consist of words with the following grammatical categories:

Word	Grammatical Category
1	A
2	B
3	C, E

The program, as it stands, contains no mechanism which automatically guards against cycles. However, if the user knows where they are likely to occur or discovers them as

---

[1]I am indebted for this example, as for other ideas too numerous to document individually, to Susumu Kuno of Harvard University.

a result of his experience with the program, he can include some special rules in his grammar which will prevent them from occurring. These rules, which we have already alluded to, are formally similar to all others except that they contain no equals sign and no right-hand side. When a P-marker is found to contain a string which matches the left-hand side of one of these rules, the program arranges that, thence forward, no other rule shall be allowed to apply to the whole string. The cycle in this latest example could not occur if the grammar contained the rule:

A B E

7.3   Transformational Grammar

We now come to the main concern of this paper which is to discuss the extent to which the program we have been describing can be made to function as a transformational analyzer. The main purpose of the examples that have been given is to show the great power of the program as a processor of symbol strings. The notion of dominance is provided for, but only in a rudimentary way. It certainly could not be claimed that the program is a tree processor in any really workable sense. But grammatical transformations are operations on trees and our investigation therefore must take the form of showing that these operations can frequently, if not always, be mimicked by string rewriting rules.

We shall take it that a transformational grammar consists of a context-free or context-sensitive phrase-structure component and a set of transformations ordered in some way. To begin with, very little will be lost if we assume that the transformational rules are simply ordered.

Consider now the first transformation in the list. In general, this may be expected to introduce phrases into the P-markers to which it applies which could not have been generated by the phrase-structure component. Let us now write some additional phrase-structure rules capable of generating these new phrases. Let us insert these rules into the grammar immediately following the first transformational rule and establish the convention that, when they are used in the analysis of the string, their output will be used only as input to the first transformation. Now treat the second transformational rule in the same way. It also can be expected to create new kinds of phrase, and phrase-structure rules can be written which would recognize these. It may be that some of the phrases formed by the second rule could also be formed by the first, and in this case, it may be possible to move the appropriate rule from its position after the first transformation to a position after the second and to mark it as providing input only for these two rules.

Notice that the rules we are proposing to construct will not constitute what has sometimes been called a *surface grammar* . The phrases they describe certainly do not belong to the base structure and many of them may not be capable of surviving unchanged into the surface structure. In general these rules describe phrases which can only have transitory existence somewhere in the generative process. Notice also that in order to describe these phrases adequately it may sometimes be necessary to extend the notion of phrase structure grammar somewhat. Consider for example the following transformation:

$$X \quad - \quad A \quad - \quad B \quad - \quad Y$$
$$1 \qquad 2 \qquad 3 \qquad 4$$

Adjoin 2 as right daughter of 3

If we make the usual assumption that a rule is applied repeatedly until no proper analyses of the P-marker remains which can be matched by its structural index, then this transformation, and many others, may produce phrases of indefinitely many types. Let us suppose that, before this transformation is applied for the first time, all possible phrases that can be dominated by the symbol "B" are describable by context-free phrase structure rules of the following form

$$B \Rightarrow \left\{ \begin{array}{c} \alpha_1 \\ \alpha_2 \\ \ldots \\ \alpha_k \end{array} \right\}$$

where the α_i are any strings. The phrase structure grammar needed to describe all the phrases that can exist after the operation of this transformation must contain the following rules, or more accurately rule schemata

$$B \Rightarrow \left\{ \begin{array}{c} \alpha_1 \\ \alpha_2 \\ \ldots \\ \alpha_k \end{array} \right\} A^*$$

where the asterisk indicates one or more repetitions of the symbol "A". If the left and right-hand sides of these rules are reversed and they are presented to the program in the proper notation, then the transformation itself can be represented by the following pair of rules:

$$B(*\$ANY.1 \ *A.2) = 2 \ B+ \ 1 \ +B$$
$$B+ \ B.1 \ +B = 1$$

Since there are no facilities for specifying dominance relations among elements on the right-hand sides of these rules, it is necessary to resort to subterfuge. The phrase dominated by the symbol "B" is reproduced in the output of this rule with copies of the symbol "A" removed from the right-hand end and the remainder bounded by the symbols "B+" and "+B". These symbols serve to delimit a part of the string which can only figure in the complete analysis of the sentence if it constitutes a phrase of type "B". The second rule removes these boundary symbols from the phrase of type "B" and, since no pointer is assigned to them, they will leave no trace in the final P-marker.

Another, and perhaps more economical, way to write recognition rules corresponding to this transformation involves conflating the additional phrase-structure rules with the reverse of the transformational rule itself to give rules of the following kind:

$$\alpha_i 1 \ *A.2 = 2 \ B+ \ 1 \ +B \ (1 \leq i \leq n)$$
$$B+ \ B.1 \ +B = 1$$

In fact, the elementary transformation for daughter adjunction that we are providing for here is more general than that often allowed by transformational grammarians. It is common to require that if some element a is adjoined as a daughter of another element b then b must have no daughters before the transformation takes place.

Sister adjunction can be treated in an analogous manner. Consider the following transformation:

$$X \quad - \quad A \quad - \quad B \quad - \quad Y$$
$$1 \qquad 2 \qquad 3 \qquad 4$$

Adjoin 2 as right sister of 4

The phrases exsisting before this transformation is carried out, and which have "B" as a constituent, can be thought of as being described by a set of rules as follows:

$$a_1 \Rightarrow B \; \alpha_1$$
$$a_2 \Rightarrow B \; \alpha_2$$
$$\cdots$$
$$a_n \Rightarrow B \; \alpha_n$$

Here the a_i are nonterminal symbols and the α_i are strings, possibly null. The grammar which describes the phrases existing after the operation of this transformation must contain, in addition, the following rules:

$$a_1 \Rightarrow B \; \alpha_1 \; \text{A*}$$
$$a_2 \Rightarrow B \; \alpha_2 \; \text{A*}$$
$$\cdots$$
$$a_n \Rightarrow B \; \alpha_n \; \text{A*}$$

The reverse transformation itself can now be represented by a set of rules as follows:

$$\text{B.1 } \alpha_i.1 \text{ A*.2 = 2 B+ 1 +B}$$

Notice that the strings referred to by the symbols "X" and "Y" in both of the above examples are unchanged by the transformation and are therefore not mentioned at all in the analysis rules. Experience shows that it is in fact rarely necessary to write separate rules for each α_i. In most cases, a transformation of this kind could be handled in the program with a rule of the following form:

$$\text{B.1 ANY.1 A*.2 = 2 B+ 1 +B}$$

This is one of a large number of cases in which it has been found that the analysis rules can be made more permissive than the original grammar suggests without introducing spurious structures and without seriously increasing the amount of time or space used by the program.

While it is possible that transformational analysis can be done in an interesting way with a program of this sort there seems to be little hope of finding an algorithm for writing analysis rules corresponding to a given transformational grammar. The following rule also involves sister adjunction but poses much more serious problems than the previous example:

$$X \quad - \quad A \quad - \quad Y \quad - \quad B \quad - \quad Z$$
$$1 \qquad 2 \qquad 3 \qquad 4 \qquad 5$$

Adjoin 2 as right sister of 4

The problem here is that a variable "Y" intervenes between "A" and "B". On the face of it, the analysis rule corresponding to this transformation would have to be somewhat as follows:

$$*\$ANY.1 \ B.2 \ *A.3 = 3 \ 1 \ 2$$

And in principle the program could carry out a rule of this kind. However the first symbol on the left-hand side of this rule will match any string whatsoever, so that, if the rule can be applied at all, it can be applied in a prodigious number of ways. But, with real grammars, it usually turns out that quite a lot can be said about the part of the sentence covered by the variable "Y" so that analysis rules can be written which are sufficiently specific to be practicable.

Deletions are notoriously troublesome in grammars of any kind because they can so easily give rise to cycles and undecidable problems. Transformational grammarians require that lexical items should only be deleted from a P-marker if there is some other copy of the same item which remains. This condition insures what they call the *recoverability* of the transformation. However, it is very important to realize that recoverability, in this sense, is a very weak condition. The requirement is that, knowing that an item has been deleted from a certain position in the P-marker, it should be possible to tell what that item was. But there is no requirement that a P-marker should contain evidence that it was derived by means of a deletion transformation or of the places in it where deletions might have taken place.

Deletions are easier to cope with in certain situations than others. Consider for example the following transformation:

$$
\begin{array}{ccccccccc}
X & - & A & - & B & - & A & - & Y \\
1 & & 2 & & 3 & & 4 & & 5
\end{array}
$$
$$\text{Delete 4.}$$

The recoverability requirement is satisfied because of the identity of the second and fourth elements in the structural index. The corresponding rule for the program might be as follows:

$$23,22, \ A.1 \ B.2 = 1 \ 2 \ 1$$

It is necessary to provide ordering information with a rule of this kind because it would otherwise be capable of operating on its own output and cycling indefinitely. But presumably this transformation can be carried out any number of times and the same therefore should be true of the corresponding analysis rule. Once again, experience shows that the grammarian almost invariably knows more about the environment in which a deletion takes place than is stated in the rule, and if this information is used carefully, analysis rules can be written which do not lead to cycles.

In principle the situation is even worse in rules of the following kind:

$$
\begin{array}{ccccccccc}
X & - & A & - & Y & - & A & - & Z \\
1 & & 2 & & 3 & & 4 & & 5
\end{array}
$$
$$\text{Delete 4}$$

Here the third element is a variable which can cover any number of nodes in the P-marker. In analysis we are therefore not only without information about how many times the rule may have been applied but we know nothing about where to insert new copies of the symbol "A" except that they must be to the right of the existing copy.

The other commonly used elementary transformations (substitutions and Chomsky-adjunction) do not present special problems. The main outstanding difficulty comes from the fact that transformational rules are ordered. We have already said that the theory of transformational grammar is in the state of continual change and this is particularly true of the part that concerns the ordering of rules. For this reason we have assumed that the rules are simply ordered in the hope that other possibilities will not be notably more difficult to deal with. We shall also make the assumption that transformational rules are all obligatory.

Consider now the following grammar

Phrase structure

1.	S	⇒	A (D) B C
2.	C	⇒	D E

Transformations

1.	A	-	B	-	X
	1		2		3
	0		2+1		3

and suppose that the program is required to analyze the string "A D B E". Since, in generation, the list of transformations is read from top to bottom it is reasonable to suppose that in analysis it should be read from bottom to top.

We may take it that the analysis rule corresponding to the second transformation is somewhat as follows:

$$\text{D.1 B.2 = 2 1}$$

This, together with the two phrase-structure rules, is sufficient to give a complete analysis of the string with this underlying P-marker:

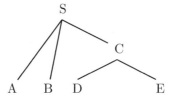

But if this is an underlying P-marker, the second transformational rule could not possibly be used to produce a derived structure from it because the first transformation, which according to our assumption is obligatory, can be applied to it giving the following result:

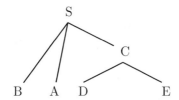

It is in fact not sufficient to scan the list of transformations from bottom to top because this procedure does not make allowance for the fact that the transformations are obligatory. To regard transformations as optional which were intended to be obligatory is in general to associate spurious base structures to some sentences. The solution for the present grammar is to use the following set of analysis rules:

```
1/0,   B D
2/1,   D.1 B.2 = 2 1
3/2,   A B
4/3,   B.1 A.2 = 2 1
       D.1 E.1 = C(1)
       A.1 $D.1 B.1 C.1 = S(1)
```

The first and third rules contain, in effect, the structural indices from the second and first transformations respectively. The first rule says that no string is acceptable as a sentence which contains "B D" as a sub-string because to this it would have been possible to apply transformation 2. The second rule reverses the effect of transformation 2. The third rule excludes any P-marker existing at this stage with a proper analysis containing "A B" as a sub-string. This is the structural index of transformation 1 which therefore should have been applied to any P-marker containing it. The fourth rule reverses the effect of transformation 1 and the remaining rules are the phrase-structure component of the grammar. Once again it turns out that what may be necessary in theory is only rarely needed in practice. Experience with this program is, so far, very limited but no cases have so far been found in which incorrect analyses have resulted from omitting rules such as those numbered one and three above.

Conclusions

It requires skill to write rules for analyzing natural sentences with the program described in this paper. A program can only properly be called a transformational parser if it can work directly with the unedited rules of the transformational grammar. But no algorithm is known, nor is it likely that one will shortly be found, which will produce from a transformational grammar a set of corresponding rules of the kind required by this program. It is not difficult to construct a transformational grammar for which no exactly corresponding set of analysis rules can be written. However, other programs have been written which, though they are still in many ways imperfect, can more reasonably be called transformational parsers. What then are the advantages of the present program?

The current version of the program is written in ALGOL and with very little regard for efficiency. But the basic algorithm is inherently a very great deal more efficient than any of its competitors. The various interpretations of an ambiguous sentence, or a sentence which seems likely to be ambiguous in the early stages of analysis, are all worked on simultaneously. At no stage can the program be said to be developing one interpretation of a sentence rather than another. If two interpretations differ only in some small part of the P-marker, then only one complete P-marker is stored with two versions of the ambiguous part. Work done on the unambiguous portion is done only once for both interpretations.

The program, though undoubtably very powerful, seems naive from the point of view of modern linguistic theory. The program embodies very little of what we know or believe to be true about the structure of natural languages. It might well be said that a computer program for analyzing natural languages is only interesting to the extent that it makes a claim about the basic form of those languages. But the program described here is intended as a tool and not as a linguistic hypothesis. There is much to be learned about natural language from ruminating on the form of universal generative grammar and trading counter-example for example. But there is also much to be learned from studying text as it actually occurs. The small amount of work that has so far been done with this program has been sufficient to suggest strongly that a set of rules derived algorithmically from a transformational grammar is unlikely to be the most effective or the most revealing analytic device.

8

From Semantics to Syntax

Language is an instrument of communication. Speakers of a common language exchange tokens and thereby influence what goes on in one another's minds in more or less predictable ways. Two people speak the same language if they not only agree on what counts as an acceptable token, but if they are also able to predict fairly accurately what effect each token will have on the other. It seems, therefore, that a linguistic theory – a model of human language – must provide for two kinds of objects corresponding to the tokens and their predictable effects respectively. These can conveniently be labeled *sentences* and *meanings*. It must also provide a characterization of the way sentences are paired with meanings.

As Lyons (1963) points out, this is not the only possible view of language. It is true that a token must be meaningful to be linguistic, but this does not entail that there is necessarily something which is its meaning. The so-called structural semanticists view meanings not as entities apart from sentences but as relations among sentences. To say that one sentence is true if and only if another is true, or that one entails another, or that one is incompatible with another, is to state, at least in part, the meanings of these sentences; it is not to state facts which are true by virtue of relations among some distinct set of entities, the true meanings.

This view is appealing because it avoids one of the traditional philosophical difficulties in discussions of meaning. The meaning of a sentence cannot be separated from its linguistic embodiment; it can be stated only in the terms of some linguistic system, which is to say, in effect, as a sentence. No principle is readily available for choosing one of a set of paraphrases and claiming that it *is* the meaning of the others. More reasonable seems to be to say that their meaning *is* the equivalence relation that unites them, and the relation of entailment that sets them off from other such sets.

But, while this view may have some short-term philosophical appeal, it is almost totally barren from the standpoint of scientific linguistics. It leaves unexplained the fact that meanings, as well as relating sentences, do affect people. More important, it fails to explain how people can correctly tell the meanings of new sentences. The number of sentences in a language is usually supposed to be infinite and the number of expressable meanings is presumably not smaller. The fact that all the members of a speech community identify essentially the same set of pairs therefore demands explanation.

It is true that meanings can never be exhibited in a pure form, but only as represented by sentences, but this is not to say that every sentence is semantically as perspicuous as every other. The sentence *The person who lived in the house at the side of theirs bought the car* means substantially the same as *The automobile was sold to their next-door neighbor* but the two sentences have almost no words in common and their grammatical structures are clearly distinct. A semantically perspicuous notation would express similar meanings in similar ways. It would be such that if one sentence entailed another, then the second could be derived from the first by applying certain very general rules.[1] There are no general rules that will derive *One of my parents had an accident today* directly from *My father fell downstairs and hurt himself badly this morning.* For a perspicuous notation, the rules could be written.

As I said at the outset, it is part of the work of linguistics to characterize the set of sentence-meaning pairs that make up a language. Since the number of such pairs is infinite, linguistic theory must enumerate them recursively; it will therefore be what is called a *generative* theory.

Many generative theories are, in principle, possible. Chomsky's theory of transformational grammar has a *base component* which characterizes a set of *base P-markers* each of which is translated into a *semantic interpretation* by a *semantic component* and into a sentence by *transformational* and *phonological components*. A base P-marker therefore corresponds to zero or more sentence-meaning pairs, and the total set generable in this way constitutes the language characterized.

An alternative plan is to make the base, or productive, component semantic. The base P-markers would then be semantic interpretations, and the transformational and phonological components would translate them into sentences.

There are several objections that can be made to both of these formulations of generative grammar (see Hays and Kay, forthcoming). Most important is the objection that they provide the worst possible basis for an attack on the problems of what Chomsky calls *performance*. A language is a set of sentence-meaning pairs, but it is also an instrument of communication. It is therefore of the essence that a speaker of a language should not only know the proper set of sentence-meaning pairs, but that he should be able effectively to translate sentences into meanings and meanings into sentences. He must be able to use his linguistic competence in performance and the linguist must, sooner or later, explain how he does this.

A linguistic theory which provides a realistic basis for the study of performance must characterize a transducer capable of translating meanings into sentences and vice versa. Chomsky's theory certainly does not do this and there is every reason to suppose that it will not be possible, in general, to construct a transducer of the required kind from the rules of a transformational grammar.

Henceforeward, I shall use the term *transductive* to refer to a linguistic theory which defines a semantic and a phonetic notation, a *transduction rule* form, an *upward transducer* or algorithm which translates phonetic expressions into semantic expressions and a *downward transducer* which translates semantic into phonetic expressions. A particular

---

[1]This should not be taken as meaning that the particular set of rules required to derive one from the other should itself be discoverable algorithmically. We must expect the semantic formalism to be such that equivalence and entailment relations will be formally undecidable.

language will be characterized by a set of transduction rules which specify the operation of both transducers.

The grammar of a language must distinguish a set of well-formed phonetic expressions, or *sentences*, and a set of well-formed semantic expressions, or *meanings*. The question of whether the set of meanings is a linguistic universal is important, but it would be premature to try to solve it now. Another important question, which must be answered at least provisionally before any further progress can be made, concerns the ranges and domains of the transducers and the way in which sets of well-formed expressions are to be defined. The simplest solution is to require that the transducers produce at least one well-formed expression as output in response to every well-formed input and that they produce no output in response to an ill-formed input.

A second possibility is to require that the transducers produce well-formed output in response to every input. In such a system, the well-formedness of an expression could be decided by translating it into one or more expressions of the other type with one transducer and translating each of these into one or more expressions of the original type with the other transducer. The expression is well formed if, and only if, it is found among the expressions resulting from the second transduction.

This plan is attractive because it offers the possibility of explaining how ungrammatical sentences are understood and how grammatical sentences can be only partially coherent, or cognitively anomalous.

A host of other possibilities suggest themselves. We can imagine a system which mapped a sentence onto meanings and non-meanings according to the various natural and anomalous interpretations it had and which mapped non-meanings sometimes onto sentences and sometimes onto non-sentences. In this case, however, the transducers themselves make no distinction between well- and ill-formed expressions and the grammar would therefore have to contain at least one extra component with a function similar to that of Chomsky's base component. But if this were found necessary in a satisfactory theory, it would weaken the claims that could be made for the transductive theory because these rest heavily on the proposition that a base component cannot be satisfactorily motivated. At this stage, it is altogether unclear which approach will be most fruitful.

The theory to be sketched shortly takes the simplest approach. Well-formed expressions are carried onto well-formed expressions and ill-formed expressions give no output.

In what follows, I shall describe a form of rules which translate semantic expressions in a notation akin to that of the predicate calculus into P-markers. The same rules, interpreted by a slightly different transducer will translate P-markers into semantic expressions. I have chosen to concentrate on the downward transduction process partly because the operation of the upward transducer is simpler, and partly to stress the difference between the view of language advocated here and the more fashionable one in which semantics is regarded as purely interpretive.

To say that we propose to write semantic expressions in a notation akin to that of the predicate calculus is, on the face of it, to say very little because the notation is rich enough to talk about objects of any kind and to describe any kind of relational structure over them. There is no limit to the number of ways in which even so simple a sentence as *The man ran* could be translated. The following are some possible candidates:

(1) ran(man)

(2) run(man) past(run)

(3) run(human) male(human) past(run)

(4) def(human) male(human) run(human) past(run)

In a sentence consisting of a subject and an intransitive verb, we are used to thinking of the verb as specifying properties predicated of the subject. Example (1) therefore seems to be a natural translation. We know however that, for many purposes, the feature of tense needs to be separated out, and this is done in (2). Here *run* must be thought of as implying no particular temporal reference. The past tense is represented by conjoining a second elementary proposition in which 'past' is predicated of 'run'. There is reason to believe that it will be profitable to separate out the feature of sex as is done in (3). The content of the English word *man* is now represented by a pair of primitives, namely 'human' and 'male'. Example (4) is an attempt to accommodate the definite article.

It is by no means clear at what point the process of factoring notions into simpler notions should stop. Outside logic itself it is difficult to find a notion so elementary that it cannot, with a little thought, be expressed as a combination of others. But this is not to say that the entire enterprise is misbegotten. It is indeed possible to state properties that semantic expressions with any real explanatory value must have and to develop a theory of the lexical structure of a language by considering examples and counter-examples and the semantic expressions that can be associated with them by a set of formal rules.

As I have said, semantic expressions must be perspicuous. If two sentences are judged to be exact paraphrases of one another, then their semantic representations must be equivalent. If one sentence logically entails another, then the semantic representation of the second should be derivable by formal rules from that of the first. This is a reasonable requirement of a semantic theory because a notion of entailment is, in fact, often crucial to deciding whether a text is well formed. Consider a fairy story which begins as follows:

> Once upon a time a lion and a unicorn decided to go hunting together. But one of the animals was afraid of the other because of what he might do when they got into the forest. It was the lion that was afraid of the unicorn.

If the second sentence is left out, the result is no longer acceptable as the beginning of a well-behaved fairy story. The sentence *It was the lion that was afraid of the unicorn* can be introduced only when it has been established that a lion and a unicorn are involved in the story, and that someone is afraid of someone else. Notice however that the following is entirely acceptable:

> Once upon a time a lion and a unicorn decided to go hunting together. The lion was afraid of the unicorn.

The sentence *The lion was afraid of the unicorn* is true if and only if the sentence *It was the lion that was afraid of the unicorn* is true. But the latter is unacceptable in at least some contexts where the former sounds entirely natural. But for the latter to be acceptable there must be some previous sentence in the text which implies that somebody is afraid of somebody. A semantic theory must therefore provide some formal mechanism for deducing *somebody is afraid of somebody* from *but one of the animals was afraid of the other*.

Another story might begin as follows:

John Doe was a school master who, at the age of seventy, fell in love with an airline hostess. The girl decided to give up her job and marry him.

If not in the best literary style, this is at least more acceptable than the following:

John Doe was a school master who, at the age of seventy, fell in love with an airline hostess. The boy decided to give up her job and marry him.

The second example sounds strange for several reasons, one of which is that no boy has been introduced into the story. There is no parallel difficulty in the first example because airline hostesses are, in general, girls. It is presumably up to the semantic component of the grammar to record this fact and to infer that one of the characters in the story is a girl because one of them is an airline hostess. The sentence *John Doe was a school master who, at the age of seventy, fell in love with an airline hostess* presumably differs in its semantic representation from *John Doe was a school master who, at the age of seventy, fell in love with a girl* in containing a few extra predicates – those necessary to make the meaning of girl more specific so that it becomes the meaning of airline hostess.

It is not the purpose of this paper to provide even the most tentative set of semantic primitives. I am concerned only with providing the formal system which will relate expressions involving semantic primitives with sentences in a real language. This is, of course, a much simpler task, but it must precede any serious work on the primitives themselves, because, in the absence of a rigorous method of associating sentences with semantic representations, there is no sure means of judging the effect of introducing or deleting this or that primitive, and the discussion rapidly loses all contact with reality. However, we cannot proceed to set up the formalism without taking notice of some more substantive issues and the most important of these concerns the relationship between the expressions we shall write and expressions in a genuine logic such as the first-order predicate calculus.

The humanist is quite right to claim that language is not logical if, by that, he means that the language of semantic representations cannot itself be a logic. Expressions in natural language can be logically equivalent without being linguistically equivalent. The sentence *It was the lion that was afraid of the unicorn* is true if and only if the sentence *The lion was afraid of the unicorn* is true. But, as we have seen, the latter can be used in places where the former is anomalous. It is, of course, possible to claim that pairs of sentences such as these should be regarded as having the same meaning and that the differences between them should be accounted for on some other basis. The grammar might, for example, contain a kind of super-syntactic component describing the way in which sentences are collected to form discourses. Or there might be a stylistic or rhetorical component, concerned with such matters as emphasis, in which these sentences would be distinguished. But, for reasons I shall present shortly, I prefer to regard these sentences as having different meanings even though they are logically equivalent.

The second reason why the language of semantic representations cannot itself be a logic is that it must be capable of expressing certain notions which must be regarded as meaningless in any logic. There must, for example, be no restriction on the ways in which predicates can be applied to other predicates and, in particular, there must be no restriction against a predicate being applied to itself. Allowing this is, of course, exactly what leads to Russell's famous paradox for, if of any one place predicate *p* the proposition *p(p)* is meaningful, then we can construct the predicate *q* such that *q(p)* is true if and only if *p(p)* is false. But, substituting *q* for *p*, we have the logical fact that *q(q)* is true if and only if *q(q)* is false.

This paradox has led logicians to reject any system in which predicates can be applied indiscriminately to other predicates and to deny the meaningfulness of such notions as self-predicability. But self-predicability is not meaningless. The word *short* is itself short and is therefore self-predicable; the word *long* is not long and is therefore not self-predicable.

It is probably true to say that Russell's paradox came to light precisely because natural languages are capable of expressing ideas which logic cannot accommodate. If such terms as 'self-predicable' and 'the set of all sets' did not sound beguilingly natural, they would never have caused any difficulty. And if they were not meaningful then it is difficult to see how they could have been so closely analyzed as to show their underlying illogicality. The point is this: Logic must be purged of contradictions if it is to be useful for its intended purpose, namely to construct arguments that can be faulted only by faulting the premises on which they are based. Such a system is just as necessary for constructing arguments about language as anywhere else. But our concern here is not with constructing a metalanguage for linguistics, but with constructing a language capable of expressing the things that people express in normal speech. It is true that we have said that the possibility of making inferences in this language by means of formal rules will be one of its crucial properties. But these inferences will have their basis in the culture and the structure of the language, and not in axioms and theorems. The examples (1)–(4) are not therefore to be rejected simply because the same word appears now as a predicate and now as an argument. But they are unsatisfactory from at least one other point of view, namely that they fail to make a necessary distinction between intension and extension. Translating the sentence *The boy saw the man* in a similar way, we might have something like:

see(human,human). male(human). male(human). young(human). past(see)

assuming, perhaps unrealistically, that the representation of 'boy' differs from that of 'man' only by the additional predicate 'young'.

This is clearly unsatisfactory because each instance of the term 'human' refers to one of two different people and there is no way of telling them apart. Another possibility is the following:

human(x). human(y). male(x). male(y). young(x). see(x,y). past(see)

Here the variables, x and y, correspond to referents. Reference is another notion that needs to be interpreted more broadly in a linguistic than a logical or philosophical context. It is clearly not profitable to think of referents as objects in the real world because it is highly unlikely that the sentence *The boy saw the man* in which the boy and the man may refer to real people is interpreted in a different way from *The unicorn saw the lion* in which the unicorn is presumably fictional. In fact, from a linguistic point of view, there is reason to suppose that a sentence like *The boy saw the man* involves more than two referents because there are also sentences like *The boy saw the man and when he did he ran away.* The word *did* in this sentence clearly refers to the same event as the word *saw.* In the sentence *The boy saw the man and so did the girl* on the other hand, the word *did* refers to a different event, though one which can have the same name.

The rules for developing P-markers will usually contain two parts, one referring to conditions that must hold in the semantic representation if the rule is applied and the other referring to conditions that must hold in the P-marker, as so far developed, and specifying additions to be made to the P-marker. The second part of a rule will look essentially like a sequence of one or more context-free phrase-structure rules of the familiar type. Let us assume for the moment that the representation of the sentence *The boy saw the man* is as follows:

$$\text{human}(x).\ \text{human}(y).\ \text{male}(x).\ \text{male}(y).\ \text{young}(x).\ \text{see}(z).\ \text{past}(z).\ z(x,y)$$

Some of the rules that might be used in producing the P-marker from this expression are as follows:

$$
\begin{array}{lll}
\text{(i)} & a(b,c) & \left| \begin{array}{ll} S & \rightarrow NP_b\ VP \\ VP & \rightarrow V_a\ NP_c \end{array} \right.
\end{array}
$$

(ii) $\text{see}(a).\text{past}(a) \mid V_a \rightarrow$ *saw*

(iii) $\text{human}(a).\text{male}(a).\text{young}(a) \mid N_a \rightarrow$ *boy*

The two parts of each rule are separated by an upright bar. Variables ($a,b,c...$) appearing in the first part of a rule can match any variables ($x,y,z...$) in the semantic expression. Rule (i) is interpreted as follows: If the semantic expression contains one variable predicated of two others and if the symbol S appears at some node in the P-marker which does not, so far, have any descendents, then the symbols NP and VP can be written against two new nodes dominated by the S. Two more new nodes are to be introduced beneath VP, labelled V and NP respectively.

The subscripts appended to certain symbols in the second half of a rule allow nodes in the P-marker to be associated with variables in the semantic expression. Thus, in rule (i), the NP node introduced below S is to be associated with the first argument of the predicate translated by this rule. Similarly, the newly introduced node V is to be associated with the predicate itself and the second NP is to be associated with the second argument of the predicate. Rule (ii) is to be interpreted as follows: If *see* and *past* are predicated of the same variable in the expression and the P-marker contains a node labelled V which has been associated with that variable, and if, furthermore, that node in the P-marker has no descendent, then a node labelled *saw* may be introduced beneath it. Interpretation of rule (iii) is similar. The *boy* can be introduced into the P-marker beneath a node labelled N provided that this has been associated by some previous rule with a variable in the semantic expression of which 'human', 'male', and 'young' are all predicated.

A fourth rule might be as follows:

$$\text{(iv) human(a).male(a)} \mid N_a \rightarrow man$$

We are assuming, perhaps unrealistically, that the representation of *boy* differs from that of *man* only by the addition of the predicate 'young'. It apparently follows that wherever rule (iii) applies rule (iv) will apply also. In principle it would be possible to avoid conflicts of this sort so that whenever the semantic properties specified by one rule included those specified by another, then the more inclusive rule would always be applied first. But this solution will not work. In the first place, since one of the main aims is to construct a model which will account for paraphrase, it must be possible to derive several different P-markers from the same semantic expression. This can only be achieved if rules are in general optional and there is little to be gained by ordering optional rules. In the present case nothing important is lost because if our assumptions about the semantic representations of *boy* and *man* were correct, then it would presumably be at least in part because we were prepared to accept any sentence containing the phrase *young man* as a paraphrase of the same sentence with this phrase replaced by *boy*. The following would presumably be included in the set of rules:

$$\text{(v) young(a)} \mid \text{ADJ}_a \rightarrow young$$

Using this rule we can produce the sentence *The young man hit the man* from the same original semantic expression.

As the rules are refined to represent more and more semantic facts about the language, the expressions that will have to be written to represent even very simple sentences are likely to become long and involved. Furthermore, since the rules are optional and since some may be applicable at many places in the same expression, the process of producing a P-marker may often block, i.e., reach a place where it cannot continue owing to lack of applicable rules, but where some parts of the expression have still not been translated. We can imagine the strategy which continues to explore different sequences of rules until it finds one which yields a translation of the expression or demonstrates that no such sequence can be found. But this is both tedious and unrealistic. If a grammar contains the rule (i) suggested above, then any two-place predicate could be used as the starting point for a P-marker. The same would presumably also have to be said of one-place predicates. Hence they will be the normal representatives of intransitive verbs. The production of a sentence could therefore begin almost anywhere.

However, expressions that adequately represent the meanings of sentences will almost certainly have to contain *rhetorical* predicates, that is, predicates that do not influence the truth value of the sentences in which they occur but which relate the information in a given sentence to a whole discourse – in other words, which present the thread of the argument.

The sentence *It was the lion that was afraid of the unicorn* differs from *It was the unicorn the lion was afraid of* in the information that must be assumed for its understanding and the information it purports to offer as new. In the first sentence, it is taken as given that someone was afraid of the unicorn; the question answered by the sentence is *Who?*. In the second sentence it is given that the lion was afraid of someone, but whom was he afraid of? The distinction comes out particularly clearly when the sentences are embedded in certain kinds of other sentences. Compare, for example, *I do not believe that it was the lion that was afraid of the unicorn* with *I do not believe it was the unicorn the lion was afraid of.* What I disbelieve is very different in the two cases. In the first case, I positively do believe that the unicorn was feared, but not necessarily by the lion; in the second, I believe that the lion was afraid, but not necessarily of the unicorn.

Consider now the sentence *I do not believe that the lion was afraid of the unicorn.* Here, what I disbelieve is either that the lion was not afraid or that the unicorn was not feared, or both. In other words, this sentence is ambiguous; it can have the meanings of either or both of the other two.

In the light of this, let us introduce the two-place rhetorical predicate 'new' and represent *It was the boy that saw the man* somewhat as follows:

human(x). human(y). male(x). male(y). young(x). see(z). z(x,y). past(z). new(x,z)

'new(a,b)' means that the predication 'b(...,a,...)', which must appear in the same conjunct, gives new information. The first rule used to generate the sentence *The boy saw the man* could now be

$$a(b,c).new(b,a) \quad \left| \quad \begin{array}{ll} S & \rightarrow NP_b \ VP \\ VP & \rightarrow V_a \ NP_c \end{array} \right.$$

However, since no transformations are to be included in the grammar so that the output of this transducer will have the same status as surface structure in transformational grammar, the *VP* node created by this rule has no obvious function outside phonology. But for phonology, the rule could be written

$$a(b,c).new(b,a) \ \left| \ S \quad \rightarrow NP_b \ V_a \ NP_c \right.$$

The cleft sentence *It was the boy that saw the man* is also generable from the expression (5). In this case, the initial rule must be something like

(5) $a(b,c).new(b,a) \ \left| \ S \quad \rightarrow it \ BE_a \ NP_b \ that \ V_a \ NP_c \right.$

If the extra nodes are needed for the phonology, the rule would have to be something like

$$a(b,c).new(b,a) \quad \left| \quad \begin{array}{ll} S & \rightarrow NP \ VP \\ NP & \rightarrow N \\ N & \rightarrow it \\ VP & \rightarrow V \ NP \\ V & \rightarrow BE_a \\ NP & \rightarrow NP_b \ S \\ S & \rightarrow NP \ VP \\ NP & \rightarrow N \\ N & \rightarrow that \\ VP & \rightarrow V_a \ NP_c \end{array} \right.$$

A slight variation of the formalism would allow

$a(b,c).new(b,a) \ | \ S \rightarrow NP(N(it)) \ VP(V(BE_a)NP(NP_bS(NP(N(that)) \ VP(V_a \ NP_c))))$

In what follows, I shall ignore phonology and assume that the simpler form of rule can be used. These can always be expanded into the more complex form if necessary.

The sentence *It was the man the boy saw* is derived from a semantic expression including 'a(b,c).new(c,a)' and the initial rule is

(6) $a(b,c).new(c,a)$ | S $\rightarrow$ *it* BE_a NP_c (*that*) NP_b V_a

The similarity between (5) and (6) can be captured if they are both replaced by

$$a(b,c).new(d,a) \quad | \quad S \quad \rightarrow \textit{it } BE_a \ NP_d \textit{ that } C_a$$
$$a(b,c).new(b,a) \quad | \quad C_a \quad \rightarrow V_a \ NP_c$$
$$a(b,c).new(c,a) \quad | \quad C_a \quad \rightarrow NP_b \ V_a$$

The symbol *BE* will be replaced in a subsequent rule by an appropriate part of the verb 'to be'. The subscript will allow the proper tense to be chosen.

A distinction between given and new, topic and comment, theme and rheme has been discovered and rediscovered from time to time throughout the history of linguistics. In many languages, like Chinese and Japanese, it is reflected in the gross syntactic structure of sentences and it must therefore by explained to beginning students. It has been a major center of attention for the Prague school because, while there is relatively free order among the major constituents of sentences in the Slavic languages, the diverse possible orders have different rhetorical effects. It is doubtful whether only one rhetorical predicate, the one I have called 'new', underlies all these distinctions. Certainly, there are others and the kind of linguistic theory advocated here would provide a very apt framework in which to study them.

The principal motivation provided so far for the predicate 'new' in this discussion, namely of marking possible starting points for the transducer, is, in a sense, a very old idea. Every semantic expression that underlies a declarative sentence must have at least one occurrence of the predicate 'new'. But this is only to recall one of the most ancient definitions of what a sentence is, namely that it introduces a new thought.

I have already remarked that, in sentences like

(7) *I believe it was Brutus that killed Caesar*

and

(8) *I believe it was Caesar that Brutus killed*

the embedded sentences are, by the usual criteria, logically equivalent but that what I am claiming to believe is different. Using the notions of given and new, (7) and (8) can be paraphrased somewhat as follows:

(9) *I believe (given that Caesar was killed, Brutus was responsible)*

and

(10) *I believe (given that Brutus killed someone, Caesar was the victim)*

Now, notice that what is given can be removed from the parentheses without change of meaning, whereas what is new cannot. (11) and (12) are not semantically distinguishable from (9) and (10).

(11) *Given that Caesar was killed, I believe (Brutus was responsible)*

(12) *Given that Brutus killed someone, I believe (Caesar was the victim)*

This suggests linking rhetorical predicates with what Ross and others call *performatives* and what the philosopher Austin calls *illocutionary acts*. Ross suggests that declarative sentences come from an underlying structure in which the highest-level sentence is something like 'I assert that S'. Austin points out that, as well as enshrining facts about the world, sentences can also change those facts. This is particularly true of sentences containing words like *promise, undertake*, and *assert*.

If we say that every sentence involves at least one performative in its semantic structure, or that every sentence is an illocutionary act, we can represent (13) and (14) as (15) and (16).

(13) *It was Brutus that killed Caesar*

(14) *It was Caesar that Brutus killed*

(15) *Brutus*(b).*Caesar*(c).*killed*(x,c).b=x

(16) *Brutus*(b).*Caesar*(c).*killed*(b,x).c=x

Clauses like $b=x$ now take the place of the 'new' predicate. The representation of sentences like (7) and (8) becomes something like (17) and (18).

(17) *Brutus*(b).*Caesar*(c).*I*(i).*killed*(x,c).*believe*(i,b =x)

(18) *Brutus*(b).*Caesar*(c).*I*(i).*killed*(b,x).*believe*(i,c =x)

Rhetorical predicates, or devices like the '=' in the above examples are crucial to the study of semantics in natural languages and serve to set those languages off against most artificial languages. Just how many of them there are is, of course, not known – probably very few. The 'new' predicate is certainly responsible for the distinction between restrictive and non-restrictive relatives, the latter being precisely those that involve new information, or, more precisely, information that purports to be new. It may also underlie the distinction between *the house is near the store* and *the store is near the house*. It almost certainly does not account for the difference between *the glass is half full* and *the glass is half empty*, or between *who am I?* and *which is me?*.

Informally, the function of a rhetorical predicate is fairly clear. When I talk to you, I normally have a construct in my mind and I want to erect a copy of it in yours. I must build the picture piece by piece, telling you where each new piece is to be placed relative to what has already been built, and checking from time to time that the construction is proceeding as I intend. Each piece comes in a sentence which also contains the necessary information about where it is to be put. It must, therefore contain old and new information to be effective – probably more old than new. What is new does not always have to be marked explicitly because it will be clear from what has been done already and the course that the construction is taking. A sentence like *It was Brutus that killed Caesar* marks what is to be taken as new very clearly, whereas the simpler sentence *Brutus killed Caesar* is relatively ambiguous.

But it would be absurd, at this stage, to make any psychological claims for the model of language sketched here. Far too many details have been left out. But, though the specific proposal made here may turn out wrong in almost every detail, and though there is no reason to claim any psychological reality for it, there is nevertheless very great importance in having models in linguistics which actually work – models of performance or, at least, performance-oriented competence. A model which claims to account for paraphrase must produce paraphrases even if some of the procedures it uses are of no eventual theoretical interest. The trouble with a purely interpretive theory of semantics is that, though one may argue about it endlessly, it is very difficult to see what it would be like to demonstrate that a grammar written according to it was wrong. In the interest of intellectual hygiene alone, it is important to study a subject as difficult as semantics with models that actually work and which therefore lay themselves open to specific attack.

Acknowledgements

I am indebted to David G. Hays of The RAND Corporation and Meyer Wolf of Michigan State University for many fruitful discussions of these ideas, but the foolishnesses are mine.

Publications referenced

Hays and Kay 1969; Lyons 1963.

9

Computational Linguistics at RAND – 1967

The linguistics project has the unique distinction at RAND of occupying uncleared space. This has the advantage of giving us a view of the ocean and the mountains from our fifth floor offices, and it means that we are more easily accessible to visitors, who do not have to be escorted and wear a badge. Linguistics projects probably receive more than their fair share of visitors because there are many people for whom the realization that they can speak a language gives them the confidence they need in their own startling and original theories of meaning, grammar, spelling, sound, human and animal communication, and the crucial importance of all this in the affairs of gods and men. Every man is an expert on linguistics. I am afraid we are sometimes a disappointment to these people. They arrive wide-eyed and expectant, and they are noticeably disappointed when their eyes do not immediately light on the thing they are looking for. "Where is it?" they plaintively ask. "Where is the translating machine?"

The word has got around that machines exist that are capable of translating from one language into another, and that either Russia or America has demonstrated intellectual and technological superiority by developing them first. There is some substance in this, but, like so many popular rumors, it is only a half-truth. There are machines that consume many thousands of words of text daily and disgorge many thousands of words in another language, but the debate about whether what they are doing should be called translation has still to be settled. What the machines do is effectively word-for-word and phrase-for-phrase substitution. The results are often unintelligible, and if there seem to be occasional flashes of brilliance, it is because the machine uses a prodigious dictionary with a great many ready-made phrases.

The RAND Corporation has no translating machine nor any plans to build one. At present, it does not even have computer programs intended to translate. In deciding, some seven years ago, to abandon machine translation as an immediately practicable goal, the linguistics project was taking a lead which was to be followed sooner or later by almost every other group and individual in the field. The day of the flamboyant project, which was confidently dedicated to putting the human translator out of work within two years, has long since passed. It is true that there are still those who claim to be working on machine translation, but far more numerous are those who have shifted from this to what they call "computational linguistics" or some similarly noncommittal term.

The reasons for the shift were twofold. On the one hand it rapidly became obvious that human language is a complicated affair and that all the centuries of careful work that have been devoted to it still leave many of the most crucial questions virtually untouched. It turns out that a language primer, however good, cannot simply be recast as a set of computer instructions, and, even if it could, some of the most difficult and important questions about the language would remain unanswered. The other important fact that came to light was that the computer processing of linguistic material is an art, and that significant progress would only be made when a great deal more experience had been gained in this art and a body of special techniques had been built up.

The first work on machine translation was done in the late forties by people who had spent the war years breaking enemy codes, often with striking success. A text in a foreign language, they argued, can be thought of as an encoded version of a text in English. To discover the rules by which a translating machine should operate is to break the code. The job should be, if anything, easier than the ones they had been accustomed to because speakers of the foreign language were available and the language could be learned. Foreign languages are not, after all, designed with the express purpose of obscuring information from speakers of English.

It is not difficult to see what is wrong with this argument. In a code, there is a systematic, although frequently complex, mapping of items with a given physical shape – letters or words – onto other items with different physical shapes. It is not surprising that, knowing some statistics about the distribution of letters and words in a language, and some statistics about the coded message, it is sometimes possible to make some inferences about the mapping. But the mapping that carries a text into its translation is determined not by physical shape alone but by the meanings which they represent. To translate a text, it is necessary to understand it; to encode a text, it is sufficient to be able to read it.

So in order to build a machine that will translate, we must be able to build a machine that can, in some sense, understand. The problem of deciding what it would be like for a machine to understand is, of course, itself a deep philosophical problem. At any rate it must be capable of teasing out ambiguities, deciding when a pair of words refer to the same thing, and coping with vagueness, ellipsis, and metaphorical usage, to name but a few.

Language is indeed very complicated, and the early attempts to build machines that would produce high-quality translations on an industrial scale, or indeed on any scale at all, were obviously premature. It became clear, however, that there was something that linguists who knew about computers could do to advance the state of their art and to bring the day of the translating machine nearer. If linguistic science was backward, it was in part because there had not been enough sufficiently clever people working on it. But, to some extent, it was also because there is such a richness of detail in language that any particular phenomenon can be expected to occur in text only in very weak dilution. The linguist has traditionally devoted a very large portion of his time and energy to searching text for examples to confirm and confute some particular hypothesis, and in addition to give him an idea of what standard usage as opposed to his own idiosyncrasies is like.

The adverse of this problem is what I like to call the 90-percent phenomenon. It seems to be the case with natural language that almost any hypothesis, however implausible, will be correct 90 percent of the time. One readily assumes that the other 10 percent will be accounted for by some minor adjustments in the theory or a more careful analysis of the data. But, in a distressingly large number of cases, a concerted program of adjustments to the theory, extending in some cases over a number of years, succeeds only in increasing the accuracy from 90 to 91 percent. I should not be surprised to learn that the part of speech of an English word can be predicted 90 percent of the time by counting the number of vowels and consonants and, let us say, the number of consonant-vowel and vowel-consonant pairs it contains and plugging these numbers into a formula involving sines, cosines, and square roots. But I should be immensely surprised to see such a thing work 99 percent of the time.

What all this means is that there is a desperate need in linguistics for data. With a computer we can accumulate large files of text of various kinds, gather statistics from it, search it for particular phenomena we are interested in, and use it to help test our more or less implausible hypotheses. To the basic file of text we can add information on grammatical or other structures derived by humans or machines. We can maintain large dictionaries in which to accumulate the information we gather about individual words, and grammars in which to store what we discover about phrases and sentences.

We at RAND were among the first to realize this need for large files of linguistic data, and we attacked the problem on two fronts. In the first place we began to build up files of text in English and Russian with and without ancillary information on grammatical and semantic structure. I shall return to this. Perhaps more important in the long run is the work we did on the general problem of storing linguistic data in a computer-usable form. It is clearly desirable that linguists should have information storage and retrieval facilities where they work, but the full utility of these can be realized only when files constructed by different people at different places can be exchanged, compared, and conflated. And this is only really practicable if there is agreement on format and encoding conventions.

Human beings are able to go to the substance of a document, hardly noticing details of page layout or typographic style. But, in computing, these are crucial matters. If a text is available on magnetic tape and also in a computer program that performs some interesting and useful operation on text, there is no guarantee that the program can be made to work on the tape at all easily. Left to themselves, everybody writes computer tapes in a different way. They use a different assignment of numbers to represent the letters; they decide how they will treat the distinction between upper and lower case letters, punctuation, titles, paragraph divisions, and so forth. One will decide to take the printed line as his unit of text and another the sentence,

One of the things that we have devoted a great deal of time to at RAND over the past two or three years is the development of a very general magnetic tape format and text encoding scheme which will provide all of the flexibility that researchers require while not imposing a great deal of extra labor on them. To use the standard we are proposing, nobody is required to record information he is not interested in, though he may occasionally do some of this out of sheer altruism. We have tried to arrange things in such a way that the computer can do most of its work with one set of codes, without making it necessary for the researcher to accept output in a single type style, or to prepare input with a single inflexible set of keyboard conventions.

Our work on formats and codes has been carried on in close cooperation with the machine translation center at the University of Grenoble in France. If they become widely adopted, it is difficult to overestimate the effect they will have on linguistic research by making more information available and freeing the time of important people to concentrate on important problems. Results to date are encouraging. The system has been adopted for one purpose or another by the very large linguistic research center at Texas, by the Machine Translation Project at the University of California at Berkeley, by a lexicographic research project at SDC, by the Chinese Society Bibliography project sponsored by the Social Science Research Council, and by the firm of Tracor in Austin, Texas.

Once agreement can be reached on the standard way of recording data, it becomes possible to think about sharing some of the programming effort. One of the reasons for abandoning machine translation as an immediate goal of computational linguistics was that too little was known, at that time, about the algorithms and techniques that will best accomplish what linguists want to do. There is, of course, no general agreement among linguists on what they want to do, but if they see any place at all for computers in their work, then there are certain basic operations which they all agree are important. It is necessary to be able to look words up in a dictionary; and the ability to parse a sentence so as to discover which word is the subject and which is the object and what word modifies what other word is fundamental. There is great utility for a program which will generate sentences at random, using some specific set of grammar rules.

There is still much to be done in the development of language processing techniques, but some of these basic operations are now fairly well understood. In the early stages, however, it was not clear how even so apparently trivial an operation as looking words up in a dictionary should be done. It is true, but by no means immediately obvious, that relatively few of the words encountered in English text can be found in exactly that form in the dictionary. In English, where this problem is less acute than in most languages, the dictionary will contain perhaps half the words. The remainder will be plural nouns from which a final "s" must be removed to give the dictionary form, third person singulars of verbs from which an "s" must also be removed, present participles from which a final "ing" must be removed, and so forth. But it cannot be assumed that "ing" is a suffix whenever it occurs finally, for there are words like "thing" and "railing". It seems, therefore, that you can only look the word up in the dictionary when you have properly identified any prefixes and suffixes it may have. But you can only identify the prefixes and suffixes when you know what the word is, and this you can only discover by looking it up in the dictionary. There are, of course, various ways of breaking out of this vicious circle, and we now have elegant and efficient dictionary look-up techniques, but they were not developed overnight, and there are a great many more difficult problems for which techniques are still required before a translating machine can be built.

If there is a standard format for recording linguistic data and some good ways of performing basic operations on them, there is no reason in principle why research groups should not exchange actual computer programs and thereby save a great deal of labor. I realize that there are still a great many caveats. Different installations have different computers, and, although the use of high-level programming languages like ALGOL and FORTRAN can reduce the apparent difference between machines, they will probably never become completely compatible. So the situation is not, and probably never will be, perfect. But we have already had a number of very encouraging experiences in exchanging programs with other groups, even though some minor modifications are nearly always required.

The history of automatic parsing – the discovery of grammatical relations among the words of the sentence – is very instructive. For a long time the only method known was to find somebody who knew the grammar of the language well and the instruction code to which a particular computer responded. He was invited, in effect, to write down what he knew about the language in that code. Each program was specialized to a particular language and a particular computer and, as more of the idiosyncrasies of the language and exceptions to the rules came to light, the programs became larger and larger till they became impossible to understand and too large to be stored in the machine. It seemed worthwhile to look for some general principles underlying the parsing process and to attempt to write a program embodying no information about the specific language. Such a program would accept as input a set of grammatical rules stated in a formal notation and apply them to a text. Programs of this kind are now available; some of the earliest ones were written at RAND. We are now reaching the stage when a fairly sophisticated grammar can be written in a powerful notation – but one which a grammarian who is not versed in the ways of computers can easily learn and handle – and applied to text by the machine.

One enterprise that the RAND linguistics project is engaged upon at the moment is a general parsing program that will handle a very sophisticated kind of grammar . It has attracted much attention among linguists recently. 1 have in mind what is called the *transformational* grammar. The program, if it is successful, will be one of the first of its kind. I think I can say what is useful about transformational grammar in the following way: It turns out to be very useful to treat sentences from two points of view. Consider the two sentences "John is easy to please" and "John is eager to please". Superficially, they both have the same grammatical structure. "John" is the subject, and "is" the main verb. The main verb has a complement in each case which is modified by a prepositional phrase. But this analysis is somewhat too facile. In "John is easy to please," we are concerned with the ease with which someone else can please John. "John" is, therefore, in some sense the object of "please". But in "John is eager to please", "John" is in the same sense the subject of "please". We are concerned with John's eagerness to be the one who pleases. We therefore say that the two sentences, though alike in their *surface* structure, are different in their *deep* structure.

Transformational grammar will sometimes say that two or more different sentences have identical deep structures so that its effect is to put sentences together in families. A sentence obviously belongs to the same family as its own passive equivalent and several other sentences which use substantially the same words and mean approximately the same thing. The deep structure can be thought of as a kind of canonical form to which a number of trivially different actual sentences can be reduced. In general, the canonical form will not itself be an English sentence but an expression in a more abstract and well-behaved language. We can, therefore, expect it to be far easier to work with than an actual sentence.

I said that the RAND linguistics project was attacking the problem of acquiring necessary linguistic data on two fronts. On the one hand it is attempting to provide a format and encoding system attractive enough to become an effective standard, and to develop some techniques and programs to work on data recorded in this way. The other thing that it has done is to make positive contributions to the data files themselves. In the near future, we expect to make available a file of some 50 million running words of Russian text taken from journals in all fields of science. The text was punched on paper tape by the Air Force for other reasons, and RAND contracted to write it on magnetic tape in the standard format. We prepared a file of one million words of text in which each sentence is accompanied by a statement of its structure. Each sentence was examined by a Russian speaker, and subjects, objects, modifiers, and the like were marked. The structures were checked by two other people before being entered in the permanent file. We are now in a position to write a parsing program for Russian and to check its results automatically against those provided by the experts.

A file of a million words of text annotated with detailed grammatical information obviously has various other uses. A linguist who is working on almost any problem in Russian can use the file as a source of examples of the kind of phenomenon he is working on. Of course, in order to do this, he has to have some means of finding his way to the examples. What we have done is to provide an information retrieval facility. This is a program which enables the linguist to write a request for words or sentences with particular properties in a simple but expressive language. In ten or fifteen minutes the program will scan the entire million words of text and find everything that meets the request, or as many as the linguist asks for.

Given such a file as this, certain kinds of linguistic analysis can be carried out automatically. Curiously enough, even so human a faculty as language has some properties which are easier to identify mechanically than by purely human means. Presented with two sentences, one perfectly unexceptional and the other grossly ungrammatical, a native speaker of the language can usually not only see the difference, but can point to the principle that the ungrammatical sentence violates. But, given two very similar ways of saying the same thing, he may sometimes feel that one is natural whereas the other is unhappy. It is perfectly clear what it means, but it sounds as though it comes from a foreigner. We talk, for example, of a "tall man" and a "tall building", but of a "high mountain". "High building" is also acceptable, but "high man", at least in this sense, is not. "High" and "tall" have the same meaning in all these phrases – something like "large in the vertical dimension" – but one is required for some words and the other for others. In the dictionary, they would be distinguished by stage directions of some sort – "said of men and buildings". But it is often very difficult to write these stage directions completely and accurately. What is the principle on which native speakers unerringly recognize the right place to use "tall" and the right place for "high"? To take an even more difficult example, how do we distinguish "royal" from "regal"?

I do not know the answers to these questions, and 1 am not going to claim that a computer can be programmed to tell me. But a computer can sometimes be programmed to produce information that throws some new light on the problem. If there is some more or less obscure property that a word or an idea like "mountain" has, and that a word like "building" does not, and if this property is crucial in determining linguistic usage, then it is reasonable to suppose that it does more than just distinguish "tall" and "high". Presumably there are other words in the language that select just the words that "tall" selects, and another set that selects what "high" selects. In other words, we hope to find what linguists call a paradigm – a pair of lists of words such that any member of the first list can occur naturally in a given grammatical construction with any member of the second.

If we set out to find paradigms in real text, we shall be faced with the well known fact that no text is ever long enough. Interesting things occur, as I have said, in too-weak dilution. But, could we imagine writing a computer program that would take what it could from the text and make some inferences to fill gaps in the paradigm? Certainly, there is nothing in the standard statistician's tool kit today that will do this job.

I am glad to be able to report some encouraging results in this area, however. In 1957, Frederick Parker Rhodes and Roger Needham of Cambridge, England, invented something called the theory of clumps. It is possible to write computer programs based on this theory which will take a list of objects classified according to a given set of properties and group the objects into natural families. There is nothing specifically linguistic about this operation; a non-linguistic example will perhaps make the idea clearer. There are a great many different types of blood disease, and it is important for a doctor to have some idea which one his patient has before he begins treatment. But, in fact, each patient looks a little different from every other, and it is often difficult to tell whether he has a new complaint or a new version of an old one. Needham took the hospital records of a large number of patients with blood diseases as objects, and the properties noted by the doctors who examined them, and then attempted to use the theory of clumps to identify the diseases. The question he asked was, "Do the facts we have about these patients classify them in any natural way?" The results were quite dramatic. Leukemia was identified immediately, and almost every other recognized ailment that was sufficiently well represented in the data was brought out. But there were also some new classes, and these became the basis of some interesting and, I am told, fruitful research. These are the kinds of results we hope to get in large numbers from our file of a million words of Russian text.

The theory of clumps has a drawback which, until last year, has kept us from using it as we should have liked. It is necessary for the computer to keep a square matrix with a row and column for every object available throughout the whole computation. Naturally, this severely limits the amount of data that can be treated. Last year, Roger Needham came to RAND for six months as a consultant and, during that time, he was able to produce a new variant to the theory of clumps. The results are substantially the same, but the square matrix is not required and the whole computation is easier. It is feasible to use this with very large amounts of data; the results we are just beginning to get from the million-word file are, as I said, extremely encouraging.

The time has come to ask where all this work is intended to lead. Having so strenuously denied that we are a machine-translation group, I must now say that machine translation is indeed one of the main ends to which we are working. A successful translating machine certainly could not be built by someone who did not have the results we are trying to achieve, and others too. The day is still far off when such a machine will go on the market, when you will be able to type a text into it, or read into a microphone and have a polished translation appear on a screen or come mellifluously phrased from a loudspeaker. But there is a need in linguistic research for computer programs that translate, albeit badly, and, in my view, the need is pressing.

What we need are programs constructed on a modular principle so that we can get some idea how some small change in linguistic theory, or in the hypotheses made about a particular language, might affect the whole theory, the whole grammar, or our whole view of translation. Descriptions of languages are extremely difficult to verify, especially when they get into questions of meaning and reference. An experimental translation program would serve as a sort of linguistic laboratory in which to try out new ideas.

Recent developments in linguistic theory as a whole make this idea of constructing an experimental machine translation system seem particularly attractive. According to the so-called *stratificational* theory of grammar, any text can be represented exhaustively in a number of different ways, each bringing out a specific kind of property that it has. Any text can be written in a phonetic transcription which, at least in principle, makes explicit exactly how it would sound. Another representation would be syntactic and would show how the words were related to one another – which was subject, which was object, which modified which other, and so forth. Then there would presumably be a semantic representation, or stratum. The idea is that this should make clear just what the text means.

Of course there are all sorts of problems connected with this. It is not immediately obvious what it would mean to have a semantic representation of a text, since this would have to be in some notation, or language, and this would have its own syntax, semantics, and so on. But 1 think we can avoid the vicious circle if we do not attempt to solve all the traditional philosophical problems of meaning with one grandiose blow. We want something which makes certain of the more obvious analytic meaning-relations explicit. A man is a human and the notion of "human" is an instance of the notion of "animal". "John bought Bill's car from him" "if and only if" "Bill sold his car to John." If "John's car is red," it is not simultaneously "blue," though it may, for example, be "powerful." (Notice that in English, if not in fact, a red and blue car is neither blue nor red; it is blue *and* red.)

It is obvious why this view of language is called "stratificational". The phonetic stratum is the most readily perceived – the closest to physical reality. A syntactic representation can be arrived at only from a spoken or written input. The semantic representation can be reached only when the syntax is known. For all I know, there may be yet higher levels to be discovered or invented. What is important is that there is a hierarchy and that the further one goes up the ladder, the less apparent the distinctions between languages become. If one text is a translation of another, it is presumably because they both convey the same meaning, which is to say, according to this view, that they have the same representation on the semantic stratum. We come, therefore, to a notion of the translation process as one in which a text is carried up through the hierarchy of strata in a series of relatively small translation steps, and then down again, but in the other language.

The idea of linguistic strata has practical as well as theoretical attractions. We may think of a translation program as being constructed out of a number of virtually independent modules, one for each stratum and one to perform the conversion between each pair of adjacent strata. More accurately, there would be two for each stratum except the topmost, because the work to be done on a given stratum would be different for the input and output languages. This structure is ideal for the kind of experimental translation system I have outlined. If it is properly designed, some of the modules can be changed or replaced while the rest are held constant, and the effects can be observed. New strata can be added and old ones deleted. In short, it makes possible a kind of experimentation in linguistics which has hitherto been regarded as impossible because, without this modular design, it would be too costly.

Machine translation is by no means the only goal of research in computational linguistics. The operations involved in arriving at the semantic representation of a text are exactly the same ones as are required for a great many other tasks. They are, for example, among the necessary ingredients of a facility that will enable a person to go to a library with a question couched in ordinary English and have a machine search the holdings for the material needed to make up an answer. From such a facility, the user expects not a stack of books on fields related to the question, but a direct answer. Clearly, there are far more than purely linguistic problems to be solved before any such system can be built, but at least there must be some sense in which the machine can be said to understand the user's question, that is, to find its semantic representation. There must also be some means of framing answers in ordinary English, that is, converting meanings to words.

It has been proposed by the World Peace Through Law Center to record the statutes of the major nations of the world in a form accessible to computers. The World Peace Through Law Center is an international organization of judges, lawyers, and teachers of law. A lawyer will immediately think of countless useful things that could be done with this file at present, and even more when our knowledge and expertise have increased a little further. The file could be used as a basis for legal information retrieval; one can imagine studies of the consistency of legal systems and of the principles that determine the applicability of particular statutes to particular cases. Whatever one does, however, it is likely to begin and end with linguistic operations like those I have suggested.

Another area in which the results of work in computational linguistics can be expected to find application is in medicine. There is work going on in the automatic analysis of psychiatric interviews and in automatic diagnosis. These problems, and many others that one could name, require sophisticated knowledge and techniques that computational linguists can hope, one day, to provide.

But, like any pure scientist – and I think that a linguist, in his better moments, has a right to call himself a pure scientist – the linguist derives his greatest stimulus from more distant goals which will probably never be reached in his lifetime, if at all. The linguist's driving force comes, I think, mainly from the hope that he may contribute to the eventual discovery of what it is that sets human language off from all other theoretically possible languages. That there is some such thing is certain. As you study language more and more, you become more and more intrigued by the different ways that languages find to do things. But you are impressed to a far greater extent by the similarities that exist among all human languages. Of all the sets of strings of sounds that might be languages and all the possible grammars that might, in principle, be written, only a very small class is actually found.

This suggests that a human being comes to the world equipped with highly specialized language-processing facilities. He is not a *tabula rasa*, a generalized problem-solving device, but a device with a great amount of built-in structure. He will develop and learn only a certain class of languages. As linguists, we must learn to characterize this class. If we were able to do this, we should be in a position to contribute not only to the practical areas I have mentioned, but also to psychology, neurophysiology, and philosophy.

Acknowledgements

Any views expressed in this paper are those of the author. They should not be interpreted as reflecting the views of The RAND Corporation or the official opinion or policy of any of its governmental or private research sponsors. Papers are reproduced by The RAND Corporation as a courtesy to members of its staff. This paper was originally presented to the RAND'S Board of Trustees Meeting held April 13th–15th, 1967, in Washington, D.C.

## 10

A Computer System to Aid the Linguistic Field Worker

The typical young modern linguist has a strong mathematical background, a disconcerting facility with erudite arguments about metaphysics and the philosophy of science, and an ability to produce on demand a dozen examples that disprove any linguistic theory or rule of grammar that you propose. When he tells someone at a party that he is a linguist and they ask him how many languages he speaks, he can answer with pride "One, I think". Only a few years ago the picture was very different. The typical young linguist had a strong background in anthropology, was a good mimic, and could hear distinctions between pairs of sounds that were actually the same, and owned seventy-five boxes of paper slips containing data that he would one day analyze, on a language that only he knew the name of and of which the last known speaker was no longer alive.

These pictures are, of course, overdrawn; there were both theoretical and practical linguists ten years ago and there still are both today but nobody should be surprised if young linguists today show more interest in creating and destroying theories than in analyzing exotic languages. For one thing, the theoretical issues have become very much more exciting; for another, theory is science and science confers prestige. But surely one of the main reasons lies in those seventy-five boxes of paper slips. They are too big to hide, presumably too valuable to throw away and a threat to the practical linguist's conscience for the rest of his life.

Consider the record of practical linguistics as it must appear to a student. A large number of people have started along the road towards a PhD in this field, have done field work for one or two summers, but have never produced a complete grammar, dictionary, or set of annotated texts. The grammars that have been produced are, for the most part, rather depressing. Out of two hundred pages, the first one hundred and fifty contain an extremely complete and detailed account of the phonology of the language, the next forty-five a more sketchy account of the morphology, and the last five a few disconnected remarks on syntax such as "In this language, the prevailing word order is subject–object–verb, but other orders are also found". Though such a grammar undoubtedly contains a large amount of information, it stops short of telling someone who might have cause to use the language how to order a glass of beer or ask the time of day.

It is in many ways remarkable that anyone has been able to produce any kind of grammar of an exotic language, single handed. The amount of data to be collected, searched, sorted, modified, copied and recopied is prodigious and boxes of paper slips are a totally inadequate tool. However, there is probably no task to which modern electronic computers are better suited, and now that such machines are becoming more widespread and the techniques for using them known to a greater number of people, there is simply no longer any excuse for investing human labor in essentially mechanical tasks. Against this point of view it is sometimes argued that it is only by repeatedly going through the data looking for patterns and searching for examples that the student can hope to become sufficiently familiar with his material to be able to analyze it competently. This argument is wholly fallacious and is, in any case, sure not to prevail. The linguist who has a computer to help him will spend no less time with his data then his less fortunate colleagues. Instead of searching through boxes of paper slips he will scan printed pages produced by the machine. The creative work of recognizing significant examples, and formulating rules will still be his to do. But when he needs examples of a certain word, morpheme, or syntactic pattern, he will be able to direct the machine to find them for him. While he is still working with his informant he can have the machine maintain a bi-lingual dictionary of which he can obtain a revised edition every week, or even every day. The dictionary can be arranged by word or morpheme and can contain, for every item, a record of every sentence containing it that has so far been collected. The computer will thereby not only make the analysis of data more efficient and the coverage more complete, but it will also make each session with the informant more productive.

A great deal of labor on the part of one or more computer programmers is required to produce the programs necessary to do all these things for the linguist, and it is therefore important that the programs should be designed with great care so that as many as possible of the linguist's needs will be foreseen and so that the resulting programs will be usable by the greatest possible number of people. With these aims in mind, Dr. Norman McQuown of the University of Chicago assisted by a programmer and with some occasional contributions from myself has been designing and constructing a comprehensive set of flexible computer programs as an aid to linguistic field work.

A general system for processing linguistic data cannot be tied to any particular alphabet. In the first place, data may be recorded in various different transcriptions, phonetic, phonemic, morphophonemic, and maybe others. In the second place, the inventory from which the sounds of the world's languages are chosen is immensely large. On the other hand, computing machinery is usually equipped with a very small character set including the digits, the letters of the alphabet in upper case only, and a few punctuation marks and special symbols. Two alternatives are thereby opened to the linguist. Either he can use a machine that has been especially modified to accommodate his data or he can adopt a set of conventions that allow him to replace each of his own symbols with a single symbol or with a string of two or more symbols from the set available on the machine. The first alternative is expensive, though not as expensive as might at first appear; the second is inconvenient but not very inconvenient because linguists are used to working with various notations. The important thing is that the computer program should be insensitive to differences of this kind. It should be capable of accepting data encoded in any reasonable way and converting it into its own internal form.

A computer can also print its results in a variety of different ways. Again, the cheapest methods allow only a very small set of characters, but other methods are available that are not very much more expensive and that allow a virtually unlimited set. Once again, programs that are going to be usable by many different linguists, working on many different languages, should be capable of taking advantage of any printing devices that happen to be available. These are properties that the programs described here have.

It is an unfortunate fact about automatic computing that the programs written for machines produced by one manufacturer cannot usually be used with those produced by another. Furthermore, even the machines made by one manufacturer can differ greatly in size and speed of operation, and there are various extra pieces of equipment that can be attached to them for special purposes. The program that we are considering is designed to be used with computers manufactured by the most prolific manufacturer, namely IBM, and with as few additional pieces of equipment as possible.

Let us consider how some of the simpler kinds of data that a linguist has to deal with might be prepared for presentation to a machine. We suppose that he has available a machine with a keyboard essentially similar to that of an ordinary typewriter which produces punched cards or tape that the computer can read. Ordinary texts, for example, stories recited by the informant, can be typed on this machine just as on an ordinary typewriter. The programming system that we are considering requires, in addition, only that the text be preceded and followed by a pair of special codes, the first of which declares it to be a text and says what language it is in, and the second of which serves only to show where it ends. In this system a word consists of any sequence of characters separated by blanks unless the first of those characters is an ampersand, in which case the sequence is taken to be a special code or instruction to the computer system. Suppose we wish to represent a text in Tzeltal, say, a story recorded by the informant. We must first invent a code which will be understood as meaning that the sequence of words immediately following is a piece of text in the Tzeltal language. This code is introduced to the computer by punching it on a special card or piece of tape that the machine will read before it encounters the main body of data. We then type this special code followed by the text of the story, and finally, the symbols "&.". "&." signals the end of a major unit of data and, as we shall see in a moment, units of this kind can be of different sizes and types and can have a more or less complex internal structure.

Suppose now that the text has been translated into Spanish, sentence by sentence. This richer body of data can be put into the system in the following way. First, type the code "&TZ" and the first sentence of the Tzeltal text. Then, type the code "&=SP" followed by the Spanish equivalent of the first sentence. They type the code "&." to show that this is the end of the first unit. We must assume that the code "&=SP" has been properly introduced to the system in the same way as the "&TZ". The second sentence followed by its Spanish translation is entered in the same way and so on until the end of the text.

The units of data may consist of three parts, or more. Each Tzeltal sentence may, for example, be accompanied by translations in both Spanish and English. Or, alternatively, there may be a Spanish translation for each sentence and also an identification number which serves to catalogue the sentence and which we can use to identify it if it has later to be modified or corrected in some way, or if we want to call for it to be printed. The machine will also be able to use these identification numbers in concordances and in dictionary entries to show where the sentences used as examples are taken from.

Let us now consider a more complex example. Suppose this time that the data consists of a bi-lingual dictionary, say, of Quiché and Spanish. A typical entry in the dictionary will consist of a Quiché word or morpheme followed by a number of Spanish equivalents, one for each of its possible meanings. For some or all of the meanings, a set of sentences together with Spanish equivalents may also be provided as examples. There are various ways in which data of this kind could be presented to the system. One possibility is as follows: Each unit begins with the special code "&QU" followed by a Quiché word or morpheme. This is followed by the code "&=SP" and a Spanish word or phrase giving the first meaning. Following this there may be any number of pairs of sentences, the first of which is preceded by the code "&CP" and the second of which is preceded by "&CPSP". The code "&CP" is followed by a Quiché sentence exemplifying the current dictionary entry in its first meaning, and the code "&CPSP" is followed by the Spanish translation of that sentence. Following the last example sentence the code "&=SP" may appear again followed by a Spanish word or phrase giving the second meaning of the Quiché word or morpheme. This, in turn, can be followed by a series of examples. Finally, the end of the dictionary entry is signaled by the code "&.".

From either one of the two kinds of data that we have described, the computer can produce concordances of various kinds. A concordance may be based on words or morphemes or, indeed, on linguistic units of various other kinds. A concordance which is based on words is a document in which each different word of the original text appears as the heading of a paragraph, with the paragraphs being arranged in alphabetical order according to their headings. The paragraph consists simply of a list of all of the different places in which the word has been found. It may take the form of a list of identification numbers or, more usually, of a list of sentences, possibly with translations. A morpheme concordance has exactly the same form except that there is one paragraph for each different morpheme. The computer can produce either kind of concordance provided that the boundaries between morphemes have been indicated in some consistent way in the original data.

Strictly speaking, there is no mechanical way of recognizing morphemes in a text, even if boundaries are marked, since the units that actually occur are allomorphs, that is, variants of morphemes. The computer system can, therefore, most easily produce a concordance based on allomorphs. Something much closer to a morpheme concordance can, however, be obtained by providing the system with a special kind of dictionary in which it can look up any given allomorph and discover what the corresponding morpheme is. Alternatively, the program can be provided with a set of morphophonemic rules it can apply to the original text to produce a new text in which every morpheme appears in a standard form. Notice that at least one of these, a list of variants of each morpheme or a list of morphophonemic rules, would, in any case, have to appear in any complete grammar of the language. Notice also that the most useful document a linguist could have to help him prepare this list would be precisely a concordance of allomorphs.

We can therefore use the computer system to help compile data which will both contribute directly to the final grammar and also to later operations with the same computer system. We shall find that this is a recurring pattern. Consider, for example, an earlier stage in the investigation when the linguist has collected some text but has not yet decided where the allomorph or morpheme boundaries fall. The computer system certainly cannot perform a morphemic analysis for him. It can, however, help him to collect evidence and counter-evidence relevant to hypotheses he may form very rapidly and painlessly. The computer can easily be instructed to locate all the words that begin or end with a certain sequence of sounds that he suspects of being a prefix or suffix, and to print each one with a small amount of surrounding context. Once the morphemic structure of a word has been decided upon, however tentatively, the proper morpheme boundaries can be automatically inserted in the word wherever it occurs throughout the entire text.

The utility of concordances in all aspects of practical linguistic research is acknowledged by almost everybody. Let us now consider the problems that attend the construction and maintenance of a bi-lingual dictionary in, say, Tzeltal and Spanish. We assume that the linguist will present new dictionary material to the system as he collects it. He will add new entries to the dictionary, new meanings to be included in existing entries, deletions and corrections. Entries do not have to be presented in any specific order because sorting items into alphabetical order is one of the tasks to which electronic computers are particularly well suited. New meanings for words already in the dictionary are typed just as though they were entirely new entries. The computer recognizes that it has two or more entries for the same word or morpheme and combines them under a single heading before the dictionary is printed. Modifications to the dictionary are made by means of a few special code words.

Material for a Tzeltal-Spanish bi-lingual dictionary is also material for a Spanish-Tzeltal dictionary, and it is clearly undesirable that the linguist should have to construct the two dictionaries separately, not only because this would be unnecessary duplication of effort, but also because an automatic system can more easily ensure that no material included in one is omitted from the other.

However, the process of inverting a bi-lingual dictionary is not quite as straightforward as it might at first appear. It is not always possible to find a single word in one language to represent each sense of a given word in another language and it is therefore often necessary to use a phrase instead. Such a phrase may begin with a substantive word such as a noun or a verb, but it may equally well begin with a semantically inconsequential word like an article or an auxiliary. For example, the Spanish translation of the Tzeltal verb "tohp'lahan" would be something like "hacer ruido fuerte al tumbar un árbol". It would be unfortunate if this were to appear under "hacer" and not under "ruido". The word "nakal" means, among other things, "sin trabajo durante un dia", but should it be listed only under "sin"? Clearly not. The simplest way to overcome this difficulty is to require the linguist to state explicitly under what Spanish headings he wants the material to appear and this can easily be done by using an additional code word. Using this device, a dictionary entry for "nakal" might appear as follows:

```
&TZ NAKAL &=SP SIN TRABAJO DURANTE UN DIA &DSP TRABAJO
&DSP DESOCUPADO &.
```

Appropriate entries would then be made under both "trabajo" and "desocupado".

There is virtually no limit to the ways one could think of to use a computer to arrange and rearrange data, to search for examples, to combine data from different sources into a single coherent file, and so forth. For example, a concordance is similar to a dictionary in that it consists of an alphabetical listing of words with a paragraph about each one. It is natural to think of combining these into a single document where all the information so far collected about a particular word could be found. As I said at the outset, the program has been designed to be as flexible as possible and, if a particular facility does not exist in the program it should require relatively little labor to introduce it.

A preliminary version of the program already exists and has been used to produce fairly extensive word and morpheme concordances in the Totenac language. But work on the program is by no means finished and there is no reason to suppose that it ever will be. As the linguists with whom we are working become more familiar with the system, as they gain more insight into the languages they are studying, and as they advance from phonology into morphonology and from morphonology into syntax, we expect the demands made of the program to become more and more sophisticated.

In its present form the program is unable to handle grammatical information of any kind. However, a completely explicit grammar of a language should be capable of serving as instruction to a machine to produce sentences in that language. Indeed, this is one of the principal tests of a well written grammar. We therefore foresee a demand for routines that will analyze and generate sentences according to the rules that the linguist proposes. But, though the possibilities of a computer system of this kind are indeed very great, its inherent limits cannot be stressed too heavily.

There are linguists who believe that computers may, in the not too distant future, be able to take over some, if not all, of the work of performing linguistic analyses, that they may, in short, be able to replace the linguist totally. Very little experimentation has been done in this direction and the few computer programs that have actually been written are, at best, rudimentary. But this is far from the aim that we have pursued on this project. We are trying simply to increase the proportion of the linguist's time during which he is doing creative, essentially non-mechanical work. We hope to make it possible for him to use the computer as an industrious, painstaking but unimaginative personal assistant. We expect that the concordances, dictionaries, tentative morpheme lists, and other documents that he directs the machine to prepare for him will be highly personal documents reflecting his own style of work. The computer will prepare bi-lingual dictionaries, but we do not expect these to be of a kind that could be immediately sent to a publisher for mass production, though this is by no means unthinkable. We expect that they will contain incidental notes about words and phrases, unverified hypotheses about morpheme structure and meaning, and so forth.

Five or ten years from now universities will doubtless still be training both theoretical and practical linguists. But the prospect facing the aspiring young practical linguist will be much more exciting. The road ahead of him will still be long and difficult, but he will, for the first time, reasonably be able to expect to pursue it into the interesting territory that lies beyond phonology and morphology. He will have a strong background in anthropology, and some knowledge about computer science, be a good mimic and a good typist, and own seventy-five thousand records of information on magnetic tape. When you ask him at a party what language he knows, he may possibly reply "FORTRAN, ALGOL, PL/I, and a little Spanish".

Acknowledgements

The views expressed in this paper are those of the author. They should not be interpreted as reflecting the views of The RAND Corporation or the official opinion or policy of any of its governmental or private research sponsors. Papers are reproduced by The RAND Corporation as a courtesy to members of its staff.

This paper was prepared for presentation at the annual symposium of the Interamerican Program on Linguistics and Language Teaching in Sao Paolo, Brazil, January 9 – 14, 1969.

11

Computational Competence and Linguistic Performance

There was a vaudeville comedian who regularly performed on the British radio during the Second World War and whose act always included a song in which he claimed to be a practioner of some totally implausible trade and bemoaned the even more implausible misfortunes that he suffered in the line of duty. The song was in rhyming couplets of approximately iambic pentameter and was sung always to the same tune. The format required the first line to state the occupation from which the ills in the ensuing recital followed, and the second line paraphrased the first in the form of a long noun phrase with preposed adjectives on the German pattern. A possible opening might be as follows:

> *I'm a dreamer up of deviance in a sentence,*
> *A deviant sentence dreamer upper, me.*
> *I find semantic readings for such nonsense*
> *As "Hueless green ideas sleep furiously."*

I am sometimes put in mind of this routine when a stranger at a party asks me where I work and what I do. I tell him that I work for the RAND Corporation and, after a preliminary exchange in which I deny any responsibility for cordless electric shavers and portable typewriters, I tell him, if I'm feeling courageous, that I'm a computational linguist. For some this response is too laconic, and I must go on to explain, with greater or less amounts of detail and illustration, that I would like to be able to contribute to a scientific theory of how human languages work and I believe that I can use a computer to help me do this. If my companion is a natural scientist, an engineer, or an accountant, then he will probably also use a computer from time to time, though he will not feel tempted to call himself a computational physicist, a computational molecular biologist, a computational heat-transfer engineer, or a computational accountant. Why do I find it necessary to dignify the implausible trade I practice with so pompous a title? The term "computational linguistics" has been made to cover a great many different activities. In the next half-hour I shall try to distinguish a small subset of these and to claim that they, at least, deserve some special recognition and the dignity of a special name. I hope I shall be able to do more than pontificate about the meaning of a term. But, if I fail, then I must ask your indulgence. One is only president once, and it is a president's prerogative to pontificate. What I really want to do is to claim that the most important part of our field is not receiving the attention it deserves, and that the bulk of our intellectual resources is being expended on secondary problems.

For some people, "computational linguistics" refers to any activity in which a computer is used for something other than arithmetic operations on integers and floating point numbers. Automatic type setting, the preparation of telephone directories, text editing, and maintaining address lists all qualify. Thousands of innocent people for whom a linguist is somebody that can converse in two or more languages would find, to their surprise, that they are computational linguists under this definition. Most of us, however, would probably prefer to say that to be a computational linguist one must first be a linguist.

If there are still linguists who, in addition to joining the quest for the golden fleece of linguistic universals that every true and noble linguist must pursue, attempt to write grammars of real languages, then we should expect at least some of them to construct and use computer programs with which to test those grammars. They will thereby become computational linguists. But in this case everyone who attempts to write a grammar of a natural language or even of some small part of one, either is or should become a computational linguist because the attempt to write a formal grammar that will adequately describe an interesting subset of a natural language without the aid of a machine is doomed to certain failure. Whatever else it may be in addition, a grammar is a set of instructions for producing or recognizing sentences and can therefore be regarded as a program for some abstract machine. The notation is typically rich and irredundant; each rule is related to many other rules in different and subtle ways; the abstract machine must be capable of exploring an immense variety of allowable paths through the rules. In short, a small grammar is several orders of magnitude more complicated than a large FORTRAN program and its writer has immeasureably more opportunities for error.

A programmer always hopes, and half believes, that the programs he writes will work perfectly the first time they are presented to the machine, historical precedents to the contrary notwithstanding. He is almost invariably disappointed and, as we all know, checking, correcting, and checking again consumes the largest proportion of any programmer's time. If a grammarian does not have the aid of a machine, then, like the programmer, he is likely to be over-optimistic about his errors and omissions. If a practical grammarian is not a computational linguist it must be through poverty or ignorance. For many people the construction and use of grammar-testing programs is the paradigm activity of a computational linguist. The purpose of such a program is to help the linguist in his every-day work and its construction requires considerable linguistic sophistication. In the same category with grammar testers we might put programs that help the field worker organize his data and find examples of phonemes, morphemes, words, and grammatical constructions that take his interest – a mechanical replacement for the traditional shoe box – a program that would seek out sets of possibly cognate words in the vocabularies of several languages, programs to aid in the construction and maintenance of dictionaries, and the like. These enterprises are all important to one linguist or another, but these programs have the same status in his affairs as do programs that solve differential equations and invert matrices in natural science and engineering or programs that prepare a balance sheet in accounting. They relieve tedium and make it possible to produce more results more accurately and with greater speed. They affect linguistics, but do not change its essential character, and they are therefore not sufficient in themselves to be the foundation of a new discipline with a catchy name.

The computer takes a much more central role in another kind of linguistic investigation, in which an attempt is made to simulate the human activities involved in learning a language and in producing and understanding discourse. If this kind of enterprise were to become of central importance in our field, as I believe it should, then computational linguistics would come to look more and more like computational psychology or, as the terminology has it, artificial intelligence. The study of language learning and of the processes whereby people say what they mean and understand what they hear, in short, of linguistic performance, belongs on the one hand to psycholinguists and phoneticians who are skilled in the art of constructing and interpreting psychological experiments and, on the other hand, to computational linguists where that term is interpreted in its best and narrowest sense, who have the skill and apparatus to build working models. In the study of linguistic performance, the canons of success are public and unequivocal: the theory accounts for a given set of phenomena just to the extent that a machine can be constructed embodying the theory, which will then reproduce the phenomena.

Many objections will doubtless be raised to this by both computational and non-computational linguists and non-linguists. The most serious opposition will come from those who claim that I am missing the point of the distinction between competence and performance. If a hard line could be drawn between competence and performance, then we would have to say that an understanding of linguistic competence is a prerequisite for any study of performance. To attempt to investigate the mechanisms of speech and understanding without first having a fairly clear idea of the important properties of language itself would be like attempting to study how people do mental arithmetic without knowing even the most elementary mathematics, or how a person contrives to keep a bicycle upright without knowing anything about mechanics. If the analogy is convincing, it is only because mathematics and mechanics are both fairly well understood. If there had been bicycles in the days before Galileo started dropping objects from the Leaning Tower of Pisa and Newton took an interest in falling apples, then it would have seemed much more reasonable to study how bicycles could be ridden without necessarily first discovering how apples fall. The investigation might have revealed many facts, some of which we should later come to see as belonging to the science of mechanics and others which would contribute to a theory of psychology and human performance. Much of the work that has been done on strategies for playing complicated games like checkers, chess, and go has involved attending to what master players say about their performance. Attempts to characterize a master player's competence independently of his performance have been made, but have been, for the most part, unsuccessful.

But we are still missing the point of the distinction between competence and performance, at least to some extent. There is in fact no hard line which distinguishes them. When we say that we are attempting to construct a theory of linguistic competence, we are saying nothing more than that we shall make certain simplifications and generalizations which, while they may distort the observed data, clear away some of the wood so that we may see the trees. Just as the natural scientist accepts the fiction of a frictionless pulley, a weightless cord, a perfect gas, an elliptical orbit, so we must accept the fiction of a speaker who never forgets, stumbles, or loses the thread of his argument. Little by little, we try to abandon the fictions. If we have a theory of weights and pulleys that accounts for the observed data fairly well, then we attempt to provide a place in the theory for friction in the pulley or for the weight of the cord, and eventually for both. In the same way in linguistics we hope slowly to absorb into competence facts which, for the present, we have agreed to ignore and which we therefore label "performance".

This is, at least in part, what linguists mean when they draw a distinction between competence and performance, but, if this were the whole story, then any attempt to study the phenomena of performance would be, by definition, absurd. If "performance" is a label we give to the phenomena we intend to ignore, then we must either ignore them or relabel them "competence". But there is another reason for setting up this distinction, namely that much of what we call "performance" and whose study we delay or leave to others, lies outside our purview as linguists.

If a person forgets, stumbles, loses track of what he is doing, or doubles back on himself in the course of speaking or, for that matter, understanding, it is presumably for the same reasons that he does so in any other kind of activity. It makes as much sense to construct a theory to account for linguistic forgetfulness or back-tracking in a sentence as it does to investigate the properties of electricity produced by a bright yellow generator or the boiling point of water on the third Sunday in the month. Forgetfulness and hesitation and backtracking are not properties of language; they are properties of human beings. Once again, we must conform to normal scientific practice and delineate a field for ourselves simplifying and distorting to some extent where necessary to preserve the boundary. The subject of our field is human language and those mental structures and processes that are associated with it in some peculiar or unique way are ours to investigate and account for.

Let me now delineate another field for which I shall temporarily use the term "computational linguistics". It will be the aim of its practitioners to fulfill Turing's old ideal of constructing a machine which, if it could communicate with us only by telephone or telegraph, would be indistinguishable from a human being. This program is no more heroic than that of any other discipline; physicists do not expect to complete the story of the physical world, nor linguists an account of linguistic competence in a finite time, and we shall not expect to see Turing's ideal realized any time soon. Like any other scientist, while keeping his eye on his ultimate heroic aim, the computational linguist will have to adopt more modest intermediate goals. To begin with he will not necessarily expect the machine to respond as promptly as a human being. He will be happy for some considerable time if the machine insists on communicating in complete sentences and stubbornly refuses to understand the more telegraphic style that is normal among real humans; he will be patient if the first version of the machine fails to show a grain of common sense and is unable to make even the simplest inferences. He *will* be studying what linguists usually call performance if only because the formalisms he adopts must provide effective procedures for obtaining semantic readings for particular strings of words, and for obtaining strings of words to correspond to particular semantic readings.

However, to say that he is concerned with linguistic performance is not to say that he is committed to do battle on all fronts at once. He will make many of the same simplifying assumptions that other linguists do, but he will feel less constrained to find linguistic universals and solutions to his problems which accord with them. The proof of his pudding is in the eating. The machine must be made to work. To be sure, human linguistic behavior is sufficiently complex that it is unlikely that any machine will be able to mimic it if it does not conform in large measure to such linguistic universals as there are. The computational linguist will be obliged to adopt formalisms to describe this and that part of his machine. But whilst the ordinary linguist is concerned to find the weakest formalism that will do the job, the computational linguist will seek the strongest formalisms possible.

One of the most important distinguishing characteristics of the computational linguist will be that he will be forced in the very early stages of his work to face facts. By this I mean simply that the machines he builds will have to be capable of acquiring and storing knowledge about the real world. There is probably no fact, real or imaginary, that we could not use to help determine whether we were in conversation with a man or a machine or which would not influence our assessment of the quality of a linguistic performance. But, I hear you cry, this means that linguistics, or rather computational linguistics, will have to encompass the whole of human knowledge. The idea is clearly absurd. Am I really proposing that we should supplant the physicist, the historian, the poet, the gourmet cook, old uncle Tom Cobly and all? The answer is – eventually, yes. But then, this is surely the aim of almost any other scientist worth his salt. Will not physics one day provide us with the ultimate explanation of everything in the universe? Or will physics have been totally absorbed by mathematics before that happens?

Yes, I am proposing that we set our sights on nothing less than the sum of human knowledge and understanding, but that our field, like everybody else's, will have its own approach to this goal. For a long time, our treatment of so-called encyclopedic facts will be essentially similar to that of a librarian – we must learn to assimilate, catalog, store, and retrieve them, taking only the minimum possible responsibility for their accuracy, value, or interest.

If we are going to build a machine whose purpose will be to simulate human behavior, there are many places that we might start. Two of the most promising seem to me to be fact retrieval, or question answering, which is receiving an increasing amount of attention, and machine translation, which is an embarrassing subject. Now, I have certainly not the slightest wish to be an embarrassment to anybody, but I do want to say a word about machine translation.

A great amount of public money has been spent on research into machine translation and there is no doubt that a proportion of that money was disbursed to incompetent people for ill-conceived projects. Machine translation is not particularly distinguished by that fact. Read almost any daily paper, especially at about this season, and you will see how sums greater by an order of magnitude than the entire outlay on machine translation continue to be spent on enterprises whose eventual value to science, the nation, and mankind is, to say the least, questionable. The remarkable fact is that little or no money, public or private, has been spent on machine translation as a vehicle of genuine scientific research. The ostensible aim of every project has been to manufacture a program or a machine that could be put to work on an industrial scale. What this has to do with research of any kind is unclear – perhaps the word has to be used to persuade university administrators that what is being done is directed towards academic rather than purely mercenary ends.

How have these projects been conducted? In the only way they could possibly have been conducted. It is clear to everybody that a translating machine must contain a large dictionary which will take a massive effort to produce. Since the machine must be delivered in two years, work on the dictionary had better begin right away. This strategy is made necessary by the time scale and the nature of the expected product, but it has the additional advantage that, while nobody knows very much about what a translating machine's dictionary should be like, they know even less about any of its other parts. Some projects reached a later stage in which grammar rules were written and some hardy souls looked forward to a day when they would engage in the enterprise known as doing the semantics. Most of the money, however, went for so-called dictionaries – a totally valueless set of properties most of which are by now mercifully lost.

It is indeed tragic that a political and intellectual climate has been created in which to declare an interest in machine translation is to attract opprobrium and repel funds. Research on machine translation has been made virtually impossible despite the fact that, given any reasonable interpretation of the terms, we must conclude that there have been almost no attempts to carry out any such research.

In my view there is no better framework within which to begin the investigation of linguistic performance than that provided by machine translation. Question answering is comparable. If question answering is not to suffer the same fate as machine translation and is to remain as a respectable vehicle for honest intellectual work, then the lessons of the past must be studied with care. The most important lesson is that extravagant claims will not only catch up with you in the end; they will effectively prevent you from doing anything of genuine interest.

Another important lesson is that a difficult inter-disciplinary task like the ones I am considering cannot be undertaken half-heartedly. I come now to the point of the second half of my title. I want to claim that linguistic performance is a worthy object for research to be undertaken today and that machine translation and question answering are excellent starting points. I also want to claim that the study of linguistic performance requires a level of computational competence far above that that has been typical in our field. We have been encouraged by our colleagues in other departments, and by the directors of our computer centers, to view the computer much as we view an airplane, a bulldozer or a dentist's drill. It is a useful tool that can be used for this and that purpose; it will operate reliably provided only that it is in the hands of a skilled operator. It differs from the aforementioned appliances in that unskilled use is unlikely to result in grievous bodily harm; it will, however, not produce any of the desired results either. Operators with the required skill are not in over-abundant supply, but regular FORTRAN classes are being given on the graduate and undergraduate level so that we should be able to find somebody who can help us.

The relationship of the computational linguist, as I am using the term, to computers and computing must, however, be different. A computational linguist is just as much a computer scientist as he is a linguist. To the extent that he is involved in the construction of psychological and linguistic theories, he must be a master of these disciplines and would never for a moment think of applying to the psychology or linguistics departments to supply him with a technician to furnish the necessary skill. To the same extent he is involved in the construction of a branch of computer science. To go into the highways and byways in search of someone who has had a FORTRAN course or has been otherwise ordained into the mysteries of programming is to condemn a project in computational linguistics to mediocrity at best, and disaster probably.

Linguistic computing is immensely difficult for several reasons. First, it involves the construction and manipulation of very complex data structures – families of trees representing the various interpretations of a syntactically ambiguous sentence, networks representing the relations among a set of semantic objects, and the like. Second, the computational linguist is usually concerned to make the computer, the paradigm example of a deterministic device, behave as though it were non-deterministic. In other words, presented with a set of alternatives, the machine must not choose one but follow each of them up independently. Techniques for inducing this kind of schizophrenia in a computer exist and are fairly well understood, but they are not trivial. Third, the computational linguist is, and will always be, a programmer's nightmare because he is always sure that he wants a program written but he can never be completely sure what he wants it to do. As I said before, the program for him is not a simple tool, it is a primary object of the research. Writing it will, therefore, involve not only skill but also artistry and good taste. The writer can never be sure what it will grow into, but he must separate in his program what is separate in the theory so that the parts can be replaced as units when the theory changes, and he must try to foresee the points of future growth so that proper provision can be made for expansion. Last but not least, linguistic programming requires good workmanship in the details. It is true that, since we are not aiming to manufacture a marketable product, we need not count the cost of every bit of storage space and every cycle of machine time. However, it is all too easy to construct a computer program, at great expense in human labor, which takes half an hour to analyse one sentence, make one inference, or make one maneuver of whatever kind it is designed for. Nondeterministic programs that operate on complex data structures can be so prodigiously expensive as to be unusable, even for research purposes.

What I conclude from all this is: first, that the study of linguistic performance constitutes a large, fascinating, and important field which is not receiving the attention it deserves; second, that the study of this field properly belongs to computational linguists but, third, that we are not doing nearly enough to equip ourselves to work in this field. We need people who are not only intelligent and have a burning interest in these problems, but have an equally strong background in linguistics, psychology and computer science. Let us attack the problem of performance with a will. Let us take a new look at some of the old problems, and notably machine translation, asking for the first time, not how computational linguistics can serve it but how it can serve computational linguistics. But, above all, let us change the name of our field to something metrically more felicitous so that bards may better chronicle our exploits. As things are, they must resort to such maneuvers as:

> *I'm as well as computational, a linguist,*
> *A calculating sentence cruncher, me.*
> *I wrote a talking program with a new twist,*
> *It speaks in California R.P.*
> *It answers riddles, wins at chess and chequers,*
> *A smarter program you will never see.*
> *But don't tell it I wrote it please, that matters*
> *Because I think it thinks that it wrote me.*

Notes

Any views expressed in this paper are those of the author. They should not be interpreted as reflecting the views of The RAND Corporation or the official opinion or policy of any of its governmental or private research sponsors. Papers are reproduced by The RAND Corporation as a courtesy to members of its staff. This paper was prepared as the presidential address to the Association for Computational Linguistics, and delivered at the Annual Meeting in Boston, Massachusetts, on May 13, 1969.

12

Performance Grammars

The study of linguistic competence, as applied to a particular language, is the attempt to characterize that subset of the Cartesian product of all possible meanings with all possible utterable sequences of sounds that are the correct sentences of the language. By talking of the *correct* sentences we do not, of course, mean to suggest that the study of linguistic competence is, in any way, involved with social norms or with rhetoric; only that it is concerned with the pairs of sounds and meanings that speakers recognize as belonging to their language rather than with the often imperfect imitations of these that human imperfection forces them to be content with in practice. The characterization of the meaning-sound pairs that constitute the language is particularly interesting if it is possible to show that the formalism in which it is stated would be inadequate to characterize other sets of pairs which do not, however, constitute human languages. To the extent that the formalism is inapplicable except to languages which either are or might plausibly be ordinary human languages, it constitutes a statement about the nature of human language as a whole.

Since language seems to be, before all else, a system in which meanings are encoded in sound, and since languages differ from one another precisely in the particular meaning-sound pairs that they contain, then the study of linguistic competence is the study of what is most essential about language and is logically prior to any other study. However, there are a great many questions that can legitimately be asked about language but which go beyond, in one way or another, the search for an abstract characterization of meaning sound pairs. It is usual to group these questions under the general heading of "performance" despite the fact that they do not exhibit any other interesting common properties. For example, questions about the sequences of sounds people actually utter as opposed to those that an ideal speaker of the language might be supposed to utter are questions about performance. If a method of characterizing languages is sought which makes it simpler to find the meanings that correspond to a particular sequence of sounds or the sequences of sounds that correspond to a particular meaning, then what is afoot is an investigation of linguistic performance. Slips of the tongue, the sets of sentences that people find difficult to understand, and segments of text which embrace more than a single sentence all belong to the study of performance. In this paper I shall discuss in very broad outline a particular kind of investigation of certain aspects of linguistic performance that interests me. I shall try to show what I think such an investigation has gained and might still gain from studies of linguistic competence and some implications that I think this work has for linguistics as a whole.

In an article in *Mind* in 1950, Alan Turing suggested as a worthy scientific goal the construction of a machine with which it would be possible to converse, presumably by telephone or telegraph, and which would be capable of masquerading as a human being. In other words, there would be no way that a person could discover, through simple conversation with the machine, that it was not a real human being. The question of whether such a machine could be constructed in principle is one with far-reaching implications, but it is a question which will not be answered soon. In any case, the attempt to build such a machine can be made interesting irrespective of whether the ultimate goal is ever reached. The capabilities that a machine would have to have in order to pass itself off as human are, of course, enormously varied. The machine must clearly be able to understand ordinary sentences and to formulate new ones to represent the meanings it has to convey.

A first step towards the design of the kind of machine Turing envisaged would be a somewhat different machine whose capabilities, while considerably more modest, would still require a measure of intellectual heroism on the part of the designers. The kind of machine I have in mind is one that would be capable of doing the so-called comprehension exercises that were once popular in the teaching of foreign languages. The student is caused to read a text in the foreign language, and is then required to answer questions, usually also in the language, about what he has read. If it were the nursery rhyme, "Jack and Jill went up the hill", then a possible question might be, "On the injuries to which of the protagonists in this story are we given the most detailed information?" But this is considerably more subtle than the questions usually asked and, in any case, it contains the word "protagonist" which a student at this level may perhaps not be expected to know. More plausible would be questions like, "What did Jack break?", "Who came tumbling after?", and possibly even "Who went to fetch what?". In this exercise the student is supposed to show that he understands that part of the language that has been taught so far, and, to the extent that he answers the questions correctly, it seems to me reasonable to claim that that is exactly what he does show. If the students were given the text of "Ten Little Indians", then one could imagine asking something like "What proportion of the original number of Indians remained alive after a big bear hugged one?". If a question of this kind brought an outrageous reply, or no reply at all, then the questioner might be led to doubt that he was in conversation with a real human being. On the other hand, he might equally well be led to doubt that he was in conversation with a machine because one thing he does expect machines to be able to do is simple arithmetic calculations. In any case, the ability to answer this kind of question correctly certainly turns on something other than purely linguistic abilities and it therefore seems reasonable to defer treatment of it until later.

Clearly, a machine that understands what people say must be capable of analyzing the grammatical structure of the utterances it receives, of representing the information that they contain in some kind of canonical form, of storing expressions in this canonical form in such a way that they can easily be retrieved, of locating those expressions that are relevant to a given question, and of constructing answers that accord with the rules of English grammar. At least in the initial stages of work on a project of this kind, there is little to be gained from drawing a distinction between utterances and sentences. If, in its initial incarnation, the machine is prepared to converse only with people who express themselves in complete sentences, this will not be accounted a major defect. From now on, I shall therefore talk of the input to the machine as though it consisted entirely of well-behaved sentences, and shall claim, nevertheless, to be engaged in a thorough-going investigation of linguistic performance. To say that we are studying performance is not to say that we abandon the right to make the kinds of idealization of our subject matter that science thrives on.

The reason for wanting to reduce the great variety of sentences that the machine must expect to canonical forms is clear. Whatever questions can be answered wholly or partly on the basis of the sentence, "John gave the book to Mary" can equally well be answered on the basis of sentences like "Mary was given the book by John", "The book was given to Mary by John" and so on. In other words, the system will be more efficient if families of sentences which are related to one another systematically but which do not differ in meaning are made to fall together at the earliest possible stage in the analysis. All the other standard arguments for distinguishing deep from surface structure also go through in the design of this kind of machine. It is clearly desirable, for example, to find a form for sentences in which the logical relationships between words and phrases are represented in a perspicuous manner. At present, it seems that the form of deep structure that will suit our purposes best will be similar to that suggested by Fillmore, but nothing of what I am saying here turns on this. Considerations that we entertain tomorrow may lead us to believe that the kind of deep structures suggested by the so-called generative semanticists will suit our purposes better.

If we are in fact able to make the machine find the deep structures that correspond to the surface strings it receives, then the efficiency of all subsequent operations will be immeasurably increased, perhaps enough to make practically feasible a project that otherwise would have been totally unthinkable. But efficiency is, in the last analysis, the only thing we can expect to gain. The ideal situation in which all strings with the same meaning would be reduced to exactly one canonical form is something we know to be unachievable. Alan Turing's most famous contribution to mathematics is a theorem, one of whose implications is that we cannot hope to construct an algorithm that will be able to tell us whether any pair of sentences do or do not have the same meaning. Strictly speaking, the theorem is to the effect that the notion of the meaning of a sentence is not entirely coherent, but this is a point to which we shall return.

In a paper entitled "From Semantics to Syntax" (Kay 1967;in this volume) I described a form of rule that would map P-markers onto expressions in a language akin to the predicate calculus. The elementary constants in that language were to be chosen from a closed set of semantic primitives. At the beginning of the paper, I argued that the semantic component of any grammar must furnish readings stated in terms of a universal alphabet of semantic primitives. I take it that, though versions of generative grammar differ in the form of semantic representations they provide, the view that they should be stated in terms of such a universal set of primitives is the one most commonly held. Despite the popularity of this view, I found it necessary in my earlier paper to

launch an attack with characteristic linguistic intemperance, on the only other view I
know which Lyons and others call *structural semantics* . I say that, "While this view
may have some short-term philosophical appeal, it is almost totally barren from the
standpoint of scientific linguistics". Well, having undertaken to build a machine that
can do comprehension exercises, I now find myself forced to retreat from my previous
position and to espouse structural semantics.

Structural semantics can be characterized briefly as follows. Because a sentence is
meaningful, we are led to suppose that there must be something that is its meaning.
However, this is not a valid inference. Furthermore, the attempt to isolate meanings from
the sentences that normally embody them invariably leads to unsatisfactory results. We
can not exhibit the meaning of any sentence otherwise than by writing one or more other
sentences in the same or a different language. It is difficult to see how this gets us any
closer to meanings in the pure state. But the structural semanticist claims that there is
no isolable entity which can reasonably be called the meaning of a word or phrase, but
words and sentences do contract relationships with other words and sentences and, if
anything is the true meaning, it is the total set of these relations. If I can say "I saw a
tulip", then I can, with equal truth, say "I saw a flower". According to the traditional
view we should say that the second sentence can be inferred from the first by virtue
of the meanings of the words. According to the structural semanticist, it is exactly the
other way about: the fact that the second sentence follows from the first is itself part of
the meanings of the words "tulip" and "flower".

Semantic primitives are an intuitively appealing notion and several arguments can
be adduced in their favor. If there is any part of linguistic theory in which it seems
reasonable to look for universals, it is surely in semantics. If it is possible to translate
sentences from one language into another, it is presumably because there is something
that is invariant as between a sentence and its translation – what we should normally
call its meaning. Semantic primitives also seem to occupy a comfortable place in the
area where semantics and syntax overlap. Whilst they belong to semantics, they can at
the same time be embedded in contextual features, transformational rules and the like.

On the other hand, the attempt to actually identify semantic primitives never leads to
satisfying results. Arguments can always be found for decomposing proposed primitives
into still more elementary units, but the process is governed by a law of diminishing
returns so that, with each new round of decomposition, the cash value of the new
primitives becomes less and less. Eventually, the process turns full circle and we have
as many primitives in the end as we had lexical items in the beginning. Like Katz and
Fodor, we find ourselves forced to establish a set of *distinguishers* along side our *semantic
markers* to capture aspects of meaning which are crucial but totally idiosyncratic.

Lyons points out in his book on structural semantics that the languages of the world
contain many sets of words whose meanings come entirely from the relations they contract with other members of the set. The color words are an obvious example. It is well
known that different cultures and different languages divide the spectrum into different
numbers of units and at different places. Furthermore, for obvious reasons, the boundaries between one color and another can never be sharply defined. The only thing that
is absolutely fixed is the sequence in which the colors are encountered as we move from

one end of the spectrum to the other. In terms of semantic primitives, there is very little that can be said about a word like "red" beyond the fact that it stands for a color and that the color in question is red.

Having claimed that meaning relations are logically prior to meaning, rather than the reverse, Lyons goes on to list a number of meaning relations which he considers to be fundamental. These contain, for example, the relation of *incompatibility* which holds between words like "black" and "white" which cannot both be true of the same thing; and *antonymy* which holds between words like "long" and "short" because to say that something is not long implies that it is short and vice versa; the relation of *hyponymy* which holds between "mammal" and "dog" because to say that Fido is a dog is to say, by implication, that he is a mammal. Other fundamental relations are those of *implication* and *equivalence* . These terms are to be understood as meaning something similar to what logicians intend by them, but there are also crucial differences. From "All men are mortal" and "Socrates is a man" we may infer that Socrates is mortal both in logic and in natural semantics. But the sentence "Two and two equal five" implies that "The moon is made of green cheese" in logic but not in semantics. In other words, by "implication" we do not mean "material implication"; just what we do mean is considerably less clear than we should like it to be.

In my view, relations such as incompatibility, antonymy, and hyponymy can all be shown to be parasitic on the notion of implication, and they can therefore be dispensed with. Suppose that our comprehending machine has been given some information about animals and that it has recorded this by storing the canonical deep structure of each of the sentences that it heard. If the machine knows that a dog is a mammal, it is presumably because it was presented with a sentence to that effect, or with a number of sentences from which the fact can be inferred. Suppose that the machine also knows that Fido is a dog and that Fido is in the living room. If we now ask the machine whether there are any mammals in the living room, it should be able to answer "yes". We could say that it does this in part on the basis of a relation of hyponymy between "mammal" and "dog" and possibly also between "dog" and "Fido" and that it makes the correct inference on the basis of these two relations together with the sentence "Fido is in the living room". But, since the machine must be capable of constructing inference schemes based on sentences, there seems to be no reason why it should also take special account of such relations as incompatibility, antonymy, and hyponymy. Relationships of these kinds can presumably only be established on the basis of sentences that the machine receives, and it is not clear that anything is to be gained by giving them special status.

What we are proposing, then, is a machine, and, by implication, the theory to underlie that machine, in which the distinction between a speaker's semantic competence and his encyclopedic knowledge of the world is totally obliterated. Intuitively, the appeal of such a scheme is considerable for no amount of introspection can reveal a distinction between semantic properties and facts about the world. The scheme is attractive to someone who wants to build the kind of machine we have had in mind because it reduces the number of parts that the machine must have. To do its job, the machine must clearly be able to remember facts and to make inferences so that it will be able to answer questions, the answer to which is not contained in any single sentence that it has stored.

The scheme is disturbing because it rests heavily on a notion of implication different from material implication and with properties which are, at best, unknown and, at worst, contradictory. But, while we may be disturbed to find that there is much illogic in the logic that underlies ordinary speech, we should surely not be altogether surprised. Indeed, much of what we know about logic was suggested to us by the very illogic of everyday language. There is nothing semantically amiss about a phrase like "the set of all sets" or a word like "self-predicability". But, as we know, the attempt to give them strict logical interpretations leads to contradictions which have, furthermore, served to illuminate the subject as a whole. The kind of logic we need for semantics is, therefore, unsatisfactory from a mathematician's point of view on at least two counts: first, it does not make use of material implication, and second, it contains no hierarchy of types.

It is worth noting that the notion of synonymy plays no part in the view of semantics I am advocating. This must surely be accounted an advantage because, while there is little difficulty in deciding whether one term is a hyponym of another, or even whether two terms are antonyms, the decision as to whether a pair of terms is synonymous or not is notoriously difficult. In the kind of scheme proposed here, we could say that a pair of terms or a pair of sentences was synonymous if, and only if, they had contracted identical relations with other terms in sentences. It is unlikely that this would ever be the case and, in any case, to verify it would be practically, if not theoretically, impossible.

There may be many people who could countenance the idea of a logic which is substantially illogical and an account of semantics that has nothing to say about synonyms. But if the design of this machine has implications for linguistic theory, they are even more fundamental than these. As I said at the outset, the goal of linguistic theory is to characterize that subset of the Cartesian product of the set of all possible meanings with a set of all utterable sounds which constitutes a given language. But, if my view of semantics is the correct one, then it no longer makes sense to talk about the set of all possible meanings. In this case, what is left for linguists to do? My answer – and I give it in all possible seriousness – is that linguists should engage in the theoretically revealing, scientifically respectable, practically useful, and altogether exciting enterprise of constructing machines of the kind we have been talking about.

It is possible to take the view that, if there is to be any interest in this enterprise at all, it will come from restrictions that the linguist places on the kinds of mechanisms and components that he allows to be used in building the machine. If no restrictions are imposed, then the machine will have the same theoretical power as a Turing machine, and the claim that it is able to talk and understand will be of relatively little interest. If, on the other hand, the mechanisms that the machine embodies are severely restricted in some way, in particular, if the power of the machine as a whole is considerably less than that of a Turing machine, then the claim that it can speak and understand becomes a much more interesting one, and the theoretical principles underlying the design of the machine become contributions to linguistic theory.

For my own part, I look forward eagerly to a time when we shall need arguments of this metaphysical refinement, but I do not expect that time to come during my life. It is true, from a purely theoretical point of view, that a machine can work properly without being based on correct principles and without revealing anything of interest about that part of the world that it is being used to model. But, it is also true that any model of human linguistic performance that can, in any reasonable sense, be said to work, is unlikely to be based on wholly fallacious principles. The argument is old and simple: if the matter is complicated, then anything that works cannot be all wrong. It is an argument that is used throughout science, and with every good reason. The current view of particle physics is accepted mainly because it works; it is a coherent story about something that it is difficult to write a coherent story about. Now, there is certainly a requirement that entities should not be multiplied beyond necessity, but it is not a difficult requirement to honor. Surely, linguistics cannot long endure if it does not learn to relax a little and to reduce the amount of its resources that it expends on self-conscious brooding over universals to a more reasonable proportion.

To the builder of mechanical models of linguistic processes, the way ahead looks hard, but the outlook is considerably different than from the point of view of theoretical linguistics. Like the linguists of the thirties, we find ourselves less concerned with characterizing languages and separating sentences from non-sentences than with making some kind of coherent statement about the sentences that do occur. Our grammars have deep structures, but there is no place in them for a base component, if by that we mean a component that is creative and not transductive. Deep structures are whatever the transductive rules yield, given the strings input to the system. If the strings do not make sense, then the machine will probably not be able to make sense of them, and there's an end to it.

The transducer uses not transformations but a highly embellished form of general rewriting rule. This is because the formalism of transformational rules does not allow one to pass from surface strings to underlying structures, but only from P-markers to other P-markers. But, since we have explicitly renounced any claim to represent linguistic universals on the part of the formalism, we have no cause to be self-conscious about this. Finally, since we do not recognize any boundary between semantics and encyclopedic knowledge, we consider that the territory we are licensed to hunt in is unrestricted. There are no linguistic facts and non-linguistic facts. But this is not over-pretentious. At the last trumpet, physics hopes to be ready with an account, in terms of elementary particles, of everything under the sun; we are proposing only to be ready with a sketch of the format that that account is stored in in the physicist's mind and some procedures that he may find useful in delivering the report.

Acknowledgements
Any views expressed in this paper are those of the author. They should not be interpreted as reflecting the views of The RAND Corporation or the official opinion or policy of any of its governmental or private research sponsors. Papers are reproduced by The RAND Corporation as a courtesy to members of its staff. This paper was prepared for presentation at the National Science Foundation Seminar on the Construction of Complex Grammars, Harvard University, Cambridge Massachusetts, June 1970.

Publications referenced
Kay 1967.

13

The MIND Translation System: A Study in Man-Machine Collaboration

WITH R. BISBEY

Abstract

The paper describes a computer-based language translation system designed and built using the MIND[1] system. The translation technique is called Human-aided Translation and differs from conventional machine translation systems in that it does not require a bilingual editor in the translation process. Instead, the system relies on a monolingual consultant to resolve ambiguities in the translation process. The system is modular in design, extensible, and independent of source and target languages. An experimental version of the system, which translates a subset of English into either Korean or Spanish, is running at The Rand Corporation.

13.1   What is a Translation Machine?

An ideal translation machine would be a black box whose primary input would be a set of texts in one language (the *source* language) and whose output would be translations of them in another (the *target* language). As a secondary input, it would accept formalized descriptions of the two languages involved so that the same black box could be used for any pair of languages for which suitable descriptions were available. In the late 1950's and early 1960's, a prodigious amount of human energy and millions of dollars were spent on attempts to build this black box. The failure of these attempts has become almost legendary. Some of the products, renamed "translation aids" or "machine-aided translation systems", were allowed to go into service. What the machine produced, since it could not qualify as translation, was passed to a professional translator to be reworked.

It is clear that the problems involved in making translations of high quality are almost as poorly understood today as they were ten years ago and the products of the best translation machine that could be built today would be barely distinguishable from those of their predecessors. But it is not clear that the mechanical translation aids into which inadequate prototypes so easily degenerate represent the most effective division of labor that can be achieved between man and machine. The purpose of this paper is to describe a method of translating which, we believe, divides that labor in a much more reasonable way.

---

[1] Management of Information through Natural Discourse

13.2 Why is Translation Difficult?

Certain kinds of translation are routinely carried out by machines. The best example comes from the world of computers themselves. Computer programs are usually written in specially designed programming languages and then automatically translated into the internal language of the machine that is to carry out the operations by another program called an *assembler, compiler* or *language conversion-program* . The problem that is solved by these programs is by no means straightforward; what we must now ask is what separates it so strongly from the problem of translating between the languages of everyday discourse.

At least two things make natural language translation more difficult than artificial-language translation. First, the grammar of a natural language is at least an order-of-

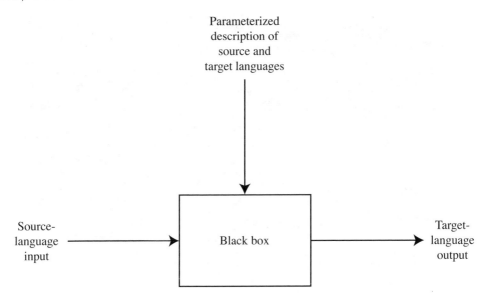

Parameterized
description of
source and
target languages

Source-
language
input

Black box

Target-
language
output

FIGURE 1 An Ideal Machine Translator

magnitude larger and more complex than the grammar of an artificial language. Second, artificial languages are generally designed to be unambiguous, whereas natural languages are massively ambiguous. A given piece of natural-language text, taken out of context, can have any number of interpretations. In the following, we briefly discuss two general types of ambiguities that occur in natural languages, *lexical* and *structural* .

Lexical ambiguities arise when a word belonging to a single grammatical category has more than one possible interpretation. In translation, lexical ambiguities can occur in both the source and target language. The word "saw" in

(1) I saw the log

is lexically ambiguous in the source language. It can mean either to see or to cut. The word "light" in

(2) Mary wore a light dress

may be lexically ambiguous because many languages distinguish between "light in color" and "light in weight".

There are three important types of structural ambiguities, ambiguities of *syntax* , *binding and scope* , and *reference and anaphora* . A structural ambiguity is called "syntactic" if a word performs different grammatical functions for different interpretations of the text. In

(3) The French bottle smells,

the words "French", "bottle", and "smells" are all syntactically ambiguous. The word "bottle", for example, functions as either a noun (meaning a glass container) or a verb (meaning the depositing of something in a bottle), depending on the interpretation of the sentence. A structural ambiguity of "binding and scope" arises whenever a given piece of text can be bound syntactically to two or more other pieces of text. The most common examples occur with conjunctions and prepositional phrases.

(4)   A bellmine is a self-contained bell or buzzer,

one must decide whether both the bell and buzzer are self-contained, or just the bell is self-contained. In

(5)   John sees the girl with the telescope

one must decide whether John is using the telescope to see the girl, or the girl has the telescope in her possession.

A third type of structural ambiguity, "reference and anaphora", arises whenever there is pronominalization as well as in other cases. Examples include:

(6)   John walked up to Bill, took $10 out of his pocket, and gave it to him.

(7)   It is interesting.

In (6), we might need to know whose pocket the $10 came from for an accurate translation. In (7). we might need to know what "it" refers to. In French, for example, (7) would be translated as either

I1 est intéressant

or

Elle est intéressant

depending on the gender of "it".

With this representative sample of the types of ambiguities, we examine the problem of building a machine translator.

13.3   Conventional Machine Translation

The conventional machine-translation system carries out the translation process in three steps (see Fig. 2). The source language is first input to an Input Analysis Routine. This routine determines all possible interpretations of the input text and outputs one analysis for each possible interpretation. The set of alternative analyses then forms the input of the second step, the Output Generation Routine. This routine generates a target-language sentence for each alternative analysis. These target-language alternatives along with the source-language input go to a *bilingual* editor who performs three basic functions. First, he reads the original source language text and chooses the appropriate translation from the alternatives. Second, he makes grammatical and stylistic changes in the translation which either were not, or could not, be expressed in the Output Generation Routine. Finally, he validates the consistency of the output.

In some ways, this is an idealization of systems that have actually been designed or built. Usually the notion of complete structural analysis does not figure in the design explicitly. Typically, however, whenever difficulties arise in the processing of the source text, there is provision for passing alternative renderings through the remainder of the system so that the editor can choose among them.

Such a system has several obvious shortcomings. First, the system requires an editor who is both bilingual and an expert in the subject matter being translated. A suitable person may be very difficult to find. Second, prodigious inefficiency results from pursuing

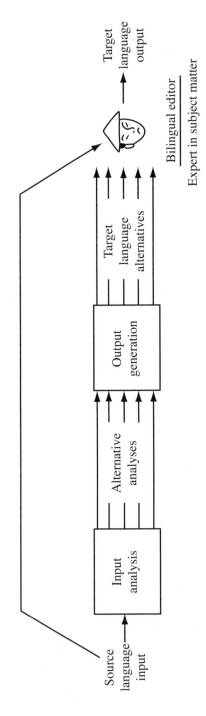

FIGURE 2 Conventional Machine Translation System

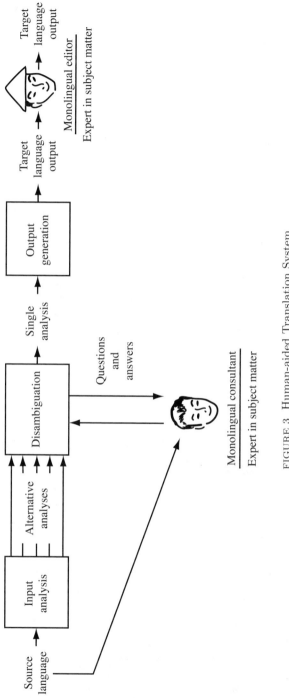

FIGURE 3 Human-aided Translation System

alternative interpretations of a sentence beyond the point in the analysis where the ambiguity is first encountered. An ambiguous sentence such as

(8) John saw the girl in the park with the telescope

requires five times as much processing by the Output Generation Routine as an unambiguous sentence because a target-language sentence must be generated for each of the five possible alternatives, even though only one of the five sentences is the correct translation. The implementor of a conventional machine translation system has three alternatives. He may choose to translate only unambiguous text (if he can find unambiguous text). He may do nothing and thus incur the degraded performance caused by ambiguities. Or, he may cause the Input Analysis Routine to ignore or not find ambiguities, and rely on the bilingual editor to find and hand translate all ambiguous text. Unfortunately, the designers and implementors of the majority of machine translation systems to date have taken this last approach. As a result, the distinction between input analysis and output generation is clouded in such systems. Input analysis usually degenerates to the gross classification of source words by syntactic category, while output generation becomes nothing more than lexical substitution and rearrangement.

13.4   Human-Aided Translation

In an attempt to circumvent many of the problems associated with conventional machine translation, the Rand Linguistics Project proposes a new approach to translation, Human-aided Translation. The intent of Human-aided Translation is to augment a human translator with functions that can clearly be performed well by a machine. Three major design goals are incorporated in the design of the system:

1. The system should not rely on a bilingual editor.
2. The system should consult a human when it does not know what to do.
3. The system should be open ended so that as more becomes known about the translation process, the system can be made to assume some of the responsibilities initially assigned to the human.

The resulting design appears in Fig. 3.

In Human-aided Translation, as in conventional machine translation, the source-language text is first input to an Input Analysis Routine, which finds all possible interpretations and outputs one analysis for each. The set of one or more possible analyses then goes to a Disambiguator, which performs two major functions. First, the Disambiguator displays the source text being processed to a monolingual consultant, providing him with the context of the information being processed. Second, in the event of multiple analyses, the Disambiguator chooses the correct interpretation by posing questions about the input text to the monolingual consultant. The consultant's responses result in the choice of a single analysis from which a target-language sentence is generated by the Output Generation Routine. The target-language output then goes to a monolingual editor, who validates its consistency and may make stylistic changes.

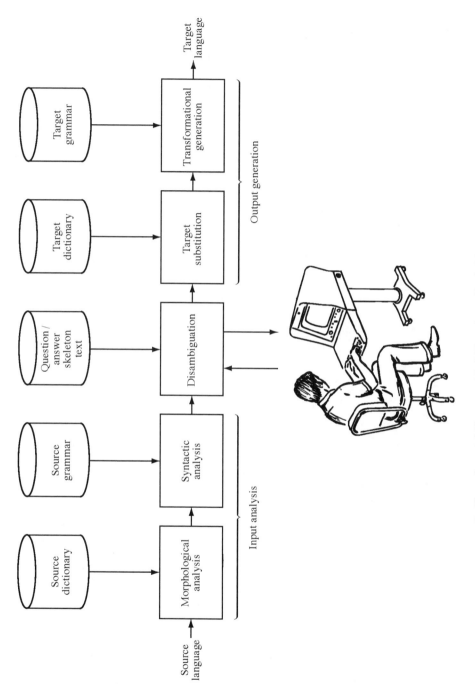

FIGURE 4 Experimental Human-aided Translator Built Using the MIND System

13.5 An Experimental Translator

In order to test the notion of Human-aided Translation, an experimental translator has been built at The Rand Corporation using the MIND System (see Fig. 4). A grammar for analyzing a modest subset of English has been written, along with grammars for generating corresponding subsets of Korean and Spanish. Some work has also been done in writing a grammar for the generation of Hungarian. English text for testing the experimental system includes excerpts from a military manual on training dogs to detect mines. Based on a very small sample of data, the experimental system compares favorably with conventional machine translation systems.

The experimental system incorporates the results of recent linguistic research on transformational grammars. Case grammars are used for analysis and generation. Each analysis of a sentence is what linguists call a *deep structure* . The programs used to carry out the analysis and generation are quite innovative and the subject of other papers (Bisbey, Kaplan and Kay 1971; Bisbey and Kay 1971). Briefly, the analysis and generation programs use the same algorithm, a generalization of Kay's (1967) Chart Parsing Algorithm. The new algorithm combines important features of both the original Kay Algorithm and an algorithm which has come into recent use, the Augmented Transition Network Parser developed by W. Woods (1970) at Bolt Beranek and Newman, Inc.

The success of Human-aided Translation is critically dependent on the Disambiguator. The Disambiguator in the MIND System communicates with the monolingual consultant by means of a television screen and keyboard. In cases of ambiguity, multiple choice questions are displayed on the terminal. The consultant answers these questions by typing the number corresponding to the correct answer. If more than one question needs to be asked, the Disambiguator minimizes the number of questions which must be asked to resolve the ambiguities. Portions of the text being translated may appear in the body of either a question or answer. In such cases, this text is underscored in the original sentence by a vertical arrow ($\uparrow$) or by a digit corresponding to the answer in which the text appears in order to make it clear what word or phrase is being referred to. Examples of questions asked by the experimental system for various ambiguous sentences are given in Figs. 5-8. Figures 5 and 6 show the handling of simple lexical ambiguities. In Fig. 5, if the monolingual consultant decides that "saw" should be interpreted as "perceive", he types "1" at the terminal. Otherwise, he types "2." Figure 7 shows an ambiguity of scope. Answers 1 and 2 determine the scope of the adjective "self-contained." When it is possible to preserve the ambiguity in the target language, answer 3 is provided as an alternative. Figure 8 shows the handling of a binding ambiguity. Here, the system paraphrases the original sentence in ways that bring out the different interpretations.

13.6 Extensions to Human-Aided Translation

Although we do not expect the work of the monolingual consultant to be burdensome, several extensions can be made to the basic design of the Human-aided Translator to reduce the amount of interaction and to more fully automate the translation process. One extension involves the resolution of target-language lexical ambiguities. Often, there is sufficient context in the target-language sentence to resolve lexical ambiguities using

```
I saw the log
   ↑↑↑
Does ''saw'' mean:

1    To perceive, or
2    To cut?

Answer?
```

FIGURE 5 Source-Language Lexical Ambiguity

```
Mary wore a light dress
            ↑↑↑↑↑
Does ''light'' mean:

1    Light in color, or
2    Light in weight?

Answer?
```

FIGURE 6 Target-Language Lexical Ambiguity

```
A bellmine is a self-contained bell or buzzer
               ↑↑↑↑↑↑↑↑↑↑↑↑↑↑ 1111    222222
Question:

1    Is only ''bell'' self-contained, or
2    Is ''buzzer'' self-contained also, or
3    Is the meaning unclear?

Answer?
```

FIGURE 7 Source-Language Scope Ambiguity

```
John saw the girl with the telescope
     111     2222 ↑↑↑↑
Should the sentence be read as:

1    saw with ...
2    girl with ...

Answer?
```

FIGURE 8 Source-Language Binding Ambiguity

the normal selective features of the grammar. For example, the English verb "to know" can be translated into two different verbs in French, either "connaître" or "savoir", depending, among other things, on the object of the verb. To simplify the matter, we can say that when the object is a person or place, "know" must be translated with the verb "connaître", as in

> He knows the professor
> Il connait le professeur.

When the object is a relative clause, the verb "savoir" must be used, e.g.,

> He knows that this is the lesson
> Il sait que ceci est la leçon.

In still other cases, either translation might be possible, e.g.,

> He knows the lesson
> Il connait la leçon
> Il sait la leçon.

In this last case, there is insufficient context to choose between translations, and a question would have to be asked to resolve the ambiguity. Thus, postponing target-language lexical disambiguation until output generation allows for the possibility that the target grammar can resolve the ambiguity. For those lexical ambiguities not resolved by context, a mechanism must be provided to allow the output generator to query the monolingual consultant. Such a mechanism has been incorporated in the experimental system and the results have been encouraging.

A second extension would be the inclusion of a semantic component able to remember facts about the text as a whole and about the universe of discourse to which the text belongs. The semantic component would answer some questions normally posed to the monolingual consultant. The incorporation of such a component could be performed on a production system in such a way as not to affect the quality of translations produced. This would be accomplished by operating the semantic component in parallel with the monolingual consultant and comparing the answers produced with those of the monolingual consultant. When the component reaches a certain level of accuracy, it could be allowed to intercept and answer certain questions. Furthermore, the data base produced by the semantic component in translating the text might later be used for question-answering, information retrieval, etc. The design of the experimental system provides for using the MIND Semantic Memory for this purpose (Kay and Su 1970, Shapiro 1971).

13.7 The Future of the System

The MIND Human-aided Translation System allocates human and mechanical resources in a way which, though it is by no means new to computer science as a whole, has never been proposed for language translation before. We are convinced that a system of this kind would be a great deal more effective than the conventional systems we have alluded to. The many aspects of human language that have always resisted any attempt to find formal or mechanical solutions need no longer be any cause for dismay. They are matters for the human consultant and the only problem concerns the best way of presenting the problems to him so the answer will be as immediate and obvious as possible.

Before something like the MIND Human-aided Translation System could be put into operation on an industrial scale, a considerable amount of work would have to be done in the development of dictionaries, schedules of grammatical rules, and skeletons of questions and answers. However, we do not believe that this is the way to derive maximum profit from these ideas. More appropriate would be to develop the more modest set of dictionary entries, rules, and skeletons that would be needed to translate a few selected texts and to use these as the basis for a series of experiments aimed at refining the interaction between the monolingual consultant and the program. The success of the system depends on reducing the number of questions that have to be asked while making those questions as straightforward as possible. Ideally, any native speaker of the source language who is familiar with the subject matter of the texts being translated would be able to serve as a consultant. It remains to be shown how close it is possible to come to this ideal. The MIND program must be regarded as a factor by which the productivity of its human collaborators can be multiplied. A relatively simple and inexpensive set of experiments would ensure that that factor was as high as possible.

Conclusion

Human-aided Translation is a new and powerful technique for natural language translation. Its important features are:

- It uses only monolinguals.
  By separating the logical function of disambiguation from editing, Human-aided Translation allows the translation process to be carried out exclusively using monolinguals rather than using more scarce and thus more valuable bilinguals.
- It is interactive.
  It knows what it does not know and asks for help in such cases rather than making precipitate assumptions resulting in errors that must be corrected later. By asking questions early in the translation process, Human-aided Translation avoids doing the unnecessary work noted in conventional translation systems.
- It is language independent.
  All language dependent features of the system are external to the translator. The same translator can be used for any pair of languages by simply changing the appropriate grammar and lexicon.
- It is modular.
  The system is compartmentalized into well-defined linguistic functions with well-defined inputs and outputs. As new and more efficient algorithms are developed for these functions, they may be incorporated into the system by simple substitution.
- It is extensible.
  Extensions such as a semantic component can be made quickly and easily without affecting the quality of translations being produced.
- It is incremental.
  The results of any step may be saved and used repeatedly as input to subsequent steps. For example, when translating a given piece of text to multiple languages,

input analysis and disambiguation need only be done once. The output can then be applied as input to the Output Generation Routine for each of any number of target languages.

- It is an optimal use of resources.
  The machine does what it does best, the repetitive application of intricately detailed rules, while the human performs what he does best, global decision-making.

Two areas merit further study and experimentation in the system. The first is the development of a semantic component for answering questions normally posed to the monolingual consultant. The development of such a component can be seen as the next logical step in a progression eventually leading to an unaided machine translation system. The second addresses the issue of human engineering. How can the machine best interrogate the consultant? What level of training is necessary or appropriate for the consultant? Questions such as these need to be answered before any full-scale translation system such as this could become operational.

By taking advantage of new possibilities associated with interactive computing, Human-aided Translation eliminates many of the problems associated with conventional machine translation and reopens the whole question of the proper place of computers in translation.

Acknowledgements
The views expressed in this paper are those of the author. They should not be interpreted as reflecting the views of The Rand Corporation or the official opinion or policy of any of its governmental or private research sponsors. Papers are reproduced by The Rand Corporation as a courtesy to members of its staff.

Publications referenced
Bisbey et al 1971; Bisbey and Kay 1971; Bisbey 1971; Kaplan 1970; Kay 1967; Kay and Martins 1970; Kay and Su 1970; Shapiro 1971; Woods 1970.

14

The MIND System

Abstract

The MIND system is a single computer program incorporating an extensible set of fundamental linguistic processors that can be combined on command to carry out a great variety of tasks from grammar testing to question-answering and language translation. The program is controlled from a graphic display console from which the user can specify the sequence of operations, modify rules, edit texts and monitor the details of each operation to any desired extent. Presently available processors include morphological and syntactic analyzers, a semantic file processor, a transformational component, a morphological synthesizer, and an interactive disambiguator.

14.1 Motivation

For the most part, linguists are unaware of the importance that computers must one day have for their subject. The exact extent of the contribution that computer models of language acquisition, speech production, speech understanding, and the like will make to theoretical linguistics is uncertain; that it will be considerable is hardly open to doubt.

To the extent that linguists attempt to produce formal descriptions of particular languages, the computer is an absolutely indispensable tool. A formal description can only be verified by checking it against actual cases. It must produce words and sentences that actually occur in the language, produce sets of sentences that native speakers accept as paraphrases of one another, answer questions correctly , or whatever. In other words, it must be possible to base a process or performance on the description and to have a speaker of the language judge it satisfactory.

One of the earliest lessons learned from computers was that human beings are curiously ill-adapted to the business of describing processes accurately and in detail. When the notion of a computer had gained some currency, but there were still few machines available, it was thought that a person could write a program to carry out a complex process and that he would be able to put it to work as soon as he could get his hands on a machine. But, while the overall design of the program may well have been correct, untold numbers of minor adjustments had invariably to be made before it would produce correct results. It is now common knowledge that the time required to produce the first draft of a program is small compared to the time needed to test it, make corrections, test again, and so on to produce a satisfactory version.

If programs are complicated, formal descriptions of natural languages, or even of small parts of them, are more so. Modern linguists have been ingenious in designing economical notations for their descriptions so that a mistake in a single character can have widespread repercussions. Furthermore, if these descriptions are thought of as specifying processes, then these processes must often be nondeterministic. What this means is that the chain of events is not, in general, uniquely specified. Starting at a given point, there are typically several different directions in which the process might continue and each of them must be pursued independently. Nondeterministic processes are fundamentally more difficult to specify than deterministic ones. Therefore, there are three options open to linguistics: It can restrict itself to theoretical and philosophical speculation about the form that linguistic descriptions should take and the consequences that this has for the human faculty of language; it can content itself with informal descriptions of particular languages as it has at times in the past; or it can accept the computer as a necessary tool of the trade. If linguistics is to make any contribution to the practical affairs of men, it is likely to be by showing how to make machines with which men will be able to communicate in everyday language. The utility of a machine with this capability would be obvious. Language translation, information storage and retrieval, the production and editing of text, and a host of other applications come readily to mind. Any such machine would necessarily incorporate a more or less complete formal description of at least one natural language. Whether machines will ever, in fact, be constructed to converse with men in their own language is open to doubt. It has even been questioned that it is a worthy goal to pursue. It is certain, though, that the success of the enterprise would depend on the success that linguists have in developing adequate formal descriptions of languages and that, in turn, rests on the use that linguists make of computers.

Linguistics is in a state of turmoil. There are a number of schools of thought, each with as many variants of the basic theoretical position as the school has adherents. Whatever seems most solid today is most likely to be overthrown tomorrow. The climate of opinion has recently become one where status is accorded only to contributions that touch the foundations of the science. Nevertheless, there is widespread, if often grudging, agreement on a number of broad issues such as: the study of the forms of words can be conducted independently of the study of sentences, and that it is useful to regard each sentence as having one or more syntactic structures; a syntactic structure has the shape of a tree, etc. In other words, there is at least some measure of agreement on the headings under which the various phases of linguistic analysis should fall – phonetics, phonology, morphology, syntax, semantics. There is less agreement on just what each of these headings covers.

In this situation, the aspiring designer of a linguistic computer system is faced with a difficult set of choices. He may decide to wait until a clearer picture of linguistic theory begins to emerge: if he adopts this policy there is no knowing how long he will have to wait. He may decide to throw in his lot with one of the contending schools; this is a particularly hazardous policy, not only because of the restlessness of modern linguistic theories, but also because few, if any, of them are readily interpretable in terms of processes that can be carried out on a computer. The third alternative is to design a kit of sufficiently versatile computational tools to build computer systems that reflect one version or another of some prevailing theory (more or less liberally interpreted by a user of the tools).

This last solution is, in many ways, ideal and it is the one that was adopted in the design of the MIND system, the subject of this talk. The system designer that follows this course must attempt to reconcile three different, and often conflicting requirements. The tools he builds must be flexible enough to be usable by the advocates of many actual and potential linguistic theories. On the other hand, they must be so well fashioned for specific purposes that it will never be unduly burdensome for a computationally naive user to adapt them to his own view of linguistic theory. Finally, each tool in the kit must be designed so as to be compatible with the rest. Just as phonograph records must turn at the same speed if they are to be playable on generally available equipment, so standards must be established covering the way in which the data will be represented, on which various cooperating programs are to operate. Many attempts to construct packages of programs which serve the needs of a diverse community of users have foundered. Attempts to design coherent sets of programs for analyzing statistical data are a case in point.

It goes without saying that the MIND system falls far short of the ideal of providing a linguistic computer system that can be all things to all men. Nevertheless, it has already been applied with some success to a considerable variety of linguistic tasks, and only the time and energy is wanting to apply it to a great many others.

14.2 The Overall Structure of the System

I began this talk by pointing out that formal descriptions of languages can only be made with the aid of a machine to verify that the description corresponds to the data. Computer programs written especially for this purpose are usually called "grammar testers," and the most notable of them was written by Joyce Friedman. Used as a tester of transformational grammars, the MIND system differs from the Friedman program mainly in its interactive facilities. The user can change any rule in the grammar at any time without disturbing the remainder, and can immediately see the effects of the change by applying the modified grammar to any basic sentence structure that takes his fancy.

The system can also be used to test grammars in a variety of different formalisms designed specifically for the task of analyzing, rather than generating sentences. An unusual feature of the system is that, despite the apparently different strategies involved, the same computer routines are used for generating and analyzing sentences. This is made possible by strictly adhering to a set of principles on which I will elaborate shortly, and which are the subject of another talk in this volume. By giving a command from his terminal, the user of the MIND system can link together several of its routines so as to make it carry out some more or less complex sequence of processes automatically. One such command causes the system to constitute itself as a question-answering machine, others as language translators of various kinds, and so on.

The set of programs that make up the MIND system can be changed very readily when the need for new facilities arises, and as superior methods of performing some of the tasks become known. This is easy because each of the principal components of the system operates, as far as possible, independently of the remainder. The only major part of the system with which all the rest interact is the so-called "master scheduler" whose job is to dictate the overall sequence of events, to locate the input data for each routine, and to determine where the output of each is to be placed. The principal components of the system, as implemented on the IBM 360, Model 65, at the Rand Corporation are:

1. The Morphological Analyzer
2. The Syntactic Processor
3. The Disambiguator
4. The Semantic Processor
5. The Output Component

Earlier in this talk, I stressed the fact that cooperation among computer programs depends, more than anything else, on the maintenance of a set of standards to which the data that passes between them must adhere. In other words, there must be well-defined formats for any data that will be treated by more than one of the programs, but these formats must nevertheless be flexible enough to allow each user of the total system the freedom he needs. The problem is particularly delicate in the design of the MIND system because the user is free to choose any one of a large number of configurations of the overall system.

The output of one program may have to serve as input for a variety of other programs, depending on the configuration. For example, when the system is used as a tester of transformational grammars, the morphological analyzer reads a series of basic sentences from the user's terminal and stores them in the machine. The output of this process is passed to the syntactic processor which applies phrase-structure and transformational rules to generate the surface forms of the sentences. These are then fed to the output program which displays them at the user's terminal. On the other hand, the system might be given a configuration corresponding to a simple translating machine in which the following was the typical sequence of events: a sentence to be translated is obtained by the morphological analyzer, either from the user's console or from a file of text. The morphological analyzer looks up each word in the text, making due provision for inflexional prefixes and suffixes, and for making changes in the basic form of a word that these some times entail. (The rules provided to the morphological analyzer would, for example, enable it correctly to associate the word "tries" with the dictionary entry of the word "try.") The output of this program, in which each word is accompanied by information about it obtained from the dictionary, now becomes the input to the syntactic processor which performs an analysis yielding one or more grammatical structures for the sentence. These are then passed to the disambiguator, whose job is to decide which grammatical structure is correct in the given context.

14.3   Syntactic Analysis and the Chart

Many of the programs in the system refer to their own files whose format is not, therefore, constrained by other components. All programs are in contact with the master scheduler which decides when to call them into operation, but which passes virtually no information to them directly nor expects any from them. Information passes from one program to another through a single common data region called the "chart." The chart is a machine representation of a directed graph with labeled vertices and edges. The labels on the nodes are of minor significance, serving mainly as an aid in checking the operation of new programs. The labels on edges are, in general, complex. The chart is interpreted as a transition network, the edges emanating from a given vertex being treated as mutually exclusive alternatives. A transition from one vertex, or state, to another corresponds approximately to left-to-right progress through a string. The chart as a whole can therefore be looked upon as a grammar which generates a set, possibly infinite in size, of strings of symbols.

Consider the sentence:

They are flying planes

This can be represented by the following trivial finite-state grammar:

They   *are*   *flying*   *planes*

or, alternatively, by the following:

(WORD *They*)   (WORD *are*)   (WORD *flying*)   (WORD *planes*)

The additional structure in the second proposal has the advantage of distinguishing edges that represent words from others that the chart might also contain.

The program that reads a sentence from the input device leaves the chart looking approximately as in the second of the above diagrams. The job of the morphological analyzer is to look each word up in a dictionary and to add the information it finds about each at the appropriate place in the chart. After this has taken place, the chart might be expected to look somewhat like Figure 1.

This is in fact a considerable simplification, but it will serve to illustrate a number of points. First, none of the original edges have been changed. The morphological analyzer, like most other components of the system, restricts itself to adding new nodes and edges to the existing chart. This policy helps assure the relative independence of programs in the system. If the morphological analyzer were to delete existing material from the chart, then other programs would be committed to the kind of analysis of the sentence made by that program. As it is, another program can modify the analysis or ignore it because the original data is still available.

Each word in the initial sentence gave rise to a single edge joining a pair of vertices. The second vertex could be reached from the first in just one way, namely by following that edge. Successful morphological analysis results in at least one, and sometimes several new paths from the first to the second vertex. In the case of a syntactically unambiguous word, one new path is added; where there is ambiguity, a new path is added for each syntactic interpretation of the word. The original edges carried a label of the form (WORD x) , where x is a word of the original sentence. The new edges

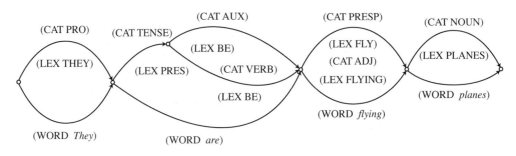

FIGURE 1

have more complex labels. Each of them has, in fact, the structure of a tree with nodes labeled by lists of so-called "attribute-value" pairs. There is, for example, an edge with the label:

This records the fact that the lexical entry "flying" can be a present participle, that is, a verb of type "PRESP."

Suppose that a text contained a phrase like "high ball" which can, but need not, be interpreted idiomatically. In a sporting context, for example, it might be intended literally, whereas, where drinking was in question, it has an interpretation that is independent of the meanings of the individual words. The initial chart would contain the following segment:

$$\circ \xrightarrow{\quad\quad\quad} \circ \xrightarrow{\quad\quad\quad} \circ$$
(WORD *high*)   (WORD *ball*)

Perceiving that an idiom might be in question, the morphological analyzer begins by adding a new edge as follows:

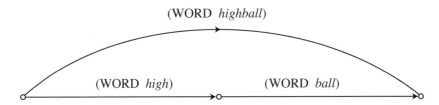

There are now two ways of traversing this section of the chart, one corresponding to the idiomatic, and one to the non-idiomatic interpretation of the phrase. The morphological analyzer now goes on to treat these two alternatives independently, adding to the chart the dictionary information appropriate to each. The result might be somewhat as follows:

Initially, each edge represents a word, and the vertices represent the spaces between them. Once analysis begins this correspondence breaks down. An idiom is represented as a single word even though it contained a space in the original text. However, this corresponds to an intuitive view of what an idiom is – a word that contains spaces.

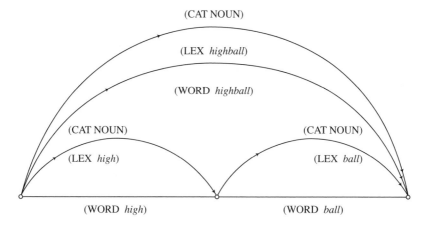

In an earlier example I represented the result of applying morphological analysis to the word "are" as follows:

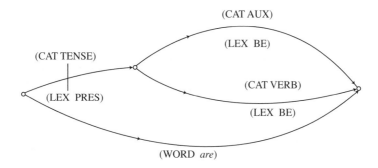

Each interpretation begins with an edge representing the tense of the verb and, since this is the same in both cases, a single edge serves for both. The two following edges represent "are" as an auxiliary and as a main verb respectively. My main concern here is not to argue for this particular analysis. Suffice to say that tense regularly appears separated from its associated verb in the deep structures of sentences. For the present, I am concerned only to point out that a word may be analyzed as a sequence of more than one segment if, for any reason, that appears to be appropriate. This is the exact inverse of what is happening in the case of idioms.

Syntactic analysis is the process in which one or more tree structures are developed for a sentence, each corresponding to one way of breaking it down into meaningful parts. Each structure is based on exactly one path through the chart that results from morphological analysis. In other words, a subsidiary effect of syntactic analysis is to choose one of the alternative analyses of each word provided by the morphological processor.

In the course of the syntactic analysis, various hypotheses will be formed about the phraseological status of various parts of the sentence. Consider, for example, the sentence

Reading books can make this work

The first two words clearly constitute the subject, and the remainder the predicate of the sentence, but both parts can be interpreted in at least two ways, each corresponding to a different syntactic analysis. Thus, "books" is either a noun modified by the adjective "reading" or it is the object of the verb "read". This gives us a distinction like that between

The reading books can make this work

and

The reading of books can make this work

The predicate is also ambiguous, its two intepretations correspond approximately to

Reading books can achieve this work

and

Reading books can cause this to work

The sentence as a whole therefore has at least four interpretations.

The syntactic analyzer will use one of a large variety of strategies, each of which will result in the various interpretations of the various parts of a sentence being developed in a characteristic order. One will seek one interpretation of the first few words under which it could function as subject of the sentence, and then attempt to interpret the remainder as a predicate compatible with that view. It would then seek alternative compatible interpretations of the predicate before seeking new hypotheses about the subject. If new hypotheses about the subject are, in fact, found, it is clearly desirable that the work of analyzing the predicate should not be repeated. Another strategy would involve exploring all possible subjects first, deferring until later the search for compatible predicates. Those for which none are found are simply abandoned. The particular strategies that can be adopted in the MIND system are discussed in detail elsewhere; what is important here is the observation that, to operate efficiently, they all require some way of recording hypotheses about the phraseological status of parts of the sentence so that they will be available for use in constructing hypotheses about larger parts at some later time.

A hypothesis about the phraseological status of part of a sentence is an alternative interpretation of it differing in no important way from the alternative interpretations of individual words obtained from the dictionary. Indeed, it is formally indistinguishable from an idiom. So, for example, the chart for the sentence

Reading books can make that work

after one hypothesis about the subject has been developed, might be as follows:

Suppose that the strategy calls for predicates compatible with this view of the subject to be sought next. The chart might then look like Figure 3. The next step is to seek alternative subjects, yielding the following Figure 4.

Finally, predicates must be sought to go with this subject. However, examination of the chart shows that the only candidates have already been found and recorded as

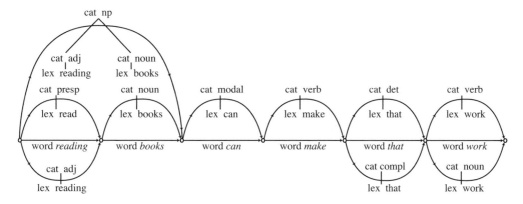

FIGURE 2

alternative interpretations of the words "can make this work ". In summary, phrases are simply ways of interpreting parts of a sentence other than as sequences of individual words.

The synthetic analysis of ordinary language can involve more than simply collecting words and phrases to make larger phrases. If no more than this were done, then it would never be possible to associate one syntactic structure with more than one sentence. However, in modern linguistics, it is usually held that syntactic structures, in general, underlie a family of sentences which mean more or less the same and which are related in a systematic way. In other words, it is the job of syntactic analysis to reduce sentences to canonical forms each of which may underlie several actual sentences. For example, the sentences

John gave some flowers to Mary

and

John gave Mary some flowers

differ in no way that is important for later processing. They are therefore assigned the same syntactic structure. The sentences

Mary was given some flowers by John
Some flowers were given to Mary by John
Some flowers were given Mary by John

might or might not be assigned the same structure, depending on the theoretical views of the linguist and the overall aims of the project. They would certainly be given more similar structures than is suggested by the different sequences of words, and "John," for example, would doubtless be identified as subject in each case. Suppose that passives were to be given the same structures as the corresponding actives and, furthermore, that their common structure was to look approximately like a decomposition of the active sentence into phrases. One structure of the sentence:

My wallet was found by the driver

might therefore be something like Figure 3.

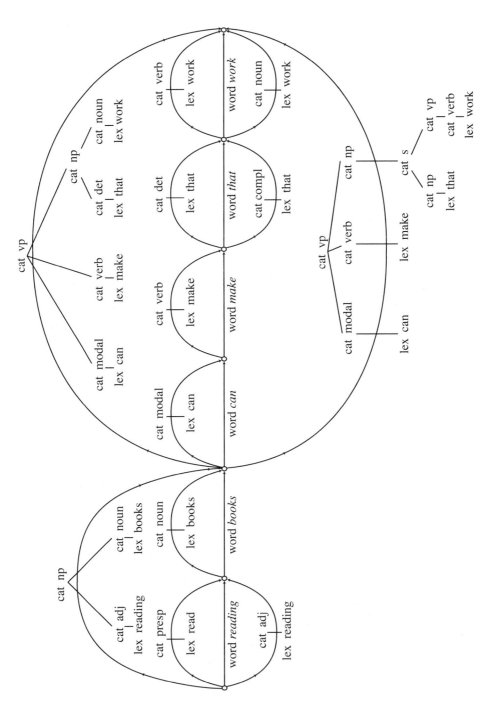

FIGURE 3

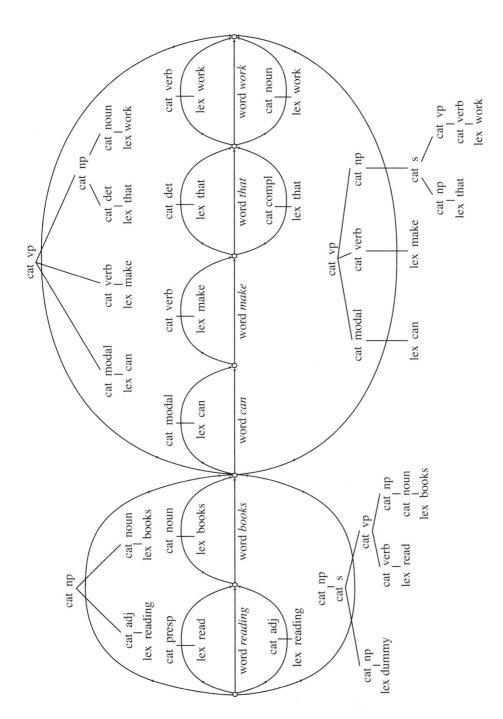

FIGURE 4

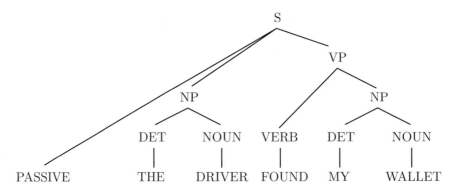

Notice that there is also a second interpretation in which the phrase "by the driver" indicates the place where the wallet was found rather than the person who found it. In this case the structure would probably be more like:

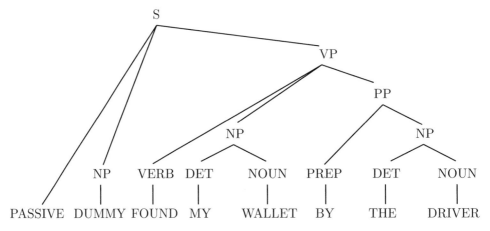

What this means is that it must be possible to represent hypotheses about the structure of a sentence in which the elements making it up appear in various orders. A grammar rule must be able to establish a new order of elements for consideration by later rules without destroying the original order. Omitting irrelevant details, this can be done in the chart as follows in Figure 5.

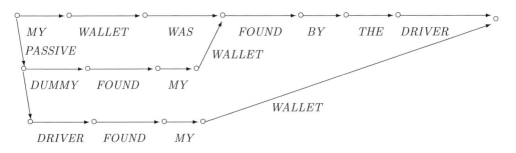

FIGURE 5

14.4 The Disambiguator

The MIND system contains a component called the "disambiguator" which is, at present, a fairly simple program but which can be expected to become considerably more elaborate in some applications of the system. In others, it will have little or nothing to do. The job of the disambiguator is to design and implement a strategy for removing the ambiguities that remain in a sentence after syntactic analysis. By saying that it designs a strategy, I mean simply that it chooses, from a set of possibilities that may sometimes be quite large, the one that seems likely to involve the least work, and implements that.

Suppose that at a given stage in the disambiguation process a considerable number of interpretations of a sentence remain in play. The program attempts to compose a question about the sentence and the text that preceded it whose answer would effectively divide this number in as many parts of approximately equal size as possible. Suppose eight alternatives are still open and one question concerns only one of them, a second question would eliminate either the first or the second group of four, and a third question would have four possible answers, each of which would eliminate all but two alternative analyses. The last question would be chosen, and the first would be considered least desirable.

How are the questions answered? Two possibilities are open, and only one of them been explored in any depth. The questions can be directed to the semantic component of the system in the hope that an answer can be found based on the understanding that has been reached of the text up to this point. Alternatively, the question can be expressed in English and directed to the user of the system. An intriguing third possibility is to do both of these, always preferring the user's answer, but comparing it with the answer supplied by the semantic program so as to verify its operation.

Consider the sentence:

They filled the tank with gas

and suppose that the system is set up to translate into French with the help of a human collaborator. The entire text is displayed on the screen, sentence by sentence, for the human to read. When this one is reached, the system might ask:

```
DOES THE WORD "TANK" REFER TO
1. A MILITARY VEHICLE, OR
2. A VESSEL FOR FLUIDS?
```

If the user types a "1," the system will translate the word as "char d'assaut," otherwise it will translate it as "tanque." It might then go on to ask:

```
DOES "GAS" REFER TO
1. GASOLINE, OR
2. VAPOR?
```

Answer number 1 will lead to the translation "essence" and number 2 to "gaz". A third question might be:

```
DOES THIS MEAN
1. "FILL WITH GAS," OR
2. "TANK WITH GAS"?
```

The correct answer to this is almost certainly number 1 which would result in "with" being translated as "de" rather than "avec". Finally, it might ask:

```
DOES "THEY" REFER TO
1. THE SOLDIERS
2. THE TANKS
3. THE SHELLS
4. THE ENEMY
     ...etc.
```

The potential answers to this question probably consist of nothing more than a list of recently used nouns. The object of the question is to determine whether "they" should be translated as "ils" or "elles". A better question would be:

```
WHAT DOES "THEY" REFER TO?
```

and this would work if the human collaborator could be counted upon to reply with a word that had actually been used in the text, or if failing this the disambiguator could recognize the answer as being a synonym of a word that had been used. The point is a delicate one because pronouns derive their gender not from the objects to which they refer, but from the words previously used to refer to those objects.

The disambiguator is a program that can be called into play by any other component in the system. Broadly speaking, it will be more effective the later it is called in the overall analysis process because more information will have been amassed to use in the construction of questions. The disambiguator will therefore be better able to profit from its ability to choose the question that will eliminate the greatest number of alternatives. Notice, that, although the word "tank" can function as a verb, this possibility was never raised by the disambiguator. This is because we imagine that the program was called after syntactic analysis, a process that eliminated this possibility. The third question – about what "with gas" modifies – arises only as a result of syntactic analysis and could not have been asked earlier.

The question of which other programs call the disambiguator, and for what purposes, involves an element of strategy. There is a trade off between calling it frequently and thereby foreclosing unproductive lines of analysis as soon as possible, and calling it rarely and late so as to minimize the total number of questions that need to be asked. Suppose that another of the sentences to be translated into French were:

He saw the girl with the telescope

If the disambiguator were called immediately after syntactic analysis, it would probably have to ask something like:

```
DOES THIS MEAN
1. "SAW WITH THE TELESCOPE" OR
2. "GIRL WITH THE TELESCOPE"?
```

But the syntactic ambiguity that this question is designed to resolve can, and indeed should, be preserved in the French. If each of the grammatical structures provided by the syntactic analyzer were pursued independently, it would emerge that there is at least one translation that can be generated from both of them. The question is simply whether the elimination of questions of this kind is worth the labor of following each analysis to a complete translation and then comparing the results. If the questions were being answered by another program, then it might be desirable to resolve this kind of ambiguity early; if they are being answered by a human, then it might be more important to minimize the number of questions asked. However, the user of the MIND system must decide these matters of policy.

14.5   Semantics

The semantic component of the MIND system is in an early stage of development. It is here that the greatest development is to be expected. The effort that has gone into the system will be justified in large measure by its use as a test bed for semantic processors. Serious work on semantics need not wait for complete grammars or dictionaries to be written but it is made immeasurably easier by an environment in which fairly large and elaborate grammars and dictionaries can be processed easily.

The principal function of the semantic component is to mediate between the chart and a semantic file which contains the systems' knowledge about the outside world. New information arrives in the form of sentences whose syntactic structures are placed in the chart by the syntactic analyzer. The semantic routines must examine these structures and modify the contents of the semantic file to include the new information. If the system is to answer users' questions, then it will be up to the semantic processor to recognize which questions require an answer, seek the necessary information in the semantic file, and either output an answer directly, or, more probably, build a new syntactic structure which will be translated into an answer by the syntactic generator.

The semantic file, in the existing processor, is a computer implementation of a directed graph with labeled vertices and edges. The processor contains primitive functions that can add and delete vertices and edges. The vertices correspond to objects that the system knows about. In other words, they are the potential referents of linguistic expressions. If more than one vertex corresponds to the same object in the external world, it is presumably because the system does not know them to be the same. Some of the vertices correspond to propositions and edges connect these to other vertices representing objects implicated in them. Some of these propositions correspond to the beliefs of the system, whereas others figure only as terms in other propositions. Thus, for example, if it is part of the system's knowledge that Bertrand Russell believed that God does not exist, then a proposition corresponding to the sentence "God does not exist" must be stored in the semantic file. However, this does not commit the system to any position on the existence of God. The vertices representing propositions the system is committed to are connected to a distinguished vertex, representing approximately "the Truth" by an edge with a special label. Edges represent relations and, whenever a particular relation is represented in the system, its inverse is also represented so that it is, in effect, possible to follow edges in both directions. Given a vertex representing a proposition, it is possible to discover if the system assents to it. It is therefore also possible to discover all the propositions that the system assents to.

There are as many approaches to the problems of semantics as there are people who have considered them. Two trends are, however, discernable. On the one hand, there are those who believe, with Chomsky and his followers, that the first requirement is for a universal semantic alphabet – a set of primitive objects or atoms – in terms of which meanings can be represented. On the other hand, there are those who hold that the meanings of words and phrases consist only of relations they contract with other words and phrases and that the search for any more fundamental kind of representation for them is futile. The second, so called "structuralist", position tends to be taken by the builders of computer models for reasons that are beyond our present scope. It is the position we took in developing the first semantic program for the MIND system.

Access to the semantic network is through vertices that are labeled with words of the language. By no means do all vertices carry such labels. Typically, a noun names a vertex corresponding to a class of objects which that noun names. The term "object" must, of course, be interpreted broadly. The word "ache" names a class of instances of "ache". A particular ache which might afflict a particular person on a particular occasion is represented by another vertex which is not directly associated with a word in the language. The association between the two vertices is established somewhat as follows:

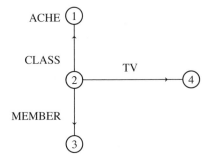

Vertex 1 – the only one with a label – represents the class of all aches. Vertex 3 represents the particular ache in question. The reason for separating these two needs no elaboration. Vertex 2 represents the proposition that the object represented by vertex 3 is a member of the class represented by vertex 1. Vertex 4 is the special point already mentioned to which all propositions are linked that count as true for the system. Vertex 2 is included in the network precisely because it may, in general, have differing statuses relative to the system's beliefs. For example, the network may also contain the information that someone does not believe that the object represented by vertex 3 is, in fact, an ache. The force of the labels "Class" and "Member" is evident. "TV" stands for "Truth Value" and will presumably be used only to label lines that terminate at vertex 4.

Consider, now, the sentence "John ran". I have shown numbers in the circles representing the vertices only to make them easier to refer to. Leaving aside the question of how the tense of the verb is to be represented, this might give rise to a structure of the following kind in the network.

The main proposition is represented by vertex 5 which is marked as being among the beliefs of the system. Vertex 3 represents the particular person who is alleged to have run on this occasion. Vertex 1 represents the class of all people named "John". Notice that proper nouns are treated as essentially similar to common nouns, such differences

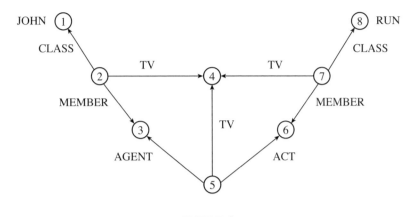

FIGURE 6

as there are being treated as a matter of syntax. The reason is simply that there are few, if any, words that are true proper nouns in a semantic sense. "John" does not uniquely identify a person and therefore differs from a phrase like 'the man" mainly in that it is not preceded by a definite article. The function of vertex 2 is the same as in the previous example.

Vertex 6 stands for the particular act of running in which John was involved and vertex 8 is the class of all acts of running. It must clearly be to vertex 8 that the word "run" is applied. It remains to argue for distinguishing vertices 5, 6, and 8. Intuitively, there is certainly a distinction between the class of acts or states that a verb names and the individual events and states that are members of that class. It is important to preserve this distinction in the network if only because of the possibility of such sentences as "Bill saw John run" and "Brutus killed Ceasar and Cassius saw it happen". What was seen, in each case, was an event like the one represented by vertex 6 and not a proposition such as vertex 5 represents. On the other hand, the sentence "Bill knew John ran" involves a reference to vertex 5 because it is the proposition, and not the event, that is believed.

I made no attempt to represent the tense of the verb in the example even though it is clearly more than a grammatical category. The reason is that, despite a great amount of effort that has been devoted to it, tense is very difficult to incorporate in a semantic model which attempts, as this one does, to keep track of the referents associated with a text. It makes no sense to have vertices with labels like "present" and "past" and to link them with propositions in some standard way. Clearly every event was present when it occurred and has been past ever since. An alternative that has been explored from time to time is to associate a specific time with each event. This is what would be required to give an accurate depiction of a set of events. But the information needed to do this is simply not obtainable from ordinary texts. The best that can be attempted – and even this is extremely difficult – is to establish a partial ordering over events. The difficulty comes from the fact that languages like English encourage great imprecision in recording even these partial orderings. Languages like Chinese treat them in an even more cavalier manner.

One of the most important questions that arises in designing a semantic file concerns the treatment of quantifiers. The reason they are so important is that sentences involving quantifiers tend to represent general statements which can be used in deducing facts from other facts. This is something that any semantic processor must be able to do because it is rare that the information it is seeking will be in the file in just the form required. Usually the correct answer to a question will be obtainable only by inference. If the system knows that John is Bill's father and Bill is Mary's father, and if it knows that the father of a person's father is that person's grandfather, then it should be able to answer the question "Who is Mary's grandfather". This ability multiplies the potential utility of each piece of information in the system by an incalculable factor.

The sentence "All men are mortal" might be represented in a semantic network somewhat as follows:

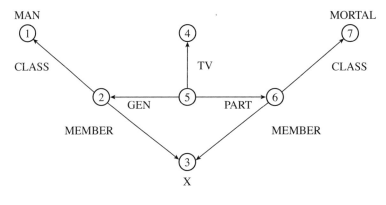

FIGURE 7

As before, vertex 4 represents the truth as the system sees it. Vertex 5 represents a proposition to which the system assents. The names "Gen" (for "General") and "Part" (for "Particular") have been chosen to represent two sides of the implication relation which, as usual in this system, must be factored into two parts so as to admit an intermediate propositional vertex. Proposition 5 is to the effect that the proposition represented by vertex 2 entails the one represented by vertex 6. Notice that neither of these is represented as being part of the program's system of beliefs. The program is committed to neither 2 nor 6 but only to the view that 2 cannot be true unless 6 is also.

Vertex 3 is labeled "x" to indicate that it is of a special kind. It represents a so-called "free variable" which can be identified with any other vertex whatsoever and assertion 5 should still hold true. The universal quantifier of standard symbolic logic is not represented, it being understood that all free variables are bound by the universal quantifier. This is all very well until sentences must be considered which involve both the universal and the existential quantifier. How is the existential quantifier to be represented and what account is taken of the order of quantifiers? In other words, how is the distinction maintained between "Everybody loves someone" and "Someone is loved by everybody"? One of many possible answers is, by means of Skolem functions. In terms of a semantic network, a Skolem function is nothing more than a specially labeled link from a node representing a variable governed by the existential quantifier to any variables governed by the universal quantifier that would have preceded it in the standard notation of the predicate calculus. So, for example, "Everybody loves somebody" might be represented as follows:

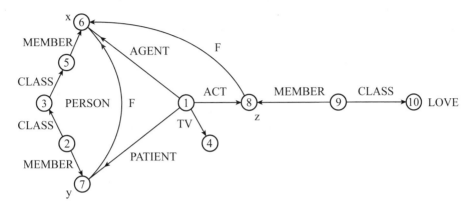

FIGURE 8

The principal proposition is represented by vertex 1 and x and y are variables governed by the universal and existential quantifiers respectively. The fact that there is an edge with the label "f" leaving vertex 7 shows that it is governed by the existential quantifier and that the vertex at the head of this edge corresponds to a preceding universal quantifier. Notice that vertex 8, representing the love that x has for y, is also represented as governed by the existential quantifier. Strictly speaking, the representation given for "John ran" should have been treated in the same manner because, according to the view I am taking here, almost every sentence describing an event involves such a quantifier. The sentence "Someone is loved by everybody" would be represented as follows:

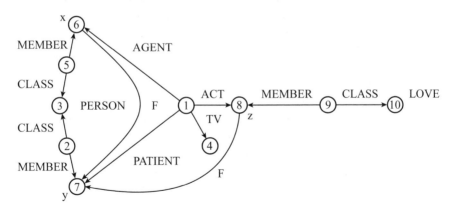

FIGURE 9

I make no particular claims for this method of expressing semantic relations; I simply want to illustrate the fact that a directed graph with labeled edges and vertices has a great amount of expressive power. In the final analysis, all that I have done is to suggest a two-dimensional notation into which English sentences might be translated. The interest of a schema of this kind comes from the operations that can be performed upon it, and this is a matter about which we can claim to know only very little. A few things, at least, are clear. I have already mentioned the ability to make inferences. How this should be approached is still a matter of debate. An increasingly strong case is being built up against the view, which seemed promising until recently, that this part of a semantic processing should be treated as essentially the same as theorem proving in mathematics. A thoroughgoing attack on theorem proving, even if we did know how to conduct it, seems likely to result in a relatively poor model of how the mind works. One difference seems to be that mathematicians are typically concerned with constructing fairly long chains of argument on the basis of a small set of premises, whereas the everyday process of understanding usually involves short chains of inference based on a great number of premises. Furthermore, the logic of ordinary thought lacks the precision of mathematical argument. Experiments with so-called "fuzzy logic", in which propositions can be more or less true have been proposed to cope with this situation, but it is not clear that they do anything about the fundamental illogicality of everyday logic. The noun phrase "the set of all sets that are not members of themselves" has nothing anomalous about it in everyday English, but it must be regarded as meaningless in logic.

It also seems clear that language cannot be understood by a purely passive being. Almost all the mechanical language processors that have been built or projected have been intended to absorb anything they were told hungrily and uncritically. Weisenbaum's "Eliza" program was a notable exception and serves admirably to stress the importance of our expectations in interpreting what we are told. What we understand is, in large measure, what we expect to hear. Without any expectations, even from one sentence to the next, a machine has little hope of filling the gaps that ordinary language leaves unfilled, or supplying the correct interpretation of ambiguous passages.

As I have said, the design of the MIND system contains no proposals on how these weighty questions are to be decided; it only provides a laboratory in which solutions can more easily be sought. The embrionic semantic component that now exists distinguishes the main semantic file from what is called "the discourse file".

14.6 The Output Component

Relatively little needs to be said about the output component because, although it appears as a separate component to the user of the system, it is, in fact, the same program as is used for syntactic analysis. A separate paper in this volume argues the essential similarity of all kinds of syntactic processing, and the function of the output component is mainly syntactic. I have already explained how syntactic processes are carried out using a special data region called the "chart" which is also the only channel of communication among the various programs in the system. The chart provides a compact way of representing a large family of strings of labeled, oriented trees provided the members of the family typically have common substrings. The construction of well-formed sentences requires just such a data structure and the operations involved are similar to those required for analysis.

Just as in analysis, there are many formalisms and techniques that might be used in sentence generation. An obvious approach, and the one that has been most used in experiments with the MIND system so far, involves using a transformational component such as is proposed in standard transformational grammar. Transformational rules are essentially different from analysis rules because they are not, in general, reversible. In other words, it is not always possible to construct a sequence of transformational rules whose effect will be the inverse of a given set. There are several reasons for this. One is that, whereas transformational rules each accept a single syntactic tree as input and deliver a single tree as output, syntactic analysis begins, not with a syntactic tree, but with a string of words. A syntactic tree is the end result of the process. This is not to say that, at a more fundamental level, the operations involved are not the same. A second reason is that the rules themselves are not sufficiently restricted for reversibility. They permit, for example, parts of a structure to be deleted without trace. It is true that injunctions against this practice have been proposed, but they have not been made precise and they are not generally assented to. In the MIND system what this means is that the same processor can be used, but a different compiler is required to translate rules from the external form in which the user writes them into the internal form required for processing.

A second important difference between transformational rules and those required for analysis concerns their ordering. Analysis rules – at least those that have so far been used in the MIND system – are either unordered or are self-ordering where, by self-ordering, I mean simply that it is one of the functions of a rule to determine what others will be tried after it. Standard transformational grammar, on the other hand, assumes that rules will be applied in a system of cycles which is the same for all grammars of this type, so that it does not need to be specified in the rules themselves. The syntactic component contains all the facilities required to insure that the rules are properly ordered; the way to invoke it is by means of a compiler that calls upon these facilities automatically as they are required. We have, for example, been working with a configuration of the MIND system in which the output component provides for a statement of the following form:

    PERFORM n FOR S;

which causes the sequence of statements beginning with number n to be applied to each subtree of the current tree whose root is labeled S. If this statement is itself numbered n, then the effect will be to cause it to be carried out recursively, thus producing the effect of the transformational cycle required in standard theory.

14.7 Summary

The MIND system contains more facilities than I have described but there would be no point in continuing the recital. It is, in any case, essential in the system that facilities can come and go as new components are added and old ones replaced. My main aim in this talk has been to show something of what it takes to make computational linguistics more productive and to ease the performance of linguistic experiments involving the computer in important ways. It is not enough to furnish a battery of powerful subroutines for the linguist to incorporate into his programs. Linguistic data and linguistic formalisms are sufficiently complex to require the composition of new processes by the experimenter while seated at the console and a number of different languages and notational devices for different aspects of the problem. Furthermore, it must, to the extent possible, be aloof from sectarian differences among scientific schools. In this enterprise, the profit comes from providing a number of specialized languages in which to state linguistic facts and to decouple these, as far as possible from the programs that will carry the processes out. Experience with the MIND system has convinced its designers and those who have worked with it that there is a vantage point from which the contending linguistic theories show more similarities than differences but which is still close enough to reality to provide a useful basis for computer programming.

15

Automatic Translation of Natural Languages

The history of man's attempt to build a translating machine for natural languages has not been illustrious. There has probably been no other scientific enterprise in which so much money has been spent on so many projects that promised so little. In the late fifties and early sixties, numerous people obtained, from one agency or another of the United States government, appreciable sums of money, in return for which they promised to deliver, in a very few years, a computer program or even an actual machine that could produce high-quality translations automatically. The events that brought these euphoric days to a sudden end are, by now, well known even to people who have no other knowledge of work in machine translation. Stimulated partly by the displeasure of some high-ranking civil servants and military officers at having received less than the best value for their money, the National Academy of Sciences in 1962 established the Automatic Language Processing Advisory Committee (ALPAC) and ordered it to investigate the entire matter of the federal sponsorship of research on machine translation.

In its report, delivered in 1963, ALPAC was as kind to the designers of automatic-translation machines as it could possibly be. It concluded that there was no possibility of producing a satisfactory translating machine in the foreseeable future and recommended that no further funds be spent on contracts that had such development in view. The committee did not, however, see the development of such machines as forever beyond the wit of man and, in fact, expressed support of the funding of research that aimed at hastening the day when it would be reasonable to let such a development contract.

Reactions to the report were predictable. For almost ten years, any application for financial support for a project involving language and computers, however modest or sound, could expect a swift and categorical refusal. None of the positive recommendations of the ALPAC report were acted upon, and a disservice may thereby have been done to many serious and inventive research workers as well as to the country. Nevertheless, although the number of research projects in computational linguistics has diminished, the discipline has attained far greater maturity. It required dedication to stay in a field that no longer had a ready source of money and whose center of interest had become an object of abuse. However, researchers were now free to look closely at the theoretical problems that stood in the way of successful machine translation. This is not to say that the profession has lost its lunatic fringe. It is not difficult to learn something about how computers are programmed, and many people know a foreign language. Those who know a little of both will always be susceptible to revelations about how a machine might be made to translate. What is to be feared is the predilection that some government agencies are apt to show for proposals that come from precisely this lunatic fringe.

The first machine-translation system to be put into full-scale operation was installed in 1964 at the Foreign Technology Division of the United States Air Force, where it remained in daily operation until 1970. It was a very ingenious machine called the Mark II translator, and it was one of the most interesting products of the early period of work on machine translation. Unfortunately, its ingenuity cannot be accounted sufficient to repay its prodigious cost. A study by Arthur D. Little, Inc. found its translations time-consuming, expensive, and of poor graphic quality; furthermore, they were not very accurate, even after human editing.

The machine made use of a so-called *photoscopic store* consisting of a glass disk, about ten inches in diameter, on which information was inscribed in concentric circles in much the same way as a movie's sound track is represented on the edge of the film. During the life of the system, a vast Russian-English dictionary of stems, prefixes, and suffixes was amassed and new disks were made periodically to incorporate the new information. The logical capabilities of the machine, however, were rudimentary. Each stem and affix on the disk was accompanied by a pair of codes indicating classes of stems and affixes that could occur before and after it. Thus, when a Russian word was sought in the dictionary, various alternative classes might be found, and the one chosen would be determined by the choice made for the item immediately preceding it.

In the heyday of machine translation, Leon Dostert at the University of Georgetown had three independent projects under his supervision. After the publication of the AL-PAC report, two of these projects continued elsewhere, though less vigorously, and were eventually quietly buried. The third was delivered as an operational system to translate Russian materials into English to the Atomic Energy Commission at Oak Ridge and to the European Atomic Energy Community (EURATOM) in Ispra, northern Italy. This system, which is usually referred to simply as the "Georgetown program," was designed for use on a standard, general-purpose computer, the IBM 7090. Its logical capabilities therefore far surpassed those of the Mark II translator, though the enhancement is not always apparent in the quality of the resulting translation.

The Georgetown program is very complicated. It consists of a large number of instructions that make use of several magnetic tapes on which various kinds of information are stored temporarily so as to make room in the main memory of the machine for other operations. In the course of translating a text, the program goes through a series of more or less well-defined steps called "dictionary lookup," "syntactic analysis,"and so on. When this program was designed, work was just beginning on the formal properties of languages and the kinds of processors they might require, and what little was known was, in any case, largely ignored by the designers of this supposedly practical system. The absence of suitable formalisms is not to blame for the scarcity of impressive results from the Georgetown and other early systems, but it is to blame for their monstrous size and complexity.

Though the Georgetown system purported to be concerned largely with syntax, it incorporated neither the notion of a grammatical rule nor the notion of a syntactic structure. The complexity of the syntactic part of the program was devoted to nothing more than resolving ambiguities in the assignment of words to grammatical classes. If a word to be translated could, in the abstract, be either an adjective or a noun, the process examined the word's context to determine in which capacity it functioned in the given sentence. The methods by which this was done were ad hoc, and they always provided a single answer to each problem regardless of genuine syntactic ambiguities in the sentence. Of course, an attempt was made to find the solution that would be correct in most cases. The grammatical classifications that were thus appended to the words in a text could be used later to determine which of a list of possible English alternatives would serve to translate the word and to help decide on the eventual order of the words in the second language. Such information about the structure of Russian and English as the program used was built into the very fabric of the program so that each attempt to modify or enhance the capabilities of the system was more difficult and more treacherous than the last. After a while, such a program becomes so complex that any further development is virtually impossible.

In the nearly ten years since the publication of the ALPAC report, much has been learned about linguistics and computer science, but few substantial inroads have been made into the basic problems that beset machine translation. Using the best knowledge that the profession has amassed, an automatic-translation system could be developed far more cheaply and easily today than was possible ten years ago, but there is little evidence that it would be able to produce translations of markedly higher quality.

It is generally agreed that any machine-translation system intended to produce results of high quality must carry out a syntactic analysis of every sentence in the text to be translated. The product of this analysis usually appears as a labeled tree representing the surface or preferably the deep structure of the sentence. Developing a structure of this kind has two important advantages. First, the function that a word or group of words fulfills in a sentence cannot usually be determined simply by examining neighboring words and phrases. It can be determined only by insuring that any function proposed for it is compatible with that proposed for every other word and phrase in the entire sentence. In other words, the most solid basis on which to assess whether a function has been correctly assigned is provided by a structural analysis of the sentence.

Tree structures are also valuable because they permit the definition of a simple but immensely powerful set of operations, known as transformations, in terms of which the structural changes that must be made to produce the sentence in another language can be stated. Suppose that a text is to be translated from a language like English in which the subject usually precedes the main verb and the object follows, into a language like Japanese in which the main verb invariably comes at the end of the sentence. The necessary adjustment in word order is easy to make if the syntactic analysis of the sentence identifies entities like subjects and objects in such a way that their relative positions can readily be altered.

Since there is no theoretical limit on the number of words that can constitute a subject or an object, the structure on which the rearrangement operations are carried out must have a way of connecting indefinitely many words into a group with a name so that it can be treated as a single item. Furthermore, subjects and objects can include other sentences with their own subjects and objects. Take the sentence, *"Claims that John had passed the examination surprised the professor."* The subject of this sentence is *"Claims that John had passed the examination,"* which contains the second sentence, *"John had passed the examination,"* which has its own subject, *"John."* The relationships of these various parts to one another can be conveniently represented in a tree diagram, as follows:

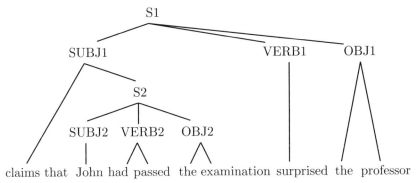

The labels Sl and S2 correspond to the first and second sentences respectively, and lines project down from each of these to labels representing the subject, verb, and object of the sentence.

Suppose, now, that the sentence is to be translated into Japanese. Two kinds of modification must be made. First, the verb of every sentence must be placed at the end, and second, whenever a subject or object includes a noun and verb that make a complete sentence, that sentence must be placed before the noun it modifies. Arranging the English words in their Japanese order, we obtain, "John the examination passed had claims the professor surprised." The tree diagram for this sentence is as follows:

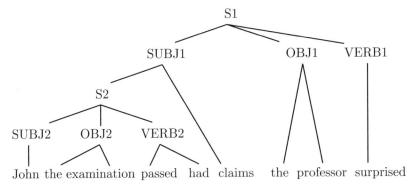

The new tree structure can be obtained from the original by treating the diagram as a mobile and changing the relative positions of items hanging from particular places.

All the mechanical-translation systems that have been put into regular use are normally described as "machine-aided" translation systems. This is because the translations they produce are not, in general, comprehensible, but must be edited, often heavily, by a person who is familiar not only with the subject matter of the document but also with both languages involved. Therefore the production of a suitable translation by one of these systems can often be complicated, time-consuming, and expensive. All graphic material must first be removed from the text, leaving an indication of where it should be reinserted in the translation. If any of the graphic material contains matter in the foreign language, this must be specially translated and the appropriate amendment made to the tables, graphs, or pictures. The textual material must be represented in a form that the computer can read, and since optical character-recognition devices are still not equal to reading print, this must be done by a human operator at the keyboard. When the automatic translation has been done, a human editor must revise the translation, the graphic material must be reinserted, and a presentable copy must be produced.

In a letter published in Science on December 17, 1971, Dr. Wallace Sinaiko described some tentative results of an informal experiment he has been conducting. In 1964, the Foreign Technology Division agreed to have a Russian paper translated for him, using the Mark II translator then in service. The Russian paper was itself a good translation of an English paper, made by a professional translator. Without any detailed knowledge of Russian, Sinaiko was thereby enabled to assess the quality of the product of the mechanical system, allowance being made for the scarcity of data (the original English paper contained only 1685 words) and the possibility that error had been introduced by the professional translator. Sinaiko was provided with the unedited output of the machine, making it easier to judge what its contribution to a satisfactory translation would have been.

Sinaiko had the same paper translated again in 1971 by the new system recently installed at the Foreign Technology Division, and he was given both the output of the machine and the final translation after human editing. In possession of two additional translations of the Russian text he had obtained from professional linguists in 1964, Sinaiko was thus able to compare the raw output of the two translation systems, the final, human-edited output of the present system, and the work of the two translators.

The techniques that Sinaiko used to compare these translations were simple and informal. The two characteristics he concentrated on were (1) untranslated words and (2) translated words that had two or more possible meanings indicated for them in the translation. The differences between the raw output of the two machine systems were insignificant. The earlier system left 1.2 percent of the words untranslated, whereas SYSTRAN failed to find English equivalents for 2.3 percent. The earlier system provided alternative translations for 6.3 percent of the words, whereas the later system provided alternatives for 5.3 percent. These types of error, if errors they are, would not be found in the work of a human translator.

A comparison of the raw output of the machine with the translation that resulted from editing showed that about 35 percent of the English words printed by the computer were altered by the editor. Every one of the approximately eighty English sentences had some editorial modifications, most of them extensive. The most interesting statistic is the following: the manual translators worked at the rate of about 450 words per hour, whereas the editors working on the SYSTRAN output worked at the rate of about 400 words per hour.

Sinaiko was careful to point out that the results of this informal experiment are anything but conclusive. However, he observes, "It is apparent that little progress has been made during recent years. Moreover I do not know of any demonstrated advantages of MT over human translations."

Earlier I stressed that, while the last ten years have seen significant advances in the ease and elegance with which linguistic operations can be programmed as well as a bewildering array of new proposals in linguistic theory, no advance has been made that promises dramatically to improve the quality of machine translations. However, there may be ways that computer technology could serve translation other than those that have already been tried. At least two other ways have recently been suggested, one capitalizing on the recent development of machines that allow human intervention in the course of the computation, and one involving special artificial languages. If I seem unduly enthusiastic about the first of these, it must be remembered that I had some part in developing the idea.

The MIND system, developed at the Rand Corporation, is a package of computer programs that can be assembled in various ways to fill several linguistic functions. A version of the system was assembled in the latter half of 1971 that is intended to take over, as much as possible, the purely routine work involved in making a translation without ever attempting to solve problems for which it is not equipped. The program contains all the components that one would expect in a full-fledged translation program. There are facilities for analyzing the morphology of words, for obtaining their definitions, and for recording for each sentence all the information furnished by the dictionary about each of its constituent words. A thorough syntactic analysis of each sentence is performed that yields a *deep structure* (in the terms of modern transformational grammar) for each sentence. Transformational rules are applied to these deep structures to produce well-formed sentences in the second language. Finally, there is a component that provides the morphologically appropriate forms for each of the words printed out.

In addition, the system contains a component called a *disambiguator* , whose job is to mediate between the other components of the system with the help of a human consultant, to whom reference is made in all cases of difficulty or unresolved ambiguity. If a word has more than one meaning and the rules supplied to the system provide no basis for deciding which one applies in a particular context, the question will be referred to the consultant. If the rules allow more than one syntactic structure for a sentence, appropriate questions will be formulated to elicit the information necessary to decide among them. If it is necessary to know what a pronoun refers to before it can be correctly translated, the consultant will be provided with a list of possible referents and invited to choose the correct one.

These are the kinds of questions that cannot, as far as we know, be solved in a purely formal way. What is noteworthy about them is that they all arise in attempting to understand the original text rather than in attempting to compose a text in the second language. This suggests that a system of the kind just outlined might function very effectively with a human consultant who is familiar only with the language of the source document and its subject matter. If that is true, such a system might be made to produce creditable translations for technical documents without the services of a human translator or bilingual editor. Whether it can, in fact, do so still remains to be seen. The results of preliminary experiments in the translation of technical manuals from English into Korean are encouraging.

In the realm of language translation, one further line of investigation seems worthy of mention. Largely because of its sheer simplicity, it has usually been ignored or ridiculed in the past. We start from the premise that there are large numbers of people who need to read documents in some foreign language, Russian for example, but who have no knowledge of the language and no desire to learn it. Furthermore, we assume that many of the Russian documents would be read by such a small number of English-speaking people that it would be very difficult to justify the cost of making a translation. Let us further suppose that, though these people are unwilling to invest the amount of time required to learn Russian, they might be prepared to spend a tenth, or possibly a quarter, of this time to learn a skill of equivalent utility. They might be willing to learn a much simpler language into which, for one reason or another, it proved very simple to translate Russian. If, for example, there were some language into which Russian texts could be mechanically translated in a simple but entirely reliable way, and if this language were also very easy for native English speakers to learn, then these people would have ready access to the foreign materials they needed.

No language with the properties just described in fact exists. But there is good reason to suppose that one could be created. If a dictionary were made that provided a counterpart for each Russian word, prefix, and suffix, and if the process of translation consisted simply of replacing the Russian words and affixes by their counterparts listed in the dictionary, a new language would have been created with the grammar of Russian but with a different vocabulary. If the vocabulary were such that each item in it corresponded to exactly one Russian item, the translation process would be completely reversible, capable of reconstituting the original text exactly. Thus, no information from the original text would ever be lost, a property that no other kind of translation has.

Suppose, now, that the items used as counterparts for Russian words were chosen, wherever possible, to be English words, or English-like words, with meanings suggestive of the meanings of the Russian words. Though it is impossible to find English words with the same meanings as some Russian words, that difficulty is encountered less in technical documents where precise equivalents are usually abundant. This method would leave it to the human reader to learn the idiosyncrasies of the most common words with the widest ranges of meanings. In return, it would relieve the human reader of his most time-consuming task, that of finding equivalents for the precise words, which, though they individually occur relatively rarely, comprise the bulk of the vocabulary encountered in technical documents.

Lest what is being proposed here be confused with some early and notoriously unsuccessful experiments in machine translation, it must be stressed that we do not expect native English speakers to be able, without training, to read texts in the curious Anglo-Russian that would emerge from this translation process. We do, however, expect that this language could be learned in much less time than Russian or any other natural foreign language. The production of these translations would be entirely mechanical, and the algorithm required is trivial, so that the cost could be extremely low. In my view, the products of a simple system of this kind would fill the needs of the Foreign Technology Division at least as well as their present system does. Furthermore, the steps that would have to be taken to extend the system to other languages are straightforward, simple and cheap.

At present, linguists are devoting more and more attention to problems of meaning. This was, of course, the principal center of interest in linguistic studies until the end of the nineteenth century when there was a temporary shift of attention to the origin and development of language. One of the most vexing aspects of the study of meaning is that there is very little agreement on the question of what the problems are that need to be solved. Since almost anything that can be thought can be said, linguists have sometimes sought to exclude meaning from their field of study lest that field become too broad and amorphous. However, it is not clear that the study of meaning entails a study of everything that can be meant any more than that the study of logic entails an examination of every true and false argument. Some students of meaning have undertaken to provide a universally valid scheme for classifying words according to their meanings as Roget did in his well-known *Thesaurus of English Words and Phrases*. Such a categorization, for all that it is purely taxonomic, might be thought of as some kind of map of the territory over which the human spirit roams, or as the basis of a universal vocabulary into which the sentences of any language could be translated. To some scholars, the study of meaning has been effectively identified with the study of informal logic. Depending on how much rigor is introduced into this kind of study, it tends to take the form of an enriched, or corrupted, version of standard logical formalisms.

One of the principal points of contention among students of meaning concerns the question of whether there is, in fact, something that can eventually be captured and examined which is the meaning of a word or sentence. Every attempt to capture such an object leads, at best, to other words and expressions, possibly in some formal notation. Presumably the best that can be said is that the new set of words and expressions provides a more transparent representation of the meaning and shows the contributions of various components explicitly. But it cannot be claimed that anything set down on paper actually is a meaning. Some scholars have reacted to this situation by noting that the fact that words and sentences are meaningful is not grounds for assuming that there must be something which is their meaning.

The meaning, as Wittgenstein said, is the use. The meaning of a word or sentence is the total set of relations that it contracts with other words and sentences. When I learn a new word or a new fact about the world, the result is to change, however imperceptibly, the meanings of all other words and sentences in my language. While this view does not broaden the scope of linguistics so that it embraces the whole of science, it does claim for it much of the territory that was previously thought of as belonging to psychology and philosophy. In this view, a person's knowledge of the world is defined by his ability to describe that knowledge in language.

By what criteria should a theory of meaning in ordinary language be judged? Each theorist, of course, has his own answer. However, many people are prepared to concede that an ultimate test of a theory of meaning would be to incorporate it in the design of a machine, thereby enabling the machine to demonstrate the same kind of linguistic competence as a human being.

Allan Turing suggested that we could claim to understand the basis of human intelligence only when we could build a machine with which human beings could communicate and which resisted every attempt on the part of an interlocutor to determine whether it was, in fact, a machine. There is a growing number of students of language, most of them, to be sure, not claiming to be linguists, for whom the adequacy of a theory of meaning must be assessed in just this way. They would claim that the studies of meaning and of intelligence are all one.

The value of this approach to the study of meaning does not depend on the validity of the specific projects that have hitherto been based on it or on how readily we expect to be able to develop machines whose performance approaches the ideal. It does depend, at least to some extent, on such fundamental epistemological questions as whether it is ultimately possible to judge the grasp of meaning that a machine or organism has attained purely on the basis of its behavior. What would it bc like to have a machine that not only could tell me that it was sorry I had a cold, but could also be sorry? Is it possible to understand the meaning of a word like "sorry" without being able to experience the emotion? To put the question somewhat differently, what conclusions would we be justified in drawing about the human faculty of language from a machine that had been enabled, by various kinds of cunning and trickery, to masquerade as a human being? Clearly there would be no necessary connection between the components of the machine and the components of human psychology. But this is to say nothing that cannot be said with equal justice of any linguistic theory that has been proposed. The test of a scientific theory must be behavioral. We cannot expect scientific models to operate for the same reasons or by the same processes as reality, but only to operate in a manner sufficiently analogous to enable us to extrapolate about reality from the behavior of the machine. Because of this ignorance of motive, the scientific value of a talking machine cannot be assessed objectively, but only on the basis of such subjective criteria as the parsimony and elegance of its structure.

The attempt to build machines that mimic human behavior belongs to a field that has come to be known as *artificial intelligence* . A contribution to that field that has recently attracted a great deal of attention is a computer program designed by Terry Winograd of M.I.T. This program enters into a conversation with its human interlocutor about a very carefully restricted domain of discourse. The program causes a picture to be displayed on a television screen depicting a table top on which a number of simple objects – cubes, balls, pyramids and boxes of various sizes and colors – are distributed. The machine can be instructed to move these objects about on the table top and it does this using its single "hand," a depiction of which can be seen entering the display from the top of the screen. It can, therefore, move only one object at once. It is possible to imagine instructions that require some ingenuity to carry out. Suppose, for example, that there are three blocks on the table and that the machine is told to stack them on top of one another. It may be that some of the blocks are initially supporting other objects which must first be removed. Obstructions must be removed from the upper face of at least two of the blocks before the stacking can begin.

Winograd's program may have to design quite a complex strategy in order to carry out a particular instruction, but, according to the view on which this work is based, it can only be said to understand an instruction fully if it can respond in this positive way. The program can also be asked questions about the disposition of the objects on the table and about its reasons for making particular moves. It may, for example, be asked, "Why did you put the green block on the red one?" to which the answer might be something like "Because you told me to stack up three blocks so that I had first to stack up two blocks."

Students of artificial intelligence have worked with diverse models from robots that use a television camera for an eye and can move from place to place negotiating obstacles to programs that prove mathematical theorems and play chess. Hitherto, few of these efforts have involved a determined attack on obviously linguistic problems. Interaction with the machine has typically been through the medium of specially designed languages but, to the extent that a wider view is taken of problems of meaning, these projects can be seen as contributing to our understanding of natural language. For Winograd, it is a matter of the first importance that his program communicate in English and he describes his work as contributing to *procedural semantics* , an explicitly linguistic enterprise. For him, the meaning of a sentence is the procedure that it sets off in the head of the hearer and he takes it as his task to replicate that process in a machine.

Any machine that processes textual data in nontrivial ways must have certain basic capabilities. It must be able to recognize words, making due allowance for the ways in which their forms vary with number, person, mood, and the like. For each word, it must be able to retrieve information about its syntactic and semantic properties from a dictionary. It must be able to distinguish the correct syntactic structure from among the several possibilities in a grammatically ambiguous sentence. The details of how these processes are carried out depends on the theoretical stance of the designer. For some purposes, a strategy that is expensive in terms of computer resources may be preferred because it is considered a better model of the human strategy or because it is more perspicuous. On the other hand, if large amounts of text are to be treated, efficiency may be a prime consideration. For one purpose, it may be necessary to have all possible analyses of every sentence whereas for another it may be desirable to seek the analysis which is, in some sense, most probably correct.

Until recently, it was thought that each set of requirements demanded a new program and that there was no end to the designing of essentially different algorithms for basic linguistic processes. While there is, of course, no way of knowing what tomorrow's revelations may bring, it now seems likely that the best algorithms will turn out to be variants of a single overall strategy. Three strategies have been proposed for obtaining so-called deep structures for arbitrary sentences. By "deep structure," I mean the kind of structure assigned to a sentence by some variant of transformational grammar. It is an attempt to make explicit the underlying logical relations among words rather than simply to label subjects, objects, and the like. There has been rivalry among the proponents of three strategies, which were thought to be fundamentally different. However, it has recently become clear that the similarities are more striking than the differences. There appears to be a common core of operations that must be part of any algorithm for syntactic analysis.

The oldest of these strategies was the subject of Stanley Petrick's doctoral thesis at M.I.T. (Petrick 1965). It is a complicated procedure divided into several different stages and drawing heavily on the details of Chomsky's formalization of transformational grammar. The other two proposals make no direct reference to this formalism. William Woods' Augmented Transition-Network Parser (Woods 1970, Woods 1971) is inspired by parts of automata theory and, in particular, by the notions of automata theory with finite numbers of discrete states and of push-down stores. Kay's chart parser (Kay 1967, Kaplan 1973) capitalizes on the notion of general rewriting rules. It is, at least in principle, possible to write equivalent grammars for programs that follow each of these three strategies. In other words, grammars can be written which would cause the three programs to deliver identical analyses of the same sentences. However, the grammars would be written in entirely different notations; furthermore, they would cause quite a different sequence of events to occur in the machine. From this point of view, grammatical formalisms take on the aspect of high-level programming languages, each of which requires a compiler to translate it into the language of a particular machine. The difference is that, in this case, the machine is not simply a general purpose digital computer, but a special machine which might be called a syntactic processor. It is not necessary to construct instances of this special machine out of pieces of hardware because a general purpose computer can be made to stimulate it by supplying it with the appropriate algorithm in a suitable programming language.

That it is possible to design a single machine with reference to which grammatical formalisms appear as high-level programming languages is, theoretically, not surprising. Indeed, it is not difficult to prove that, if the formalism is adequate for syntactic analysis at all, then it must be possible to solve the problem in this way. What is interesting is that the proposed syntactic processor turns out to have a simple and elegant design and that this approach to the problem of syntactic analysis is efficient and practical. The difference between the syntactic processor and the general purpose computer is the difference between the theoretically adequate machines that are the object of mathematical study and the machines that are manufactured by engineers.

It will take time to discover the cash value of something like the syntactic processor. At best, it will be shown to incorporate important components of the human faculty of language. At worst, it will be a useful piece of engineering. In any case, it belongs to the field of computational linguistics.

The strategy of syntactic analysis is a real problem on which some modest headway has been made. But it is not a problem that belongs obviously either to linguistics or to computer science and it would probably never have arisen in the normal course of work in either of these disciplines. The same can be said of many problems in semantics. The computational linguist, however, sees problems of meaning in a different light from other linguists. To him, the meaning of a sentence is, as I have said, a process – a program that will be carried out in the head of the hearer. The computational linguist is, above all, a specialist in the processes of language and he is coming more and more to see semantics as the field in which his main contribution will be made.

Publications referenced
ALPAC 1966; Kaplan 1973; Kay 1967; Petrick 1965; Woods 1970; Woods and Kaplan 1971.

16

Morphological Analysis

A computer program that is intended to carry out nontrivial operations on texts in an ordinary language must start by recognizing the words that the text is made up of. This is the procedure I call *morphological analysis* . It is necessary because the linguistically interesting properties of words cannot be discovered by examining the words themselves but are associated with them in an essentially arbitrary manner. Therefore, there must be a list – what we call a *dictionary* – to define the mapping of words into linguistically interesting properties and a process to look words up in this dictionary.

Many computer programs have been written in which morphological analysis consists of nothing more than accepting any unbroken string of letters encountered in a text as a word and referring it to a dictionary. This means that, in addition to what is usually found there, the dictionary must contain plural forms of nouns, all the forms of every verb, regular or irregular, all adverbs, and so forth. A machine dictionary of English constructed on these principles would contain four to six times as many entries as a standard dictionary but some of these entries could presumably consist of little more than a reference to the standard form of the word - the singular of the noun, the infinitive of the verb, or whatever. A modern computer could easily accommodate a dictionary of English enlarged in this way and it is an attractive thing to do if only because it reduces the problem of morphological analysis almost to triviality. The increase in the size of the dictionary is more alarming in the case of a highly inflected language. There are, however, many languages for which this solution is unthinkable and many for which it is clearly undesirable. In ancient Greek, Latin, and Sanskrit, for example, it was not customary to leave spaces between words so that

Galliaestomnesdi
visainpartestres

would have been a reasonable way for Caesar to write what would be printed as

Gallia est omnes divisa in partes tres

in a modern edition. Many languages, like German, admit compounding as a productive part of the grammar so that words like

Lebensversicherungsgesellschaftsangestelter

meaning "employee of a life insurance society" can be freely invented. Under these circumstances, the policy of referring unbroken strings of letters to the dictionary will clearly be inadequate.

In general, therefore, it is necessary to recognize lexical items in a text otherwise than by the simple fact that they are bounded by spaces or other non-alphabetic characters. The possibility of words being juxtaposed without any explicit boundary must be admitted and it may even be desirable to divest the space of its special status as a separator altogether and treat it like any other member of the alphabet. This opens the possibility of treating many kinds of idioms and fixed phrases as ordinary words that happen to contain spaces or other non-alphabetic characters.

But there is more to morphological analysis than recognizing lexical items in a connected text in the absence of explicit boundary markers. In general, when lexical items are conjoined, they undergo some change of form. In English, for example, the plural of nouns is regularly formed adding an *s*. But, if the noun ends in *j, s, x, z, sh*, or *ch*, an *e* is introduced before the *s*. If the singular form ends in *y*, then this is replaced by *ies* in the plural. These changes are specified in a chapter of the grammar called morphographemics which is much more copious in some languages than in English. In Sanskrit, for example, morphographemic rules are applied when one word is written after another and not only when grammatical affixes are appended. Thus, for example,

rajendra

is written instead of

raja indra

because of a grammatical rule requiring *a+i* to be replaced by *e* wherever it occurs. Notice that rules of this kind make the use of spaces to delimit words almost impossible because, in a case like this, there is no non-arbitrary way of assigning the *e* to the first or the second word.

I have been treating grammatical items like inflexional affixes on a level with other lexical items. This seems reasonable, at least for the immediate purpose which is simply to decompose a text into items that are small enough to constitute a finite list in the description of the language and which are composed into larger items by productive processes. The trouble is that texts consist of more than a concatenation of lexical items occasionally modified by the action of morphographemic rules. Words undergo productive processes formally different from, though functionally identical to, the adjunction of other lexical items. The plural that is represented in English by adding an *s* appears in other languages by the repetition of a syllable or part of a syllable with or without some change in the vowel of that syllable. In addition to prefixing and suffixing, some languages admit infixing, a process by which the string of characters representing one lexical item is interrupted by a second item. In fact, the complete variety of the morphological processes used in the languages of the world has never been surveyed.

In the remainder of this paper, I shall outline a procedure for morphological analysis of which it is not too unreasonable to hope that it will accommodate most of the languages of the world while, at the same time, being efficient enough to be considered for inclusion in practical computer systems in competition with more specialized methods that have been proposed. The procedure I shall outline has the additional advantage that it can be made to blend in an interesting way with syntactic processes that can be expected to follow.

Morphographemic rules are made available to the procedure in the form of a set of string-rewriting rules whose job is to reduce the lexical items in a text to canonical forms which can then be referred to a dictionary.

For example, a rule approximately of the form

$$ied \rightarrow y + ed$$

would transform the word *tried* into *try+ed*. The "+" represents a boundary between a pair of lexical items; operationally, it will be a lexical item in its own right and will occur as part of no other lexical item.

Consider the string

He tried the fuses

The morphographemic rewriting component of the system proposes three forms for the word *tried* and two for the word *fuses* so that a total of six strings are delivered to the next component of the system. Only one of these, namely

He try+ed the fuse+s

is correct. If more rewriting rules had been applied, a great many more strings would have resulted. In fact, if each of the words in a longer sentence were given two forms by the rewriting rules, then 1024 different strings would be generated.

Clearly, what is required is the ability to work with expressions with something like the following form:

He tr(i/y+)ed the fus(es/+s)

in which the parentheses include alternative substrings separated by slashes. This should be more than just a notational convention but should reflect the inner workings of a system in which the amount of material generated and the amount of processing to be done on it is more nearly proportional to the sum than the product of the ambiguities.

Let the string to be analyzed be represented in a diagram of the following kind:

o—o—o—o—o—o—o—o—o—o—o—o—o—o—o—o—o
  H   E   sp   T   R   I   E   D   sp   T   H   E   sp   F   U   S   E   S

This kind of diagram is what I call a chart. Each letter labels an edge. There is an initial and a final vertex and the remaining vertices correspond to the points in the string at which a pair of letters meet. When the rewriting process is complete, the chart will look like this:

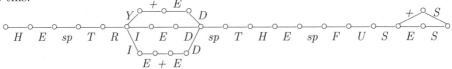

Each of the six strings that the morphological rewriting component must produce for this example is represented by a path from left to right through the chart. Instead of rewriting in the strict sense, the rules have caused new edges and vertices to be added to the chart. A rule like

$$ied \rightarrow y + ed$$

is interpreted as an instruction to look for instances of the string *ied* and introduce a new path from the vertex before *i* to the vertex following *d* with labels *y*, *+*, *e*, and *d*.

There are many simple ways of representing the same logical structure that a chart diagram represents inside a computer. One is to represent each edge by a quadruple ⟨label, character, alternate, successor⟩. Each edge has a unique label which, in the computer, can be the index of the edge in a set of three parallel arrays in which the other components are stored. The second component is the letter or other character represented by the edge. The alternate is the label of another edge incident from the same vertex. A vertex, in this representation, is simply the set of edges incident from it. The index of the first of these to be put in the chart serves also as the index of the vertex. The remaining edges are found by taking the alternate of the first edge as the second edge, the alternate of the second as the third, and so on until an edge is encountered that has no alternate. The chart displayed above, in which three rewriting rules have been applied to the string *He tried the fuses* is represented as follows:

Label	Character	Alternate	Successor
1	H	0	2
2	E	0	3
3	sp	0	4
4	T	0	5
5	R	0	6
6	I	19	7
7	E	0	8
8	D	0	9
9	sp	0	10
10	T	0	11
11	H	0	12
12	E	0	13
13	sp	0	14
14	F	0	15
15	U	0	16
16	S	0	17
17	E	28	18
18	S	0	0
19	Y	23	20
20	+	0	21
21	E	0	22
22	D	0	9
23	I	0	24
24	E	0	25
25	+	0	26
26	E	0	27
27	D	0	9
28	+	0	29
29	S	0	0

The first 18 entries represent the characters of the original string. The only changes that have been made to these are in the "alternate" column for entries 6 and 17. These correspond to the first characters of substrings to which rules have applied. Entry 6, for example, has 19 as its alternate and entries 19 through 22 represent the string *y+ed*. The successor of entry 22 is 9 indicating that *y+ed* is a replacement for the *ied* in entries 6, 7, and 8, the last of which also has 9 as its successor. The string *ied* was, in fact, rewritten by two different rules so that entry 19 also has an alternate and entries 23 through 27 represent the output of the second rule. Entry 6 is the head of an alternate chain that also contains 19 and 23, and these are indeed three edges that are all incident from the same vertex, a vertex that we can think of as represented by the number 6.

The chart comes close to achieving the economy desired of the rewriting component of the system. Notice, however, that there are still three separate edges labeled *d* preceding the second space. In order to see why this must be so, consider the following more abstract example:

1. Rewrite *a* as *d* when it precedes *b*
2. Rewrite *b* as *c* when it follows *a*

If the initial string is *ab*, then the rewriting process must deliver three strings, namely *ab*, *ac* and *db*. The set does not include *dc*. Now look at the diagrammatic representation. Interpreting the rules in the most straightforward way, one might expect to get

But this does include a path representing the string *dc*. If phrases like *when it precedes* ... and *when it follows* ... are excluded from the rules, so that we must say:

1a. Rewrite *ab* as *ac*
2a. Rewrite *ab* as *db*

we not only stress the mutual incompatibility of the two rules, but also produce a situation in which the most natural interpretation of the rules gives the correct result. We now get

It is possible for rules to operate on characters resulting from the application of previous rules. A compact statement of the rules of Sanskrit morphology would capitalize on this possibility to a large extent. In English, it might never be used in a realistic system, but it is not difficult to manufacture examples that are not hopelessly implausible even in English. Consider a word like *cruddily*. One rule might rewrite this as *cruddy+ly* and a second rule might then rewrite this as *crud+y+ly*. Part of the input to the second rule is the final *y* of *cruddy* which the first rule introduced. In the chart, this would appear as follows:

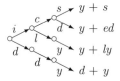

What this means is that, when substrings are being considered as candidates for rewriting, every path through the chart must be considered, including those that arise as a result of previous rewriting. This brings up the basic problem of syntactic analysis, namely, how can one guarantee that every possibility will be explored once, but no more than once. A full discussion of this problem is beyond the scope of this paper and I shall therefore limit the discussion to one simple but very general technique which can be modified in innumerable ways in the interests of efficiency.

Let us consider just four rewriting rules taken from the morphological section of a hypothetical English recognition grammar:

$$
\begin{aligned}
i\,e\,s &\rightarrow y + s \\
i\,e\,d &\rightarrow y + e\,d \\
i\,l\,y &\rightarrow y + l\,y \\
d\,d\,y &\rightarrow d + y
\end{aligned}
$$

A considerable amount of space and, as we shall see, work, can be saved by representing the rules also in diagrammatic form. Although it is in many ways similar to a chart, I shall use the term *transition network* , or simply *network* to refer to this diagram so that it will be easy to refer to both in the same context. For the same reason, I shall refer to the lines in a transition network as *arcs* rather than edges. A network representing these four rules would be as follows:

In this representation, if several rules begin in the same way, the similar parts are only represented once and if the similar initial parts of a set of rules are matched against a set of edges, this will be a partial test of all the rules in the set. In the computer, this can be represented as follows:

Label	Character	Alternate	Successor	Replacement
1	I	7	2	
2	E	5	3	
3	S	4	0	$\rightarrow Y + S$
4	D	0	0	$\rightarrow Y + ED$
5	L	0	6	
6	Y	0	0	$\rightarrow Y + LY$
7	D	0	8	
8	D	0	9	
9	Y	0	0	$\rightarrow D + Y$

All parts of the network can be reached from arc number 1. The set of alternates of arc number 1 correspond to sets of rules that differ in their very first character.

We are now ready to consider how a transition network can be applied to a chart in such a way as to allow all applicable rules to be identified and carried out exactly once. Like almost all non-deterministic procedures, this involves the use of a list of tasks that still remain to be done at any given moment during the execution of the procedure. This list is sometimes referred to as a *stack* because it is usual to maintain the policy of never removing from it any but the last entry made so that the last task remembered will always be the first to be carried out, and the word "stack" is reserved for lists that are used in this way. I shall use another term, namely *task list* , because I do not wish to suggest any such discipline. Indeed, it is a feature of this procedure that the tasks on the list can be carried out in any order whatsoever without altering the eventual result.

An entry on the task list is a triple ⟨arc, edge, vertex⟩. When the task is carried out, an attempt will be made to match the arc to the edge. If this completes the matching of the left-hand side of a rule with a substring in the chart, then some new material will be introduced into the chart beginning at the vertex named in the triple and ending at the vertex which is the successor of the named edge.

In greater detail, the task specified by the triple ⟨a, e, v⟩ is carried out as follows:

1. Let b be the alternate of a. If b is not zero, create a new task ⟨b, e, v⟩ and put it on the task list.

2. Consider the edge e and any other edges that there may be on its alternate chain in turn. Let d be the current edge. Carry out the process described below for each new edge d. In other words, first let $d = e$, then set d to the alternate of d on each occasion unless d has an alternate of 0, in which case, stop.

   If they are the same and the arc has a replacement, then introduce a new sequence of edges into the chart to represent the replacement starting at vertex v and ending at the vertex which is the successor of d. Whether or not there is a replacement, if the arc has a successor s and the edge has a successor t, then create a new task ⟨s, t, v⟩ and put it on the task list.

It will be clear from this that a task can create any number of new tasks and this is why it is necessary to keep a list of them.

The entire process is set in motion by putting on the task list a task ⟨l, w, w⟩ for each vertex w in the chart. Recall that, for such purposes as this, a vertex is represented by the label of its first edge and, initially, there will be exactly one edge incident from each vertex. I might, therefore, just as well have said that a task is created for each edge in the chart. Tasks are now removed from the list and carried out until none remain.

The procedure, as described so far, will result in the rules being applied to the characters of the initial string and all possible results obtainable in this way being added to the chart. However, there is no provision for applying rules to substrings that arise, in whole or in part, from the application of other rules. Part of the problem can be solved by adding a new task ⟨l, n, n⟩ for each new vertex n that is added to the list as a result of applying a rule. In fact, the initial task list and these later additions would all be covered by a general requirement that a task ⟨l, n, n⟩ is created for every vertex n added to the chart, initially or later. But there remains the problem of ensuring that, when new edges are introduced incident from existing vertices, all processes that should apply to that edge do in fact apply. The difficulty is that at least some tasks will already have been applied to the edges incident from that vertex and will, by now, have disappeared without trace. A simple example will show how this can arise.

Suppose that the initial chart is as follows:

$$\circ\!\!-\!\!-\!\!\circ\!\!-\!\!-\!\!\circ$$
$$a\quad b$$

and that the rules are as in the following network:

The initial task list is as follows:

Arc	Edge	Vertex
1	1	1
1	2	2

The first task is removed from the list and carried out. Since arc number 1 has an alternate, a new task is put on the list. Since we are assuming that the order of the task list is immaterial, let us add the new task at the head of the list so that we now have:

Arc	Edge	Vertex
2	1	1
1	2	2

The current edge has no alternates so that it is the only one to be considered in this task. The label on the edge is a and the label on the arc is b. These do not match and the task therefore comes to an end. The next task is $\langle 2, 1, 1 \rangle$. Arc 2 has no alternate so that no new task has to be created for it. There is only one edge to be considered and arc 2 does, in fact, have the same symbol as edge 1. There is no replacement but both arc and edge have successors. A new task is therefore created, and we place it, as before, at the head of the list, which is now as follows:

Arc	Edge	Vertex
3	2	1
1	2	2

This new task is now immediately removed from the list to be carried out. Once again, there is only one edge to consider and its character is b. This does not match the c on the arc and the task therefore terminates. Notice that there are now no tasks on the list with vertex number 1 so that there is no longer any possibility of adding new edges at that vertex. The one task remaining will cause a new edge to be added at vertex 2 which could have been successfully used by the task just completed. But it is now too late. To complete the story, task $\langle 1, 2, 2 \rangle$ is now started, leaving the task list empty. The arc and edge match and a replacement is made giving the following as the final chart:

$$\overset{\displaystyle c}{\circ\!\!-\!\!-\!\!\circ\!\!\frown\!\!\circ}$$
$$a\quad b$$

This problem can be solved in a variety of ways. Most of them consist in carefully controlling the order in which items are removed from the task list. For reasons that will emerge later, I shall here propose an alternative solution. With each vertex in the chart, there will be associated a *wait list* which will simply be a list of things to be done to any new edge added at that vertex. An entry on a wait list will be a couple ⟨arc, vertex⟩. Whenever a new edge is added at the given vertex, a new task will be created for each item on the wait list, the required triple being formed by adding the new edge to the couple on the wait list. It remains only to describe how new entries are made on a wait list. This is done in a third step which we now add to the description of how tasks are carried out.

3. Add the couple ⟨a, v⟩ to the wait list of the vertex to which e belongs *if it is not already there.*

In the example just considered, this will cause, among other things, a couple ⟨3, 1⟩ to be placed on the wait list for vertex 2. When the new edge representing the character c is appended to this vertex, a new task will automatically be created, namely ⟨3, 3, 1⟩, where 3 is taken to be the label of the new edge. When this task is carried out, it will lead immediately to the addition of a new edge at vertex 1 and the final chart will have the desired final form, namely:

The principal problems that arise in dictionary consultation concern (1) what to look up, and (2) how to store and gain access to the dictionary. The problem of what to look up is the problem of deciding which of the substrings that the chart contains at the end of the rewriting process should be referred to the dictionary. We shall see that the approach we take to the second of these problems is strongly conditioned by the solution we adopt to the first.

One of the earliest solutions to the problem of what to look up was the following: start at the beginning of the string and find the longest word in the dictionary that can be matched beginning at that point. Then repeat the process starting with the first unmatched character. This so-called *longest-match* procedure is easy to fault. In a word like *underivable*, it will surely recognize *under* as the longest initial component and go on to forage for something in the dictionary to match *ivable*. Furthermore, the scheme would doubtless have to be modified before it could be applied to data presented in the form of a chart because there could be more than one longest matching initial substring if they lay on different paths. Almost any process applied to a chart will necessarily have to be nondeterministic. But it is easy to see that the process of dictionary consultation must, in any case, be nondeterministic because there are many cases of morphological ambiguity. In English, there are a few words like *ellipses* that are derivable from more than one stem; in this case *ellipse* and *ellipsis*. In other languages, such examples are much easier to find. The word *conti* in Italian is the plural of both *conto* and *conte* and there are many other words like it.

It seems, then, that nothing less than a procedure that exhausts the *coverings* of all the strings in the chart will have the generality we require. By a covering of a string I mean a segmentation of the string into non-overlapping substrings each of which is an entry in the dictionary. The English word *interminable* has only one correct segmentation that would be deemed correct in most texts, but it has at least two coverings by the English lexicon, for it is not only *in + terminate + able*, but also *inter + mine + able*. The second analysis might possibly be considered correct in a text on mining containing a sentence like *These strata are not interminable with presently available machinery.*

Logically, there is little to distinguish dictionary consultation from the application of rewriting rules. In one case strings of characters are rewritten by other strings of characters whereas, in the other, they are rewritten by strings of items of a fundamentally different kind, namely words or the lexical descriptions of words. The principal difference is that dictionary consultation is a process that does not apply to its own results; the input always consists of characters and the output of words. But there are practical considerations that are usually adduced to distinguish dictionary consultation as a special process.

Dictionaries are very large relative to many of the other bodies of data that a linguistic computer program must treat and it has therefore usually been impossible to accommodate them in the rapid-access store of a computer. Reference to external files is notoriously slow and therefore expensive and special techniques are often necessary to make it practical. Now, machines are getting larger and they are frequently designed so that the rapid-access store appears to be much larger than it actually is. But, leaving these facts aside, we nevertheless find that the format I suggested for the rewriting rules can readily be generalized to accommodate a dictionary, and in ways that yield practical and efficient systems.

The heart of the idea is to conflate the initial parts of strings when they are the same so that the whole set of strings is stored in the form of a tree. The only disadvantage that this has as a storage scheme for dictionaries is that, especially near the root of the tree, an arc can have an inordinate number of alternatives so that an appreciable amount of time would have to be expended in searching through them. In English, for example, there are words beginning with each of the 26 letters of the alphabet so that it would take an average of 13 trials to find the initial letter of a word. There are a variety of ways to overcome this problem. The following is a somewhat simplified version of one that has proved efficient, both in time and storage. The method combines the representation in the form of a tree with the well known technique of binary search.

Sort the dictionary into alphabetical order and choose a word from somewhere near the center of the resulting list. This word – the whole word and not just its first letter – will occupy the root of the tree. Suppose the word is *man*. Divide the dictionary in two at this point and choose a second word from near the center of the list of words that preceded *man*. This will occupy a node connected to the root by a line labeled with a zero. Suppose the word is *fortune*. Now consider only the words that precede *fortune* in the list, pick a word from near the middle, and connect it to the node for *fortune* with a line also labeled with a zero. Proceed in this manner until the first word in the dictionary is appended to the end of the chain. What we have now is a diagram of the following kind:

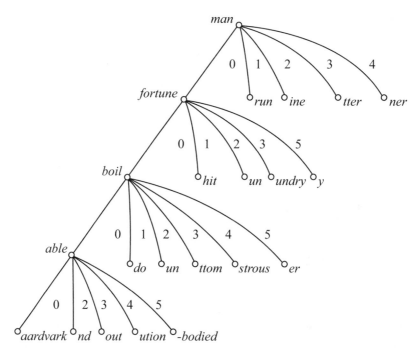

The remainder of the dictionary now consists of five lists: the words following *man*, the words between *fortune* and *man* and so on. Consider first the words that follow *man* in alphabetical order. Divide this into four sublists according to the length of the initial substrings that the words share with *man*. Thus, there will be a sublist of words beginning with the letters *man*, a sublist beginning with *ma* but not having an *n* in the third place, a sublist beginning with *m* but without an *a* in position 2, and a sublist of words that follow *man* in the dictionary but which share no initial substring with it. Now remove the shared initial substrings from the beginnings of the members of these lists – three letters from the members of the first list, two from the second, and so forth. The fourth list remains unchanged. Observe that the alphabetical ordering of the lists is preserved because the same initial substring is removed from the beginning of all the words in a given sublist. Now choose a (truncated) word from near the center of each sublist and connect it to the node for *man* by a link labeled with a number one greater than the number of letters in the initial substring just removed from it. For example, if *matter* is chosen from the third list, it is first truncated to *atter* and is then used to label a node connected to the root of the tree by a link labeled with a 3. Repeat this process for each of the five lists, adding new nodes below each of the existing ones. The result will look something like this:

Each word in the tree (except *aardvark*) is connected by a link labeled "0" to a subtree of words all of which precede it in alphabetical order. All other links lead from a word to a subtree of words that follow it in the alphabet. A link labeled n connects a word to alphabetically later words that differ from it in the nth position, but not before.

Each of the words so far accommodated in the tree was chosen from the center of some sublist. These sublists are now installed below the corresponding words in exactly the same way.

It is an entirely straightforward matter to look words up in a dictionary stored in this way. The algorithm is as follows:

1. Let w be the word to be looked up and v be, initially, the root of the tree.
2. If w occupies node v, then announce success; otherwise continue.
3. If w precedes the word at node v in alphabetical order, then let $n = 0$ and skip to step 6.
4. Let n equal the first position, counting from left to right, at which w differs from the word at node v.
5. Remove the first *n-1* characters from w.
6. If there is a link labeled n below v, let v be the node at the end of that link and return to step 2; otherwise announce that the word is not in the dictionary.

The method is readily recognizable as a variant of the familiar technique known as binary search. The principal difference lies in the treatment of words that share initial characters. This modification makes possible considerable economies in storage space because common initial substrings are only stored in one place. However, the variation also leads to interesting economies in the work that must be done to identify words in character strings stored in the form of a chart.

Suppose the rewriting procedure is changed to allow for two kinds of task, the original rewriting tasks and what I shall call *dictionary tasks* . A dictionary task will be represented on the task list by a quadruple ⟨node, edge, vertex, position⟩ in which the edge and vertex fill the same roles as in the rewriting task but, instead of an arc representing part of a rewriting rule, there is a dictionary node. Position is a number giving the number of characters of the substring that labels the dictionary node which have already been matched. A dictionary task ⟨n, e, v, p⟩ is carried out as follows:

Whenever a dictionary task is carried out, a character in the dictionary is compared with the characters associated with each of the edges incident from a given vertex. Paths in the chart may diverge, but the process of looking up substrings in the dictionary is one process up to the point of divergence.

The principal advantage of this data structure for a dictionary is that it minimizes the cost of referring different possible analyses of the same word to the dictionary in cases where the differences occur mainly at the end. The algorithm for looking words up also combines with the string-rewriting strategy I have proposed in a happy manner. The organization also allows new words to be added to the dictionary in a straightforward manner without disturbing the existing structure – nothing more than a new link and a single new node at the bottom of the tree is ever required. A simple recursive strategy will restore the dictionary to the form of a simple alphabetical list. The method of

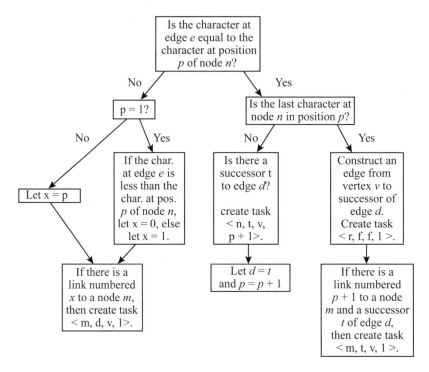

constructing a tree of this kind from an alphabetical list that I have described was designed to make the structure clear and not as an algorithm for incorporation in a computer program. However, algorithms do exist, which are beyond the scope of this paper, for performing this operation simply and efficiently. But the principal advantages of doing morphological analysis in this way have still to be stated.

The use of wait lists makes it possible, as I have already remarked, to relax any restrictions there might otherwise have been on the order in which tasks awaiting execution are selected. If processing is allowed to continue, the same results are guaranteed to emerge. What this means is that there can be complete freedom in designing strategies that will increase the probability of reaching a satisfactory solution early in which case the option of abandoning the remaining tasks is open. For example, dictionary tasks might always be given priority over morphographemic rewriting tasks on the principle that a lexical item identified in the text in its standard dictionary form is likely to have been correctly identified, especially if it occurs between non-alphabetic characters. Tasks operating on parts of the chart further to the right might be given priority over those further to the left simply because they are nearer to reaching a conclusion. It would even be possible to augment the grammar in such a way as to allow individual rules to give an explicit priority to the tasks they create. I do not want to urge any one of these policies here, but merely to stress that the basic algorithm leaves the field entirely open.

Perhaps more important is the fact that other tasks, unconnected with morphological analysis, can be interleaved freely between those that have been mentioned. The chart was originally designed for use in syntactic analysis (Kay 1967) and recent work suggests that syntactic analysis can profitably be performed as a set of independent, self-synchronizing tasks as suggested here. If these tasks are intermixed with those required for morphological analysis, the range of possibilities for driving towards a likely solution while foreclosing none of the possibilities allowed by the grammar is greatly extended. What I am proposing is, in the large, obvious: do first what is likely to lead earliest to a successful conclusion and put off other things until later. The particular organization I have suggested is attractive because it seems likely to lead to this goal without any attendant increase in programming complexity. Indeed, these principles are likely to make for greater perspicuity of the resulting program.

Publications referenced
Kay 1967.

17

Syntactic Processing and Functional Sentence Perspective

This paper contains some ideas that have occurred to me in the course of some preliminary work on the notion of reversible grammar. In order to make it possible to generate and analyze sentences with the same grammar, represented in the same way, I was led to consider restrictions on the expressive power of the formalism that would be acceptable only if the structures of sentences contained more information than American linguists have usually been prepared to admit. I hope to convey to you some of my surprise and delight in finding that certain linguists of the Prague school argue for the representation of this same information on altogether different grounds.

17.1 Reversible Grammars

For me, a grammar is not so much a set of well-formedness conditions on strings of words as a relation between strings of words (sentences) and structures. Usually it is constructive in the sense that there is a device that interprets it to convert either structures into sentences (a *generator*) or sentences into structures (a *parser*). A grammar for which both a generator and a parser can be found is what I call *reversible* and, of course, what I am interested in is not so much particular reversible grammars as a formalism which guarantees reversibility for any grammar that adheres to it. Context-free grammars are clearly reversible in this sense and transformational grammars are clearly not. Augmented Transition Networks (ATNs) are reversible provided some quite reasonable restrictions are placed on the operations that can be performed on registers. This is not to say that it is a trivial matter to obtain a generator from an arbitrary ATN grammar.

It goes without saying that the composition of a generator and a parser interpreting the same reversible grammar on the same sentence or structure does not, in general, perform the identity transformation. Frequently, sentences are ambiguous and structures often correspond to sets of more than one grammatical paraphrase. Parsing followed by generation of each member of the resulting set of structures will therefore yield the grammatical paraphrases of the original under all grammatical interpretations.

The practical advantages of a reversible grammar are obvious. A program that engages in any kind of conversation must both parse and generate and it would be economical to base both processes on the same grammar. But, to me, the theoretical appeal is stronger. It is plausible that we have something in our heads that fills the function I am ascribing to grammar, though I am not insensitive to the claims of those who deny this. But it is altogether implausible that we have two such things, one for parsing and one for generation, essentially unrelated to one another.

A *left-to-right generator* is one that deposits words into the output string one after another, in left-to-right sequence. A *left-to-right parser* is one that examines the words of the input string one after another, from left to right. A left-to-right reversible grammar is one for which there is a left-to-right generator and a left-to-right parser. Once again, it is clear that context-free grammars, in the usual notation, meet the requirements. ATN grammars probably do not. They certainly do not if we exclude the possibility of entirely reworking the grammar and presenting it in an entirely new form to the generator. The kind of grammar I have in mind would require no such reworking. Intuitively, the notion is a simple one. It is very like an ATN in that it analyses sentences by moving through a network, examining the input string at each transition and, if the current symbol meets the conditions specified for the transition, assigning it to a register. The generator would also move through the network, making exactly the same transitions, but depositing the contents of registers into the string at each step.

17.2   The Processor

Generators and parsers for the kind of reversible grammar I have in mind could be implemented in a great variety of ways. One of the simplest I know would be to use a version of the General Syntactic Processor (GSP). GSP contains:

1. a *grammar* in the form of a transition network, that is, a directed graph in which the permissible transitions between *states* are represented by *arcs*, each labeled with a more or less complicated set of *actions* which determine the applicability of the arc and cause side effects, such as the assignment of values to registers,

2. an *agenda* of *tasks* to be carried out,

3. a *chart* , that is, a directed graph consisting of vertices and edges which represents the sentence being analyzed or generated together with component parts – phrases, intermediate derivations, or whatever – which, together with the agenda, completely encapsulates the state of the entire processor at any given point in its operation,

4. a set of *scheduling* rules whose job is to determine the order in which the tasks on the agenda will be carried out, and

5. the interpreter itself.

Edges in the chart are either *complete* or *incomplete* . Complete edges represent completely specified words or phrases and, if there is a path through the chart from one edge to another, it is because the first precedes the second in temporal, or left-to-right, sequence. If there is no path from one to another, then they belong to alternative hypotheses about the structure of the sentence. So, the sentence "they are flying planes" has, let us say, two analyses, each consisting of a noun phrase followed by a verb phrase. But there is no path between the phrases in one analysis and those in the other. The verb phrase in one analysis consists of the verb "are" followed by the noun phrase "flying planes", which are therefore adjacent on the same path, but there is no path from either of them to the verb phrase they make up because this is an alternative analysis of the same set of words.

An incomplete edge represents part of a phrase together with an indication of what would have to be added to complete it. For example, an incomplete noun phrase might include the string "the big black" plus an indication that a following noun, possibly preceded by some more adjectives, would complete it. A special kind of incomplete edge is an *empty edge* . Empty edges are successors of themselves. In other words, they are always incident from and to the same vertex, reflecting the fact that they represent no part of the sentence, but merely the potential for finding some structural component. The specification of how an incomplete edge can be completed takes the form of one or more arcs in the grammar, each paired with a direction – *left* or *right*. If the direction is right, then completion can be achieved by following sequences of arcs incident *from* the given state; if it is left, then arcs incident *to* the state must be followed.

The interpreter uses the scheduling rules to choose an item on the agenda which it then carries out. If all the tasks that were ever put on the agenda in the course of generation or analysis were carried out in an arbitrary order, then all results that the grammar allowed would be obtained sooner or later. The scheduling rules formalize strategies of one kind and another. They are presumably designed so as to shorten the time required to reach a result which is, in some sense, acceptable, at which time the remaining entries on the agenda can simply be abandoned.

The typical task is an attempt to apply an arc from the grammar to an edge in the chart. If the arc applies successfully, new material will be added to the chart. In generation, the new material typically consists of one or two new edges constituting a sequence with the same end points as those of the initial edge. Usually, no more than one of the newly introduced edges will be incomplete. Thus, there might be a task in which an arc applied to the noun-phrase edge representing "big black dog" and which resulted in the complete article "the" and the incomplete noun phrase "big black dog". In parsing, the task specifies one or two edges, one of which is incomplete. The idea is to attempt to take the complete edge at least one step nearer to completion by incorporating the other edge. If only one edge is specified, then the new edge will have the same end points as the original, but will presumably be differently labeled.

Within this version of GSP, top-to-bottom, left-to-right parsing, in the manner of an ATN parser, proceeds broadly as follows:

1. Whenever, as the result of introducing a new edge into the chart, a new sequence consisting of an incomplete edge followed by a complete one comes into existence, put a new task on the agenda for each of the "category" arcs named on the incomplete edge. When one of these tasks is executed, the arc will be applied to the complete edge giving rise, if successful, to a new edge, complete or incomplete.

2. Whenever a new incomplete edge is introduced that names a "Pop" or "Jump" arc, create tasks that will cause these to be carried out.

3. Place an empty sentence edge before the first word of the sentence.

The process starts with step 3, which immediately causes a sequence of instances of steps 1 and 2.

An incomplete edge represents a stack frame in the ATN processor. It is labeled with a set of registers and it spans a portion of the chart representing the part of the string so far analyzed. "Category" arcs are applied to an incomplete edge and a complete edge immediately to its right. If successful, the result is a new incomplete edge. "Pop" arcs produce a complete edge, in exchange for an incomplete one. "Jump" arcs produce an incomplete edge in exchange for an incomplete edge, the differences being in the arcs that specify how to proceed towards completion, and possibly in the label.

It turns out that the mechanism of recursive calls that "Push" and "Pop" arcs provide for is embraced by the devices already described. Suppose that sentences are to be analyzed as consisting of a noun phrase followed by a verb phrase and that a noun phrase, say "the big black dog" has somehow been recognized at the beginning of the sentence. This means that there will be a complete edge representing this noun phrase and an incomplete sentence edge which has the same end points with an arc specifying that a verb phrase with a singular, third-person verb, is to follow. Since the grammar contains a subnetwork giving the structure of verb phrases, an empty edge labeled with the category "verb phrase" is introduced following that incomplete sentence provided there is not one already there. In due course, this will presumably cause a complete verb phrase to appear. The general principle is this: whenever an incomplete edge specifies a "category" arc for which there is a corresponding subnetwork, an empty edge is created following that one for each of the initial arcs in the subnetwork in the hope that this will lead to the creation of a new complete edge that the "category" arc can be successfully applied to.

17.3   The Use of Registers

The principal problem with this simple plan, when applied to reversible grammars, is that the registers cannot be guaranteed to have the necessary contents at the time required. One of the strengths of the ATN formalism is that it allows the parser to "change its mind". The canonical example is the passive construction. The first verb phrase in the sentence is assigned to the subject register. But when a passive verb – part of the verb "be" and a transitive past participle – has been encountered, the contents of the subject register are simply transferred to the object register. If a "by" phrase follows, its object will later go into the subject register. In this way, a great deal of backing up is avoided.

In generating a passive sentence, it is clear that the first step cannot be to deposit the contents of the subject register in the first position. An alternative might be to decide which register to use in filling the first position by examining a "voice" register, using the object instead of the subject register if its value is "passive". But this would require us to assign a value to the voice register in parsing before the relevant evidence is in. It would work only if the contents of the voice register were changed at the same time as the passive verb was recognized and the contents of the subject register were moved to the object register. It could indeed be made to work, but the solution is unsatisfactory because it does not reflect any general principle that carries over to other cases. More important, it violates a principle that must be regarded as fundamental for the achievement of reversibility in general, namely that each elementary operation that an arc in the grammar can specify must have two systematically related interpretations, for use in generation and parsing respectively.

Another solution would be to assign the first noun phrase to a neutral register when it is encountered in parsing, and only to copy it into the subject or object registers when it was finally established which one it belonged in. This neutral register would have to be reflected directly in the structure assigned to the sentence because it would be from there that the first noun phrase in the sentence would have to be taken by the generator. One advantage of this scheme is that a passive marker would no longer be required in the structure of passive sentences. Instead, the voice of a sentence would be determined by the generator on the basis of which register – subject or object – had the same contents as the special neutral register. The general principle behind this strategy is that the contents of a register are never changed in the course of either generation or parsing. This is the solution I advocate.

A name is needed for the neutral register, and *topic* , or *theme* , suggest themselves immediately. But consider the case of cleft sentences like "It was Brutus that killed Caesar" and "It was Caesar that Brutus killed" and assume, for the sake of the argument, that these are to be handled as main clauses and not by the relative-clause mechanism. Once again the underlying grammatical function of the first phrase is not known when the parser first encounters it. The problem can be solved by the same device, but of all the names one might choose for the neutral register, "topic" is least appropriate in this instance. Something like *focus* or *comment* would be more to the point. What, then, of datives? Consider "He gave Fido a bone" and "He gave Fido to Mary". The problem here is the noun phrase following the verb. In neither case can we argue that it is either the topic or the focus of the sentence.

17.4   Functional Sentence Perspective

The most satisfying solution to these problems is to be found in the work of the Prague school of linguists, particularly Mathesius, Firbas, Danes, and Sgall. The basic notion is that of the *Functional Sentence Perspective* according to which topic and focus are two regions in the scale of *communicative dynamism* along which each of the major constituents of a sentence are ordered. In the unmarked case each succeeding constituent in the surface string has a higher degree of communicative dynamism. The point on the scale at which one passes from topic to focus may or may not be marked. In speech, special stress can be used to mark any element as the focus; in writing, several devices like clefting fill the same role.

Communicative dynamism correlates with a number of other notions that are more familiar in this part of the world. Elements that are low on this scale are the ones that are more *contextually bound*, which is to say that they involve presuppositions about the preceding text. In "It was Brutus that killed Caesar", "that killed Caesar" is the topic and it clearly involves the presupposition that someone killed Caesar. In an unmarked sentence, like "Brutus killed Caesar", it is not clear whether the dividing line between topic and comment falls before or after the verb; there are nevertheless three degrees of communicative dynamism involved.

According to this view, the difference between "He gave Fido to Mary" and "He gave Mary Fido" is not in what is topic and what is focus but simply in the positions that "Mary" and "Fido" occupy on the scale of communicative dynamism. Consider the sentences:

1. John did all the work, but they gave the reward to Bill.
2. John did all the work, but they gave Bill the reward.
3. They were so impressed with the work that they gave Bill a reward.
4. They were so impressed with the work that they gave a reward to Bill.

I claim that (2) and (4) are less natural than (1) and (3) when read with even intonation. Sentence (5), with underlining for stress, is, of course, quite natural, and (6) is questionable.

5. John did all the work, but they gave <u>Bill</u> the reward.
6. John did all the work, but they gave a <u>reward</u> to Bill.

The claim is simply that the last item carries the greatest communicative load, represents the most novel component of the sentence.

This is consistent with the observation that dative movement is at best awkward when the direct object is a pronoun, as in

7. I gave him it.

and it becomes more awkward when the indirect object is more ponderous, as in

8. I gave the man you said you had seen it.

In fact, it is consistent with the observation that ponderous constituents tend to be deferred, using such devices as extraposition. It is in the nature of pronouns that they are contextually bound, and the complexity of large constituents presumably comes directly from the fact that they tend to convey new information.

What this suggests is a formalism in which the structure of a phrase is a list of attributes named for grammatical functions, whose values are words or other phrases. They are ordered so as to show their positions on the scale of communicative dynamism and there is provision for a marker to be introduced into the list explicitly separating the topic from the focus. Considering only the sentence level, and simplifying greatly, this would give examples like the following, using "/" as the marker:

[Subject:John Verb:gave Dir-obj:(the candy) Indir-obj:Mary] ⇒
"John gave the candy to Mary"
[Indir-obj:Mary Verb:gave Dir-obj:(the candy) Subject:John] ⇒
"Mary was given the candy by John"
[Verb:gave Dir-obj:(the candy) Indir-obj:Mary / Subject:John] ⇒
"It was John that gave Mary the candy" or "<u>John</u> gave Mary the candy"
[Subject:John Verb:gave Dir-obj:(the candy) / Indir-obj:Mary] ⇒
"It was Mary that John gave the candy to"

[Dir-obj:(the candy) Subject:John Verb:gave Indir-obj:Mary] $\Rightarrow$
"What John did with the candy was give it to Mary"

The implications for reversible syntactic processing seem to be as follows: The familiar set of registers, named for the most part for the names of grammatical functions, are supplemented by three others called *topic* , *focus* and, say, *marker*. *Marker* will have a value only when the sentence is marked in the sense I have been using. *Topic* and *focus* will contain ordered lists of elements. The structure of a passive sentence, for example, will be recognizable by the fact that it is unmarked and has a patient (dative, or whatever) as the first item on its topic list. The parser will place the first noun phrase in a "standard" sentence on this list and only copy it into some other register later. The generator will unload the first item into the string and decide later what form of verb to produce.

The ill-formedness of the ideas I have tried to present here is clear for all to see. I have so far acquired only the most tenuous grasp of what the Czech linguists are doing, and while I should publicly thank Petr Sgall for his patience in explaining it to me, it is only right that I should also apologise for the egregious errors I have doubtless been guilty of. But whatever errors of detail there may be, one important point will, I hope, remain. The notions of topic and focus are clearly well motivated in theoretical linguistics, and the richer notion of functional sentence perspective probably is also. I have been led to these same notions for purely technical reasons arising out of my desire to build a reversible syntactic processor.

Publications referenced
Firbas 1964; Kaplan 1973; Mathesius 1929.

## 18

Overview of Computer Aids in Translation

Abstract

There are many ways in which computers could and probably should be applied to the problems of language translation, but fully automatic machine translation is not one of them. I shall explain why this is so and describe some of the recent advances in computer technology and how they could be put at the disposal of translators to multiply their effectiveness and enhance the quality of their working lives. Translators in different environments have different needs, and well-designed tools must be capable of adapting to different requirements and styles of work. Their functions should not be limited to the actual activity of translation.

I am a computer person. I design algorithms, and I want to tell you about what goes on inside machines. The reason it is important to do so is precisely because translation is the sort of creative, non-mechanical, essentially human, thing we have been talking about this morning. It is precisely because I believe this that I think machines have a very important role to play. I do not want to argue as one well might, that a potter who makes fine pottery ought not to use an electric kiln because pottery is an art, an essentially human thing, and you can't make a good pot unless you put the logs into the fire yourself. I am reminded constantly of how difficult it is to handle these linguistic problems. I was in the London underground a few weeks ago, and I found that in the short time since I had been there they have posted a new regulation everywhere. It says "dogs must be carried," and I hadn't brought mine with me. We have heard how difficult translation can be and anyone who doubts it has not only not tried to translate, he probably hasn't tried to write anything in his own language. To translate one's own thoughts into a written form which can be read and easily understood is surely the same kind of task.

There are different kinds of translations and different levels of difficulty. If we try to solve the problem in a general sense, if we try to provide a device we technologists think the translator should use, we are almost sure to be wrong about what we produce. If somebody says you should use this for your job because it will improve your specific working conditions, then necessarily a large number of other translators will be doing something which is slightly different and they will have every right to take exception to that solution and reject it.

Many problems arise with translation. There may not be enough people to do them.

One of the problems is that the consumers of the translations are often far from the people that produce them. The producers make one set of decisions about what shall be translated and the consumers have another set of criteria for what they need. Thus, the translation done may be too much of the wrong things and too little of the right. You may not be able to get translation done fast enough. If you are in Canada and the equivalent of the Congressional Record must be produced by tomorrow morning, getting it that fast is difficult. If you are flying from the east to the west of Canada, the weather report that tells you about the inclement conditions in Vancouver must be translated into the language of the pilot. You may not be able to get the translations done cheaply enough. We have all been told often enough and we will be told again before we leave that translators aren't paid enough. I believe that they are not; but they may be too expensive for what we have in mind. And you may not be able to get your translations done well enough. Here again, if you go to a country like Canada or Finland, laws must be translated into two languages. The rules of the game are such that a lawyer can use either text in pleading his case, whichever one he thinks he will be able to argue most favorably for his client. Under those conditions, one is prepared to pay rather highly for a very good translation, since the legal system depends in a large sense on how well it is done. So we must stress these different needs, depending on what our background is and what the job is that we have to do.

I take it to be the case that one of the most important problems of the intelligence community is getting translations done when they need them and not when they don't need them. A second consideration is getting them done cheaply enough. If you examine the European economic community, the priorities are quite different. Their job is to get the translations done whenever they need to be done and the question of the quality of the translations is not very important. You see, the reason for translating in the European economic community is not because somebody is going to read it, but because a requisition, written in Danish for a dozen pencils, will slight the importance of the other four languages unless it is also translated into those languages before it is filed. So the important thing is to have the legal equivalent of a translation, perhaps the same length as the original, etc.

The sorts of problems that we face are different in each case and there are many dimensions in which they differ. I want to concentrate on a particular characteristic here. The curve for this characteristic extends on the right from the Bar Hillel concept of fully automatic high quality machine translation (where everything is automated) and it extends on the extreme left (which for some reason or other I don't think Bar Hillel invented a suitable term for) to what I have called HTLGI which stands for Human Translation Like God Intended. Now the main point that I want to bring out is that among all the problems in the world to which people have applied computing, translation has been treated in a completely unique way. Problems in physics, weather control, statistics, bank accounts, payrolls, and insurance have been handled quite differently from the way translation has been handled. As we progress along a line from the point where the human does everything to the point where the machine does everything, it is clear that the problems we have to solve become not only more difficult but also invade what is essentially a human creative domain. What has our response been? It has been to ignore almost entirely the things that people have known how to do for quite a long time and to concentrate entirely on something which we knew we couldn't do in the first place. It's a really quite remarkable phase of human history, and it is not surprising that we hear people say, "You can't automate this job, isn't it ridiculous. Can't you see what you are doing? Why don't you people wake up?" We have heard it this morning in somewhat more gentlemanly terms. However, there are many tasks along the line that can accomplish useful things. The reason for doing so is precisely because translation needs very specialized, able, artistic people. But nevertheless, it does contain a number of tasks which are frankly burdensome and routine. Therefore, we must try and separate the routine tasks from the rest so that they can be handled in machines using technology we know how to use and whose development does not require great research effort. The idea of putting a computer at the disposal of every translator is, I agree, absolutely fantastic. It's just about as ridiculous as the idea of providing every one of them with an electric typewriter, which we would clearly never consider doing. Because everybody knows that a translator couldn't afford an electric typewriter; and in order to get a computer terminal or even a complete computer for that matter, he would have to spend very nearly as much as on an electric typewriter. So to this extent, what I am saying may appear a little unreal. I am talking to the small segment of translators for whom the notion of purchasing their own electric typewriter is at least a consideration.

I don't think the technology has reached the point at which linking all translators to a monster computer in Washington is the right way to go. The assertion that networking has not reached the point at which a few hundred computers could be tied together in a network is probably wrong. I think it is well within the bounds of possibility. To give you an example that applies in Europe: In many countries it is a legal requirement that any television set sold should contain particular circuitry. It will not be of use to most people this year or next year, but the circuitry must be there to enable you to connect the television set not only to an antenna but also to your telephone. In London today, if your TV includes this feature, you can dial a number, tune your television set to a particular channel which is not showing other things, and have displayed on the screen one of ten sets of information, such as the weather, the football results, the stock market, etc. You press a button to choose which of the ten sets you want. Typically you will be given another choice of subsets of information from which you may select one by pressing the button. In this way you work down a tree until you find yourself looking at stock prices for a particular kind of commodity or whatever it is you happen to be interested in. This system contains all the components that are needed for a network system. The display you get on your particular TV is not necessarily the same that anybody else is getting on theirs. It uses exactly the same kind of technology as is used in the ARPA network and is potentially available to everybody who buys a television set in England. There is no reason why this same technology should not link together a device costing (approximately) the same amount as an electric typewriter and which you can sit on the kitchen table which is small enough so that you can move it when you want to eat.

Why do such devices cost less today? Is it really true that the cost of such useful things is going down in this field unlike anywhere else? Usually when somebody tells us that a cost is going down, there is some sort of hidden trick – there is a different way of accounting being introduced or some other explanation. Well, there are several good reasons. One is that computers are now produced in larger numbers. And, indeed, if you will join us in purchasing them, we might be able to give you a discount price and make them at even less cost. They are being produced by a technique similar to photography. You can now make a circuit – and I am simplifying this only a little bit – by taking a photograph of the design for that circuit, developing the photograph in a certain way, and then using that developed photograph to reproduce the circuit. I have simplified somewhat, but this photographic process exists, though it requires very carefully designed optics which are quite expensive. It costs several thousand dollars to take one of these photographs and to get one iteration of that circuit. But if you are going to make several thousand components that contain the circuit then the expensive job needs to be done only once and the rest is mass production. Now you can buy the electronic part of a computer for a price which actually is related to little more than what it costs to ship from one place to another, pay the managing director, etc. Elements of this sort dominate the cost of the item. The materials and production cost is lost in the noise, as we say. This is central to the computer and the rest is composed of elements like the television tube.

Let's talk for a moment about the television tube. It has a device at the back which shoots electrons at a screen and most terminals on the market today have specially wired equipment which produces characters. So all you need is to select which character you want to display and where on the screen you want it placed. Now an alternative way is to substitute for this special wiring, a memory section computer in which you store a series of digits having one of two possible states representing black or white areas on the screen in the form of the character you wish displayed. This section of memory is scanned at the same rate as the surface of the tube. Any design from this part of memory is displayed on the tube. Why, you may ask, wasn't this simple solution to the problem used before? Why was specially wired hardware constructed for the tube? The answer is that ways of producing this circuitry cheaply were not available before. The notion of setting aside several thousand words of memory just for the purpose of producing a display was regarded as very prodigal. Now it has become not only a feasible thing to do, but probably the cheapest way to achieve the result. The point I am making is we have learned how to gain tremendous power in the computer by taking away something we had before and by doing things in what would have been originally the most obvious way though too expensive at the time. Now the most obvious way has also become the cheapest. For this reason, it's possible in the near future, to put into the home of the translator not only a terminal but a complete computer which will display on the screen absolutely any characters, so that if some part of what he is producing should be in boldface, it will appear in boldface not only in the printed copy but on the screen. Or it will be in italics or Cyrillic or Greek or whatever. Furthermore, it will be cheaper than with the telegram letters that look as though they come from a deity who set computing aside from the rest of the world.

The most important thing to concern ourselves with is not a matter of cost but rather one of insuring that any device put in translators' homes has the functions the translator really needs. And here we are up against an important problem that pervades all of computing. The hardware, i.e., the chips, the screens, etc. have been developing at an immense rate. The kind of good taste that is required to write the programs by which these devices will give people the service they need in the way that they want it has not developed at anything like the same rate. For example, it is typically the case that when you sit down at one of these devices the first line you type appears at the top of the screen, the next line appears immediately under it, and so on until you reach the bottom of the screen. In which case the line at the top of the screen disappears being replaced by the one immediately below and everything is pushed up, the new lines appearing at the bottom. What the designers of this method have succeeded in doing is to make an extremely flexible device with cathode ray display, behave just like an inflexible typewriter. And now since everyone for a long time printed only in upper case, almost everything that you run across now has, by dint of considerable expertise and ingenuity, been reduced to the level of a typewriter. One of the things that we must do is to influence, in a way that I cannot entirely describe, the design of these devices so that they are not reduced to some other device that we don't need to replace. If it does exactly what we had before then the replacement is presumably considerably less effective.

One of the things a translator must be able to do is to point at what he is working on. Pointing is something that comes to us very early and it's a very natural way to indicate things. Anybody who has used a text editor can appreciate, in an intellectual sense, the fact that it is nice not to have to retype everything just because you change a word. But finding your way around in computer stored text simply takes more effort than it ought to. You have to tell the machine (in a language which it thought up) where the word is that you want to change. You can see it there, you can point to it, but the confounded machine has to be told in a sort of perverse kind of way how to get itself to that position before you can change it. Now we have known for a long time how to make devices that enable you to point. So we must require that technology produce terminals and computers that enable us to point by simply pointing to them and not by describing the place as though we were blind. As example of an interesting data point, my wife who is a travel agent works in an office that had a set of terminals installed which are supposed to be the latest thing for the travel business. They enable you to rent Hertz cars in Hawaii, to get hotels in Bora Bora, to change from flights on United Airlines to flights on American Airlines going by way of Singapore instead of Paris, etc. In order to do this, you must type a set of instructions to the machine which would be "Greek" to anyone. In this system you do not call London, London; you do not call San Francisco, San Francisco; you do not call Los Angeles, Los Angeles; and obviously you call Montreal by a three letter code which, as you would expect, being Montreal, begins with a Y.

Codes and directions in impossible semi-mathematical-looking languages are not a necessary part of computing. They arise from the fact that the algorithm designers spend most of their time worrying about how we look this word up, how we manage to insert a word in the middle of this text without having to move everything around a lot, how we make it efficient, and if somebody wants to find a particular string in a text, how are we going to find it without using too much time. These are important questions and they are extremely challenging. They have a lot of interesting intellectual content, but they have little to do with the face the system presents to the human user. They say absolutely nothing about how easy it will be for him to remember what it is he must do in order to cause these things to happen. The computer scientists, until recently and for that matter continuing today, have had no encouragement to think in these terms. So when you get a text editor or a translation system to handle your own private glossary, you may find you must learn a set of codes which actually aren't necessary unless you have been careful and have insisted on getting only what you require. It seems to me that translators can be helped in many different ways but the first thing to be done is to provide text editing. Secondly, we must provide a method of maintaining one's own personal glossary, the famous shoeboxes, only now it is inside the machine. Thirdly, we must establish a method of exchanging the contents of the shoeboxes with other colleagues. This is a service that a set of machines on a network can reasonably provide. I am not talking about putting something in a big central dictionary where there must be a person who verifies that everything is correct, that it meets government specifications, and that it's in the correct fonts, etc. I am talking about a simple way to distribute among colleagues messages of the form – has anyone handled a problem like this before; or a method for disseminating among colleagues things which they feel fairly sure will be of general utility such as making the shoeboxes available to a large community.

Certain things are cheap and easy to have like a computer terminal with display. More expensive is a device which will actually produce nice camera-ready copy from the translation you produce or from a text you are editing. But there is no reason why such a device should be on the kitchen table. Indeed, there is no reason why the translator, having finished, should not direct the printing to be done at the place where it is needed via a network system. If you have 500 translators in the field, there is no reason why you should have 500 printing stations and then wait for the U.S. mail. It would be quicker, simpler, and far more efficient if the translator simply sent over the network the electronic version of what he had produced. The network can consist of nothing more than the telephone lines. It could then be printed on a high-quality device of which you need only one and which can, therefore, be in a central place.

The bottom line is that what stands between us and automating parts of translation that need to be automated is not technological. The technological problems have in very large measure been solved. What is needed is an infusion of good taste which can come only through users accepting the fact that you can expect your requirements to be fulfilled. There is no reason why you should use something that is difficult to use, that requires special codes, that enable things to be deleted when they should have been preserved, that enables you to make mistakes which you didn't intend, and that makes you nervous to use because you might blow a fuse in Washington if you hit the wrong button.

19

The Proper Place of Men and Machines in Language Translation

Abstract

The only way in which the power of computers has been brought to bear on the problem of language translation is machine translation, that is, the automation of the entire process. Machine translation is an excellent research vehicle but stands no chance of filling actual needs for translation which are growing at a great rate. In the quarter century during which work on machine translation has been going on, there has been considerable progress in relevant areas of computer science. However, advances in linguistics, important though they may have been, have not touched the core of this problem. The proper thing to do is therefore to adopt the kinds of solution that have proved successful in other domains, namely to develop cooperative man-machine systems. This paper proposes a *translator's amanuensis*, incorporating into a word processor some simple facilities peculiar to translation. Gradual enhancements of such a system could eventually lead to the original goal of machine translation.

The world is badly in need of translators. Almost nobody denies this. The number of pairs of languages between which translations must be made and the number and types of documents involved is constantly increasing. There is not enough money to invest the profession with the status that would attract more people to it and that it certainly deserves. But we are fortunate to be children of the age of computers and it is to them that we naturally turn. A computer is a device that can be used to magnify human productivity. Properly used, it does not dehumanize by imposing its own Orwellian stamp on the products of the human spirit and the dignity of human labor but, by taking over what is mechanical and routine, it frees human beings for what is essentially human. Translation is a fine and exacting art, but there is much about it that is mechanical and routine and, if this were given over to a machine, the productivity of the translator would not only be magnified but his work would become more rewarding, more exciting, more human. It is altogether right that we should look to the computer. Indeed, if the need for translation is as great as it is said to be, the computer is our only hope.

When the computer is improperly used, its effects are, of course, quite different. This happens when the attempt is made to mechanize the non-mechanical or something whose mechanistic substructure science has not yet been revealed. In other words, it happens when we attempt to use computers to do something we do not really understand. History provides no better example of the improper use of computers than machine translation. Of the impressive list of exploits that computer scientists and computational linguists have engaged in over the past twenty years, the only one that has ever succeeded in firing the imagination of translators and their employers has been machine translation. But here the success of machine translation ends. It fires the imagination but it does not, except under very special circumstances, produce useful results.

The late Bar Hillel, a most vociferous critic of machine translation, characterized the ideal towards which inventors in this field strive as *Fully Automatic High-Quality Translation (FAHQT)*. The machine would be one which, without human intervention except perhaps at the input keyboard, could render a more or less arbitrary text in one language into a text of equal quality in another. It is surely a worthy ideal and one which has attracted a regrettably small number of linguists and computer scientists. Even if it is never achieved, it provides an incomparable matrix in which to study the workings of human language. Whether it is achieved or not, other useful, if more modest, inventions may well emerge as by-products of the attack on FAHQT provided only that the work is conducted in a healthy intellectual environment. The trouble is that no such environment exists today.

To understand language is to understand how it *works*. Enlightening remarks about it will therefore often be best expressed in terms of *processes*. I take this to mean that important contributions to linguistics are likely to be more and more in the spirit of Artificial Intelligence. A manifesto for this point of view is out of place here. What is to the point is that translation embraces every facet of language while providing a task whose criteria of success, for all their problems, are remarkably well defined. In science in general, and artificial intelligence in particular, the proper rôle of computers is quite different from any they can play in engineering or any enterprise directed towards the fulfillment of immediate and practical needs. Here they are properly applied to what is not understood with the expectancy that, as much by their frequent and resounding failures as by anything else, they will illuminate the boundaries of our ignorance. Engineering pays heavily for the very failures that science can best profit from.

The need for translated texts will not be filled by a program of research that devotes all of its resources to a distant ideal, and linguists and computer experts will be denied the proper rewards of their labors if they must promise to reach the ideal by some specific time. A healthy climate for FAHQT will be one in which a variety of different though related goals are being pursued with equal vigor for the intellectual and practical benefits that they may bring.

There was a long period – for all I know, it is not yet over – in which the following comedy was acted out nightly in the bowels of an American government office with the aim of rendering foreign texts into English. Passages of innocent prose on which it was desired to effect this delicate and complex operation were subjected to a process of vivisection at the hands of an uncomprehending electronic monster that transformed them into stammering streams of verbal wreckage. These were then placed into only slightly more gentle hands for repair. But the damage had been done. Simple tools that would have done so much to make the repair work easier and more effective were not to be had presumably because of the voracious appetite of the monster, which left no resources for anything else. In fact, such remedies as could be brought to the tortured remains of these texts were administered with colored pencils on paper and the final copy was produced by the action of human fingers on the keys of a typewriter. In short, one step was singled out of a fairly long and complex process at which to perpetrate automation. The step chosen was by far the least well understood and quite obviously the least apt for this kind of treatment.

Government and bureaucracy may be imbued with a sad fatalism that forces it to look to the future as destined to repeat the follies of the past, but we can surely take a moment to wonder at the follies of the past and nostalgically to muse about what a kinder and more rational world would be like.

The case against machine translation as a solution to practical problems is overwhelming and has been made many times. I do not propose to repeat it in any detail here. It will, however, be worth a few words to make a *prima facie* case for the implausibility of practical machine translation if only so that the contrast with realistic approaches to the problem will be more striking. I will go on to outline what some of these might be. I shall make some specific proposals, but I should like it to be clearly understood that I do not believe that they represent the only course to follow. They are intended only to illustrate my main point which is this: There is a great deal that computer scientists and linguists could contribute to the practical problem of producing translations, but, in their own interests as well as those of their customers, they should never be asked to provide an engineering solution to a problem that they only dimly understand. By doing only what can be done with absolute surety and reliability now and by going forward from there in short, carefully measured steps, very considerable gains can be virtually guaranteed to all concerned.

19.1 The *Prima Facie* Case Against Machine Translation

It is not difficult to convince oneself that fully automatic machine translation is no more a serious answer to any practical problem today than it ever was. But to do so responsibly and scientifically requires examination of a lot of evidence and the careful design and performance of a number of experiments. It is clearly pure irresponsibility to attempt to assess any particular translation system on the basis of intuitive reactions to a so-called *demonstration* in which one examines what the line printer delivers and listens to ingenious attempts to explain the tenuous relationship this bears to, say, English. But it is reasonable and easy to consider what *prima facie* case can be made just on the basis of the advertising. This section contains two related arguments against the plausibility of machine translation as an industrial enterprise, one from the point of view of linguistics and the other from that of computer science.

19.2 Machine Translation and Linguistics

Let us look for a moment at a particular problem – one of the prodigious set that the designer of any machine-translation system has to face. Almost any member of the set would serve my purpose, so I will take one of the oldest and most hackneyed, namely how to choose a translation for a pronoun. To state it in this way is, of course, already a gross simplification because no translator or translation system worth its salt chooses translations for pronouns or, for that matter, any other isolated words. But the simplification will take nothing from the very elementary point I want to make.

Consider the following pair of sentences:

- Since the dictionary is constructed on the basis of the text that is being processed, <u>it</u> need refer to only a small amount of context to resolve ambiguities.
- Since the dictionary is constructed by a native speaker of the language, <u>he</u> need refer to only a small amount of context to resolve ambiguities.

Suppose that these are both translations from some other Indo-European language so that, in all probability, the underlined *it* and *he* correspond to the same word in the original; in French, the word would be *il*, for example. Now, it is entirely possible that automatic translation systems could be found that would get the translations of both sentences right. But it is almost inconceivable that one could be found that would get them right for the right reasons or that it would systematically solve problems of this kind correctly. If such a system did exist, we could not expect to find its designer in a gathering of this kind because he would surely be a person of such saintly modesty and so retiring a nature as to prevent his ever making his results known to others. He would die in poverty and obscurity. A person with normal human weaknesses who had the key to this problem could confidently be expected to claim the crown that linguistics is eager to bestow on him. Pronominal reference is, after all, among the most vexing problems in linguistics. Much the same can be said of innumerable other problems on whose solution the success of machine translation turns. If any of them had in fact been solved, we should not have to purchase an expensive system to find out about it and commercial or proprietary interest would not long hide it from us.

We are forced to one of two conclusions. Either some essentially *ad hoc* solution to these difficulties has been found and built into the systems that are offered for sale, or these systems do not really solve the problems at all. *Ad hoc* solutions tend to be based on case-by-case analyses of what linguists call *surface* phenomena, essentially strings of words, and on real or imagined statistical properties of particular styles of writing and domains of discourse. In scientific and technical texts, for example, one runs less risk of error by translating the French pronouns *il* and *elle* as *it*, rather than *he* and *she*, especially in contexts like *il est possible que....* In *Il est convaincu que...*, on the other hand, *he* is a better bet. These facts are listed in the functional equivalent of a dictionary of *words in context* to which new entries are continually brought. The cash value of each new addition is slightly less than that of the one before as the contribution to the device as a whole slowly approaches its asymptote.

In fact, such little documentary evidence as the proprietors of past machine-translation systems have been prepared to release has typically pointed with evident pride to the great number of *ad hoc* devices that they contain and has made the incontestable point that any enhancement of the system in the future will require more and more and more of the same. I will come shortly to the question of what is wrong with engineering products that rest on *ad hoc* devices rather than sound theory.

19.3 Machine Translation and Computer Science

The *prima facie* case against operational machine translation from the linguistic point of view will be to the effect that there is unlikely to be adequate engineering where we know there is no adequate science. A parallel case can be made from the point of view of computer science, especially that part of it called *Artificial Intelligence* . To translate is to re-express in a second language what has been understood by reading a text. Any purported solution to the problem that does not involve understanding in some sense is, at best, *ad hoc* and therefore subject to the linguistic objections already alluded to. A large part of the field of artificial intelligence is given over to building models on the basis of which to attempt some explication of this notion of understanding but no serious worker in this field has ever claimed to be able to provide the theoretical support required by any practical enterprise, least of all one so embracing as language translation.

There are also some points about past performance that deserve to be made from the computer scientist's point of view. There is, for example, the question of programming style and technique. The designers of machine translation systems have been intensely concerned with a property of their programs they call *efficiency* . Here is how the argument goes: These systems would not be required at all if there were not large quantities of text to be translated so that if one program took only slightly more computer time than another, it could soon involve a great deal of extra cost when put into operation. This is the main justification for the fact that there has been little or no use of higher-level programming languages. The lower-level assembly languages that have been used give the programmer direct access to the most basic facilities in his machine so that they cannot be less powerful than higher-level languages. Given a program in a higher-level language, it is almost always possible to produce a translation into assembly language that requires less machine time to run. This is not to say that it will not be a difficult, error-prone, and time-consuming operation to do so. Against this obvious advantage of assembly languages must be set their equally obvious disadvantage, namely that they are arch-enemies of clarity and perspicuity. My claim will be that a program written in assembly language is much more likely to embody an *ad hoc* solution to a problem than one written in a higher-level language. This is only to be expected. Assembly languages give equal status to every detail in the specification of the program so that there is no way in which the overall plan that the program embodies can emerge. Consequently, a program that would seem simple in another language is almost guaranteed to look bewilderingly complex in assembly language. A program such as machine translation would require, one that would be complex by any imaginable standard, would be beyond imagination in assembly language. In programming, as in any kind of writing, the most complex ideas require the greatest clarity and skill for their exposition. But programming differs from everyday communication in that the languages available differ greatly in expressive power and the choice among them severely conditions the clarity that can be achieved. Every computer scientist is taught, but only comes truly to appreciate as a result of bitter experience, that programs are written for a human as well as a mechanical audience and the most important member of that audience is himself. A programmer who writes in assembly language is necessarily giving us less than his best at the highest possible price.

Efficiency, in computer programming, is itself a complex and subtle matter. It is true that it is affected by such issues as the language that a program is written in, but these effects are, at worst, linear. More realistically speaking, they are sublinear because a very large proportion of the time taken for any large program to run is accounted for by a very small proportion of the code. Standard practice, therefore, is to write a program in a language that displays its structure as clearly as possible and to rewrite carefully selected small portions of it in assembly language only when experience has clearly demonstrated that the effort involved in doing this would amply repay the effort.

Truly significant gains in efficiency invariably come from adjustments to the algorithm itself, that is, to the overall strategy that the program employs. Consider a simple example. The words of a text are to be looked up in a dictionary. There are a great many strategies that could be used, all of which would produce identical results for the same words and the same dictionary, but at very different cost in machine time. The dictionary could be searched from the top for each separate word in the text. Binary search, hashing, or one of the innumerable variants of these could be used. A method that has been popular with the designers of machine-translation systems is to sort the words of the text into alphabetical order so that a single pass through the resulting list and the dictionary locates all relevant entries. These are then sorted back into the order of the text.

Quite independently of the machine or the programming system used to implement them, these techniques can all be analyzed in terms of the way the time they take is related to the length of the text and the size of the dictionary. If there are m entries in the dictionary and n words in the text, if the dictionary is not ordered in any especially helpful way, and if almost all the words are in the dictionary, then the first method requires each of the n words in the text to be compared with about half the words in the dictionary so that the time involved will vary with both m and n; in other words, it will be proportional to mn. Putting the dictionary in order by frequency could conceivably improve things to the point where the average word is found in the first $log\ m$ entries, which would make the technique as efficient as binary search. A suitably chosen hashing scheme removes the effect of m altogether so that, at least from this point of view, this method is better than either of the others. The technique that requires sorting proceeds in three steps, two sorts and the comparison with the dictionary. The comparison with the dictionary is linear, but sorting n items takes on the order of $n\ log\ n$ steps by the best known methods, which means that the time taken by the comparison is not significant. This is a simple classic case where the considerations determining the best solution are well known. In reality, the choice is often difficult and text-book solutions are not available.

There is a branch of computer science called *analysis of algorithms* that is devoted to the assertions of this kind that can be made about computational methods. What is important about such assertions is that they characterize the cost of a technique *as a function of* the data it will be applied to. Differences in the functions that characterize competing techniques are altogether more significant than the purely linear differences that programming languages and coding practice can affect. If techniques *A, B,* and *C* all achieve the same results when applied to an input of size s and the time taken by A varies with s^2, B with s, and C with $\log s$, then C is best and A is worst and, unless s is very small, the implementation details are beside the point. If C takes 10 steps for a certain case, then B will take about 1000, and A, 1,000,000. When the differences are as great as these – and they often are – the cost of the individual steps is irrelevant. Any program that purports to translate natural text must clearly be orders of magnitude more complex than one that simply looks words up in a dictionary. It will always be susceptible of improvement, at least in a theoretical sense, not only in the quality of the results it delivers, but also in the efficiency of the algorithms it incorporates. To be continually improvable in this way, a program must be perspicuous and robust. It must be perspicuous so that there is never any doubt about the role that each of its parts plays in the overall structure and robust so that it can be changed in important ways without fear of damage. Perspicuity and robustness are clearly two sides of the same coin. They are the high ideals to which the art of programming is continually striving and which it never achieves.

19.4 The Statistical Defense

It is immediately clear why *ad hoc* solutions should be offensive to a scientist. His job is, in a sense, precisely to reveal as principled and orderly what had previously been *ad hoc*. But what we must attend to is whether these solutions should upset an engineer or someone whose primary concern is getting a job done and, if so, to what extent. Two arguments are commonly made for *ad hoc* solutions to the problems of machine translation. The first is a simple statistical claim that can be dismissed almost as easily as it can be stated. The second is what I shall refer to as the *sorcerer's apprentice* argument. The statistical argument rests on the fact that something can be complex and subtle without the complexities and subtleties being spread uniformly through it. Linguistics requires of its practitioners remarkable virtuosity in constructing examples of problems such as no existing or proposed computer system could possibly solve. But the claim is that we do not have to solve them so long as they do not crop up very often. We may not have an algorithm that will identify the antecedent of a pronoun whenever a human reader could but, if we can devise a method that will identify it most of the time, that will be good enough.

An algorithm that works most of the time is, in fact, of very little use unless there is some automatic way of deciding when it is and when it is not working. If it were able to draw a proofreader's attention to all the cases of pronominal reference that were in doubt so that these, and only these, would have to be examined by a human reader, and if a high proportion of the cases were known to be correctly handled, then the utility of the technique would be clear. But the statistical argument is usually stated in the weaker form.

Suppose that a good, reliable translation of a text is required and that a computer program is available that translates pronouns correctly 90 per cent of the time. If there were some way to tell which 10 per cent of the pronouns had been wrongly translated, it would be sufficient to examine these to verify the correctness of the translation (ignoring, for simplicity, other possible sources of error). But since this cannot be done,

100 per cent of the pronouns must be examined. To find a pronoun and check that it is correctly translated is expensive relative to making the correction. Therefore, it does not matter very much if the program is right 90, 99, 80, or 50 per cent of the time. The amount of work that it leaves for the repairman is essentially the same. Somebody may claim, however implausibly, that 10 per cent of pronouns occur in contexts where the translation is not crucial. This would be a useful thing to know just in case these were precisely the instances that the machine translated incorrectly but no such argument has been, or is likely to be, upheld.

The real situation is much worse because there is more to translation than pronouns. A great many decisions of essentially the same difficulty must be made in the course of translating a single sentence. If there is reason to expect each of them to be correct 90 per cent of the time, there need only be seven of them in a stretch of text to reduce the expectation of translating it correctly to below 50 per cent.

The moral is clear. The overall efficiency of a translation system, human or electronic, is directly related to its reliability. If it falls short of the acceptable standard, *to any degree whatsoever*, it might as well fail grossly because the burden it places on the proofreader will be very large, and not notably different in either case. The efficiency of a translation system, like any other, must be assessed over all its components, human and mechanical.

19.5   The Sorcerer's Apprentice Defense

The Sorcerer's Apprentice argument is to the effect that the kind of incomplete theory that linguists and computer scientists have been able to provide is often a worse base on which to build practical devices than no theory at all because the theory does not know when to stop. When a theory proposes questions about the data to which it can provide only partial answers, it is often better that the question should never have been asked.

Consider the following version of an often quoted sentence:

> *The man looked at the girl with the telescope.*

It will be pointed out that this can be translated word-for-word into French, and innumerable other languages, and gives a perfectly adequate result. It is, of course, ambiguous in various ways because of the different roles that the prepositional phrase can play in the syntactic structure. But French admits exactly parallel ambiguities so that any effort spent trying to decide whether the girl had the telescope or the man had it and used it to see her with, is wasted. In fact, such an effort can serve only to jeopardize the translation because, if it results in any but a word-for-word translation of this sentence, there is an unnecessary risk that it will be wrong.

On the other hand, if the sentence had been

> *The man looked at the girl with penetrating eyes.*

the question of whose eyes were involved would suddenly have been important because no acceptable word-for-word translation is possible; we are forced to choose between *aux yeu* and *de ses yeux. Avec* is a good translation for *with* in neither case. What algorithm will tell a translator that this case needs analysis whereas the first one does not? Perhaps the absence of an article before *penetrating eyes* gives the clue. This would indicate that

He looked at the girl with affection.

requires analysis. Unfortunately for the argument, it does not.

The main problem with the sorcerer's-apprentice argument is that the decision that a sentence could be translated without analysis can only be made after the fact. Analysis shows that there is more than one interpretation of a sentence at some level and further analysis shows that there is a single translation that is compatible with each of them. In short, the algorithm required to decide when analysis is required would have to use the results of the very analysis it is designed to avoid.

What the sorcerer's-apprentice argument does suggest is that the process of translation should proceed in the following nondeterministic fashion. Whenever the information needed to make a choice reliably is not available, all possibilities should be followed up independently. Furthermore, when an essentially arbitrary choice must be made, say between a pair of synonymous words, these possibilities should also be held open. Under this policy, a given sentence of input would yield a family of sets of sentences in the target language. The members of each set are presumed equivalent and the sets are distinguished by the different patterns of decisions that led to their production. If, by happy chance, there is a sentence that belongs to every set in the family, then it is presumably the safest, and possibly even the best, translation. Consider, for example, the following somewhat contrived French sentence:

Ils signeront le document pourvu que leur gouvernement accepte.

Possible translations, classified by family, are

I

- *They will sign the document supplied that their government accepts.*
- *They will sign the document furnished that their government accepts.*
- *They will sign the document provided that their government accepts.*
- *They are going to sign the document supplied that their government accepts.*
- *They are going to sign the document furnished that their government accepts.*
- *They are going to sign the document provided that their government accepts.*
- *etc.*

II

- *They will sign the document provided that their government accepts.*
- *They will sign the document on condition that their government accepts.*
- *They will sign the document only if their government accepts.*
- *They are going to sign the document provided that their government accepts.*
- *They are going to sign the document on condition that their government accepts.*
- *They are going to sign the document only if their government accepts.*
- *etc.*

The two translations come from two quite different analyses of the original. It could be only as a result of a quite remarkable chance that a pair of interpretations as different as these should fall together. They would not have done so, for example, if *accepter* had been a verb that showed a difference between its indicative and subjunctive forms or if a feminine or a plural noun had taken the place of *document.* However, since the sentences involving the phrase *provided that* belong to both sets, the choice of a translation can be narrowed to them because this neutralizes the ambiguity.

This technique does not depend on there being a sentence that appears in every member of the family. Whenever a single sentence occurs in more than one set, they can be reduced to a single set containing only the intersection of the originals. There are optimal ways of choosing sets to conflate so as to reduce the choice that must eventually be made to a minimum. Furthermore, it is not difficult to devise extensions of the procedure. If the sets in the family of translations are labeled in some way for the places in the analysis where a decision was made in the course of their production, then the differences between pairs of translations can be ascribed to specific sets of decisions. If there is no translation that belongs to all the sets, then the number and the difficulty of the decisions that need to be made to make the choice can be minimized. This is a topic I shall return to. For the moment, the point to note is that the observation on which the sorcerer's apprentice argument is based tends to maximize the amount of computation to be done – just the inverse of their original intent.

19.6 The Translator's Amanuensis

I come now to my proposal. I want to advocate an incremental approach to the problem of how machines should be used in language translation. The word *approach* can be taken in its original meaning as well as the one that has become so popular in modern technical jargon. I want to advocate a view of the problem in which machines are gradually, almost imperceptibly, allowed to take over certain functions in the overall translation process. First they will take over functions not essentially related to translation. Then, little by little, they will approach translation itself. The keynote will be modesty. At each stage, we will do only what we know we can do reliably. Little steps for little feet!

19.6.1 Text Editing

The easy way to prepare a piece of text is the way this one was prepared, that is, with a text-editing program on a computer. It does not matter whether it is done on a very small and personal computer that fits under the table in your office or on a large time-sharing machine, except that the latter is apt to be expensive. It matters very much that the design of the editor should be in the best possible taste, and it makes some difference whether the facilities include a screen that the writer can point at when he wishes to draw the program's attention to a particular place. People who have worked with bad editors soon retreat to the security of their typewriter or a pencil; anyone who has worked with a good one cannot be dragged away with a team of wild horses.

So, one thing to do would be to get a good editor and give it to your translators. If you could only do one thing, this would probably be the best. But you would do better to find an inventive computer scientist with good taste and to have him design a special editor which, in its earliest incarnations, would do little more than the program he would design for anyone else. But the design would be flexible and make provision for various kinds of extension. The kind of computer scientist I have in mind will expect to see the initial product in operation for a while before he makes detailed proposals for the extensions and he will probably want to see various alternative forms of each extension in use before any one is adopted.

Let us be specific. The device I am about to describe, which I call *The Translator's Amanuensis* , does not exist and probably never will. It is not the result of a careful program of design so that its details are ill specified, and what is specified I have invented only to illustrate the kind of avenue that seems most fruitful to follow and to avoid a long sequence of conditional sentences I should otherwise have to write.

Suppose that the translators are provided with a terminal consisting of a keyboard, a screen, and some way of pointing at individual words and letters. The display on the screen is divided into two windows. The text to be translated appears in the upper window and the translation will be composed in the bottom one. Fig. 1 shows how the screen might appear before the translation process begins. Both windows behave in the same way. Using the pointing device, the translator can *select* a letter, word, sentence, line, or paragraph and, by pressing the appropriate key, cause some operation to be visited upon it.

There are various styles of work that a translator might adopt using this device. One that I shall pursue briefly here involves first copying the entire text to be translated into the bottom window. It thereby becomes, so to speak, the first draft of the translation. Little by little, words, phrases and sentences will be replaced by true translations until, in the end, little or nothing of the original remains in the bottom window. This somewhat unconventional procedure has the advantage of making it possible for the machine to maintain detailed linkages between the original and the translation so that it has a detailed idea of what corresponds to what.

In Fig. 2, the words *indicated by* have been selected because it has been decided that they constituted too literal a translation. The translator now gives the REPLACE command, say by striking R on the keyboard, and the selected word is replaced by a symbol showing that subsequent characters will be accepted as a new insertion at that place. In this case, the translator types *of* and the display is adjusted to show the amended text.

This recital could be continued indefinitely. Basically, what I am describing is an editor of a kind that has become quite common. Now, let us consider how this device might be made to give special service to a translator. In line with the incremental approach, I will start simple. A relatively trivial addition would be a dictionary. The translator selects a word or sequence of words and gives a command to cause them to be looked up. In Fig. 3, the word *spécificateur* has been selected. When the lookup command is given, a new smaller window appears at a place indicted by the user. This new window gives the effect of overlaying some portion of the windows already present. In this case, the new window contains a deceptively simple dictionary entry for the selected word.

The simplicity of the dictionary entry is a feature of the system. We should think

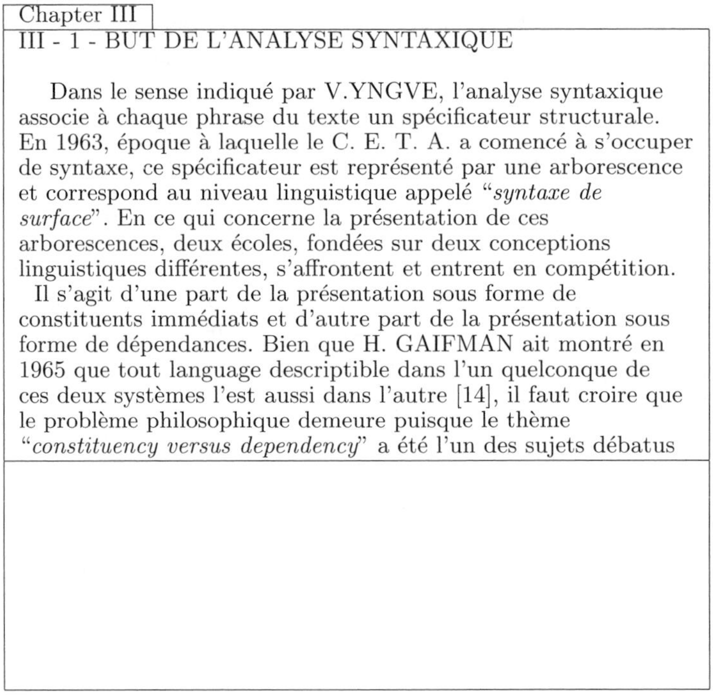

Chapter III

III - 1 - BUT DE L'ANALYSE SYNTAXIQUE

Dans le sens indiqué par V.YNGVE, l'analyse syntaxique associe à chaque phrase du texte un spécificateur structurale. En 1963, époque à laquelle le C. E. T. A. a comencé à s'occuper de syntaxe, ce spécificateur est représenté par une arborescence et correspond au niveau linguistique appelé *"syntaxe de surface"*. En ce qui concerne la présentation de ces arborescences, deux écoles, fondées sur deux conceptions linguistiques différentes, s'affrontent et entrent en compétition.

Il s'agit d'une part de la présentation sous forme de constituents immédiats et d'autre part de la présentation sous forme de dépendances. Bien que H. GAIFMAN ait montré en 1965 que tout language descriptible dans l'un quelconque de ces deux systèmes l'est aussi dans l'autre [14], il faut croire que le problème philosophique demeure puisque le thème *"constituency versus dependency"* a été l'un des sujets débatus

FIGURE 1 The Initial Display

of the dictionary that the system has on file as being large and highly structured, growing on a daily basis as its deficiencies are revealed. To consult an entry, the user of the system is therefore provided with special tools. He is first shown only a gross summary of what the entry contains. By pointing to a subentry in that summary, he can obtain information on the next level of structure in a new window. The strange symbols following the words *Syntax* and *Semantics* in Fig. 3 represent text which will be included if the user points to them. The text that then appears may contain other instances of this symbol, and so on. The translator can thus cause the entry to develop in the direction indicated by the text on hand. At any time, he can return to a higher level by pointing at some part of the corresponding window that still remains exposed. If, in the course of translating a text, a word or phrase is looked up a second time, the display will show, not just the top-level entry, but the situation that was obtained when the same entry was consulted previously. This is on the theory that the same part of the dictionary is apt to be most relevant. The example given in the illustration is unrealistically simple; we must envisage many levels of structure and a greater investment of effort in the corresponding system design.

The translator can edit dictionary entries with the same commands that he uses for the translation itself. These amendments may be temporary, serving essentially as notes on the vocabulary of the particular document and the terminological decisions that have been made. They can also be more permanent, providing instant information to other translators with similar problems. Communication of this sort, across time as well as space is one of the most crucial functions that computers can serve.

Chapter III

III - 1 - BUT DE L'ANALYSE SYNTAXIQUE

Dans le sense indiqué par V.YNGVE, l'analyse syntaxique associe à chaque phrase du texte un spécificateur structurale. En 1963, époque à laquelle le C. E. T. A. a comencé à s'occuper de syntaxe, ce spécificateur est représenté par une arborescence et correspond au niveau linguistique appelé *"syntaxe de surface"*. En ce qui concerne la présentation de ces arborescences, deux écoles, fondées sur deux conceptions linguistiques différentes, s'affrontent et entrent en compétition. Il s'agit d'une part de la présentation sous forme de constituents immédiats et d'autre part de la présentation sous forme de dépendances. Bien que H. GAIFMAN ait montré en 1965 que tout language descriptible dans l'un quelconque de ces deux systèmes l'est aussi dans l'autre [14], il faut croire que le problème philosophique demeure puisque le thème *"constituency versus dependency"* a été l'un des sujets débatus

III - 1 - AIMS OF SYNTACTIC ANALYSIS

In the sense indicated by V.YNGVE, syntactic analysis associates with each sentence of a text un spécificateur structurale. En 1963, époque à laquelle le C. E. T. A. a comencé à s'occuper de syntaxe, ce spécificateur est représenté par une arborescence et correspond au niveau linguistique appelé *"syntaxe de surface"*. En ce qui concerne la présentation de ces arborescences, deux écoles, fondées sur deux conceptions linguistiques différentes, s'affrontent et entrent en compétition. Il s'agit d'une part de la présentation sous forme de constituents immédiats et d'autre part de la présentation sous forme de dépendances. Bien que H. GAIFMAN ait montré en 1965 que tout language descriptible dans l'un quelconque de ces deux systèmes l'est aussi dans l'autre [14], il faut croire que le problème philosophique demeure puisque le thème *"constituency versus dependency"* a

FIGURE 2 Selection

I take it that words selected for reference to the dictionary will not have to be in their citation form. The computer will be able to apply rules of morphological analysis to determine the proper dictionary heading for itself. While this is not trivial, it is one of the few parts of linguistic analysis that is well understood. Furthermore, it should be possible to look up compounded words and sequences suspected of constituting an idiom or fixed phrase.

The machine's dictionary can be used in a variety of ways. Suppose, for example, that a word is put in the local store – that part of the dictionary that persists only as long as this document is being worked on – if it occurs in the text significantly more frequently than statistics stored in the main dictionary indicate. A phrase will be noted if it occurs two or three times but is not recognized as an idiom or set phrase by the dictionary. By examining the contents of this store before embarking on the translation, a user may hope to get a preview of the difficulties ahead and to make some decisions in advance about how to treat them. These decisions, of course, will be recorded in the store itself. In the course of doing this or, indeed, for any reason whatever, the translator

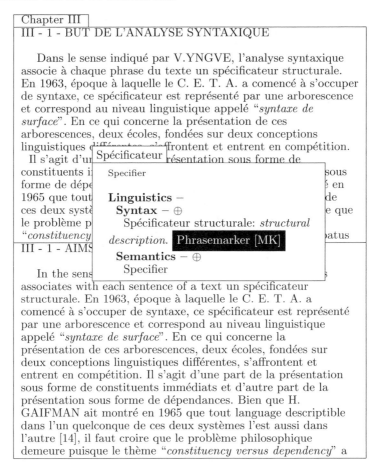

Chapter III

III - 1 - BUT DE L'ANALYSE SYNTAXIQUE

Dans le sense indiqué par V.YNGVE, l'analyse syntaxique associe à chaque phrase du texte un spécificateur structurale. En 1963, époque à laquelle le C. E. T. A. a comencé à s'occuper de syntaxes, ce spécificateur est représenté par une arborescence et correspond au niveau linguistique appelé "syntaxe de surface". En ce qui concerne la présentation de ces arborescences, deux écoles, fondées sur deux conceptions linguistiques différentes, s'affrontent et entrent en compétition.

Il s'agit d'une part de la présentation sous forme de constituents immédiats et d'autre part de la présentation sous forme de dépendances. Bien que H. GAIFMAN ait montré en 1965 que tout language descriptible dans l'un quelconque de ces deux systèmes l'est aussi dans l'autre, il faut croire que le problème philosophique demeure puisque le thème "constituency versus dependency" a gardé son statut

Specificateur

Specifier

Linguistics −
　Syntax − ⊕
　　Spécificateur structurale: *structural description.* Phrasemarker [MK]
　Semantics − ⊕
　　Specifier

III - 1 - AIMS

In the sense indiqué par V.YNGVE, l'analyse syntaxique associes with each sentence of a text un spécificateur structurale. En 1963, époque à laquelle le C. E. T. A. a comencé à s'occuper de syntaxe, ce spécificateur est représenté par une arborescence et correspond au niveau linguistique appelé "syntaxe de surface". En ce qui concerne la présentation de ces arborescences, deux écoles, fondées sur deux conceptions linguistiques différentes, s'affrontent et entrent en compétition. Il s'agit d'une part de la présentation sous forme de constituents immédiats et d'autre part de la présentation sous forme de dépendances. Bien que H. GAIFMAN ait montré en 1965 que tout language descriptible dans l'un quelconque de ces deux systèmes l'est aussi dans l'autre [14], il faut croire que le problème philosophique demeure puisque le thème "constituency versus dependency" a

FIGURE 3 Looking up Terms

can call for a display of all the units in the text that contain a certain word, phrase, string of characters, or whatever. After all, the most important reference to have when translating a text is the text itself.

If the piece of text to be translated next is anything but entirely straightforward, the translator might start by issuing a command causing the system to display anything in the store that might be relevant to it. This will bring to his attention decisions he made before the actual translation started, statistically significant words and phrases, and a record of anything that had attracted attention when it occurred before. Before going on, he can examine past and future fragments of text that contain similar material.

Most editing programs allow the writer to insert an arbitrary symbol of his own choosing at various places in the text and, at some later time, to cause all instances of that symbol to be replaced by some other word or symbol. This comes close to filling an important need that translators have. It turns out that a particularly vexing problem of technical translation is that of vocabulary control. That you should translate a technical term in one language by the proper technical term in the other language is important, but it is less important than that you should translate it always in the same way. One way to achieve this would be to make up a symbol, containing some otherwise unused character, and then to make replacements when the translation was complete. The device envisaged here goes further.

Chapter III

III - 1 - BUT DE L'ANALYSE SYNTAXIQUE

Dans le sense indiqué par V.YNGVE, l'analyse syntaxique associe à chaque phrase du texte un spécificateur structurale. En 1963, époque à laquelle le C. E. T. A. a comencé à s'occuper de syntaxe, ce spécificateur est représenté par une arborescence et correspond au niveau linguistique appelé *"syntaxe de surface"*. En ce qui concerne la présentation de ces arborescences, deux écoles, fondées sur deux conceptions linguistiques différentes, s'affrontent et entrent en compétition.
Il s'agit d'une part de la présentation sous forme de constituents immédiats et d'autre part de la présentation sous forme de dépendances. Bien que H. GAIFMAN ait montré en 1965 que tout language descriptible dans l'un quelconque de ces deux systèmes l'est aussi dans l'autre [14], il faut croire que le problème philosophique demeure puisque le thème *"constituency versus dependency"* a été l'un des sujets débatus

III - 1 - AIMS OF SYNTACTIC ANALYSIS

In the sense of V.YNGVE, syntactic analysis associates with each sentence of a text a [**2** structural description]. In 1963, the time when C. E. T. A. started concerning itself with syntax, this [**2** structural description] took the form of a tree and corresponded to the linguistic level called "surface structure". As for the [presentation] of these trees, two schools, based on two different linguistic conceptions, confronted one another and began to compete. On the one hand there was the [presentation] in the form of immediate constituents and, on the other, the [presentation] in the form of [dependency]s. Bien que H. GAIFMAN ait montré en 1965 que tout language descriptible dans l'un quelconque de ces deux systèmes l'est aussi dans l'autre [14], il faut croire que le problème philosophique demeure puisque le thème *"constituency versus dependency"* a été l'un des sujets débatus

---

FIGURE 4 Morphology and Lexical Alternatives

I suppose that the user of the system has available a special pair of brackets that he can insert in the text; in the examples they appear square and bold. They appear on his screen but will not be printed in the final translation. They are used as follows. If it is, for the moment, unclear how a word or technical phrase should be treated, the tentative translation is enclosed in these special brackets. They can be used in the translation itself or in dictionary entries. When the same word or phrase turns up again, the bracketed phrase is explicitly copied into the new position, thus maintaining an association among ail the places where it is used. If the contents of such a pair of brackets is changed, the contents of ail the others that are linked to it change automatically in the same way. Notice that this is a considerably finer instrument than the replacement facility of standard text-editing programs because the changes effect only those occurrences of a word or phrase that have been explicitly associated. Furthermore, if inflectional material belonging to one of these bracketed words or phrases is written in a standard, regular form outside the brackets – as in the case of the word *dependency* in Fig. 4 – the appropriate form of the word can be constructed when the final version is settled on. Once again, this calls for the application of morphological rules, this time in the generative direction.

Fig. 4 also illustrates another possible variant of this device. If more than one translation is being considered for a particular term, possibly because both are suggested in the dictionary, the fact is recorded by displaying a bold numeral just after the open bracket. If the translator points at this, the next possibility is taken, both in this and the other places in the text that are linked to it. In this way he can rapidly switch back and forth between variants without having to type.

19.7   Machine Translation

There is no early limit to the facilities that could, and probably should, be added to the translator's amanuensis. Rather than prolonging the rehearsal, let us look at where the process might end. I began by proposing an incremental approach to machine translation, so it is machine translation that must come at the bottom of the list. But, if it is to avoid the objections made by myself and others, it must be machine translation in a new form.

I propose that one of the options that should be offered to a user of the hypothetical system I have been describing, at a fairly early stage, be a command that will direct the program to translate the currently selected unit. What will happen when this command is given will be different at different stages of the system's development. But a user of the system will always be empowered to intervene in the translation process to the extent that he himself specifies. If he elects not to intervene at all, a piece of text purporting to translate the current unit will be displayed in the lower window of his screen. He will be able to edit this in any way he likes, just as post-editors have done in the past. Alternatively, he may ask to be consulted whenever the program is confronted with a decision of a specified type, when certain kinds of ambiguities are detected, or whatever. On these occasions, the system will put a question to the human translator. He may, for example, ask to be consulted on questions of pronominal reference.

The only difference between the translation facilities of the translator's amanuensis and previous machine-translation systems that can be seen from a user's point of view is that here the translator has his say while the translation is under way whereas previously he had to wait. If this scheme can be made to work, as I claim it can, its many advantages are collectively overpowering.

The kind of translation device I am proposing will always be under the tight control of a human translator. It is there to help increase his productivity and not to supplant him. It will never resort to *ad hoc* measures that have not been explicitly sanctioned by him. In its normal and recommended mode of use, it will appeal to him rather than being forced back on unfounded guesses. After the system has been under development for a while, its users will either still be using it as a clerical aid, or they will be consigning considerable amounts of the actual translation work to it. The usage will remain mainly clerical only if the best efforts invested in the translation facilities failed to make them useful or economical. In other words, this system will certainly be able to undertake whatever present systems are able to undertake reliably and if that proves to be very little, the inference is clear. But there is reason to hope that it will undertake more. A system that never reached the stage of proposing translations would still be of inestimable value in automatically producing the final copy, looking up words and phrases faster and in a larger and constantly growing dictionary than would be possible any other way, in keeping notes about vocabulary usage and the like.

There are several important reasons to expect better performance of a system that allows human intervention as opposed to one that will brook no interference until all the damage has been done. First, the system is in a position to draw its human collaborator's attention to the matters most likely to need it. It is clearly important that he should give special attention to matters for which the designers of the system were unable to provide satisfactory algorithmic solutions. A wrong answer in these cases does nothing but mislead. It is far better that the labor and ingenuity spent on developing the machine's ability to make bad guesses should be employed more productively.

The second point is related. The decisions that have to be made in the course of translating a passage are rarely independent. The outcome of one decision typically determines whether certain other decisions will have to be faced at all. A wrong decision at the beginning of such a chain leads the system to ask questions of the data before it that do not even make sense; whatever answer is given, it is bound to be wrong. Cascading errors of this kind are common in language processing. In the kind of system proposed here, they will not happen except when the human member of the team makes an error, or when he consigns too much to the machine. In the standard case, he will be consulted when the first decision in the chain is reached and will direct the machine along the right lines.

A third point concerns the machine's use of history. One of the most important facilities in the system is the one that keeps track of words and phrases that are used in some special way in the current text. It is a device that should probably be extended in a variety of ways to cover more than just vocabulary usage. By means of this, the translator is able to make a decision on the first occasion that a difficulty arises that will determine how both he and the machine treat it on all subsequent occasions. In other words, the man and the machine are collaborating to produce not only a translation of a text but also a device whose contribution to that translation is being constantly enhanced. A post-editor who changes something at the beginning of a translation must expect to make essentially the same change many more times before he finishes. This is not to say that a machine-translation program could not be devised that modified its behaviour in the light of experience. However, such a system would be especially liable to the last objection made, namely that bad decisions made early lead to worse decisions later. It is bad enough that ill-founded decisions made early in the processing of a sentence should be allowed to engender other ones later; to extend this policy over an entire text is to invite disaster. The system proposed here will accumulate only experience of what was agreed upon between both human and mechanical members of the team, the mechanical always deferring to the human.

The translator's amanuensis will not run before it can walk. It will be called on only for that for which its masters have learned to trust it. It will not require constant infusions of new *ad hoc* devices that only expensive vendors can supply. It is a framework that will gracefully accommodate the future contributions that linguistics and computer science are able to make. One day it will be built because its very modesty assures its success. It is to be hoped that it will be built with taste by people who understand languages and computers well enough to know how little it is that they know.

20

Functional Grammar

The term *functional grammar* has been used before, notably by Dik (1978). I risk adding to the number of its meanings here, and thus debasing its value, only because it is peculiarly apt for this new employment. I propose to outline a new grammatical formalism which, if it can be successfully developed, will be worthy of the name *functional* on three counts. First, it is required to *function* as part of a model of language production and comprehension. The formalism is interpretable by an abstract machine whose operation is intended to model the syntactic processing of sentences by speakers and hearers indifferently. This is not to say that it is not also intended to represent a speaker's grammatical competence. Secondly, the formalism ascribes to every sentence, word, and phrase, a *functional description* which differs from the structural description of better known formalisms mainly by stressing the function that a part plays in a whole rather than the position a part occupies in a sequence of others. The names of grammatical categories, like *S, NP,* and *VP* will therefore play a secondary role to terms like *subject, object,* and *modifier* . Thirdly, properties that distinguish among logically equivalent sentences will have equal importance with properties that they share. In other words, this will be a functionalist view of grammar in which notions like *topic* and *focus, given* and *new* will have equal status with *subject* and *predicate, positive* and *negative.*

For the most part, theoretical linguists see a grammar as an abstract device characterizing the presumably infinite set of sentences of a language, that is, differentiating the sentences from other strings which are not sentences. Computational linguists, on the other hand, have usually taken a grammar to be a transducer showing how a meaning comes to be represented as a string of words or, more frequently, how a string of words is analyzed to reveal its meaning. Functional grammar has both aspects. It can also be said to be a transducer whose input is a more or less incomplete account of the syntactic relations among the parts of a sentence and whose output is one or more accounts which are complete according to the theory. Given a more or less incomplete description, it verifies that it describes a legal grammatical object – a word, phrase, or sentence – and adds such additional detail as the grammar allows. If it is not a legal grammatical object, no output is produced. If it is, one or more descriptions are produced, each an enrichment of the original, but reflecting different grammatical interpretations.

The ideal speaker comes to the syntactic processor wanting a sentence with a certain meaning; the processor's job is to complete his picture of the sentence by supplying appropriate words and phrases. The ideal hearer has a complete description of the words in the sentence but needs descriptions of the phrases and the meaning of the whole to complete the picture. A more realistic hearer starts with a picture including imperfectly heard words and some notions about what is being said and needs details filled in in a variety of places. In any case, the process consists in applying the grammar to a functional description to yield a more complete functional description or, if the description does not correspond to a grammatical object, the null functional description.

Functional Descriptions

Intuitively, a description is a set of properties. The objects it describes are those that share just those properties. Generally speaking, to add new properties to a description is to reduce the number of objects in the set described. In fact, there is a duality in the set-theoretic properties of descriptions and those of their extensions, that is, the sets of objects described. Thus, the empty description applies to all objects; the union of two descriptions applies to the intersections of the sets they individually describe; and the intersection of a pair of descriptions applies to the union of the two original sets of objects. Functional descriptions are defined in such a way as to preserve these intuitive properties. So, suppose that $F(s_1)$ ... $F(s_4)$ describe sentences (1) – (4) respectively.

(1) Brutus killed Caesar

(2) Cassius killed Caesar

(3) John hit Caesar

(4) John wrote a book

(5) ... killed Caesar

(6) John ...

(7) John killed Caesar

$F(s_5) = F(s_1) \cap F(s_2)$ is a description of all the sentences that have the predicate *killed Caesar* and $F(s_6) = F(s_3) \cap F(s_4)$ is a description of all sentences of which *John* is the subject. $F(s_7) = F(s_5) \cup F(s_6)$ describes sentence (7).

A simple functional description consists of a possibly empty set of *patterns* and a list of attributes with associated values. I shall come to the form and function of patterns shortly. For the moment, we shall consider the attribute-value pairs.

The attributes in a functional description must be distinct from one another so that if a functional description F contains the attribute a, the phrase "the a of F" uniquely identifies a value. An attribute is a *symbol*, that is, a string of letters. A value is a symbol or another functional description. In the notation I shall use, symbols are to be interpreted as representing attributes when they are immediately followed by an "=" sign or when they are written inside angle brackets. Otherwise, they are values. So, in (8), ALPHA and BETA are attributes and GAMMA is a value.

(8) [ALPHA = BETA = GAMMA]

The list of attribute-value pairs in a functional description is written in square brackets, the members of each pair separated by the equal-sign. No significance attaches to the order in which the attribute-value pairs are written. Thus, (9) might be a description, albeit a very simple one, of the sentence *He saw her*. In what follows, I shall use uppercase letters for true atomic values and lowercase ones as an informal surrogate for complex values whose details are either irrelevant or readily inferrable from the context.

$$(9) \quad \begin{bmatrix} \text{CAT} & = \text{S} \\ \text{SUBJ} & = \begin{bmatrix} \text{CAT} & = \text{PRON} \\ \text{GENDER} & = \text{MASC} \\ \text{CASE} & = \text{NOM} \\ \text{NUMBER} & = \text{SING} \\ \text{PERSON} & = 3 \end{bmatrix} \\ \text{DOBJ} & = \begin{bmatrix} \text{CAT} & = \text{PRON} \\ \text{GENDER} & = \text{FEM} \\ \text{CASE} & = \text{ACC} \\ \text{NUMBER} & = \text{SING} \\ \text{PERSON} & = 3 \end{bmatrix} \\ \text{VERB} & = \text{SEE} \\ \text{TENSE} & = \text{PAST} \\ \text{VOICE} & = \text{ACTIVE} \end{bmatrix}$$

$$(10) \quad \begin{bmatrix} \text{CAT} & = \text{S} \\ \text{PROT} & = \begin{bmatrix} \text{CAT} & = \text{PRON} \\ \text{GENDER} & = \text{MASC} \\ \text{NUMBER} & = \text{SING} \\ \text{PERSON} & = 3 \end{bmatrix} \\ \text{GOAL} & = \begin{bmatrix} \text{CAT} & = \text{PRON} \\ \text{GENDER} & = \text{FEM} \\ \text{NUMBER} & = \text{SING} \\ \text{PERSON} & = 3 \end{bmatrix} \\ \text{VERB} & = \text{SEE} \\ \text{TENSE} & = \text{PAST} \end{bmatrix}$$

$$(11) \quad \begin{bmatrix} \text{CAT} & = \text{S} \\ \text{SUBJ} & = \text{PROT} = \begin{bmatrix} \text{CAT} & = \text{PRON} \\ \text{GENDER} & = \text{MASC} \\ \text{CASE} & = \text{NOM} \\ \text{NUMBER} & = \text{SING} \\ \text{PERSON} & = 3 \end{bmatrix} \\ \text{DOBJ} & = \text{GOAL} = \begin{bmatrix} \text{CAT} & = \text{PRON} \\ \text{GENDER} & = \text{FEM} \\ \text{CASE} & = \text{ACC} \\ \text{NUMBER} & = \text{SING} \\ \text{PERSON} & = 3 \end{bmatrix} \\ \text{VERB} & = \text{SEE} \\ \text{TENSE} & = \text{PAST} \\ \text{VOICE} & = \text{ACTIVE} \end{bmatrix}$$

If the values of SUBJ and DOBJ are reversed in (9), and the value of VOICE changed to PASSIVE, it becomes a description of the sentence *She was seen by him*. However, in both this and the original sentence, he is the protagonist (PROT), or logical subject, and she the goal (GOAL) of the action, or logical direct object. In other words, both sentences are equally well described by (10). In the sense of transformational grammar (10) shows a *deeper* structure than (9). However, in functional grammar, if a given linguistic entity has two different descriptions, a description containing the information in both can be constructed by the process of *unification* which we shall examine in detail shortly. The description (11) results from unifying (9) and (10).

A pair of descriptions is said to be *incompatible* if they have a common attribute with different symbols, or incompatible descriptions, as values. Grammatically ambiguous sentences have two or more incompatible descriptions. Thus, the sentence *He likes writing books* might be described by (12) or (13). Incompatible simple descriptions $F_1...F_k$ can be combined into a single *complex* description $\{F_1...F_k\}$ which describes the union of the sets of objects that its components describe. The notation allows common parts of components to be factored in the obvious way, so that (14) describes all those objects that are described by *either* (12) or (13).

(12)
$$
\begin{bmatrix}
\text{CAT} & = \text{S} \\
\text{SUBJ} & = \text{he} \\
\text{DOBJ} & = \begin{bmatrix}
\text{CAT} & = \text{NP} \\
\text{HEAD} & = \text{books} \\
\text{MOD} & = \begin{bmatrix} \text{CAT} & = \text{PRESP} \\ \text{LEX} & = \text{WRITE} \end{bmatrix}
\end{bmatrix} \\
\text{VERB} & = \text{LIKE} \\
\text{TENSE} & = \text{PRES} \\
\text{VOICE} & = \text{ACTIVE}
\end{bmatrix}
$$

(13)
$$
\begin{bmatrix}
\text{CAT} & = \text{S} \\
\text{SUBJ} & = \text{he} \\
\text{DOBJ} & = \begin{bmatrix}
\text{CAT} & = \text{NP} \\
\text{HEAD} & = \begin{bmatrix}
\text{CAT} & = \text{S} \\
\text{VERB} & = \begin{bmatrix} \text{CAT} & = \text{PRESP} \\ \text{LEX} & = \text{WRITE} \end{bmatrix} \\
\text{DOBJ} & = \begin{bmatrix} \text{CAT} & = \text{NP} \\ \text{HEAD} & = \text{books} \end{bmatrix}
\end{bmatrix}
\end{bmatrix} \\
\text{VERB} & = \text{LIKE} \\
\text{TENSE} & = \text{PRES} \\
\text{VOICE} & = \text{ACTIVE}
\end{bmatrix}
$$

(14)
$$
\begin{bmatrix}
\text{CAT} & = \text{S} \\
\text{SUBJ} & = \text{he} \\
\text{DOBJ} & = \begin{bmatrix}
\text{CAT} = \text{NP} \\
\left\{
\begin{bmatrix}
\text{HEAD} & = \text{books} \\
\text{MOD} & = \begin{bmatrix} \text{CAT} & = \text{PRESP} \\ \text{LEX} & = \text{WRITE} \end{bmatrix}
\end{bmatrix}
\begin{bmatrix}
\text{HEAD} = \begin{bmatrix}
\text{CAT} & = \text{S} \\
\text{VERB} & = \begin{bmatrix} \text{CAT} & = \text{PRESP} \\ \text{LEX} & = \text{WRITE} \end{bmatrix} \\
\text{DOBJ} & = \begin{bmatrix} \text{CAT} & = \text{NP} \\ \text{HEAD} & = \text{books} \end{bmatrix}
\end{bmatrix}
\end{bmatrix}
\right\}
\end{bmatrix} \\
\text{VERB} & = \text{LIKE} \\
\text{TENSE} & = \text{PRES} \\
\text{VOICE} & = \text{ACTIVE}
\end{bmatrix}
$$

The use of braces to indicate alternation between incompatible descriptions or sub-descriptions provides a compact way of describing large classes of disparate objects. In fact, as we shall see, given a few extra conventions, it makes it possible to claim that the grammar of a language is nothing more than a complex functional description.

Unification

A string of atoms enclosed in angle brackets constitutes a *path* and there is at least one that identifies every value in a functional description. The path $\langle a_1\, a_2...a_k \rangle$ identifies the value of the attribute a_k in the functional description that is the value of $\langle a_1\, a_2...a_{k-1} \rangle$. It can be read as *The a_k of the a_{k-1} ... of the a_1*. Paths are always interpreted as beginning in the largest functional description that encloses them. Attributes are otherwise taken as belonging to the small enclosing functional description. Accordingly,

$$\left[A \;\; = \left[B \;\; = \langle C \rangle = X \right] \right] \equiv \left[\begin{array}{ll} A & = \left[B \;\; = X \right] \\ C & = \langle A\ B \rangle \end{array} \right]$$

A pair consisting of a path in a functional description and the value that the path leads to is a *feature* of that functional description. If the value is a symbol, the pair is a *basic feature* of the description. Any functional description can be represented as a list of basic features. For example, (15) can be represented by the list (16).

$$(15) \left[\begin{array}{lll} \text{CAT} & = \text{S} \\[4pt] \text{SUBJ} & = \text{PROT} & = \left[\begin{array}{ll} \text{CAT} & = \text{PRON} \\ \text{GENDER} & = \text{MASC} \\ \text{CASE} & = \text{NOM} \\ \text{NUMBER} & = \text{SING} \\ \text{PERSON} & = 3 \end{array} \right] \\[4pt] \text{DOBJ} & = \text{GOAL} & = \left[\begin{array}{ll} \text{CAT} & = \text{PRON} \\ \text{GENDER} & = \text{FEM} \\ \text{CASE} & = \text{ACC} \\ \text{NUMBER} & = \text{SING} \\ \text{PERSON} & = 3 \end{array} \right] \\[4pt] \text{VERB} & = \left[\begin{array}{ll} \text{CAT} & = \text{VERB} \\ \text{WORD} & = \text{SEE} \end{array} \right] \\[4pt] \text{TENSE} & = \text{PAST} \\ \text{VOICE} & = \text{ACTIVE} \\[4pt] \text{ASPECT} & = \left[\begin{array}{ll} \text{PERFECT} & = + \\ \text{PROGRESSIVE} & = - \end{array} \right] \end{array} \right]$$

It is in the nature of functional descriptions that they blur the usual distinction between features and structures. (15) shows descriptions embedded in other descriptions, thus stressing their structural properties. Rewriting (15) as (16) stresses the componential nature of descriptions.

The possibility of viewing descriptions as unstructured sets of features makes them subject to the standard operations of set theory, thereby bestowing on them that most salient property of descriptions in general discussed in reference to (1) – (7). However, it is also a crucial property of functional descriptions that they are not closed under set-theoretic operations. Specifically, the union of a pair of functional descriptions is not, in general, a well-formed functional description. The reason is as follows: The requirement that a given attribute appear only once in a functional description implies a similar constraint on the set of features corresponding to a description. A path must uniquely identify a value. But if the description F_1 has the basic feature $\langle a \rangle = x$ and the description F_2 has the basic feature $\langle a \rangle = y$ then either $x = y$ or F_1 and F_2 are incompatible and their union is not a well-formed description. So, for example, if F_1 describes a sentence with a singular subject and F_2 describes a sentence with a plural subject, then $S_1 \cup S_2$, where S_1 and S_2 are the corresponding sets of basic features, is not well formed because it would contain both $\langle \text{SUBJ NUMBER} \rangle = \text{SINGULAR}$ and $\langle \text{SUBJ NUMBER} \rangle = \text{PLURAL}$.

(16)

$$
\begin{aligned}
\langle \text{CAT} \rangle &= \text{S} \\
\langle \text{SUBJ CAT} \rangle &= \text{PRON} \\
\langle \text{SUBJ GENDER} \rangle &= \text{MASC} \\
\langle \text{SUBJ CASE} \rangle &= \text{NOM} \\
\langle \text{SUBJ NUMBER} \rangle &= \text{SING} \\
\langle \text{SUBJ PERSON} \rangle &= 3 \\
\langle \text{PROT CAT} \rangle &= \text{PRON} \\
\langle \text{PROT GENDER} \rangle &= \text{MASC} \\
\langle \text{PROT CASE} \rangle &= \text{NOM} \\
\langle \text{PROT NUMBER} \rangle &= \text{SING} \\
\langle \text{PROT PERSON} \rangle &= 3 \\
\langle \text{DOBJ CAT} \rangle &= \text{PRON} \\
\langle \text{DOBJ GENDER} \rangle &= \text{FEM} \\
\langle \text{DOBJ CASE} \rangle &= \text{ACC} \\
\langle \text{DOBJ NUMBER} \rangle &= \text{SING} \\
\langle \text{DOBJ PERSON} \rangle &= 3 \\
\langle \text{GOAL CAT} \rangle &= \text{PRON} \\
\langle \text{GOAL GENDER} \rangle &= \text{FEM} \\
\langle \text{GOAL CASE} \rangle &= \text{ACC} \\
\langle \text{GOAL NUMBER} \rangle &= \text{SING} \\
\langle \text{GOAL PERSON} \rangle &= 3 \\
\langle \text{VERB CAT} \rangle &= \text{VERB} \\
\langle \text{VERB WORD} \rangle &= \text{SEE} \\
\langle \text{TENSE} \rangle &= \text{PAST} \\
\langle \text{VOICE} \rangle &= \text{ACTIVE} \\
\langle \text{ASPECT PERFECT} \rangle &= + \\
\langle \text{ASPECT PROGRESSIVE} \rangle &= -
\end{aligned}
$$

When two or more simple functional descriptions are compatible, they can be combined into one simple description describing those things that they both describe, by the process of unification: Unification is the same as set union except that it yields the null set when applied to incompatible arguments. The "=" sign is used for unification, so that $\alpha = \beta$ denotes the result of unifying α and β. (17) – (19) show the results of unification in some simple cases.

(17)
$$
\begin{bmatrix} \text{CAT} & = \text{VERB} \\ \text{LEX} & = \text{RUN} \\ \text{TENSE} & = \text{PRES} \end{bmatrix}
=
\begin{bmatrix} \text{CAT} & = \text{VERB} \\ \text{NUM} & = \text{SING} \\ \text{PERS} & = 3 \end{bmatrix}
\Rightarrow
\begin{bmatrix} \text{CAT} & = \text{VERB} \\ \text{LEX} & = \text{RUN} \\ \text{TENSE} & = \text{PRES} \\ \text{NUM} & = \text{SING} \\ \text{PERS} & = 3 \end{bmatrix}
$$

(18)
$$
\begin{bmatrix} \text{CAT} & = \text{VERB} \\ \text{LEX} & = \text{RUN} \\ \text{TENSE} & = \text{PRES} \end{bmatrix}
=
\begin{bmatrix} \text{CAT} & = \text{VERB} \\ \text{TENSE} & = \text{PAST} \\ \text{PERS} & = 3 \end{bmatrix}
\Rightarrow \text{NIL}
$$

(19)
$$
\begin{bmatrix} \text{PREP} & = \text{MIT} \\ \text{CASE} & = \text{DAT} \end{bmatrix}
=
\begin{bmatrix} \text{CAT} & = \text{PP} \\ \text{HEAD} & = \begin{bmatrix} \text{CAT} & = \text{NP} \\ \text{CASE} & = \langle \text{CASE} \rangle \end{bmatrix} \end{bmatrix}
\Rightarrow
\begin{bmatrix} \text{CAT} & = \text{PP} \\ \text{PREP} & = \text{MIT} \\ \text{CASE} & = \text{DAT} \\ \text{HEAD} & = \begin{bmatrix} \text{CAT} & = \text{NP} \\ \text{CASE} & = \langle \text{CASE} \rangle \end{bmatrix} \end{bmatrix}
$$

The result of unifying a pair of complex descriptions is, in general, a complex description with one term for each compatible pair of terms in the original descriptions. Thus $\{a_1 \ldots a_n\} = \{b_1 \ldots b_m\}$ becomes a description of the form $\{c_1 \ldots c_k\}$ in which each c_h $(1 \le h \le k)$ is the result of unifying a compatible pair $a_i = b_j$ $(1 \le i \le m, 1 \le j \le n)$. This is exemplified in (20).

$$(20) \quad \left\{ \begin{bmatrix} \text{TENSE} & = \text{PRES} \\ \text{FORM} & = \text{is} \end{bmatrix} \right\} = \begin{bmatrix} \text{CAT} & = \text{VERB} \\ \text{TENSE} & = \text{PAST} \end{bmatrix} \Rightarrow \begin{bmatrix} \text{CAT} & = \text{VERB} \\ \text{TENSE} & = \text{PAST} \\ \text{FORM} & = \text{was} \end{bmatrix}$$

Unification is the fundamental operation underlying the analysis and synthesis of sentences using functional grammar and there will be abundant examples of its use in the sequel.

Patterns and Constituents

We come now to the question of recursion in the grammar and how constituency is represented. I have already remarked that functional grammar deliberately blurs the distinction between structures and sets of features. It is clear from the examples we have considered so far that some parts of a description of a phrase typically belong to the phrase as a whole whereas others belong to its constituents. For example, in (15) the value of SUBJ is the description of a constituent of the sentence whereas the value of ASPECT is not. The purpose of patterns is to identify constituents and to state constraints on the order of their occurrence. (21) is a version of (15) that specifies the order. (SUBJ VERB DOBJ) is a pattern stating that the values of the attributes SUBJ, VERB and DOBJ are descriptions of constituents and that they occur in that order.

$$(21) \quad \begin{bmatrix} \text{(SUBJ VERB DOBJ)} & & \\ \text{CAT} & = \text{S} & \\ \text{SUBJ} & = \text{PROT} & = \begin{bmatrix} \text{CAT} & = \text{PRON} \\ \text{GENDER} & = \text{MASC} \\ \text{CASE} & = \text{NOM} \\ \text{NUMBER} & = \text{SING} \\ \text{PERSON} & = 3 \end{bmatrix} \\ \text{DOBJ} & = \text{GOAL} & = \begin{bmatrix} \text{CAT} & = \text{PRON} \\ \text{GENDER} & = \text{FEM} \\ \text{CASE} & = \text{ACC} \\ \text{NUMBER} & = \text{SING} \\ \text{PERSON} & = 3 \end{bmatrix} \\ \text{VERB} & = \begin{bmatrix} \text{CAT} & = \text{VERB} \\ \text{WORD} & = \text{SEE} \end{bmatrix} \\ \text{TENSE} & = \text{PAST} & \\ \text{VOICE} & = \text{ACTIVE} & \\ \text{ASPECT} & = \begin{bmatrix} \text{PERFECT} & = + \\ \text{PROGRESSIVE} & = - \end{bmatrix} \end{bmatrix}$$

Equivalently, the description could have contained many other sets of patterns, for example, those in (22) – (26).

(22) (SUBJ VERB ...) (... VERB DOBJ)

(23) (SUBJ ... DOBJ) (... VERB ...)

(24) (... SUBJ ... DOBJ) (# VERB ...)

(25) (... SUBJ ... VERB ... DOBJ)

(26) (... SUBJ ... VERB ...) (... DOBJ)

If an attribute or, more generally, a path, appears in one or more patterns, then its value is the description of a constituent. If more than one constituent is named in the same pattern, then they must appear in the phrase or sentence in the order given. If a pair of attributes or paths is separated by dots, other constituents, specified in other patterns, may optionally intervene. Adjacent attributes or paths specify adjacent constituents and an attribute or path that begins (or ends) a pattern names a constituent that occurs first (or last). The symbol # signifies exactly one constituent specified in another pattern. Consider now examples (27) – (29) in which the order of the constituents is not uniquely specified.

(27) (... SUBJ ... VERB DOBJ ...) (... MOD ...)

(28) (... SUBJ ...) (... VERB ...) (... DOBJ ...)

(29) (... NOM ...) (... ACC ...) (... DAT ...) (# VERB ...)

(27) says that SUBJ precedes VERB and VERB precedes DOBJ but allows MOD, presumably an adverbial modifier, to occur before or after SUBJ or at the end of the sentence. (28) allows SUBJ, VERB and DOBJ to occur in any order relative to one another. (29) specifies NOM, ACC, DAT, and VERB as constituents. The only constraints it places on the order is that the verb must be in second position.

Clearly, patterns, like attribute-value pairs, can be incompatible thus preventing the unification of descriptions. This is the case in examples (30) – (32).

(30) (... SUBJ ... VERB ...) (... VERB ... SUBJ ...)

(31) (# SUBJ ...) (SUBJ ...)

(32) (... SUBJ VERB ...) (... SUBJ DOBJ ...)

If the name of a path or an attribute is preceded by an asterisk in a pattern, the corresponding value must be unified with a value specified in another pattern in order to establish compatibility between them. Thus, for example, while the patterns in (33) are incompatible, those in (34) are not. Unifying a pair of descriptions each containing one of the patterns in (33) will result in the unification of SUBJ and PROT.

(33) (SUBJ VERB ...) (PROT VERB ...)

(34) (*SUBJ VERB ...) (PROT VERB ...)

As we have seen, the functional descriptions of sentences and phrases may have other descriptions embedded in them that describe their constituents. However, the outer description is also taken as applying to each of these constituents. Thus, if G is a functional description that fills the role of a grammar which, when unified with a sentence description F, reveals it to have constituents with descriptions $F_1...F_n$, then these are also unified with G, and so on recursively. As we shall see, it follows from this that patterns can only be usefully employed in complex descriptions. Consider, for example, the description (35), which is roughly equivalent to the phrase-structure rule given in (36).[1]

$$(35) \quad \left\{ \begin{array}{l} \left[\begin{array}{l} \text{(SUBJ VERB ...)} \\ \text{CAT} = \text{S} \\ \text{SUBJ} = \left[\text{CAT} = \text{NP} \right] \\ \text{PRED} = \left[\text{CAT} = \text{VERB} \right] \\ \left\{ \begin{array}{l} \left[\text{SCOMP} = \text{NONE} \right] \\ \left[\begin{array}{l} \text{(... SCOMP)} \\ \text{SCOMP} = \left[\text{CAT} = \text{S} \right] \end{array} \right] \end{array} \right\} \end{array} \right] \\ \left[\text{CAT} = \text{NP} \right] \\ \left[\text{CAT} = \text{VERB} \right] \end{array} \right\}$$

(36) $S \rightarrow SUBJ{:}NP \ VERB{:}VERB \ (SCOMP{:}S)$

Example (35) describes *either* sentences *or* verbs *or* noun phrases. Nothing is said about the constituency of the verbs or noun phrases described – they are terminal constituents. The sentences have either two or three constituents depending on the choice made in the embedded alternation. All constituents must match the description (35). Since the first constituent has the feature [CAT = NP], it can only match the second term in the main alternation. Likewise, the second constituent can only match the third term. If there is a third constituent, it must match the first term in the alternation, because it has the feature [CAT = S]. It must therefore also have two or three constituents which (35) also describes. It is for this reason that patterns make sense only in complex descriptions. For the same reason, context-free grammars make sense only if some of the symbols are terminal and there is some nonrecursive expansion for every symbol. If (35) consisted only of the first term in the outer alternation, it would have a null extension because the first term, for example, would be required to have the incompatible features [CAT = NP] and [CAT = S]. On other hand, if the inner alternation were replaced by its second term, so that [SCOMP = NONE] were no longer an option, then the description would correspond to the rule (37), whose derivations do not terminate.

(37) $S \rightarrow SUBJ{:}NP \ VERB{:}VERB \ SCOMP{:}S$

---

[1]This is, in fact, more like a tagmemic rule including, as it does, the relation that each constituent bears to the phrase, as well as its category.

Example (35) is a recursive definition and a trivial example of the way a functional description can be used to characterize an infinite class of sentences and thus serve as the grammar of a language. Generally speaking, grammars will take the form of alternations each clause of which describes a major category; that is, they will have the form exhibited in (38).

(38)
$$
\left\{
\begin{array}{l}
\begin{bmatrix} \text{CAT} & = C_1 \\ & \cdot \\ & \cdot \\ & \cdot \end{bmatrix} \\[2mm]
\begin{bmatrix} \text{CAT} & = C_2 \\ & \cdot \\ & \cdot \\ & \cdot \end{bmatrix} \\[2mm]
\begin{bmatrix} \text{CAT} & = C_3 \\ & \cdot \\ & \cdot \\ & \cdot \end{bmatrix} \\[2mm]
\cdot \\ \cdot \\ \cdot
\end{array}
\right\}
$$

A Grammar of Simple Sentences

In this section, I examine (51), the sentence part of a simple grammar covering such sentences as (39) – (50).

(39) *Jesus wept*

(40) *Brutus killed Caesar*

(41) *Caesar was killed by Brutus*

(42) *They gave Socrates hemlock*

(43) *They gave hemlock to Socrates*

(44) *?They gave to Socrates hemlock*

(45) *Socrates was given hemlock by them*

(46) *?Socrates was given by them hemlock*

(47) *Hemlock was given to Socrates by them*

(48) *Hemlock was given by them to Socrates*

(49) *Socrates was given hemlock*

(50) *Hemlock was given to Socrates*

Specifically, the sequence of word descriptions corresponding to (39) results from unifying (52) with (51); (40) and (41) from unifying (53) with (51); (42) through (48) from unifying (54) with (51); and (49) and (50) from unifying (55) with (51).

(51)
$$
\begin{bmatrix}
\text{CAT} = \text{S} \\
(\text{SUBJ V} \ldots) \\
\text{FV} = \begin{bmatrix} \text{INFLEXION} = \langle \text{SUBJ INFLEXION} \rangle \end{bmatrix} \\
\text{VERB} = \begin{bmatrix} \text{CAT} & = \text{VERB} \\ \text{LEX} & = \text{ANY} \end{bmatrix} \\
\left\{
\begin{bmatrix}
\text{PROT} & = \text{NONE} \\
\text{VERB} & = \begin{bmatrix} \text{VOICE} = \text{PASSIVE} \end{bmatrix}
\end{bmatrix}
\\
\begin{bmatrix}
\text{PROT} = \begin{bmatrix} \text{CAT} & = \text{NP} \\ \text{LEX} & = \text{ANY} \end{bmatrix} \\
\left\{
\begin{bmatrix}
(\text{PROT V} \ldots) \\
\text{VERB} = \begin{bmatrix} \text{VOICE} = \text{ACTIVE} \end{bmatrix}
\end{bmatrix}
\\
\begin{bmatrix}
(\ldots \text{V} \ldots \text{BY-OBJ} \ldots) \\
\text{BY-OBJ} = \begin{bmatrix} \text{CAT} & = \text{PP} \\ \text{PREP} & = \text{by} \\ \text{OBJ} & = \langle \text{PROT} \rangle = \text{ANY} \end{bmatrix} \\
\text{VERB} = \begin{bmatrix} \text{VOICE} = \text{PASSIVE} \end{bmatrix}
\end{bmatrix}
\right\}
\end{bmatrix}
\right\}
\\
\left\{
\begin{bmatrix} \text{GOAL} = \text{NONE} \end{bmatrix}
\\
\begin{bmatrix}
(\ldots \text{GOAL} \ldots) \\
\text{GOAL} = \begin{bmatrix} \text{CAT} & = \text{NP} \\ \text{LEX} & = \text{ANY} \end{bmatrix} \\
\left\{
\begin{bmatrix} \text{BENEF} = \text{NONE} \end{bmatrix}
\\
\begin{bmatrix}
\text{BENEF} = \begin{bmatrix} \text{CAT} & = \text{NP} \\ \text{LEX} & = \text{ANY} \end{bmatrix} \\
\left\{
\begin{bmatrix}
(\ldots \text{BENEF} \ldots \text{GOAL} \ldots) \\
\begin{bmatrix}
(\ldots \text{V} \ldots \text{TO-OBJ} \ldots) \\
\text{TO-OBJ} = \begin{bmatrix} \text{CAT} & = \text{PP} \\ \text{PREP} & = \text{to} \\ \text{OBJ} & = \langle \text{BENEF} \rangle = \text{ANY} \end{bmatrix}
\end{bmatrix}
\end{bmatrix}
\right\}
\end{bmatrix}
\right\}
\end{bmatrix}
\right\}
\\
\left\{
\begin{bmatrix}
\text{V} = \text{FV} = \text{VERB} = \begin{bmatrix} \text{TENSE} & = \langle \text{TENSE} \rangle = \text{ANY} \\ \text{VOICE} & = \text{ACTIVE} \end{bmatrix}
\end{bmatrix}
\\
\begin{bmatrix}
\text{VERB} = \begin{bmatrix} \text{VOICE} = \text{PASSIVE} \end{bmatrix} \\
\text{V} = \begin{bmatrix}
\text{CAT} & = \text{VG} \\
\text{V1} & = \langle \text{FV} \rangle = \begin{bmatrix} \text{CAT} & = \text{VERB} \\ \text{LEX} & = \text{be} \\ \text{TENSE} & = \langle \text{TENSE} \rangle = \text{ANY} \end{bmatrix} \\
\text{V2} & = \langle \text{VERB} \rangle = \begin{bmatrix} \text{TENSE} = \text{PASTP} \end{bmatrix}
\end{bmatrix}
\end{bmatrix}
\right\}
\end{bmatrix}
$$

(52)
$$
\begin{bmatrix}
\text{CAT} & = \text{S} \\
\text{PROT} & = \begin{bmatrix} \text{LEX} = \text{Jesus} \end{bmatrix} \\
\text{GOAL} & = \text{NONE} \\
\text{BENEF} & = \text{NONE} \\
\text{VERB} & = \begin{bmatrix} \text{LEX} = \text{weep} \end{bmatrix} \\
\text{TENSE} & = \text{PRES}
\end{bmatrix}
$$

(53) $\begin{bmatrix} \text{CAT} & = \text{S} \\ \text{PROT} & = \begin{bmatrix} \text{LEX} = \text{Brutus} \end{bmatrix} \\ \text{GOAL} & = \begin{bmatrix} \text{LEX} = \text{Caesar} \end{bmatrix} \\ \text{BENEF} & = \text{NONE} \\ \text{VERB} & = \begin{bmatrix} \text{LEX} = \text{kill} \end{bmatrix} \\ \text{TENSE} & = \text{PRES} \end{bmatrix}$

(54) $\begin{bmatrix} \text{CAT} & = \text{S} \\ \text{PROT} & = \begin{bmatrix} \text{LEX} = \text{They} \end{bmatrix} \\ \text{GOAL} & = \begin{bmatrix} \text{LEX} = \text{hemlock} \end{bmatrix} \\ \text{BENEF} & = \begin{bmatrix} \text{LEX} = \text{Socrates} \end{bmatrix} \\ \text{VERB} & = \begin{bmatrix} \text{LEX} = \text{give} \end{bmatrix} \\ \text{TENSE} & = \text{PRES} \end{bmatrix}$

(55) $\begin{bmatrix} \text{CAT} & = \text{S} \\ \text{PROT} & = \text{NONE} \\ \text{GOAL} & = \begin{bmatrix} \text{LEX} = \text{hemlock} \end{bmatrix} \\ \text{BENEF} & = \begin{bmatrix} \text{LEX} = \text{Socrates} \end{bmatrix} \\ \text{VERB} & = \begin{bmatrix} \text{LEX} = \text{give} \end{bmatrix} \\ \text{TENSE} & = \text{PRES} \end{bmatrix}$

No claims are made for the theoretical soundness of the analysis represented in (51), which was designed only to elucidate the formalism. In particular, it should not be taken as implying an argument in favor of eliminating *VP*.

(51) contains six alternations, five of which represent choices that the speaker must make in the course of framing a sentence. Indeed, there is a strong family resemblance between grammatical descriptions in this formalism and *systems* that Halliday (1961, 1967-8) uses to represent such sets of choices. (51), for example, corresponds closely to the system (56).

(56) $\left\{ \begin{array}{l} \begin{bmatrix} -\text{without protagonist} \\ -\text{with protagonist} \begin{bmatrix} -\text{active} \\ -\text{passive} \end{bmatrix} \end{bmatrix} \\ \begin{bmatrix} -\text{without goal} \\ -\text{ with goal} \begin{bmatrix} -\text{without beneficiary} \\ -\text{with beneficiary} \begin{bmatrix} -\text{indirect object} \\ -\text{prepositional object} \end{bmatrix} \end{bmatrix} \end{bmatrix} \end{array} \right.$

The sixth alternation is different only in that, as we shall see, the choice to be made here is determined entirely by the choices made at the other five.

The first four terms in (51) state that any object meeting this description will be a sentence whose first two constituents are a subject and a verb, that the values of the paths ⟨FV INFLEXION⟩ and ⟨SUBJ INFLEXION⟩ will be equal and that VERB – to be distinguished from V – will have the feature [CAT = VERB] and a non-null value for the attribute LEX. ANY is not a true *symbol* in the sense defined above. In the first place, any description containing ANY is deemed to be incomplete. I will give an example to illustrate the point of this shortly. Secondly, if a pair of descriptions are unified, one with the feature $\langle \alpha \rangle =$ ANY and the other with the feature $\langle \alpha \rangle = v$, where v is not NONE, the result will have the feature $\langle \alpha \rangle = v$. In other words, ANY is a "wild card" that will match any substantive, non-null, value.

The remainder of (51) consists of three alternations. The first of these says that any sentence meeting the description will either have no protagonist, in which case it will have the feature $\langle$VERB VOICE$\rangle =$ PASSIVE, or its protagonist will be a noun phrase with a substantive value for the attribute LEX. The embedded alternation says that a sentence with a protagonist can be either active or passive. In the first case, the protagonist is a constituent which immediately precedes the verb and in the second, there will be a constituent called BY-OBJ somewhere after the verb. This BY-OBJ will be a prepositional phrase with preposition *by* and the protagonist of the sentence as object. If the sentence is active, it is implicit that the values of PROT and SUBJ will be unified because the patters (SUBJ V ...) and (PROT V ...) must be unified.

The second major alternation in (51) states that, if the sentence has a value for the GOAL attribute, then that value describes a constituent which is a noun phrase with a substantive value for the LEX attribute. Furthermore, only if there is a goal can there be a beneficiary. If there is a beneficiary, it must be a substantive noun phrase which can either precede the goal in the sentence or be the object of the preposition *to* following the goal. If the beneficiary precedes the goal, it will follow the verb as indirect object in active sentences and be the subject of passive sentences, for otherwise there would not be a substantive subject. If there is no beneficiary, the goal is the subject in passive sentences.

The last alternation provides the correct value for the V-attribute according as the sentence is active or passive. In an active sentence, V, the surface verb, FV, the finite verb, and VERB, the "deep" verb are all the same and the values are unified and given the tense attribute of the sentence. In a passive sentence, V is a verbal group consisting of two verbs. The first is an appropriately tensed form of *be* and the second is the past participle of the value of VERB. The first of these is the finite verb and the one whose INFLEXION must be unified with that of the subject.

Consider now the sentences that could be generated from the description (57) which makes no mention of the attribute BENEF.

(57) $\begin{bmatrix} \text{CAT} & = \text{S} \\ \text{PROT} & = \begin{bmatrix} \text{LEX} = \text{They} \end{bmatrix} \\ \text{GOAL} & = \begin{bmatrix} \text{LEX} = \text{hemlock} \end{bmatrix} \\ \text{VERB} & = \begin{bmatrix} \text{LEX} = \text{give} \end{bmatrix} \\ \text{TENSE} & = \text{PRES} \end{bmatrix}$

They seem to include (60) – (63), in which "???" represents a beneficiary with the feature [LEX = ANY] supplied by the grammar, as well as (58) and (59).

(58) *They gave hemlock*

(59) *Hemlock was given by them*

(60) *They gave ??? hemlock*

(61) *They gave hemlock to ???*

(62) *??? was given hemlock by them*

(63) *Hemlock was given to ??? by them*

More accurately, (57) describes all the sentences that can be obtained from (60) – (63) by replacing "???" with a noun phrase. It is precisely to exclude such cases as these that the special symbol ANY is provided in the formalism. In (51), either an explicit value for BENEF must be provided in the initial description of a sentence, or the description that results from unifying it with the grammar will be deemed incomplete.

While it is indeed the case that (51) correctly describes (39) – (50), it also describes such sentences as (64) – (67).

(64) *Jesus gave*

(65) *Brutus wept Caesar*

(66) *Caesar was given by Brutus*

(67) *Hemlock was wept to Socrates*

I shall describe a simple way of excluding these here and another, which may be preferable, in the following section. The simplest solution is to employ essentially the same device as is used in (51) for subject-verb agreement and include in the grammar something like (68). This requires appropriate values in the lexical entry for each verb. The entries for the verbs in the examples would be somewhat as in (69) – (71).

$$(68) \quad \left[\text{VERB} = \begin{bmatrix} \text{PROT} & = \langle \text{PROT} \rangle \\ \text{GOAL} & = \langle \text{GOAL} \rangle \\ \text{BENEF} & = \langle \text{BENEF} \rangle \end{bmatrix} \right]$$

$$(69) \quad \begin{bmatrix} \text{CAT} & = \text{VERB} \\ \text{LEX} & = \text{weep} \\ \text{GOAL} & = \text{NONE} \end{bmatrix}$$

$$(70) \quad \begin{bmatrix} \text{CAT} & = \text{VERB} \\ \text{LEX} & = \text{kill} \\ \text{BENEF} & = \text{NONE} \end{bmatrix}$$

$$(71) \quad \begin{bmatrix} \text{CAT} & = \text{VERB} \\ \text{LEX} & = \text{give} \end{bmatrix}$$

This guarantees that *weep*, for example, can only be the verb of a sentence that has the feature [GOAL = NONE] which, according to the grammar, implies that it must also have the feature [BENEF = NONE]. The principal disadvantage of this solution is that it replicates large amounts of the sentence structure within the description of the verb.

Some More Complex Phenomena

In this section, I give a brief sketch of how functional grammar accounts for the phenomena that require unbounded-movement rules of transformational grammar. Specifically, I shall consider (1) topicalization and relativization; (2) subject raising.

Suppose that the grammar describes noun phrases somewhat as in (72) and phrases of category $\overline{S}$ as in (73). The "↑" symbol provides a way of referring to levels in the constituent structure above the one to which the current description is being applied. Suppose that a given noun phrase is the direct object of the comment of the relative of the direct object of the comment of the matrix sentence; that is, it is the value of the path ⟨COMMENT DOBJ REL COMMENT DOBJ⟩ and that the grammar is now being unified with that noun phrase. ⟨↑REL⟩ refers to the higher-level constituent – presumably a noun phrase – in whose REL it is embedded. In other words, it refers to the value of ⟨COMMENT DOBJ⟩ in the matrix sentence. ⟨↑REL HEAD⟩ refers to the HEAD of that noun phrase. DOBJ refers to the lower sentence, in which the current noun phrase fills the role of direct object, that is, to the value of ⟨COMMENT DOBJ REL COMMENT⟩. In general, if ⟨$\alpha_1...\alpha_i\alpha_{i+1}...\alpha_n$⟩ is the path that identifies the current constituent, and α_{i+1} does not occur in ⟨$\alpha_{i+2}...\alpha_n$⟩, then ↑ α_{i+1} refers to the value of ⟨$\alpha_1...\alpha_i$⟩.

(72)
$$
\begin{bmatrix}
\text{CAT} = \text{NP} \\
\left\{
\begin{array}{l}
\begin{bmatrix}
\text{(TOPIC COMMENT)} \\
\text{TOPIC} = \begin{bmatrix} \text{CAT} = \text{NP} \\ \text{GAP} = \text{ANY} \end{bmatrix} \\
\text{COMMENT} = \begin{bmatrix} \text{CAT} = \overline{S} \end{bmatrix}
\end{bmatrix} \\
\begin{bmatrix}
\text{(ART HEAD ...)} \\
\text{ART} = \begin{bmatrix} \text{CAT} = \text{DEF} \end{bmatrix} \\
\text{HEAD} = \begin{bmatrix} \text{CAT} = \text{NOUN} \end{bmatrix} \\
\left\{
\begin{array}{l}
\begin{bmatrix} \text{REL} = \text{NONE} \end{bmatrix} \\
\begin{bmatrix} \text{(... REL)} \\ \text{REL} = \begin{bmatrix} \text{CAT} = \text{S} \end{bmatrix} \end{bmatrix}
\end{array}
\right\} \\
\langle\rangle = \langle\uparrow \text{ COMMENT TOPIC}\rangle = \begin{bmatrix} \text{GAP} = ? \end{bmatrix}
\end{bmatrix}
\end{array}
\right\}
\end{bmatrix}
$$

(73)
$$
\begin{bmatrix}
\text{CAT} = \overline{S} \\
\text{(... COMMENT)} \\
\text{COMMENT} = \begin{bmatrix} \text{CAT} = \text{S} \end{bmatrix} \\
\left\{
\begin{array}{l}
\begin{bmatrix} \text{TOPIC} = \text{NONE} \end{bmatrix} \\
\text{TOPIC} = \langle\uparrow \text{ COMMENT TOPIC}\rangle = \text{ANY} \\
\text{(TOPIC ...)}
\end{array}
\right\}
\end{bmatrix}
$$

For present purposes, I take it that main and relative clauses, among others, belong to the category $\overline{S}$ whose constituents are an optional TOPIC and an obligatory COMMENT. A noun phrase is either a determiner followed by a noun or, to provide for relative clauses, a noun phrase as the value of TOPIC followed by an $\overline{S}$ as the value of COMMENT. Alternatively, a noun phrase can simply be unified with the TOPIC of the lowest constituent in whose COMMENT it is embedded and with the feature [GAP = ?].

The sign "?", occurring as the value of an attribute, is a meta-symbol each instance of which represents a different symbol not otherwise occurring in the description. By requiring that the value of GAP be unique in this way, we ensure that a given TOPIC be unified with at most one *NP* in the way just described; that is, that there should be only one trace, or *gap* corresponding to it. The grammar would therefore describe the sentence *The soup the boys liked* somewhat as in (74). The same sequence of words is described in (75) as a noun phrase. Notice that the COMMENT of (75) is just (74).

(74)
$$
\begin{bmatrix}
\text{CAT} = \overline{S} \\[4pt]
\text{TOPIC} = \begin{bmatrix} \text{CAT} = \text{NP} \\ \text{GAP} = \text{x} \\ \text{... The soup} \end{bmatrix} \\[12pt]
\text{COMMENT} = \begin{bmatrix} \text{CAT} = \text{S} \\ \text{PROT} = \text{The boys} \\ \text{VERB} = \text{like} \\ \text{GOAL} = \langle \text{TOPIC} \rangle \end{bmatrix}
\end{bmatrix}
$$

(75)
$$
\begin{bmatrix}
\text{CAT} = \text{NP} \\
\text{TOPIC} = \langle \text{COMMENT TOPIC} \rangle \\[4pt]
\text{COMMENT} = \begin{bmatrix}
\text{CAT} = \overline{S} \\[4pt]
\text{TOPIC} = \begin{bmatrix} \text{CAT} = \text{NP} \\ \text{GAP} = \text{x} \\ \text{... The soup} \end{bmatrix} \\[12pt]
\text{COMMENT} = \begin{bmatrix} \text{CAT} = \text{S} \\ \text{PROT} = \text{The boys} \\ \text{VERB} = \text{like} \\ \text{GOAL} = \langle \text{TOPIC} \rangle \end{bmatrix}
\end{bmatrix}
\end{bmatrix}
$$

Suppose, now, that the lexical entry for a relative pronoun is (76). According to (72), it is a noun phrase with neither TOPIC nor HEAD constituents; its description must therefore be unified with that of a TOPIC higher in the constituent structure. Since relative pronouns themselves function as TOPICS of $\overline{S}$'s. there must be some noun phrase in the corresponding COMMENT with which they are also unified. The description of *the soup that the boys liked* will therefore also be (75).

This analysis covers – it is tempting to say *predicts* – Pied Piping. Thus (77) describes the sentence *In the house the boys live* and (78) describes the noun phrase *The house in which the boys live*. The relative pronoun in the prepositional phrase is unified with the TOPIC of the outer noun phrase *the house* to give, as TOPIC of the $\overline{S}$, a description for *in the house*. This is then unified with the value of the LOC attribute in the S on the understanding that prepositional phrases, like noun phrases, may be unified with higher TOPICS just in case they have no local constituents.

(76)
$$
\begin{bmatrix}
\text{CAT} = \text{NP} \\
\text{LEX} = \text{Rel} \\
\text{TOPIC} = \text{HEAD} = \text{ANY}
\end{bmatrix}
$$

(77)
$$
\begin{bmatrix}
\text{CAT} = \overline{S} \\[4pt]
\text{TOPIC} = \begin{bmatrix} \text{CAT} = \text{PP} \\ \text{GAP} = \text{x} \\ \text{PREP} = \text{in} \\ \text{OBJ} = \text{the house} \end{bmatrix} \\[18pt]
\text{COMMENT} = \begin{bmatrix} \text{CAT} = \text{S} \\ \text{PROT} = \text{The boys} \\ \text{VERB} = \text{live} \\ \text{LOC} = \langle \text{TOPIC} \rangle \end{bmatrix}
\end{bmatrix}
$$

(78)
$$
\begin{bmatrix}
\text{CAT} = \text{NP} \\
\text{TOPIC} = \langle \text{COMMENT TOPIC} \rangle \\[4pt]
\text{COMMENT} = \begin{bmatrix}
\text{CAT} = \overline{S} \\[4pt]
\text{TOPIC} = \begin{bmatrix} \text{CAT} = \text{PP} \\ \text{GAP} = \text{x} \\ \text{PREP} = \text{in} \\ \text{OBJ} = \text{the house} \end{bmatrix} \\[18pt]
\text{COMMENT} = \begin{bmatrix} \text{CAT} = \text{S} \\ \text{PROT} = \text{The boys} \\ \text{VERB} = \text{live} \\ \text{LOC} = \langle \text{TOPIC} \rangle \end{bmatrix}
\end{bmatrix}
\end{bmatrix}
$$

The "↑" device also suggests a solution to a large class of problems for which *Raising* rules are invoked in transformational grammar. If the grammar in (51) were expanded to provide for sentential complements as values of the attribute SCOMP, it is easy to see how it would interact appropriately with lexical entries such as (79) and (80).

(79)
$$
\begin{bmatrix}
\text{CAT} = \text{VERB} \\
\text{LEX} = \text{expect} \\
\text{↑VERB} = \begin{bmatrix} \text{BENEF} = \text{NONE} \end{bmatrix} \\[4pt]
\left\{ \begin{bmatrix} \langle \text{↑VERB GOAL} \rangle = \text{NONE} \\ \langle \text{↑VERB SCOMP SUBJ} \rangle = \langle \text{↑VERB PROT} \rangle = \text{ANY} \end{bmatrix} \right. \\
\left. \begin{bmatrix} \langle \text{↑VERB SCOMP SUBJ} \rangle = \langle \text{↑VERB GOAL} \rangle = \text{ANY} \end{bmatrix} \right\}
\end{bmatrix}
$$

(80)
$$
\begin{bmatrix}
\text{CAT} = \text{VERB} \\
\text{LEX} = \text{persuade} \\
\text{↑VERB} = \begin{bmatrix} \text{BENEF} = \text{NONE} \end{bmatrix} \\
\langle \text{↑VERB SCOMP SUBJ} \rangle = \langle \text{↑VERB GOAL} \rangle = \text{ANY}
\end{bmatrix}
$$

Example (79) requires that the phrase in which *expect* functions as VERB have the feature [BENEF = NONE] and that the SUBJ of the SCOMP of that phrase be unified with the value of PROT if the value of GOAL is NONE; otherwise with the value of GOAL. In other words, the subject of the complement will be the description of *John* in the description of *John expected to go*, and *Mary* in *John expected Mary to go*. (80), on the other hand, requires the phrase in which *persuade* functions as VERB to have a substantive value for the GOAL attribute, which is unified with the subject of the complement.

The lexical entries of *weep* and *kill* can be restated as (81) and (82) on the analogy of (79) and (80), thus avoiding the disadvantage of my previous proposal, namely that much of the sentential structure is restated as part of the description of the verb.

(81) $\begin{bmatrix} \text{CAT} = \text{VERB} \\ \text{LEX} = \text{weep} \\ \uparrow\text{VERB} = \begin{bmatrix} \text{GOAL} = \text{NONE} \end{bmatrix} \end{bmatrix}$

(82) $\begin{bmatrix} \text{CAT} = \text{VERB} \\ \text{LEX} = \text{kill} \\ \uparrow\text{VERB} = \begin{bmatrix} \text{BENEF} = \text{NONE} \end{bmatrix} \end{bmatrix}$

So, for example, (81) causes any constituent in which *weep* is the VERB to be unified with [GOAL = NONE].

Conclusion

It is the business of syntax to state constraints on the relations that words and phrases contract by virtue of their position in sentences. One of the principal attractions of functional grammar is that it states these constraints simply and explicitly. In other words, the constraints are not manifested only in objects that can be produced by following a set of rules that constitute the grammar. A good *prima facie* case can therefore be made for functional grammar as the form in which a child stores the grammatical knowledge he acquires. The null grammar describes all possible languages and to reduce the range of languages described is, generally speaking, to add new features to the current set. Delicate interactions such as those that occur between the members of ordered sets of rules are largely absent.

One of the advantages that I claimed for functional grammar at the outset was that it places the logical relations that words and phrases contract on an equal footing with relations that expound communicative functions. It is noteworthy that those linguists that have given equal weight to these two aspects of language have not, for the most part, constructed formal theories. This is accounted for partly by current fashion. But it is also due to a fundamental conflict between the demands of formalization and the clarity that comes from keeping statements about grammatical relations separate when they are exponents of separate kinds of meaning relations. This is the kind of clarity that presumably motivates Halliday's systems in which grammatical phenomena are collected together more because of similarities in what they expound than because of the way they interact in a carefully articulated generative scheme.

A frontal attack on the design of a formalism to meet both sets of requirements all too easily compounds previous errors and results in a device of wondrous complexity (see, for example, Hudson 1971). I hope that the formalism proposed here may be simple enough in its basic design to avoid this danger. It treats of one kind of entity only, namely functional descriptions. Grammatical constructions, lexical entries, and the grammar itself are known to the formalism only through this one type of representation. Unification is the only operation that is used, and it is also simple and intuitive, for it is nothing more than a slight embellishment of the notion of set union.

Publications referenced
Bresnan 1978; Dik 1978; Halliday 1961; Halliday 1967-68; Hudson 1971.

## 21

Algorithm Schemata and Data Structures in Syntactic Processing

Abstract

The space in which models of human parsing strategy are to be sought is large. This paper is an exploration of that space, attempting to show what its dimensions are and what some of the choices are that the psycholinguist must face. Such an exploration as this may provide some protection against the common tendency to let some choices go by default.

A notion of *configuration tables* is used to locate algorithms on two dimensions according as (1) they work top-down or bottom-up, and (2) they are directed or undirected. The algorithms occupying a particular place in this two dimensional space constitute an *algorithm schema* . The notion of a *chart* is used to show how to limit the amount of work a parser must do by ensuring that nothing is done more than once. Finally, the notion of an *agenda* is introduced to show how a rich variety of psychological strategies can be combined in a principled way with a given algorithm schema to yield an algorithm.

Interest in context-free grammars and associated parsing techniques has recently been rekindled among theoretical linguists and psycholinguists. A number of reasons for this suggest themselves. Chomsky's program for linguistics values a grammar more highly the more constrained the theoretical framework in which it is written. It is only by assuming that the human linguistic faculty is specialized for a narrow class of languages that we may hope to explain the prodigious feats of language learning accomplished by even the dullest of children in their first six years. So goes the argument. Generally, the most desirable constraints have been held to be those that place a theory low on the scale of weak generative power. In other words, the larger the class of languages that a theory cannot characterize at all – provided this class contains no natural languages – the better the theory.[1] However, determined attempts to modify tranformational grammar so as to reduce its weak generative power in a reasonably motivated manner have been largely unsuccessful. The overall theory remains relatively unconstrained. Bids for explanatory adequacy on its behalf continue to be based almost entirely on lists of *constraints* . These are more or less arbitrary from the point of view of the theory, and appended to it as riders and footnotes.

---

[1]This is not an accurate characterization of Chomsky's own current view.

At the same time, it came to be recognized that the so-called *proofs* made by early generative grammarians of the proposition that natural languages are not context free had been accepted far too eagerly (see, for example, Gazdar 1979a and 1979b). Context-free grammars occupy a low position in the hierarchy of weak generative power and they have the additional advantages of conceptual simplicity and susceptibility to algorithmic treatment. This last is not, of course, a requirement for a theory of linguistic competence but, *ceteris paribus*, a competence theory that also makes claims about the nature of linguistic performance is to be preferred.

Bresnan (1978) and others have pointed out that much of the machinery of transformations was not only unnecessary but also inappropriate even for such established and apparently natural uses as passivization. Bresnan proposed eliminating large numbers of transformational rules in favor of much weaker lexical redundancy rules. The only transformations that would remain according to this proposal would be *unbounded-movement* rules, such as topicalization and relativization, or possibly just a single *WH-movement* rule. With so much of the burden removed from it, the idea of eliminating the heavy machinery of transformations altogether becomes increasingly attractive.

At the same time, various new theories of grammar have been developed by computational linguists. While often not strictly context free, their grammars were of a sufficiently similar kind to be processed by minor variants of context-free algorithms. A sadly neglected early contribution to this line of development was that of Gilbert Harman (1963) whose theory made use of phrase-marker trees with complex symbols at the nodes and conventions by which features of dominating nodes were inherited by their descendents. Far more influential were the Augmented Transition Network (ATN) grammars of Woods and Kaplan (1971). These are not equivalent to context-free grammars but, like Harman's scheme, they arise by making relatively minor changes to the basic context-free formalism, mainly in the direction of permitting operations on complex symbols. Fairly straightforward and easily understood processing strategies can be used. Because of their susceptibility to algorithmic treatment, the ATN grammars have been proposed as a theory of linguistic performance (see, for example Kaplan (1972 and 1978), Wanner, Kaplan and Shiner (1975) and Wanner and Maratsos (1978).

A psychological model of sentence production or comprehension based on context-free grammar or a related formalism will seek to make predictions about the computational resources required for these activities. It must therefore be related to specific computational strategies. However, the number of parsing and generation algorithms available is large and there is no reason to suppose that it will not grow indefinitely. It seems, therefore, that a psycholinguist interested in syntax must conduct his investigations in a very large space having as three of its dimensions the linguistic theory, the particular language description within that theory, and the processing algorithms. In principle, at least, he may look to theoretical linguists for some guidance in exploring the first two of these dimensions. He should expect to receive some assistance with the third from computer scientists in general and computational linguists in particular. For the most part, however, very little such assistance has been forthcoming.

I think there are two reasons for this. First, most work by computer scientists, for example that quoted in Kimball (1973), has been done with a view to the formalization of programming languages and the automatic analysis of programs written in them. The first requirement of a programming language is that it should not admit syntactic, or indeed any other, ambiguities. Furthermore, the languages are usually designed so as to make it possible for a parser to make local choices on the basis of strictly limited contexts. As a result, the parsing algorithms that have been explored have been of a highly specialized kind, by no means appropriate for application to natural languages.

Second, computer scientists and computational linguists have usually approached questions of syntactic processing as engineers in search of algorithms that would achieve processing economies of one kind or another. While it is true that this line of attack could, in principle, produce plausible psychological models, there is no *a priori* reason to suppose that an investigation guided entirely by questions of efficiency on existing computers will ever lead in this direction. Griffiths and Petrick (1965) provided a useful classification of existing parsing algorithms and restatements of canonical members of each class in an ingenious form designed to highlight their salient features and to provide some basis for comparison, mostly from the point of view of computational efficiency.

If, as I shall argue at the end of this paper, the notion of an algorithm as normally conceived is an inappropriate component of a model of linguistic performance, then a great deal of groundwork must still be laid before any substantial results in the psycholinguistic investigation of syntax can be expected. In some respects, my aim in this paper will be similar to that of Griffiths and Petrick (1965) in that I shall attempt to provide a conceptual vantage point from which to view a variety of different processing strategies and to assess the properties that distinguish them. I shall also discuss canonical representations of classes of algorithms. However, unlike Griffiths and Petrick, I shall not attempt to remove the mechanisms for achieving nondeterminism from the representations. In fact, I hold nondeterminism to be the crucial dimension along which systems that countenance ambiguity must be judged. Accordingly, there will be three major sections to the paper.

In section 2, I shall review the principal classes of syntactic processing methods that have been proposed.[2] While it is true that my main concern will be with parsing, I shall begin with some consideration of sentence generation. I do this mainly to introduce some basic notions and to show that it is all of a piece with parsing when viewed from an appropriate vantage point. I shall concentrate heavily on those properties of a syntactic processor that guarantee that it will do everything that must be done when processing a sentence, leaving until later the question of how to avoid duplication of effort. Following a practice that has become common, especially in the psychological literature, I shall assume a fairly general back-up strategy to provide for non-determinism. To achieve a representation of classes of processing strategies, suppressing unnecessary detail, I shall make use of what I call *algorithm schemata* which differ from algorithms as usually conceived in that the sequence of events is not always uniquely specified, though the function eventually computed is.

Section 3 will be devoted to showing the error of so cavalier an approach to ambi-

---

[2]I shall not consider predictive analysis which, while it can be assimilated to the framework to be developed, requires grammars to be cast in a special form, thereby raising problems that are beyond the scope of this paper.

guity and non-determinism. I shall show that it is not sufficient to simply assume some unspecified backup strategy and that, when this problem is given a central position in the assessment of processing techique, a different picture of the problem emerges. In particular, judgments of the probable computational costs of this or that strategy or grammatical device must be made afresh in the light of processing models that take nondeterminism seriously. The properties of a syntactic processor that enable it to avoid unnecessary computation steps will be a major concern in this section.

In section 4, I shall briefly consider how the algorithm schemata of the first two sections relate to specific algorithms and processing strategies. I shall urge the adoption of an algorithm schema, rather than any specific algorithm, in the construction of computer programs and psychological models of syntactic processing. The schema can be simulated by a particular algorithm, but this higher-order algorithm will have various properties that recommend it over the more well-known first-order algorithms.

21.1   Configuration Tables and Algorithm Schemata

For expository purposes, context-free grammars are usually described in terms of a top-down sentence-production process in which rules are applied to *derivation strings* to produce new derivation strings. The sequence of derivation strings involved is a *derivation* of the sentence. The process starts with a special derivation string consisting of just the initial symbol of the grammar. A derivation string to which no further rules can be applied is a *sentence*.

If it is required to obtain structures for the strings produced, one of a variety of modified versions of the basic procedure must be used. Suppose, for example, that syntactic structures, whether partial or complete, are represented by labeled bracketings, or *phrase markers*, $[\beta_1...\beta_k]_\alpha$ in which α is a non-terminal symbol and the β_i, $(1 \leq i \leq k)$ are either terminal symbols or other labeled bracketings. Partial structures will contain subexpressions of the form $[?]_\alpha$, called *open boxes* , to indicate nonterminals whose substructure has yet to be developed. Given a symbol α, it will sometimes be convenient in the discussion that follows to use $\mathcal{F}(\alpha)$ to refer to the open box $[?]_\alpha$ in case α is non-terminal, and otherwise to α itself.

The production process starts with the expression $[?]_S$ on the first line of the derivation. A new line is derived from an old one by applying the *transition rule* (1):

(1)   Select one open box $[?]_\alpha$ on the line and a rule $\alpha \rightarrow \beta_1 ... \beta_k$ from the grammar. Create a new configuration replacing the open box with $[\mathcal{F}(\beta_1) ... \mathcal{F}(\beta_k)]_\alpha$

Given the grammar shown in (2), such a structural derivation for the sentence *radio broadcasts pay* is shown in (3).

(2)							
1.	S	$\rightarrow$	NP VP	5.	VP	$\rightarrow$	V
2.	NP	$\rightarrow$	A N	6.	A	$\rightarrow$	pay, radio, ...
3.	NP	$\rightarrow$	N	7.	N	$\rightarrow$	broadcasts, pay, radio, ...
4.	VP	$\rightarrow$	V NP	8.	V	$\rightarrow$	broadcasts, pay, radio, ...

Each line in (3) shows, in the *Rule* column, the number of the grammar rule by which it was obtained and, in the *Parent* column, the number of the line giving the immediately preceding state of the process. In this case, the entry in the *Parent* column always refers to the immediately preceding line. This will not be true of the tables we shall consider later.

(3)

#	Parent	Rule	Configuration
1	0		$[?]_S$
2	1	1	$[[?]_{NP}[?]_{VP}]_S$
3	2	2	$[[[?]_A[?]_N]_{NP}[?]_{VP}]_S$
4	3	6	$[[[radio]_A[?]_N]_{NP}[?]_{VP}]_S$
5	4	7	$[[[radio]_A[broadcasts]_N]_{NP}[?]_{VP}]_S$
6	5	5	$[[[radio]_A[broadcasts]_N]_{NP}[[?]_V]_{VP}]_S$
7	5	5	$[[[radio]_A[broadcasts]_N]_{NP}[[pay]_V]_{VP}]_S$

(4)

#	Parent	Rule	Configuration
1	0		$[?]_S$
2	1	1	$[[?]_{NP}[?]_{VP}]_S$
3	2	2	$[[[?]_A[?]_N]_{NP}[?]_{VP}]_S$
4	2	3	$[[[?]_N]_{NP}[?]_{VP}]_S$
5	3	6	$[[[pay]_A[?]_N]_{NP}[?]_{VP}]_S$
6	3	6	$[[[radio]_A[?]_N]_{NP}[?]_{VP}]_S$
7	4	7	$[[[broadcasts]_N]_{NP}[?]_{VP}]_S$
8	4	7	$[[[pay]_N]_{NP}[?]_{VP}]_S$
9	4	7	$[[[radio]_N]_{NP}[?]_{VP}]_S$
10	3	6	$[[[pay]_A[broadcasts]_N]_{NP}[?]_{VP}]_S$
11	3	6	$[[[pay]_A[pay]_N]_{NP}[?]_{VP}]_S$
12	3	6	$[[[pay]_A[radio]_N]_{NP}[?]_{VP}]_S$
13	7	4	$[[[broadcasts]_N]_{NP}[[?]_V[?]_{NP}]_{VP}]_S$
14	7	5	$[[[broadcasts]_N]_{NP}[[?]_V]_{VP}]_S$
15	8	4	$[[[pay]_N]_{NP}[[?]_V[?]_{NP}]_{VP}]_S$
16	8	5	$[[[pay]_N]_{NP}[[?]_V]_{VP}]_S$
17	9	4	$[[[radio]_N]_{NP}[[?]_V[?]_{NP}]_{VP}]_S$
18	9	5	$[[[radio]_N]_{NP}[[?]_V]_{VP}]_S$
19	10	4	$[[[pay]_A[broadcasts]_N]_{NP}[[?]_V[?]_{NP}]_{VP}]_S$
20	10	5	$[[[pay]_A[broadcasts]_N]_{NP}[[?]_V]_{VP}]_S$
21	11	4	$[[[pay]_A[pay]_N]_{NP}[[?]_V[?]_{NP}]_{VP}]_S$
22	11	5	$[[[pay]_A[pay]_N]_{NP}[[?]_V]_{VP}]_S$
23	12	4	$[[[pay]_A[radio]_N]_{NP}[[?]_V[?]_{NP}]_{VP}]_S$
24	12	5	$[[[pay]_A[radio]_N]_{NP}[[?]_V]_{VP}]_S$
25	13	8	$[[[broadcasts]_N]_{NP}[[broadcasts]_V[?]_{NP}]_{VP}]_S$
26	13	8	$[[[broadcasts]_N]_{NP}[[pay]_V[?]_{NP}]_{VP}]_S$
27	13	8	$[[[broadcasts]_N]_{NP}[[radio]_V[?]_{NP}]_{VP}]_S$
28	14	8	$[[[broadcasts]_N]_{NP}[[broadcasts]_V]_{VP}]_S$
29	14	8	$[[[broadcasts]_N]_{NP}[[pay]_V]_{VP}]_S$
30	14	8	$[[[broadcasts]_N]_{NP}[[radio]_V]_{VP}]_S$

The derivation process just described is not an algorithm in the strict sense of the word because it does not specify the sequence of steps to be followed exactly. Rather it is an *algorithm schema*. The transition rule (1) does not specify which open box should be chosen or which of the rules expanding α is to be applied. However, all algorithms derived from this schema by determining these choices generate the same sentences, though possibly with different derivations. Suppose rule (1) is revised to read:

(5) Select one open box $[?]_\alpha$ on the line. For *each* rule $\alpha \to \beta_1 \ldots \beta_k$ in the grammar, create a new configuration, replacing the open box $[?]_\alpha$ with $[\mathcal{F}(\beta_1) \ldots \mathcal{F}(\beta_k)]_\alpha$

The result is an algorithm schema for producing all the sentences in the language of the grammar and the process will clearly terminate only in the degenerate case of a grammar like (2) that generates a finite language. The first thirty lines of a table generated according to this schema from the grammar (2) is shown in (4).

(3) and (4) are simple cases of *configuration tables* . Each line in such a table is a complete record of the *state* of a process at a particular moment. In other words, each line either represents a final state in the process or contains all the information necessary to take the next step. The outputs of the computation chronicled in a configuration table are typically configurations that have a certain syntactic property. In the case of structural derivations like (3) and (4), a line containing no open boxes is part of the output. Generally speaking, several different steps can be taken independently from a given state, as in (4), and in these cases, the process as a whole is said to be *non-deterministic* . It is therefore no longer the case that each rule in a configuration table is derived from the one above it and for this reason a *Parent* column is printed in each table. It is there entirely for expository purposes, as is the *Rule* column, and plays no role in the algorithm. All the processes I shall examine below are non-deterministic.

It is also generally true that configuration tables belong to equivalence classes the members of each of which show the computation of a single function of the same inputs. There are two reasons for this. First, while all lines with a given parent must follow the parent line, the transition rules impose no constraint on the way they are ordered relative to one another. Second, the transition rules in accordance with which the process passes from state to state may be underdetermined, as in the case of the standard sentence-production derivations with which we started. (1) specifies that an open box is to be replaced by a new subexpression, but the choice of the open box to replace is open. There is an implicit claim that the results will be the same whichever choice is made.

21.1.1 Bottom-up Production

Sentence production can also be described in terms of bottom-up operations on *coverings*. A covering is simply a sequence of phrases made up of the words in the string. So, for example, the sentence *I know the girl he married* has one covering consisting of a pronoun, a verb, and a noun phrase, and another consisting of a pronoun, a verb, two noun phrases, and another verb. It also has others. More precisely, a covering of a string is a sequence of phrase markers the labels on whose terminal nodes, when concatenated in the order of the sequence, constitute the string. It will usually be implicit that the coverings we are considering are constructed according to the rules of a particular grammar. The string of symbols obtained by reading off the root labels from a covering is a *root string* so that the two coverings of the sentence *I know the girl he married* just mentioned correspond to the root strings *PRON V NP* and *PRON V NP NP V*. Clearly every derivation string relative to a grammar is the root string for some covering, but covering strings are not necessarily also derivation strings. For example, *I know the girl he married* can be seen as the concatenation of the sentence *I know* and the topicalized sentence *the girl he married*. Accordingly, it has a covering whose root string is *S S* even though this would presumably not be a line in its derivation by any reasonable grammar. Similarly, relative to the grammar (2), the sentence *radio broadcasts pay* has a covering consisting of a sentence ($[[[radio]_N]_{NP}[[broadcasts]_v]_{VP}]_S$) followed by verb phrase ($[[pay]_V]_{VP}$), but no derivation *S VP*.

(6)

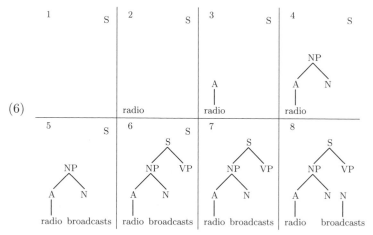

If the root string of a covering relative to a given grammar contains a substring that matches the right-hand side of a rule, a new covering relative to that grammar can be produced by replacing the corresponding subsequence of trees with a single tree whose root is labeled with the symbol on the left-hand side of the rule and whose immediate descendants are that subsequence of trees. The new covering is a reduction of the original one. Consider the sentence *I know the girl he married* once more. As we saw, an intuitively reasonable grammar would give it a covering with the root string *PRON V NP NP V*. Assuming a rule that rewrites *VP*'s as *V*'s, *PRON V NP NP VP* and *PRON VP NP NP V* are both reductions of this. Assuming another rule that expands *S* into *NP NP V*, the first of these has the further reduction *PRON V 5*. The bottom-up procedure aims to produce a string from which a root string consisting of the initial symbol of the grammar can be obtained by a series of reductions.

A fairly straightforward method of bottom-up generation makes use of a *reachability* table which shows, for every non-terminal symbol α in a grammar, the set $\mathcal{R}(\alpha)$ of terminal and non-terminal symbols each of which can be the first element in a string dominated by α. The reachability table for the grammar in (2) is as follows:

(7)

α	$\mathcal{R}(\alpha)$
S	NP, A, N, broadcasts, pay, radio
NP	A, N, broadcasts, pay, radio
VP	V, broadcasts, pay, radio
A	pay, radio, ...
N	broadcasts, pay, radio, ...
V	broadcasts, pay, radio, ...

The overall goal is to construct a sentence and accordingly the initial configuration consists of the open box $[?]_\alpha$. Whereas in (3) and (4), a configuration is a single phrase marker, we shall henceforth be working with configurations that are sequences of *terms* each of which is a phrase marker. A term that contains at least one open box will be called *active* ; others are *inactive* . The interpretation is as follows: the part of the sequence to the right of a given term shows the current state of progress towards filling the first open box in that term. So, for example, in the sequence $[?]_S[?]_{NP}[radio]_N$, the noun *radio* will fill the open box in the noun phrase, either alone or with other material yet to be obtained, and that will go towards filling the sentence. Thus, a well-formed configuration can contain at most one inactive term which must be in the final position.

The sequence of terms that make up a configuration are portions of a single tree structure that will eventually be constructed. The top node first term in a configuration will become the root of the final tree. Nonterminal symbols in a term that have no structure below them are the open boxes. Terms that contain open boxes are "looking for" other terms to dominate and they are therefore said to be *active* . If one term precedes another in a configuration, the latter will eventually come to be dominated by one such nonterminal in the former, that is, it will "fill the open box". (6) gives a graphic representation of the first eight configurations in the table (9). Notice that lines 5 and 6 in (9) each contain three terms and that squares 5 and 6 in (6) each contain three disconnected subtrees. Left-to-right ordering in the table corresponds to top-to-bottom ordering in the diagrams. The aim of the procedure will always be to conflate pairs of adjacent subtrees, building new structure below the upper one or above the lower one when necessary.

Suppose $[?]_\alpha$ is the first open box of the last term in the configuration. Using the reachability table, a terminal t is chosen that could be initial in a phrase of type α. If the grammar contains the rule $\alpha \to t$, then t can simply be used to fill the open box. In other words, a new configuration is created replacing the last two terms by $[t]_\alpha$ (See, for example, lines 3, 8, and 11 in (9)). Otherwise, a rule of the form $\beta \to \gamma_1 \ldots \gamma_k$ is found in the grammar, such that β can be initial in a phrase of type α and $\gamma = t$. t is replaced as the last term in the configuration by $[\mathcal{F}(\gamma_1)...\mathcal{F}(\gamma_k)]_\beta$. A rule of the required form must exist, given the way the terminal was chosen using the reachability table. If the term contains other open boxes, new terminals are chosen and the process repeats until they are all full. If the last term in a configuration contains no open boxes, it is inactive and is treated as though it were the most recently chosen terminal. The aim now becomes that of incorporating this term in the one that immediately precedes it in the configuration.

In summary, the process is governed by three transition rules:

(8)   1. **Append a terminal symbol**: If the last term in the configuration is active, let $[?]_\alpha$ be the first open box it contains. Select a terminal $t \in \mathcal{R}(\alpha)$ and create a new configuration by appending t to the current one.

2. **Find a dominating non-terminal**: If the last term is inactive, consider two adjacent terms g_i and g_{i+1}, of the current configuration. If g_{i+1} is of category α (i.e. it consists of the terminal α or an expression of the form $[...]_\alpha$) and $[?]_\beta$ is the first open box in g_i, for each rule $\gamma \to \delta_1 \ldots \delta_n$ such that $\gamma = \beta$

or $\gamma \in \mathcal{R}(\beta)$ and $\alpha = \delta_1$, create a new configuration replacing g_{i+1} with g_{i+1} $\mathcal{F}(\delta_2)...\mathcal{F}(\delta_n)]_\gamma$.

3. **Incorporate completed subgoal**: If the last term is inactive, consider two adjacent terms g_i and g_{i+1}, of the current configuration. If g_{i+1} is of category α and the first open box in g_i is $[?]_\alpha$, replace that open box with g_{i+1} and delete g_{i+1} from the configuration.

Rule 1 can apply only in circumstances in which rules 2 and 3 do not. Rules 2 and 3, however, do not exclude one another and, when both apply to the same configuration, the values chosen for i must be the same. The reason is easy to see. The application of each destroys the conditions of applicability of the other so that, if both lines of attack are to be explored, the rules must be applied simultaneously. In the examples in this paper, i is systematically chosen to be as large as possible. One result of this, which will be of interest in the next section, is that rules 2 and 3 will invariably be applied to a pair of terms the first of which is active, as the rules require, and the second of which is inactive. But if rules 2 or 3 can be applied in more than one place, that is, for more than one value of i, then only one is chosen and the choice is arbitrary. This is because applications of the rules to different terms is independent. To see that this is true, consider three adjacent terms ... $t_i\ t_{i+1}\ t_{i+2}$ ... of a configuration and suppose that transition rule 2 applies to both pairs $\langle t_i, t_{i+1} \rangle$ and $\langle t_{i+1}, t_{i+2} \rangle$. If it is applied to the first pair, t_{i+1} will be replaced by a new term u of the form $[t_{i+1}]_\alpha$ for some α. Since t_{i+1} is the first term dominated by α in u, the first open box in u is the same as the first open box in t_{i+1}. Applying rule 2 to the pair $\langle u, t_{i+2} \rangle$ will therefore be the same as applying it to $\langle t_{i+1}, t_{i+2} \rangle$. Suppose, on the other hand, that rule 2 is applied first to $\langle t_{i+1}, t_{i+2} \rangle$. In this case, t_{i+1} is unchanged and application to the first pair is therefore unaffected. An exactly parallel argument applies to rule 3 and to combinations of the two.

(9) is a configuration table showing how these transition rules can be used to generate the sentence *radio broadcasts pay*, in one of its syntactic readings, using the grammar (2). The column headed *TR* gives the number of the transition rule employed.

(9)

#	TR	Par	R	Configuration
1				$[?]_S$
2	1	1		$[?]_S radio$
3	2	2	6	$[?]_S[radio]_A$
4	2	3	2	$[?]_S[[radio]_A[?]_N]_{NP}$
5	1	4		$[?]_S[[radio]_A[?]_N]_{NP}broadcasts$
6	2	5	1	$[?]_S[[[radio]_A[?]_N]_{NP}[?]_{VP}]_S broadcasts$
7	3	6		$[[[radio]_A[?]_N]_{NP}[?]_{VP}]_S broadcasts$
8	2	7	7	$[[[radio]_A[?]_N]_{NP}[?]_{VP}]_S[broadcasts]_N$
9	3	8		$[[[radio]_A[broadcasts]_N]_{NP}[?]_{VP}]_S$
10	1	9		$[[[radio]_A[broadcasts]_N]_{NP}[?]_{VP}]_S pay$
11	2	10	8	$[[[radio]_A[broadcasts]_N]_{NP}[?]_{VP}]_S[pay]_V$
12	2	11	5	$[[[radio]_A[broadcasts]_N]_{NP}[?]_{VP}]_S[[pay]_V]_{VP}$
13	3	12		$[[[radio]_A[broadcasts]_N]_{NP}[[pay]_V]_{VP}]_S$

21.1.2 Bottom-up Parsing

Bottom-up sentence production is something of a *tour de force*. It is essentially a procedure of *synthesis by analysis* – a parsing procedure in which the string is constructed so as to ensure that the first hypothesis made about its structure at each step turns out right. The fully fledged parsing procedure can be derived from that just given with very few modifications. This time, however, the process is non-deterministic because it must countenance ambiguities.

I shall follow the usual practice in discussing parsing procedures of assuming that the terminals have been looked up in the lexicon in a previous step so that the data consists not of a string of terminals but a string of alternative lexical entries each of which is a family of degenerate phrase markers of the form $[t]_\alpha$, where t is a terminal and α a *pre-terminal* symbol. After lexical lookup, the sentence *radio broadcasts pay* takes on essentially the following form.

$$\left\{ \begin{array}{c} [radio]_A \\ [radio]_N \\ [radio]_V \end{array} \right\} \left\{ \begin{array}{c} [broadcasts]_V \\ [broadcasts]_N \end{array} \right\} \left\{ \begin{array}{c} [pay]_A \\ [pay]_N \\ [pay]_V \end{array} \right\}$$

Only the first two transition rules of the production procedure in (8) require modification. They must now read:

(10)   1. **Append a terminal symbol**: If the last goal in the list is active, let $[?]_\alpha$ be the first open box it contains. For each lexical entry $[w_i]_\beta$ of the next word in the string, $[w_i]$, such that such that $\beta = \alpha$ or $\beta \in \mathcal{R}(\alpha)$, create a new line in the table in which the open box is replaced by $[w_i]_\beta$.

      2. **Find a dominating non-terminal**: Consider two adjacent terms g_i and g_{i+1}, of the current configuration. If g_{i+1} is of category α and $[?]_\beta$ is the first open box in g_i, then for all rules $\gamma \to \delta_1 \ldots \delta_n$ such that $\gamma = \beta$ or $\gamma \in \mathcal{R}(\beta)$, and $\alpha = \delta_1$, create a new configuration replacing g_{i+1} with $g_{i+1} \mathcal{F}(\delta_2)...\mathcal{F}(\delta_n)]_\gamma$.

Rule 1 adds a terminal – or more strictly, a preterminal – to the end of a configuration whose current last term contains open boxes, that is, that represents a subtree with nonterminal symbols that dominate no substructure. The only lexical interpretations of the terminal that need be considered are those that can be dominated by the first nonterminal in the subtree that is still in need of substructure. Rule 2 builds some additional structure on top of the lower of a pair of adjacent subtrees with a view to eventually conflating them. (by rule 3).

Complete analyses appear in the table as lines that contain no active terms. (11) is a configuration table showing the analysis of the sentence *radio broadcasts pay* using the grammar in (2). The entries in the Pos. column show the serial number of the last terminal considered. Where transition rule 1 has been applied, the number of the relevant grammar rule is also given. In transition rule 2, rules of grammar are chosen in accordance with two criteria: (i) The symbol on the left-hand side of the rule must be reachable from the symbol beneath which it is eventually to be inserted ($\gamma = \beta$ or $\gamma \in \mathcal{R}(\beta)$) and (ii) the first symbol on the right-hand side of the rule must match a particular symbol already established in the configration ($\alpha = \delta_1$).

(11)

#	TR	Pos	Par	R	Configuration
1		0	0		$[?]_S$
2	1	1	1		$[?]_S[radio]_A$
3	1	1	1		$[?]_S[radio]_N$
4	2	1	2	2	$[?]_S[[radio]_A[?]_N]_{NP}$
5	2	1	3	3	$[?]_S[[radio]_N]_{NP}$
6	1	2	4		$[?]_S[[radio]_A[?]_N]_{NP}[broadcasts]_N$
7	2	1	5	1	$[?]_S[[[radio]_N]_{NP}[?]_{VP}]_S$
8	3	2	6		$[?]_S[[radio]_A[broadcasts]_N]_{NP}$
9	1	2	7		$[?]_S[[[radio]_N]_{NP}[?]_{VP}]_S[broadcasts]_V$
10	2	2	8	1	$[?]_S[[radio]_A[broadcasts]_N]_{NP}[?]_{VP}]_S$
11	2	2	9	4	$[?]_S[[[radio]_N]_{NP}[?]_{VP}]_S[[broadcasts]_V[?]_{NP}]_{VP}$
12	2	2	9	5	$[?]_S[[[radio]_N]_{NP}[?]_{VP}]_S[[broadcasts]_V]_{VP}$
13	1	3	10		$[?]_S[[[radio]_A[broadcasts]_N]_{NP}[?]_{VP}]_S[pay]_V$
14	1	3	11		$[?]_S[[[radio]_N]_{NP}[?]_{VP}]_S[[broadcasts]_V[?]_{NP}]_{VP}[pay]_A$
15	1	3	11		$[?]_S[[[radio]_N]_{NP}[?]_{VP}]_S[[broadcasts]_V[?]_{NP}]_{VP}[pay]_N$
16	3	2	12		$[?]_S[[[radio]_N]_{NP}[broadcasts]_V]_{VP}]_S$
17	2	3	13	4	$[?]_S[[[radio]_A[broadcasts]_N]_{NP}[?]_{VP}]_S[[pay]_V[?]_{NP}]_{VP}$
18	2	3	13	5	$[?]_S[[[radio]_A[broadcasts]_N]_{NP}[?]_{VP}]_S[[pay]_V]_{VP}$
19	2	3	14	2	$[?]_S[[[radio]_N]_{NP}[?]_{VP}]_S[[broadcasts]_V[?]_{NP}]_{VP}[[pay]_A[?]_N]_{NP}$
20	2	3	15	3	$[?]_S[[[radio]_N]_{NP}[?]_{VP}]_S[[broadcasts]_V[?]_{NP}]_{VP}[[pay]_N]_{NP}$
21	3	2	16		$[[[radio]_N]_{NP}[broadcasts]_V]_{VP}]_S$
22	3	3	18		$[?]_S[[[radio]_A[broadcasts]_N]_{NP}[[pay]_V]_{VP}]_S$
23	3	3	20		$[?]_S[[[radio]_N]_{NP}[?]_{VP}]_S[[broadcasts]_V[[pay]_N]_{NP}]_{VP}$
24	3	3	22		$[[[radio]_A[broadcasts]_N]_{NP}[[pay]_V]_{VP}]_S$
25	3	3	23		$[?]_S[[[radio]_N]_{NP}[[broadcasts]_V[[pay]_N]_{NP}]_{VP}]_S$
26	3	3	25		$[[[radio]_N]_{NP}[[broadcasts]_V[[pay]_N]_{NP}]_{VP}]_S$

It is the second of these criteria that is characteristic of a bottom-up process since it ensures that new non-terminals are introduced only when at least one branch connecting them to a terminal symbol has already been constructed. The first criterion characterizes the process as *directed* and it serves only to prevent the creation of certain phrases for which there is known to be no place in a higher-level structure. This process is also directed to the extent that transition rule 1 requires the terminal selected to be in the reachability set of a particular non-terminal symbol $\beta = \alpha$ or $\beta \in \mathcal{R}(\alpha)$. The *undirected* process that results from removing these conditions, though less efficient, is not only viable, but represents the type of bottom-up procedure that has most often been proposed. The complete set of transition rules for an undirected bottom-up parser would be as in (12):

(12)   1. **Append a terminal symbol**: If the last term in the configuration is active and there remain terminals in the string to be considered, create a new configuration for each lexical alternative of the next one and append it to the end of the configuration.

      2. **Find a dominating non-terminal**: If the last term is inactive, and g_i is of category α and a term of the current configuration, other than the last, then for all rules $\gamma \rightarrow \delta_1 \ldots \delta_n$ such that $\alpha = \delta_i$, replace g_i with $g_u \, [\mathcal{F}(\delta_2)\ldots\mathcal{F}(\delta_n)]_\gamma$. This operation is inhibited if the sum of terminals and open boxes in a new configuration were greater than the number of words in the analyzed string.

      3. **Incorporate completed subgoal**: If the last term is inactive, consider two adjacent terms g_i and g_{i+1}, of the current configuration. If g_{i+1} is of category α and the first open box in g_i is $[?]_\alpha$, replace that open box with g_{i+1} and delete g_{i+1} from the list.

The modification to rule 2 that inhibits the production of configurations with more open boxes than can be filled by the remainder of the string under analysis is called the *shaper* test and is due to Kuno and Oettinger (1964). It is needed here to ensure that the process will terminate even if the grammar contains *left-recursive* groups of rules. A rule of the form $\alpha \to \alpha$ ... constitutes such a group by itself. In general, a left-recursive group is of the form

$$
\begin{array}{ccl}
\alpha_1 & \to & \alpha_2 \, ... \\
\alpha_2 & \to & \alpha_3 \, ... \\
. & \to & . \\
. & \to & . \\
. & \to & . \\
\alpha_i & \to & \alpha_1 \, ...
\end{array}
$$

Top-down strategies are notoriously unstable in the presence of such rules unless restrained by something like the shaper test. We make the usual assumption that the grammar contains no cyclic sets of nonbranching rules, that is, there are no sets of the form:

$$
\begin{array}{ccl}
\alpha_1 & \to & \alpha_2 \\
\alpha_2 & \to & \alpha_3 \\
. & \to & . \\
. & \to & . \\
. & \to & . \\
\alpha_i & \to & \alpha_1
\end{array}
$$

The initial configuration consisting of the single term $[?]_S$ can be usefully eliminated from the configuration table for undirected bottom-up parsing provided that a configuration is entered in the table for each lexical entry of the first item in the string before the process begins. The complete configuration table for *radio broadcasts pay* using grammar (2) contains 72 configurations. A more modest example appears later in the paper at (25).

21.1.3 Top-down Parsing

We come finally to top-down parsing which is illustrated, in its directed variety, in (15). As before, the initial configuration is $[?]_S$. The transition rules are the same as in (10) except for the second which now reads as follows:

(13)   2. **Find a dominating non-terminal**: If the last term is inactive, consider two adjacent terms g_i and g_{i+1}, of the current configuration. If g_{i+1} is of category α and $[?]_\beta$ is the first open box in g_i, then for all rules $\beta \to \delta_1 \, ... \, \delta_n$ such that $\alpha = \gamma_1$ or $\alpha \in \mathcal{R}(\gamma_1)$, replace the first open box $[?]_\beta$ in g_i with g_{i+1} $\mathcal{F}(\delta_2)...\mathcal{F}(\delta_n)]_\beta$. As before, the operation is inhibited if the sum of terminals and open boxes in a new configuration would be greater than the number of words in the string being analyzed.

An undirected top-down parser differs in that the selection of the grammar rule to be applied does not make use of the reachability table. The appropriate transition rule is given in (14).

(14)   2. **Find a dominating non-terminal**: If the last term is inactive and g_i is a term in the current configuration and $[?]_\beta$ is the first open box that it contains, then for all rules $\beta \to \gamma_1 \dots \gamma_n$, replace the open box $[?]_\beta$ with $[\mathcal{F}(\delta_2)\dots\mathcal{F}(\delta_n)]_\beta$. The operation is inhibited if the sum of terminals and open boxes in a new configuration would be greater than the number of words in the string being analyzed.

(15)

#	T.R.	Pos.	Par.	R	Configuration
1		0	0		$[?]_S$
2	1	1	1		$[?]_S[radio]_A$
3	1	1	1		$[?]_S[radio]_N$
4	2	1	2	1	$[[?]_{NP}[?]_{VP}]_S[radio]_A$
5	2	1	3	1	$[[?]_{NP}[?]_{VP}]_S[radio]_N$
6	2	1	4	2	$[[[?]_A[?]_N]_{NP}[?]_{VP}]_S[radio]_A$
7	2	1	5	3	$[[[?]_N]_{NP}[?]_{VP}]_S[radio]_N$
8	3	1	6		$[[[radio]_A[?]_N]_{NP}[?]_{VP}]_S$
9	3	1	7		$[[[radio]_N]_{NP}[?]_{VP}]_S$
10	1	2	8		$[[[radio]_A[?]_N]_{NP}[?]_{VP}]_S[broadcasts]_N$
11	1	2	9		$[[[radio]_N]_{NP}[?]_{VP}]_S[broadcasts]_V$
12	3	2	10		$[[[radio]_A[broadcasts]_N]_{NP}[?]_{VP}]_S$
13	2	2	11	4	$[[[radio]_N]_{NP}[[?]_V[?]_{NP}]_{VP}]_S[broadcasts]_V$
14	2	2	11	5	$[[[radio]_N]_{NP}[[?]_V]_{VP}]_S[broadcasts]_V$
15	1	3	12		$[[[radio]_A[broadcasts]_N]_{NP}[?]_{VP}]_S[pay]_V$
16	3	2	13		$[[[radio]_N]_{NP}[[broadcasts]_V[?]_{NP}]_{VP}]_S$
17	3	2	14		$[[[radio]_N]_{NP}[[broadcasts]_V]_{VP}]_S$
18	2	3	15	5	$[[[radio]_A[broadcasts]_N]_{NP}[[?]_V]_{VP}]_S[pay]_V$
19	1	3	16		$[[[radio]_N]_{NP}[[broadcasts]_V[?]_{NP}]_{VP}]_S[pay]_A$
20	1	3	16		$[[[radio]_N]_{NP}[[broadcasts]_V[?]_{NP}]_{VP}]_S[pay]_N$
21	3	3	18		$[[[radio]_A[broadcasts]_N]_{NP}[[pay]_V]_{VP}]_S$
22	2	3	20	3	$[[[radio]_N]_{NP}[[broadcasts]_V[[?]_N]_{NP}]_{VP}]_S[pay]_N$
23	3	3	22		$[[[radio]_N]_{NP}[[broadcasts]_V[[pay]_N]_{NP}]_{VP}]_S$

21.1.4   Rule-Selection Tables

When expressed in terms of configuration tables, the differences between bottom-up and top-down parsing appear quite small. In (11), the transition from line 2 to line 4 uses rule 2 because the terminal at the end of the configuration on line 2 is of category A and rule 2 permits this to be immediately incorporated in a higher-level phrase, namely an NP. The reachability table guarantees that there is a place for this at the beginning of a sentence. A top-down strategy applies a rule that expands the symbol S, secure in the knowledge that the first symbol on the right-hand side of that rule can have an adjective on its left-most branch. Notice, however, that the only difference between the two strategies resides in the way the rules are chosen and not in any other detail of how the configuration table develops. A single set of transition rules could be written for both kinds of procedure if it were made to depend on a *Rule-Selection Table* instead of a reachability table.

A Rule-Selection Table is an m x n array, where m is the number of non-terminal symbols in the grammar that are not pre-terminals and n is the total number of non-terminals. The cell $\mathcal{S}_{\alpha,\beta}$ of a rule-selection table $\mathcal{S}$ contains the list of grammar rules to be used in transition rule 2 when α is the *upper* symbol and β is the *lower*. In other words, α is the label of the first open box in a term and the immediately following term in the configuration is $\mathcal{F}(\beta)$. For a top-down procedure, these rules will all be of the form $\alpha \rightarrow \gamma_1 \dots \gamma_n$. If the procedure is undirected, all rules whose left-hand symbol is α will be on the list. If it is directed, the list will contain only those for which $\beta = \gamma_1$ or $\beta \in \mathcal{R}(\gamma_1)$. (16) is a rule-selection table specifying a directed top-down procedure for grammar (2). The directed top-down procedure would have 2,3 in place of 2 and 3 in the NP row. The table for an undirected top-down procedure has the same value in every non-null cell of a given row. Conversely, the table for an undirected bottom-up procedure procedure has the same value in every non-null cell of a given column. For a bottom-up procedure, the rules will all be of the form $\gamma \rightarrow \delta_1 \dots \delta_n$ where $\delta_1 = \beta$. In the directed case, only rules for which $\gamma = \alpha$ or $\gamma \in \mathcal{R}(\alpha_1)$ will be included.

(16)

	S	NP	VP	A	N	V
S		1		1	1	
NP				2	3	
VP						4,5
A						
N						
V						

We can now write a general set of transition rules that implements whatever strategy the rule-selection table provided to it dictates:

(17) 1. **Append a terminal symbol**: If the last term in the configuration is active, let $[?]_A$ be the first of them. If there remain terminals in the string to be considered, then for each lexical alternative of the next terminal $[t]_\beta$ such that $\beta \in \mathcal{R}(\alpha)$ that can be on a left branch of α, create a new configuration by appending $[t]_\beta$ to the end of the current one.

2. **Find a dominating non-terminal**: If the last term is inactive, consider two adjacent terms g_i and g_{i+1}, of the current configuration. If $g_{i+1} = \mathcal{F}(\alpha)$ and $[?]_\beta$ is the first open box in g_i, for each rule $\gamma \rightarrow \delta_1 \dots \delta_n$ in $S_{\beta,\alpha}$, create a new configuration introducing $[\mathcal{F}(\delta_1)\dots\mathcal{F}(\delta_n)]_\gamma$ between g_i and g_{i+1}.

3. **Incorporate completed subgoal**: If the last term is inactive, consider two adjacent terms g_i and g_{i+1}, of the current configuration. If $g_{i+1} = \mathcal{F}(\alpha)$ and the first open box in g_i is $[?]_\alpha$, replace that open box with g_{i+1} and delete g_{i+1} from the list.

A word of explanation is in order about the second of these transition rules which, unlike corresponding transition rules in previous schemes, is formulated so as to intro-duce a new term that does not replace any existing ones. In the top-down scheme, it was possible to eliminate an open box in this step because the rules were chosen precisely to provide contents for such a box. In the bottom-up scheme, an existing item could be incorporated into the newly introduced structure because the structures were chosen with a view to making that possible. However, the rules supplied by the rule-selection table may be such as to allow neither possibility. We therefore leave the incorporation of existing material to a later application of rule 3. An alternative solution would have been to recognize three cases of rule 2 according as (i) $\beta = \gamma$, (ii) $\alpha = \delta_1$ but $\beta \neq \gamma$, or (iii) neither of the above. Clearly, it would also be possible to give special treatment to the case in which $\beta = \gamma$ and $\alpha = \delta_1$ for, under these circumstances both g_i and g_{i+1} could be incorporated in the new structure. The solution I have adopted, while it makes for more lines in the configuration table, is the simplest. More important, we shall see that it leads to important generalizations in the next section.

(18)

	S	NP	VP	A	N	V
S		1		2	1	
NP				2	3	
VP						4,5
A						
N						
V						

By now it should be clear that the distinction between top-down and bottom-up procedures is not primary. Rule tables can generally be assembled in a large number of ways only some of which correspond to either top-down or bottom-up procedures. Perhaps these procedures should be characterized as *middle-out* . (18) is a trivial example, based on (2). According to this table, sentences beginning with N will be analyzed by a procedure whose first move is top-down, whereas the analysis of those beginning with A will begin bottom-up.

The conditions under which a rule-selection table properly represents a given grammar are quite straightforward. Clearly, the rules in the cell $\mathcal{S}_{\alpha,\beta}$ must be chosen from the set $\mathcal{G}_{\alpha,\beta} = \gamma \rightarrow \delta_1...\delta_n \| \gamma \in \mathcal{R}(\alpha), \beta \in \mathcal{R}(\delta_1)$ In other words, the symbol on the left-hand side of each rule must be reachable from the upper symbol and the lower symbol must be reachable from the first symbol on the right-hand side of the rule. Suppose now that $\mathcal{G}_{\alpha,\beta}$ contains the pair

(19) $\kappa \rightarrow \lambda_1...\lambda_m$

$\mu \rightarrow \nu_1...\nu_n$

and that

(20) $\mu \in \mathcal{R}(\lambda_1)$

Only one member of the pair must be included in $\mathcal{R}_{\alpha,\beta}$ because leaving both in the set will give rise to redundancies in the analysis process. To see that this is true, it is sufficient to consider how they would apply to a configuration of the form

$$... \ [?]_\alpha \mathcal{F}(\beta) \ ...$$

Clearly two new configurations would be produced as follows:

(21) $... \ [?]_\alpha [[?]_{\lambda_1} \mathcal{F}(\lambda_2) \ ... \ \mathcal{F}(\lambda_m)]_\kappa \mathcal{F}(\beta) \ ...$

(22) $... \ [?]_\alpha []_\mu \mathcal{F}(\nu_1) \ ... \ \mathcal{F}(\nu_n) \mathcal{F}(\beta) \ ...$

but, since $\mu \in \mathcal{R}(\lambda_1)$, (22) must also arise, directly or indirectly from (21).

Proper values for $\mathcal{S}_{\alpha,\beta}$ are therefore those that are derived from $\mathcal{G}_{\alpha,\beta}$ by deleting one member of any pair of rules standing in the relation (19) and (20) and continuing to do this until no such pairs remain. The table corresponding to a bottom-up strategy is arrived at by systematically removing the rule corresponding to the first member of the pair in (19) and the top-down strategy, by removing the second member.

21.1.5 The Efficiency Question

It is often supposed that the most efficient parsers use top-down methods. So long as the discussion is confined to undirected strategies, there is doubtless some broad statistical validity to the claim though it is easy to construct grammars and strings that falsify it in general. The intuition on which it is based is presumably this: The undirected bottom-up strategy has the property that every substring that can be construed as a phrase is identified as such, completely without regard to context. So, for example, the last two words of *radio broadcasts pay* would appear in several lines of the configuration table as a sentence. This does not happen when a top-down procedure is used. In this case, a phrase is sought only when a string of symbols could occur to its right – though possibly not the one actually there – that would complete a sentence containing that phrase. In other words, the search for a phrase of a given category at a given place in the string is undertaken by a top-down parser only if such a phrase could be combined with phrases already found into a legal structure for a sentence beginning with the words of the string under analysis up to the current point. On the other hand, an undirected top-down parser can postulate phrases, and phrases within those phrases, that cannot accomodate even the very next word to be examined. For example, a more ample grammar than (1) would provide for sentences beginning with infinitives, gerunds, and topicalized prepositional phrases, and a top-down parser would attempt all these expansions of the initial $[?]_S$ even though no sentence beginning with phrases of these types could also begin with the word *radio*.

Stronger claims can be made for directed strategies. A situation that favors one or the other kind of undirected parsing method favors all directed methods as against them. Consider, as in transition rule 2, an adjacent pair of items, g_i and g_{i+1} in a configuration, g_i being active with $[?]_\alpha$ as its first open box and g_{i+1} being inactive and of category β. The top-down strategy is to fill the open box in g_i with a string of new open boxes and to continue doing this until the first member of the most recently introduced string is $[?]_\beta$. The number of steps in this process is determined by the grammar and the shaper test together, if the rules involved contain no cycles, and otherwise by the shaper test alone. In any case, once it is set in motion, it takes no further cognizance of the symbols in the string. Thus, if the rules involved do contain cycles or the operation takes place in the early part of a long string, a long train of events may take place without reference to the string being analyzed. Ignoring possible interventions by the shaper, rules of the form $\gamma \to \beta...$ must be applied at least once during the processing, given that β is the category of the next terminal, for this is precisely what the reachability table (or the rule-selection table) guarantees to parsers employing directed methods. Let us call these *bottom* rules because they complete the bottom end of a left branching path from the upper symbol, α, to the lower symbol, β.

Under the same initial conditions, a bottom-up procedure starts by applying the bottom rules against the possibility that the same left branching path can be constructed in the reverse order. If successful, this process will finish by applying *top* rules of the form $\alpha \rightarrow$ .... But it may not be successful, and therein lies the crucial difference. The left branch will not necessarily be constructed by the bottom-up procedure because the next rule applied after the bottom rule will be the next one in this sequence only if the bottom rule is nonbranching. Otherwise, the second symbol on its right-hand side becomes a new upper symbol whose corresponding lower symbol is the next terminal in the string. In general, the next upward step in the construction of a left branch will be taken only when the most recent symbol has been established at the root of a complete phrase, without open boxes. For every new rule application – every invocation of transition rule 2 – made in the bottom-up process, a corresponding application of the same rule, with a view to establishing a phrase at the same place in the overall structure, will be made by the top-down process. The reverse, however, is not true.

Suppose, for example, that the string to be analyzed is *alpha beta gamma delta*, the words belonging to the categories A, B, C, and D respectively. The input to the parser will therefore be $[alpha]_A[beta]_B[gamma]_C[delta]_D$. Let the grammar be as in (23).

(23) 1. S $\rightarrow$ P D
       2. P $\rightarrow$ Q C
       3. Q $\rightarrow$ A B

The string has one structure which is readily discovered by all the methods we have discussed with about equal ease. Now consider what happens if the category of the second word is changed so that the string is no longer accepted by the grammar. The first symbol continues to be reachable from the initial symbol of the grammar, S. The top-down strategy proposes rule 2 because the first symbol in the string is also reachable from Q. Then rule 3 is invoked. Its first symbol matches, the second one fails to match, and the process comes to an end, two rules having been considered. The bottom-up strategy calls for rule 3 to be the first one considered. Its first symbol matches the first item in the string, but the second one fails, bringing the whole process to an end after only one rule has been considered. The example could have been constructed so as to make the chain of rules needlessly invoked in the top-down procedure of any desired length.

Contrary to intuitions deriving from better understood undirected methods, it is therefore possible to assert that bottom-up directed methods are superior to all others within this framework. This is falsified only in situations where short sentences must be parsed using grammars with long rules for these are the cases where the functional load born by the shaper is high. Under these circumstances, the shaper may be in a position to curtail the construction of a left branch before the bottom rule is applied often enough to recommend the top-down method. This argument in favor of directed bottom-up parsing methods does not rest on an analysis of the worst case that can arise because, as far as is known, the methods discussed here cannot be distinguished in that way. The claim is to the effect that such differences in performance as do arise will invariably favor the directed bottom-up technique. *Pace* the use of the shaper, no case can be constructed in which, say, directed top-down parsing fares better.

21.2   The Chart

In the last section, our aim was to abstract from a large class of syntactic-processing algorithms those properties of them that ensure that all the processing is done that has to be. We now turn to the problem of eliminating unnecessary repetition of parts of the computation. By far the major part of this repetition comes from a phenomenon that the simple example used was carefully designed to avoid. The phenomenon is this: if a particular initial segment of a long string is analyzable as a phrase of a given type, but in more than one way, then any computation aimed at recognizing phrases in the remainder of the string will be repeated once for each analysis. This is because no mechanism has been provided for recognizing when the phrases required to advance a particular configuration already exist in another.

Consider the sentence *Failing students looked hard*. The first two words can be construed as a noun phrase in two ways meaning approximately *students that fail* and *the failing of students*. Likewise, the second pair of words can be construed as a verb phrase in two ways with the meanings *looked intently* and *looked difficult to do*. These constructions are provided for in the grammar (24). According to this grammar, therefore, the sentence has four structures, each construction of the subject being combinable with each construction of the predicate. But, whereas the parsing strategies so far examined would discover each construction of the subject only once, they would reanalyze the predicate independently for each of these.

$$
\begin{array}{rlcll}
(24) & 1. & S & \rightarrow & NP\ VP \\
& 2. & NP & \rightarrow & A\ N \\
& 3. & NP & \rightarrow & PRP\ N \\
& 4. & VP & \rightarrow & V\ A \\
& 5. & VP & \rightarrow & V\ AV \\
\end{array}
\qquad
\begin{array}{rlcll}
6. & A & \rightarrow & \text{failing, hard, ...} \\
7. & PRP & \rightarrow & \text{failing, ...} \\
8. & N & \rightarrow & \text{students, ...} \\
9. & V & \rightarrow & \text{looked, ...} \\
10. & AV & \rightarrow & \text{hard, ...} \\
\end{array}
$$

In (25) I show the analysis by the undirected bottom-up strategy. The two constructions of the subject are established in lines 7 and 8. A following verb phrase is postulated for each construction of the subjects in lines 9 and 10 and the verb *looked* is adjoined to each of these configurations in lines 11 and 12. Each of these configurations has two offspring corresponding to the two constructions of the predicate that will eventually be found. From this point on, four lines of development are pursued independently to the final results in lines 29 through 32. Lines 17, 19, 21, and 23 are derived from their parent lines by exactly parallel moves. Those terms that serve to differentiate these lines, but which are not affected by the operation, are therefore brought forward unchanged to lines 22 and 24. These unchanged terms are, in an important sense, *equivalent*, and the new terms introduced are equivalent to one another in the same sense. In this section, I shall first explicate this notion of equivalence and then propose a new data structure, called a *chart* , a kind of well-formed substring table,[3] to replace configuration tables. A chart admits only one member of an equivalence class of terms and, when transition rules are defined on it corresponding to those defined for configuration tables in the last section, redundant operations are therefore naturally eliminated.

---

[3]See Kuno (1965).

(25)

#	TR	Pos	Par	R	Configuration
1		1	0		$[failing]_A$
2		1	0		$[failing]_{PRP}$
3	2	1	1	2	$[[failing]_A[?]_N]_{NP}$
4	2	1	1	3	$[[failing]_{PRP}[?]_N]_{NP}$
5	1	2	3		$[[failing]_A[?]_N]_{NP}[students]_N$
6	1	2	4		$[[failing]_{PRP}[?]_N]_{NP}[students]_N$
7	3	2	5		$[[failing]_A[students]_N]_{NP}$
8	3	2	6		$[[failing]_{PRP}[students]_N]_{NP}$
9	2	2	7	1	$[[[failing]_A[students]_N]_{NP}[?]_{VP}]_S$
10	2	2	8	1	$[[[failing]_{PRP}[students]_N]_{NP}[?]_{VP}]_S$
11	1	3	9		$[[[failing]_A[students]_N]_{NP}[?]_{VP}]_S[looked]_V$
12	1	3	10		$[[[failing]_{PRP}[students]_N]_{NP}[?]_{VP}]_S[looked]_V$
13	2	3	11	4	$[[[failing]_A[students]_N]_{NP}[?]_{VP}]_S[[looked]_V[?]_A]_{VP}$
14	2	3	11	5	$[[[failing]_A[students]_N]_{NP}[?]_{VP}]_S[[looked]_V[?]_{AV}$
15	2	3	12	4	$[[[failing]_{PRP}[students]_N]_{NP}[?]_{VP}]_S[[looked]_V[?]_A]_{VP}$
16	2	3	12	4	$[[[failing]_{PRP}[students]_N]_{NP}[?]_{VP}]_S[[looked]_V[?]_{AV}]_{VP}$
17	1	4	13		$[[[failing]_A[students]_N]_{NP}[?]_{VP}]_S[[looked]_V[?]_A]_{VP}[hard]_A$
18	1	4	13		$[[[failing]_A[students]_N]_{NP}[?]_{VP}]_S[[looked]_V[?]_A]_{VP}[hard]_{AV}$
19	1	4	14		$[[[failing]_A[students]_N]_{NP}[?]_{VP}]_S[[looked]_V[?]_{AV}[hard]_A$
20	1	4	14		$[[[failing]_A[students]_N]_{NP}[?]_{VP}]_S[[looked]_V[?]_{AV}[hard]_{AV}$
21	1	4	15		$[[[failing]_{PRP}[students]_N]_{NP}[?]_{VP}]_S[[looked]_V[?]_A]_{VP}[hard]_A$
22	1	4	15		$[[[failing]_{PRP}[students]_N]_{NP}[?]_{VP}]_S[[looked]_V[?]_A]_{VP}[hard]_{AV}$
23	1	4	16		$[[[failing]_{PRP}[students]_N]_{NP}[?]_{VP}]_S[[looked]_V[?]_{AV}]_{VP}[hard]_A$
24	1	4	16		$[[[failing]_{PRP}[students]_N]_{NP}[?]_{VP}]_S[[looked]_V[?]_{AV}]_{VP}[hard]_{AV}$
25	3	4	17		$[[[failing]_A[students]_N]_{NP}[?]_{VP}]_S[[looked]_V[hard]_A]_{VP}$
26	3	4	20		$[[[failing]_A[students]_N]_{NP}[?]_{VP}]_S[[looked]_V[hard]_{AV}]_{VP}$
27	3	4	21		$[[[failing]_{PRP}[students]_N]_{NP}[?]_{VP}]_S[[looked]_V[hard]_A]_{VP}$
28	3	4	24		$[[[failing]_{PRP}[students]_N]_{NP}[?]_{VP}]_S[[looked]_V[hard]_{AV}]_{VP}$
29	3	4	25		$[[[failing]_A[students]_N]_{NP}[[looked]_V[hard]_A]_{VP}]_S$
30	3	4	26		$[[[failing]_A[students]_N]_{NP}[[looked]_V[hard]_{AV}]_{VP}]_S$
31	3	4	27		$[[[failing]_{PRP}[students]_N]_{NP}[[looked]_V[hard]_A]_{VP}]_S$
32	3	4	28		$[[[failing]_{PRP}[students]_N]_{NP}[[looked]_V[hard]_{AV}]_{VP}]_S$

21.2.1 Undirected Parsing

In what follows, I shall describe two ways of representing in a chart the data that a parsing procedure operates on, one appropriate to undirected and the other to directed parsing. This section is devoted to the first of these. I shall first provide fairly direct translations into the new formalism of the undirected strategies described in the last section. I shall then go on to consider the case in which the grammar is represented as a rule-selection table so that the top-down and bottom-up cases will not have to be distinguished. Of course, the information contained in a rule selection table is largely degenerate in the undirected case. However, we shall see that a nondegenerate table – one designed for a directed procedure – can be combined with chart operations appropriate to undirected processing. The result is a *partially directed* strategy which is not only viable but, in some ways, attractive. If a degenerate rule-selection table – one intended for undirected parsing – is used with chart operations appropriate to directed parsing, the result is simply an inefficient version of undirected parsing with no redeeming features.

I shall refer to the number of terminal symbols represented in a term as the length of that term. Open boxes do not count as terminals so that, for example, $[?]_{NP}$ and $[[?]_{Adj}[?]_N]_{NP}$ both have lengths of 0; $[[radio]_{Adj}[?]_N]_{NP}$ has length 1, and $[[radio]_{Adj}[broadcasts]_N]_{NP}$ has length 2. The length of a sequence or a configuration will be the sum of the lengths of the terms in it. The *locus* of a term in a configuration is simply the sum of the lengths of the terms that precede it in the configuration.

Intuitively, the locus captures the notion of position in the sentence; two terms have the same locus if they follow the same sequence of words. The first term in a configuration has a locus of 0.

The undirected processing strategies we have considered have the property that the only terms that need be considered when creating a new term with a given locus are exisiting terms with the same or greater loci. This is trivially true of undirected top-down strategies because all constructed terms – that is, all non-terminals – have locus 0. Configurations are of three types: (i) Those consisting of a single inactive term, (ii) Those consisting of a sequence of active terms, and (iii) Those consisting of a sequence of active terms followed by a single inactive term. Now, a crucial fact about a configuration table arising from an undirected procedure is that the configurations making it up are just those that can be constructed from the terms in it, and their loci, subject to the constraints just mentioned. In other words, the set of entries in a configuration table can be generated knowing only the set of different terms that it contains and the loci of each.

Table (25) is a configuration table showing the analysis of *failing students looked hard* by the undirected bottom-up method and grammar (24). A corresponding chart is given at (26). It contains all the terms in (25), and gives the locus and length of each. Now, (26) contains 8 inactive terms with locus 0, two terminals from the initial string, two noun phrases, one for each interpretation of the subject of the sentence, and four different analyses of the complete sentence. These contribute 8 configurations to (25). 8 different sequences of active terms can be constructed such that the first one has locus 0, four with one member and four with two. 16 sequences can be constructed from active terms followed by a single inactive term.

(26)

#	Locus	Length	Term
1	0	1	$[failing]_A$
2	0	1	$[failing]_{PRP}$
3	1	1	$[students]_N$
4	2	1	$[looked]_V$
5	3	1	$[hard]_A$
6	3	1	$[hard]_{AV}$
7	0	1	$[[failing]_A[?]_N]_{NP}$
8	0	1	$[[failing]_{PRP}[?]_N]_{NP}$
9	0	2	$[[failing]_A[students]_N]_{NP}$
10	0	2	$[[failing]_{PRP}[students]_N]_{NP}$
11	0	2	$[[[failing]_A[students]_N]_{NP}[?]_{VP}]_S$
12	0	2	$[[[failing]_{PRP}[students]_N]_{NP}[?]_{VP}]_S$
13	2	1	$[[looked]_V[?]_{AV}]_{VP}$
14	2	1	$[[looked]_V[?]_V]_{VP}$
15	2	2	$[[looked]_V[hard]_{AV}]_{VP}$
16	2	2	$[[looked]_V[hard]_V]_{VP}$
17	0	3	$[[[failing]_A[students]_N]_{NP}[[[looked]_V[hard]_{AV}]_{VP}]_{VP}]_S$
18	0	3	$[[[failing]_{PRP}[students]_N]_{NP}[[[looked]_V[hard]_{AV}]_{VP}]_{VP}]_S$
19	0	3	$[[[failing]_A[students]_N]_{NP}[[[looked]_V[hard]_A]_{VP}]_{VP}]_S$
20	0	3	$[[[failing]_{PRP}[students]_N]_{NP}[[[looked]_V[hard]_A]_{VP}]_{VP}]_S$

The unambiguous terminals *students* and *looked* are each final members of two of these as are the two verb phrases representing alternative structures of the predicate. Each of the two lexical entries for *hard* is the final member of four sequences. The resulting 32 sequences are precisely the ones that make up the configuration table (25). For undirected strategies, then, a pair of similar terms are equivalent for present purposes if they have the same locus. Table (26) contains only one representative of each equivalence class.

A natural way to represent a chart is as a directed graph. The graph for a sentence of *n* words has *n+1* vertices. Terms label edges, and all the terms with a given locus label edges incident from the vertex for that locus. An edge is said to be active or inactive depending on the status of the term that labels it. A term with locus *i* and length *j* is incident to the vertex for locus *i+j*. (27) is the graph corresponding to the table (26). The active edges are shown as thicker lines. Arrowheads are not used in the diagrams in this paper because all edges are either oriented from left to right, or loop back to the same vertex.

(27)

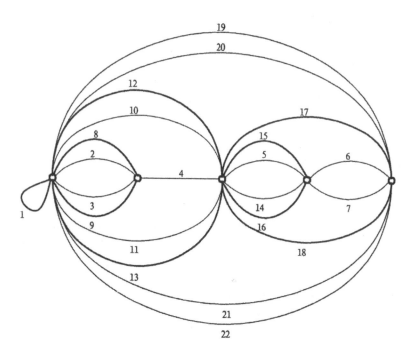

It remains to restate the transition rules for undirected parsing so that they apply to a chart instead of a configuration table. The new set of transition rules need have no member corresponding to rule 1 in the old sets. The chart must contain an entry for each lexical entry of each word in the string being analyzed and the locus of each of these is determined simply by the position in the string of the word. Each of these is the sole member of an equivalence class and they can simply be entered in the chart before the analysis proper begins. In (26), they are lines 1 through 6.

For bottom-up parsing, rule 1 of the new set, corresponding to the old rule 2, is:

(28)   1. **Find a dominating non-terminal**: Let e_i be an inactive edge of category α incident from a vertex v. For all rules of the form $\beta \to \gamma_1 ... \gamma_n$ in the grammar such that $\gamma_1 = \alpha$, introduce a new edge e, with the term $[a[?]_{\gamma_2} ... [?]_{\gamma_n}]_\beta$, incident from and to v, provided there is no such edge in the chart already.

The replacement for Rule 3 must be constrained to apply at only one place in a configuration in the same way. Rule 2 in the new system is thus:

(29)   2. **Incorporate completed subgoal**: Let e_a and e_i be adjacent active and inactive edges. e_a is incident from vertex v and e_i is incident to vertex w. Let $[?]_\alpha$ be the first open box in e_a. If e_i is of category α, create a new edge between v and w whose term is that of e_a with the first open box replaced by the term of e_{i+1}.

Both these rules are applied to all qualifying edges or pairs of edges, including any that arise as a result of applying these rules. All but the initial six entries in (25) will be seen to be generable by these rules and, as we have seen, (25) contains the same information as (26). Unnecessary steps in the computations have, however, been eliminated because each locus-term pair is computed only once.

Rule 1 for top-down parsing is:

(30)   1. **Find a dominating non-terminal**: Let e_a be an active edge whose first open box is $[?]_\alpha$ incident to a vertex v. For all rules of the form $\alpha \to \beta_1 ... \beta_n$ in the grammar introduce a new edge incident from and to v whose term is the term of e_a with the first open box replaced by $[[?]_{\beta_1} ... [?]_{\beta_n}]_\alpha$, provided there is no such edge in the chart already.

(31) and (32) show charts generated by this method for the same example. I have already remarked that all terms in a top-down configuration table have locus zero. If the transition rules are translated directly, as I have just done, the chart therefore offers little advantage. The reason for this is that, when the transition rule (32) is applied, the new phrase marker is created which fills an open box in a structure with locus 0. In the bottom-up case, the newly introduced phrase marker was not immediately engulfed by a higher structure; in fact it engulfed a lower one and the result could have any locus. The decision to write this transition rule so as to amalgamate the new phrase marker into an existing term is made in the interests of efficiency. As we saw, the procedure that makes use of a rule-selection table inserts a new term into the sequence, leaving it to a later application of the old rule 3 to perform the amalgamation. However, it now appears that the minor logical confusion that comes from confounding the functions of the two transition rules leads to considerable inefficiencies in the chart method.

The procedure that uses a rule-selection table must apply to an adjacent pair of edges, the first active and the second inactive in spite of the fact that the active edge influences the result only in top-down methods and the inactive edge only in bottom-up methods. By excluding pairs both of which are active we implement the policy established previously of applying rule 1 only to one pair of terms in a configuration.

(31)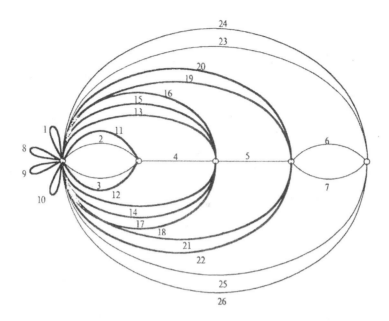

(32)

#	Locus	Length	Term
1	0	0	$[\,]_S$
2	0	1	$[failing]_A$
3	0	1	$[failing]_{PRP}$
4	1	1	$[students]_N$
5	2	1	$[looked]_V$
6	3	1	$[hard]_A$
7	3	1	$[hard]_{AV}$
8	0	0	$[[?]_{NP}[?]_{VP}]_S$
9	0	0	$[[[?]_A[?]_N]_{NP}[?]_{VP}]_S$
10	0	0	$[[[?]_{PRP}[?]_N]_{NP}[?]_{VP}]_S$
11	0	1	$[[[failing]_A[?]_N]_{NP}[?]_{VP}]_S$
12	0	1	$[[[failing]_{PRP}[?]_N]_{NP}[?]_{VP}]_S$
13	0	2	$[[[failing]_A[students]_N]_{NP}[?]_{VP}]_S$
14	0	2	$[[[failing]_{PRP}[students]_N]_{NP}[?]_{VP}]_S$
15	0	2	$[[[failing]_A[students]_N]_{NP}[[?]_V[?]_A]_{VP}]_S$
16	0	2	$[[[failing]_A[students]_N]_{NP}[[?]_V[?]_{AV}]_{VP}]_S$
17	0	2	$[[[failing]_{PRP}[students]_N]_{NP}[[?]_V[?]_A]_{VP}]_S$
18	0	2	$[[[failing]_{PRP}[students]_N]_{NP}[[?]_V[?]_{AV}]_{VP}]_S$
19	0	3	$[[[failing]_A[students]_N]_{NP}[[looked]_V[?]_A]_{VP}]_S$
20	0	3	$[[[failing]_A[students]_N]_{NP}[[looked]_V[?]_{AV}]_{VP}]_S$
21	0	3	$[[[failing]_{PRP}[students]_N]_{NP}[[looked]_V[?]_A]_{VP}]_S$
22	0	3	$[[[failing]_{PRP}[students]_N]_{NP}[[looked]_V[?]_{AV}]_{VP}]_S$
23	0	4	$[[[failing]_A[students]_N]_{NP}[[looked]_V[hard]_A]_{VP}]_S$
24	0	4	$[[[failing]_A[students]_N]_{NP}[[looked]_V[hard]_{AV}]_{VP}]_S$
25	0	4	$[[[failing]_{PRP}[students]_N]_{NP}[[looked]_V[hard]_A]_{VP}]_S$
26	0	4	$[[[failing]_{PRP}[students]_N]_{NP}[[looked]_V[hard]_{AV}]_{VP}]_S$

For this method, the required rule is given in (33) and (34) and (35) repeat the example with this method.

(33)   1. **Find a dominating non-terminal**: Let e_a and e_z be adjacent active and inactive edges, e_a being incident from v and e_i being incident to w. Let $[?]_\alpha$ be the first open box in e_a and let β be the category of e_i. For all rules $\gamma \to \delta_1...\delta_n$ in $\mathcal{S}_{\alpha,\beta}$, introduce a new edge between v and w and with the term $[[?]_{\delta_i}...[?]_{\delta_n}]_\gamma$, provided there is no such edge in the chart already.

(34)

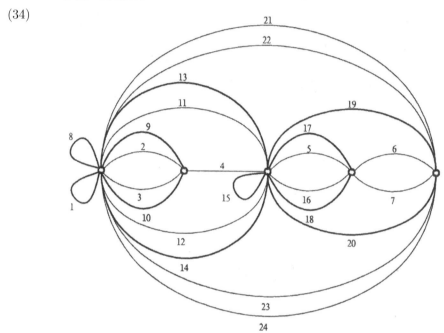

Examination of (34) is instructive. All applications of transition rule 1 cause a term of length 0 to be introduced and these are recognizable in the graph as active edges that are incident to and from the same vertex. Other edges are either initial lexical edges or arise from applications of rule 2. For this particular example, it is not necessary to state whether the rule-selection table used corresponds to a top-down or a bottom-up strategy because the results are the same in both cases. This, however, is an artifact of the trivial grammar used. The chart does, however, accord equal advantages to both methods both here and in general. Furthermore, nothing turns on whether a rule-selection table is in fact used; the crucial requirement is that the functions of the two transition rules should remain dissociated.

There is one respect in which the chart procedures using a rule-selection table fails to reflect the top-down parsing strategy accurately. This arises when there are sets of left-recursive rules. Careful examination of the transition rules shows that the phrases will not be built in a strictly top-to-bottom order in this case but that the phrases constructed in the bottom cycle of such a set of rules will be produced first. The topmost member of the set of phrases will then serve as a terminal and the cycle will repeat.

(35)

#	Locus	Length	Term
1	0	0	$[]_S$
2	0	1	$[failing]_A$
3	0	1	$[failing]_{PRP}$
4	1	1	$[students]_N$
5	2	1	$[looked]_V$
6	3	1	$[hard]_A$
7	3	1	$[hard]_{AV}$
8	0	0	$[?]_{NP}$
9	0	1	$[[failing]_A[?]_N]_{NP}$
10	0	1	$[[failing]_{PRP}[?]_N]_{NP}$
11	0	2	$[[failing]_A[students]_N]_{NP}$
12	0	2	$[[failing]_{PRP}[students]_N]_{NP}$
13	0	2	$[[[failing]_A[students]_N]_{NP}[?]_{VP}]_S$
14	0	2	$[[[failing]_{PRP}[students]_N]_{NP}[?]_{VP}]_S$
15	2	1	$[?]_{VP}$
16	2	1	$[[looked]_V[?]_{AV}]_{VP}$
17	2	1	$[[looked]_V[?]_A]_{VP}$
18	2	2	$[[looked]_V[hard]_{AV}]_{VP}$
19	2	2	$[[looked]_V[hard]_A]_{VP}$
20	0	3	$[[[failing]_A[students]_N]_{NP}[[[looked]_V[hard]_{AV}]_{VP}]_{VP}]_S$
21	0	3	$[[[failing]_{PRP}[students]_N]_{NP}[[[looked]_V[hard]_{AV}]_{VP}]_{VP}]_S$
22	0	3	$[[[failing]_A[students]_N]_{NP}[[[looked]_V[hard]_A]_{VP}]_{VP}]_S$
23	0	3	$[[[failing]_{PRP}[students]_N]_{NP}[[[looked]_V[hard]_A]_{VP}]_{VP}]_S$

This happens because the zero-length edge introduced by transition rule 2 for each rule in the set is the same each time; it incorporates nothing from the edges on the basis of which it was introduced. There will be only one such edge for each rule in the left-recursive set regardless of how many cycles of the set take place at a given point in the analysis. The only move open, once such an edge has been established is therefore to pursue the downward path. One consequence of this is that the shaper test is no longer required because the deviation from the top-down strategy occurs in just such a way as to break the vicious cycle.

21.2.2 Directed Parsing

Representing the state of a parsing device by means of a chart can bring the same advantages to directed as to undirected parsing. However, the chart must be used differently because the equivalence classes of terms that are of interest now are not simply those that have the same locus. The point is best illustrated by a string with more than one left branching structure. Consider the sentence *Can openers work* which, punctuation aside, can be read as an assertion about can openers or a question about openers. The first word presumably has two lexical entries, one as a modal verb, and the other as a noun. In its capacity as a modal, we may assume it can be an auxiliary and, as a noun, it can become a noun phrase. I shall refrain from attempting to write explicit context-free rules for the relevant parts of English grammar. Relations between concision and verisimilitude have already been sufficiently strained in this paper.

Using a reachability. or rule-selection, table, the parser posits an initial noun phrase on the basis of the first noun and an auxiliary on the basis of the modal. Four questions now arise: (i) Can the modal begin an auxiliary? (ii) Can the noun begin a noun phrase? (iii) Can the modal begin a noun phrase? and (iv) Can the noun begin an auxiliary? But clearly only the first two of these are proper questions to be considered as part of a directed strategy. Now, it is true that a number of questions that an undirected parser would have to consider are avoided. An undirected top-down parser would, for example establish hypotheses – configurations – that could only be borne out if the first word was a determiner, an infinitive or, indeed, any category that can begin a sentence. Each of these would be eventually ruled out when neither lexical entry for the first word matched them. Similary, an undirected bottom-up parser, observing that *can* can be a main verb, would go on to discover that *can openers* is a verb phrase.

The reason that two irrelevant questions arise is that the chart puts all terms with a given locus on the same footing. In the purportedly directed procedure we are now investigating, grammar rules will therefore be applied to all terms with a given locus provided the reachability table sanctions their application to any term with that locus. As more phrases are formed, more unnecessary work is done. Later in the analysis, it will emerge that the first two words, *can openers* constitute a noun phrase and, at that point, the question of whether this could be initial in an auxiliary will be considered. In short, a procedure that uses a reachability, or rule-selection, table together with the chart-management regime just decribed, is only partially directed.

I shall now show that the chart representation can easily be made to support fully directed context-free parsers. The crucial observation has just been made, namely that terms with the same locus do not constitute the interesting equivalence classes for directed processing. Each class must now contain terms at a given locus and with a given category. But, the full generality of the chart representation will be preserved only if there continues to be a vertex corresponding to each locus. This is the vertex to which terms whose successors have that locus will be incident. For ease of reference, I shall call these *locus vertices* . Those from which edges representing terms of a certain category are incident will be called *term vertices* . Two kinds of edge will also be required. The *term edges*, familiar from the last section, will always be incident from *term vertices*. Inactive term edges will be incident to locus vertices and active term edges to term vertices. The term vertices for a given locus will be accessible from the corresponding locus vertex by following a *category edge* whose label, instead of being a term, will simply be the category characteristic of the term vertex in question.

Each lexical entry for a string to be parsed is represented in the new chart by a pair consisting of a category edge followed by a term edge. The category edges for the i-th word are incident from locus vertex i. If α is a category of the i-th word, a category edge will be constructed from the locus edge i to the term vertex $i : \alpha$, and from there a term edge, labeled with the lexical entry, will be constructed to the locus vertex $i+1$. Suppose now that an arbitrary inactive term is to be entered into the chart at locus L. Let its length be i,and its category α. The edge that it labels will be incident from the term vertex $L : \alpha$, and to the locus vertex $L+1$. If vertex $L : \alpha$ did not previously exist, it would be necessary, at the same time, to create a category edge giving access to that vertex from the locus vertex L.

The parsing procedure starts when an active edge labeled with the open box $[?]_S$ is entered into the chart, incident from and to the locus vertex 0. From this point on, the process is governed by (36).

(36) 1. **Find a dominating non-terminal**: Let e_a be an active edge incident from vertex v to the vertex w, and e_i an inactive edge of category ϵ incident from w. Let L be the locus of w or, more strictly, of the edges incident from w. (If e_i is a category edge, ϵ is its label and L is the name of the vertex w; if e_i is a term edge, its label is of the form $[...]_\epsilon$ and the label of w is $L : \epsilon$). Let the term of e_a be of category α and its first open box be $[?]_\beta$. For each rule $\gamma \to \delta_1...\delta_n \in \mathcal{R}_{\alpha,\beta}$, create whatever is not already present in the chart of the following structure: (i) the term vertex $L : \gamma$, (ii) a term edge with the same label as e_a from v to $L : \gamma$, (iii) a term edge labeled $[\mathcal{F}(\delta_1) ... \mathcal{F}(\delta_n)]_\gamma$ from $L : \gamma$ to $L : \epsilon$, and (iv) a category edge labeled γ from w to $L : \gamma$.

2. **Extend Active Edge**: Let e_a, be an active edge incident from vertex v to the locus vertex L, and e_i a category edge labeled α incident from L to $L : \alpha$. If $[?]_\alpha$ is the first open box in e_a, create a new edge whose term is the same as that of e_a from v to $L : \alpha$.

3. **Incorporate completed subgoal**: Let e_a be an active edge incident from vertex v to the term vertex $L : \alpha$, and e_i a term edge of category α incident from $L : \alpha$ to x. If $[?]_\alpha$ is the first open box in e_a, create a new edge whose term is that of e_a, with the first open box replaced by the label of e_i incident from v and to x.

(37) and (38) show the results of analyzing *failing students looked hard* using the grammar at (24) and the directed bottom-up method. Each transition rule operates on a pair consisting of an active edge and an immeadiately following inactive edge and, wherever a rule is applicable to such a pair, it must be applied before the process is complete. A measure of the amount of work done by the procedure at each vertex is therefore given by the product of the number of active edges incident to it and the number of inactive vertices incident from it. The sum of these measures for this example is 24. The comparable result for (34) and (35), the undirected counterpart of this procedure is 28. The small difference in the results is due mainly to the triviality of the example. Directed methods, and particularly directed bottom-up methods, come into their own in the face of structures with long left branches.

I believe that the superiority of directed bottom-up parsing methods has not been generally appreciated. However, I also believe that they may not always be appropriate or that the advantages that they offer over simpler undirected methods may not be enough to recommend them in all circumstances. One argument for simpler techniques is based on the presumed nature of natural languages. The number of categories that linguists have thought it right to use in their grammars has usually been very small[4] and the left branches that are constructed without repeating symbols are very short so that, empirically, the advantages of the directed schemes are minimal.

The value of the information in the reachability or rule-selection tables is further debased if rules are stored as transition networks. This method of representing rules has the advantage of conflating subsequences of symbols that occur in more than one rule.

---

[4]Gazdar (1979a and 1979b) are notable exceptions to this.

In particular, if the right-hand sides of a pair of rules have a common initial substring, then any work that a parser does comparing these symbols against a string contributes to the matching of both rules. However, such a pair of rules may well have different symbols on the left-hand side so that there is no reason to suppose that they would be called upon under similar circumstances by a directed parser.

(37)

#	Left	Right	Term
1	0	0:A	A
2	0:A	1	$[failing]_A$
3	0	0:PRP	PRP
4	0:PRP	1	$[failing]_{PRP}$
5	1	1:N	N
6	1:N	2	$[students]_N$
7	2	2:V	V
8	2:V	3	$[looked]_V$
9	3	3:A	A
10	3:A	4	$[hard]_A$
11	3	3:AV	AV
12	3:AV	4	$[hard]_{AV}$
13	0	0:S	S
14	0:S	0:A	$[?]_S$
15	0:S	0:PRP	$[?]_S$
16	0	0:NP	NP
17	0:S	0:NP	$[[?]_{NP}[?]_{VP}]_S$
18	0:NP	0:A	$[[?]_A[?]_N]_{NP}$
19	0:NP	0:PRP	$[[?]_{PRP}[?]_N]_{NP}$
20	0:NP	1	$[[failing]_A[?]_N]_{NP}$
21	0:NP	1	$[[failing]_{PRP}[?]_N]_{NP}$
22	0:NP	1:N	$[[failing]_A[?]_N]_{NP}$
23	0:NP	1:N	$[[failing]_{PRP}[?]_N]_{NP}$
24	0:NP	2	$[[failing]_A[students]_N]_{NP}$
25	0:NP	2	$[[failing]_{PRP}[students]_N]_{NP}$
26	0:S	2	$[[[[failing]_A[students]_N]_{NP}]_{NP}[?]_{VP}]_S$
27	0:S	2	$[[[[failing]_{PRP}[students]_N]_{NP}]_{NP}[?]_{VP}]_S$
28	0:S	2:VP	$[[[[failing]_A[students]_N]_{NP}]_{NP}[?]_{VP}]_S$
29	2:VP	2:V	$[[?]_V[?]_A]_{VP}$
30	0:S	2:VP	$[[[[failing]_{PRP}[students]_N]_{NP}]_{NP}[?]_{VP}]_S$
31	2:VP	2:V	$[[?]_V[?]_{AV}]_{VP}$
32	2:VP	3	$[[looked]_V[?]_A]_{VP}$
33	2:VP	3	$[[looked]_V[?]_{AV}]_{VP}$
34	2:VP	3:A	$[[looked]_V[?]_A]_{VP}$
35	2:VP	3:AV	$[[looked]_V[?]_{AV}]_{VP}$
36	2:VP	4	$[[looked]_V[hard]_A]_{VP}$
37	2:VP	4	$[[looked]_V[hard]_{AV}]_{VP}$
38	0:S	4	$[[[failing]_A[students]_N]_{NP}[[looked]_V[hard]_A]_{VP}]_S$
39	0:S	4	$[[[failing]_A[students]_N]_{NP}[[looked]_V[hard]_{AV}]_{VP}]_S$
40	0:S	4	$[[[failing]_{PRP}[students]_N]_{NP}[[looked]_V[hard]_A]_{VP}]_S$
41	0:S	4	$[[[failing]_{PRP}[students]_N]_{NP}[[looked]_V[hard]_{AV}]_{VP}]_S$

(38)

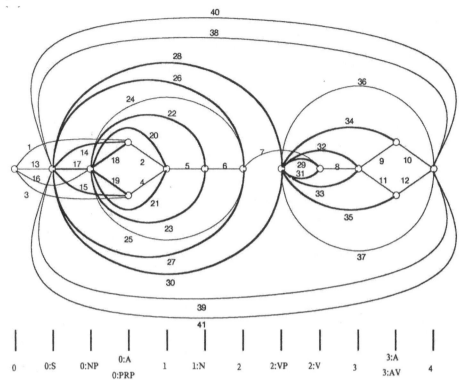

Finally, as I pointed out at the outset, the current interest in context-free processing techniques is due in part to the fact that they can often be applied to grammatical formalisms that are not strictly context free, for example, various formalisms involving complex symbols. Under these circumstances, the appropriateness of directed processing methods is governed in large measure by whether it is easy, or indeed possible, to construct reachability tables or rule-selection tables within these formalisms.

21.3 The Agenda

An algorithm schema becomes an algorithm when all the choices that must be made in executing it are determined. The indeterminacy arises because the transition rules we have considered call for some action to be taken whenever an edge of a certain kind is created or, more importantly, whenever a pair consisiting of an active edge followed by an inactive edge comes into being. The actions that take place under these circumstances can easily give rise to new instances of the same kinds of circumstance. In other words, each step in the process can produce the conditions for more than one subsequent step. Clearly, entering one new edge into a chart can increase by an arbitrary amount the number of active-inactive pairs that there are. It is therefore a fundamental feature of parsing that the material to be processed is amassed, during certain phases of the enterprise, faster than it can be treated.

A classical response to this problem is through recursion. Suppose there is a procedure whose job is to add new edges to the chart and then rehearse the new situations thus created to which transition rules must be applied. It applies the rules, calling itself recursively to add new edges as needed. In general, some number of edges or pairs of edges will be waiting for treatment by transition rules. The queue is maintained by the recursion mechanism. What results is a so-called *depth first* algorithm in which the most recently proposed task is always the next one to be carried out. In parsing, the result is that one, essentially arbitrary, hypothesis about the grammatical structure of the string at hand is pursued relentlessly until it either succeeds or can be pursued no further.

Another technique which preserves the conceptual clarity and operational simplicity of the chart involves a list of *tasks* called an *agenda* and a policy for managing it. A task is simply an edge, or pair of edges – whatever the transition rules require. Whenever new edges are added to the chart, any new tasks that can be created as a result, are added to the agenda. If they are always added to the front of the agenda and are also removed from the front of the agenda for execution, the same depth-first strategy just described results. If they are added to one end of the agenda, but removed from the other, so that the agenda serves as a queue in the usual sense, the result is a *breadth-first* strategy in which, roughly speaking, equal time is given to each currently open hypothesis. Work on a given hypothesis is resumed only when those corresponding to all others have been cycled through.

The agenda, like the other data structures I have proposed, has the appeal of leaving as many options as possible open. Observe that, if the aim of the parsing exercise is to discover all the structures of a potentially ambiguous string of symbols, tasks can be removed from the agenda in any order whatsoever, in as nearly a random way as can be contrived, without influencing the results eventually arrived at or the time taken to reach them. All the tasks must be done and the cost of executing a given task is not affected by the others on the agenda. If, on the other hand, some significance is attached to the order in which solutions are arrived at, then the policies governing the management of the chart become crucially important. Suppose one holds, for example, that the grammar that represents a person's linguistic competence assigns some number of interpretations to a string but that only certain of these will be recognized under conditions of actual performance. Presumably such facts would be explained by positing a specific parsing algorithm or the agenda-management policy that gives rise to that algorithm.

Before pursuing this line too far, we shall do well to assess what the true value of an algorithm as opposed to an algorithm schema actually is. The important fact is that computers, as they exist today, are algorithmic machines *par excellence*. They require algorithms to direct their operations and they are, in principle, able to execute all algorithms indifferently. But machines can be envisaged, and some are being built, which force some reassessment of the notion of an algorithm in the direction suggested in this paper. The main reason for requiring that the order of events be exactly specified is that the computer can do only one thing at once and everything turns on knowing what that shall be. If a machine were able to do more than one thing at once and, if the outstanding tasks were independent of one another, then a number of them could be underway at any moment and no importance would attach to whether one was finished before or after another. Such a machine might be thought of as having a number of work stations at each of which tasks of the same kind could be done. But some could be faster and some slower; some work stations could be removed from service and others introduced without influencing the outcome. The interest of all this for present purposes has nothing to do with possible future directions in computer science but simply with the very real possibility that algorithms, narrowly construed, are not necessarily what is required as mental models. Indeed, the proposition that the brain is patterned after the computer that we know today is, *prima facie*, implausible.

On the other hand, a standard computer can be set to predict something of the behavior of mental models which countenance the simultaneous execution of several tasks. For example, suppose it was proposed that syntactic tasks all took unit time and that some fixed number, say k, of them could be in process at any time. A computer model of this behavior would maintain a main agenda and a secondary agenda. Tasks would be taken from the secondary agenda in any convenient order for execution and, as new tasks were produced, they would be appended to the main agenda. When the secondary agenda was exhausted, k tasks would be chosen from the main agenda according to a policy laid down as part of the model and transferred to the secondary agenda. If the main agenda only contained k or less tasks, they would all be transferred. The model would predict that the time taken to analyze a string would be proportional, not to the number of tasks executed, but to the number of times the secondary agenda was replenished from the main agenda. The explanatory power of a model which specifies more is surely greater than one that specifies less, but this is not to say that a model is to be preferred that makes von Neumann seem to have invented the brain.

Psychological experiments aimed at obtaining data about syntactic processing strategies are carefully designed to control for any possible intrusion by other mental processes, particularly semantic effects. It seems reasonable and, indeed, it is often observed, that the syntactic reading that first suggests itself to a subject is conditioned by previous context, the meanings of the words involved, and so on. A psychological model must eventually explain this behavior as well as what happens when these effects are, as far as possible, avoided. A model that took the form of an algorithm, in the narrow sense, would be poorly placed to do this. In fact, the advocate of such a model would be forced into the position that the strategies used in controlled psychological experiments were unrelated to those used in understanding sentences in context. A model based on the agenda can associate priorities with tasks in more or less complex ways and thus ascribe the variation observed in experimental results to a variety of sources. The simpler experiments reveal what the priorities are when there is little or no semantic contribution but, when the time comes to give an account of that contribution, the work will center on how the priorities are computed and not on designing a completely new algorithm.

An objection that might be raised against a psychological model based on charts and agendas is that it assumes that the result of every intermediate result involved in the overall computation is remembered and equally accessible at any later time. Indeed, the conceptual clarity of this way of doing things comes largely from the fact that there are almost no state variables in the abstract machine. The quantities that such variables would contain in other processors here become permanent parts of a data structure. This argument would be persuasive against a proposal that charts and agendas as described here be accorded the status of a psychological model. But that would be an absurd proposal. High on the long list of additions that would have to be made to it before it could fill that role would be a model of short term memory that would have a notion of time and of the intervals of time during which particular parts of each data structure were accessible. But the notion of time would not be taken over uncritically from the instruction counter of the computer. In short, what I have presented here is what I claimed it would be, namely a framework within which parsers, conceptual and actual, can be designed and constructed. The choices that it invites the designer to make are motivated by inherent properties of the problem of syntactic processing and not by more or less irrelevant considerations from automata theory and electrical engineering.

Publications referenced

Bresnan 1978; Frazier 1978; Frazier and Fodor 1978; Gazdar 1979a; Gazdar 1979b; Griffiths and Petrick 1965; Harman 1963; Kaplan 1972; Kaplan 1978; Kay 1977; Kimball 1973; Kuno and Oettinger 1962; Kuno 1965; Marcus 1978; Woods and Kaplan 1971. Wanner et al. 1975; Wanner and Maratsos 1978.

22

When Meta-Rules are not Meta-Rules

I want to exploit an analogy between phonological rules and meta-rules in Generalised Phrase Structure Grammar (GPSG) resulting in an alternative for the model usually presented of the role meta-rules play. It should have consequences for the way we assess grammars of that type as mental models and particularly for the kinds of parser that might be appropriate for them. In brief, I shall advocate a model in which meta-rules are viewed as constituting a transducer that intervenes between the ordinary rules and the strings of constituents they describe much as phonological rules intervene between the lexicon and the strings of phonetic matrices that make up an utterance.

Phonological[1] rules are usually stated from the speaker's point of view, that is, they are designed to take strings of canonical lexical headings as input and to deliver textual strings as output. The reasons for this are not clear, but they are probably related to the fact that, whereas utterances are primary data, lexical forms are under the linguist's control so that they can be manipulated to make the rules more convenient. It is therefore generally the case that, up to free variation, things can be arranged so that a string of lexical forms is unambiguously translatable into a textual string whereas a textual string may correspond to large numbers of lexical strings. It is not a trivial matter to find a hearer's equivalent for a set of phonological rules of this kind and, in its absence, the designer of a parser or recognition model has two alternatives: he can expand the lexicon to include all possible variants, or allomorphs, of each morpheme, annotating each with the characteristics of the environments in which it could legitimately be used. Alternatively, he can design a new set of rules from scratch, not systematically related to those assumed used by the speaker or included in the competence model.

The usual descriptions of GPSG are based on a model in which meta-rules are used as much as in the allomorph approach to phonology, every possible variant of the basic set of rules being assembled in a working grammar before any processing is undertaken, whether by speaker or hearer. This is the obvious strategy to follow because it requires a very few new kinds of object to be posited – essentially only the meta-rules themselves. In addition, once the working grammar has been assembled, analysis is set on an equal

---

[1]Computational linguistics has usually been more concerned with graphological, orthographic, or spelling, than with phonological rules. In this paper, I shall continue to use phonological terminology for the sake of the status it confers while taking examples mainly from orthography for the sake of their familiarity and ease of statement.

footing with generation. This is important to the adherents of GPSG, who take seriously their commitment to treat the hearer as a first-class citizen.

Other approaches to the treatment of meta-rules would not have these advantages because the problem of reversing syntactic meta-rules is every bit as difficult as the parallel problem in phonology. The approach I shall advocate requires a considerable array of unfamiliar devices and kinds of objects. To that extent it is less appealing. However, the standard approach is also not without its disadvantages. The conceptual simplicity of the "allorule" approach is bought at some considerable expense to the language learner, who presumably must engage in a major processing effort when modifications are made to his grammar, especially if they affect the meta-rules. In fact, the more he knows about the language, the more and the faster the complexity of that processing step increases. From the learner's standpoint, simplicity comes with being able to treat rules and meta-rules as unit-cost items.

The cost incurred in theory by the language learner is paid in an obvious and straightforward way by the computational linguist who is using a generation or parsing program as a tool in perfecting a grammar, for he must presumably repeat the computation of a new working grammar after every change that he makes. Another potential disadvantage of the standard allorule approach is that the number of working rules required for a realistic grammar of a language may turn out to be unmanageably large. One of the most striking formal properties of GPSG is certainly the great combinatoric power of its meta-rules. Precise statements cannot be made about this power because it has yet to be decided how the ability of meta-rules to apply their own output, and that of other rules, should be limited. However, it is at least clear that meta-rules are interesting only to the extent that they retain a considerable amount of combinatoric power.

The alternative view of meta-rules that I propose in this paper does not avoid all the disadvantages of the standard theory. For efficient use, it also requires considerable preprocessing of the grammar, though differing amounts of this can be traded off against the efficiency of the generation and parsing processes. Certainly, it does not require the working grammar to be recomputed whenever a new meta-rule is proposed. Just what the relative costs of the two schemes will turn out to be is far from clear. For the moment I will be content to claim only that this scheme offers greater flexibility to infant and algorithm designer alike.

Limitations on the ordering of meta-rule applications is a topic that has received too little attention from the proponents of GPSG. It is a pressing issue if only because the claim that the grammars are in fact context-free turns upon being able to show, at the very least, that the number of rules they contain is finite. Meta-rules have the form of general rewriting rules which, if allowed to apply without restraint, would not support this assumption. In the absence of guidance from the theoreticians, the writer of a computer program for generation or analysis is forced to take some sort of stand on the issue, and those with which I am familiar have imposed what seems to be the minimal restriction, namely that rules may apply each to the output of the one before and in any order, but no meta-rule may be applied more than once to the same rule.

It is presumably appropriate for a technician to make only minimal assumptions while awaiting clarification from those endowed with theoretical insight. But the *use-*

once proposal is flagrantly implausible. As far as I know, no such principle has been made in all the illustrious rule-making history of our subject. It requires more mechanism for its execution than any other proposal I have heard; in all but the simplest cases, it necessitates the use of a computer to determine just what working rules a given basic rule gives rise to; it is remarkably brittle in the sense of producing very sweeping changes in the working grammar as a result of apparently trivial changes in the basic grammar; in short, of all the proposals that might meet the basic theoretical requirement, it is the most powerful and the least manageable.

In the balance of this paper, I shall assume that meta-rules are simply ordered, just as the phonological rules of almost any theory are considered to be. This makes for a weaker device and therefore involves a much stronger empirical claim: on that basis alone, it would be regarded as superior in many quarters. This proposal has the practical advantage of making the outcome of applying a set of meta-rules to a given set of context-free rules a simple and intuitive matter, with the concomitant advantage for grammarian and infant alike that grammars become altogether less brittle. The proposals I have to make are much easier to carry through under this assumption about meta-rule application, though it turns out that they do not turn on it crucially. However, from my point of view, the use-once proposal is about as bad as any that could be readily imagined because it would give rise to data structures that would be unmanageably large and expensive to compute.

22.1 A Straw Man

Logically speaking, nothing turns on whether we think of the rules of the working grammar as being computed once for all before they are needed or as being worked out on demand in the course of sentence generation and analysis. The mechanism that is responsible for applying meta-rules can be thought of as a transducer interposed between that store of grammar rules and the generation or analysis device, from the point of view of which it is immaterial whether the computation is being repeated each time a rule is required, or has been done in advance and the results stored away.

There are also other logically possible ways of obtaining the effects for which meta-rules were devised. One possibility is to regard meta-rules as applying to strings of constituents in the course of parsing. The following example gives a rough sketch of how this might go. Consider the meta-rule[2]

(1) $VP \rightarrow V\ NP\ ... \Rightarrow VP \rightarrow V_{[form:passive]} \cdots (PP_{[case:by]})$

which is normally described as taking as input a rule such as

(2) $VP \rightarrow V\ NP\ PP^*$

and delivering as output

(3) $VP \rightarrow V_{[form:passive]}\ PP^*\ (PP_{[case:by]})$

Suppose that some form of chart parser is to be used and the sentence to be analysed is *The job could be done in a week by a good technician.* After some number of steps, we

---

[2]Since I am not concerned with semantics, I am not adopting the notation for rules and meta-rules preferred by the proponents of GPSG, preferring one that follows more traditional lines.

may assume that the chart contains among others, the edges shown in Fig. 1.

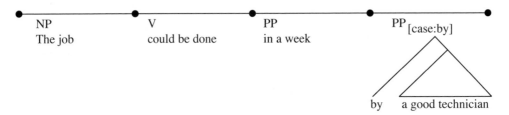

FIGURE 1 An early stage in the analysis of a sentence

The rule needed to take the next step is clearly (3), the passive VP rule. But suppose that no working grammar has been constructed by applying metarules to rules so that no passive VP rule is available. Instead a minor variant, which we may write as (4), of the meta-rule (1) is applied directly to the chart, rewriting the sequence $V\ PP\ PP_{[case:by]}$ as $[_{vp}V\ NP\ PP^*]_{vp}$ as in Fig. 2.

(4) $V \ldots PP_{[case:by]} \rightarrow [_{vp}V\ NP\ PP^*]_{vp}$

The role of the subscripted brackets, which are entered in the chart explicitly, is to ensure that the sequence $V\ NP\ PP$ that they enclose be incorporable into the sentence structure only in a manner that the meta-rule sanctions. The subscript inside the first bracket states the requirement that the material matching the specification inside the brackets must be analysed as VP. The subscript outside the second bracket says that VP will be labelled as a VP when it is entered in the chart, rather than as some other non-terminal symbol specified in the meta-rule. In short, the sequence must be analysed as a VP and can function as a VP in larger structures. More generally, a meta-rule of the form (5) will allow any sequence of constituents in the chart that fits the pattern to be rewritten as (6).

(5) $\alpha \rightarrow \beta \Rightarrow \gamma \rightarrow \delta$

(6) $[_\gamma\beta]_\alpha$

If β is a single constituent of category γ, or can be reduced to one by the application of other rules, then it can be labelled as belonging to category α and incorporated into larger structures as such. In other words, for every pair of categories γ and α, there is a rewriting rule of the form

(7) $[_\gamma\gamma]_\alpha \rightarrow \alpha$

The heavy loops labelled **VP** in Fig. 2 are active edges.[3] The one at the right-hand end of the $[_{VP}$ edge is introduced with the purpose of finding a VP-analysis of the bracketed material. A corresponding active edge would be introduced following any such open bracket according to this scheme. In the present case, it gives rise, in due course, to the VP edge shown at the top of the diagram. The other active **VP** edge is the one that would be introduced in the normal course of the parsing. The dotted lines represent associations between constituents that would be established by the semantic

---

[3]For a discussion of this terminology, and of chart parsing in general, see Kay (1977).

component of the rules and which are beyond our scope. Roughly, they represent either constituency or semantic identity.

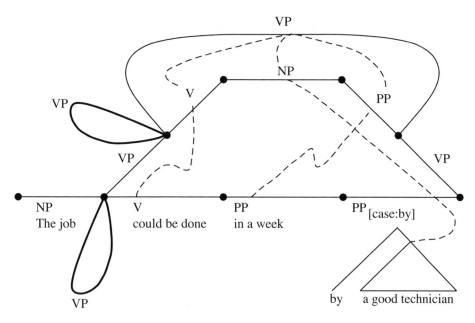

FIGURE 2 A later stage in the analysis of a sentence

The use that is being made of the chart here is unconventional in rewriting strings as other strings and not simply as single symbols. It was in fact just in order to permit such operations that charts were first proposed in Kay (1967). Meta-rules are placed on an even footing with context-free rules and made to look for all the world like the local transformations of yesteryear. However, by applying meta-rules without regard to which context-free rules will apply to their output, such a technique runs into serious difficulties that the above example does not bring out sharply enough. They are made immediately clear by a so-called linking meta-rule[4] that introduces "slashed" categories. I take this to be somewhat as follows:

(8) $X \rightarrow ...Y... \Rightarrow X/Z \rightarrow ...Y/Z...$

where X, Y and Z are variables ranging over suitable categories. In reading a rule like this, it is to be understood that the first and second set of dots, "..." that appear on the left side correspond to the first and second set on the right side. Situations in which such unspecified strings occurred in different orders in the two parts of the rule would require additional notational devices which we shall not need. The problem with this is that the unspecified strings occur at the ends of the pattern to be matched so that if the specified central element is found in the ith position of a string of n constituents, there are i-1 places before the ith position where the rule could begin matching and n-i following the ith position where it could finish matching for a total of $(j$-$1)$ $(n$-$i)$ times.

---

[4]See Gazdar, Pullum and Sag (1981).

Furthermore, a realistic grammar would doubtless contain many meta-rules that would provoke this kind of behaviour and, since many of them could be applied to the output of others, their explosive effects would be multiplied. If this is added to the already known sources of combinatory explosion that characterise the parsing process, the result will clearly be impracticable.

To one regularly involved with parsing techniques, the problem just identified has a familiar ring. It arises because a mechanism that converts one thing into another – a rewriting rule or transducer – is being used in an *undirected* [5] manner, that is, without regard to whether the results will be useful in some other part of the process. In a later section, I shall show how a directed version of the technique just discussed can be made to work. By way of preparation, I now turn to the analogous problem in phonology.

22.2 Phonological and Graphological Rules

There is a large and interesting class of phonological rules that can be systematically restated in a way that not only permits them to be incorporated in a recognition model but allows for unexpectedly efficient processing by speaker and hearer alike. The translation process produces a finite-state transducer, similar to a finite-state machine except in that its transactions carry two labels instead of one, each label referring to one of the two tapes to which the machine is connected. A standard finite-state machine is said to *accept* a tape if the characters on it match the labels on a sequence of transitions taken from its state-transition diagram starting in the initial state and ending in one of a set of designated *final* states. If no such sequence can be found, the tape is rejected. A finite-state transducer, for us, is just like this except that it accepts or rejects *pairs* of tapes. Accordingly, its transitions are labelled with pairs of symbols. Provision is made for transitions in which the symbol to be matched against one or other of the tapes is empty, in which case the corresponding tape is ignored when the transition is taken. This provision is necessary if it is to be possible to accept pairs of tapes of unequal length.

The transition diagram for a simple transducer is shown in Fig. 3. This machine embodies a greatly simplified version of the rules governing the spelling of the endings of regular plural nouns and third person singular verbs in English, and the changes in spelling that occur when certain endings are appended to a word that ends in "y". For the purpose of the example, I assume that lexical entries are written with a twenty-eight-letter alphabet consisting of the lower case letters plus two special characters, S and Y. The plural or 3rd-person ending is the only lexical entry spelled with the S, and the Y is used for the last letter of words like *flY* and *emptY*.

In the interests of simplicity, I have nowhere shown more than one transition between a given pair of states but have written all the labels on such a set of transitions against a single arc. The word *others* is used in the diagram as a shorthand for a list of up to 26 labels of the form $x{:}x$ where x is a lower case letter that does not appear explicitly as the label on any other transition from that state. So, for example, the *others* label on the arc from and to state 0 stands for 23 transitions, $a{:}a$ ... $r{:}r$, $t{:}t$, $u{:}u$, $v{:}v$, $w{:}w$,

---

[5] For a discussion of the notions of directed and undirected rule application in parsing, see Griffiths and Petrick (1965) and Kay (1980).

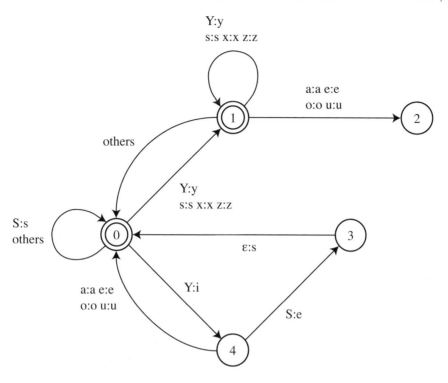

FIGURE 3 A transducer for morphographemic rules

$y{:}y$, whereas the one from state 1 to state 0 stands for 19 transitions, because $a{:}a$, $e{:}e$, $o{:}o$, and $u{:}u$ are missing in addition as they label transitions from that state to state 2. State 0 is the initial state and double circles indicate final states.

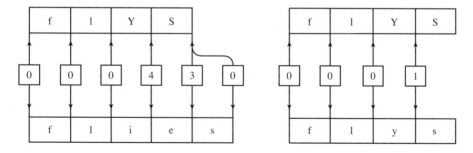

FIGURE 4 The operation of the morphographemic transducer

The transducer works in an extremely simple way, which is illustrated in Fig. 4. The upper tape is assumed to contain a sequence of lexical items and the lower a putative textual string. The diagram on the left shows the states that the machine would pass through in the course of accepting a pair of tapes with the string *flYs* on the first and *flies* on the second, namely 0, 0, 4, 3, 0. The boxes in the centre of the diagram show the state of the machine when it is in the position indicated by the upper and lower arrows. Notice that the last transition moves only the lower tape; the symbol ϵ in Fig. 3 is the *empty* symbol and causes the corresponding tape to be ignored. The diagram on the right demonstrates that the machine does *not* accept the pair *flYS* and *flys* because there is no transition from state 1 for the pair *S:s*.

A more traditional way to capture the facts enshrined in this transducer would be in a set of ordered rules such as the following:

1. S → es/**Sibilant**__
2. S → es/Y__
3. S → s
4. Y → y/__i
5. Y → i/__**Vowel**
6. Y → y

where **Sibilant** = {s, x, z}
and **Vowel** = {a, e, i, o, u}

Kaplan and I designed an algorithm for deriving a transducer from such a set of rules. This algorithm operates in two stages. In the first, a transducer is built for each of the rules in the set. The details of this stage are not relevant to our present concerns. I shall describe a new one, designed for use with meta-rules in a later section. In the second stage, these machines are composed, two at a time, until only one remains. The composition operation is applicable to any pair of transducers and will also have a role to fill in the techniques to be proposed for handling meta-rules.

The fact that transducers can be composed, so that a cascade of arbitrarily many can be reduced to one simple machine that can be modelled by an extremely simple computer program is one of their most appealing characteristics. Another is that, unlike ordered sets of rewriting rules, they have no essential directionality, that is, that same machine can be used with equal ease and efficiency in generation and analysis. Instead of reading a pair of tapes and accepting or rejecting them, the machine reads one tape and writes the other. The result consists of whatever has been written on the output tape when the input tape has been exhausted and the machine is in a final state. The process is fundamentally non-deterministic so that, if more than one output tape can be set in correspondence with the given input tape, they can all be found. Those that fail to carry the machine into a final state are simply ignored.

I said in the introduction to this paper that lexical strings usually translate unambiguously into textual strings but the reverse does not hold. Notice that even the very simple transducer discussed above, and whose transition diagram is given in Fig. 3, allows the following correspondences:

flYS   flies
flYes   flies
flies   flies

The strings on the left, viewed as canonical lexical forms, can each be paired with only one textual string, namely *flies*. However, this can be paired with three lexical strings. If more rules were added to the grammar, we should expect the number of lexical strings corresponding to a given textual string to increase. It should apparently follow from this that analysis would be a fundamentally less efficient process than generation, even if carried out with one and the same transducer, because a significant proportion of the intermediate results produced by the transducer would not match anything in the lexicon. But this depends, once again, on whether the analysis is done in a directed manner.

Let us make the reasonable assumption that the word analyser stores the canonical forms of lexical entries in the form of a tree. Such an arrangement, suitable for recognising just the words in the sentence "Fiction flies in the face of fact" is depicted in the upper left corner of Fig. 5. The point is that, whenever two entries share some initial characters, these are represented only once.

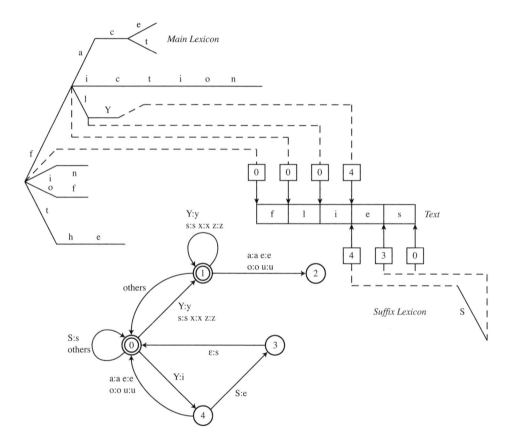

FIGURE 5 Word recognition

Using such a tree, it is a straightforward matter to conduct an incremental search for lexical entries in parallel with the operation of the transducer, so that any non-deterministic path on which the latter embarks can be curtailed as soon as it requires a character in the lexicon that cannot be found there. The fundamental notion is to use the lexical tree in place of one of the transducer's tapes. An example will make this clear.

At the top of Figure 5 is the main lexical tree, and at the bottom right is a second lexicon which contains the single entry "S". The bottom left of the figure is simply a reproduction of Figure 3 and the figure as a whole shows how the tree-structured lexicon and the transducer conspire in the recognition of the word "flies" which is laid out on the tape represented in the centre of the figure. Just as in Figure 4, little boxes with numbers in them are used to show the various states of the transducer. The transducer is in state 0 before reading the first character of the text and its other pointer is to the root node of the larger lexical tree. After reading f from the text tape, it remains in state 0 and its lexical pointer moves over the character f in the tree. The machine also remains in state 0 as both pointers move over the character l. From the current lexical node, the only possible move is over the character Y. The transducer can pair this with an i in the text by moving to state 4, as the figure shows. The entry fl in the lexicon has now been provisionally recognised. The recognition is only provisional because the transducer is not in a final state. Since flY is a word that allows, among others, the suffix S, we now replace the main lexicon with a suffix lexicon which, for the sake of simplicity, we assume to contain this suffix alone. The depictions of the transducer's states are now shown below that of the text tape. The transducer remains in state 4 while the lexicon change takes place. It then advances to state 3 over e on the text tape and S in the suffix lexicon. Finally, the transducer advances from state 3 to state 0, reading s from a text tape and ignoring the dictionary. The recognition of the word "flies" is thus completed.

The point of this somewhat protracted example has been to show how the dictionary, if made available in a suitable form, can be used to direct the operation of the transducer so that, instead of producing all candidate lexical strings that the spelling rules would allow and looking each of them up independently in the lexicon, it uses the transducer to evaluate a predicate on a pair of objects, one the text string, and the other a path through the dictionary trees. I shall now show how this same strategy can be applied to syntactic rules and meta-rules.

22.3   Context-Free Rules as Transition Networks

We saw in the last section how one of the transducer's tapes can be replaced with a tree-structured lexicon. Since the finite-state transducers are non-deterministic devices, nothing fundamental changes when a tape where every cell has a unique successor is replaced by a tree whose nodes may have more than one. If the tape and the transition diagram of the transducer permit more than one branch of the tree to be followed, the non-deterministic process simply splits and independent paths are followed for each possible branch of the tree.

In adapting this scheme to syntactic analysis, the first step we take is to replace the *other* tape – the text tape – with a branching data structure, namely the chart. The second is to replace the tree-structured lexicon with a tree-structured version of the basic grammar, that is the context-free rules of the grammar, untreated by meta-rules. Finally, we must convert the meta-rules into a transducer that can mediate between these two data structures. The first step need not detain us; the second will occupy us only briefly, and the third will require more discussion.

At the heart of almost any parser is a process in which rules are sought which could be applied to an initial subsequence of a particular string of constituents. In a directed parser, only a certain subset of the rules in the grammar is considered, typically those that expand a certain non-terminal symbol; in a non-directed parser, all rules are eligible. Suppose that there are n eligible rules, as follows:

$$1. \quad \alpha_1 \quad \rightarrow \quad \beta_1$$

$$.$$
$$.$$
$$.$$

$$n. \quad \alpha_n \quad \rightarrow \quad \beta_n$$

The object of the step, then, is to determine which members of the set $\{\beta_1...\beta_n\}$ are initial subsequences of the string at hand. This problem is logically indistinguishable from that of identifying the first word of a text in a lexicon, and the procedure can often be expedited by arranging the members of the set $\{\beta_1...\beta_n\}$ in just the kind of tree structure described in the last section. Such a representation is particularly appropriate if, as in the case of GPSG, the rules make use of the Kleene star and other devices borrowed from the formalism of regular expressions. Under these circumstances, the tree structures that figure in the above discussion become finite-state transition networks. This is a desirable move to make, independently of the considerations raised here, because finite-state machines are inherently more amenable to computational processes than regular expressions. If the following were the only eligible rules, the transition network might be as in Fig. 6.

1.	S	$\rightarrow$	NP VP
2.	NP	$\rightarrow$	DET ADJ* NP
3.	NP	$\rightarrow$	NP REL
4.	NP	$\rightarrow$	NP PP*
5.	VP	$\rightarrow$	V NP PP*

The heavier lines, whose labels end in an arrow, represent the symbols on the left-hand side of the rule; we shall take up the function of these shortly.

22.4   Meta-Rules as Transducers

Figure 7 is a transducer which embodies the information in the two meta-rules we have considered, namely (1) and (8). I shall make at least a *prima facie* case for this claim after first explaining the few additional notational devices in the diagram.

The symbol φ is simply a shorthand device. It matches any categorial symbol and it is to be understood that a transition over a pair $\varphi : \varphi$ is allowable only if the same unspecified category level appears both in the lexicon and in the chart; in other words, it is implicit that the symbols matched by such a pair are the same.

The labels in some transitions make use of subscripts. These constitute a fundamentally new device added to the structure of transducers to allow them to represent meta-rules. Towards the end of this paper, I shall propose a more general mechanism to replace subscripts; however, they will satisfy our present needs and their intuitive appeal is more immediate. The purpose of the subscripts is to coordinate unspecified substrings on the two tapes. If some number of symbols on the upper tape is matched by

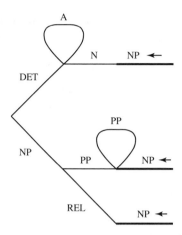

FIGURE 6 A transition network for grammar rules

symbols in the transition diagram with a given subscript, say i, then that same number of symbols on the lower tape must also be matched by symbols with that subscript. Furthermore, if a symbol on the upper tape, say x, is matched by φ_i, and this is the kth symbol on the upper tape matched by a symbol with the subscript i, then the kth symbol on the lower tape that matches a symbol with subscript i must also be x. So, consider the paths that lead from the initial state $\langle 0, 0 \rangle$ to the final state $\langle 3, 2 \rangle$ in Fig. 7. These in fact correspond to the situations in which both the passive and linking meta-rules apply. The transitions from state $\langle 1, 0 \rangle$ are the ones that actually match slashed categories on the lower tape, the one incident to state $\langle 2, 1 \rangle$ for the case where the NP gap will occur in the *by* prepositional phrase of the passive construction, the one incident to state $\langle 1, 1 \rangle$ for all other cases. Three looping transitions are encountered along this path, two labelled $\epsilon : \varphi_1$, and one labelled $\varphi_1 : \epsilon$. The convention governing subscripts requires that the number of times this last one is traversed be the same as the total number of times either of the other two is traversed. Furthermore, since the subscripted symbol is always φ, the symbols traversed on the upper tape by these loops must be the same symbols, and in the same order, as those traversed by loops on the lower tape. In particular, a string $V\ NP\ x\ y\ z\ VP \leftarrow$ on the upper tape will match $V\ x$ $y\ z\ PP/NP_{[case:by]}$ on the lower tape, whereas the same upper tape would not match V $x\ y\ PP/NP_{[case:by]}$ or $V\ w\ x\ y\ z\ PP/NP_{[case:by]}$.

The reason for naming the states of Fig. 7 with pairs of numbers rather than more simply will be made clear shortly. For the moment, it may be illuminating to note the following facts about these pairs.

1. If the current state of the machine has a label with ω in the first position, the linking meta-rule is not being applied.

2. If the current state has a label with ω in the second position, the passive meta-rule is not being applied.

3. If the label of the current state is a pair of digits, the possibility of applying neither meta-rule has been foreclosed.

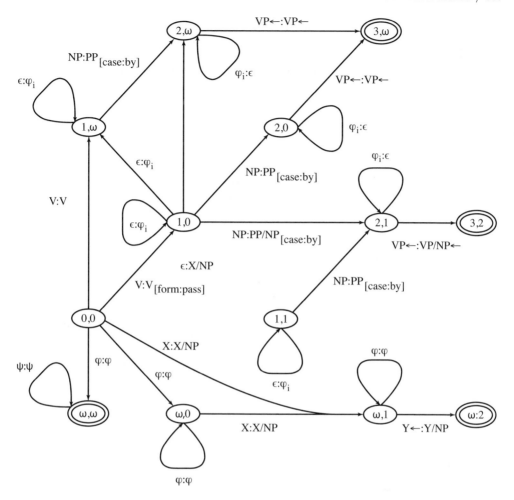

FIGURE 7 A meta-rule transducer

Accordingly, the transducer has four final states corresponding to the four possible combinations of meta-rule applications. The state labels also permit the following generalizations:

4. A digit other than 0 in the first position of a label indicates that the current rule application can go through only if the linking meta-rule is applied.

5. A digit other than 0 in the second position of a label indicates that the current rule application can go through only if the passive meta-rule is applied.

Particular digits can be interpreted according to the table in Fig. 8.

Figure 9 is an example, parallel to the phonological one shown in Fig. 5, of the transducer in operation. On the left of the figure is a simple grammar organised in the form of a tree. Dashed lines connect a sequence of nodes in this tree to depictions of the transducer as it moves through the states $\langle 0,0 \rangle$, $\langle 1,0 \rangle$, $\langle 2,1 \rangle$, $\langle 2,1 \rangle$, $\langle 3,2 \rangle$. The sequence of constituents encountered in the chart is *V, PP/NP, PP*. The last transition, from

First position	
State	Interpretation
0	Initial state
1	Last pair was $V{:}V$ – committed to passive
2	Last pair was NP:*by*-phrase of passive
3	Passive completed
Second position	
State Interpretation	
0	No slashed category seen
1	One slashed category seen
2	Linking meta-rule complete

FIGURE 8 Key to the states of the meta-rule transducer

state $\langle 2,1 \rangle$ to state $\langle 3,2 \rangle$, is treated somewhat specially; the second symbol named in the transition is not compared with the label on an edge in the chart, like the preceding ones, because the symbol ends with the character "←". All such symbols are interpreted by the parser as the labels of new edges to be inserted into the chart, that is as the output of successful rule applications. Accordingly, in making this last transition, the parser completes the analysis of the sequence *V PP/NP PP* as a constituent of category *VP/NP*.

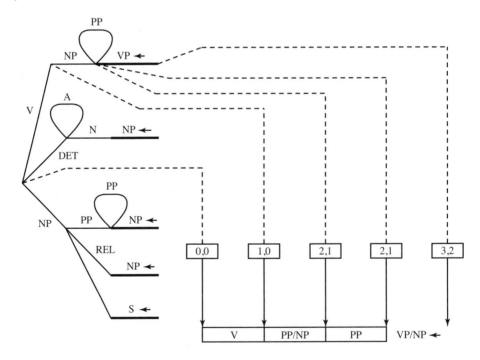

FIGURE 9 Using a meta-rule transducer

22.5 Constructing Meta-Rule Transducers

It remains to explain how a transducer can be constructed for an individual meta-rule and how a set of these can then be combined into a single transducer. As I pointed out earlier, meta-rules have the structure.

(9) $\alpha \to \beta \Rightarrow \gamma \to \delta$

and β and δ are regular expressions. By concatenating $\alpha \leftarrow$ and $\gamma \leftarrow$ (both single symbols) on the ends of β and δ respectively, we reduce the meta-rule to a simple pair of regular expressions. On the principle that computation is easier with finite-state machines (FSMs) than with regular expressions, and that the end result of the present computation will be a member of the same family of devices as FSMs, we next convert these regular expressions to a pair of FSMs, F_l and F_r, corresponding to the left and right sides of the meta-rule. An algorithm for doing this can be found in any elementary text on automata theory. The only modification required for the present purpose is to allow for subscripts. Whenever a variable is encountered in the course of carrying out the algorithm that is intended to match a substring of unspecified length, it will naturally be translated as though it were a simple variable covering a single symbol, but annotated with a Kleene star to show that it can be repeated any number of times. It must also receive a subscript, different from any used in any other rule or on the same side of the present rule. Any other occurrences of the same variable on the other side of the rule must have the same subscript.

I shall use the passive meta-rule to illustrate the process. Once the basic pair of FSMs has been constructed, the process continues as illustrated in Fig. 10. The transition diagram of F_l is shown as (a), that of F_r as (b), and the resulting transducer as (c). If S_l is the state set of F_l, and S_r the state set of F_r, then the transducer we shall construct will have states corresponding to a subset of $S_l \times S_r$. The problem of constructing the transducer therefore reduces to one of deciding, for a given state $\langle p, q \rangle \in S_l \times S_r$, what transitions will be incident from it and at which states each of them will terminate. The obvious strategy is to start with the initial state, and then consider in turn hitherto untreated states at the end of which already constructed transitions terminate. We thus avoid constructing transitions for states that are not reachable, directly or indirectly, from the initial state.

Consider a state $\langle p, q \rangle$. The transducer will be in this state when enough of the rule tree has been examined to carry F_l into state p and enough edges in the chart have been examined to carry F_r into state j. We therefore take each of the transitions t_l that can be made from state p in F_l in conjunction with each of the transitions t_r that can be made from state j in F_r. Suppose that t_l terminates at state m and t_r at state n, then the transducer must have a transition from $\langle p, q \rangle$ over the symbol pair $t_l : t_r$. to the state $\langle m, n \rangle$.

This procedure covers all but two kinds of circumstance. The first arises when one of the states is final even though further transitions are possible from the other. In other words, the left and right sides of the meta-rule can match strings of different lengths so that one reaches a final state before the other. What is required is a way of allowing the FSM that is scanning the shorter string to mark time while the other one catches up.

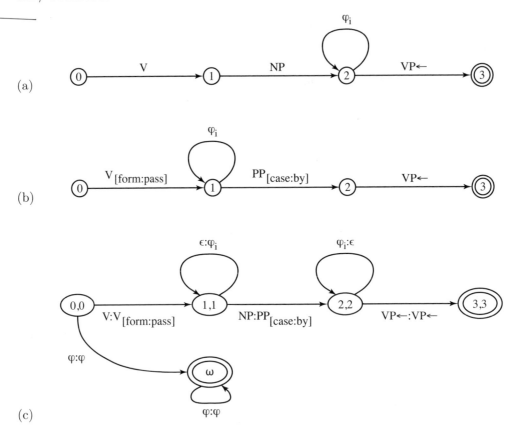

FIGURE 10 The construction of a meta-rule transducer

This is easily done by providing every final state with one additional transition, labelled with the null symbol, ϵ, leaving and returning to the same state. The null symbols from the machine that reaches its final state first will be paired with enough symbols to carry the other machine into a final state. By convention, we abstain from adding transitions to the transducer that leave and enter the same state and are labelled $\epsilon : \epsilon$, for these clearly embody no information.

The other special circumstance that must be provided for arises when one of the transitions in the pair is a subscripted symbol. These are not paired with symbols from the other FSM in constructing the transducer; the other member of the pair is always the null symbol, ϵ. Notice that these subscripted symbols always loop back to the same state from which they start. Thus, suppose that t_l is a transition to and from state p over φ_i. Regardless of t_r, the only transition to which it contributes will be from $\langle p, q \rangle$ over $\varphi_i : \epsilon$ and back to $\langle p, q \rangle$.

The final step in the construction process is to add a transition from the initial state of the transducer to a special final state labelled ω, and two transitions to and from that state, labelled $\omega : \omega$ and $\psi : \psi$. The ψ transitions match only the symbols that come from the left-hand sides of rules, that is symbols whose last character we have systematically written as "$\leftarrow$". The effect of this addition is to allow a non-deterministic alternative at the initial state which, if taken, causes the transducer to carry any rule whatsoever into itself. When the transducers for the various rules are composed, this will cause a result to be produced in which each individual meta-rule is treated as optional. If it were omitted, a successful transduction would be possible only in the case where the rule applied in the chart came from applying *all* the meta-rules.

22.6 Composing Transducers

The final step in the process of creating a single transducer capable of mimicking an ordered set of meta-rules is to compose the individual transducers produced in the manner just outlined into a single machine. The algorithm I shall describe composes a pair of transducers. Its result can be characterised more specifically as follows. Suppose M_i and M_2 are transducers and T_1, T_2 and T_3 are tapes such that M_1 accepts the pair $\langle T_1, T_2 \rangle$ and M_2 accepts the pair $\langle T_2, T_3 \rangle$, then M_3 accepts the pair $\langle T_1, T_3 \rangle$. Furthermore, the pairs of tapes that M_3 accepts are completely characterised in this way.

The procedure for composing transducers has a strong family resemblance to the one just described for obtaining a transducer from a pair of FSMs representing the two sides of a meta-rule. Once again, the state-set of the resulting machine will correspond to a subset of the Cartesian product of the state sets of the component machines. The principal step is therefore one of determining what transitions will leave a state $\langle p,\ q \rangle$ in this set. Consider a pair of transitions, $a{:}b$ leaving state p and entering state x in the first machine and $c{:}d$ leaving state q and entering state y in the second, and assume temporarily that subscripts and instances of the variable φ are not involved. In order for the composed machine to make a transition corresponding to this pair, one of the following propositions must clearly be true:

$$
\begin{array}{ll}
\text{(i)} & \text{b} = \text{c} \\
\text{(ii)} & \text{b} = \epsilon \\
\text{(iii)} & \text{c} = \epsilon
\end{array}
$$

Condition (i) simply states that, if the two component machines are to make a move in parallel, and that move requires them both to examine their common tape, T_2, then they must both find the same symbol there. Conditions (ii) and (iii) state that one of the machines can read any symbol whatever on the shared tape if, in the same move of the transducer, the other machine ignores the shared tape.[6] If condition (i) obtains, a transition is introduced in the composed machine from $\langle p,\ q \rangle$ over $a{:}d$ to $\langle x,\ y \rangle$. Condition (ii) is one in which the first tape can move independently of the second tape; a transition is therefore introduced from $\langle p,\ q \rangle$ over $a{:}\epsilon$ to $\langle x,\ q \rangle$. Condition (iii) is the obverse of this; a transition is introduced from $\langle p,\ q \rangle$ over $\epsilon{:}d$ to $\langle p,\ y \rangle$.

The unsubscripted variable φ adds little complication to this basic scheme. Rather than discuss each case in detail, I provide a table in Fig. 11 of the ways in which some representative pairs of transitions compose.

Finally we must consider the treatment of subscripts in the composition process. As I pointed out earlier, it is in respect of the subscripts that the formalism proposed here as

---

[6]It is, of course possible for all three conditions to obtain. For reasons too detailed to pursue here, the simplest machine is obtained when this is regarded as a situation in which condition (i) obtains, the other two being ignored.

Upper from from p to x	Lower from from q to y	Result	to
a:b	c:d		
a:b	b:d	a:d	$\langle x, y \rangle$
ϵ:b	b:c	a:ϵ	$\langle x, y \rangle$
a:ϵ	c:d	a:ϵ	$\langle x, q \rangle$
a:b	ϵ:d	ϵ:d	$\langle p, y \rangle$
a:b	c:ϵ	a:ϵ	$\langle x, y \rangle$
a:ϵ	ϵ:d	a:d	$\langle x, y \rangle$
φ:b	c:d	φ:d	$\langle x, y \rangle$
a:φ	c:d	a:d	$\langle x, y \rangle$
a:b	φ:d	a:d	$\langle x, y \rangle$
a:b	c:φ	a:φ	$\langle x, y \rangle$
$\varphi : \varphi$	c:d	c:d	$\langle x, y \rangle$
a:b	$\varphi : \varphi$	a:b	$\langle x, y \rangle$

FIGURE 11 Key to the states of the meta-rule transducer

a replacement for meta-rules differs from the one Kaplan and I proposed for phonology. Not surprisingly, it is also in respect of the subscripts that most of the subtlety in dealing with the formalism arises. It is for this reason that I announced the replacement of the original subscripts by a somewhat more general mechanism. The reason for deferring the introduction of that mechanism until now is that, while subscripts capture the information in a single meta-rule quite adequately, they are unable to represent one additional piece of information that must be included in the kind of composed machine we are about to consider. The point will be most readily made with an example.

Figure 12 shows the result of first composing two transducers (a) and (b) to form a single machine (c), and then of composing this with a third (d) to give a final result (e). Only when such a cascade of compositions is considered can the inadequacies of the basic scheme be revealed.

Notice that the subscripts in Fig. 12 take the form of expressions such as $[i \leftarrow D]$. For each symbol x in a subscript of the form $[x \leftarrow Y]$, we assume that the transduction mechanism is furnished with a *buffer* of symbols and the subscripts are each interpreted as operations on the buffer they name. The buffers obey a strict queue discipline, that is, the symbols are removed in the order in which they were inserted. Furthermore, it will invariably be the case that all the symbols in the buffer at any given time were put there under direction of subscripts associated with the same tape. A subscript $[x \leftarrow Y]$ is interpreted as follows:

1. If buffer i is empty or if the symbols it currently contains came from interpreting subscripts associated with the same tape as the current one, insert the symbol Y into it.

2. If the symbols in the buffer came from interpreting subscripts associated with the other tape, remove the next symbol from the buffer and allow the current transition to succeed just in case that symbol is Y.

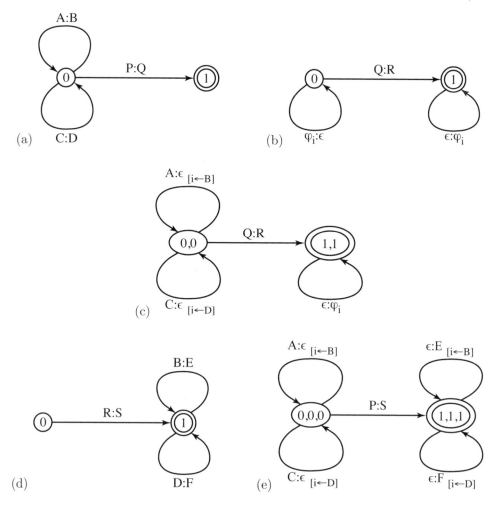

FIGURE 12 Composition of transducers

All the buffers are required to be empty at the end for the pair of tapes to be accepted. The net effect is to require that each tape presents the same sequence of symbols to each buffer; however, those symbols are not read from the tapes themselves but are explicitly named in the label of the transition. This move is necessary because composition effectively removes intermediate tapes from the cascade, so that the symbols that would have been associated with subscripts in the original proposal may no longer be on any tape in the resulting machine. This modification preserves just the symbols required to make the subscripting scheme work as explicit parts of the structure of the transducer.

Let us examine Fig. 12 in somewhat greater detail. (a) is a machine that accepts a pair of tapes if the first consists of a string over $\{A,\ B\}$ terminated by P, and A on the first tape maps onto B on the second, C onto D, and P onto Q. (b) carries a tape containing any αQ onto one containing $R\alpha$, where α is an arbitrary string. The result of composing these, (c), carries a string over $\{A, B\}$ terminated by P onto a string consisting of R followed by Cs and Ds corresponding one for one with the As and Bs on the first tape. It would, for example, accept $AACAP$ and $RBBDB$. Composition with (d) simply replaces R with S, B with E, and D with F, so that (c) would accept $AACAP$ and $SEEFE$. Figure 13 shows this transduction with a diagram similar to the ones I have used previously, augmented to show the contents of the i-buffer between each pair of transitions. The final composite machine, (e), can therefore be characterised as carrying a string over $\{A, B\}$ terminated by P onto a string consisting of S followed by Es and Fs corresponding one for one with the As and Bs on the first tape.

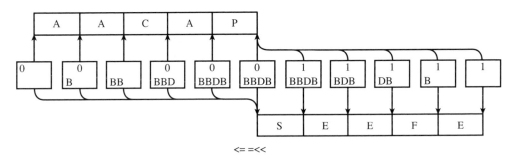

FIGURE 13 Transduction with one buffer

Consider now how transducers (a) and (b) in Fig. 12 compose to give (c). In particular continue the move in which the transition $A{:}B$ in (a) combines with $\varphi : \epsilon$ to give $A_{i\leftarrow B} : \epsilon$. Except for the subscript, this is as prescribed by the table in Fig. 11, and the subscript comes from taking the subscript on φ_i and combining it with the symbol B that the first machine of the pair would have matched against its lower tape in this transition. Instead, this symbol is stored in a buffer to be matched against a symbol at some other position in the lower tape of the composed machine. This is just the kind of movement operation for which subscripts were devised.

Conclusion

I have shown that meta-rules are not essentially meta-rules in that they can do their appointed job without being applied to other rules. Instead they are taken as specifications of transducers that have the effect of making a string of constituents to which a derived rules could apply look to the relevant portion of the parser like a string to which a basic rule would apply. Since, in this scheme, meta-rules are not really meta-rules, the cost of acquiring a new context-free rule, or modifying or deleting an old one is very small. The cost of altering the stock of meta-rules is considerably more difficult to assess. To get the best performance from the generation and parsing machinery, the meta-rules must not only be transformed into transducers, but these must then be composed into a single transducer. If performance is a paramount consideration, then this composition step must be repeated whenever the stock of meta-rules changes. However, a number of tradeoffs are possible. Since composition is a pairwise process, it would be possible to preserve certain intermediate results to speed up possible later recompilation steps. Notice also that the parsing strategy suggested here does not require that the meta-rules be represented by a single transducer, or even that any composition of transducers is undertaken at all. It is therefore possible to imagine a number of strategies that a language learner might follow involving, for example, composing the transducers for an adjacent pair of rules only when they had proved themselves in the field for some time.

Publications referenced

Gazdar 1979; Gazdar 1979; Gazdar et al. 1981; Griffiths and Petrick 1965; Kay 1967; Kay 1977; Kay 1980.

23

Functional Unification Grammar: A Formalism for Machine Translation

Abstract

Functional Unification Grammar provides an opportunity to encompass within one formalism and computational system the parts of machine translation systems that have usually been treated separately, notably analysis, transfer, and synthesis. Many of the advantages of this formalism come from the fact that it is monotonic allowing data structures to grow differently as different nondeterministic alternatives in a computation are pursued, but never to be modified in any way. A striking feature of this system is that it is fundamentally reversible, allowing a to translate as b only if b could translate as a.

23.1 Overview

23.1.1 Machine Translation

A classical translating machine stands with one foot on the input text and one on the output. The input text is analyzed by the components of the machine that make up the left leg, each one feeding information into the one above it. Information is passed from component to component down the right leg to construct the output text. The components of each leg correspond to the chapters of an introductory textbook on linguistics with phonology or graphology at the bottom, then syntax, semantics, and so on. The legs join where languages are no longer differentiated and linguistics shades off into psychology and philosophy. The higher levels are also the ones whose theoretical underpinnings are less well known and system designers therefore often tie the legs together somewhere lower down, constructing a more or less *ad hoc* bridge, pivot, or transfer component.

We cannot be sure that the classical design is the right design, or the best design, for a translating machine. But it does have several strong points. Since the structure of the components is grounded in linguistic theory, it is possible to divide each of these components into two parts: a formal description of the relevant facts about the language and an interpreter of the formalism. The formal description is data whereas the interpreter is program. The formal description should ideally serve the needs of synthesis and analysis indifferently. On the other hand we would expect different interpreters to be required in the two legs of the machine. We expect to be able to use identical interpreters in corresponding places in all machines of similar design because the information they embody comes from general linguistic theory and not from particular languages. The scheme therefore has the advantage of modularity. The linguistic descriptions are independent of the leg of the machine they are used in and the programs are independent of the languages to which they are applied.

For all the advantages of the classical design, it is not hard to imagine improvements. In the best of all possible worlds, there would only be one formalism in which all the facts about a language – morphological, syntactic, semantic, or whatever – could be stated. A formalism powerful enough to accommodate the various different kinds of linguistic phenomena with equal facility might be unappealing to theoretical linguists because powerful formal systems do not make powerful claims. But the engineering advantages are clear to see. A single formalism would straightforwardly reduce the number of interpreters to two, one for analysis and one for synthesis. Furthermore, the explanatory value of a theory clearly rests on a great deal more than the restrictiveness of its formal base. In particular, the possiblity of encompassing what had hitherto been thought to require altogether different kinds of treatment within a single framework could be theoretically interesting.

Another clear improvement on the classical design would result from merging the two interpreters associated with a formalism. The most obvious advantage to be hoped for with this move would be that the overall structure of the translating machine would be greatly simplified, though this would not *necessarily* happen. It is also reasonable to hope that the machine would be more robust, easier to modify and maintain, and altogether more perspicuous. This is because a device to which analysis and synthesis look essentially the same is one that is fundamentally less time dependent, with fewer internal variables and states; it is apt to work by monitoring constraints laid down in the formal description and ensuring that they are maintained, rather than carrying out long and complex sequences of steps in a carefully prescribed order.

These advantages are available in large measure through a class of formal devices that are slowly gaining acceptance in linguistics and which are based on the relations contracted by formal objects rather than by transformations of one formal object into another. These systems are all procedurally monotonic in the sense that, while new information may be added to existing data structures, possibly different information on different branches of a nondeterministic process, nothing is ever deleted or changed. As a result, the particular order in which elementary events take place is of little importance. Lexical Functional Grammar and Generalized Phrase-Structure Grammar share these relational and monotonic properties. They are also characteristics of Functional Unification Grammar (FUG) which I believe also has additional properties that suit it particularly well to the needs of experimental machine-translation systems.

The term *experimental* must be taken quite seriously here though, if my view of machine translation were more generally held, it would be redundant. I believe that all machine translation of natural languages is experimental and that he who claims otherwise does his more serious colleagues a serious disservice. I should not wish any thing that I say in this paper as a claim to have solved any of the myriad problems that stand between us and working machine translation systems worthy of the name. The contribution that FUG might make is, I believe, a great deal more modest, namely to reformalize more simply and perspicuously what has been done before and which has come to be regarded, as 1 said at the outset "classical".

23.1.2 Functional Unification Grammar

FUG traffics in descriptions and there is essentially only one kind of description, whether for lexical items, phrases, sentences, or entire languages. Descriptions do not distinguish among levels in the linguistic hierarchy. This is not to say that the distinctions among the levels are unreal or that a linguist working with the formalism should not respect them. It means only that the notation and its interpretation are always uniform. Either a pair of descriptions is incompatible or they are combinable into a single description.

Within FUG, every object has infinitely many descriptions, though a given grammar partitions the descriptions of the words and phrases in its language into a finite number of equivalence classes, one for each interpretation that the grammar assigns to it. The members of an equivalence class differ along dimensions that are grammatically irrelevant – when they were uttered, whether they amused Queen Victoria, or whether they contain a prime number of words. Each equivalence class constitutes a lattice with just one member that contains none of these grammatically irrelevant properties, and this *canonical* member is the only one a linguist would normally concern himself with. However, a grammatical irrelevancy that acquires relevance in the present context is the description of possible translations of a word or phrase, or of one of its interpretations, in one or more other languages.

A description is an expression over an essentially arbitrary basic vocabulary. The relations among sets of descriptions therefore remain unchanged under one-for-one mappings of their basic vocabularies. It is therefore possible to arrange that different grammars share no terms except for possible quotations from the languages described. Canonical descriptions of a pair of sentences in different languages according to grammars that shared no terms could always be unified into a single description which would, of course. not be canonical. Since all pairs are unifiable, the relation that they establish between sentences is entirely arbitrary. However, a third grammar can be written that unifies with these combined descriptions only if the sentences they describe in the two langauages stand in a certain relation to one another. The relation we are interested in is, of course, the translation relation which, for the purposes of the kind of experimental system I have in mind I take to be definable for isolated sentences. Such a *transfer* grammar can readily capture all the components of the relation that have in fact been built into translation systems: correspondences between words and continuous or discontinuous phrases, use of selectional features or local contexts, case frames, reordering rules, lexical functions, compositional semantics, and so on.

23.2 The Formalism

23.2.1 Functional Descriptions

In FUG, linguistic objects are represented by *functional descriptions* (FDs). The basic constituent of a functional description is a *feature* consisting of an *attribute* and an associated *value* . We write features in the form $a = v$, where a is the attribute and v, the value. Attributes are arbitrary words with no significant internal structure. Values can be of various types, the simplest of which is an *atomic value* , also an arbitrary word. So $Cat = S$ is a feature of the most elementary type. It appears in the descriptions of sentences, and which declares that their *Category* is *S*. The only kinds of non-atomic values that will concern us here are *constituent sets, patterns* and FDs themselves.

A FD is a Boolean expression over features. We distinguish conjuncts from disjuncts by the kinds of brackets used to enclose their members; the conjuncts and disjuncts of $a = p,\ b = q,\ and\ c = r$ are written

$$\begin{bmatrix} a = p \\ b = q \\ c = r \end{bmatrix} \text{ and } \begin{Bmatrix} a = p \\ b = q \\ c = r \end{Bmatrix}$$

respectively. The vertical arrangement of these expressions has proved convenient and it is of minor importance in that braces of ordinary variety are used for a different purpose in FUG, namely to enclose the members of constituent sets. The following FD describes all sentences whose subject is a singular noun phrase in the nominative or accusative cases:

$$(1) \quad \begin{bmatrix} Cat = S \\ \\ Subj = \begin{bmatrix} Cat = NP \\ Num = Sing \\ \begin{Bmatrix} Case = Nom \\ Case = Acc \end{Bmatrix} \end{bmatrix} \end{bmatrix}$$

It is a crucial property of FDs that no attribute should figure more once in any conjunct, though a given attribute may appear in feature lists that are themselves the values of different attributes. This being the case, it is always possible to identify a conjunct or disjunct in a FD by giving a sequence of attributes $\langle a_1...a_k \rangle$. a_1 is an attribute in the FD whose value v_1 is another FD. The attribute a_2 is an attribute in v_1 whose value is an FD, and so on. Sequences of attributes of this kind are referred to as *paths* . If the FD contains disjuncts, then the value identified by the path will naturally also be a disjunct.

We sometimes write a path as the value of an attribute to indicate that that value of that attribute is not only equal to the value identified by the path but that these values are one and the same, in short, that they are *unified* in a sense soon to be explained. Roughly, if more information were acquired about one of the values so that more features were added to it, the same additions would be reflected in the other value. This would not automatically happen because a pair of values happened to be the same. So, for example, if the topic of the sentence were also its object, we might write

$$\begin{bmatrix} Object = v \\ Topic = \langle Object \rangle \end{bmatrix}$$

where v is some FD.

Constituent sets are sets of paths identifying within a given FD the descriptions of its constituents in the sense of phrase-structure grammar. No constituent set is specified in example (1) above and the question of whether the subject is a constituent is therefore left open.

Example (2), though still artificially simple, is more realistic. It is a syntactic description of the sentence *John knows Mary*. Perhaps the most striking property of this description is that descriptions of constituents are embedded one inside another, even though the constituents themselves are not so embedded. The value of the *Head* attribute describes a constituent of the sentence, a fact which is declared in the value of the *CSet* attribute. We also see that the sentence has a second attribute whose description is to be found as the value of the Subject of the Head of the Head of the sentence. The reason for this arrangement will become clear shortly.

$$
(2) \quad \begin{bmatrix} \text{Cat} = \text{NONE} \\ \text{Head} = \begin{bmatrix} \text{Cat} = \text{NONE} \\ \text{Head} = \begin{bmatrix} \text{Cat} = \text{Verb} \\ \text{Head} = \text{NONE} \\ \text{Tense} = \text{Pres} \\ \text{Word} = \text{know} \\ \text{Subj} = \begin{bmatrix} \text{Cat} = \text{NONE} \\ \text{Head} = \begin{bmatrix} \text{Cat} = \text{Noun} \\ \text{Head} = \text{NONE} \\ \text{Pers} = 3 \\ \text{Word} = \text{John} \\ \text{Art} = \text{NONE} \end{bmatrix} \end{bmatrix} \\ \text{Obj} = \begin{bmatrix} \text{Cat} = \text{NONE} \\ \text{Head} = \begin{bmatrix} \text{Cat} = \text{Noun} \\ \text{Head} = \text{NONE} \\ \text{Pers} = 3 \\ \text{Word} = \text{Mary} \\ \text{Art} = \text{NONE} \end{bmatrix} \end{bmatrix} \end{bmatrix} \\ \text{CSet} = \begin{bmatrix} \langle \text{Head} \rangle \ \langle \text{Head Obj} \rangle \end{bmatrix} \\ \text{Pat} = \begin{bmatrix} \langle \text{Head} \rangle \ \langle \text{Head Obj} \rangle \end{bmatrix} \end{bmatrix} \\ \text{CSet} = \begin{bmatrix} \langle \text{Head Head Subj} \rangle \ \langle \text{head} \rangle \end{bmatrix} \\ \text{Pat} = \begin{bmatrix} \langle \text{Head Head Subj} \rangle \ \langle \text{head} \rangle \end{bmatrix} \end{bmatrix}
$$

In example (2), every conjunct in which the CSet attribute has a value other than *NONE* also has a substantive value for the attribute *Pat*. The value of this attribute is a regular expression over paths which restricts the order in which the constituents must appear. By convention, if no pattern is given for a description which nevertheless does have constituents, they may occur in any order. We shall have more to say about patterns in due course.

23.2.2 Unification

Essentially the only operation used in processing FUG is that of *unification*, the paradigm example of a monotonic operation. Given a pair of descriptions, the unification process first determines whether they are compatible in the sense of allowing the possibility of there being some object that is in the extension of both of them. This possibility would be excluded if there were a path in one of the two descriptions that led to an atomic value while the same path in the other one led to some other value. This would occur if, for example, one described a sentence with a singular subject and the other a sentence with a plural subject, or if one described a sentence and the other a noun phrase. There can also be incompatibilities in respect of other kinds of value. Thus, if one has a pattern requiring the subject to precede the main verb whereas the other specifies the other order, the two descriptions will be incompatible. Constituent sets are incompatible if they are not the same.

We have briefly considered how three different types of description behave under unification. Implicit in what we have said is that descriptions of different types do not unify with one another. Grammars, which are the descriptions of the infinite sets of sentences that make up a language, constitute a type of description that is structurally identical to an ordinary FD but is distinguished on the grounds that it behaves slightly differently under unification. In particular, it is possible to unify a grammar with another grammar to produce a new grammar, but it is also possible to unify a grammar with a FD, in which case the result is a new FD. The rules for unifying grammars with grammars are the same as those for unifying FDs with FDs. The rules for unifying grammars with FDs, however, are slightly different and the difference lies in the ability of FUG to describe structures recursively and hence to provide for sentences of unbounded size. The rule for unifying grammars with FDs requires the grammars to be unified – following the rules for FD unification – with *each individual* constituent of the FD.

$$
(3) \quad
\left\{
\begin{array}{l}
\left[
\begin{array}{l}
\mathrm{Head} = \left[\mathrm{Head} = \left[\mathrm{Cat} = \mathrm{V} \right] \right] \\[4pt]
\mathrm{CSet} = \left[\left\{ \langle \mathrm{Head\ Head\ Subj} \rangle \langle \mathrm{Head} \rangle \right\} \right] \\[4pt]
\mathrm{Pat} = (\langle \mathrm{Head\ Head\ Subj} \rangle \langle \mathrm{Head} \rangle)
\end{array}
\right] \\[24pt]
\left[
\mathrm{Head} =
\left[
\begin{array}{l}
\mathrm{Cat} = \mathrm{V} \\[4pt]
\left\{
\begin{array}{l}
\mathrm{Obj} = \mathrm{NONE} \\[4pt]
\mathrm{Obj} = \left[\mathrm{Cat} = \mathrm{NP} \right]
\end{array}
\right\} \\[4pt]
\mathrm{CSet} = \mathrm{NONE}
\end{array}
\right]
\right] \\[24pt]
\left[
\mathrm{Head} =
\left[
\begin{array}{l}
\mathrm{Cat} = \mathrm{N} \\
\mathrm{CSet} = \mathrm{NONE}
\end{array}
\right]
\right]
\end{array}
\right\}
$$

By way of illustration, consider the grammar in (3). Like most grammars, it is a disjunction of clauses, one for each (non-terminal) category or constituent type in the language. The first of the three clauses in the principal disjunction describes sentences as having a head whose head is of category *V*. This characterization is in line with so called $\overline{X}$-theory, according to which a sentence belongs to the category $\overline{\overline{X}}$. In general, a phrase of category $\overline{X}$, for whatever X, has a *head* constituent of category X, that is, a category with the same name but one less bar. $\overline{X}$ is built into the very fabric of the version of FUG illutrated here where, for example, a sentence is by definition a phrase whose head's head is a verb. The head of a sentence is a $\overline{V}$, that is, a phrase whose head is of category V and which has no head of its own. A phrase with this description cannot unify with the first clause in the grammar because its head has the feature [Head = NONE].

Of sentences, the grammar says that they have two constituents. It is no surprise that the second of these is its head. The first would usually be called its subject but is here characterized as the subject of its verb. This does not imply that there must be lexical entries not only for all the verbs in the language but that there must be such an entry for each of the subjects that the verb might have. What it does mean is that the subject must be unifiable with any description the verb gives of its subject and thus provides automatically both for any selectional restrictions that a verb might place on its subject but also for agreement in person and number between subject and verb. Objects are handled in an analogous manner. Thus, the lexical entries for the French verb forms *connait* and *sait* might be as follows:

$$
\begin{bmatrix}
\text{Cat} = \text{V} \\
\text{Lex} = \text{connaitre} \\
\text{Tense} = \text{Pres} \\
\text{Subj} = \begin{bmatrix} \text{Pers} = 3 \\ \text{Num} = \text{Sing} \\ \text{Anim} = + \end{bmatrix} \\
\text{Obj} = \begin{bmatrix} \text{Cat} = \text{NP} \end{bmatrix}
\end{bmatrix}
$$

$$
\begin{bmatrix}
\text{Cat} = \text{V} \\
\text{Lex} = \text{savoir} \\
\text{Tense} = \text{Pres} \\
\text{Subj} = \begin{bmatrix} \text{Pers} = 3 \\ \text{Num} = \text{Sing} \\ \text{Anim} = + \end{bmatrix} \\
\text{Obj} = \begin{bmatrix} \text{Cat} = \text{S} \end{bmatrix}
\end{bmatrix}
$$

Each requires its subject to be third person, singular and animate. Taking a rather simplistic view of the difference between these verbs for the sake of the example, this lexicon states that *connait* takes noun phrases as objects, whereas *sait* takes sentences.

23.3 Translation

23.3.1 Syntax

Consider now the French sentence *Jean connait Marie* which is presumably a reasonable rendering of the English sentence *John knows Mary*, a possible functional description of which was given in (2). I take it that the French sentence has an essentially isomorphic structure. In fact, following the plan laid out at the beginning of the paper, let us assume that the functional description of the French sentence is that given in (2) with obvious replacements for the values of the *Lex* attribute and with attribute names x in the English grammar systematically replaced by *F-x* in the French. Thus we have *F-Cat, F-Head*, etc. Suppose now, that. using the English grammar and a suitable parsing algorithm, the structure given in (2) is derived from the English sentence, and that this description is then unified with the following transfer grammar:

$$
\begin{bmatrix}
\text{Cat} = \langle \text{F-Cat} \rangle \\[2mm]
\left\{
\begin{aligned}
&\begin{bmatrix} \text{Lex} = \text{John} \\ \text{F-Lex} = \text{Jean} \end{bmatrix} \\
&\begin{bmatrix} \text{Lex} = \text{Mary} \\ \text{F-Lex} = \text{Marie} \end{bmatrix} \\
&\begin{bmatrix} \text{Lex} = \text{know} \\ \left\{ \begin{aligned} &\text{F-Lex} = \text{connaitre} \\ &\text{F-Lex} = \text{savoir} \end{aligned} \right\} \end{bmatrix}
\end{aligned}
\right\}
\end{bmatrix}
$$

The first clause of the principal conjunct states a very strong requirement, namely that the description of a phrase in one of the two languages should be a description of a phrase of the same category in the other language. The disjunct that follows is essentially a bilingual lexicon that requires the description of a lexical item in one language to be a description of that word's counterpart in the other language. It allows the English verb *know* to be set in correspondence with either *connaitre* or *savoir* and gives no means by which to distinguish them. In the simple example we are developing, the choice will be determined on the basis of criteria expressed only in the French grammar, namely whether the object is a noun phrase or a sentence.

This is about as trivial a transfer grammar as one could readily imagine writing. It profits to the minimal possible extent from the power of FUG. Nevertheless, it should already do better than word-for-word translation because the transfer grammar says nothing at all about the order of the words or phrases. If the English grammar states that pronominal objects follow the verb and the French one says that they precede, the same transfer grammar, though still without any explicit mention of order, will cause the appropriate "reordering" to take place. Similarly, nothing more would be required in the transfer grammar in order to place adjectives properly with respect to the nouns they modify, and so forth.

23.3.2 Semantics

It may be objected to the line of argument that I have been pursuing that it requires the legs of the translating machine to be tied together at too low a level, essentially at the level of syntax. To be sure, it allows more elaborate transfer grammars than the one just illustrated so that the translation of a sentence would not have to be structurally isomorphic with its source, *modulo* ordering. But the device is essentially syntactic. However, the relations that can be characterized by FUG and similar monotonic devices are in fact a great deal more diverse than this suggests. In particular, much of what falls under the umbrella of semantics in modern linguistics also fits conveniently within this framework. Something of the flavor of this can be captured from the following example. Suppose that the lexical entries for the words *all* and *dogs* are as follows:

$$
\begin{bmatrix}
\text{Cat} = \text{Det} \\
\text{Lex} = \text{all} \\
\text{Num} = \text{Plur} \\
\text{Def} = + \\
\text{Sense} = \begin{bmatrix}
\text{Type} = \text{all} \\
\text{Prop} = \begin{bmatrix}
\text{Type} = \text{Implies} \\
\text{P1} = \begin{bmatrix} \text{Arg} = \langle \text{Sense Var} \rangle \end{bmatrix} \\
\text{P2} = \begin{bmatrix} \text{Arg} = \langle \text{Sense Var} \rangle \end{bmatrix}
\end{bmatrix}
\end{bmatrix}
\end{bmatrix}
$$

$$
\begin{bmatrix}
\text{Cat} = \text{N} \\
\text{Lex} = \text{dog} \\
\text{Art} = \begin{bmatrix}
\text{Num} = \text{Plur} \\
\text{Sense} = \langle \text{Sense} \rangle
\end{bmatrix} \\
\text{Sense} = \begin{bmatrix}
\text{Prop} = \begin{bmatrix}
\text{P1} = \begin{bmatrix} \text{Type} = \text{Pred} \end{bmatrix} \\
\text{P2} = \begin{bmatrix} \text{Pred} = \text{dog} \end{bmatrix}
\end{bmatrix}
\end{bmatrix}
\end{bmatrix}
$$

When the first of these is unified with the value of the *Arg* attribute in the second as required by the grammar, the result is as follows:

$$
\begin{bmatrix}
\text{Cat} = \text{N} \\
\text{Lex} = \text{dog} \\
\text{Art} = \begin{bmatrix}
\text{Cat} = \text{Det} \\
\text{Lex} = \text{All} \\
\text{Def} = + \\
\text{Num} = \text{Plur} \\
\text{Sense} = \langle \text{Sense} \rangle
\end{bmatrix} \\
\text{Sense} = \begin{bmatrix}
\text{Type} = \text{All} \\
\text{Prop} = \begin{bmatrix}
\text{Type} = \text{Implies} \\
\text{P1} = \begin{bmatrix}
\text{Type} = \text{Pred} \\
\text{Pred} = \text{dog} \\
\text{Arg} = \langle \text{Sense Var} \rangle
\end{bmatrix} \\
\text{P2} = \begin{bmatrix} \text{Arg} = \langle \text{Sense Var} \rangle \end{bmatrix}
\end{bmatrix}
\end{bmatrix}
\end{bmatrix}
$$

This, in turn, is readily interpretable as a description of the logical expression

$$\forall q.dog(q) \wedge P(q)$$

It remains to provide verbs with a sense that provides a suitable value for P, that is, for $\langle$Sense Prop P2 Pred$\rangle$. An example would be the following:

$$
\begin{bmatrix}
\text{Cat} = \text{V} \\
\text{Lex} = \text{barks} \\
\text{Tense} = \text{Pres} \\
\text{Subj} = \begin{bmatrix} \text{Pers} = 3 \\ \text{Num} = \text{Sing} \\ \text{Anim} = + \end{bmatrix} \\
\text{Obj} = \text{NONE} \\
\text{Sense} = \begin{bmatrix} \text{Prop} = \begin{bmatrix} \text{P2} = \begin{bmatrix} \text{Pred} = \text{bark} \end{bmatrix} \end{bmatrix} \end{bmatrix}
\end{bmatrix}
$$

Conclusion

It has not been possible in this paper to give more than an impression of how an experimental machine translation system might be constructed basesd on FUG. I hope, however, that it has been possible to convey something of the value of monotonic systems for this purpose. Implementing FUG in an efficient way requires skill and a variety of little known techniques. However, the programs, though subtle, are not large and, once written, they provide the grammarian and lexicographer with an immense wealth of expressive devices. Any system implemented strictly within this framework will be reversible in the sense that, if it translates from language A to language B then, to the same extent, it translates from B to A. If the set S is among the translations it delivers for a, then a will be among the translations of each member of S. I know of no system that comes close to providing these advantages and I know of no facility provided for in any system proposed hitherto that is not subsumable under FUG.

## 24

Parsing in Functional Unification Grammar

Language is a system for encoding and transmitting ideas. A theory that seeks to explain linguistic phenomena in terms of this fact is a *functional* theory. One that does not misses the point. In particular, a theory that shows how the sentences of a language are all generable by rules of a particular formal system, however restricted that system may be, does not explain anything. It may be suggestive, to be sure, because it may point to the existence of an encoding device whose structure that formal system reflects. But, if it points to no such device, it simply constitutes a gratuitous and wholely unwelcome addition to the set of phenomena to be explained.

A formal system that is decorated with informal footnotes and amendments explains even less. If I ask why some phenomenon, say relativization from within the subject of a sentence, does not take place in English and am told that it is because it does not take place in any language, I go away justifiably more perplexed that I came. The theory that attempts to explain things in this way is not functional. It tells me only that the source of my perplexity is more widespread than I had thought. The putative explanation makes no reference to the only assertion that is sufficiently self-evident to provide a basis for linguistic theory, namely that language is a system for encoding and transmitting ideas.

But, surely there is more to functionalism than this. To fill their role as systems for encoding and transmitting ideas, languages must first be learnable. Learnability is a functional propeprty and language learning needs to be explained. But what is involved here is a derivative notion of function. A satisfactory linguistic theory will at least make it plausible that children could learn to use language as a system for encoding and transmitting ideas. It will *not* show how a child might learn to distinguish sentences from nonsentences, a skill with little survival value and one for which evolution probably furnished no special equipment.

It follows that any reasonable linguistic theory will be functional. To use the word to characterize one particular theory, as I shall shortly do, must therefore be accounted pretentious. However, while it is true that the label has been used before, it is manifestly untrue that linguistic theories have typically been functional. Just recently, there has been a partial and grudging retreat from the view that to formalize is to explain. This has not been because of any wisdepread realization of the essential vacuity of purely formal explanations, but for two other reasons. The first is the failure of the formalists to produce workable criteria on which to distinguish competing theories, and the second is the apparent impossibility of constructing theories whose most cogent remarks are made within the formalism rather than in footnotes and amendments. The search for sources of constraint to impose on formal grammar has led to an uneasy alliance with the psychologists and a belated rekindling of interest in parsing and other performance issues (for some discussion, see Gazdar 1982; Kaplan 1972, 1973, 1978; Kay 1973, 1977, 1979).

My aim in this polemic is not to belittle the value of formalisms. Without them linguistics, like most other scientific enterprises, would be impotent. It is only to discredit them as an ultimate basis for the explanation of the contingent matters that are the stuff of science. What I shall describe under the banner of functional unification grammar is indeed a formalism, but one which has been designed to accommodate functionally revealing, and therefore explanatorily satisfying, grammars.

24.1   Functional Unification Grammar

A functionally adequate grammar must either be a particular transducer, or some kind of data structure that more general kinds of transducer – generators and parsers – can interpret. It must show not only what strings can be associated with what meanings, but how a given meaning can be expressed and a given utterance understood. Furthermore, it cannot take logic as the measure of meaning, abjuring any responsibility for distinctions that are not readily reflected in the predicate calculus. The semantic side of the transducer must traffic in quantifiers and connectives, to be sure, but also in topic and emphasis and given and new. Functional grammar will, therefore, at the very least, adopt some form of *functional* sentence perspective.

In practice, I take it that the factors that govern the production of a sentence typically come from a great variety of different sources, logical, textual, interpersonal, and so forth. In general, each of these, taken by itself, underdetermines what comes out. When they jointly overdetermine it, there must be priorities enabling a choice to be made among the demands of the different sources. When they jointly undetermine the outcome, the theory must provide defaults and unmarked cases. The point is that we must be prepared to take seriously the claim that language in general, and individual utterances in particular, fill many different *functions* and these all impact the theory, even at the syntactic level.

I have outlined a broad program for linguistic theory, and the possibility of carrying it through rests on our being able to design clean, simple formalisms. This applies to the formal descriptions by which words, phrases, sentences, grammars, and languages are known and also to the operations that the theory allows to be performed on these descriptions.

Much of the character of the theory I shall outline comes from the set-theoretic properties that are imputed to descriptions of all kinds in everyday life. These properties do not, in fact, carry over to the descriptions provided for in most linguistic formalisms. In this theory, there is no limit on how detailed a description can be and no requirement that everything in it should serve some grammatical end. Generally speaking, to add more detail to a description is to narrow the class of objects described, and to remove material from a description is to widen its coverage. In fact, descriptions and the sets of things they refer to are duals of one another with respect to the operations of set theory. In other words, the intersection of a pair of descriptions describes the union of the sets of objects that they describe separately and the union of a pair of descriptions describes the intersection of the corresponding pairs of sets. These are properties we are entitled to look for in anything to which the term "description" is seriously applied.

Descriptions are sets of *descriptors* and prominent among the kinds of object that go to make up the sets are pairs consisting of an attribute, like *number*, with an associated value, like *singular*. An important subclass of attributes consists of grammatical *functions* like *Subject, Modifier*, and *Connective*.

The claim that this theory makes on the word "functional" in its title is therefore supported in three ways. First, it gives primary status to those aspects of language that have often been called functional; logical aspects are not privileged. Second, it describes linguistic structures in terms of the function that a part fills in a whole, rather than in terms of parts of speech and ordering relations. Third, and most important for this paper, it requires its grammars to *function*, that is, they must support the practical enterprises of language generation and analysis.

24.2   Compilation

The view that a grammar is a data structure that can be interpreted by one or more transducers has some attractions over the one that would have it actually be a transducer. On the one hand, while the grammar itself remains the proper repository of linguistic knowledge, and the formalism, an encapsulation of formal linguistic universals, the language-independent transducer becomes the embodiment of a theory of performance. But there is no reason to suppose that the same transducer should be reversible, taking responsibility for both generation and parsing. While the strongest hypothesis would indeed provide only one device, a more conservative position would separate these functions. This paper takes the conservative position. Given that generation and parsing are done by different transducers, a strong hypothesis would have both transducers interpret the same grammar; a more conservative position would associate a different formalism with each transducer and provide some mechanism for ensuring that the same facts were represented in each. This paper takes the conservative position. Specifically, the position is that that the generator operates directly on the canonical form of the grammar – the competence grammar – and that the parser operates on a translation of this grammar into a different formalism. This paper will concentrate on how this translation is actually carried out; it will, in short, be about machine translation between grammatical formalisms.

The kind of translation to be explored here is known in computer science as *compilation* , and the computer program that does it is called a *compiler* . Typically, compilers are used to translate programs from so-called *high-level* programming languages like FORTRAN or ALGOL, into the *low-level* languages that directly control computers. But, compilers have also proved very useful in other situations.

Whatever the specific application, the term "compilation" almost always refers to a process that translates a text produced by a human into a text that is functionally equivalent, but not intended for human consumption. There are at least two reasons for doing this. One is that those properties of a language that make for perspicuity and ease of expression are very different from those that make for simple, cheap, reliable computing. Put simply, computers are not easy to talk to and it is sometimes easier to use an interpreter. It is economical and efficient for man and machine to talk different languages and to interact through an intermediary. The second reason has to do with flexibility and is therefore also economic. By compilation, the programming enterprise is kept, in large measure, independent of particular machines. Through different compilers, programs can be made to run on a variety of computers, existing or yet to be invented. All in all, compilers facilitate the business of writing programs for computers to execute. The kind of compiler to be described here confers practical benefits on the linguist by facilitating the business of obtaining parsing grammars. It does this by making the enterprise essentially indistinguishable from writing competence grammars.

It is possible to say things in the native language of a computer that never should be said, because they are either redundant or meaningless. Adding zero to a number, or calculating a value that is never used, is redundant and therefore wasteful. Attempting to divide a number by zero makes no sense and an endless cycle of operations prevents a result ever being reached. These things can almost always be assumed to be errors on the part of the programmer. Some of these errors are difficult or impossible to detect simply by inspecting the program and emerge only in the course of the actual computation. But some errors can be dealt with by simply not providing a way of committing them in the higher-level language. Thus, an expression $n/0$, meaning the result of dividing n by 0, would be deemed outside the language, and the compiler would not be able to translate a program that contained it. The general point is this: compiling can confer additional benefits when it is used to translate one language into a *subset* of another. In the case of programming languages, the idea is to exclude from the subset useless constructions.

This benefit is easy to appreciate in the linguistic case. As I have said, competence grammars are written in a formal language designed to enshrine restrictions that have been found characteristic of the human linguistic faculty, in short, linguistic unversals. The guarantee that performance grammars reflect these same universals can be provided by embedding them in the language of those grammars. But, it can also be provided by deriving the performance grammars from the competence grammars by means of a process that is guaranteed to preserve all important properties. The language of the performance grammar is relatively unconstrained and would allow the expression of theoretically unmotivated things, but the translation procedure ensures that only a properly motivated subset is used. This strategy clearly makes for a stronger theory by positing a close connection between competence and performance. It has the added advantage of freeing the designer of the performance formalisn of any concern for matters already accounted for in the competence system.

24.2.1 Attributes and Values

As I have already pointed out, functional unification grammars know things by their *functional descriptions* (FDs). A *simple* FD is a set of *descriptors* and a descriptor is a *constituent set* , a *pattern* , or an attribute with an associated value. I shall come to the form and function of constituent sets and patterns shortly. For the moment, we consider only attribute-value pairs. The list of descriptors that make up an FD is written in square brackets, no signifance attaching to the order. The attributes in an FD must be distinct from one another so that if an FD F contains the attribute a, it is always possible to use the phrase "the a of F" to refer unambiguously to a value.

An attribute is a *symbol* , that is, a string of letters. A value is either a symbol or another FD. The equal sign, "=", is used to separate an attribute from its value so that, in $\alpha = \beta$, α is the attribute and β the value. Thus, for example, (1) might be an FD, albeit a simple one, of the sentence *he saw her*.

$$(1) \quad \begin{bmatrix} \text{CAT} & = \text{S} \\ \text{SUBJ} & = \begin{bmatrix} \text{CAT} & = \text{PRON} \\ \text{GENDER} & = \text{MASC} \\ \text{CASE} & = \text{NOM} \\ \text{NUMBER} & = \text{SING} \\ \text{PERSON} & = 3 \end{bmatrix} \\ \text{DOBJ} & = \begin{bmatrix} \text{CAT} & = \text{PRON} \\ \text{GENDER} & = \text{FEM} \\ \text{CASE} & = \text{ACC} \\ \text{NUMBER} & = \text{SING} \\ \text{PERSON} & = 3 \end{bmatrix} \\ \text{VERB} & = \text{SEE} \\ \text{TENSE} & = \text{PAST} \\ \text{VOICE} & = \text{ACTIVE} \end{bmatrix}$$

$$(2) \quad \begin{bmatrix} \text{CAT} & = \text{S} \\ \text{PROT} & = \begin{bmatrix} \text{CAT} & = \text{PRON} \\ \text{GENDER} & = \text{MASC} \\ \text{NUMBER} & = \text{SING} \\ \text{PERSON} & = 3 \end{bmatrix} \\ \text{GOAL} & = \begin{bmatrix} \text{CAT} & = \text{PRON} \\ \text{GENDER} & = \text{FEM} \\ \text{NUMBER} & = \text{SING} \\ \text{PERSON} & = 3 \end{bmatrix} \\ \text{VERB} & = \text{SEE} \\ \text{TENSE} & = \text{PAST} \end{bmatrix}$$

If the values of SUBJ and DOBJ are reversed in (1), and the value of VOICE changed to PASSIVE, it becomes an FD for the sentence *She was seen by him*. However, in both this and the original sentence, *he* is the protagonist (PROT), or logical subject, and *she* the goal (GOAL) of the action, or logical direct object. In other words, both sentences are equally well described by (2). In the sense of transformational grammar (2) shows a *deeper* structure than (1). However, in functional unification grammar, if a given linguistic entity has two different FDs, a single FD containing the information in both can be constructed by the process of *unification* which we shall examine in detail shortly. The FD (3) results from unifying (1) and (2).

$$(3) \quad \begin{bmatrix} \text{CAT} & = \text{S} \\ \text{SUBJ} = \text{PROT} & = \begin{bmatrix} \text{CAT} & = \text{PRON} \\ \text{GENDER} & = \text{MASC} \\ \text{CASE} & = \text{NOM} \\ \text{NUMBER} & = \text{SING} \\ \text{PERSON} & = 3 \end{bmatrix} \\ \text{DOBJ} = \text{GOAL} & = \begin{bmatrix} \text{CAT} & = \text{PRON} \\ \text{GENDER} & = \text{FEM} \\ \text{CASE} & = \text{ACC} \\ \text{NUMBER} & = \text{SING} \\ \text{PERSON} & = 3 \end{bmatrix} \\ \text{VERB} & = \text{SEE} \\ \text{TENSE} & = \text{PAST} \\ \text{VOICE} & = \text{ACTIVE} \end{bmatrix}$$

A pair of FDs is said to be *incompatible* if they have a common attribute with different symbols, or incompatible FDs, as values. Grammatically ambiguous sentences have two or more incompatible FDs. Thus, for example, the sentence *He likes writing books* might be described by (4) or (5). Incompatible simple FDs $F_1...F_k$ can be combined into a single *complex* FD $\{F_1...F_k\}$ which describes the union of the sets of objects that its components describe. The notation allows common parts of components to be factored in the obvious way, so that (6) describes all those objects that are described by *either* (4) or (5).

$$(4) \quad \begin{bmatrix} \text{CAT} & = \text{S} \\ \text{SUBJ} & = \text{he} \\ \text{DOBJ} & = \begin{bmatrix} \text{CAT} & = \text{NP} \\ \text{HEAD} & = \text{books} \\ \text{MOD} & = \begin{bmatrix} \text{CAT} & = \text{PRESP} \\ \text{LEX} & = \text{WRITE} \end{bmatrix} \end{bmatrix} \\ \text{VERB} & = \text{LIKE} \\ \text{TENSE} & = \text{PRES} \\ \text{VOICE} & = \text{ACTIVE} \end{bmatrix}$$

(5)
$$
\begin{bmatrix}
\text{CAT} & = \text{S} \\
\text{SUBJ} & = \text{he} \\
\text{DOBJ} & =
\begin{bmatrix}
\text{CAT} & = \text{NP} \\
\text{HEAD} & =
\begin{bmatrix}
\text{CAT} & = \text{S} \\
\text{VERB} & =
\begin{bmatrix}
\text{CAT} & = \text{PRESP} \\
\text{LEX} & = \text{WRITE}
\end{bmatrix} \\
\text{DOBJ} & =
\begin{bmatrix}
\text{CAT} & = \text{NP} \\
\text{HEAD} & = \text{books}
\end{bmatrix}
\end{bmatrix}
\end{bmatrix} \\
\text{VERB} & = \text{LIKE} \\
\text{TENSE} & = \text{PRES} \\
\text{VOICE} & = \text{ACTIVE}
\end{bmatrix}
$$

(6)
$$
\begin{bmatrix}
\text{CAT} & = \text{S} \\
\text{SUBJ} & = \text{he} \\
\text{DOBJ} & =
\begin{bmatrix}
\text{CAT} = \text{NP} \\
\left\{
\begin{aligned}
&\begin{bmatrix}
\text{HEAD} & = \text{books} \\
\text{MOD} & =
\begin{bmatrix}
\text{CAT} & = \text{PRESP} \\
\text{LEX} & = \text{WRITE}
\end{bmatrix}
\end{bmatrix} \\
&\begin{bmatrix}
\text{HEAD} & =
\begin{bmatrix}
\text{CAT} & = \text{S} \\
\text{VERB} & =
\begin{bmatrix}
\text{CAT} & = \text{PRESP} \\
\text{LEX} & = \text{WRITE}
\end{bmatrix} \\
\text{DOBJ} & =
\begin{bmatrix}
\text{CAT} & = \text{NP} \\
\text{HEAD} & = \text{books}
\end{bmatrix}
\end{bmatrix}
\end{bmatrix}
\end{aligned}
\right\}
\end{bmatrix} \\
\text{VERB} & = \text{LIKE} \\
\text{TENSE} & = \text{PRES} \\
\text{VOICE} & = \text{ACTIVE}
\end{bmatrix}
$$

The use of braces to indicate alternation between incompatible FDs or sub-FDs provides a compact way of describing large classes of disparate objects. In fact, as we shall see, given a few extra conventions, it makes it possible to claim that the grammar of a language is nothing more than a single complex FD.

24.2.2 Unification

A string of atoms enclosed in angle brackets constitutes a *path* and there is at least one that identifies every value in an FD. The path $\langle a_1 a_2 ... a_k \rangle$ identifies the value of the attribute a_k in the FD that is the value of $\langle a_1 a_2 ... a_{k-1} \rangle$. It can be read as *The a_k of the a_{k-1} ... of the a_1*. Paths are always interpreted as beginning in the largest FD that encloses them. Attributes are otherwise taken as belonging to the smallest enclosing FD. Accordingly,

(7)
$$\left[A = \left[B = \langle C \rangle = X\right]\right] = \begin{bmatrix} A & = \left[B = X\right] \\ C & = \langle A\ B \rangle \end{bmatrix}$$

A pair consisting of a path in an FD and the value that the path leads to is a *feature* of the object described. If the value is a symbol, the pair is a *basic feature* of the FD. Any FD can be represented as a list of basic features. For example, (8) can be represented by the list (9).

It is the nature of FDs that they blur the usual distinction between features and structures. Example (8) shows FDs embedded in other FDs, thus stressing their structural properties. Rewriting (8) as (9) stresses the componential nature of FDs.

(8)
$$\begin{bmatrix} \text{CAT} & = \text{S} \\ \\ \text{SUBJ} = \text{PROT} & = \begin{bmatrix} \text{CAT} & = \text{PRON} \\ \text{GENDER} & = \text{MASC} \\ \text{CASE} & = \text{NOM} \\ \text{NUMBER} & = \text{SING} \\ \text{PERSON} & = 3 \end{bmatrix} \\ \\ \text{DOBJ} = \text{GOAL} & = \begin{bmatrix} \text{CAT} & = \text{PRON} \\ \text{GENDER} & = \text{FEM} \\ \text{CASE} & = \text{ACC} \\ \text{NUMBER} & = \text{SING} \\ \text{PERSON} & = 3 \end{bmatrix} \\ \\ \text{VERB} & = \begin{bmatrix} \text{CAT} & = \text{VERB} \\ \text{WORD} & = \text{SEE} \end{bmatrix} \\ \text{TENSE} & = \text{PAST} \\ \text{VOICE} & = \text{ACTIVE} \\ \\ \text{ASPECT} & = \begin{bmatrix} \text{PERFECT} & = + \\ \text{PROGRESSIVE} & = - \end{bmatrix} \end{bmatrix}$$

It is the possibility of viewing FDs as unstructured sets of features that makes them subject to the standard operations of set theory. However, it is also a crucial property of FDs that they are not *closed* under set-theoretic operations. Specifically, the union of a pair of FDs is not, in general, a well-formed FD. The reason is this: The requirement that a given attribute appear only once in an FD implies a similar constraint on the set of features corresponding to an FD. A path must uniquely identify a value. But, if the FD F_1 has the basic feature $\langle \alpha \rangle = x$ and the FD F_2 has the basic feature $\langle \alpha \rangle = y$ then either $x = y$ or F_1 and F_2 are incompatible and their union is not a well-formed FD. So, for example, if F_1 describes a sentence with a singular subject and F_2 describes a sentence with a plural subject, then $S_1 \bigcup S_2$, where S_1 and S_2 are the corresponding sets of basic features, is not well formed because it would contain both $\langle \text{SUBJ NUMBER} \rangle$ = SINGULAR and $\langle \text{SUBJ NUMBER} \rangle$ = PLURAL.

(9)
$$
\begin{aligned}
\langle\text{CAT}\rangle &= \text{S} \\
\langle\text{SUBJ CAT}\rangle &= \text{PRON} \\
\langle\text{SUBJ GENDER}\rangle &= \text{MASC} \\
\langle\text{SUBJ CASE}\rangle &= \text{NOM} \\
\langle\text{SUBJ NUMBER}\rangle &= \text{SING} \\
\langle\text{SUBJ PERSON}\rangle &= 3 \\
\langle\text{PROT CAT}\rangle &= \text{PRON} \\
\langle\text{PROT GENDER}\rangle &= \text{MASC} \\
\langle\text{PROT CASE}\rangle &= \text{NOM} \\
\langle\text{PROT NUMBER}\rangle &= \text{SING} \\
\langle\text{PROT PERSON}\rangle &= 3 \\
\langle\text{OBJ CAT}\rangle &= \text{PRON} \\
\langle\text{OBJ GENDER}\rangle &= \text{FEM} \\
\langle\text{OBJ CASE}\rangle &= \text{ACC} \\
\langle\text{OBJ NUMBER}\rangle &= \text{SING} \\
\langle\text{OBJ PERSON}\rangle &= 3 \\
\langle\text{GOAL CAT}\rangle &= \text{PRON} \\
\langle\text{GOAL GENDER}\rangle &= \text{FEM} \\
\langle\text{GOAL CASE}\rangle &= \text{ACC} \\
\langle\text{GOAL NUMBER}\rangle &= \text{SING} \\
\langle\text{GOAL PERSON}\rangle &= 3 \\
\langle\text{VERB CAT}\rangle &= \text{VERB} \\
\langle\text{VERB WORD}\rangle &= \text{SEE} \\
\langle\text{TENSE}\rangle &= \text{PAST} \\
\langle\text{VOICE}\rangle &= \text{ACTIVE} \\
\langle\text{ASPECT PERFECT}\rangle &= + \\
\langle\text{ASPECT PROGRESSIVE}\rangle &= -
\end{aligned}
$$

When two or more simple FDs are compatible, they can be combined into one simple FD describing those things that they both describe, by the process of unification. Unification is the same as set union except that it yields the null set when applied to incompatible arguments. The "=" sign is used for unification, so that $\alpha = \beta$ denotes the result of unifying α and β. Examples (10) – (12) show the results of unification in some simple cases.

(10)
$$
\begin{bmatrix} \text{CAT} & = \text{VERB} \\ \text{LEX} & = \text{RUN} \\ \text{TENSE} & = \text{PRES} \end{bmatrix}
=
\begin{bmatrix} \text{CAT} & = \text{VERB} \\ \text{NUM} & = \text{SING} \\ \text{PERS} & = 3 \end{bmatrix}
\Rightarrow
\begin{bmatrix} \text{CAT} & = \text{VERB} \\ \text{LEX} & = \text{RUN} \\ \text{TENSE} & = \text{PRES} \\ \text{NUM} & = \text{SING} \\ \text{PERS} & = 3 \end{bmatrix}
$$

(11)
$$
\begin{bmatrix} \text{CAT} & = \text{VERB} \\ \text{LEX} & = \text{RUN} \\ \text{TENSE} & = \text{PRES} \end{bmatrix}
=
\begin{bmatrix} \text{CAT} & = \text{VERB} \\ \text{TENSE} & = \text{PAST} \\ \text{PERS} & = 3 \end{bmatrix}
\Rightarrow \text{NIL}
$$

(12)
$$
\begin{bmatrix} \text{PREP} & = \text{MIT} \\ \text{CASE} & = \text{DAT} \end{bmatrix}
=
\begin{bmatrix} \text{CAT} & = \text{PP} \\ \text{HEAD} & = \begin{bmatrix} \text{CAT} & = \text{NP} \\ \text{CASE} & = \langle\text{CASE}\rangle \end{bmatrix} \end{bmatrix}
\Rightarrow
\begin{bmatrix} \text{CAT} & = \text{PP} \\ \text{PREP} & = \text{MIT} \\ \text{CASE} & = \text{DAT} \\ \text{HEAD} & = \begin{bmatrix} \text{CAT} & = \text{NP} \\ \text{CASE} & = \langle\text{CASE}\rangle \end{bmatrix} \end{bmatrix}
$$

The result of unifying a pair of complex FDs is, in general, a complex FD with one term for each compatible pair of terms in the original FDs. Thus $\{a_1...a_n\} = \{b_1...b_m\}$ becomes an FD of the form $\{c_1...c_k\}$ in which each c_h $(1 \leq h \leq k)$ is the result of unifying a compatible pair $a_i = b_j$ $(1 \leq i \leq m, 1 \leq j \leq n)$. This is exemplified in (13).

$$(13) \quad \left\{ \begin{bmatrix} \text{TENSE} & = \text{PRES} \\ \text{FORM} & = \text{is} \end{bmatrix} \atop \begin{bmatrix} \text{TENSE} & = \text{PAST} \\ \text{FORM} & = \text{was} \end{bmatrix} \right\} = \begin{bmatrix} \text{CAT} & = \text{VERB} \\ \text{TENSE} & = \text{PAST} \end{bmatrix} \Rightarrow \begin{bmatrix} \text{CAT} & = \text{VERB} \\ \text{TENSE} & = \text{PAST} \\ \text{FORM} & = \text{was} \end{bmatrix}$$

Unification is the fundamental operation underlying the analysis and synthesis of sentences using functional unification grammar.

It is important to understand the difference between saying that a pair of FDs are *equal* and saying that they are *unified*. Clearly, when a pair of FDs has been unified, they are equal; the inverse is not generally true. To say that a pair of FDs A and B are unified is to say that A and B are *two names for one and the same description*. Consequently, if A is unified with C, the effect is to unify A, B and C. On the other hand, if A and B, though possibly equal, are not unified, then unifying A and C does not affect B and, indeed, if A and C are not equal, a result of the unification will be to make A and B different. A crucial consequence of this is that the result of unifying various pair of FDs is independent of the order in which the operations are carried out. This, in its turn, makes for a loose coupling between the grammatical formalism as a whole and the algorithms that use it.

24.2.3 Patterns and constituent sets

We come now to the question of recursion in the grammar and how constituency is represented. I have already remarked that functional unification grammar deliberately blurs the distinction between structures and sets of features. It is clear from the examples we have considered so far that some parts of the FD of a phrase typically belong to the phrase as a whole, whereas others belong to its constituents. For example, in (7), the value of SUBJ is the FD of a constituent of the sentence, whereas the value of ASPECT is not. The purpose of constituent sets and patterns is to identify constituents and to state constraints on the order of their occurrence. Example (14) is a version of (8) that specifies the order. (SUBJ VERB DOBJ) is a pattern stating that the values of the attributes SUBJ, VERB, and DOBJ are FDs of constituents and that they occur in that order. As the example illustrates, patterns appear in FDs as the values of attributes. In general, the value is a list of patterns, and not just one as in (14). The attribute *pattern* is distinguished, its value being the one used to determine the order of the immediate constituents of the item being described. The attribute *C-set* is also distinguished, its value being a single list of paths identifying the immediate constituents of the current item, but imposing no order on them. Here, as elsewhere in the formalism, one-step paths can be, and usually are, written without enclosing angle-brackets.

(14)

$$
\begin{bmatrix}
\text{C-set} & = \text{(SUBJ VERB OBJ)} \\
\text{Pattern} & = \text{(SUBJ VERB OBJ)} \\
\text{CAT} & = \text{S} \\
\text{SUBJ = PROT} & = \begin{bmatrix} \text{CAT} & = \text{PRON} \\ \text{GENDER} & = \text{MASC} \\ \text{CASE} & = \text{NOM} \\ \text{NUMBER} & = \text{SING} \\ \text{PERSON} & = 3 \end{bmatrix} \\
\text{DOBJ = GOAL} & = \begin{bmatrix} \text{CAT} & = \text{PRON} \\ \text{GENDER} & = \text{FEM} \\ \text{CASE} & = \text{ACC} \\ \text{NUMBER} & = \text{SING} \\ \text{PERSON} & = 3 \end{bmatrix} \\
\text{VERB} & = \begin{bmatrix} \text{CAT} & = \text{VERB} \\ \text{WORD} & = \text{SEE} \end{bmatrix} \\
\text{TENSE} & = \text{PAST} \\
\text{VOICE} & = \text{ACTIVE} \\
\text{ASPECT} & = \begin{bmatrix} \text{PERFECT} & = + \\ \text{PROGRESSIVE} & = - \end{bmatrix}
\end{bmatrix}
$$

The patterns are templates that the string of immediate constituents must match. Each pattern is a list whose members can be

1. *A path.* The path may have as its value
    a. *An FD.* As in the case of the constituent set, the FD describes a constituent.
    b. *A pattern.* The pattern is inserted into the current one at this point.
2. *A string of dots.* This matches any number of constituents.
3. *The symbol #.* This matches exactly one arbitrary constituent.
4. *An FD.* This will match any constituent whose description is unifiable with it. The unification is made with a *copy* of the FD in the pattern, rather than with the FD itself, because the intention is to impute its properties to the constituent, but not to unify all the constituents that match this part of the pattern.
5. *An expression of the form (* fd), where fd is an FD.* This matches zero or more constituents, provided they can all be unified with a copy of *fd.*

The ordering constraints in (14) could have been represented by many other sets of patterns, for example, those in (15).

(15) (SUBJ VERB ...) (... VERB DOBJ)
    (SUBJ ... DOBJ) (... VERB ...)
    (... SUBJ ... DOBJ) (# VERB ...)
    (... SUBJ ... VERB ... DOBJ)
    (... SUBJ ... VERB ...) (... DOBJ)

The pattern (16) requires exactly one constituent to have the property [TRACE = NP]; all others must have the property [TRACE = NONE].

(16) ((* [TRACE = NONE]) [TRACE = NP] (* [TRACE = NONE]))

Clearly, patterns, like attribute-value pairs, can be incompatible thus preventing the unification of FDs. This is the case in examples in (17).

(17) (... SUBJ ... VERB ...) (... VERB ... SUBJ ...)
    (# SUBJ ...) (SUBJ ...)
    (... SUBJ VERB ...) (... SUBJ DOBJ ...)

The last of these could be a compatible pair just in case VERB and DOBJ were unified but the names suggest that the first would have the feature [CAT = VERB] and the other [CAT = NP], ruling out this possibility.

The value of the *C-set* attribute covers all constituents. If two FDs are unified, and both have *C-set* attributes, the *C-set* attribute of the result is the intersection of these. If a member of the pair has no such attribute, the value is taken from the other member. In other words, the universal set of constituents can be written by simply omitting the attribute altogether. If there are constituents, but no patterns, then there are no constraints on the order in which the constituents can occur. If there are patterns, then each of the constituents must be assimilated to all of them.

24.2.4 Grammar

A functional unification grammar is a single FD. A sentence is well formed if a constituent-structure tree can be assigned to it each of whose nodes is labeled with an FD that is compatible with the grammar. The immediate descendents of each node must be properly specified by constituent-sets and patterns.

Generally speaking, grammars will take the form of alternations, each clause of which describes a major category, that is, they will have the form exhibited in (18).

$$(18) \quad \left\{ \begin{array}{l} \begin{bmatrix} \text{CAT} = & c_1 \\ & \vdots \end{bmatrix} \\ \begin{bmatrix} \text{CAT} = & c_2 \\ & \vdots \end{bmatrix} \\ \begin{bmatrix} \text{CAT} = & c_3 \\ & \vdots \end{bmatrix} \\ \vdots \end{array} \right\}$$

Example (19) shows a simple grammar, corresponding to a context-free grammar containing the single rule (20).

$$(19) \left\{ \begin{bmatrix} (\text{SUBJ VERB} \ldots) \\ \text{CAT} = \text{S} \\ \text{SUBJ} = \begin{bmatrix} \text{CAT} = \text{NP} \end{bmatrix} \\ \left\{ \begin{bmatrix} \text{SCOMP} = \text{NONE} \end{bmatrix} \\ \begin{bmatrix} (\ldots \text{SCOMP}) \\ \text{SCOMP} = \begin{bmatrix} \text{CAT} = \text{S} \end{bmatrix} \end{bmatrix} \right\} \\ \begin{bmatrix} \text{CAT} = \text{NP} \end{bmatrix} \\ \begin{bmatrix} \text{CAT} = \text{VERB} \end{bmatrix} \end{bmatrix} \right\}$$

(20) S → NP VERB (S)

FD (19) describes *either* sentences *or* verbs *or* noun phrases. Nothing is said about the constituency of the verbs or noun phrases described – they are treated as terminal constituents. The sentences have either two or three constituents depending on the choice made in the embedded alternation. All constituents must match the FD (19). Since the first constituent has the feature [CAT = NP], it can only match the second term in the main alternation. Likewise, the second constituent can only match the third term. If there is a third constituent, it must match the first term in the alternation, because it has the feature [CAT = S]. It must therefore also have two or three constituents which (19) also describes. If (19) consisted only of the first term in the outer alternation, it would have a null extension because the first term, for example, would be required to have the incompatible features [CAT = NP] and [CAT = S]. On other hand, if the inner alternation were replaced by its second term, so that [SCOMP = NONE] were no longer an option, then the FD would correspond to the rule (21), whose derivations do not terminate.

(21) S → NP VERB S

24.3   The Parser

24.3.1   The General Syntactic Processor

As I said at the outset, the transducer that is used for generating sentences operates on grammars in essentially the form in which they have been given here. The process is quite straightforward. The input is an FD that constitutes the specification of a sentence to be uttered. The more detail it contains, the more closely it constrains the sentence that will be produced. The transducer attempts to unify this FD with the grammar. If this cannot be done – that is, if it produces a null result because of incompatibilities between the two descriptions – there is no sentence in the language that meets the specification. If the unification is successful, the result will, in general, be to add detail to the FD originally provided. If the FD that results from this step has a constituent set, the process is repeated, unifying each constituent in turn with the grammar. A constituent that has no constituents of its own is a terminal that must match some entry in the lexicon.

Parsing is by no means so straightforward. Grammars, as I have characterized them, do not, for example, enable one to discern, in any immediate way, what properties the first or last word of a sentence might have. It is mainly for this reason that a compiler is required to convert the grammar into a new form. Compilation will result in a set of *procedures* , or miniature programs, designed to be embedded in a general parsing program which will call upon it at the appropriate time.

The general program, a version of the *General Syntactic Processor* , has been described in several places. The basic idea on which it is based is this. There are two principal data structures, the *chart* , and the *agenda* . The chart is a directed graph each of whose edges maps onto a substring of the sentence being analyzed. The chart therefore contains a vertex for each of the possible end points of such substrings, $k + 1$ vertices for a sentence of k words. Vertices are directed from left to right. The only loops that can occur consist of single edges incident from and to the same vertex.

Each word in the sentence to be parsed is represented by an edge labeled with an FD obtained by looking that word up in the lexicon. If the word is ambiguous, that is, if it has more than one FD, it is represented by more than one edge. All the edges for the ith word clearly go from vertex $i - 1$ to vertex i. As the parser identifies higher-order constituents, edges with the appropriate FDs are added to the chart. A particular analysis is complete when an edge is added from the first to the last vertex and labeled with a suitable FD, say one with the feature [CAT = S].

The edges just alluded to are all *inactive* ; they represent words and phrases. *Active* edges each represent a step in the recognition process. Suppose a phrase with c constituents is recognized. Since the only knowledge the parser has of words and phrases is recorded in the chart, it must be the case that the constituent edges are entered in the chart before the process of recognizing the phrase is complete, though the recognition process can clearly get underway before they are all there. If the phrase begins at vertex v_i, the chart will contain c vertices (possibly among others) beginning at v_i, each ending at a vertex where one of the constituents ends. The one that ends where the final constituent ends is the one that represents the phrase itself. That one is inactive. The remainder are *active* edges and each records what is known about a phrase when only the first of so many of its constituents have been seen, and also what action must be taken to incorporate the next constituent to the right. The label on an active edge therefore has two parts, an FD describing what is known about the putative phrase, and a *procedure* that will carry the recognition of the phrase one step further forward. It is these procedures that constitute the parsing grammar and that the compiler is responsible for constructing.

Parsing proceeds in a series of steps in each of which the procedure on an active edge is applied to a pair of *fds*, one coming from that same active edge, and the other from an inactive edge that leaves the vertex where the active edge ends. In other words, if a and i are an active and an inactive edge respectively, a being incident to the vertex that i is incident from, the step consists in evaluating $P_a(f_a, f_i)$, where f_a and f_i are the FDs on a and i, and P_a is the procedure. The step is successful if f_i meets the requirements that P_a makes of it, one of which is to unify it with the value of some path in a copy of f_a. This copy then becomes part of the label on a new edge beginning where f_a begins and ending where f_i ends. The requirements imposed on f_i, the path in the copy of f_a

with which it is unified, and the procedure to be incorporated in the label of the new edge, are all built in to P_a. The last step completes the recognition of a phrase, and the new edge that is produced is inactive and therefore has no procedure in its label.

This process is carried out for every pair consisting of an active followed by an inactive edge that comes to be part of the chart. Each successful step leads to the introduction of one new edge, but this edge may result in several new pairs. Each new pair produced therefore becomes a new item on the agenda which serves as a queue of pairs waiting to be processed.

The initial step in the recognition of a phrase is one in which the active member of the pair is incident from and to the same vertex – the same vertex from which the inactive edge is also incident. This is reasonable because active edges represent a snapshot of the process of recognizing a phrase when it is still incomplete. The initial active edge is therefore a snapshot of the process before any work has been done. These edges constitute the only cycles in the chart. Their labels clearly contain a process, but no FD. The question that remains to be answered is how these initial active edges find their way into the chart.

Suppose the first step in the recognition of all phrases, of whatever type, is carried out by a single procedure. I leave open, for the moment, the question of whether this is true of the output of the functional grammar compiler. This process will be the only one ever found in the label of initial, looping, active edges. If a looping edge is introduced at every vertex in the chart labeled with this process, then the strategy I have outlined will clearly cause all substrings of the string that are phrases to be analysed as such, and all the analyses of the string as a whole will be among them. This technique corresponds to what is sometimes called undirected, bottom-up parsing.[1] If there are several different processes that can begin the recognition of a phrase, then a loop must be introduced for each of them at each vertex. Undirected top-down parsing is modeled by a strategy in which the only loops introduced initially are at the first vertex and the procedures in their labels are those that can initiate the search for a sentence. Others are introduced as follows: when the FD that a given procedure is looking for on an inactive edge corresponds to a phrase rather than a lexical item, and there is no loop at the relevant vertex that would initiate the search for a phrase of the required type, one is created.

24.3.2 The Parsing Grammar

The parsing grammar, as we have seen, takes the form of a set of procedures each of which operates on a pair of FDs. One of these FDs, the *matrix FD*, is a partial description of a phrase, and the other, the *constituent FD*, is as complete a description as the parser will ever have of a candidate for inclusion as constituent of that phrase. There may be various ways in which the constituent FD can be incorporated. Suppose, for example that the matrix is a partial FD of a noun phrase and that it already contains the description of a determiner. Suppose, further, that the edge representing the determiner ends where the current active edge ends. The current procedure will therefore be a specialist in noun-phrase constituents that follow initial determiners. Offered a constituent FD that describes an adjective, it will incorporate it into the matrix FD as a modifier and create

---

[1]See Kay 1980 for a fuller discussion of these terms.

a new active edge whose label contains, possibly, itself, on the theory that what can follow a determiner can also follow a determiner and an adjective. But, if the constituent FD describes a noun, that must be incorporated into the matrix as its head. At least two edges will produced in this case, an inactive edge representing a complete noun phrase and an active edge labeled with a procedure that specializes in incorporating prepositional phrases and relative clauses.

We have seen that the process of recognizing a phrase is initiated by an active edge that loops back to its starting vertex, and which has a null FD in its label. For the case of functional grammar, all such loops will be labeled with the same procedure, one capable of recognizing initial members of all constituents and building a matrix FD that incorporates them appropriately. Thus, for example, if this procedure is given a constituent FD that is a determiner description, it will put a new active edge in the chart whose FD is a partial NP description incorporating that determiner FD.

The picture that emerges, then, is of a network of procedures, akin in many ways to an augmented transition network (ATN: Woods 1969). The initial procedure corresponds to the initial state and, in general, there is an arc connecting a procedure to the procedures that it can use to label the new active edges it introduces. The arc that is followed in a particular case depends on the properties that the procedure finds in the constituent FD it is applied to.

Consider the situation that obtains in a simple English sentence in the active voice after a noun phrase, a verb, and a second noun phrase have been seen. Three different grammar procedures are involved in getting this far. Let us now consider what would face a fourth procedure. If the verb is of the appropriate kind, the question of whether the second noun phrase is the direct or the indirect object is still open. If the current constituent FD is a noun phrase, then one possible way to continue the analysis will accept that noun phrase as the direct object and the preceding one as the indirect object. But, regardless of what the constituent FD is, another possibility that must be explored is that the preceding noun phrase was in fact the direct object. Let us assume that what can follow is the same in both cases; in ATN terms, a transition is made to the same state. A grammar procedure that does this is given below in (22).

```
(22)  [1]    (PROG   ((OLDMATRIX MATRIX)
      [2]             S1)
      [3]            (SELECTQ (PATH 4 CAT)
      [4]               (NP)
      [5]               (NIL (SETQ S1 T))
      [6]               (GO L1))
      [7]            (AND S1 (NEWPATH 4 CAT)
      [8]                    (QUOTE NP)))
      [9]            (ASSIGN 3 IOBJ)
      [10]           (ASSIGN 4 DOBJ)
      [11]           (TO S/DOBJ)
      [12]    L1     (SETQ MATRIX OLDMATRIX)
      [13]           (ASSIGN 3 DOBJ)
      [14]           (TO S/DOBJ)
      [15]    OUT)
```

The procedure is written in Interlisp, a general programming language, but only a very small subset of the language is used and the salient points about the example will be readily understood with the help of the following remarks. The major idiosyncracy of the language for present expository purposes is that the name of a function or procedure, instead of being written before a parenthesized list of arguments, is written as the first item within the parentheses. So what would normally be written as $F(x)$ is written (F x).

The heart of the procedure is in lines 3 through 6, which constitute a call on the function SELECTQ. SELECTQ examines the value of the CAT attribute of the constituents FD, as specified by the first argument, [PATH 4 CAT]. This returns the value of the ⟨CAT⟩ path of the fourth, that is, the current constituent.[2] The SELECTQ function can have any number of arguments, and the remaining ones give the action to be taken for various values of the first one. All but the last give the action for specific values, or sets of values, and the last says what is to be done in all other cases. In (22), the specific values are NP (line 4), and NIL (line 5). The nonspecific case is given in line 6: (GO L1). Now let us examine these cases more closely.

The last case is the most straightforward. If the value of the constituent FD has some value other than NP, or NIL for its CAT attribute, then it must describe something other than a noun phrase. NP is the value it would have if it did describe a noun phrase, and NIL is a purely conventional value which the procedure finds when the attribute is absent altogether. The only other possibility is that the attribute has some other substantive value, like VP. If this happens, the instruction (GO L1) is executed, causing processing to resume at line 12. The first thing that is done here, (SETQ MATRIX OLDMATRIX), is of minor interest, and we will return to it shortly. After this, only two instructions remain, on lines 13 and 14. The effect of the first of these, (ASSIGN 3 DOBJ), is to unify the description of the third constituent of the phrase – the noun phrase immediately preceding the phrase that this procedure examines – with the value of the path DOBJ. In short, it implements the hypothesis that that constituent was the direct object. The instruction (TO S/DOBJ), intentionally reminiscent of the language of ATNs, causes a new active edge to be created, labeled with the procedure S/DOBJ.

In the remaining cases, the constituent either has, or could be given, the feature [CAT = NP]. These are the cases in which the current constituent could be the direct, and the preceding constituent the indirect, object. However, if the value of the CAT attribute of the current constituent is NIL, it must be assigned the value NP before the hypothesis is acted upon and the procedure sets the local variable S1 to T (Interlisp's own name for "true") in line 5 to remind it to do this. It is actually done by the instructions on lines 7 and 8; if S1 has a non-null value, the instruction (NEWPATH 4 CAT) (QUOTE NP)) is carried out, causing NP to become the new value of the CAT attribute of the constituent FD. Setting and testing the local variable S1 is an efficiency measure, enabling the cost of the NEWPATH operation to be avoided when the required value is already in place.

The instructions on lines 9 and 10 are similar to the one on line 13. They cause the

---

[2]The functions PATH, NEWPATH, and ASSIGN all take an indefinite number of arguments which, since the functions are all fexprs, are unevaluated. The first argument is a constituent-number and the remainder constitute a path.

third and fourth constituents to be assigned the functions IOBJ and DOBJ, respectively. (TO S/DOBJ) then causes a new active edge to be created as before. The procedure then goes on to do what it would have done in the default case described above. But it must first restore the FDs to the condition they were in when the procedure was entered, and this is the purpose of the instruction (SETQ MATRIX OLDMATRIX) on line 12.[3] The original matrix FD was preserved as the value of the temporary variable OLDMATRIX in line 1 and the constituent FD is embedded in the same data structure by a subterfuge that is best left unexamined.

If, in the case we have just examined, the grammar made no provision for constituents following the direct object, the instruction (TO S/DOBJ), appearing on lines 11 and 14 would have been replaced by (DONE). This has the effect of creating an inactive edge labeled with the current matrix FD. More realistically, the procedure should probably have both instructions in both places, on the theory that material can follow the direct object, but it is optional.

Before going on to discuss how procedures of this kind can be compiled from functional grammars, a few words are in order on why procedures like (22) have the particular structure they have. Why, in particular, is the local variable S1 used in the way it is rather than simply embedding the (NEWPATH 4 CAT) (QUOTE NP)) in the (SELECTQ) instruction? The example at (23) will help make this clear. The procedure succeeds, and a transition to the state NEXT is made, just in case the current constituent has the feature [CAT = NP] and [ANIMATE = NONE]. If attribute CAT in the constituent FD has the value NIL, then as we have seen, the function NEWPATH must be called to assign the value NP to this attribute. However, there is no point in doing this if the other requirements of the constituent are not also met. Accordingly, in this case, the procedure verifies the feature [ANIMATE = NONE] before making any reassignments of values.

(23) [1]   (PROG   ((OLDMATRIX MATRIX)
      [2]   S2 S1)
      [3]   (SELECTQ (PATH 1 CAT)
      [4]   (NP)
      [5]   (NIL (SETQ S1 T))
      [6]   (GO OUT))
      [7]   (SELECTQ (PATH 1 ANIMATE)
      [8]   (NONE)
      [9]   (NIL (SETQ S2 T))
      [10]   (GO OUT))
      [11]   (AND S2 (NEWPATH 1 ANIMATE)
      [12]   (QUOTE NONE))
      [13]   (AND S1 (NEWPATH 1 CAT)
      [14]   (QUOTE NP))
      [15]   (TO NEXT)
      [16]   OUT)

---

[3]Argumentative Lisp programmers may find this construction unconvincing on the grounds that OLDMATRIX in fact preserves only a pointer to the data structure and not the data structure itself. They should subside, however, on hearing that the data structure is an association list and the only changes made to it involve CONSing new material on the beginning, thus masking old versions.

A second point that may require clarification involves instructions like [ASSIGN 3 DOBJ] which can cause the assignment of constituents other than the current one to grammatical functions – attributes – in the matrix FD. In principle, all such assignments could be made when the constituent in question is current, in which case no special instruction would be required and it would not be necessary to use numbers to identify particular constituents. These devices are the cost of some considerable gains in efficiency. A situation that illustrates this is now classic in discussions of ATN grammars. Suppose that the first noun phrase in a sentence is to be assigned to the SUBJ attribute if the sentence is active, and to the DOBJ attribute if it is passive. The voice of the sentence is not known at the time the noun phrase is encountered. A perfectly viable solution to the problem this raises is to make both assignments, in different active edges, and to unify the corresponding value with that of the VOICE attribute. When the voice is eventually determined, only the active edge with the proper assignment for the first noun phrase will be able to continue. But, in the mean time, parallel computations will have been pursued redundantly. The numbers that appear in the ASSIGN instructions serve as a temporary label and enable us to defer the decision as to the proper role for a constituent.

24.4   The Compiler

The compiler has two major sections. The first part is a straightforward application of the generation program to put the grammar, effectively, into disjunctive normal form. The second is concerned with actually building the procedures.

A grammar is a complex FD, typically involving a great many alternations. As with any algebraic formula involving *and* and *or*, it can be restructured so as to bring all the alternations to the top level. In other words, if F is a grammar, or indeed any complex FD, it is always possible to recast it in the form $F_1 \vee F_2 \ldots F_n$, where the $F_i (1 \leq i \leq n)$ each contain no alternations. This remains true even when account is taken of the alternations implicit in patterns, for if the patterns in an FD do not impose a unique ordering on the constituents, then each allowable order is a different alternative.

Now, the process of generation from a particular FD, f, effectively selects those members of $F_1 \ldots F_n$ that can be unified with f, and then repeats this procedure recursively for each constituent. But F is, in general, a conjunct containing some atomic terms and some alternations. Ignoring patterns for the moment, the procedure is as follows:

1. Unify the atomic terms of F with f. If this fails, the procedure as a whole fails. Some number of alternations now remain to be considered. In other words, that part of F that remains to be unified with f is an expression F' of the form $(a_{1,1} \vee a_{1,2} \ldots a_{1,k_1}) \wedge (a_{2,1} \vee a_{2,2} \ldots a_{2,k_2}) \ldots (a_{n,1} \vee a_{n,2} \ldots a_{n,k_n})$.
2. Rewrite as an alternation by *multiplying out* the terms of an arbitrary alternation in F', say the first one. This gives an expression F'' of the form $(a_{1,1} \wedge (a_{2,1} \vee a_{2,2} \ldots a_{2,k_2}) \wedge (a_{n,1} \vee a_{n,2} \ldots a_{n,k_n})) \vee (a_{1,2} \wedge (a_{2,1} \vee a_{2,2} \ldots a_{2,k_2}) \wedge (a_{n,1} \vee a_{n,2} \ldots a_{n,k_n})) \ldots (a_{1,k} \wedge (a_{2,1} \vee a_{2,2} \ldots a_{2,k_2}) \wedge (a_{n,1} \vee a_{n,2} \ldots a_{n,k_n}))$
3. Apply the whole procedure (steps 1-3) separately to each conjunct in F''.

If f is null, then there are no constraints on what is generated and the effect is to enumerate all the sentences in the language, a process that presumably only terminates in trivial cases. Unconstrained generation does terminate, however, if it is applied only to a single level in the constituency hierarchy and, indeed, the effect is to generate precisely the disjunctive normal form of the grammar required by the compiler.

It remains to spell out the alternatives that are implicit in the patterns. This is quite straightforward and can be done in a separate part of the procedure applied to each of the FDs that the above procedure delivers. The basic idea is to generate all permutations of the constituent set of the FD and to eliminate those that do not match all the patterns. This process, like the one just described, can be considerably streamlined. Permutations are generated in an analog of alphabetical order, so that all those that share a given prefix are produced together. But, if any such prefix itself violates the requirements of the patterns, the process is truncated and the corresponding suffixes are not generated for them.

The result of this phase of the compilation is a list of simple FDs, containing no alternations, and having either no pattern, or a single pattern that specifies the order of constituents uniquely. Those that have no pattern become lexical entries and they are of no further interest to the compiler. It seems likely that realistic grammars will give rise to lists which, though quite long, are entirely manageable. If a little care is exercised and list-processing techniques are used in a thoroughgoing manner, a great deal of structure turns out to be shared among members of the list.

When FDs are simplified in this way, an analogy between them and phrase structure rules begins to emerge. In fact, a simple FD F of this kind could readily be recast in the form $F \rightarrow F_1 \ldots F_k$ where $F_1 \ldots F_k$ are the subdescriptions identified by the terms in the pattern taken in the order given there. The analogy is not complete because the items that make up the right-hand side of such a rule cannot be matched directly against the left-hand sides of other rules. A rule of this kind can be used to expand a given item, not if its left-hand side is that item, but if it can be *unified* with it.

The second phase of the compiler centers around a procedure which, given a list of simple FDs, and an integer n, attempts to find an attribute, or path, on the basis of which the nth constituent of those FDs can be distinguished. In the general case, the result of this process is (1) a path A, (2) a set of values for A, each associated with the subset of the list of FDs whose n^{th} constituent has that value of A, and (3) a residual subset of the list consisting of FDs whose n^{th} constituent has no value for the attribute A. The procedure attempts to find a path that minimizes the size of the largest of these sets. The residual set cannot be distinguished from the other sets on the basis of the chosen path; in other words, for each member R of the residual set, a new member can be added to each of the other sets by adding a path with the appropriate value to a copy of R. The same procedure is applied to each of the resulting sets, with the same constituent number, until the resulting sets cannot be discriminated further. The overall result of this is to construct a discrimination tree that can be applied to an FD to determine in which of the members of the list it could be incorporated as the nth constituent.

The discrimination procedure also has the responsibility of detecting features that are shared by all the FDs in the list provided to it. For this purpose, it examines the whole FD and not just the nth constituent. Clearly, if the list is the result of a previous discrimination step, there will always be at least one such feature, namely the path and value on the basis of which that previous discrimination was made. The discrimination procedure thus collects almost all the information required to construct a grammar procedure. All that is lacking is information about the other procedures that a given one must nominate to label active chart edges that it produces. This in its turn is bound up with the problem reducing equivalent pairs of procedures to one. Before going on to these problems, we shall do well to examine one further example of a grammar procedure to see how the operation of the discrimination process is reflected in its structure.

The procedure below, (24), shows the reflexes of all the important parts of the procedure. It is apparent that two sets of FDs have been discriminated on the basis that the discriminating path was CAT. If the value of the path is VERB, a further discrimination is made on the basis of the TRANSITIVE attribute of the third constituent. If the constituent is a transitive verb, the next active arc will be labeled with the procedure V-TRANS, and if intransitive with V-INTRANS. If the category is AUX, the next procedure will be AUX-STATE. This discrimination is reflected in lines 5–23. Lines 3 and 4 reflect the fact that all the FDs involved have the subject in first position, and that subject is singular. The instruction (OR (UNIFY (SUBJ) (1)) (GO OUT)), for example, says that either the value of the subject attribute can be unified with the first constituent or the procedure terminates without further ado.

```
(24)  [1]   (PROG   ((OLDFEATURES FEATURES)
      [2]            S1 S2)
      [3]            (OR (UNIFY (SUBJ) (1)) (GO OUT))
      [4]            (OR (UNIFY SING (SUBJ NUM)) (GO OUT))
      [5]            (SELECTQ (PATH 3 CAT)
      [6]               (VERB (GO L2))
      [7]               (AUX (GO L1))
      [8]               (NIL (SETQ S1 T))
      [9]               (GO OUT))
      [10]           (NEWPATH 3 CAT (QUOTE VERB))
      [11]  L2       (SELECTQ (PATH 3 TRANSITIVE)
      [12]              (PLUS (GO L4))
      [13]              (MINUS (GO L3))
      [14]              (NIL (SETQ S2 T))
      [15]              (GO OUT))
      [16]           (NEWPATH 3 TRANSITIVE (QUOTE PLUS))
      [17]  L4       (TO V-TRANS)
      [18]           (SETQ FEATURES OLDFEATURES)
      [19]           (AND S2 (NEWPATH 3 TRANSITIVE (QUOTE MINUS))
      [20]  L3       (TO V-INTRANS)
      [21]           (OR S1 (GO OUT))
      [22]           (NEWPATH 3 CAT (QUOTE AUX))
      [23]  L1       (TO AUX-STATE)
      [24]  OUT)
```

It remains to discuss how a procedure is put in touch with its successor procedures.

In the examples I have shown, instructions like (TO V-INTRANS) provide more or less mnemonic names for the procedures that will be used to label new active edges but, in doing so, I was exercising expository license. When the time comes to insert a name like this into the procedure, the discrimination process is invoked recursively to compile the procedure in question. Having done this, it compares the result with a list of previously compiled procedures. If, as frequently happens, it finds that the same procedure has been compiled before, it uses the old name and throws away the result of the compilation just completed; otherwise it assigns a new name. The effect of this is to substantially reduce the total number of procedures required. In ATN terms, the effect is to conflate similar tails of the transition networks. If this technique were not used, the network would in fact have the form of a tree.

Conclusion

The compilation scheme just outlined is based on the view, expressed at the outset, that the competence grammar is written in a formalism with theoretical status. This is the seat of linguistic universals. Since the parsing grammar is tightly coupled to this by the compiler, the language that it is written in is of only minor theoretical interest. The obvious choice is therefore a standard programming language. It is not only relatively straightforward to compile the grammar into such a language, as I hope to have shown, but the result can then be further compiled into the language of a particular computer. The result is therefore an exceedingly efficient parser. But there is a concomitant inefficiency in the research cycle involved in developing the grammar. This comes from the fact that the compilation itself is a long and very time-consuming enterprise.

Two things can be said to mitigate this to some extent. First, the parsing and generation grammars do indeed describe exactly the same languages, so that much of the work involved in testing prototype grammars can be done with a generator that works directly and efficiently off the competence grammar. The second point is this: it is not in fact necessary to compile the whole grammar in order to obtain an entirely satisfactory parser. Suppose, for example, that every constituent is known to have a value for the attribute CAT. Some such assumption is almost always in order. Suppose, further, that a parsing grammar is compiled ignoring completely all other attributes; in other words, the compiler behaves as though any attribute-value pair in the grammar that did not mention CAT was not there at all. The resulting set of parsing procedures clearly recognizes at least all the sentences of the language intended, though possibly others in addition. However, the results of the parsing process can be unified with the original grammar to eliminate false analyses.

Publications referenced

Gazdar 1979a; Gazdar 1979b; Kaplan 1972; Kaplan 1973; Kaplan 1978; Kay 1973; Kay 1977; Kay 1979; Kay 1982; Woods 1970.

25

Parsing in a Free Word Order Language

WITH LAURI KARTTUNEN

We will start with a review of some facts about Finnish. The conventional wisdom about Finnish word order is that it is free because the language has a rich inflectional system. The syntactic role that a given constituent plays in the sentence is often uniquely determined by its form. It is not necessary for comprehension to mark it with position. The standard reference book on Finnish gives only one general directive concerning word order: "One should avoid ordering words in a way that may lead to a misunderstanding or give rise to distracting associations in the mind of the hearer or the reader" (Ikola, 1968:301). This conversational maxim suggests that syntax itself places no constraints on word order. This is seemingly true for major constituents at sentence level. For example, all the six possible permutations of the three words *Esa* (Sg Nom), *luki* "read" (Past Sg 3rd), and *kirjan* "book" (Sg Gen) are grammatical sentences in Finnish. Only the last of the six sounds a bit strange in isolation, but one can imagine contexts where it might fit.

(1) *Esa luki kirjan.*   *Kirjan Esa luki.*   *Luki Esa kirjan.*
  Esa kirjun luki.   *Kirjan luki Esa.*   *?Luki kirjan Esa.*
  Esa read a/the book.

The looseness of ordering constraints on sentence level does not extend to all syntactic categories. The order of constituents in a noun phrase, for example, is almost as fixed in Finnish as it is in English. There are constraints on sentence level as well. They just happen not to rule out any of the permutations in a case as simple as (1). The fact that one can distinguish the subject from the object in these examples by looking at the case endings is certainly not unrelated to the fact that the language allows the order to vary, but the two properties do not always go together.

It would be a mistake to conclude from this data that the order does not matter. In fact it matters a great deal. Although the examples in (1) are equivalent in the sense that they express the same proposition, it is obvious to anyone who speaks the language that these sentences are generally not interchangeable. In particular discourse situations some sound more natural than others. There are also intonational differences. We leave out the last example because we are not sure of its status. The remaining five seem to fall naturally into two groups. We have tried to find translations that have roughly the same conversational function in English as their counterparts in Finnish.

(2) NEUTRAL: (a) *Esa luki kirjan.*   Esa read a book.
                (b) *Kirjan luki Esa.*   The book was read by Esa.
     CONTRASTIVE: (c) *ESA kirjan luki.*   It was ESA who read the book.
                (d) *KIRJAN Esa luki.*   It was a BOOK that Esa read.
                (e) *LUKI Esa kirjan.*   Esa DID read a book.

The capitals here indicate that the contrastive sentences seem to require an emphatic stress and intonation peak on their first constituent. The presence and the location of emphasis in (2c-e) is made obligatory by word order. These sentences sound distinctly un-Finnish if one emphasizes some noninitial constituent: *?Esa KIRJAN luki. ?Esa kirjan LUKI.* (Heinamaki, 1980). In that respect (2a,b) are different. They allow optional emphasis on any constituent: *ESA luki kirjan, Kirjan LUKI Esa, Esa luki KIRJAN*, etc.

There are also subtler differences. Although the examples in (2a,b) are synonymous, and in some intuitive sense neutral, they address different topics. Sentence (2a) would be a natural answer to the question *What did Esa read?*; (2b) would sound right only as an answer to *Who read the book?*. In contexts where there is no recent mention of either Esa or the book, for example, in answering a question like *What happened?*, (2a) sounds more natural.

In Finnish word order and emphasis obviously encode distinctions that in English are associated with other sorts of structural differences. The alternation between the SVO and OVS orders in (2a) and (2b) has intuitively very much the same feel to it as the difference between active and passive in English. The two sentences express the same fact but differ with respect to how that fact is viewed, whether it is seen as a fact about Esa or as a fact about the book. We use the term topic to describe the discourse function of the first constituent in (2a,b). Another word for the same concept is theme.[1]

The conclusion we draw from examples of this sort is that it would not be very interesting to write a grammar for Finnish that postulates some fixed underlying order from which various surface orders are generated by means of an uninterpreted scrambling transformation. It would be equally unilluminating to account for the variation by means of numerous phrase structure rules even if they are derived from a small set of basic rules in a systematic way. In either case one is left with the task of indicating how the ultimate surface configurations differ from one another with regard to topic, emphasis, and other such matters. It is not difficult to produce a grammar that generates all possible orders. It is more challenging to try to explain what the different configurations express.

Discourse functions like topic are notoriously fuzzy, but they are more relevant for word order in Finnish than structural categories, such as NP, V, VP, or traditional syntactic functions, subject and object and the like. The observations we have made here are hardly new, but we are not familiar with any grammars of Finnish that successfully integrate the description of word order phenomena with the rest of syntax. The problem is particularly difficult in standard transformational grammar. In that framework basic syntactic functions are associated with fixed positions in the underlying phrase structure

---

[1]Preposed constituents in English sentences such as *The BOOK Esa read* are not topics in this sense of the term, although the preposing rule is commonly known as *Topicalization* (Chafe 1976; Prince 1981).

trees. There is no natural way to assign discourse roles, because they depend not on the application of particular transformations but on the resulting surface configuration.

It seems to us that an adequate solution should have two features. First of all, it should have a system of syntactic representation that does not assign syntactic roles exclusively on the basis of structural configurations. Second, it should provide a way to constrain configuration variation by statements that mention discourse roles in addition to principles that refer to syntactic functions and categorial properties of constituents. The framework we use has been described in a number of papers by Martin Kay under the label *functional grammar* . We refer to it here as *functional unification grammar* in order to avoid confusion with other uses of the old term and because unification plays a central role in our grammar.

The organization of this paper is as follows. First, we present some data from Finnish with an informal account of word order phenomena. Then comes a formal grammar for the same data written in the style and notation discussed in Kay's paper "Parsing in functional unification grammar" (in this volume). We illustrate the workings of the grammar by showing some output from a generator that takes as input a functional description of a sentence and produces from it every realization of the sentence that the grammar allows. Finally, we describe briefly how one turns the generator into a parser that does the reverse operation, that is, a machine that produces for any input sentence all and only the functional descriptions allowed by the grammar.

25.1 Data

Let us start by looking at the data more closely. We concentrate here on simple transitive sentences and discuss the positioning of subject and object, adverbs, and auxiliary verbs. There are of course many other types of sentences in Finnish, but the principles that determine word order do not vary significantly from one type to another.

25.1.1 Topic

The data in (2) seem to pattern as follows. Each sentence has a topic: some nominal constituent located immediately in front of the finite verb. In a simple transitive sentence the subject and the object noun phrase are equally eligible to serve as topics. Because it is more common in Finnish for subjects to be topics than for objects, the SVO order

(2a) *Esa luki kirjan.* Esa read the book.

is statistically more frequent than the OVS order[2]

(2b) *Kirjan luki Esa.* The book was read by Esa.

We see no reason to assume that either one of the two sentences should be syntactically derived from the other or from some canonical underlying configuration by changing the order. It would certainly be mistaken to argue that the OVS order must be transformationally derived from SVO because it is less frequent. This would be analogous to saying that there must be a passive transformation in English because active sentences are more common than passive.

---

[2] According to Hakulinen and Karlsson (1982) there are about five instances of SVO for one occurrence of OVS in Finnish texts.

Nevertheless, a grammar of Finnish would be incomplete if it did not in some manner give preference to the SVO order. We do this by designating subject as the default topic of this construction. There are obviously many discourse contexts that are neutral with regard to the choice of topic. For example, if one is using the sentence *Esa read the book* to answer the question *What happened yesterday?*, there need not be any reason at all to take Esa as topic except a bias in the language itself. It is in such cases where default assignments play a role in determining word order. By making subject be the default topic, we give the SVO order preference over OVS whenever the context allows it. We do not assume that there is a single underlying order or an underlying pairing of syntactic and discourse roles.

It is important to recognize in this context that the assignment of default topic depends on particular constructions. For example, in existential sentences (e.g., *There are books on the table*) the subject is not the default topic in Finnish (or English) and its natural place is at the end of the sentence rather than in the beginning.

25.1.2 Contrast

In addition to a topic, a sentence may have an initial emphatic constituent that plays a different role. For the lack of a better term, we call it *contrast* . *Contrasted focus* (Chafe, 1976) and *initial focus* are other names for the same function.

(2) (c) *ESA kirjan luki.*   It was ESA who read the book.
     (d) *KIRJAN Esa luki.*   It was the BOOK that Esa read.
     (e) *LUKI Esa kirjan.*   Esa DID read the book.

In some contexts it might be better to translate the first two sentences in English as topicalized constructions: "By ESA the book was read", "The BOOK Esa read". The initial constituents in these sentences play a conversational role that is very similar to the focus NP in the cleft construction.

Like the corresponding English sentences, (2c) and (2d) implicate that the contrasted NP picks out one individual from some contextually determined set of alternatives. It does not introduce a new individual to the discourse. There is an implication that the referent and the set of other possible choices are already part of the context of discourse. By saying that the sentence is true of the particular individual, (2c) and (2d) imply it is not true of the others. For example, (2c) implicates that, of the people under consideration, only Esa read the book. (2d) suggests that Esa read just the book and not any of the other things.

It is not clear how this account should be extended to cover (2e), where the emphasis is on the verb.[3] The alternatives here consist of Esa either reading or not reading the book. Sentence (2e) is an emphatic way of saying that the former is the true one. The appearance of the finite verb in the contrast position is always a mark of disagreement. It implies that the addressee holds the opposite view.

Because of the implied contrast, sentences of this sort are commonly used in rebuttals. For example, (2d) could be uttered to deny a preceding assertion that Esa read

---

[3]Heinamaki (1980) and Hakulinen & Karlsson (1981) do not mention finite verbs among constituents that can be contrasted (focused on) but we are inclined to think that they should be included here.

something other than the book. It could also be used to continue a sentence like *Esa had a magazine and a book*, with the implication that Esa did not read the magazine.

Note that in a framework that postulates SVO as the underlying word order for Finnish, it would not be possible to attribute the parallel contrastive interpretations of (2c) and (2d) to any particular transformation. The SOV order in (2c) would have to be generated by a rule that moves the verb to the end of the sentence, the OSV order of (2d) by a rule that moves the object to the beginning. This is essentially what is proposed by Hakulinen and Karlsson (1979:308-9). They use the term *Topicalization* for the preposing rule and *Verb Movement* for the postposing rule. We regard this as an unfortunate choice of terminology, because it doesn't indicate that the discourse role associated with the first position in these cases is one of contrast. What intuitively is the topic (theme) of the sentence is designated not by the initial constituent but by the immediately following one. We will discuss the question of verb placement shortly.

It is interesting in this connection that the contrasted constituent can also take on a number of clitics that occur only in sentence-initial position. Of these the most important one is the question clitic *-ko* shown in (3).

(3) (a) *ESAKO kirjan luki?*   Was it ESA who read the book?
     (b) *KIRJANKO Esa luki?*   Was it a BOOK that Esa read?
     (c) *LUKIKO Esa kirjan?*   Did Esa read a book?

Only the last one is a neutral *yes/no* question; the others carry the same implication as their declarative counterparts. They present the referent of the initial NP as a member of some contextually determined range of alternatives and implicate the sentence is true only of one of them. Because the same order of constituents exists even without the question particle, there is no reason to assume that there is a special fronting rule for *yes/no* questions in Finnish. This also applies to *wh*-questions:

(4) (a) *KUKO luki kirjan?*   Who read a book?
     (b) *KUKA kirjan luki?*   Who was it who read the book?
     (c) *MINKÄ Esa luki?*   What did Esa read?

In all of these cases the same word order can be found in noninterrogative sentences.

25.1.3 Nonemphatic contrast

Sentential adverbs, such as *eilen* "yesterday" and *kotona* "at home," and *sangyssa* "in bed," can occur anywhere except between the verb and topic.

(5) (a) *Esa luki kirjan eilen.*   Esa read the book yesterday.
     (b) *Esa luki eilen kirjan.*   Esa read the book yesterday.
     (c) *??Esa eilen luki kirjan.*
     (d) *Eilen Esa luki kirjan.*   Yesterday Esa read a book.

As the last example indicates, they can also occur in contrast position preceding topic without necessarily being emphatic. In principle a sentence can contain any number of such adverbs and they can occur alone scattered in allowable adverb positions or in groups of two or more, as in (6).

(6) (a) *Eilen Esa luki kotona kirjan sangyssa.*   Yesterday Esa read at
     (b) *Esa luki eilen kotona sangyssa kirjan.*   home a book in bed.

The prosodic pattern in sentences like (5d) and (6a) is sensitive to the position of the verb. If the verb is nonfinal, as in these examples, the contrasted adverb need not carry any special emphasis. But if the verb is moved to the end of the sentence, the adverb becomes emphatic and the prosodic pattern changes accordingly.

(7) *EILEN Esa kirjan luki.*   It was YESTERDAY that Esa read the book.

Emphatic contrast signals that (7) is a rebuttal of a preceding contrary statement. Emphasis on the contrasted constituent and the final position of the verb are a sign of disagreement.

The question now arises whether examples like (2c) and (2d) have initial emphasis because they begin with a contrasted element or because they end with the verb. If it is the latter, then the sentences in (8) should be just as good as those in (9).

(8)   (a)   *Kirjan Esa luki eilen.*   The BOOK Esa read yesterday.
      (b)   *?Esa kirjan luki eilen.*   It was Esa who read the book yesterday.

(9)   (a)   *KIRJAN Esa eilen luki.*   The BOOK Esa read yesterday.
      (b)   *ESA kirjan eilen luki.*   It was ESA who read the book yesterday.

The contrasted element clearly carries obligatory emphasis in (9), where the verb is final. All of the verb-final cases, (9a), (9b), and (7), are sentences that one would say only to contradict another speaker. Of the two examples in (8), where the verb is nonfinal, at least the former could be uttered without special emphasis on the first noun phrase, and it need not be a case of disagreement. It seems that the difference between emphatic and nonemphatic contrast is a matter of degree. The more emphasis there is, the stronger the suggestion that the statement would become false if the contrasted term were replaced by something else, say the term just mentioned by the other speaker.

25.1.4   Final position

There is a tendency in Finnish as well as English for heavy constituents to gravitate to the end of the sentence.

(10) *Esa luki eilen Chomskyn uuden kirjan Hallitsemisesta ja Sitomisesta.*
     Esa read yesterday Chomsky's new book about Government and Binding.

The end is also the unmarked position for constituents that introduce some new individual or put some already mentioned character to a surprising new relation. Heavy phrases that contain a lot of descriptive material typically also introduce new things to the discourse. They could be expected to come at the end for that reason alone.

Although final noun phrases do not necessarily designate novel individuals, there is a clear preference for new things to be introduced last. This tendency is exploited in Finnish to make up for the lack of definite and indefinite articles. Because a reference to a new entity would appear in the final position, one way to mark something as old is not to mention it there. Although the two sentences in (11) are actually both ambiguous from the point of view of English, it is likely that "the book" is the correct translation in (11a) and "a book" in (11b).

(11) (a)   *Esa luki kirjan eilen.*   Esa read the book yesterday.
      (b)   *Esa luki eilen kirjan.*   Esa read a book yesterday.

25.1.5 Order of verbs

There are two auxiliaries in Finnish: the negative verb *ei*, which is inflected for person and number but not for tense, and the verb *ole* for perfect tense. The latter is similar to *have* in English. *Ei* and *ole* control the form of the next element in the verbal chain very much as English auxiliaries do. The negative verb requires that next verb to be either a present negated form or a past participle. The choice depends on whether the tense of the sentence is present or past. The perfect auxiliary requires that the main verb be a past participle. A sentence may thus have three inflected verbs.

(12) *Esa ei ole lukenut kirjaa.*   Esa hasn't read the book.

The order is fixed: Negative < Perfect < Main Verb, but the elements do not have to be contiguous. The chain may be broken by intervening adverbs or noun phrases:

(13) *El Esa ole kirjaa lukenut.*   No, Esa hasn't read the book.

Except for the fact that *ei* and *ole* often do occur next to each other, there does not seem to be any motivation in Finnish to regard the string *ei ole* as a constituent analogous to Aux in English. There also does not seem to be any evidence for a structure involving stacked VPs or Vs. There is no phenomenon in Finnish similar to VP-deletion in English. Other elements in the sentence can freely intervene between *ei ole* and *lukenut* as long as their order remains the same. We assume that the structure is flat and consists maximally of three elements: FiniteVerb, TensedVerb, and MainVerb. The negative verb can only be FiniteVerb. If that role is played by *ole*, it is also TensedVerb at the same time, but it is never MainVerb. Anything that can serve as MainVerb can also play the other two roles. Thus in a simple sentence the same verb is simultaneously FiniteVerb, TensedVerb, and MainVerb.

It is interesting to note that it is the main verb rather than the negative or perfect auxiliary that has to appear in the final position in sentences such as (14) that show emphatic contrast.

(14) (a) *EILEN Esa oli kirjan lukenut.* It was YESTERDAY that Esa had read the book.
   (b) *KIRJAA Esa ei eilen lukenut.* It was the BOOK that Esa didn't read yesterday.

25.1.6 Focus of negation

One important feature of negative sentences is that the focus of the negation may be marked by emphasis. This is the case also when the negative verb itself is in the initial contrasted position, as in (15). In that position it carries emphasis only in the absence of any marked focus, as in (15a). If the sentence contains an emphasis peak to mark the focus of negation (15b-d), the negative verb itself is unstressed regardless of its position. The data here suggest that the focus peak can be anywhere in the sentence, but actually there are restrictions.[4]

---

[4] As Heinamaki (1980) points out, negation cannot focus on the topic in cases like *Ei KIRJAA Esa lukenut* "No, the BOOK Esa didn't read", although (15b) and (15c) are both grammatical. The initial placement of negation is irrelevant here because the judgments remain the same even if *ei* comes after the topic: *KIRJAA ei lukenut Esa* versus *ESA ei lukenut kirjaa, Esa ei lukenut KIRJAA.* Similar asymmetries in the assignment of negative focus show up in other constructions, for example in existential clauses: *Ei TALOSSA kissoja ole* "There are no cats in the HOUSE" verses *Ei KISSOJA talossa ole* "There are no CATS in the house". The latter proposition can only be expressed by changing

(15) (a) *Ei Esa kirjaa lukenut.*   No. Esa DIDN'T read a book.
     (b) *Ei ESA kirjaa lukenut.*   No, ESA didn't read the book.
     (c) *Ei Esa KIRJAA lukenut.*   No, Esa didn't read the BOOK.
     (d) *Ei Esa kirjaa LUKENUT.*   No, Esa didn't READ the book.

It is important for the semantics to distinguish the cases in (15) from those in (16), where the sentence does contain negation but the contrast is on some other constituent.

(16) (a) *ESA kirjaa ei lukenut.*   ESA is the one who didn't read the book.
     (b) *KIRJAA Esa ei lukenut.*   The BOOK Esa didn't read.

One indication of the difference is that (16b) could be used in a dialogue like (17), where (15c) could not appear.

(17) Spker A: *Esa ei lukenut lehtea.*   Esa didn't read the paper.
     Spker B: *KIRJAA Esa ei lukenut.*   The BOOK Esa didn't read.
             *(*Ei Esa KIRJAA lukenut.)*   (No, Esa didn't read the BOOK.)

In this context (15c) would be out of place. Sentences with contrasted negation are appropriate responses only to affirmative statements. Sentence (15c) could be used as a partial denial of (18); so could (16b).

(18) *Esa luki kirjan ja lehden.*   Esa read the book and the paper.

In a context like this one, (15c) and (16b) are equally appropriate. They both entail that (18) is false, but only the former signals that it is in direct conflict with the preceding statement.

Because initial negation is in many ways a special case, it may be a mistake to view it as contrast. A better analysis remains to be worked out.

25.1.7   Crossing clause boundaries

Objects and adverbs from infinitival and participial clauses can also appear in the beginning of the main sentence as topics or in the contrast position, but they do not play any syntactic role in the main clause. For example, cases like (19b) and (19c) show that the object of the infinitive can be the topic or the contrast of the entire sentence. (There is no good English translation for sentence (19b)).

(19) (a) *Esa halusi lukea kirjan.*   Esa wanted to read the book.
     (b) *Kirjan halusi lukea Esa.*   The one who wanted to read the book was Esa.
     (c) *KIRJAN Esa lukea halusi.* The BOOK Esa wanted to read.

More than one element can be outside of the rest of the infinitival clause, at least as long as they occupy designated positions (contrast, topic) in the main sentence. However, it does not seem possible to freely interleave constituents from infinitival clauses with elements of the main clause. Examples such as (20b) sound very marginal if not completely unacceptable.

(20) (a) *Esa halusi lukea kirjan kotona.*   Esa wanted to read the book at home.
     (b) *?Kirjan halusi kotona Esa lukea.*

---

the order to *Ei talossa KISSOJA ole.* It appears that negation cannot focus on the topic unless it is the unmarked default topic – that is, the subject in transitive sentences, locative in existential sentences. This is an interesting problem for future research.

If it is true that the mixing of elements from different clauses is possible only in cases like (19b,c), which can be described in the same way as long-distance dependencies in English, then configurational variation in Finnish is clause-bound and affects only sister constituents. It would obviously be much harder to account for examples such as (20b), where the elements of the infinitival clause *lukea kirjan kotona* "to read the book at home" are scattered all over the main sentence. We leave the matter open for now.

25.1.8   Other sentence types

So far we have discussed only simple transitive sentences, because they are sufficient to illustrate all the word order phenomena that we are trying to account for in our sample grammar. There are of course many other sentence types in Finnish. The most important are as follows:

(21) Simple intransitive   *Esa nukkuu kotona.*   Esa sleeps at home.
   Impersonal transitive   *Kirja luettiin.*   The book was read.
   Impersonal intrans.   *Taalla tanssitaan.*   There is dancing here.
   Existential   *Pihalla juoksee poikia.*   There are boys running in the yard
   Possessive   *Esalla on rahaa.*   Esa has money.
   Necessive   *Esan taytyy mukkua.*   Esa must sleep.

Each of these sentence types shows just as much variation in word order as simple transitive sentences do in accordance with the same principles. The differences arise from the fact that in some cases the default topic of the construction is something other than the subject. For example, in possessive sentences the possessor, syntactically an adverbial, usually plays the role of the topic. In existential sentences it is most often the locative phrase, though the subject is in principle just as eligible. Since the subjects of existential sentences typically introduce new individuals to the discourse, they tend to occur in last position, leaving the topic slot for the locative phrase. The default order for *There are boys running in the yard*, composed of *poikia* "boys" (Pl Partitive), *juoksee* "run" (Pres Sg 3rd), and *pihalla* "in the yard," is LOC V S, as shown in (21). However, the S V LOC order in (22a) and LOC S V in (22b) orders are just as grammatical.

(22)(a) *Poikia juoksee pihalla.*   As for boys, there are some running in the yard.

   (b) *PIHALLA poikia juoksee.* It is in the YARD where there are some boys running

In both cases the topic is boys, in the latter case the adverb is contrasted. We expect that our grammar of simple transitive sentences could easily be extended to include these types of constructions.

25.1.9   Summary

From the foregoing discussion of Finnish it is possible to disengage four propositions that are important to our present concerns.

1. There are languages whose word order is substantially free, if, by that, we mean that once it has been established that a certain sequence of phrases constitutes a sentence, it is also known that most of their permutations have the same status.

2. Finnish and other free word order languages also have a strong permutation property in that the members of a set of permutations are equivalent in more than

simple wellformedness. In particular, they are logically equivalent, although they may differ with respect to the preferred resolution of quantifier scope ambiguities and other such matters we have not discussed here.

3. In Finnish, and, as far as we know, in other free word order languages, the members of a set of permutations are rarely if ever equivalent in all respects. In particular, there are important functional properties relating to topic, contrast, and the distinction between given and new which distinguish them.[5] In that respect, Finnish is a configurational language.

4. The placement of constituents may be constrained by a mixed set of criteria. Some may refer to discourse roles, others to syntactic roles or just to grammatical categories. It seems unlikely that one can make sense of the configurational variation in a language like Finnish except as an interplay of many different principles.

We distinguish two discourse roles: topic and contrast. We interpret *Topic* in the traditional way. An expression in that role serves to identify an individual or individuals that is to be tagged with the proposition expressed by the sentence. It indicates what the sentence is about. The underlying intuition is that, whenever possible, we tend to associate a proposition with some individual that it involves and view it as a fact about *Theme*, which is often used in the same sense.

There is no standard term corresponding to our *Contrast* , but similar characterizations have been given elsewhere for the role itself. There is a suggestion that the expression in that role designates one of several mutually exclusive alternatives. These may but need not be explicitly given in the discourse. By referring to only one of them, the sentence creates an implication that the others lack whatever the relevant property happens to be.

The same two discourse roles, topic and contrast, are of course just as relevant for English as for Finnish. Topic is one of the differences between active and passive. Contrast is needed, for example, to explain the fact that *The BOOK John read* can be used as a correction but not as a continuation to *John read the magazine*. The difference is that surface configurations in English encode syntactic relations as well as discourse functions, whereas in Finnish they are for the most part only used for the latter purpose.

Our findings about constituent order in Finnish can be summarized as follows:

(23) (a) Topic immediately precedes FiniteVerb.
      (b) Contrast (if any) is first and immediately precedes Topic.
      (c) Contrast is more emphatic if MainVerb comes last.
      (d) Only final NPs introduce new discourse referents.
      (e) FiniteVerb precedes TensedVerb, if they are distinct.
      (f) TensedVerb precedes MainVerb, if they are distinct.
      (g) Adverbs can occur in any position not ruled out by other constraints.

---

[5]The distinction between logical and functional aspects of meaning can be nicely drawn in *situation semantics* – see Barwise and Perry, 1982. The basic idea is that meanings are relations between types of situations. In particular, the meaning of a declarative sentence S is a relation between situations that are assertions of S and situations that are described by them. In Finnish, changes of word order typically affect only the domain but not the range of this relation. The set of situations described by a sentence is unaffected by configurational changes, but the set of discourse situations varies.

These principles account for the data we have considered, but we are aware that some of them need to be refined further and there are other constraints we are not going to pursue here. Instead, we will show how ordering constraints of this sort are integrated with the rest of syntax in functional unification grammar.

25.2   A unification grammar for Finnish

We use the notation described in Kay's paper in this book. In Functional Unification Grammar, each grammatical phrase of a language has a functional representation or description (FD) consisting of attribute-value pairs. The set of possible attributes ranges from phonological to semantic properties. Here are some of the properties that appear in our grammar for Finnish.

(24) Phonological   Emphasis
      Morphological   Case, Number, Person, Tense, Voice
      Semantic   Positive, Aspect, Quantity
      Structural   Cat(egory), Pattern (alias $), Branching
      Syntactic   Subject, Object, Adverb
      Pragmatic   Topic, Contrast, New

The values can be either atomic designators (Yes, No, Nom, Sg, Past, NP, etc.) or functional descriptions. They can be designated indirectly by specifying paths that lead to them. For example, the FD of FiniteVerb might contain the pair [Number = Sg]. If the grammar requires Subject to agree with FiniteVerb in Number, then the FD of Subject may contain the pair [Number = (FiniteVerb Number)] (pronounced: "Number is FiniteVerb's Number"). Alternatively, Subject might be specified with [Number = Sg] and FiniteVerb with [Number = (Subject Number)]. These are equivalent ways of expressing the fact that the two constituents have been unified with respect to Number.

The values of syntactic and functional attributes are typically FDs. For example, the FD of the sentence *John read the book* would contain the pair

$$(25) \quad \left[\text{SUBJECT} = \begin{bmatrix} \text{CAT} & = \text{NP} \\ \text{LEX} & = \text{JOHN} \end{bmatrix} \right]$$

The similarities between our framework and Lexical Functional Grammar (Kaplan and Bresnan 1980) are obvious. One important difference is that in functional unification grammar the information about constituent structure is not expressed by means of phrase structure rules in the grammar. The dominance hierarchy of mother and daughter nodes is represented separately from the left-to-right order of sister nodes. The latter is encoded as the value of a special pattern attribute ($). This results in a deliberate blurring of the distinction between constituents and properties. It is not important as far as phrases are concerned, because it is a trivial matter to recover a unique phrase structure tree from a fully specified functional representation. It does make a difference in the grammar. Since patterns can be arbitrarily loose or strict with respect to order, it is easy to allow configurational variation. In that respect unification grammar is similar to the immediate-dominance/linear-precedence (ID/LP) variant of Generalized Phrase Structure Grammar (Gazdar and Pullum 1982). The complete functional description for *Esa slept* is given in (26).

(26)
$$
\begin{bmatrix}
\text{TYPE} & = \text{Non Terminal} \\
\text{Cat} & = \text{S} \\
\$ & = ((\text{Subject}) (\text{MainVerb})) \\
\text{Tense} & = \text{Past} \\
\text{Perfect} & = \text{No} \\
\text{Positive} & = \text{Yes} \\
\text{Polarity} & = \text{Positive} \\
\text{Contrast} & = \text{NONE} \\
\text{Topic} & = (\text{Subject}) \\
\text{Subject} & = \begin{bmatrix}
\text{TYPE} & = \text{Terminal} \\
\text{Cat} & = \text{NP} \\
\text{Quantity} & = \text{All} \\
\text{Nominal} & = \text{NONE} \\
\text{Determiner} & = \text{NONE} \\
\text{Branching} & = \text{No} \\
\text{New} & = \text{No} \\
\text{Emphasis} & = \text{No} \\
\text{ProDrop} & = \text{No} \\
\text{Person} & = (\text{MainVerb Person}) \\
\text{Number} & = (\text{MainVerb Number}) \\
\text{Case} & = \text{Nom} \\
\text{LEX} & = \text{Esa}
\end{bmatrix} \\
\text{FiniteVerb} & = (\text{TensedVerb}) \\
\text{TensedVerb} & = (\text{MainVerb}) \\
\text{MainVerb} & = \begin{bmatrix}
\text{TYPE} & = \text{Terminal} \\
\text{Cat} & = \text{Verb} \\
\text{Tense} & = \text{Past} \\
\text{Positive} & = \text{Yes} \\
\text{Polarity} & = \text{Positive} \\
\text{Subject} & = (\text{Subject}) \\
\text{TenseMood} & = \text{Past} \\
\text{Branching} & = \text{No} \\
\text{Person} & = \text{3rd} \\
\text{Number} & = \text{Sg} \\
\text{Emphasis} & = \text{No} \\
\text{Subcat} & = \text{Intransitive} \\
\text{Voice} & = \text{Active} \\
\text{Object} & = (\text{Object}) \\
\text{LEX} & = \text{sleep}
\end{bmatrix} \\
\text{Adverb} & = \text{NONE} \\
\text{Branching} & = \text{Yes} \\
\text{Emphasis} & = \text{No} \\
\text{LEX} & = \text{NONE} \\
\text{Object} & = \text{NONE}
\end{bmatrix}
$$

The functional description in (26) is fully specified in the sense that it specifies a single sentence. An important feature of unification grammar is that removing parts of such specifications results in FDs that describe sets of sentences. For example, if the properties [Perfect = No], [Positive = Yes] are left out, the resulting FD describes a set of sentences containing *Esa slept, Esa didn't sleep, Esa has slept, Esa hasn't slept.* Another way to loosen up a description is to introduce alternations. If we change (26) by replacing [Contrast = NONE] with the alternation

(27)
$$\left\{ \begin{array}{l} [\ \text{Contrast} \quad = \text{NONE}\ ] \\ [\ \text{Contrast} \quad = (\text{FiniteVerb})\ ] \end{array} \right\}$$

we get an FD representing the set *Esa slept, Esa DID sleep.*

Loosely specified patterns that do not prescribe a unique order or constituents have the same effect as explicit alternations. For example, the pattern (... FiniteVerb ... TensedVerb ... MainVerb ...) specifies that the three constituents it mentions have to occur in the given order, but they need not be contiguous. The ellipses marked by three dots match any sequence of constituents. Thus the pattern actually matches a large set of possible sequences.

One can think of a grammar as a very loose functional description that simultaneously describes all the phrases of the language. There is no formal distinction in this theory between a grammar and an FD for a single unambiguous phrase except that the latter by definition contains no alternations.

A section of our Finnish grammar is given in (28). It deals for the most part with verb inflection and subject-verb agreement. The top of the description, [Cat = S], indicates that it pertains to sentences. The first alternation says in effect that a sentence either has the property [Tense = Present] or [Tense = Past]. The second alternation forces a choice between two clusters of properties, one headed by [Positive = Yes], the second by [Positive = No]. In the former case FiniteVerb and TensedVerb are the same; in the latter case FiniteVerb is the tenseless negative verb. The last alternation in the diagram involves a choice between personal (active) and impersonal (passive) voice. In the active, the sentence must have a grammatical subject with certain agreement properties. In the passive, there is no such requirement. The pattern ((#[New = No]) #1) in the middle of (28) incorporates the idea that NPs introduce new discourse referents only in the last position. It attributes the property [New = No] to all but the last immediate constituent. This is not a satisfactory solution, but it serves us here as example of a nontrivial pattern. One way to test the correctness of a grammar of this sort is to take a partial description of a sentence and to produce from it all realizations that the grammar allows. We have used such a generator extensively in the course of our investigation. The generator takes as input an incomplete FD and systematically explores every admissible way of expanding it. It produces a sequence of fully specified FDs from which one can extract a constituent structure tree or just a list of FDs that represent the words, as our generator does. These are turned over to another generator, which augments the stem with appropriate morphological suffixes and prints out the actual Finnish word. Our syntactic generator was written by Martin Kay; the morphological generator for Finnish is the work of Lauri Karttunen, Rebecca Root, and Hans Uszkoreit (1981).

(28) $\begin{bmatrix} \text{Cat} = \text{S} \\[4pt] \left\{ \begin{array}{l} Present \\ \left[\text{Tense} = \text{Present} \right] \\ Past \\ \left[\text{Tense} = \text{Past} \right] \end{array} \right\} \\[4pt] \$ = (\ldots \text{FiniteVerb} \ldots \text{TensedVerb} \ldots \text{Mainverb} \ldots) \\[4pt] \left\{ \begin{array}{l} Positive \\ \begin{bmatrix} \text{Positive} & = \text{Yes} \\ \text{Polarity} & = \text{Positive} \\ \text{Finiteverb} & = \text{TensedVerb} \end{bmatrix} \\ Negative \\ \begin{bmatrix} \text{Positive} & = \text{No} \\ \text{Polarity} & = \text{Negative} \\ \text{Finiteverb} & = \begin{bmatrix} \text{LEX} & = \text{not} \\ \text{Tense} & = \text{NONE} \end{bmatrix} \end{bmatrix} \end{array} \right\} \\[4pt] \left\{ \begin{array}{l} NonPerfect \\ \begin{bmatrix} \text{Perfect} & = \text{No} \\ \text{TensedVerb} & = \text{Mainverb} \end{bmatrix} \\ Perfect \\ \begin{bmatrix} \text{Perfect} & = \text{Yes} \\ \text{TensedVerb} & = \begin{bmatrix} \text{LEX} = \text{have} \end{bmatrix} \\ \text{MainVerb} & = \begin{bmatrix} \text{Tense} & = \text{NONE} \\ \text{TenseMood} & = \text{PastPart} \\ \text{Number} & = (\text{TensedVerb Number}) \end{bmatrix} \end{bmatrix} \end{array} \right\} \\[4pt] \$ = ((\# \begin{bmatrix} \text{New} = \text{No} \end{bmatrix}) \ \#\text{I}) \\[4pt] \text{FiniteVerb} = \begin{bmatrix} \text{Cat} & = \text{Verb} \\ \text{Positive} & = (\text{Positive}) \end{bmatrix} \\[4pt] \text{TensedVerb} = \begin{bmatrix} \text{Cat} & = \text{Verb} \\ \text{Tense} & = (\text{Tense}) \\ \text{Positive} & = (\text{Positive}) \\ \text{Number} & = (\text{FiniteVerb Number}) \end{bmatrix} \\[4pt] \text{MainVerb} = \begin{bmatrix} \text{Cat} & = \text{Verb} \\ \text{Subject} & = (\text{Subject}) \\ \text{Object} & = (\text{Object}) \end{bmatrix} \\[4pt] \left\{ \begin{array}{l} Personal \\ \begin{bmatrix} \text{MainVerb} = \begin{bmatrix} \text{Voice} = \text{Active} \end{bmatrix} \\ \text{Subject} = \begin{bmatrix} \text{Case} & \text{Nom} \\ \text{Number} & (\text{FiniteVerb Number}) \\ \text{Person} & (\text{FiniteVerb Person}) \end{bmatrix} \\ \$ = (\ldots \text{Subject} \ldots) \end{bmatrix} \\ Impersonal \\ \begin{bmatrix} \text{MainVerb} & = \begin{bmatrix} \text{Voice} & = \text{Passive} \\ \text{Number} & = \text{Pl} \end{bmatrix} \\ \text{Subject} & \text{NONE} \end{bmatrix} \end{array} \right\} \end{bmatrix}$

A sample of output from the generator is given in (29). It shows (to a Finn) that the subject-verb agreement part of the grammar in (28) is descriptively adequate. The input description for the generator leaves the values of Positive, Perfect, and Subject's

Number unspecified. Since these three attributes are required by the grammar and each has two possible values, the generator produces eight sentences: *The small child sleeps.* *The small children sleep.* *The small child doesn't sleep,* etc. The most striking feature of the example is that the two auxiliary verbs, *ei* and *ole* that are not mentioned in the input FD at all, appear in the output where they should with the right inflectional endings.

(29) Input description:

$$
\begin{bmatrix}
\text{Cat} & = \text{S} \\
\text{Tense} & = \text{Past} \\
\text{Contrast} & = \text{NONE} \\
\text{Topic} & = (\text{Subject}) \\
\text{Subject} & = \begin{bmatrix}
\text{Cat} & = \text{NP} \\
\text{Nominal} & = \begin{bmatrix} \text{Nominal} & [\text{LEX} = \text{child}] \\ \text{Attribute} & [\text{LEX} = \text{small}] \end{bmatrix} \\
\text{Determiner} & = \text{NONE}
\end{bmatrix} \\
\text{MainVerb} & = [\text{LEX} = \text{sleep}] \\
\text{Object} & = \text{NONE} \\
\text{Adverb} & = \text{NONE}
\end{bmatrix}
$$

Output:

Pieni lapsi nukkui
Pienet lapset nukkuivat
Pieni lapsi oli nukkunut
Pienet lapset olivat nukkuneet
Pieni lapsi ei nukkunut
Pienet lapset eivät nukkuneet
Pieni lapsi ei ollut nukkunut
Pienet lapset eivät olleet nukkuneet

The FD in (30) contains the part of the grammar that deals with Topic and Contrast. Except for the given/new distinction, discussed previously, it incorporates all the ordering principles listed in (23). The section of grammar displayed in (30) consists of two alternations, one for Topic, the other for Comment. The first part says that a sentence either has a topic or it does not. The latter alternative is for constructions we have not discussed here, for example, imperatives. If there is a Topic, it can be either Subject, Object, or Adverb. The preferred choice is listed first; it is the one that the generator tries out first. (In that sense, Subject is the default selection for Topic.) Furthermore, the choice of Object or Adverb for that role is limited by an additional requirement. Either there is no Subject, or Subject serves as Contrast, or Subject introduces a new individual to the discourse. The position of Topic depends on whether FiniteVerb serves as Contrast. If it does, then FiniteVerb comes first and Topic immediately behind it. Otherwise they come in the opposite order.

The second alternation in (30) pertains to Contrast. If there is Contrast, either Finite-Verb, Subject, Object, or Adverb serves in that role. If the verb is selected, it is always emphasized. Otherwise emphasis depends on the position of the MainVerb. If MainVerb comes last, Contrast carries emphasis. The position of Contrast is immediately in front of Topic. The expression "PART(Topic NIL)(Contrast NIL)" at the end means that Contrast and Topic have to be distinct, unlike FiniteVerb, TensedVerb, and MainVerb.

(30)

$$
\left[
\begin{array}{l}
\left\{
\begin{array}{l}
Topic \\
\left[
\begin{array}{l}
\left\{
\begin{array}{l}
\left[Topic = Subject \right] \\
\left[
\begin{array}{l}
\left\{
\begin{array}{l}
\left[Subject = \text{NONE} \right] \\
\left[Subject = Contrast \right] \\
\left[Subject = \left[New = Yes \right] \right]
\end{array}
\right\} \\
\left\{
\begin{array}{l}
\left[Topic = Object \right] \\
\left[Topic = Adverb \right]
\end{array}
\right\}
\end{array}
\right]
\end{array}
\right\} \\
\left\{
\begin{array}{l}
No\ VerbContrast \\
\left[\$ = (\ldots\ Topic\ FiniteVerb\ \ldots) \right] \\
VerbContrast \\
\left[\$ = (FiniteVerb\ Topic\ \ldots) \right]
\end{array}
\right\}
\end{array}
\right] \\
NoTopic \\
\left[
\begin{array}{ll}
Topic & = \text{NONE} \\
\$ & = (FiniteVerb\ \ldots)
\end{array}
\right]
\end{array}
\right\} \\
\left\{
\begin{array}{l}
NoContrast \\
\left[
\begin{array}{ll}
Contrast & = \text{NONE} \\
Emphasis & = No \\
\$ & = (Topic\ \ldots)
\end{array}
\right] \\
Contrast \\
\left[
\begin{array}{l}
\left\{
\begin{array}{l}
VerbContrast \\
\left[
\begin{array}{ll}
Contrast & = FiniteVerb = \left[Emphasis = Yes \right] \\
Emphasis & = Under
\end{array}
\right] \\
OtherContrast \\
\left[
\begin{array}{l}
\left\{
\begin{array}{l}
\left[Contrast = Subject \right] \\
\left[Contrast = Object \right] \\
\left[Contrast = Adverb \right]
\end{array}
\right\} \\
\left\{
\begin{array}{l}
NoEmphasis \\
\left[
\begin{array}{ll}
Emphasis & = No \\
\$ & = (\ldots\ MainVerb\ \#1)
\end{array}
\right] \\
Emphasis \\
\left[
\begin{array}{ll}
Contrast & = \left[Emphasis = Yes \right] \\
Emphasis & = Under \\
\$ & = (\ldots\ MainVerb)
\end{array}
\right]
\end{array}
\right\}
\end{array}
\right]
\end{array}
\right\} \\
\$ = (Contrast\ Topic\ \ldots) \\
\text{PART}\ (Topic\ \text{NIL})(Contrast\ \text{NIL})
\end{array}
\right]
\end{array}
\right\}
\end{array}
\right]
$$

As one can see by comparing the two sections of the grammar in (28) and (30), the information of the left-to-right order of constituents comes from several places in the grammar. The value of the pattern attribute typically is a list of patterns, such as (... MainVerb ...), (... Finite-Verb ...TensedVerb ... MainVerb ...), (Subject ...), each of which expresses some ordering constraint. These need to be checked for consistency and merged into a single pattern in order to extract a phrase structure tree for the sentence. In our system this is done by the generator as the phrase is produced. If the patterns are inconsistent, the merge fails and nothing is generated. Sometimes the merge produces alternatives. If the position of some constituent is not uniquely determined, the generator tries out all possibilities and produces multiple output.

The first part of (31) contains an FD for *Esa read the book* which leaves Topic and Contrast unspecified. The second part shows the output from the generator, which contains all the six possible permutations. (The morphological analyzer prints words that have the feature [Emphasis = Yes] in capitals.)

(31) Input description:

$$
\begin{bmatrix}
\text{Cat} & = \text{S} \\
\text{Tense} & = \text{Past} \\
\text{Perfect} & = \text{No} \\
\text{Positive} & = \text{Yes} \\
\text{Subject} & = \begin{bmatrix} \text{LEX} = \text{Esa} \end{bmatrix} \\
\text{MainVerb} & = \begin{bmatrix} \text{LEX} & = \text{read} \\ \text{Aspect} & = \text{Perfective} \end{bmatrix} \\
\text{Adverb} & = \text{NONE} \\
\text{Object} & = \begin{bmatrix} \text{Cat} & = \text{NP} \\ \text{Nominal} & = \begin{bmatrix} \text{LEX} = \text{book} \end{bmatrix} \\ \text{Determiner} & = \text{NONE} \\ \text{Quantity} & = \text{All} \\ \text{Number} & = \text{Sg} \end{bmatrix}
\end{bmatrix}
$$

Output:

> *Esa luki kirjan*
> *LUKI Esa kirjan*
> *LUKI kirjan Esa*
> *KIRJAN Esa luki*
> *ESA kirjan luki*
> *Kirjan luki Esa*

One useful aspect of the grammar we have sketched is its modularity. Although the grammar can be represented as a single FD with many alternations, the parts are relatively independent from one another and can be constructed separately.

25.3   Parser

We now turn to the question of what provisions, if any, a parser must make in order to accommodate a language like Finnish. We begin by considering this question from the point of view of context-free phrase structure grammar without arguing the merits of this kind of grammar for these or any other languages. We are interested in it because it is the simplest and best understood kind of grammar, and one for which a great variety of parsing strategies have been proposed. Functional Unification Grammar, while it is not context-free, does belong to the class of phrase structure grammars in the sense that sentences are assigned recursive constituent structures directly, and these are not modified in the course of the generation process as they would be in, for example, transformational grammar. The daughters of a given node are determined by the label of the parent node without reference to context. The formalism fails to be context-free because node labels are not taken from a closed set. As we shall see, the parsing strategies devised for context-free grammar can therefore be carried over virtually unchanged to grammars of this new kind.

At the heart of any context-free parsing algorithm is a step in which it must be decided of a particular string of words and phrases, or of a prefix of such a string, whether or not it matches the right-hand side of a rule in the grammar. Let us call this the matching step. Parsers differ considerably in how the many matching steps that must be taken are scheduled relative to one another and in the schemes used for representing the strings of words and phrases. Matching steps, however, differ only in minor details such as the number of rules considered at a time and possible special treatment for sets of rules whose right-hand sides begin the same way, thus allowing for some economy in the matching process.

If free word order languages present a special problem in the design of parsing strategies, it is clearly in the matching step that the problem arises. But it is not difficult to see that what these languages present is in fact more of an opportunity than a fundamental problem because, in the last analysis, it is always possible to provide a separate rule for each possible order of constituents. The opportunity is to work with a much smaller grammar by embodying the permutation property in the algorithm itself. This also provides no fundamental problem.

Let us assume the parser gains access to the grammar through the intermediary of a set of functions that obtain rules with particular properties on demand. Thus, if a rule is required to match a string beginning with a determiner or to expand a node labeled NP, these requirements are supplied as arguments to the proper function and any rules meeting them are returned as the value. This much is standard practice. It is clearly a straightforward matter to arrange for the function to manufacture ordered context-free rules of the familiar kind from a data base containing rules whose right-hand sides are not completely specified as to order. There is no reason why a parser should be restricted to a single way of accessing the rules in its grammatical data base. A rule allowing one constituent ordering can be represented in the usual way, while the set resulting from generating all permutations of unordered rules could be stored in the more compact form and expanded only as required. The artifice of access functions serves to dissociate these essentially administrative concerns from the body of the parsing program.

The fact that the permutations of a given sequence of constituents generally are not equivalent in all respects seems to support the view that the grammar of free word order languages should not be treated in any special way in parsing. Although permuting the constituents of a sentence leaves its logical form unchanged, it does affect other semantic or pragmatic properties so that the rules for the different permutations would have to differ otherwise than in their order. This is not an entirely convincing argument, because the semantic and pragmatic distinctions do not necessarily have to be associated with individual rules of grammar but can be assigned to an interpretive component that works on the resulting constituent structures. This point was well made in respect of lexical functional grammar by P-K. Halvorsen (1983).

Functional unification grammar has the property – which some will consider an advantage and some a liability – of leaving open a large number of different approaches to the parsing of free word order languages. As we have seen, it is convenient within this formalism to separate a grammar into a number of components. The categorial component can be separated from the logical component, and both of these can be distinct from a functional component. Compositional semantics can be described within the formalism, and this can constitute a separate component of the grammar. In this last case, the advantages of keeping the components separate are particularly clear because we should expect the semantic component to be largely universal, allowing itself to be combined through unification with categorial and other components from the grammars of particular languages.

The designer of a parsing strategy for functional unification grammar has the option of obtaining initial structures for sentences using only one of the components and of obtaining more complete descriptions by later unifying these with other components of the grammar. The only requirement is that the component, or components, used in the first stage of the analysis should contain information on constituent sets because, without these, it is impossible to tell which functional roles are filled by distinct constituents. Notice that the components incorporated in the first-order parser need not contain the ordering information represented in patterns even if the word order of the language concerned is narrowly specified. The result of putting these patterns in a component of the grammar with which structures are unified later is that the initial parsing will be conducted as though there were no constraints on word order, and analyses in which the constraints were violated would be eliminated in later steps. This would almost certainly not be the recommended strategy because of the large number of pseudo-ambiguities that would remain after the end of the first stage. Generally speaking, the parser that incorporates only one component will be less constrained and will therefore recognize a greater number of spurious structures, which will fail to unify with other components of the grammar. On the other hand, these structures will be simpler and more easily identified than if the grammar were of the more highly constrained variety resulting from the unification in advance of several components.

A context-free rule has the form $A \rightarrow B_1...B_n$ where A is a nonterminal category label and $B_1...B_n$ are arbitrary category labels. A functional unification grammar is not made up of rules, but it is possible to extract a set of rules from it which are very similar to that of context-free rules. These rules have the form $F \rightarrow P_1...P_n$, where F is a functional description and $P_1...P_n$ are paths identifying parts of that description. For example, the following would be a possible rule.

$$(32) \begin{bmatrix} \text{Cat} & = \text{S} \\ \text{Subject} & = \begin{bmatrix} \text{Cat} = \text{NP} \end{bmatrix} \\ \text{Verb} & = \begin{bmatrix} \text{Cat} & = \text{V} \\ \text{Number} & = \text{(Subject Number)} \\ \text{Person} & = \text{(Subject Person)} \end{bmatrix} \end{bmatrix} \rightarrow \text{(Subject)(Verb)}$$

This says that any phrase whose description can be unified with the one given can be accommodated in the constituent structure in such a way as to dominate a pair of other constituents, the first of which is its subject and the second of which is its verb. Each of these can, of course, have a description of arbitrary complexity, which will also be part of the description of the dominating node. There are therefore indefinitely many labels that a phrase could have while still meeting the conditions required for the application of this rule. Notice that this rule provides for agreement in person and number between the subject and the verb. Although this does not require essentially non-context-free devices, it does suggest a way in which the formalism might incorporate them. The reader may wish to verify, for example, that the grammar in (33) generates the well-known non-context-free language $a^n b^n c^n$. In this case the essential property is the Daughter feature, which must have the same value for all nodes at the same level in the structure of any sentence, but a different one for each level. The description of a node domainating three terminals, for example, must have the feature [Daughter = [Daughter = [Daughter = NONE]]].[6]

Although the form of these rules is not identical to that of a context-free rule and although grammars can be written with them that have more generative power, they can clearly be incorporated in a parser of essentially the same design as would be used with a context-free grammar. It is perhaps worth noting an implication of this, namely that functional unification grammar has less generative power than context-sensitive grammar because it is well known that the same parsing strategies are not applicable to these. The question we now briefly address is that of deriving a set of rules of the kind just suggested, with or without ordered right-hand sides, from a grammar expressed in the standard way.

It turns out that an algorithm that will produce rules from a functional unification grammar is a minor variant of the unification algorithm itself. The simplest kind of unification algorithm produces a result which is in disjunctive normal form. To produce a result in a more compact form would require the use of complex algebraic simplification techniques. However, as a model of human sentence production, a generator of descriptions in disjunctive normal form may be particularly apt because we assume

---

[6]The feature Char assures that only a appears as a terminal under A, similarly for B and C. All lower level constituents agree with their dominating node with respect to this feature except for terminal nodes, which pick it up as their lexical realization. Every nonterminal node has a Daughter property whose value is a list that in effect encodes the length of the longest branch it dominates. Thus a node that dominates only a terminal symbol has the feature [Daughter = NONE]; the node immediately above has the feature [Daughter = [Daughter = NONE]], and so on.

that the speaker will abandon the process as soon as the first term has been produced. While the grammar will generally allow a variety of ways of expressing a given idea, the speaker is interested in finding only one of them, which is to say that he is only interested in one term of the expression. This assumes, of course, that a careful speaker controls the quality of his linguistic output by providing more complete descriptions to the linguistic generator and not by generating several alternatives among which he then makes a choice.

(33)

$$
\left\{
\begin{array}{l}
Top \\
\begin{bmatrix}
\text{Cat} & = \text{Top} \\
\text{A} & = \begin{bmatrix} \text{Cat} & = \text{Middle} \\ \text{Char} & = \text{a} \end{bmatrix} \\
\text{B} & = \begin{bmatrix} \text{Cat} & = \text{Middle} \\ \text{Char} & = \text{b} \end{bmatrix} \\
\text{C} & = \begin{bmatrix} \text{Cat} & = \text{Middle} \\ \text{Char} & = \text{c} \end{bmatrix} \\
\$ & = (\text{A B C}) \\
\text{TYPE} & = \text{NonTerminal}
\end{bmatrix} \\
Middle \\
\begin{bmatrix}
\text{Cat} = \text{Middle} \\
\text{Daughter} = (\text{Daughter Daughter}) \\
\left\{
\begin{array}{l}
NonBranching \\
\begin{bmatrix}
\text{Daughter} & = \text{NONE} \\
\text{x} & = \begin{bmatrix} \text{Cat} = \text{Terminal} \end{bmatrix} \\
\$ & = (\text{x})
\end{bmatrix} \\
Branching \\
\begin{bmatrix}
\text{Daughter} & = \text{ANY} \\
\text{x} & = \begin{bmatrix} \text{Cat} = \text{Terminal} \end{bmatrix} \\
\text{X} & = \begin{bmatrix} \text{Cat} & = \text{Middle} \\ \text{Char} & = (\text{Char}) \end{bmatrix} \\
\$ & = (\text{x X})
\end{bmatrix}
\end{array}
\right\} \\
\text{TYPE} = \text{NonTerminal}
\end{bmatrix} \\
Terminal \\
\begin{bmatrix}
\text{Cat} & = \text{Terminal} \\
\text{TYPE} & = \text{Terminal} \\
\text{LEX} & = (\text{Char})
\end{bmatrix}
\end{array}
\right\}
$$

For the present purposes, in any case, a generator of disjunctive normal forms will be ideal and we shall indeed need all the terms in the expressions that it produces. However, the essentially recursive step in which the grammar is unified with constituents below the top-level node is disabled. The result is a device that does nothing more than reduce the grammar itself to disjunctive normal form, providing a separate description of each possible phrase type. These descriptions can be made into the rules we require by simply extracting their patterns and making them the right-hand sides of the rules. Unordered rules are obtained by curtailing the normal unification process so as not to include the patterns. In this case the right-hand sides of the rules are provided by the constituent sets.

The details of the process by which a functional description is reduced to disjunctive normal form need not concern us here. They are part of the stock in trade of computer scientists, especially in artificial intelligence. The following broad outline will be sufficient. The functional description has the structure of a tree with attribute-value pairs labeling terminal nodes and either "and" or "or" labeling the nonterminal nodes. Each term in the disjunctive normal form also has such a tree structure, but since all the nonterminals are labeled "and", it would be possible to replace them all with a single nonterminal node. Each tree that represents one of these terms can be derived from the tree for the original expression by simply selecting certain arcs and nodes from it. The top node must be included. If a node labeled "and" is included, then the arcs extending downward from it, and the nodes to which these lead, must also be included. If a node labeled "or" is included, then exactly one of the arcs leading downward from it, and the node to which this leads, must be included. Arcs and nodes must be included only if they satisfy these requirements. It emerges that the terms of the resulting expression, and therefore the rules of the parsing grammar, differ from one another with respect to the choice of a downward arc from at least one "or" node.

What, then, is the appropriate strategy for a "mildly configurative" language like Finnish, where many, but not all, of the orderings of a constituent set are generally allowable? We have outlined straightforward procedures for automatically constructing more or less traditional rules spelling out each possible order individually. Such rules can then be compiled into a transition network that can be made the basis of very efficient analysis procedures. However, the number of such rules that would have to be generated, and the storage space they would consume, would make this an attractive alternative only if all the rules were very short. But we have seen that Finnish has largely flat structures at the sentence level where word order is least constrained; the rules would therefore be long and the size of the corresponding set of ordered rules unthinkably large.

The preferred analysis strategy for a language like Finnish would therefore make use of unordered rules, each annotated with the corresponding patterns taken from the functional unification grammar. Those patterns are then brought into play by the parser at the time the rule is matched against a segment on the string. Let us suppose that each of the patterns associated with a rule is converted into the form of a finite-state machine. Since patterns are written in the language of regular expressions, we know that automata theory has standard techniques for doing this. These are now used in the parser's matching step as follows. The first item in the string to be matched is first compared with the members of the constituent set for the rule to verify that, considerations of order aside, it could belong to a phrase sanctioned by this rule. If it is found, the matching member of the constituent set is removed so that it will not also be allowed to match against subsequent items. Needless to say, this is done in a non-deterministic manner so that what is done in this matching step does not affect others. It is next verified that each of the finite-state machines produced from the patterns associated with the rule can be advanced to a new state over this item. If this can be done for each of the machines, the matching step proceeds to the next character with the reduced constituent set and new states for each of the pattern machines. A string meeting the specifications of the rule has been identified when the constituent set is empty and each of the finite-state machines is in a final state.

What is in fact being done in this procedure is that that particular part of the fully expanded set of rules required for the particular case on hand is computed on demand and the string to be matched is used to direct the computation in a straightforward way so that it can proceed quite efficiently. In fact, in all but the most perverse situations, which must be especially constructed to make a point, this version of the matching step required very little more computation than one that worked from a grammar containing the fully expanded set of ordered rules. The number of patterns associated with a given rule is quite small and each of them can be made deterministic using algorithms that are a standard part of automata theory. On occasion, it may even be possible to combine some of the finite-state machines associated with a rule into a single machine without encountering much of a combinatorial explosion. In short, the overall strategy leaves room for space versus time trade-offs of several kinds so that it is readily adapted to a variety of practical needs.

We conclude that formalisms like that of functional unification grammar justify two of the principal claims made for them, namely that they enable a perspicuous account to be given of the so-called functional aspects of language and that they provide a firm basis for performance models and computational procedures. Free word order languages like Finnish cannot be described in a revealing way within a framework that contains only ordered rules or that does not allow separate statements to be made about logical and functional aspects of the language that nevertheless interact so that each constrains the other in a well-defined way. In addition to this, we have shown that a framework in which revealing descriptions of the languages are possible does not lead to intractable parsing problems.

Publications referenced

Barwise and Perry 1982; Chafe 1976; Gazdar and Pullum 1982; Hakulinen and Karlsson 1979; Hakulinen and Karlsson 1980; Halvorsen 1983; Heinamaki 1980; Ikola, ed. 1968; Kaplan and Bresnan 1982; Karttunen et al. 1981; Prince 1981.

## 26

Structure Sharing with Binary Trees

WITH LAURI KARTTUNEN

Many current interfaces for natural language represent syntactic and semantic information in the form of directed graphs where attributes correspond to vectors and values to nodes. There is a simple correspondence between such graphs and the matrix notation linguists traditionally use for feature sets.

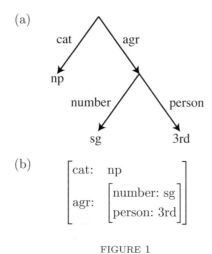

(a)

(b)

$$\begin{bmatrix} \text{cat:} & \text{np} \\ \text{agr:} & \begin{bmatrix} \text{number: sg} \\ \text{person: 3rd} \end{bmatrix} \end{bmatrix}$$

FIGURE 1

The standard operation for working with such graphs is unification. The unification operation succeeds only on a pair of compatible graphs, and its result is a graph containing the information in both contributors. When a parser applies a syntactic rule, it unifies selected features of input constituents to check constraints and to build a representation for the output constituent.

Problem: proliferation of copies

When words are combined to form phrases. unification is not applied to lexical representations directly because it would result in the lexicon being changed. When a word is encountered in a text. a copy is made of its entry, and unification is applied to the copied graph, not the original one. In fact, unification in a typical parser is always preceded by a copying operation. Because of nondeterminism in parsing, it is, in general, necessary to preserve every representation that gets built. The same graph may be needed again when the parser comes back to pursue some yet unexplored option. Our experience suggests that the amount of computational effort that goes into producing these copies is much greater than the cost of unification itself. It accounts for a significant amount of the total parsing time.

In a sense, most of the copying effort is wasted. Unifications that fail typically fail for a simple reason. If it were known in advance what aspects of structures are relevant in a particular case, some effort could be saved by first considering only the crucial features of the input.

Solution: structure sharing

This paper lays out one strategy that has turned out to be very useful in eliminating much of the wasted effort. Our version of the basic idea is due to Martin Kay. It has been implemented in slightly different ways by Kay in Interlisp-D and by Lauri Karttunen in Zeta Lisp. The basic idea is to minimize copying by allowing graphs to share common parts of their structure. This version of structure sharing is based on four related ideas:

- Binary trees as a storage device for feature graphs
- "Lazy" copying
- Relative indexing of nodes in the tree
- Strategy for keeping storage trees as balanced as possible

Binary trees

Our structure-sharing scheme depends on representing feature sets as binary trees. A tree consists of cells that have a content field and two pointers which, if not empty, point to a left and a right cell respectively. For example. the content of the feature set and the corresponding directed graph in Figure 1 can be distributed over the cells of a binary tree in the following way.

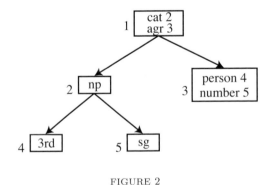

FIGURE 2

The index of the top node is 1; the two cells below have indices 2 and 3. In general, a node whose index is n may be the parent of cells indexed $2n$ and $2n+1$. Each cell contains either an atomic value or a set of pairs that associate attribute names with indices of cells where their value is stored. The assignment of values to storage cells is arbitrary; it doesn't matter which cell stores which value. Here, cell 1 contains the information that the value of the attribute **cat** is found in cell 2 and that of **agr** in cell 3. This is a slight simplification. As we shall shortly see, when the value in a cell involves a reference to another cell, that reference is encoded as a relative index.

The method of locating the cell that corresponds to a given index takes advantage of the fact that the tree branches in a binary fashion. The path to a node can be read off from the binary representation of its index by starting after the first 1 in this number and taking 0 to be a signal for a left turn and 1 as a mark for a right turn. For example, starting at node 1, node 5 is reached by first going down a left branch and then a right branch. This sequence of turns corresponds to the digits 01. Prefixed with 1, this is the same as the binary representation of 5, namely 101. The same holds for all indices. Thus the path to node 9 (binary 1001) would be LEFT-LEFT-RIGHT as signalled by the last three digits following the initial 1 in the binary numeral (see Figure 6).

Lazy copying

The most important advantage is that the scheme minimizes the amount of copying that has to be done. In general, when a graph is copied, we duplicate only ... The operation that replaces copying in this scheme starts by duplicating the topmost node of the tree that contains it. The rest of the structure remains the same. Other nodes are modified only if and when destructive changes are about to happen. For example, assume that we need another copy of the graph stored in the tree in Figure 2. This can be obtained by producing a tree which has a different root node, but shares the rest of the structure with its original. In order to keep track of which tree actually owns a given node, each node carries a numeral tag that indicates its parentage. The relationship between the original tree (generation 0) and its copy (generation 1) is illustrated in Figure 3 where the generation is separated from the index of a node by a colon.

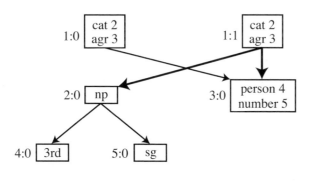

FIGURE 3

If the node that we want to copy is not the topmost node of a tree. we need to duplicate the nodes along the branch leading to it.

When a tree headed by the copied node has to be changed. we use the generation tags to minimize the creation of new structure. In general, all and only the nodes on the branch that lead to the site of a destructive change or addition need to belong to the same generation as the top node of the tree. The rest of the structure can consist of old nodes. For example. suppose we add a new feature. say [gender: fem] to the value of **agr** in Figure 3 to yield the feature set in Figure 4.

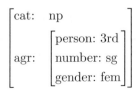

FIGURE 4

Furthermore. suppose that we want the change to affect only the copy but not the original feature set. In terms of the trees that we have constructed for the example in Figure 3, this involves adding one new cell to the copied structure to hold the value *fem*, and changing the content of cell 3 by adding the new feature to it.

The modified copy and its relation to the original is shown in Figure 5. Note that one half of the structure is shared. The copy contains only three new nodes.

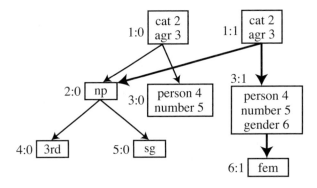

FIGURE 5

From the point of view of a process that only needs to find or print out the value of particular features, it makes no difference that the nodes containing the values belong to several trees as long as there is no confusion about the structure.

Relative addressing

Accessing an arbitrary cell in a binary tree consumes time in proportion to the logarithm of the size of the structure, assuming that cells are reached by starting at the top node and using the index of the target node as an address. Another method is to use relative addressing. Relative addresses encode the shortest path between two nodes in the tree regardless of where they are. For example, if we are at node 9 in Figure 6a below and need to reach node 11, it is easy to see that it is not necessary to go all the way up to node 1 and then partially retrace the same path in looking up node 11. Instead, one can stop going upward at the lowest common ancestor, node 2, of nodes 9 and 11 and go down from there.

(a)   (b)

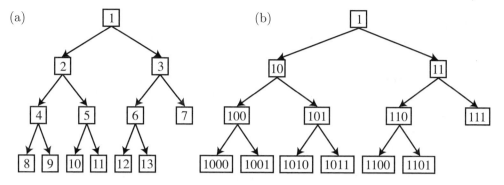

FIGURE 6

With respect to node 2, node 11 is in the same position as 7 is with respect to 1. Thus the relative address of cell 11 counted from 9 is 2,7 – "two nodes up, then down as if going to node 7". In general, relative addresses are of the form ⟨up,down⟩ where ⟨up⟩ is the number of links to the lowest common ancestor of the origin and ⟨down⟩ is the relative index of the target node with respect to it. Sometimes we can just go up or down on the same branch; for example, the relative address of cell 10 seen from node 2 is simply 0,6; the path from 8 or 9 to 4 is 1,1.

As one might expect, it is easy to see these relationships if we think of node indices in their binary representation (see Figure 6b). The lowest common ancestor 2 (binary 10) is designated by the longest common initial substring of 9 (binary 1001) and 11 (binary 1011). The relative index of 11, with respect to 7 (binary 111), is the rest of its index with 1 prefixed to the front.

In terms of number of links traversed, relative addresses have no statistical advantage over the simpler method of always starting from the top. However, they have one important property that is essential for our purposes: relative addresses remain valid even when trees are embedded in other trees; absolute indices would have to be recalculated.

Figure 7 is a recoding of Figure 5 using relative addresses.

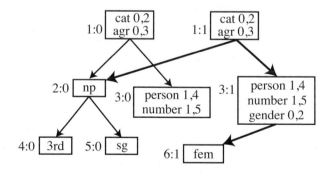

FIGURE 7

Keeping trees balanced

When two feature matrices are unified, the binary trees corresponding to them have to be combined to form a single tree. New attributes are added to some of the nodes; other nodes become "pointer nodes," i.e., their only content is the relative address of some other node where the real content is stored. As long as we keep adding nodes to one tree, it is a simple matter to keep the tree maximally balanced. At any given time, only the growing fringe of the tree can be incompletely filled. When two trees need to be combined, it would, of course, be possible to add all the cells from one tree in a balanced fashion to the other one but that would defeat the very purpose of using binary trees because it would mean having to copy almost all of the structure. The only alternative is to embed one of the trees in the other one. The resulting tree will not be a balanced one; some of the branches are much longer than others. Consequently, the average time needed to look up a value is bound to be worse than in a balanced tree.

For example, suppose that we want to unify a copy of the feature set in Figure 1b, represented as in Figure 2 but with relative addressing, with a copy of the feature set in Figure 8.

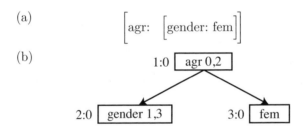

FIGURE 8

Although the feature set in Figure 9a is the same as the one represented by the right half of Figure 7, the structure in Figure 9b is more complicated because it is derived by unifying copies of two separate trees, not by simply adding more features to a tree, as in Figure 7. In 9b, a copy of 8b has been embedded as node 6 of the host tree. The original indices of both trees remain unchanged. Because all the addresses are relative, no harm comes from the fact that indices in the embedded tree no longer correspond to the true location of the nodes. Absolute indices are not used as addresses because they change when a tree is embedded. The symbol -> in node 2 of the lower tree indicates that the original content of this node – gender 1.3 – has been replaced by the address of the cell that it was unified with, namely cell 3 in the host tree.

In the case at hand, it matters very little which of the two trees becomes the host for the other. The resulting tree is about as much out of balance either way. However, when a sequence of unifications is performed, differences can be very significant. For example, if A. B, and C are unified with one another, it can make a great deal of difference, which of the two alternative shapes in Figure 10 is produced as the final result.

When a choice has to be made as to which of the two trees to embed in the other, it is important to minimize the length of the longest path in the resulting tree. To do this

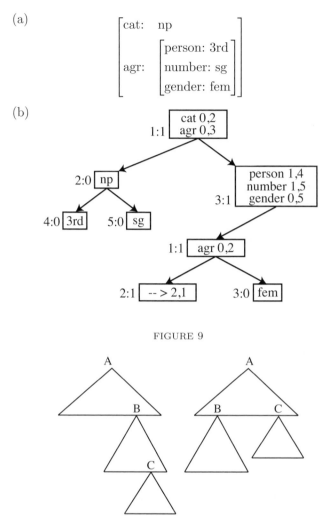

FIGURE 9

FIGURE 10

at all efficiently requires additional information to be stored with each node. According to one simple scheme, this is simply the length of the shortest path from the node down to a node with a free left or right pointer. Using this, it is a simple matter to find the shallowest place in a tree at which to embed another one. If the length of the longest path is also stored, it is also easy to determine which choice of host will give rise to the shallowest combined tree.

Another problem which needs careful attention concerns generation markers. If a pair of trees to be unified have independent histories, their generation markers will presumably be incommensurable and those of an embedded tree will therefore not be valid in the host. Various solutions are possible for this problem. The most straightforward is to relate the histories of all trees at least to the extent of drawing generation markers from a global pool. In Lisp, for example, the simplest thing is to let them be CONS cells.

Conclusion

We will conclude by comparing our method of structure sharing with two others that we know of: R. Cohen's immutable arrays and the idea discussed in Fernando Pereira's paper at this meeting. The three alternatives involve different trade-offs along the space/time continuum. The choice between them will depend on the particular application they are intended for. No statistics on parsing are available yet but we hope to have some in the final version.

Acknowledgements

This research, made possible in part by a gift from the Systems Development Foundation. was also supported by the Defense Advanced Research Projects Agency under Contracts N00039-80-C-0575 and N00039-84-C-0524 with the Naval Electronic Systems Command. The views and conclusions contained in this document are those of the author and should not be interpreted as representative of the official policies, either expressed or implied, of the Defense Advanced Research Projects Agency, or the United States government. Thanks are due to Fernando Pereira and Stuart Shieber for their comments on earlier presentations of this material.

27

Unification in Grammar

A number of grammatical formalisms that are currently gaining popularity are based on a notion of unification that differs slightly from the one used in logic programming. The differences are such as to make logic programming, at least as commonly practiced, relatively unsuitable for grammatical description. However, the minor modification on which these formalisms appear to be converging has a great many desirable properties. Most important among these is that the notion of a completely specified formula is missing.

Introduction

Language is an abstraction from observed processes of communication and ratiocination. A particular language is abstracted from a subset of such processes and a grammar is a characterization of such a subset. One of the major goals of linguistics in recent times has been to design ways of writing grammars that do justice to their essentially procedural nature while not ascribing more to linguistic processes than the evidence supports.

Transformational grammar is based on a carefully articulated process of sentence generation which is, however, explicitly dissociated from the processes that occur when language is used. By ignoring these processes it closes itself off from an important potential source of evidence about the nature of language. At the other extreme, augmented transition network grammars contain a detailed specification of the sequence of events that must be followed to analyze each individual sentence. Much of the detail that they contain is therefore without empirical motivation. Context-free grammars occupy a middle ground in that they are associated with a simple and effective class of well behaved procedures which leaves open most of the underdetermined questions, such as the specific order of low-level events. However, context-free grammar was long thought not to have the expressive power necessary to capture natural linguistic processes, and it is still generally agreed that the formalism requires supplementing in various ways if it is to be capable of capturing important generalizations and stating the facts in an irredundant manner.

Such considerations as these have led to the development over the last few years of several new linguistic formalisms with associated interpretive procedures that can be specified without laying out specific sequences of events. These include Generalized Phrase-Structure Grammar (GPSG), Lexical Functional Grammar (LFG), and Functional Unification Grammar (FUG). All of them are phrase-structure grammars in the sense that they assign constituent-structure trees to sentences and determine the kinds of constituents that a phrase can have solely on the basis of that phrase's grammatical description. They are also all *monotonic* in that the processes involved in their interpretation can add information to existing structures but never require an existing structure to be modified. Monotonicity is a property of context-free grammars and also of definite-clause grammars and, in the latter, much of what makes this property important is clearly exhibited. Definite-clause grammars are nonprocedural in the usual sense of not determining a unique sequence of events.[1] However, when offered almost unmodified to a standard Prolog interpreter, sequences of events are generated that result in sentences being generated and analyzed.

These facts about definite-clause grammars come as no surprise to habitual Prolog users who are the constant beneficiaries of a monotonic formal system. Typically, these people resist allowing their activities to lead them into Prolog's embarrassing periphery where monotonicity no longer holds. Monotonicity is a feature of Prolog because it is a feature of the principal operation on which Prolog is based, namely unification. This is an operation that compares a pair of expressions and determines whether they could be descriptions of the same object or state of affairs. If they could not, it declares as much and this is its only result. If they could, it constructs a new expression, in general more specific than either of the originals, because it contains all the details from both of them. The unification operation is also at the heart of the new grammatical formalisms just mentioned. However, the grammatical version of the operation differs in some important details from the logical version. In this paper, I propose to explore why unification has come to fill so central a role and also why the linguists prefer to work with their own version. To this end, I shall construct examples using a "pedagogical" formalism, which I will call *Simple Unification Grammar* (SUG), which is none of the above, but which shares the relevant properties of all of them.

27.1 Simple Unification Grammar

Like all the formalisms under discussion, SUG associates a *functional description* (FD) with every word and phrase. This is a complex object that takes the place of the simple grammatical label or category of phrase-structure grammar. A FD is a list of names called *attributes* each of which has a value associated with it. Several kinds of value are possible but, for the moment, we will restrict our attention to two, namely unanalyzable *atoms* and FD's. I will write attributes to the left of an '=' sign and the corresponding value to the right. The FD in Fig. 1 describes the sentence *All dogs chase cats* according to the grammar in Fig. 2.

Each rule has a left and a right-hand side separated by an arrow. The left-hand side is a functional description, possibly preceded by the negation sign '−', and the right-hand side is a Boolean expression over three types of primitive, namely

1. FDs,

---

[1] A sequence of events is. of course, implicit, if one supposes that the grammars will be interpreted by a Prolog program in the usual way. However. this is clearly not the only procedure. or even the one obviously to be preferred.

2. A constituency expression consisting of the word *Constituent:* followed by a sequence of one or more *paths.*
3. An ordering expression consisting of the word *Order:* followed by a sequence made up of paths and zero or more occurrences of '...'.

A path is a sequence of words enclosed in angle brackets. It is simply a means of identifying a value within the FD; if $[a_1 = [a_2 = \ldots [a_n = v] \ldots]]$, then the path written $\langle a_1 a_2 \ldots a_n \rangle$ has the value v in that FD. Paths in FUG fill much the same role as variables do in logic programming, namely to link sets of unified values. When a location in a FD is occupied by a path that identifies some other location, the two values are unified. Usually, we write the value itself in one place and paths identifying that place in all others where the value is unified with that one. The advantage of this scheme is that it makes it possible to stipulate identity between parts of a FD without allowing for special expressions to establish equality between variables and values.

$$
\left[\begin{array}{ll}
\text{Cat} & = \text{NONE} \\
\text{Head} & = \left[\begin{array}{ll}
\text{Cat} & = \text{NONE} \\
\text{Head} & = \left[\begin{array}{ll}
\text{Cat} & = \text{Verb} \\
\text{Head} & = \text{NONE} \\
\text{Tense} & = \text{Pres} \\
\text{Word} & = \text{chase} \\
\text{Subj} & = \left[\begin{array}{ll}
\text{Cat} & = \text{NONE} \\
\text{Head} & = \left[\begin{array}{ll}
\text{Cat} & = \text{Noun} \\
\text{Head} & = \text{NONE} \\
\text{Pers} & = 3 \\
\text{Word} & = \text{dogs} \\
\text{Art} & = \left[\begin{array}{ll}
\text{Cat} & = \text{Det} \\
\text{Word} & = \text{all} \\
\text{Case} & = \text{Nom} \\
\text{Num} & = \text{Plur}
\end{array}\right]
\end{array}\right]
\end{array}\right] \\
\text{Obj} & = \left[\begin{array}{ll}
\text{Cat} & = \text{NONE} \\
\text{Head} & = \left[\begin{array}{ll}
\text{Cat} & = \text{Noun} \\
\text{Head} & = \text{NONE} \\
\text{Pers} & = 3 \\
\text{Word} & = \text{cats} \\
\text{Art} & = \left[\begin{array}{ll}
\text{Cat} & = \text{NONE} \\
\text{Case} & = \text{Acc} \\
\text{Num} & = \text{Plur}
\end{array}\right]
\end{array}\right]
\end{array}\right]
\end{array}\right]
\end{array}\right]
\end{array}\right]
$$

FIGURE 1 A functional description

If the label of a word or phrase is unifiable with the left hand side of a rule, then that rule must be applied to it. Where an alternation appears on the right of the rule, at least one of its clauses must apply; where a conjunct appears, all its clauses must apply. The notion of unification involved is straightforward. A pair of FDs is unifiable just in case there is no attribute with a value in one of them that cannot be unified with its value in the other. Atoms, of course, unify only with themselves. The result of the operation is a FD with the union of the attributes of the contributors. The value of each attribute has its original value if it comes from only one of the contributors, and otherwise the result of unifying the corresponding input values. Thus, FDs differ from more familar expressions in two ways: first, corresponding subexpressions are identified by name rather than position, and second, each FD behaves as though it had indefinitely many subexpressions, all but a finite subset having empty values.

One virtue of the attribute-value scheme is that of convenience. It is possible to work with linguistic descriptions in this formalism without having to remember the exact layout of every possible expression. More importantly, it is necessary to include in an expression only those parts that will appropriately restrict its possibilities of unification with other expressions. There is in FUG no notion of a completely specified FD just as, in everyday life, there is no notion of a complete description of a object – it is always possible to add more detail. This means, for example, that it is possible to supplement the supposedly complete FD constructed by unification by the syntactic component of a grammar with semantic or other information, also by unification.

1. $[\ ] \rightarrow$ ([Head = NONE] **and** ([Cat = noun] [Cat = verb])) **or**
   ($\sim$[Head = NONE] **and** [Cat = NONE])

2. [Head = [Cat = Verb]] $\rightarrow$ *Order:* <Head> ...

3. $\sim$[Head = [Cat = Verb]] $\rightarrow$ *Order:* ... <Head>

4. [Head = [Head = [Cat = Verb]]] $\rightarrow$ [Head = [Head = [Subj = [Head = [Arg = [Case = Nom]]]]]] **and**
   Constituent: <Head Head Subj>

5. $\left[\text{Head} = \begin{bmatrix}\text{Cat = Verb} \\ \text{Obj} = \begin{bmatrix}\text{Cat = NP}\end{bmatrix}\end{bmatrix}\right] \rightarrow$ [Head = [Obj = [Head = [Art = [Case = Acc]]]]] **and**
   Constituent: <Head Obj>

6. [Head = [Art = [Cat = Det]]] $\rightarrow$ *Constituent:* <Det>

FIGURE 2 A Simple Unification Grammar

Rather than give an explanation of the formalism, I will summarize what the rules in Fig. 2 say. This will provide enough detail for present purposes.

1. An item either has NONE as the value of its Head attribute, indicating that it is a word, or it has some other value for that attribute indicating that it is a phrase. A word must have a Cat attribute with the value det, noun, or verb and a phrase must have NONE for that attribute. Since the FD on the left of the rule is empty it will unify with anything and the rule therefore applies to all words and phrases: It has the status of a redundancy rule.

2. If the Head of a phrase is a verb, then the phrase is a verb phrase and its Head is its first member. If there are other members, they take the position of the dots.

3. The Head of a phrase that is not a verb phrase comes last. For the present grammar, this covers sentences and noun phrases.

4. A phrase whose Head is a verb phrase is a sentence so that it has a verb as the Head of its Head. The subject of this verb is a constituent of the sentence and its article, described by the value of its Head's Art attribute, has the property [Case = Nom].

5. If a verb phrase has an object, then the article of that object has the property [Case = Acc], and the object itself is a constituent of the verb phrase.

6. If a noun phrase has a Head whose article has the property [Cat = Det], then that article is a constituent of the noun phrase.

Rule one implements a principle known in linguistics as X-bar theory. I do not intend to argue for this theory but only to use it to illustrate the flexibility of the formalism. What the theory says is that every phrase has a distinguished constituent called its *head*. If a phrase has something with the grammatical category X as its head, then it is an X-phrase. Since a sentence has a verb phrase as its head, it might more strictly be referred to as a *verb-phrase phrase*. The theory is implemented here by representing categories explicitly only in the descriptions of lexical items. Thus, a sentence is a phrase whose head's head is a verb.

The lexical entry for a word is an FD, or several FDs if it is grammatically ambiguous. Fig. 3 gives some lexical entries to go with the preceding examples. Notice that the grammar embeds the description of a determiner within that of the noun it determines and ascribes properties in respect of which a determiner and a noun agree to the more deeply embedded of the two. It follows that *dog* can be used only with a singular determiner and *dogs* only with a plural. A determiner like *the* has no "Num" attribute in its lexical entry and can therefore be used with either singular or plural nouns. *Fido* is a proper noun and has a lexical entry that prevents a determiner from occurring with it. An analogous strategy is used for encoding the frames and agreement information of verbs. The description of a verb within the description of a sentence contains the description of the subject of the sentence, and the object if there is one. These must therefore be unifiable with the appropriate parts of the lexical description of the particular verb. *Chases* and *chase* require singular and plural subjects respectively, whereas the past-tense forms *slept* and *ate* agree with subjects of either number. Both forms of *chase* exclude the possibility of a null object (incorrectly, as it happens); *slept* excludes the possibility of an object, and *ate* can be used transitively or intransitively.

It is not difficult to show that the weak generative capacity of SUGs, like the others in the class we are considering, exceeds that of context-free grammars – it is, for example, possible to write a grammar that generates the language $a^n b^n c^n$. Very probably, these grammars have the same weak generative power as Definite-Clause grammars. But their value does not come from this. One of their principal advantages is that, as well as the traditional constituent structure that they obviously assign to sentences, they also assign a label to each node in these trees that typically contains the labels of all the nodes that it dominates. As the example just explored illustrates, this structure is far

$$\begin{bmatrix} \text{Cat} & = \text{Noun} \\ \text{Word} & = \text{dog} \\ \text{Art} & = \begin{bmatrix} \text{Cat} & = \text{Det} \\ \text{Num} & = \text{Sing} \end{bmatrix} \end{bmatrix} \begin{bmatrix} \text{Cat} & = \text{Noun} \\ \text{Word} & = \text{dogs} \\ \text{Art} & = \begin{bmatrix} \text{Cat} & = \text{Det} \\ \text{Num} & = \text{Plur} \end{bmatrix} \end{bmatrix}$$

$$\begin{bmatrix} \text{Cat} & = \text{Noun} \\ \text{Word} & = \text{Fido} \\ \text{Art} & = \begin{bmatrix} \text{Cat} = \text{NONE} \end{bmatrix} \end{bmatrix} \begin{bmatrix} \text{Cat} & = \text{Noun} \\ \text{Word} & = \text{sheep} \end{bmatrix}$$

$$\begin{bmatrix} \text{Cat} & = \text{Verb} \\ \text{Word} & = \text{chases} \\ \text{Obj} & = [\text{Cat} = \text{NP}] \\ \text{Subj} & = [\text{Head} = [\text{Art} = [\text{Num} = \text{Sing}]]] \end{bmatrix} \begin{bmatrix} \text{Cat} & = \text{Verb} \\ \text{Word} & = \text{chase} \\ \text{Obj} & = [\text{Cat} = \text{NP}] \\ \text{Subj} & = [\text{Head} = [\text{Art} = [\text{Num} = \text{Plur}]]] \end{bmatrix}$$

$$\begin{bmatrix} \text{Cat} & = \text{Verb} \\ \text{Word} & = \text{slept} \\ \text{Obj} & = \text{NONE} \end{bmatrix} \begin{bmatrix} \text{Cat} & = \text{Verb} \\ \text{Word} & = \text{ate} \end{bmatrix}$$

FIGURE 3 Lexical entries

from isomorphic with that of the constituent tree. This *functional structure* plays a role reminiscent of the deep structures of transformational grammar, and its value is argued for extensively and persuasively in Bresnan (1982). I have attempted to show how agreement, and various other phenomena that are lexically bound can be treated naturally within a formalism of this class.

The rules of SUG function strictly as constraints on the kinds of structures that a language allows. I have already pointed out that there is no notion of a completely specified FD, a fact that I shall exploit in the next section where we shall see that an existing grammar can be made to play host to important additional information. The grammar in Fig. 2, while too small to reveal important generalizations in a convincing way, gives clear indications of some of the ways in which this might be done. Rules 2 and 3, for example specify the ordering relations for the language by restricting the position of the head of a phrase. If these rules were removed, the grammar would be that of a free word order language. Rules 2 and 3 also state the generalization that the value of a head attribute always describes a constituent. Rules 4 and 5 specify that subjects and objects are constituents without saying anything about how they are ordered relative to others.

27.2   Semantics

I now hope to show that the benefits of unification go well beyond those just outlined. Let us augment the lexical entries for *all* and *dogs* so that they become as shown in Fig 4. Lower-case italic letters are used as variables. They are used here in an inessential way simply to indicate when two values are unified. Unbound variables are never used. Observe what will happen now when, following rule 4, these two words are incorporated in a noun phrase. The determiner's description is unified with the value of the *Art* property of the noun, causing the variable p to take on the value of the *Meaning* property of the determiner unified with the value of the meaning property of the noun.

$$
\begin{bmatrix}
\text{Cat} & = \text{Det} \\
\text{Word} & = \text{all} \\
\text{Num} & = \text{Plur} \\
\text{Meaning} & =
\begin{bmatrix}
\text{Type} & = \text{all} \\
\text{Var} & = q \\
\text{Prop} & =
\begin{bmatrix}
\text{Type} & = \text{Implies} \\
\text{P1} & = [\text{Arg} = q] \\
\text{P2} & = [\text{Arg} = q]
\end{bmatrix}
\end{bmatrix}
\end{bmatrix}
$$

$$
\begin{bmatrix}
\text{Cat} & = \text{Noun} \\
\text{Word} & = \text{dogs} \\
\text{Art} & =
\begin{bmatrix}
\text{Num} & = \text{Plur} \\
\text{Meaning} & = p
\end{bmatrix} \\
\text{Meaning} & = p =
\begin{bmatrix}
\text{Prop} & =
\begin{bmatrix}
\text{P1} & =
\begin{bmatrix}
\text{Type} = \text{Pred} \\
\text{Pred} = \text{dog}
\end{bmatrix}
\end{bmatrix}
\end{bmatrix}
\end{bmatrix}
$$

FIGURE 4 Semantic lexical entries

This unification gives the following result:

$$
\begin{bmatrix}
\text{Type} & = \text{all} \\
\text{Var} & = q \\
\text{Prop} & =
\begin{bmatrix}
\text{P1} & =
\begin{bmatrix}
\text{Type} & = \text{and} \\
& \begin{bmatrix}
\text{Pred} & = \text{dog} \\
\text{Arg} & = q
\end{bmatrix}
\end{bmatrix} \\
\text{P2} & = \begin{bmatrix} \text{Arg} = q \end{bmatrix}
\end{bmatrix}
\end{bmatrix}
$$

Without going into elaborate detail, this can be seen as description of the logical expression

$$\forall q \; dog(q) \wedge P(q)$$

The predicate P remains to be specified. It would come to be specified if the noun phrase "all dogs" became the subject of the verb "ate", and the lexical entry of "ate" were provided with a *Meaning* as follows:

$$
\begin{bmatrix}
\text{Cat} & = \text{Verb} \\
\text{Word} & = \text{sleep} \\
\text{Meaning} & = r \\
\text{Subj} & = [\text{Meaning} = r = [\text{Prop} = [\text{P2} = [\text{Pred} = \text{eat}]]]]
\end{bmatrix}
$$

The meaning of the verb is unified with that of the subject, and P2 of the Prop of that meaning is unified with [Pred = eat]. It is not difficult to see that the result of this is effectively

$$\forall q \; dog(q) \wedge eat(q)$$

27.3   Control structure

I have tried to make a strong argument for monotonic processes in grammatical analysis. Before an audience of logic programmers, the argument probably does not need to be urged particularly strongly. What doubtless requires more justification here is building special programs to carry out these monotonic processes when Prolog lies readily at hand. The argument that is most frequently made for not using Prolog is based on the claim that the most straigthforward implementations – those using recursive descent in the spirit of standard definite-clause processors – generally require an amount of time that is exponentially related to the length of the sentence analyzed, whereas a chart parser such as I in fact use requires only polynomial time. As the linguistic coverage of the grammar and the length of the sentences analyzed get large, this may become an issue. But they are not an issue for me, nor are they likely to become important in the near future. Prolog programmers usually claim that the time taken by their parsing programs on actually occurring sentences is acceptable for all practical purposes, and I see no reason to take issue with this.

It is also argued that, if a case can be made for something other than straightforward recursive-descent analysis, this does not also constitute an argument against Prolog as the implementation system of preference because Prolog readily accommodates other strategies. I find this less persuasive, especially in a context where a model being constructed is intended to serve as a psychological model of human language processing. Monotonicity makes for grammars with sufficient power to describe natural languages without building into them commitments about how they are to be processed which do not belong there. But this is not to say that they do not belong somewhere and that they are not a proper object of linguistic investigation. Indeed, one of the benefits of removing all such issues from the grammars of particular languages to the linguistic faculty that is presumably common to the speakers of all languages should make it more readily available to be studied in the manner it deserves. If this is one of the aims of computational linguistics, then one of the strengths of Prolog, namely that it frees the programmer from many of the usual concerns about control structure, becomes a weakness.

Conclusion

I have tried to display some of the advantages of grammatical formalisms that construct functional structures for sentences by means of a strictly monotonic process based on unification. To an audience of logic programmers, it should not be necessary to urge this case particularly strongly. However, the principal argument for the formalisms in this class does not flow automatically from simply embedding a grammar in a logic programming system. There are two important reasons for this: First, logic programming systems do impose strong constraints on the order of the events that make up the linguistic process. But, for the linguist, this order is an empirical matter. Even if the only aim were to analyze or generate sentences efficiently, without regard to psychological reality, it is possible to show that the strategies usually embodied in programming systems are extremely costly when faced with certain kinds of ambiguity. Second, the standard mathematical notion, which distinguishes the parts of an expression and, in particular, the arguments to a function, by their serial order relative to one another does not serve linguistic ends nearly as well as the attribute-value notation. One reason for this is simple if shallow, namely that large numbers of arguments are easier to keep track of if they are named and if irrelevant ones are not mentioned at all. But more important is the fact that naming arguments gives rise to the situation in which expressions are never completely specified so that more detail can always be added to an existing grammar without affecting what is already there.

Publications referenced
Bresnan 1982.

28

Machine Translation will not Work

Panelist Statement

Large expenditures on fundamental scientific research are usually limited to the hard sciences. It is therefore entirely reasonable to suppose that, if large sums of money are spent on machine translations, it will be with the clear expectation that what is being purchased is principally development and engineering, and that the result will contribute substantially to the solution of some pressing problem.

Anyone who accepts large (or small) sums on this understanding is either technically naive or dangerously cynical. It may certainly be that

1. machine translation could provide a valuable framework for fundamental research;
2. texts in highly restricted subsets of natural language could be devised for particular purposes and translated automatically;
3. computers have an important role to fill in making translations;
4. translations of extremely low quality may be acceptable on occasion.

However,

1. the fundamental research is so far from applicability,
2. the language subsets are so restricted,
3. the useful computer technologies are so different from machine translation,
4. the quality of the translations that can be produced of natural texts by automatic means is so low, and
5. the occasions on which those translations could be useful are so rare,

that the use of the term in these cases can only result in confusion if not deception.

A determined attempt was made to bring machine translation to the point of usability in the sixties. It has become fashionable to deride these as "first generation" systems and to refer to what is being done now as belonging to the second or third generation. It should surely be possible for those who think that the newer systems can succeed where the earlier ones failed, to point to problems that have been solved since the sixties that are so crucial as substantially to change our assessment of what can be achieved. We know a good deal more about programming techniques and have larger machines to work with; we have more elegant theories of syntax and what modern linguists are pleased to call semantics; and there has been some exploratory work on anaphora. But, we still have little idea how to translate into a closely related language like French or German, English sentences containing such words as "she", "it", "not", "and", and "of". Furthermore, such work as has been done on these problems has been studiously ignored by all those currently involved in developing systems.

Unfortunately, the sums that are being spent on MT in Europe and Japan are large enough to make virtually inevitable the production of a second ALPAC report sometime in the next few years. This will inevitably have a devastating effect on the whole field of computational linguistics, everywhere in the world. The report will be the more devastating for the fact that much of the money has in fact been spent frivolously, and much of the work has been incompetent, even by today's limited standards.

## 29

The Linguistic Connection

Set theory is the sole foundation of the whole edifice of mathematics, or so I have been given to understand. Sequences are constructed from ordered pairs in a fairly obvious way, and ordered pairs result from an artifice that can only cause the lay observer to put his hand on his wallet. In computing, on the other hand, sequences have always been treated as primitive. Sets are represented by an arbitrary permutation of their members. They are sets, and not sequences, only in as much as the algorithms that operate on them are expected to produce equivalent results regardless of the permutation chosen. Now, I take it that an important effect of connectionism will be to bring computing more into line with mathematics by giving first-class status to sets.

This is doubtless good news for the mathematician, for the theoretical computer scientist, and possibly for many others. But, in the linguist, it seems, on the face of it, to be cause for modified rapture, at best. Language is probably the most striking example of a two-dimensional object in this three-dimensional world. Its most obvious property is its sequentiality. But, this has been said before, for example by those who offered computational linguists string processing languages like COMIT and SNOBOL as the tools most obviously fitting their needs, and sophisticated people are no longer beguiled by the argument. According to the more enlightened view, sequentiality is a very superficial property of language. By applying the rules of syntax, we are able to uncover the richer, more revealing, multidimensional structures that lie behind it, and which are closer to the essence of language. In fact, there has been much interest in recent times in languages that are alleged to have a much more set-like character than English has, in that many of the permutations of a sentence often constitute a logical, or semantic, equivalence class.

Linguists have organized their subject in various ways, a familiar one being by level of abstraction. Phonetics is about the sounds people make when they talk and what they do to make them. Some would have it that there is so little abstraction in phonetics that it should not properly count as part of linguistics at all. Phonology talks about how the raw material of phonetics is organized into basic symbols of the most basic kind, about allowable sequences of these symbols, and about the way in which the phonetic forms of particular basic symbols are conditioned by the environment. This is all unrepentantly sequential, except when the discussion turns to such things as intonation and stress.

Morphology and lexicology are more abstract in the simple sense that they take the organization that phonology imposes on the primary material as primitive, and impose a further level of organization on that. Morphology is about how lexical items, themselves represented by sequences of phonologically defined units, are arranged to make words. It is mostly a matter of sequence, but morphology is sometimes conspicuously "nonconcatenative", to use the word that McCarthy (1979, 1981) coined in connection with Semitic languages. However, though morphology is sometimes not simply a matter of just which sequences of morphemes do make up words, and with what properties, it is inescapably a matter of how the phonetic or phonological material supplied by morphemes is arranged into a sequence so as to form a word.

The next level of abstraction is syntax, the way in which words are collected to form sentences. Just about all of the multifarious formal theories of grammar that have been proposed have been particularly strong in the facilities they provided for describing the proper ordering of words in a sentence, though it is widely recognized that there may be some ethnocentrism in this, for formal linguists have been speakers of languages where word order plays a predominant role. But it was not so in traditional informal grammar which took Latin as a model for all languages. Formalists are now in search of less strongly sequential paradigms as they attempt to account for so-called *free word order* and *nonconfigurational languages* .

By the time we reach the next level of abstraction, that of semantics, essentially no reflection of the ordering of the initial phonetic material remains. But, by this time, it is also possible to claim that the territory that falls most clearly within the purview of linguists has already been traversed. Linguistics makes contact with the real world at two points: the sounds that people utter and the meanings that are associated with them – phonetics and semantics. At all of the intervening levels of abstraction, the reflexes of the temporal ordering of the sounds is usually strongly in evidence.

If the picture I have painted of language is substantially correct, and if I have not misunderstood the nature of the connectionist revolution in computing too grossly, it seems that we may have to conclude that the human linguistic faculty, if not human intelligence at large, have more in common with the von Neumann machine than with the connection machine and that my colleagues and I will regretfully not be part of this new adventure. But now, let us see if we cannot find another side to the coin.

For all that language gives up its sequentiality grudgingly and into the brighter set-theoretic world only as its identity is confounded with that of intelligence at large, it nevertheless remains remarkably *context-free* . I say "remarkably" because we know from mathematics that context free languages are a subset – a small subset in some sense – of the theoretically possible languages. What this means for language users and computational linguists is that one can analyze any part of the sequence of phonemes, morphemes, words or whatever, with the expectation that, if the analysis of the whole string incorporates an analysis of that part, then the analysis one has already made will fill the requirement. Given that the subject and the object of the sentence do not overlap, the analysis of each of them can proceed in parallel. This is the property of language that makes chart parsers an attractive option.

Chart parsers in general, and so-called *active* chart parsers in particular, are fundamentally exercises in parallel computing. If, along with the chart, there is usually a second data structure called the *agenda* , it is simply to facilitate the simulation of this parallel architecture on sequential machines. But what is going on in chart parsing is much better understood if one thinks of each vertex in the chart as an autonomous device responsible for delivering all phrases that begin with the word at that vertex. The process of finding these phrases is dependent on similar work going on at other vertices only to the extent that, when phrases are delivered at other vertices, it may become possible to recognize others that begin here. But the relationships are *intrinsic*, to use the term in the linguist's special sense. In other words, these relationships are not dictated by some general algorithm or external set of principles, but by the obvious requirement that computations that require a particular piece of information cannot be completed until that information is available.

Some twenty years ago, when local networks were a relatively new thing, I harnessed the nocturnal energies of several machines at the Xerox Palo Alto Research Center to just such a task, more for fun than enlightenment. Of course, it worked. Furthermore, if the speed had been multiplied by a substantial factor, it would have been quite fast. The idea behind what I did was simple and obvious. An active edge consisted of a message from one machine to another asking for any phrases with a certain description that appeared at that other vertex. An inactive edge was a phrase already found that enabled a given machine to answer such requests. Each machine kept old requests against the possibility of finding phrases later with which to amplify its answer to previous requests. Each machine also had a complete copy of the grammar so that there could be no contention over access to it.

So, if the sentence to be analyzed was "Brutus killed Caesar", three machines would have been assigned and the talk on the net might have been somewhat like this:

1. a. From *Brutus* to *killed*: need a singular, 3rd. person VP.
   b. From *killed* to *Caesar*: need a NP.
2. From *Caesar* to *killed*: herewith one NP, namely "Caesar", ending where the sentence ends.
3. From *killed* to *Brutus*: herewith one VP, namely "V(killed) NP(Caesar)", ending where the sentence ends.

The *Brutus* machine is now in a position to deliver an analysis of the whole string. The ordering of the work into these three stages is intrinsic. In particular the *killed* machine cannot honor the request for a VP until information about the NP to its right is in. However, *killed* does not wait to be asked for a VP to send out its request for a NP. Each machine goes to work building whatever it can in a bottom up manner, just in case it may prove useful. So, if there had been a fourth machine to the right of 'Caesar', then 'Caesar' would have asked it for VP's in the hope of building sentences with them, even though no request for sentences was destined to reach it from the left.

This approach to syntactic analysis falls down because of a property of languages that I have not mentioned so far, namely that they all assiduously avoid center embedding in favor of strongly left- or right-branching structures. It is easy to see that, if syntactic structures were more or less well balanced trees, the time that my parallel device would require to find a single analysis of a sentence of n words would be of order $\log(n)$. But, if the most richly developed part of each subtree is almost always on its righthand side, as in English, then the intrinsic ordering of the processes will be such as to make this scheme essentially similar to standard sequential ones. If the language is predominently right recursive, then it will rarely be possible for a machine to finish its work before all, or almost all, the machines to its right. The situation is no better for left-recursive languages.

One further remark may be in order before I leave the question of chart parsing. Chart parsers exploit the grossly context-free nature of natural languages in a dynamic programming scheme that avoids, to a large extent, doing the same computation more that once. The chart is a record of the computations that have been attempted, and the results they produced, together with an index that makes it easy to check the record before repeating the work. It does a great deal to speed the business of finding all the structures that a grammar allows for a given sentence. But it is just as bad as a psychological model as it is good as a computational technique. If we had charts in our head, we would never be led down the garden path, and we should have no difficulty in reanalyzing the early part of a long sentence, possibly several times, to reconcile it with what occurred much later. But we do not seem to be able to do this. The evidence, such as it is, is all to the effect that linguistic problems are solved on the basis of very local information and that it proceeds much faster than even the chart model suggests. The connection machine may be able to provide a model that accounts for some greater speed, but locality and sequentiality remain.

There may be reason to suspect that the most obviously linguistic aspects of language processing – those that concern phonology, morphology, and syntax – are even more sequential even than the best known linguistic theories make them seem. It has often been pointed out that intonation and speech rhythm betray an organization of utterances into phrases of a different kind than emerges from considerations of syntax and semantics. It turns out that it is more natural to pause at some points in an utterance than at others, but these places are not always at syntactic boundaries. So we may have to countenance two different phrasings. Indeed, we may have to go further, because it has also been claimed that there is an *informational*, or *functional*, organization to discourse which does not respect the boundaries of either of the other two that I have mentioned. In Prague, this is known as the *functional sentence perspective* and it has to do with the differential treatment that a speaker gives to information he supposes his interlocutor to know already, as against the information that he is explicitly offering as new. These things are poorly understood, but the claim of those who do battle with them is that they are based on essentially sequential, local patterns in the text.

So far, my attempt to find another side to the coin has failed. Furthermore, those who know me well may be beginning to suspect that I am talking against myself because I have for a long time been singing the song of monotonicity in linguistics, calling for the banishment of all that is essentially procedural. Many current linguistic theories attract attention largely for having abandoned *derivations* in favor of systems of *constraints* . Examples are Lexical Functional Grammar, Generalized Phrase-Structure Grammar and its derivatives, and my own Functional Unification Grammar. Government Binding theory seems to me to be moving fast in the same direction and I suspect that it would be profitable to formulate a notational variant of it in which such procedural notions as "move-α" give way to a static system of constraints.

There are at least two advantages that constraint-based systems like these have over derivation-based systems, such as transformational grammar, at least in its older forms. The first is that it achieves a cleaner and more thoroughgoing separation of competence from performance, and the other is that it gives first-class status to methods of computing with only partial information. The second of these has also been touted as one of the strengths of the connectionist approach. The situation with the first is less clear. Consider the case of what I will refer to generically as *unification grammar* .

The view of scientific philosophy that prevails among linguists focuses a lot of attention on a Utopian situation in which they are called upon to choose between two descriptively perfect grammars. They prepare themselves for this challenge by setting up metrics that will be ready for immediate application when this need arrises. I take it that, *ceteris paribus*, a competence grammar will be preferred if it more readily supports some plausible theory of competence. In the long run, it will be even more to be preferred if it supports the *right* theory of competence. Now, a competence grammar that is based on a calculus in which operations have to be carried out in a specific, very carefully orchestrated way, is less likely to have this property than one in which no reliance is placed on carefully ordered sequences of operations. One might counter that the carefully ordered sequence could be just the one that people in fact follow so that the competence grammar could go into immediate service as a performance grammar without substantial change. But this is clearly a forlorn hope if only because the sequence of operations that a speaker and a hearer must perform are unlikely to be ordered in the same way. The constraint-based systems of grammar that have been proposed, on the other hand, are hospitable to a variety of different processing strategies. The freedom that this gives to performance theorists also extends to computational linguists with more practical aims in mind; they are much freer to bring their ingenuity and expertise as computer scientists to bear.

The constraint-based grammars that are now in vogue are based on unification and, to a lesser extent, on related operations, such as generalization and subsumption. These are logical operations, in a strong sense of the word, as evidenced by the fact that unification is also a basic operation of logic programming in general, and Prolog in particular. Logic programming, and computation with constraint-based grammars, rests heavily on implementing the notion of a *logical variable* , as opposed to what programmers have usually called "variables", and which are really names of storage locations. The values of logical variables, unlike the contents of storage locations, do not change over time, at least on one path through a nondeterministic process. Unification is an operation as a result of which it sometimes comes to light that sets of two or more variables refer to the same thing. Henceforward, any constraints imposed on the value of one of the variables, as a result of its appearance in one expression, must be consonant with those imposed upon other members of the set through their appearance in other expressions. If these conditions are violated at the outset, the unification operation does not go through. I do not know what would be involved in modeling this situation in something like the connection machine, but such uninformed speculations as I have allowed myself on the subject, together with occasional remarks from others who know better than I, suggest that this is not entirely in the connectionist spirit.

The skepticism I have expressed here on the matter of connectionism in linguistics is based to some extent on facts and to some extent on speculation on matters where I believe the evidence to be inconclusive. If I were wrong about most of the matters in the second class, it may be that the role of connectionism in linguistics could be very great. It seems to me that our way is clear. Arguments along the lines of those I have outlined should not be used against the attempt to apply connectionist ideas to linguistics. Quite the contrary. Connectionism should be pursued vigorously in the hope that, if nothing else, it will shed light on these areas of uncertainty, most of which have resisted attack for far too long a time.

Publications referenced
McCarthy 1979; McCarthy 1981.

## 30

Nonconcatenative Finite-State Morphology

In the last few years, so called *finite-state* morphology, in general, and *two-level* morphology in particular, have become widely accepted as paradigms for the computational treatment of morphology. Finite-state morphology appeals to the notion of a finite-state transducer, which is simply a classical finite-state automaton whose transitions are labeled with pairs, rather than with single symbols. The automaton operates on a pair of tapes and advances over a given transition if the current symbols on the tapes match the pair on the transition. One member of the pair of symbols on a transition can be the designated null symbol, which we will write ε. When this appears, the corresponding tape is not examined, and it does not advance as the machine moves to the next state.

Finite-state morphology originally arose out of a desire to provide ways of analyzing surface forms using grammars expressed in terms of systems of ordered rewriting rules. Kay and Kaplan (1981) observed that finite-state transducers could be used to mimic a large class of rewriting rules, possibly including all those required for phonology. The importance of this came from two considerations. First, transducers are indifferent as to the direction in which they are applied. In other words, they can be used with equal facility to translate between tapes, in either direction, to accept or reject pairs of tapes, or to generate pairs of tapes. Second, a pair of transducers with one tape in common is equivalent to a single transducer operating on the remaining pair of tapes. A simple algorithm exists for constructing the transition diagram for this composite machine given those of the original pair. By repeated application of this algorithm, it is therefore possible to reduce a cascade of transducers, each linked to the next by a common tape, to a single transducer which accepts exactly the same pair of tapes as was accepted by the original cascade as a whole. From these two facts together, it follows that an arbitrary ordered set of rewriting rules can be modeled by a finite-state transducer which can be automatically constructed from them and which serves as well for analyzing surface forms as for generating them from underlying lexical strings.

A transducer obtained from an ordered set of rules in the way just outlined is a *two level* device in the sense that it mediates directly between lexical and surface forms without ever constructing the intermediate forms that would arise in the course of applying the original rules one by one. The term *two-level morphology* , however, is used in a more restricted way, to apply to a system in which no intermediate forms are posited, even in the original grammatical formalism. The writer of a grammar using a two-level formalism never needs to think in terms of any representations other than the lexical and the surface ones. What he does is to specify, using one formalism or another, a set of transducers, each of which mediates directly between these forms and each of which restricts the allowable pairs of strings in some way. The pairs that the system as a whole accepts are those that are rejected by none of the component transducers, modulo certain assumptions about the precise way in which they interact, whose details need not concern us. Once again, there is a formal procedure that can be used to combine the set of transducers that make up such a system into a single automaton with the same overall behavior, so that the final result is indistinguishable from that obtained from a set of ordered rules. However it is an advantage of parallel machines that they can be used with very little loss of efficiency without combining them in this way.

While it is not the purpose of this paper to explore the formal properties of finite-state transducers, a brief excursion may be in order at this point to forestall a possible objection to the claim that a parallel configuration of transducers can be combined into a single one. On the face of it, this cannot generally be so because there is generally no finite-state transducer that will accept the intersection of the sets of tape pairs accepted by an arbitrary set of transducers. It is, for example, easy to design a transducer that will map a string of x's onto the same number of y's followed by an arbitrary number of z's. It is equally easy to design one that maps a string of x's onto the same number of z's preceded by an arbitrary number of x's. The intersection of these two sets contains just those pairs with some number of x's on one tape, and that same number of y's followed by the same number of z's on the other tape. The set of second tapes therefore contains a context-free language which it is clearly not within the power of any finite-state device to generate.

Koskenniemi overcame this objection in his original work by adopting the view that all the transducers in the parallel configuration should share the same pair of read-write heads. The effect of this is to insist that they not only accept the same pairs of tapes, but that they agree on the particular sequence of symbol pairs that must be rehearsed in the course of accepting each of them. Kaplan has been able to put a more formal construction on this in the following way: Let the empty symbols appearing in the pairs labeling any transition in the transducers be replaced by some ordinary symbol not otherwise part of the alphabet. The new set of transducers derived in this way clearly do not accept the same pairs of tapes as the original ones did, but there is an algorithm for constructing a single finite-state transducer that will accept the intersection of the pairs they all accept. Suppose, now, that this configuration of parallel transducers is put in series with two other standard transducers, one which carries the real empty symbol onto its surrogate, and everything else onto itself, and another transducer that carries the surrogate onto the real empty symbol, then the resulting configuration accepts just the desired set of languages, all of which are also acceptable by single transducers that can be algorithmically derived from the originals.

It may well appear that the systems we have been considering properly belong to finite-state phonology or graphology, and not to morphology, properly construed. Computational linguists have indeed often been guilty of some carelessness in their use of this terminology. But it is not hard to see how it could have arisen. The first step in any process that treats natural text is to recognize the words it contains, and this generally involves analyzing each of them in terms of a constituent set of formatives of some kind. Most important among the difficulties that this entails are those having to do with the different shapes that formatives assume in different environments. In other words, the principal difficulties of morphological analysis are in fact phonological or graphological. The inventor of two-level morphology, Kimmo Koskenniemi, in fact provided a finite-state account not just of morphophonemics (or morphographemics), but also of morphotactics. He took it that the allowable set of words simply constituted a regular set of morpheme sequences. This is probably the more controversial part of his proposal, hut it is also the less technically elaborate, and therefore the one that has attracted less attention. As a result, the term "two-level morphology" has come to be commonly accepted as applying to any system of word recognition that involves two-level, finite-state, phonology or graphology. The approach to nonconcatenative morphology to be outlined in this paper will provide a more unified treatment of morphophonemics and morphotactics than has been usual.

I shall attempt to show how a two-level account might be given of nonconcatenative morphological phenomena, particularly those exhibited in the Semitic languages. The approach I intend to take is inspired, not only by finite-state morphology, broadly construed, but equally by autosegmental phonology as proposed by Goldsmith (1979) and the autosegmental morphology of McCarthy (1979). All the data that I have used in this work is taken from McCarthy (1979) and my debt to him will be clear throughout.

TABLE I

| | Perfective | | Imperfective | | Participle | |
	Active	Passive	Active	Passive	Active	Passive
I	katab	kutib	aktub	uktab	kaatib	maktuub
II	kattab	kuttib	ukattib	ukattab	mukattib	mukattab
III	kaatab	kuutib	ukaatib	ukaatab	mukaatib	mukaatab
IV	?aktab	?uktib	u?aktib	u?aktab	mu?aktib	mu?aktab
V	takattab	tukuttib	atakattab	utakattab	mutkattib	mutakattab
VI	takaatab	tukuutib	atakaatab	utakaatab	mutakaatib	mutakaatab
VII	nkatab	nkutib	ankatib	unkatab	minkatib	munkatab
VIII	ktatab	ktutib	aktatib	uktatab	muktatib	muktatab
IX	ktabab		aktabib		muktabib	
X	staktab	stuktib	astaktib	ustaktab	mustaktib	mustaktab
XI	ktaabab		aktaabib		muktaabib	
XII	ktawtab		aktawtib		muktawtib	
XIII	ktawwab		aktawwib		muktawwib	
XIV	ktanbab		aktanbib		muktanbib	
XV	ktanbay		aktanbiy		muktanbiy	

I take it as my task to describe how the members of a paradigm like the one in Table I might be generated and recognized effectively and efficiently, and in such a way as to capture and profit from the principal linguistic generalizations inherent in it. Now this is a slightly artificial problem because the forms given in Table I are not in fact words, but only verb stems. To get the verb forms that would be found in Arabic text, we should have to expand the table very considerably to show the inflected forms that can be constructed on the basis of each of the stems shown. However, there is every reason to suppose that, though longer and greatly more complex in detail, that enterprise would not require essentially different mechanisms from the ones I shall describe.

The overall principles on which the material in Table I is organized are clear from a fairly cursory inspection. Each form contains the letters "ktb" somewhere in it. This is the root of the verb meaning "write". By replacing these three letters with other appropriately chosen sequences of three consonants, we would obtain corresponding paradigms for other roots. With some notable exceptions, the columns of the table contain stems with the same sequence of vowels. Each of these is known as a *vocalism* and, as the headings of the columns show, these can serve to distinguish perfect from imperfective, active from passive, and the like. Each row of the table is characterized by a particular pattern according to which the vowels and consonants alternate. In other words, it is characteristic of a given row that the vowel in a particular position is long or short, or that a consonant is simple or geminate, or that material in one syllable is repeated in the following one. McCarthy refers to each of these patterns as a *prosodic template* , a term which I shall take over. Each of them adds a particular semantic component to the basic verb, making it reflexive, causative, or whatever. Our problem will therefore involve designing an abstract device capable of combining components of these three kinds into a single sequence. Our solution will take the form of a set of one or more finite-state transducers that will work in parallel like those of Koskenniemi (1983), but on four tapes rather than just two.

There will not be space, in this paper, to give a detailed account, even of all the material in Table I, not to mention problems that would arise if we were to consider the full range of Arabic roots. What I do hope to do, however, is to establish a theoretical framework within which solutions to all of these problems could be developed.

We must presumably expect the transducers we construct to account for the Arabic data to have transition functions from states and quadruples of symbols to states. In other words, we will be able to describe them with transition diagrams whose edges are labeled with a vector of four symbols. When the automaton moves from one state to another, each of the four tapes will advance over the symbol corresponding to it on the transition that sanctions the move.

I shall allow myself some extensions to this basic scheme which will enhance the perspicuity and economy of the formalism without changing its essential character. In particular, these extensions will leave us clearly within the domain of finite-state devices. The extensions have to do with separating the process of reading or writing a symbol on a tape, from advancing the tape to the next position. The quadruples that label the transitions in the transducers we shall be constructing will be elements each consisting of two parts, a symbol, and an instruction concerning the movement of the tape. I shall use the following notation for this. An unadorned symbol will be read in the traditional way, namely, as requiring the tape on which that symbol appears to move to the next position as soon as it has been read or written. If the symbol is shown in brackets, on the other hand, the tape will not advance, and the quadruple specifying the next following transition will therefore clearly have to be one that specifies the same symbol for that tape, since the symbol will still be under the read-write head when that transition is taken. With this convention, it is natural to dispense with the ε symbol in favor of the notation "[ ]", that is, an unspecified symbol over which the corresponding tape does not advance. A symbol can also be written in braces, in which case the corresponding tape will move if the symbol under the read-write head is the last one on the tape. This is intended to capture the notion of *spreading* , from autosegmental morphology, that is, the principle according to which the last item in a string may be reused when required to fill several positions.

A particular set of quadruples, or *frames* , made up of symbols, with or without brackets or braces, will constitute the *alphabet* of the automata, and the "useful" alphabet must be the same for all the automata because none of them can move from one state to another unless the others make an exactly parallel transition. Not surprisingly, a considerable amount of information about the language is contained just in the constitution of the alphabet. Indeed. a single machine with one state which all transitions both leave and enter will generate a nontrivial subset of the material in Table I. An example of the steps involved in generating a form that depends only minimally on information embodied in a transducer is given in Table II.

Table II

```
(a)              ┌───┐
                 │ k │ t   b                          [ ]
                 │ V │ C   C   V   V   C   V   C        V
                 │ a │ i                              [a]
                 │ a │                                 a
                 └───┘

(b)              ┌───┐
             V   │ C │ V   V   C   V   C                k
                 │ a │ i                                C
             a   │ k │                                 [ ]
                 └───┘                                  k

(c)              ┌───┐
         k       │ t │ b                                t
     V   C       │ C │ V   C   V   C                    C
                 │ a │ i                               [ ]
     a   k       │ t │                                  t
                 └───┘

(d)              ┌───┐
         k   t   │ b │                                 [ ]
     V   C   C   │ V │ C   V   C                        V
                 │ a │ i                                a
     a   k   t   │ a │                                  a
                 └───┘
```

```
(e)                          k    t    b                   {b}
              V    C    C    V    C    V    C                C
                                  a    i                    [ ]
              a    k    t    a    b                          b
```

```
(f)                          k    t    b                   [ ]
              V    C    C    V    C    V    C                V
                                  a    i                     i
              a    k    t    a    b    i                     i
```

```
(g)                          k    t    b                    b
              V    C    C    V    C    V    C                C
                                  a    i                    [ ]
              a    k    t    a    b    i    b                b
```

```
(h)                          k    t    b
         V    C    C    V    C    V    C
                             a    i
         a    k    t    a    b    i    b
```

The eight steps are labeled (a) – (h). For each one, a box is shown enclosing the symbols currently under the read-write heads. The tapes move under the heads from the right and then continue to the left. No symbols are shown to the right on the bottom tape, because we are assuming that the operation chronicled in these diagrams is one in which a surface form is being generated. The bottom tape – the one containing the surface form – is therefore being written and it is for this reason that nothing appears to the right. The other three tapes, in the order shown, contain the root, the prosodic template, and the vocalism. To the right of the tapes, the frame is shown which sanctions the move that will be made to advance from that position to the next. No such frame is given for the last configuration for the obvious reason that this represents the end of the process.

The move from (a) to (b) is sanctioned by a frame in which the root consonant is ignored. There must be a "V" on the template tape and an "a" in the current position of the vocalism. However, the vocalism tape will not move when the automata move to their next states. Finally, there will be an "a" on the tape containing the surface form. In summary, given that the prosodic template calls for a vowel, the next vowel in the vocalism has been copied to the surface. Nondeterministically, the device predicts that this same contribution from the vocalism will also be required to fill a later position.

The move from (b) to (c) is sanctioned by a frame in which the vocalism is ignored. The template requires a consonant and the frame accordingly specifies the same consonant on both the root and the surface tapes, advancing both of them. A parallel move, differing only in the identity of the consonant, is made from (c) to (d). The move from (d) to (e) is similar to that from (a) to (b) except that, this time, the vocalism tape does advance. The nondeterministic prediction that is being made in this case is that there will be no further slots for the "a" to fill. Just what it is that makes this the "right" move is a matter to which we shall return. The move from (e) to (f) differs from the previous two moves over root consonants in that the "b" is being "spread". In other words, the root tape does not move, and this possibility is allowed on the specific grounds that it is the last symbol on the tape. Once again, the automata are making a nondeterministic decision, this time that there will be another consonant called for later by the prosodic template and which it will be possible to fill only if this last entry on the root tape does not move away. The moves from (f) to (g) and from (g) to (h) are like those from (d) to (e) and (b) to (c) respectively.

Just what is the force of the remark, made from time to time in this commentary, that a certain move is made *nondeterministically* ? These are all situations in which some other move was, in fact, open to the transducers but where the one displayed was carefully chosen to be the one that would lead to the correct result. Suppose that, instead of leaving the root tape stationary in the move from (e) to (f), it had been allowed to advance using a frame parallel to the one used in the moves from (b) to (c) and (c) to (d), a frame which it is only reasonable to assume must exist for all consonants, including "b". The move from (f) to (g) could still have been made in the same way, but this would have led to a configuration in which a consonant was required by the prosodic template, but none was available from the root. A derivation cannot be allowed to count as complete until all tapes are exhausted, so the automata would have reached an impasse. We must assume that, when this happens, the automata are able to return to a preceding situation in which an essentially arbitrary choice was made, and try a different alternative. Indeed, we must assume that a general backtracking strategy is in effect, which ensures that all allowable sequences of choices are explored.

Now consider the nondeterministic choice that was made in the move from (a) to (b), as contrasted with the one made under essentially indistinguishable circumstances from (d) to (e). If the vocalism tape had advanced in the first of these situations, but not in the second, we should presumably have been able to generate the putative form "aktibib", which does not exist. This can be excluded only if we assume that there is a transducer that disallows this sequence of events, or if the frames available for "i" are not the same as those for "a". We are, in fact, making the latter assumption, on the grounds that the vowel "i" occurs only in the final position of Arabic verb stems.

Consider, now, the forms in rows II and V of Table I. In each of these, the middle consonant of the root is geminate in the surface. This is not a result of spreading as we have described it, because spreading only occurs with the last consonant of a root. If the prosodic template for row II is "CVCCVC", how is it that we do not get forms like "katbab" and "kutbib" beside the ones shown? This is a problem that is overcome in McCarthy's autosegmental account only at considerable cost. Indeed, it is a deficiency of that formalism that the only mechanisms available in it to account for gemination are as complex as they are, given how common the phenomenon is.

Within the framework proposed here, gemination is provided for in a very natural way. Consider the following pair of frame schemata, in which c is an arbitrary consonant:

$$
\begin{array}{cc}
c & [c] \\
C & G \\
[\,] & [\,] \\
c & c
\end{array}
$$

The first of these is the one that was used for the consonants in the above example except in the situation for the first occurrence of "b", where it was being spread into the final two consonantal positions of the form. The second frame differs from this in two respects. First, the prosodic template contains the hitherto unused symbol "G". for "geminate", and second, the root tape is not advanced. Suppose, now, that the prosodic template for forms like "kattab" is not "CVCCVC", but "CVGCVC". It will be possible to discharge the "G" only if the root template does not advance, so that the following "C" in the template can only cause the same consonant to be inserted into the word a second time. The sequence "GC" in a prosodic template is therefore an idiom for consonant gemination.

Needless to say, McCarthy's work, on which this paper is based, is not interesting simply for the fact that he is able to achieve an adequate description of the data in Table I, but also for the claims he makes about the way that account extends to a wider class of phenomena, thus achieving a measure of explanatory power. In particular, he claims that it extends to roots with two and four consonants. Consider, in particular, the following sets of forms:

ktanbab   dhanraj

kattab   dahraj

takattab   tadahraj

Those in the second column are based on the root /dhrj/. In the first column are the corresponding forms of /ktb/. The similarity in the sets of corresponding forms is unmistakable. They exhibit the same patterns of consonants and vowels, differing only in that, whereas some consonant appears twice in the forms in column one, the consonantal slots are all occupied by different segments in the forms on the right. For these purposes, the "n" of the first pair of forms should be ignored since it is contributed by the prosodic template, and not by the root.

Given a triliteral and a quadriliteral root, the first pair are exactly as one would expect – the final root consonant is spread to fill the final consonantal slot in the prosodic template only in the case of the shorter form. The structure of the second and third forms is equally straighforward, but it is less easy to see how our machinery could account for them. Once again, the template calls for four root consonants and, where only three are provided, one must do double duty. But in this case, the effect is achieved through gemination rather than spreading so that the gemination mechanism just outlined is presumably in play. That mechanism makes no provision for gemination to be invoked only when needed to fill slots in the prosodic template that would otherwise remain empty. If the mechanism were as just described, and the triliteral forms were "CVGCVC" and "tVCVGCVC" respectively, then the quadriliteral forms would have to be generated on a different base.

It is in cases like this, of which there in fact many, that the finite-state transducers

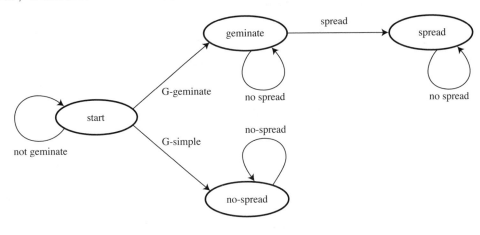

FIGURE 1

play a substantive role. What is required in this case is a transducer that allows the root tape to remain stationary while the template tape moves over a "G", provided no spreading will be allowed to occur later to fill consonantal slots that would otherwise be unclaimed. If extra consonants are required. then the first priority must be to let them occupy the slots marked with a "G" in the template. Fig. 1 shows a schema for the transition diagram of a transducer that has this effect. I call it a "schema" only because each of the edges shown does duty for a number of actual transitions. The machine begins in the "start" state and continues to return there so long as no frame is encountered involving a "G" on the template tape. A "G" transition causes a nondeterministic choice. If the root tape moves at the same time as the "G" is scanned, the transducer goes into its "no-spread" state, to which it continues to return so long as every move over a "C" on the prosodic tape is accompanied by a move over a consonant on the root tape. In other words, it must be possible to complete the process without spreading consonants. The other alternative is that the transducer should enter the "geminate" state over a transition over a "G" in the template with the root tape remaining stationary. The transitions at the "geminate" state allow both spreading and nonspreading transitions. In summary, spreading can occur only if the transducer never leaves the "start" state and there is no "G" in the template, or there is a "G" on the template which does not trigger gemination. A "G" can fail to trigger gemination only when the root contains enough consonants to fill all the requirements that the template makes for them.

One quadriliteral case remains to be accounted for, namely the following:

ktaabab   dharjaj

According to the strategy just elaborated, we should have expected the quadriliteral form to have been "dhaaraj". But, apparently this form contains a slot that is used for vowel lengthening with triliteral roots, and as consonantal position for quadriliterals. We must therefore presumably take it that the prosodic template for this form is something like "CCVXCVC" where "X" is a segment, but not specified as either vocalic or consonantal. This much is in line with the proposal that McCarthy himself makes. The question is, when should it be filled by a vowel, and when by a consonant? The data in Table I is, of course, insufficient to answer the question, but a plausible answer that strongly suggests itself is that the "X" slot prefers a consonantal filler *except* where that would result in gemination. If this is true, then it is another case where the notion of gemination, though not actually exemplified in the form, plays a central role. Supposing that the analysis is correct, the next question is, how is it to be implemented? The most appealing answer would be to make "X" the exact obverse of "G", when filled with a consonant. In other words, when a root consonant fills such a slot, the root tape must advance so that the same consonant will no longer be available to fill the next position. The possibility that the next root consonant would simply be a repetition of the current one would be excluded if we were to take over from autosegmental phonology and morphology, some version of the *Obligatory Contour Principle (OCP)* (Goldsmith 1979) which disallows repeated segments except in the prosodic template and in the surface string. McCarthy points out that roots like /smm/, which appear to violate the OCP, can invariably be reanalyzed as biliteral roots like /sm/ and, if this is done, our analysis, like his, goes through.

The OCP does seem likely to cause some trouble when we come to treat one of the principal remaining problems, namely that of the forms in row I of Table I. It turns out that the vowel that appears in the second syllable of these forms is not provided by the vocalism, but by the root. The vowel that appears in the perfect is generally different from the one that appears in the imperfect, and four different pairs are possible. The pair that is used with a given root is an idiosyncratic property of that root. One possibility is, therefore, that we treat the traditional triliteral roots as consisting not simply of three consonants, but as three consonants with a vowel intervening between the second and third, for a total of four segments. This flies in the face of traditional wisdom. It also runs counter to one of the motivating intuitions of autosegmental phonology which would have it that particular phonological features can be represented on at most one lexical tier, or tape. The intuition is that these tiers or tapes each contain a record of a particular kind of *articulatory gesture*; from the hearer's point of view, it is as though they contained a record of the signal received from a receptor that was attuned only to certain features. If we wish to maintain this model, there are presumably two alternatives open to us. Both involve assuming that roots are represented on at least two tapes in parallel, with the consonants separate from the vowel.

According to one alternative, the root vowel would be written on the same tape as the vocalism; according to the other, it would be on a tape of its own. Unfortunately, neither alternative makes for a particularly happy solution. No problem arises from the proposal that a given morpheme should, in general, be represented on more than one lexical tape. However, the idea that the vocalic material associated with a root should appear on a special tape, reserved for it alone, breaks the clean lines of the system as so far presented in two ways. First, it separates material onto two tapes, specifically the new one and the vocalism, on purely lexical grounds, having nothing to do with their phonetic or phonological constitution, and this runs counter to the idea of tapes as records of activity on phonetically specialized receptors. It is also at least slightly troublesome in that that newly introduced tape fills no function except in the generation of the first row of the table. Neither of these arguments is conclusive, and they could diminish considerably in force as a wider range of data was considered.

Representing the vocalic contribution of the root on the same tape as the vocalism would avoid both of these objections, but would require that vocalic contribution to be recorded either before or after the vocalism itself. Since the root vowel affects the latter part of the root, it seems reasonable that it should be positioned to the right. Notice, however, that this is the only instance in which we have had to make any assumptions about the relative ordering of the morphemes that contribute to a stem. Once again, it may be possible to assemble further evidence reflecting on some such ordering, but I do not see it in these data.

It is only right that I should point out the difficulty of accounting satisfactorily for the vocalic contribution of verbal roots. It is only right that I should also point out that the autosegmental solution fares no better on this score, resorting, as it must, to rules that access essentially non-phonological properties of the morphemes involved. By insisting that what I have called the *spelling* of a morpheme should, by definition, be its only contribution to phonological processes, I have cut myself off from any such *deus ex machina*.

Linguists in general, and computational linguists in particular, do well to employ finite-state devices wherever possible. They are theoretically appealing because they are computationally weak and best understood from a mathematical point of view. They are computationally appealing because they make for simple, elegant, and highly efficient implementations. In this paper, I hope I have shown how they can be applied to a problem in nonconcatenative morphology which seems initially to require heavier machinery.

Publications referenced

Goldsmith 1979; Kay and Kaplan 1981; Koskenniemi 1983; Leben 1973; McCarthy 1979; McCarthy 1981.

31

Head-Driven Parsing

There are clear signs of a "Back to Basics" movement in parsing and syntactic gener-ation. Our Latin teachers were apparently right. You should start with the main verb. This will tell you what kinds of subjects and objects to look for and what cases they will be in. When you come to look for these, you should also start by trying to find the main word, because this will tell you most about what else to look for.

In the early days of research on machine-translation, Paul Garvin advocated the application of what he called the "Fulcrum" method to the analysis of sentences. If he was the last to heed the injunctions of his Latin teacher, it is doubtless because America followed the tradition of rewriting systems exemplified by context-free grammar and this provided no immediate motivation for the notion of the *head* of a construction. The European tradition, and particularly the tradition of Eastern Europe, where Garvin had his roots, tend more towards dependency grammar, but away from that of mathematical formalization which has been the underpinning of computational linguistics.

But the move now is towards linguistic descriptions that put more information in the lexicon so that grammar rules take on a more schematic quality. Little by little, we moved from rules like

(1) *VP1 → VP2 NP*
      CaseOf(VP2) = Dative
      CaseOf(NP) = Dative

to rules that attain greater abstraction through the use of logical variables (or the equivalent), like

(2) *VP1 → VP2 NP*
      ObjCase(VP2) = Case
      CaseOf(NP) = Case

where the underlined Case is to be taken as the name of a variable. From there , it was a short step to

(3) *VP1 → VP2 X*
      ComplementOf(VP2) = X

or even

(4) *VP1 → VP2 X*

$ComplementStringOf(VP2) = \underline{X}$

Given rule (2), the parser knows what case the noun must have only after it has encountered the verb. Rules (3) and (4) do not even tell it that the complement must be a noun phrase. In (4) we cannot even tell how many complements there will be. For most parsers, the problem is masked in these examples by the fact that they apply rules from left to right so that the value of the variable $\underline{X}$ is known by the time it is needed. In rule (4a), the matter is different.

(4a) $VP1 \rightarrow \underline{X}\ VP2$
        $ComplementStringOf(VP2) = \underline{X}$

Needless to say, these things have not gone unnoticed, least of all by the participants in this conference. It has been noted, for example, that definite-clause grammars can be adjusted so as to look for heads before complements and adjuncts. If the head of a sentence is a verb phrase, then it is sufficient to write (6) instead of (5).

(5)   *s(Left/Right)* :–
       np(Left/Middle),
       vp(Middle/Right)

(6)   *s(Left/Right)* :–
       vp(Middle/Right),
       np(Left/Middle)

A rule that expands the verb phrase would be something like (7).

(7)   *vp(Left/Right)* :–
       verb(Left/Middle),
       np(Middle/Right)

This time, the order is the usual one because the head is on the left.[1]

Of course, all this works if *Left*, *Middle*, and *Right* are something like word numbers that provide random access to the parts of the sentence. To make the system work with difference lists, we need something more, for example, as in (8).

(8)   *s(Left/Right)* :–
       append(X, Middle, Left),
       vp(Middle/Right), *np(Left/Middle)*

The reason for the addition is that the parser, embodied here in the set of rules themselves, has no way to tell where the verb phrase will begin. It must therefore consider all possible positions in the string, an end which, against all expectation, is accomplished by the *append* predicate. If *append* is not needed when something like word numbers are used, it is because the inevitable search of the string is being quietly conducted by the Prolog system as it searches its data base, rather than being programmed explicitly.

The old-fashioned parser had no trouble finding the beginnings of things because they were always immediately adjacent, either to the boundaries of the sentence, or to another phrase whose position was already known. Given the sentence

I sold my car to a student of African languages whom I met at a party

---

[1] We have now moved to the Prolog convention of using capitalized names for variables.

and given appropriate rules, the head-driven parser will correctly identify "my car" as the direct object of "sold". But it will also consider for this role at least the following:

(9) *a student*
     a student of African
     a student of African languages
     a student of African languages whom I met
     a student of African languages whom I met at a party
     African
     African languages
     African languages whom I met
     African languages whom I met at a party
     languages
     languages whom I met
     languages whom I met at a party
     a party

It will reject them only when it fails to extend them far enough to the left to meet the right-hand edge of the word "sold". Likewise, the last four entries on the list will be constructed again as possible objects for the preposition "of". As we shall see, this problem is not easy to set aside.

Of course, definite-clause grammars have other problems, when interpreted directly by a standard Prolog processor. The most notorious of these is that, in their classical form, they cycle indefinitely when provided with a grammar that involves left recursion. However this can be overcome by using a more appropriate interpreter such as the one given in Appendix A of this paper. It does not touch the question of the additional work that has to be done in parsing a sentence.

Two solutions to the problem suggest themselves immediately. One is to use an undirected bottom-up parsing strategy, and the other is to seek an appropriate adaptation of chart parsing to a directed, head-driven, strategy. The first solution works for the simple reason that the problem we are facing simply does not arise in undirected bottom-up processing. There is no question of finding phrases that are adjacent to, or otherwise positioned relative to, other phrases. The strategy is a purely opportunistic one which finds phrases wherever, and whenever, its control strategy dictates. A simple chart parser with these properties is given in Appendix B. It accepts only unary and binary rules, but this is not a real restriction because these binary rules can function as meta-rules that interpret the more general of the actual grammar according to something like the following scheme. Real rules have a similar format to that used in the program in Appendix A, namely

$$rr(Mother, [L_1, L_2...L_n], Head, [R_1, R_2...R_m])$$

L_1 ... L_n are the non-head (complement) daughters of 'Mother' to the left of the head, and R_1 ... R_m are those to the right. For convenience, we give the ones on the left in the reverse of the order in which they actually appear so that the one nearest to the head is written first. We define the binary rule predicate referred to in the algorithm somewhat as follows:

$$rule(p(Mother, L, Rest), Head, Next) :-$$
$$rr(p(Mother, L, Head, [Next \,|Rest]).$$
$$rule(p(Mother, Rest, [\,]), Next, Head) :-$$
$$rr(p(Mother, [Next \,|Rest], Head, [\,]).$$
$$rule(p(Mother, L, T), p(Mother, L, [H|T]), H).$$
$$rule(p(Mother, H, p(Mother, L, [H|T]), [\,])).$$

One special unary rule is required, namely

$$rule(Mother, p(Mother, [\,], [\,])).$$

The scheme is reminiscent of categorial grammar. *p(Category, Left, Right)* is a partially formed phrase belonging to the given *Category* which can be completed by adding the items specified by the *Left* list on the left, and the *Right* list on the right.

This scheme has a certain elegance in that the parser itself is simple and does not reflect any peculiarities of head-driven grammar. Only the simple meta-rules given above are in any way special. Furthermore, the performance properties of the chart parser are not compromised. On the other hand, this inactive chart parser cannot be extended to make it into an active chart parser in a straightforward manner as our second solution requires. This is the crux of the matter that this paper addresses.

Suppose that the verb has been located that will be the head of a verb phrase, but that it remains to identify one or two objects for it on the right. A standard active chart parser does this by introducing active edges at the vertex to the right of the verb which will build the first object if the material necessary for its construction is available, or comes to be available. As the construction procedes, active edges stretch further and further to the right until the construction is complete and the corresponding inactive edge is introduced. This works only because the phrase can be built incrementally starting from the left, that is, starting next to the phrase to which it must be adjacent. But this strategy is not open to the head-driven parser which must begin by locating, or constructing the head of the new phrase. The rest of the phrase must then be constructed outwards from the head. We are therefore forced to modify the standard approach.

We propose to enrich the notion of a chart so that instead of simply active and inactive edges, it contains five different types of object. Edges can be *active* and *inactive*, but they can also be *pending* or *current*. This gives four of the five kinds. The fifth we shall refer to simply as a *seek*. It is a record of the fact that phrases with a given label are being sought in a given region of the chart. A seek contains a label and also identifies a pair of vertices in the chart. It is irrelevant at the level of generality of this discussion whether we think of the seek as actually being located in, or on, one of the vertices, or being representable as a transition between them. A condition that the chart is required to maintain is that edges with the same label as that of a seek, both of whose end points lie within the region of the seek, must be current. Edges which are not so situated must be pending. The standard chart regime never calls for information in a chart to change, but that is not the case here. When a new seek is introduced, pending edges are modified to become current as necessary to maintain the above invariant.

The fundamental rule (Henry Thompson's term) of chart parsing is that an action is taken, possibly resulting in the introduction of new edges, whenever the introduction of a particular new edge brings the operative end of an active edge together, at the same vertex, with an end of an inactive edge. If the label on the inactive edge is of the kind that the active edge can consume, a new edge is introduced, possibly provoking new applications of the fundamental rule. The fundamental rule also applies in our enriched charts, but only to current edges – pending edges are ignored by it.

Suppose once again that a verb has been identified and that we are now concerned to find its sisters to the right. The verb can have been found only because there was a seek in existence for verbs covering the region in which it was found, and this, in its turn, will have come about because seeks were extant in that region for higher-level phrases, notably verb phrases. The objects we are now interested to locate must lie entirely in a region bounded on the left by the verb itself and, on the right, by the furthest right-hand end of a VP seek that includes the verb. Accordingly, a new seek is established for NP's in this region. The immediate effect of this will be to make current any pending edges in that region that are inactive and labeled NP, or active and labeled with a rule that forms NP's.

It remains to discuss how active edges, whether current or pending, are introduced in the first place. The simplest solution seems to be to do this just as it would be in an undirected, bottom-up parser. Whenever a current inactive edge is introduced, or a pending one becomes current, active edges are introduced, one for each rule that could accept the new item as head. However, these do not become current until a need for them emerges higher in the structure, and this is signaled by the introduction of a seek.

Consider, for example, the sentence *the dog saw the cat* and assume that *dog, saw,* and *cat* are nouns, *saw* is also a transitive verb, and that the grammar contains the following rules:

    rule(s(s(NP, VP)), [np(NP)], vp(VP), [ ]).
    rule(vp(vp(V, NP)), [ ], v(v), [np(NP)]).
    rule(np(np(D, N)), [det(D)], n(N), [ ]).

The sequence of events involved in parsing the sentence with a parser that follows a simple shift reduce regime, would be as follows:

1. *Add pending for det(det(the)) from 0 to 1, Left = [ ], Right = [ ]*
2. *Add pending for n(n(dog)) from 1 to 2, Left = [ ], Right = [ ]*
3. *Add edge for v(v(saw)) from 2 to 3, Left = [ ], Right = [ ]*
4. *Add edge for vp(vp(v(saw), _653)) from 2 to 3, Left = [ ], Right = [np(_653)]*
5. *Add edge for vp(vp(v(saw), _653)) from 2 to 3, Left = [ ], Right = [s(_653)]*
6. *Add pending for n(n(saw)) from 2 to 3, Left = [ ], Right = [ ]*
7. *Add pending for det(det(the)) from 3 to 4, Left = [ ], Right = [ ]*
8. *Add edge for n(n(cat)) from 4 to 5, Left = [ ], Right = [ ]*
9. *Add edge for np(np(_690,n(cat))) from 4 to 5, Left = [det(_690)], Right = [ ]*
10. *Add edge for det(det(the)) from 3 to 4, Left = [ ], Right = [ ]*
11. *Add edge for np(np(det(the),n(cat))) from 3 to 5, Rule = r4 / 1, Left = [ ], Right = [ ]*

12. *Add edge for vp(vp(v(saw),np(det(the),n(cat)))) from 2 to 5, Left = [ ], Right = [ ]*

13. *Add edge for s(s(_1507,vp(v(saw),np(det(the),n(cat))))) from 2 to 5, Left = [np(_1507)], Right = [ ]*

14. *Add edge for n(n(dog)) from 1 to 2, Left = [ ], Right = [ ]*

15. *Add edge for np(np(_2014,n(dog))) from 1 to 2, Left = [det(_2014)], Right = [ ]*

16. *Add edge for det(det(the)) from 0 to 1, Left = [ ], Right = [ ]*

17. *Add edge for np(np(det(the),n(dog))) from 0 to 2, Left = [ ], Right = [ ]*

18. *Add edge for s(s(np(det(the),n(dog)),vp(v(saw),np(det(the),n(cat))))) from 0 to 5, Left = [ ], Right = [ ]*

Result = [s(s(np(det(the),n(dog)),vp(v(saw),np(det(the),n(cat)))))].

We write *add edge ...* when the edge being added is current. Notice that the edge for the word *saw*, construed as a verb, is initially introduced as current, because the goal is to find a sentence and a seek is therefore extant for S, VP, and V, covering the whole string. The N edge for *saw*, however, is pending. In step 4, the active edge is introduced that will consume the object of *saw* when it is found. This introduces a seek for NP and N between vertex 3 and the end of the sentence. For this reason, when *cat* is introduced in step 8, it is as a current edge. Notice, however, the *the*, in step 7, is introduced as pending, because it is not the head of a NP. However, the introduction of the active NP edge in step 9 causes the edge for *the* to be made current, and this is what happens in step 10. The active S edge in step 13 activates the search for an NP before the verb so that all the remaining edges are introduced as current. At the end of the process all pending edges have been made current except the one corresponding to the nominal interpretation of *saw*.

The Prolog code that implements this strategy is considerably more complicated than that for the techniques discussed earlier, and I have therefore not included it.

I believe that the strategy I have outlined is the natural one for anyone to adopt who is determined to work with a head-driven active chart parser. However, it is entirely unclear that the advantages that it offers over the simple undirected chart parser are worth its considerable added expense in complexity. Notice that, if one of the other nouns in the sentence just considered also had a verbal interpretation, the search for noun phrases would have been active everywhere. The longer the sentence, and therefore the more pressing the need for high performance, the more active regions there would be in the string and the more nearly the process as a whole would approximate that of the undirected technique. This should not, of course, be taken as an indictment of head-driven parsing, which is interesting for reasons having nothing to do with performance. It does, however, suggest that the temptation to claim that it is also a natural source of efficiency should be resisted.

Appendix A – A Parser-Generator for Head-Driven Grammar

This is a simple head-driven recursive-descent parser. There is a distinction between the top level **parse** predicate and the **syntax** predicate to eliminate inessential arguments to the top level call, and also because the program can, with only minor modifications in syntax, be used as a generator. The predicate head is assumed to be defined as part of the grammar. It is true of a pair of grammatical labels if the second can be the head (of the head, of the head...) of the first. Having hypothesized the label of the eventual lexical head of a phrase that will satisfy the current goal, **syntax** calls **range** to find a word in the string with that label. If such a word is found, its position in the string will be given by the **HRange** (head range) difference list and it must, in any case, lie within the range of the string given by **Maxl** and **Maxr**. The **build** predicate constructs phrases with the given putative head so long as their labels stand in the **head** relation to the goal.

```
/*********************************************************************
* parse(String, Result)                                           *
*                                                                 *
* String is a list of words                                       *
* Struct is the structure (nondeterministically) returned if the parse *
* succeeds                                                        *
*********************************************************************/
parse(String, Struct)
syntax(String/[ ]/Struct, String/[ ]).
/*********************************************************************
* syntax((L/R/Goal, Maxl/Maxr)                                    *
*                                                                 *
* G is the Goal for the parser                                    *
* L/R is a DL giving the bounds of the phrase satisfying the goal *
* Maxl/Maxr gives the string bounds for the current search.       *
*                                                                 *
*********************************************************************/


syntax(Range/Goal, Max) :-
    head(Goal, Head)                % Find lexical head for Goal
    range(HRange/Head, Max),        % Associate Head with actual
                                    % word and string position.
    build(Range/Goal, HRange/Head, Max). % Build bottom up based on Head.


/*********************************************************************
* range((L/R)/Head, MaxL/MaxR)                                    *
*                                                                 *
* True of (1) position L/R in the string                          *
*         (3) with grammatical description Head                   *
*         (4) somewhere in the string range MaxL/MaxR (parsing)   *
*********************************************************************/
%
% Whole maximum range explored.
% =============================
range(_, X/X) :- !, fail.
```

```
%
% Next word in maximum range is the required head.
% ================================================
```

```
range(L/R/Head, L/_) :- dict(L/R, Head).
%
% Try again one place to the right.
% ================================
range(Head, [H|T]/MaxR) :-
  range(Head, T/MaxR).
```

```
/***********************************************************************
* build\((GL/GR)/Goal, (HL/HR)/Head, MaxL/MaxR)                       *
*                                                                     *
* Build phrases bottom up based on the Head located in the string at  *
* HL/HR. The location of the phrase found will be GL/GR and it must    *
* fall in the range MaxL/MaxR.                                        *
***********************************************************************/
build(X, X, _).                              % Current head is result.
build(GL/GR/Goal, HL/HR/Head, MaxL/MaxR) :- % Find rule matching Head
  rr(Lhs, Left, Head, Right), head(Goal, Lhs).
  build_left(Left, LL/HL, MaxL/HL)           % Check left daughters
  build_right(Right, HR/RR, HR/MaxR)         % and right daughters.
  build(GL/GR/Goal, LL/RR/Lhs, MaxL/MaxR).% Try building further on that
build_left([ ], X/X, _). build_left([H|T], L/R, MaxL/MaxR) :-
  syntax(HL/R/H, MaxL/MaxR),
  build_left(T, L/HL, MaxL/HL). build_right([ ], X/X, _).
build_right([H|T], L/R, MaxL/MaxR) :-
  syntax(L/HR/H, MaxL/MaxR),
  build_right(T, HR/R, HR/MaxR).
```

Appendix B – A Simple Inactive Chart Parser

This is a chart version of a nondeterministic shift-reduce parser. Vertices of the chart are constructed from left to right, one on each recursive call to **parse/3**. A vertex is a list of edges headed by a number which is provided for convenience in printing. An edge takes the form [**label, next-vertex**]. The predicate **build_edge** is given a word and its successor vertex and returns a completed vertex. It succeeds once for each entry that the word has in the dictionary and, for each one, calls **build_edge1**. This can succeed in three ways, all of which are collected into the list of edges contributing to the current vertex by virtue of the **setof** construction. The three possibilities are (1) The word's lexical entry itself labels an edge; (2) A unary rule applies to the entry, and its left-hand side labels an edge, and (3) A binary rule matches the entry and an entry in the next vertex (**member([Label, Next1], Next)**). Each new label is passed to **build-edge1** to be processed in the same manner as the original lexical entry.

```
parse(String, Result) :-
   parse(String, [0], Result}.

parse([ ], V, V).
parse([Word|Rest], [N|Next], Vertex) :-
   setof(Edge, build_edge(Word, [N|Next], Edge), V),
   M is N+1,                            % Next vertex number
   parse(Rest, [M|V], Vertex)           % [M|V] is the vertex

build_edge(Word, Next, Edge) :-
   dict(Word, Entry),                   % Dictionary lookup
   build_edge1(Entry, Next, Edge).

build_edge1(Entry, Next, [Entry, Next]).   % Shift.
build_edge1(Entry, Next, Edge) :-          % Reduce one item
   rule(Lhs, Entry),
   build_edge1(Lhs, Next, Edge).
build_edge1(Entry, [N|Next], Edge) :-      % Reduce two items
   member([Label, Next1], Next),
   rule(Lhs, Label, Entry),
   build_edge1(Lhs, Next1, Edge).
```

## 32

Machines and People in Translation

It is useful to distinguish a narrower and a wider use for the term "machine translation." The narrow sense is the more usual one. In this sense, the term refers to a batch process in which a text is given over to a machine from which, some time later, a result is collected which we think of as the output of the machine translation process. When we use the term in the wider sense, it includes all the process required to obtain final translation output on paper. In particular, the wider usage allows for the possibility of an interactive process involving people and machines.

Machine translation, narrowly conceived, is not appropriate for achieving engineering objectives. Machine translation, narrowly conceived, provides an extremely rich framework within which to conduct research on theoretical and computational linguistics, on cognitive modeling and, indeed, a variety of scientific problems. I believe that it provides the best view we can get of human cognitive performance, without introducing a perceptual component. When we learn more about vision, or other perceptual modalities, this situation may change. Machine translation, narrowly conceived, requires a solution to be found to almost every imaginable linguistic problem, and the solutions must be coherent with one another, so that it is a very demanding framework in which to work.

During the last twenty years – the period we are focusing on – there have been essentially no advances in the field of linguistics of sufficient size or significance as to affect our ability to build working machine translation systems. We remain today at essentially the same place we were in at the time when the ALPAC report was written. Furthermore, I doubt whether many professional linguists would be disposed to contest this. If this claim is right, then we have no reason to expect to be able to build significantly better machine translation systems today than we could then. This is construing the term narrowly. But, if we construe the term widely, we can hope to do better, thanks to improvements that have occurred in computer science and related fields because, while it is clear that fully automatic machine translation can only be as successful as the linguistic theory on which it is based, semi-automatic methods rest on a much wider set of factors. In the wide conception, the problem is not so much to build a machine that can translate as to bring about as good an impedance match as possible between man and machine when they are working jointly on translation.

Seeking this impedance match brings up a great many important questions, few of which have been addressed. They are not questions of morphological analysis, of building chart parsers, or transfer components and pivot languages. They are a new set of problems including such questions as how best to involve monolingual people in the course of the total translation process – how to use people that know a lot about the subject of the text being translated, but only one of the languages involved. How can we make a system which, when faced with ambiguities or vague formulations, knows how to present questions to a person in a natural way so as to get them resolved? It should be possible to put the questions in the same kind of language that one person would naturally use, and not the one used inside the system. How can we provide to a translator, or to a person who is collaborating with a machine on translation, access method to the linguistic and other information that will make the job easier? How, for example, can we best give him access to other translations that have been made with the same kind of technical terminology as in the current document? How can we give him access to the encyclopedic information about the subject matter of documents? What can we do to put him in touch with other people that could provide assistance of one kind or another? What can we do to insure that, once he has negotiated with the machine over the proper rendering of a particular technical phrase, that he will not have to repeat that negotiation when the same phrase crops up again? In what ways can we benefit from situations in which the same document has to be translated into several languages? In the EEC, it frequently happens that a document has to be translated into eight languages, but I have yet to hear the suggestion that the French translation might profitably be taken into account when preparing the German version. Might we not at least provide more intelligent text editing facilities to translators so that they could call for every instance of the word "kid" to be replaced by "child", and automatically have "kids" to be replaced by "children"?

Above all, everything that the human collaborator is called upon to do must be such as to honor his sense of professionalism and his intelligence. We must by all means never put a professional translator in the position of clearing up after an incompetent machine day after day, because, if we do that, we will rapidly achieve the situation where the number of professional translators, already very small, is reduced even further.

## 33

Semantic Abstraction and Anaphora

WITH MARK JOHNSON

Abstract

This paper describes a way of expressing syntactic rules that associate semantic formulae with strings, but in a manner that is independent of the syntactic details of these formulae. In particular we show how the same rules construct predicate argument formulae in the style of Montague grammar (Thomason 1974), representations reminiscent of situation semantics (Barwise and Perry 1983) and of the event logic of Davidson (1967), or representations inspired by the discourse representations proposed by Kamp (1981). The idea is that semantic representations are specified indirectly using semantic construction operators, which enforce an abstraction barrier between the grammar and the semantic representations themselves. First we present a simple grammar which is compatible with the three different sets of constructors for the three formalisms. We then extend the grammar to provide one treatment that accounts for quantifier raising in the three different semantic formalisms.

Grammars specifying the relationship between strings and semantic representations often have details of these representations embedded in them. We show how grammar rules can be written in a form which, by abstracting away from details of the semantic representation, acquires greater modularity and hence theoretical perspicuity and practical robustness. In particular, we believe that the approach helps clarify the relationship between apparently disparate theories of semantic representation.[1] The basis of our proposal is that each grammatical rule should contain, or be paired with, an expression written in terms of semantic construction operators. Different operations can be associated with these operators and, depending on the set in force at a given time, the effect of interpreting the expression will be to construct a representation in one semantic formalism or another. The set of operators contains members corresponding to such notions as *composition, conjunction,* etc. The set is small and independent of the semantic formalism. The operations are associated with the operators independently of the grammar and they determine the form of the semantic representation.

---

[1] The kind of separation between the grammar and the details of the semantic representation proposed here also appears in the examples of Pereira and Shieber (1987) and in Lexical-Functional Grammar (see Fenstad 1987). Our use of different sets of semantic constructors with a single grammar is novel, as far as we are aware.

We present three different sets of semantic constructors here, which we have dubbed the *predicate-logic* , the *sets-of-infons* and the *discourse-representation* constructors. We begin by introducing the constructors used in this paper: no claims are made for their general sufficiency. Not all of the constructors are relevant to all semantic theories and those not needed for a particular one are given degenerate definitions. The simplest kind of construction operator is the identity function which maps every input i onto just one output, namely i.

The operators are the following:

external(S, EF) relates a semantic representation S and an external form EF, e.g. a representation that constitutes the parser's output. The internal and external forms are distinguished because the (internal) representation S will, in general, contain information that plays a role in the process of analyzing a sentence (e.g. for anaphora tracking) but that is not part of the logical form (EF) of the sentence as a whole.

atom(S, Prop) specifies that the content of the (internal) semantic representation, S, is the atomic proposition *Prop*. This is used to construct the semantic values for lexical entries, for example.

conjoin(S1, S2, S12) relates three semantic representations. It specifics that the content of $S12$ is constructed by conjoining $S1$ and $S2$. This operator occurs crucially in the semantics of indefinite determiners.

new_index(S, I) specifies that the content of S is I, a referential index for a non-anaphoric NP. The form of a referential index is defined by the particular semantic theory.

accessible_index(S, I) specifies that the content of S is a referential index I of some noun phrase that is a potential antecedent of an anaphor. Constraints on accessible indices are defined by the particular semantic theory.

While the primitives discussed in this paper have relatively simple definitions, in other more elaborate theories they may involve nontrivial computation. For example, the *compose* primitive might impose certain discourse consistency requirements arising from a more restrictive theory of discourse structure than those described here.

A key insight of the Discourse Representation and Situation Semantics accounts, but originating with Karttunen (1976), is that anaphoric and quantificational domains coincide. Thus, in (1), *it* can be co-indexed with *a donkey* only if *a donkey* is interpreted as having wide scope.

(1)   Every man kicked a donkey. It developed blue bumps.

The relationship between these sentences is one of (semantic) *precedence* , and we call the operator that relates the corresponding semantic representations *compose*:

compose(S1, S2, S12) specifies that the information in the representation $S12$ is the information in $S1$ followed by the information in $S2$. Compose defines an ordering of semantic operations that particular semantic theories may or may not be sensitive to. (In this paper, the Montague constructors are not sensitive to this ordering, while the other two types of semantic representations are.)

When *a donkey* is interpreted as having narrow scope with respect to *every man* in (1), the reference marker introduced by a donkey is located in a context subordinate to the sentence as a whole, and hence not accessible to anaphors in the following discourse. To provide for this, we introduce the following operator:

subordinate(S,SubName,Sub) specifies that *S* contains an anaphorically and quantificationally subordinate representation *Sub*, which has the "name" *SubName*. The *SubName* would be distinguished from *Sub* in non-extensional theories of meaning, where a meaning is distinguished from its propositional content (say), as in the sets-of-infons representation described below.

We turn now to the grammar without quantifier-raising. We formulate both the grammar and the semantic constructors in pure Prolog (exploiting the syntactic sugar of *Definite Clause Grammar* (Pereira and Shieber 1987, pp. 70–79) because it is expressive enough for our purposes and is widely used in work of this kind (see, *inter alia* Colmerauer 1982, Abramson and Dahl 1989, and McCord 1986.).

33.1   A Grammar using Semantic Constructors

The grammar generates simple transitive clauses and subject-relative clauses that do not involve long-distance dependencies. It is based on the Montague-style grammars presented in Chapter 4 of Pereira and Shieber (1987), and the treatments of agreement, Wh-dependencies, etc., presented there could also be incorporated without difficulty.

```
/******************************************************************
 * Operators:                                                     *
 *    ^    for lambda abstracts,                                  *
 *    --> for implication.                                        *
 ******************************************************************/
:- op(950, xfy, ^).

:- op(300, xfx, -->).

parse(String,ExtSem) :- external(IntSem,ExtSem), s(IntSem,String,[]).


/******************************************************************
 * The grammar                                                    *
 ******************************************************************/

s(S) --> np(VP^S), vp(VP).
np(NP) --> det(N1^NP), n1(N1).
n1(N) --> n(N).
n1(X^S) --> n(X^S1), rc (X^S2), {conjoin (S1,S2,S)}.
vp(X^S) --> v(X^VP), np(VP^S)
rc(VP) --> [that], vp(VP).
```

```
v(X^Y^S) --> [Verb], {verb(Verb,X^Y^Pred), atom(Pred,S)}.
n(X^S) --> [Noun], {noun(Noun,X^Pred),new_index (X,S1), atom(Pred,S2),
            compose(S1,S2,S)}.
det((X^Hes)^(X^Scope)^S) --> [Det], {determiner(Det, Res^Scope^S)}.
np((X^S1)^S) --> [Pronoun], {pronoun(Pronoun), accessible_index(X,S2),
            compose(S1,S2,S)}.


/*********************************************************************
 * The lexicon                                                      *
 *********************************************************************/

pronoun(he).
pronoun(she).
pronoun(him).
pronoun(her).
pronoun(iL).

verb(likes, X^Y^likes(X,Y)).
verb(saw, X^Y^see(X,Y)).
verb(beats, X^Y^beat(X,Y)).
verb (owns, X^Y^own (X,Y).

noun(woman, X^woman(X)).
noun(man, X^man(X)).
noun(donkey, X^donkey(X)).

determiner(a,Res^Scope^S) :- conjoin(Res,Scope,S).
determiner(every,Res0^Scope^S) :- compose(S1, S2, S),
                                  subordinate(Res, ResName, S1),
                                  compose(Res0, Res1, Res),
                                  subordinate(Scope, ScopeName, Res1),
                                  atom(ResName --> ScopeName, S2).
```

Most of the grammar should be familiar, even if it is somewhat more pedantically expressed than is usual. Following Pereira and Shieber (who were in turn inspired by Montague), VP and N meanings are represented by terms of the form X^S, where X represents a referential index and S represents an S meaning. NP meanings are represented by terms of the form VP^S (or equivalently, (X^S0)^S), where VP represents a VP meaning, X a referential index, and S and S1 represent S meanings. All manipulation of semantic values is performed by constructor primitives, rather than by explicit construction of terms. For example, the N1 production that introduces relative clauses invokes `conjoin` explicitly to conjoin the semantic values of the N and the relative clause to yield the semantic value of the N1. The sharing of the referential index X between the N and the VP is performed in the grammar alone, since it is a syntactic rather than semantic property of the construction.

The semantic component of the production that introduces lexical nouns has two parts. S0 represents the atomic predicate `Pred` associated with the lexical meaning of the noun. S2 represents the fact that X is a (possibly new) referential index. The component S of the semantic value associated with the noun contains all of the information in S0 and S2.

The production introducing (lexical) pronouns requires that the referential index X of the pronoun be accessible in S0, and specifies that the S component is the composition of S0 and the S0 component of the VP meaning. (Recall that the semantic representations of pronouns, like all NP's, are terms of the form VP^S, so the S0 is a component of the meaning of the VP or V phrase that this pronoun is an argument of.)

Undoubtedly the most complex component of the grammar is the lexical entry for *every*. Because the structure of the lexical entries for all anaphoric scope-inducing quantifiers will be similar to the entry for *every*, we explain it in some detail.

The quantification induced by the determiner *every* is described in terms of the determiner's *restriction*, which defines the entities that the quantification ranges over, and its *scope*, the component of the expression quantified over. (2) indicates the components of the utterance corresponding to the restriction and the scope of the quantifier *every* in the absence of quantifier-raising.

(2)   Every man that saw a donkey kicked it.
                     Restrictor   Scope

The grammars presented here identify the restrictor and the scope of a determiner in the syntax; e.g. quantifier-raising arises from the grammar permitting multiple assignments of components of the utterance to the restrictions and scopes of the determiners of that utterance.

The semantic value associated with the lexical entry for a determiner in the grammars presented here is a term of the form *Res^Scope^Sentence*, where *Res* is the semantic value associated with the restrictor and *Scope* is the semantic value associated with the scope. A grammar directly constructing predicate-logic style semantic representations would assign the lexical entry in (3) to the determiner *every*, where '$\Rightarrow$' is interpreted as the implication operator in semantic representations (see Pereira and Shieber 1987).

(3)   *determiner(every, Res^Scope^(Res$\Rightarrow$Scope))*.

This lexical entry does not suffice for our purposes, since it provides no information about the relative anaphoric scope relationships between the restrictor, the scope, and that portion of the utterance external to the quantificational expression as a whole.

Anaphors in opaque quantificational expressions can refer to entities superordinate to the quantificational expression, but in general anaphors outside of an opaque quantificational expression cannot refer to entities introduced in either the restriction or scope of the quantificational expression.[2] Anaphors in the scope of an opaque quantificational expression can refer to entities introduced in the restriction of that expression (e.g. as

---

[2]There are exceptions to this: for example, anaphors can refer to proper names introduced in the restrictor or scope of opaque determiners. Within the framework described below, this can be treated by adding a new semantic construction operator `add_top_level`, which adds a referential index to the most superordinate level.

in (3) above), but anaphors in the restriction cannot refer to entities introduced in the scope.

The `compose` and `subordinate` predicates in the lexical entry for *every* in the grammar presented above express subordination relationships that describe the behavior of opaque determiners. The semantic representation `S` is the composition of `S1` and `S2`, where `S2` is the semantic atom `ResName⇒ScopeName`. `Res` is subordinate to `S1`, and is itself the composition of `Res0` and `Res1`, where `Res0` is the semantic representation of the restrictor. `Scope` is subordinate to `Res1`, and is the semantic representation of the scope. The diagram in Figure 1 sketches the relationship between the various semantic entities mentioned in the lexical entry for *every*. Subordination relationships are depicted by vertical lines (the name of the subordinate space is written alongside the line), and composition relationships are indicated by V-shaped diagonals.

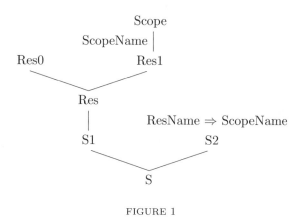

FIGURE 1

33.2   The Predicate-Logic Constructors

These constructors build a *predicate-logic* type of semantic representation in a fairly transparent fashion. Pronouns are treated as free variables, there are no constraints on their distribution, and anaphoric binding is not treated. Thus the definitions of the constructors `new_index`, `accessible_index`, `compose` and `subordinate` have degenerate definitions.

A property is identical with the term representing it:

```
atom(Prop, Prop).
```

The conjunction of `P` and `Q` is represented by the term `P&Q`.

```
conjoin(P,P,P&Q).
```

There are no constraints on new indices.

```
new_index(_,_).
```

There are no constraints on accessible indices.

```
accessible_index(_,_).
```

Sequencing is unimportant.

    compose(P,P,P).

A Subordinate space can be introduced freely.

    subordinate (_,Sub,Sub).

Internal and external forms are identical.

    external(P,P).

The grammar described above and the predicate-logic constructors yield analyses such as the following:

    ?- p([a, man, owns, a, donkey], S).
    S = man(X)&donkey(Y)&own(X,Y)
    ?- p([every,man,that,owns,a,donkey,beats, it],S).
    S = (man(X)&donkey(Y)&own(X,Y)) ⇒ beat(X,Z)

Roughly this latter form might be interpreted as: if X is a man and Y is a donkey and X owns Y, then there is a Z such that X beats Z.

33.3   The *Sets-of-Infons* Constructors

The constructors for the *sets-of-infons* and for the *discourse-representation* both constrain anaphora by requiring that the referential indices provided by the accessible_index constructor be indices that were introduced by new_index in some earlier representation (where precedence is defined by the compose constructor). This entails that the internal form of these semantic representations encode information about preceding representations. Both constructors thread this information using the difference-list technique described in Johnson and Klein (1986).

The primitive element of the *sets-of-infons* representation is inspired by the *infons* of Situation Semantics (Barwise and Perry 1983). We represent an infon as a term of the form Sit:P, which means that P is true in the situation Sit. For example, Kim's sleeping in situation s0 is represented by s0:sleep(kim). For simplicity arbitrarily named constants (like the *gensyms* of Lisp) are used as the names of situations in this representation: this has the disadvantage that the definitions of the external and subordinate constructors are not declaratively specified.[3]

The internal form of a *sets-of-infons* representation has three components. We represent them in Prolog with a term of the form @(Sits, InfonsIn, InfonsOut). The first is a stack whose top element is the situation currently being defined, and whose other elements are the situations superordinate to this one (as defined by the subordinate constructor). The second component is the set of all infons introduced in representations preceding this one. The infons in this list associated with the current or a superordinate situation provide the information needed for the accessible_index constructor. The third component of the representation is the set of infons introduced in preceding representations with the addition of any infons added to the representation by the semantic representation constructor. In describing the term @(Sits, InfonsIn, InfonsOut), we use the names InfonsIn and InfonsOut to stress the fact that they constitute a difference list.

---

[3]All that is required is that there is an infinite stock of situation names, so e.g. integers could have been used as situation names at the expense of a slight complication of the representation's data structures.

```
:- op( 900, xfx, : ).
atom(P, @([Sit|_],Is,[(Sit:P)|Is])).
compose(@(Ss,IOs,I1s), @(Ss,I1s,I2s), @(Ss,IOs,I2s)).
conjoin(I1, I2, I12) :- compose(I1, I2, I12).
subordinate(@([Sit|Sits],IOs,I1s), Sit, @(Sits, IOs, I1s)) :- gensym(Sit).
new_index(Index,S) :- atom(i(Index),S).
accessible_index(Index,@(Ss,Is,Is)) :- member(Sit:i(Index),Is),member(Sit,Ss).
external(@([Sit], [ ], Is), Sit:Is) :- gensym(Sit).
```

The atom constructor introduces a new atomic proposition P as an infon Sit:P, where Sit is the situation currently being constructed. Notice that InfonsOut is the same as InfonsIn but for the addition of (Sit:P).

The compose constructor threads the difference list of infons through both of the representations, so the composed representation contains all of the infons added to the sets of infons composed. The conjoin constructor is equivalent to the compose constructor.

The subordinate constructor introduces a new subordinate representation by pushing a new situation name Sit on to the list of (now superordinate) situations. The difference list of infons is threaded through the subordinate representation so that any infons added to it will appear in the superordinate representation as well.

The new_index constructor adds an atom of the form i(Index) to the representation S: no constraints are placed on Index.

The accessible_index[4] constructor is satisfied for a referential index Index if Index was introduced by new_index to a preceding non-subordinate representation, i.e. if the context contains an infon Sit:i(Index), where Sit is the current or a superordinate situation name.

The external(Internal, External) predicate initializes Internal to have no superordinate situations and no preceding context, and returns the list of infons associated with this Internal representation as its external form.

When these constructors are used with the grammar defined above, the following analyses are obtained:

```
?- p([a,man,owns,a,donkey],S).
S = s0:[S0:own(X,Y),s0:i(Y),s0:donkey(Y),S0:i(X),s0:man(X)]
```

This can be paraphrased as: Situation $s0$ contains individuals X and Y; in $s0$ X is a man, Y is a donkey and X owns Y.

```
?- p([every,man,owns,a,donkey],S).
S = s0:[S0:s1⇒s2,S2:own(X,Y),s2:i(Y),s2:donkey(Y),s1:i(X),S1:man(X)]
```

This can be paraphrased as: Situation $s0$ contains the fact that all situations of type $s1$ are also situations of type $s2$. A situation is of type $s1$ if it contains individuals X and Y, and X is a man and Y is a donkey. A situation is of type $s2$ if X owns Y.

```
?- p([every,man,that,owns,a,donkey,beats,it],S).
S = s0:[s0:s1 ⇒ s2,s2:beat(X,Y),s1:own(X,Y),s1:i(Y),s1:donkey(Y),
       s1:i(X),s1:man(X)]
```

---

[4]The predicate member used here, and elsewhere in this paper, has its standard logical definition: viz: member(X, [X | _]). member(X, [_, L]) :- member(X, L). If this definition is used with the grammars and constructors given in this paper, the SLD selection rule of Prolog may lead to non-termination. It is in general necessary to delay the evaluation of the member predicate until its second argument is instantiated, which can be done using the freeze primitive of Prolog II.

This can be paraphrased as: Situation $s0$ contains the fact that all situations of type $s1$ are also situations of type $s2$. A situation is of type $s1$ if it contains individuals X and Y, X is a man, Y is a donkey and X owns Y. A situation is of type $s2$ if X beats Y.[5]

33.4   The Discourse-Representation Constructors

The representations built by these constructors are inspired by the "box representations" of Kamp's (1981) Discourse Representation Theory. A discourse representation "box" is represented by the list of items that constitute its contents. A representation is a difference-pair of the lists of the representations of the currently open boxes (i.e. the current box and all superordinate boxes), as in Johnson and Klein (1986). In Prolog, we use the binary '−' operator to separate the two members of the pair.

```
atom(P, [B|Bs]-[[P|B]|Bs]).
compose(B0s-B1s, B1s-B2s, B0s-B2s).
conjoin(P1, P2, P) :- compose(P1, P2, P).
subordinate([[ ]|B0s]-[B|B1s], B, B0s-B1s).
new_index(Index, C) :- atom(i(Index), C).
accessible_index(Index, Bs-Bs) :- member(B,Bs), member(i(Index),B).
external([[ ]]-[S], S).
```

The `atom` constructor introduces a new atomic proposition P by adding it to the current box, i.e. the first element of the list of open boxes.

The `compose` constructor threads the difference list representing the open boxes through both compose representations of the items being composed in the same way that the compose constructor of the sets-of-infons representations does. The `conjoin` constructor is equivalent to the `compose` constructor.

The `subordinate` constructor introduces an empty subordinate box onto the list of currently open boxes. The "name" B of the subordinate box is the list of atoms it contains.

The `new_index` constructor adds an atom of the form `i(Index)` to the semantic representation: no constraints are placed on `Index` (as in the sets-of-infons representation).

The `accessible_index` constructor is satisfied by a referential index `Index` if `Index` is introduced by `new_index` in a preceding non-subordinate representation, i.e. if one of the superordinate boxes contains `i(Index)`.

The `external(Internal,External)` predicate initializes `Internal` to have exactly one open box (empty), and returns the contents of that box as its external form.

With these constructors, the parser yields the following semantic values for the test sentences.

```
?- p([a,man,owns,a,donkey],S).
S = [own(X,Y),donkey(Y),i(Y),man(X),i(X)]
```

This representation is true just in case there are two individuals X and Y, X is a man and Y is a donkey, and X owns Y.

---

[5]The grammar and the sets-of-infons constructors also generate an additional reading in which the man that owns the donkey beats himself; i.e. *it* is taken as anaphorically dependent on *every man*. Simple extensions to the grammar (e.g. requiring the index of a pronoun to differ from the index of all c-commanding NPs) or the semantics (e.g. requiring the gender of the pronoun to agree with its antecedent's gender) would rule out this spurious analysis.

```
?- ([every,man,owns,a,donkey],S).
S = [[man (X),i(X)] ⇒ [own(X,Y),donkey(Y),i(Y)]]
```

This representation is true just in case for all individuals X such that X is a man there is an individual Y such that Y is a donkey and X owns Y.

```
?- p([every,man,that,owns,a,donkey,beats,it],S).
S = [[own(X,Y),donkey(Y),i(Y),man(X),i(X)] ⇒ [beat(X,Y)]]
```

This representation is true just in case for all individuals X and Y such that X is a man and Y a donkey and X owns Y, it is also true that X beats Y.

33.5   Extending the Grammar to Handle Quantifier-Raising

In this section we sketch a syntactic account of quantifier-raising inspired by the implementation of Cooper-storage (Cooper 1983) presented in Pereira and Shieber (1987), to which we refer the reader for details. Each syntactic constituent is associated with a list of quantifiers that are "in storage" (this corresponds in an LF-movement account of quantifier-scope to being raised out of this constituent). Quantificational determiners add items to the quantifier store, and at S nodes, quantifiers are removed from the store and applied to the semantic representation. The quantifier-store of nodes at which quantifiers are neither added nor removed is the shuffle of the quantifier-stores of its children.[6] The grammar presented below is simply the grammar presented above with the addition of quantifier-storage. The lexical entries for this grammar are the same as the above, and so are not listed here.

```
q(String, Analysis) :- external(S, Analysis), s(S, [ ], String, [ ]).
s(S,Qs) ⇒ np(VP^S1,Qnp), vp(VP,Qvp), {shuffle(Qnp,Qvp,Q1s),
        apply_some(Q1s,S1,Qs,S)}.
np(NP,Qnp) ⇒ det(N1^NP,Qdet), n1(N1,Qn1), {append(Qdet,Qn1,Qnp)}.
n1(N,Qn) ⇒ n(N,Qn).
n1(X^S,Qn1) ⇒ n(X^S1,Qn), rc(X^S2,Qrc), {conjoin(S1,S2,S),
        shuffle(Qn,Qrc,Qn1)}.
vp(X^S,Qvp) ⇒ v(X^VP,Qv), np(VP^S,Qnp), {shuffle(Qv,Qnp,Qvp)}.
rc(X^S2,Qrc) ⇒ [that], vp(X^S1,Qvp), {apply_some(Qvp,S1,Qrc,S2)}.
np((X^S1)^S,[ ]) ⇒ [Pronoun],{pronoun(Pronoun), accessible_index(X,S2),
        compose(S1,S2,S)}.
v(X^Y^S,[ ]) ⇒ [Verb], {verb(Verb,X^Y^Pred), atom(Pred,S)}.
n(X^S, [ ]) ⇒ [Noun], {noun(Noun,X^Pred), compose(S1,S2,S),
        atom(Pred,S1), new_index(X,S2)}.
det((X^Res)^(X^Scope)^Scope, [Quant]) ⇒ [Det],
        {determiner(Det,Res^Quant)}.
```

The proposition shuffle(L1, L2, L3) is true just in case L3 is a list that can be seen as having been constructed in a sequence of steps in each of which the next available item is taken from either L1 or L2 and added to the end. So long as items remain on both L1 and L2, it is immaterial which of them supplies the next member of L3. What is important is that the

---

[6]Treating the quantifier-store as a syntactic feature can express many properties of LF-movement accounts, such as quantificational islandhood, etc., without the explicit construction of additional representations.

members of L1 and L2 should all be on L3, and in their original order. This relationship is assured by the following Prolog clauses:

```
shuffle([ ], [ ], [ ]).
shuffle([Q|Q1s],Q2s,[Q|Q3s]) :- shuffle(Q1s,Q2s,Q3s).
shuffle(Q1s,[Q|Q2s],[Q|Q3s]) :- shuffle(Q1s,Q2s,Q3s).
```

The first clause asserts that the proposition is true of three empty lists, and serves to terminate the recursion implicit in the other two. The second clause says that, if Q2s and Q3s are suffixes of a pair of lists to be shuffled, and that shuffling them gives Q1s, then the item that precedes Q1s in the final result can come from the first list, that is, it can be the item preceding Q1s. The third clause says that, alternatively, the item preceding Q1s can come from the second list.

The grammar also makes use of the predicate apply_some(Quants, OldSemanticValue, UnappliedQuants, NewSemanticValue) which is true if applying zero or more quantifiers from the beginning of the list *Quants* to a given *OldSemanticValue* yields *NewSemanticValue* and leaves a suffix of that list of quantifiers, namely *UnappliedQuants* still unapplied. It can be defined with the following pair of clauses, the first of which terminates the sequence of applications and the second of which applies the next quantifier in sequence.

```
apply_some(Qs,P,Qs,P).
apply_some([P^Qp|Qs],P,Q1s,P1) :- apply_some(Qs,Qp,Q1s,P1).
```

The new grammar can be used with the three different semantic constructors presented above. Using the Predicate-Logic constructors, it yields results like the following:

```
?- q([a,man,owns,a,donkey],S).
S = donkey(Y)&man(X)&own(X,Y);
S = man(X)&donkey(Y)&own(X,Y)
```

This example has two (semantically-equivalent) representations corresponding to the two scope possibilities for the two existentially quantified NPs.

```
?- q([every,man,owns,a,donkey],S).
S = donkey(Y)&man(X) ⇒ own(X,Y);
S = man(X) ⇒ (donkey(Y)&own(X,Y))
```

In this example the two non-equivalent representations correspond to the two different scope possibilities for the quantified NPs. These readings paraphrase as: There is a donkey *Y* and for each man *X*, *X* owns *Y*, and For each man *X* there is a donkey *Y* and *X* owns *Y*.

```
?- q([every,man,that,owns,a,donkey,beats,it],S).
S = donkey(Y)&(man(X)&own(X,Y)) ⇒ beat(X,Z);
S = (man(X)&donkey(Y)&own(X,Y)) ⇒ beat(X,Z)
```

In this example the two non-equivalent representations correspond to the two different scope possibilities for the quantified NPs. These readings paraphrase as: There is a donkey *Y* and for each man *X* such that *X* owns *Y* it is the case that *X* beats *Y*, and For each man *X* and donkey *Y* such that *X* owns *Y*, it is the case that *X* beats *Y*.

Using the sets-of-infons constructors, we get the following results:

```
?- q([every,man,owns,a,donkey],S).
```

```
S = s0:[s0:s1⇒s2,s2:own(X,Y),s1:i(X),s1:man(X),s0:i(Y),s0:donkey(Y)];
S = s0:[s0:s1⇒s2,s2:own(X,Y),s2:i(Y),s2:donkey(Y),s1:i(X),s1:man(X)]
```

The scope possibilities are indicated here by the situation in which the noun phrases are interpreted. The first reading displayed corresponds to the quantifier-raised interpretation, which paraphrases as: Situation *s0* contains the individual *Y*, the fact that *Y* is a donkey, and the fact that for all ways of making *s1* true, *s2* is also true, where *s1* contains the individual *X* and the fact that *X* is a man, and *s2* contains the fact that *X* owns *Y*. Since *Y* is in *s0*, under this reading it is a potential antecedent for anaphors in following sentences.

The second reading differs from the first in that the NP *a donkey* is interpreted in the subordinate situation *s1* instead of *s0*. As well as causing *a donkey* to be quantificationally subordinate to *every man*, this also makes *a donkey* unavailable as a potential antecedent for anaphors in following sentences. We can therefore account for the fact that under normal intonation *a donkey* is interpreted as having wide scope over *every man* in the following discourse fragment (4).

(4) Every man saw a donkey. It had a bushy tail.

We now consider one of the famous "donkey" sentences:

```
?- q([every,man,that,owns,a,donkey,beats,it],S).
S = s0:[s0:s1⇒s2,s2:beat(X,Y),s1:own(X,Y),s1:i(X),s1:man(X),s0:i(Y),
     s0:donkey(Y)];
S = s0:[s0:s1⇒s2,s2:beat(X,Y),s1:own(X,Y),s1:i(Y),s1:donkey(Y),
     s1:i(X),s1:man(X)]
```

The first reading displayed again corresponds to the quantifier-raised interpretation, which paraphrases as: Situation *s0* contains an individual *Y*, and the facts that *Y* is a donkey and that every way of making *s1* true also makes *s2* true, where *s1* contains the individual *X* and the facts that *X* is a man and *X* owns *Y*, and *s2* contains the fact that *X* beats *Y*.

Finally, the discourse-representation constructors yield the following:

```
?- q([every,man,owns,a,donkey],S).
S = [[i(X),man(X)] ⇒ [own(X,Y)],i(Y),donkey(Y)]
S = [[i(X),man(X)] ⇒ [own(X,Y),i(Y),donkey(Y)]]
```

These representations are direct notational variants of the two set-of-infons representations of this sentence given above. The truth conditions of the first reading correspond to the wide-scope interpretation of a donkey, and can be paraphrased as: There is a donkey *Y*, and for every man *X*, *X* owns *Y*.

```
?- q([every,man,that,owns,a,donkey,beats,it],S).
S = [[own(X,Y),i(X),man(X)] ⇒ [beat(X,Y)],i(Y),donkey(Y)];
S = [[own(X,Y),i(Y),donkey(Y),i(X),man(X)] ⇒ [beat(X,Y)]]
```

Again, these representations are direct notational variants of the two sets-of-infons representations of this sentence given above. The truth conditions of the first reading correspond to the wide-scope interpretation of a donkey, and can be paraphrased as: There is a donkey *Y*, and for every man *X* such that *X* owns *Y*, *X* beats *Y*. The same correlation between quantificational scope and anaphoric scope holds with these constructors, as expected.

Conclusion

We have worked out a scheme for computing the logical forms of sentences incrementally in the course of parsing them which we believe achieves an unprecedented level of abstraction of the semantic from the syntactic parts of the grammar. The very incrementality of the scheme might be used to argue against it. Given the prevalence of scope ambiguities, the interests of computational efficiency may be best served by a scheme that delays all semantic computation until the parsing is complete so as not to work unnecessarily on phrases that turn out not to be capable of incorporation in a complete analysis of the sentence. Hobbs and Shieber (1988) adopt such a scheme apparently on the grounds of greater perspicuity. In any case, the modifications that need to be made to our scheme are entirely trivial, requiring only the introduction of a modest amount of symbolic computation. Basically, the idea is to use operations which, instead of returning pieces of the final logical form incrementally and nondeterministically, return expressions that will exhibit this nondeterministic behavior when evaluated later. The later evaluation will, of course, be as specified by the definitions we have given. In short, we believe that the abstractions we have created effectively isolate the syntactic rules both from the corresponding semantic formalism and from the architecture of the system by which both of them will be interpreted.

Publications referenced

Abramson and Dahl 1969; Barwise and Perry 1983; Colmerauer 1982; Cooper 1983; Davidson 1967; Fenstad et al 1987 Hobbs and Shieber 1988; Johnson and Klein 1986 Kamp 1981; Karttunen 1976; McCord 1986; Pereira and Shieber 1987; Thomason 1974.

34

Computational Linguistics

The term "computational linguistics" is regularly given a variety of constructions, from very narrow to very broad. The broader reading covers any activity that links computers together with ordinary language. The narrower reading refers to scientific enterprise that shares with linguistics at large the aim of explaining the phenomenon of language but draws inspiration from computer science.

For those who hold the broad view, any primarily linguistic enterprise in which computers play an important role belongs to computational linguistics. Preeminent are enterprises in which the computer is a tool, serving in an unabashedly subservient capacity. Generally speaking, two computer applications are involved, one in which what we may refer to as "linguistic technology" is applied to some practical problem, and one in which computers are applied to problems that arise in the study of language itself.

Perhaps the most obvious, if not the most successful, attempt to apply linguistic technology, is in machine translation. As of this writing, the only clearly successful machine-translation systems are those that treat text in a language that is so constrained as to be arguably not a true natural language at all. Such a system translates Canadian weather reports between English and French, automatically rejecting some proportion as being in too rich a language for it to handle. Other systems are used to translate maintenance manuals that have been specially prepared in a contrived subset of a natural language. These successes are clearly no more to be belittled than they are to be heralded as presaging the imminent success of machine translation as a whole.

A second area of application for linguistic technology that has received much attention is so called natural-language "front ends" for database systems. Motivation for these efforts comes from three observations: (i) the potential subject matter of databases covers the whole range of human thought; consequently, (ii) the range of messages that the user of a database system may need to communicate to it is very large, and (iii) people who typically use these systems are influential and important, but they know little of formal language systems and are generally impatient with them. Great advantages are therefore thought to attach to designing systems that can interact in the common language of their users.

Compared with machine translation, it is more difficult to measure the success of these attempts to build database systems that talk the user's language. Undoubtedly, the part of the language that the best of them can use effectively is always a tiny subset of the total language. On the other hand, it is often claimed that users of computer systems that have even a severely impoverished natural language capability adapt to these systems rapidly, willingly, and almost imperceptibly. In the matter of language, people do not have very high expectations of machines, and are grateful for any help they can get. Nevertheless, the requirements placed on natural language front ends increases as the power and flexibility of other means of communications, such as those provided by graphic and window systems, grows. The designers of the "Q & A" system, which provides for interaction in ordinary language as an alternative to a more formal notation, report that users usually drift from the natural toward the more formal language as they gain experience.

The contribution that linguistic technology can make to information retrieval of the more classical variety is less equivocal. Generally speaking, the proportion of the burden that the technology has been expected to carry has been smaller. For the most part, a query is treated as a set, rather than a sequence, of words, so that there is no attempt to make the machine understand it in any serious sense. It is, or is treated as, a list of key terms, or it is a Boolean expression over such terms, and the object of the enterprise is to assess the relevance of individual documents to the query on the basis of how closely that query describes the vocabulary in them. Even at their best, these are anything but delicate tools, and there has been a continuing effort to improve them with appropriate infusions of linguistic technology.

There are two obvious moves that can be made, both having to do with normalizing essentially incidental differences in the way individual vocabulary items are used. First, it is possible to use one of several techniques of morphological analysis to reduce variation in the forms of words. Differences between singular and plural nouns, or between present and past tense verbs, are important for the role a word plays in a particular sentence, but are only a distraction if what we are interested in is the way the subject matter of a document as a whole is reflected in its vocabulary.

The second kind of normalization removes noise due to the essentially uninformative use of a given word in preference to another with the same meaning. The idea is to replace individual words in queries, and in the descriptions by which a system knows documents, by designators of synonym sets in a thesaurus rather than individual words. While these noise reduction tactics doubtless contribute something to the effectiveness of information retrieval systems, it seems that efforts invested in them rapidly reach the point of diminishing returns.

Morphological analysis and thesauri are more generally familiar today through a range of software products intended as aids to writers that are presently flooding the market. Good techniques for morphological analysis are essential in present-day spelling checkers and correctors if only to keep the size of the dictionary that must be stored within reasonable bounds. The need is more apparent when the language involved is more highly inflected, as in the case of French or, more strikingly, Finnish, or where it makes wholesale use of compounds written as a single word, as in Russian and most of the Germanic languages apart from English. A typical French verb has on the order of 30 forms and, if one counts cliticized forms like "digamelo", a Spanish form has a great many more. The need to store these explicitly is eliminated in most cases by the proper use of morphological analysis.

Still within the broad construction of computational linguistics is a range of applications of computer techniques to problems that arise within linguistics itself. These are similar to computer applications that one finds in physics, engineering, or accounting in the sense that they automate, and therefore simplify and accelerate jobs that would otherwise be done by other methods. A field worker is collecting data on a new language. He or she must organize files of texts, lexical entries, and sets of grammar rules in varying stages of development. The field worker wants to be able to search for examples of words, constructions, suffixes, and the like, and having the material and a few general-purpose programs on a computer obviously makes this more convenient. Until recently, literary scholars and linguistic field workers made heavy use of printed concordances prepared by computer, but the wider availability of personal computers has made interactive techniques more attractive.

A related field of endeavor in which even larger concordances have long been part of the stock in trade, is lexicography. Many of the best general purpose dictionaries either are more or less directly derived from a major historical dictionary such as the *Oxford English Dictionary*, the *French Littre*, or the recently completed *Trésor* de la *Langue Francaise*. The principal aim of these works is to record the first use of each word in the language, in each of its meanings. Traditionally, the work of creating such a dictionary starts with the compilation of a huge file of citations, generally collected by an army of dedicated amateur volunteers. Only a small proportion of these find their way into the eventual work. The job of assembling the entries requires an expert and a large table on which he or she plays an elaborate game of lexical solitaire with the slips. The compilers of the *Trésor* de la *Langue Francaise*, noting that dedicated amateur volunteers are in diminishing supply, used computers to collect citations from selected books and periodicals in French, of which the full text was prepared in machine-readable form especially for this purpose. Attempts have also been made to build computational replacements for the large table, but this has been considerably less successful if only because so much seems to turn on being able to hold a great deal in view at the same time.

On the borderline between the territories covered by the broad and the narrow constructions of the term "computational linguistics" are the uses the linguists make of computers to help verify the details of a grammar, or other closely reasoned piece of linguistic description. To the extent that much of linguistics, especially in the United States, is taking on a more formal character, the activity of writing a grammar takes on the character of constructing a computer program. In particular, it becomes an activity that is susceptible to innumerable errors that can only be eliminated by applying it to large numbers of examples. This is tedious and, like the construction of the grammar itself, it is prone to error. But, unlike the construction of the grammar, it is an activity much of which can readily be automated. Today, probably very few people would undertake to construct a formal grammar of even a modest part of a language without a program that could generate sentences from it in accordance with arbitrary specifications, and analyze strings of words to discover what, if any, structures it assigned to them. Grammar checking programs, specialized for the phonological and syntactic aspects of grammar, have been in routine use for 20 years or more, and they are now coming to have some currency among students of semantics.

In its narrow construction, "computational linguistics" refers to a field in which the computer plays a more essential role. It is not a tool in the usual sense of the term, and its job is not to alleviate tedium. But it is the generic computer – the computer as an abstract entity, rather than as a physical machine – that occupies this central position. Most computational linguists in fact work with real computers but, under the narrow construction, this is, strictly speaking, nonessential. According to this construction of the term, the computer is naturally of interest to a student of language because it is the only example, other than ourselves, of a semiotic engine. It is the only device that, clearly, unequivocally, and nontrivially, operates with symbols. Though there are many obvious differences between the uses that people and computers make of symbols, there is also much in common and therefore strong reason to hope that linguistics and computer science would have much to learn from each other.

Against this view, it has sometimes been argued that modern computers have been designed in accordance with certain basic ideas which, while they make for simplicity and economy, are essentially arbitrary choices among a potentially very large set of candidates. The machine that von Neumann envisaged, and that we all now use, was elegant in its simplicity and sequential in its operation. But there is no reason to suppose that the human mind, or its language-processing component, shares these characteristics.

This is a mistaken argument which comes from viewing the physical machines we work with every day, rather than the abstract machines that we can construct mathematically and that we can model inside the physical machines, as the objects of primary interest as models of human language processing. Perhaps the most remarkable thing about the digital computer is that, as far as we know, it can be used to compute absolutely anything that can be computed, given enough resources. If a machine of a different kind would naturally compute something in a manner which is not natural for this machine, one of the things that is nevertheless computable for it is what the other machine would do to carry out the original computation in its preferred way. More simply put, a general computing machine can simulate the operation of any other computing machine, general or specialized.

Having said this, it is important to recognize that there have been few, even among those whose primary allegiance is to computational linguistics as a pure science, who have dedicated themselves to the kind of program that this suggests. Until recently, for example, scant attention was given to the possibility that a considerable amount of parallel processing might be involved in the production and understanding of language. One possible way of accounting for this apparent oversight might be as follows: Since the inception of so called "generative linguistics" with Chomsky, great, and possibly unwarranted, importance has been accorded to what is referred to as the "productivity" of natural language, that is, the ability that people are presumed to have to produce and understand sentences that have never been used before. If this claim about the nature of language is taken seriously, it is easy to argue from it that there can be no upper bound on the number of sentences in a language, or on the length of a single sentence. Almost all of formal and computational linguistics has been informed by a perceived need to remain true to these beliefs. From this it follows that the complexity of the process of producing or understanding a sentence will be essentially that of a serial system, if any limit at all is placed on the amount of parallelism that the system as a whole is capable of.

While parallelism has not been a central focus of interest in computational linguistics, much of what has been done has, in fact, led to processing strategies that are essentially parallel. A prime example is the method of analyzing the syntactic structure of sentences referred to as "chart parsing". Like most parsing methods, this is a technique in which words are combined to form phrases according to rules supplied in a grammar, and phrases are combined into larger phrases, until complete sentences emerge. When a sentence is grammatically ambiguous, or contains ambiguous substrings, some of the phrases that are recognized may not be compatible with others, and some may play no role in the structure, or structures, eventually recognized covering the whole string. But, at least during the early stages of the process, these phrases are on an equal footing with all others. Now, the recognition of a larger phrase cannot be completed until all the smaller phrases that are part of it have been constructed. But, this is the only constraint that needs to be placed on the order in which work on the different parts of the sentence structure is conducted. The chart parser is designed to allow arbitrary orders in a serial implementation, and would naturally extend to allowing work on different phrases to go on simultaneously in a parallel machine.

In contrast to the view that computational linguists have been too much influenced by the nature of the machines that happen to be available to them, it is pointed out that language in fact has an ineluctably serial nature in that it is spoken and perceived linearly and, indeed, quite slowly, through time. The evidence suggests that the understanding process proceeds essentially in real time. In other words, enough of the understanding process keeps pace with the flow of words that little of the detailed history of what was said needs to be retained. Halfway through a long sentence, the actual words that occurred at the beginning of it may be forgotten without the understanding of the whole being compromised. This sort of observation has led to a reaction to such things as chart parsing in favor of so called "deterministic" methods of syntactic analysis. These methods never recognize a sentence as ambiguous, and their adherents claim that this is realistic because people almost never recognize ambiguities either. Each choice that must be made in the course of the analysis is considered carefully and, once made, cannot be retracted.

The increasingly easy access to fast and truly parallel machines has caused a new wave of excitement to spread through the community of computational linguists, even affecting some hitherto purely theoretical linguists. The movement goes by the name of *connectionism* and puts its faith in the possibility of building working models of large networks of neurons. Remarkably, the idea is growing that such networks may relieve linguists of much of the burden that they previously welcomed, because these neural models will be naturally imbued with the power to learn, so that the question of what form internal linguistic representations take will automatically be solved by them. Hard evidence to support these expectations has not yet been revealed, at least to this writer. Furthermore, they seem to fly in the face of the belief commonly held by generative linguists that linguistic processing in general, and the acquisition of language in particular, are handled by specialized mental mechanisms, possibly by a special part of the brain, and that the linguistic feats that small children show themselves to be capable of could not be achieved by general-purpose devices of whatever kind. Whatever the truth may be on this matter, the appeal to self-organizing networks of elementary neurons seems a curiously naive and primitive form of reductionism.

If computational linguistics, narrowly construed, is, in essence, theoretical linguistics inspired by computer science, then it is reasonable to ask what notions from computer science have been influential in it. One of these is compilation – the idea of *mapping* or *translating* information from one formalism to another. This is the process that computer programs usually undergo before the instructions that make them up are carried out. A text in Pascal, FORTRAN, or whatever, is automatically translated into another language – usually the native machine language of the computer – and it is this new text that then guides the operation of the machine. In a strictly formal sense, programming languages are usually equivalent to one another in that what can be stated in one can be stated in the other, though not necessarily with the same facility. But, for compilation to be possible, this is not necessary. It is enough that the expressive power of the target language should be at least that of the source language.

It is generally in the interest of the designers of computer languages that they should have as much expressive power as possible, and it is therefore not surprising that they all turn out to be essentially equivalent. Generative linguists, on the other hand, consider it to be in their interest to design formalisms with the minimal power adequate to their purposes. The reason is this: If the language in which a linguist wrote grammars had the full expressive power of a standard programming language, then it would embody no claims about the nature of human language. But, if it were weaker, then the fact that it was nevertheless equal to the task of linguistic description on a large scale would reflect something about language as a whole and not just the subject matter of the current text. This is a somewhat simplified version of the argument and, even more precisely stated, it is far from uncontroversial. But it will serve our immediate purposes in this form.

Now, in the 1950s and 1960s, the argument was made by Chomsky, Postal, and others, that natural languages could not be context-free, on the grounds that the number of rules involved would be unthinkably large, possibly even infinite. If the number were finite, but absurdly large, then it would be uninteresting to claim that the languages were context-free because the sets of essentially unrelated rules that a person would have to learn would be beyond all reasonable bounds. After an interval of almost 20 years, Gazdar has argued that natural languages are in fact context-free and that the grammars involved can be made manageable by expressing them in a different notation which can be shown to be equivalent to the original one, essentially through a process of compilation. If Gazdar's claim is true, it is interesting in that it places a limit on the expressive power of the language needed to describe the syntax of a natural language. But it is also interesting because it suggests that there are other generalizations about the nature of natural syntax encoded in the compilation rules that relate the new notation to the basic notion of context-free grammars. Presumably, the new notation and the associated compiler would not have the same beneficial effects for arbitrary context-free languages, but only for those having some yet to be investigated properties that natural languages apparently possess. However, the possibility of compilation relations among languages weakens any claim that one might be tempted to make about the psychological reality of particular rules being individually represented in the brain.

Perhaps a more striking example is to be found in recent work in computational phonology. For a long time, phonologists of widely differing theoretical persuasions have described the phenomena of interest to them by means of ordered lists of rewriting rules each of which applies to the output of the one above it in the list. Arguments among phonologists have made crucial reference to the rules, their relative order, and to characteristics that the string would have to have when it emerged from a given stage in the cascade. Differing measures of psychological reality were imputed to these things by the protagonists. Recently it has been shown that the information a rule expresses can be restated in almost all circumstances in the form of a particular kind of automaton called a *Finite-state transducer* . If the output of one finite-state transducer is the input to another one, then there is a way of automatically constructing a new transducer that is equivalent to the original pair, and which eliminates the intervening string altogether. If this operation is repeated enough times, it clearly has the effect of reducing the entire phonological description to a single transducer which is not related in any essential way to the original set of rules, and contains no reflex of any intermediate stages that might occur in the derivation of a word. Constructing this transducer is a compilation process which turns out to be crucial to building effective working models of the phonological process and which calls into question much of the argumentation that was based on particular members of the set of original rules.

It could still turn out that the expressive power of the rules was strictly less than that of the transducers, and the suggestions that this would make for the nature of the underlying reality are interesting. Suppose one were to argue that something like the transducer representation was necessary for efficient processing in people just as in computers, and that this therefore best reflected the internal representation of the processing information. How then could one account for the fact that the full expressive power of this representation scheme was apparently not used? One appealing possibility might be that the learning of such a system of information required a simpler and more concise initial representation related to the eventual one through a process of compilation. The question of how such a hypothesis might be verified must, unfortunately, be left as an exercise for the reader.

Something of the structure of computational linguistics has emerged from the above discussion. Generally speaking, its structure is parallel to that of theoretical linguistics. Language is generally studied at several different levels of abstraction. It makes contact with the physical world through the sounds that people utter when they talk, and through the objects and events in the world that they refer to in what they say. Unlike these things, the abstract models that linguists build to elucidate the nature of language are entirely discrete. When people discuss the words they use, they speak with confidence about this sound being the same or different from that one because language seems to require that the continuously varying stream of input that impinges on the ears be broken into discrete segments, and that each segment be assigned to one of a small number of classes called "phonemes". Phonemes are an abstraction belonging to linguistics, just over the border from the continuously varying outside word.

Phonemes are related through a more or less complex mapping onto small linguistic entities like words, or stems and endings. These entities fall in the purview of lexicology for their meanings, of morphology for the way in which they combine with one another, and of phonology for the relations they contract with strings of phonemes. We have already remarked how, with a view to making the relation between morphemes and phonemes computable, computational linguists have been led to restate traditional phonological rules in terms of finite-state transducers. Morphology also sometimes appeals to finite-state models, but here they seem rather less satisfactory. One difference between finite-state devices and more expressive models is the latter, as well as being able to cover a wider class of phenomena, also say more about each item they describe. In particular, while a finite-state morphological model would limit itself to distinguishing allowable from impossible sequences of prefixes, stems, and suffixes, a context-free model would also assign a structure to each allowable sequence, reflecting something about how it might be understood. A context-free model would say that the word "unknowable" had a structure that could be represented as (un(know able)) rather than, say ((un know) able) because it means "not knowable" rather than "capable of being unknown". Some words are ambiguous in this respect. For example, an "untieable knot" is either a knot that cannot be tied or a knot that can be untied. A finite-state model would have no way of reflecting this ambiguity.

To the extent that morphology is simply a matter of describing possible sequences of morphemes and assigning meaningful structures, it does not look very different from syntax, which attempts to solve these problems on the level of words, and it does not call for any special computational devices. However, there are at least two reasons why this may be too simple a view of morphology. One is that morphemes may be related to one another in ways other than by concatenation. For example, one might want to say that otherwise identical sentences that meant different things because of the intonational contour with which they were pronounced, contained different intonational morphemes, but that these morphemes were expressed simultaneously with a sequence of others. Tone and intonation play different roles in different languages and, in some, the argument that it can be used as part of the representation of morphemes is more cogent. More striking ways of combining morphemes are found in Semitic languages where one morpheme can be represented by the consonants in a word, another by the vowels, and a third by the pattern by which these are arranged. So, "kataba" and "kutiba" both have to do with the verb that means "to write", whose root is the consonant sequence "ktb", but whereas "kataba" is active, "kutiba" is passive. "Kattaba" is also active because it uses the same vowels, and it is based on the same root, and so has to do with writing. But the meaning in this case is "to cause to write", the difference being reflected systematically in the doubling of the middle consonant. Predictably, "kuttiba" is the perfect form of this verb. Examples of so called "nonconcatenative" morphology such as these have helped spur the development of so called "autosegmental" phonology and morphology in linguistics, and of generalizations of the model based on finite-state transducers in computational linguistics.

The second reason for not allowing the distinction between morphology and syntax to be lost has to do with the status that should be accorded to the notion of a word within linguistics. Psychologically speaking, words seem to be just as real as morphemes, and possibly a great deal more so. Ask someone the name of an object or how to say something, and you will get a word or a sequence of words – never a morpheme. To eliminate morphology would be to deny words any status. Furthermore, there may be internal evidence from within morphology for the distinctive status of the word, though this is not the place to pursue it in detail. According to one view, words are not formed by assembling entities of a basically different kind, namely morphemes; they are formed from other words. "Unthinkable" is not formed from "unthink" because, among other things, "unthink" is not a word. "Unthinkable" is formed from the word "thinkable". This clearly leads to a quite different view of the kinds of processes involved in producing and recognizing words that have only just begun to be explored.

Without doubt, the most thoroughly explored topic in computational linguistics has been syntax in general, and syntactic analysis, or *parsing* , in particular. This may be partly because there is a related area of concern to computer scientists who must provide for the syntactic analysis of programs in higher-level programming languages in order that they can be processed automatically. The parsing problem has well-defined boundaries and a rich mathematical structure.

For the most part, work on parsing has concentrated on discovering the structures that are assigned to sentences by what can broadly be characterized as phrase-structure grammars. With this term, I mean to capture the notion of grammars which describe sentences as recursive structures of phrases, and which describe phrases directly in terms of the words and other phrases that make them up. I mean to set these apart from grammatical theories like transformational grammar in which the status of a putative phrase is partially dependent on relations that it contracts with other putative phrases. In transformational grammar, the notion of a derivation plays a crucial role. It is a carefully controlled sequence of steps leading to the construction of a sentence or analysis of a sentence.

Context-free grammar is the canonical example of a phrase-structure grammar. In recent times, there has been a move to extend the power of context-free grammar so as to increase its expressive power and ability to capture appropriate generalizations, while preserving its character as a phrase-structure formalism and its desirable computational properties. More specifically, the new formalisms continue to use rules of the form

$$a \rightarrow b_1...b_k$$

to express that a phrase with the grammatical description a can consist of a sequence of words or phrases with the description $b_1...b_k$. The rule is context free in the sense that it makes no reference to the context in which the phrase meeting the description a occurs. If the a and $b_1...b_k$ are atomic, unanalyzable symbols, then the grammar as a whole is context-free in the classical sense. The newer formalisms allow them to be expressions, possibly involving variables, so that it would, for example, be possible to write a rule of the general form

Sentence → Subject Predicate

but where Subject and Predicate were expressions in some suitable formalism, and to include the requirement that the subject and the predicate should agree in person and number. This would probably be done by including variables in the Subject and Predicate expressions that must be instantiated to the person and number of the phrases. It is generally regarded as important that the formalism should preserve the property of monotonicity that context-free grammar has and which requires, in essence, that, a rule of the form $a \rightarrow b_1...b_k$ should allow descriptions $b_1...b_k$ to be computed from any description matching a, and that a should be computable from the set of descriptions matching to $b_1...b_k$. In other words, the rule should be usable impartially in generation or recognition.

The most notable extensions of context-free grammars that have these properties replace atomic symbols as descriptions with expressions involving variables, as we have said. It then uses an operation known as *unification* as the way in which the description given in a rule is compared with the descriptions of actual words and phrases. Two expressions can be unified if, by consistently replacing variables in them, one can obtain the same expression. Suppose that the grammatical description of the word "they" were [Pronoun, third-person, plural] and that the rule in the grammar contained the expression [Pronoun, x, y], where x and y are variables. The two expressions can clearly be made the same by replacing x with "third-person" and y with "plural". The grammatical description of the word "ran" might be [Verb, Past, x, y] where x and y represent the person and the number of the verb, but are variables in this case because the word "ran" is uncommitted as to person and number. Suppose now that the grammar contained a rule of somewhat the following form

[Sentence] → [Pronoun x y] [Verb w x y]

This could be applied to the sequence "they ran", instantiating w to "Past", x to "third-person", and y to "plural".

Unification is a considerably more interesting and powerful operation than can be made plain in this brief exposition, and it constitutes possibly the best example of work initiated in computational linguistics being taken over into the mainstream of theoretical linguistics. Unification provides a major part of the theoretical underpinning of such grammatical theories as Functional Unification Grammar, Generalized Phrase-Structure Grammar, and Lexical Functional Grammar.

The most important school of linguistic thought that is left apparently untouched by these developments, is Government Binding theory, the most recent successor to early trnasformational grammar. This is based on the view that what distinguishes one language from another is not so much a list of rules that constitute its grammar as a set of parameters that govern the operation of an abstract device which, however complex it might be, does not vary from one language to another. Despite the widespread appeal of this view, it has informed relatively little work in computational linguistics. Two reasons for this suggest themselves immediately. One is the sheer complexity of the enterprise. The abstract device that must be simulated is an order of magnitude more complex than any phrase-structure formalism that has been proposed, and it does not obviously have the monotonicity property, so that the ability to generate sentences says nothing about whether one might be able to analyze them, or how. The other reason is that Government Binding theory presents a disconcertingly mobile target in that, as the theory develops, the basic architecture of the abstract machine changes. This is in marked contrast to work on phrase-structure grammars where new rules are proposed and old ones replaced, but the underlying mechanism that interprets the rules remains unchanged over fairly long periods. Nevertheless, there has been growing interest in recent years in so-called "principle-based" parsing and the most interesting suggestion that emerges from some of it is that the lines that separate it from work in phrase-structure and unification may be less strongly drawn than had been thought earlier.

The two major areas of computational linguistics that remain to be discussed are semantics and discourse. Some informed observers would doubtless say that semantics has long been an area of vigorous activity in computational linguistics, whereas others would say that it had received scant attention. The difference depends on what one takes the proper content of semantics to be and how much of it one believes belongs in the purview of linguistics. That there is such a difference of opinion should be no surprise, because semantics, like phonology, is close to the border at which linguistics makes contact with the physical world. There has been a great deal of work within the artificial intelligence community on "knowledge representation," natural inference, naive physics, and the like, which some might say was all part of the semantics of natural language. However, most of this work is directed toward gaining a deeper understanding of beings that can perceive, reason, and plan, and is not directly related to their specifically linguistic abilities.

The term "semantics" also has narrower constructions that put it squarely within linguistics. According to the most widely understood of these, semantics is concerned with the logical structure of sentences. Specifically, it studies the mechanisms that are used in natural languages that fill roles comparable to those of quantifiers, variable bindings, negation, and the like, in logic. There is much debate about the kind of logic to which natural languages are most closely related – whether it is extensional or intentional, modal, or whatever. But this work has had relatively little impact on computational linguistics where the semantic work that has been done has been inspired more from artificial intelligence. The same is true of lexical semantics, a branch of linguistics that is presently enjoying rapid, if belated, growth.

Discourse is the field that studies those aspects of a text extending beyond the scope of a single sentence that gives it coherence. It involves, for example, the circumstances under which a pronoun can be successfully used to refer back to something introduced into the discourse earlier. This is clearly a very important area of study, but it has so far received relatively little attention, doubtless because of its extreme difficulty. However, a major part of the work that has been done has been within the framework of computational linguistics.

35

Ongoing Directions in Computational Linguistics

This is the fifteenth International Conference on Computational Linguistics. It is arguably the fifteenth COLING, although we only adopted the name of a Swedish hobo as our nickname after the third meeting.

Since the first meeting in 1965, this is only the third time that we have returned to a country where we had been before. The first time was in 1984, when we returned to the United States, and the second in 1988, when we returned to Hungary. This year we return to France, where the second conference was held in 1967.

For those who, like me, have been associated with these meetings since the beginning, it is a privilege and an enormous pleasure to return to France, and to a conference organized under the auspices of the University of Grenoble. It is too little recognized how much the field of computational linguistics owes to this country and to that university. My predecessor, the chairman of the International Committee on Computational Linguistics, the late Professor Bernard Vauquois and the machine translation center that he founded in Grenoble, have done more to shape our field than any other single person or center. They were the only major academic research group to live through the dark ages that followed the ALPAC report, and their Ariane system has become the model for the great majority of the commercial machine translation systems that have ever been built. Professor Vauquois and his students and colleagues have been missionaries for, and tireless teachers of, computational linguistics for thirty years, establishing new research centers as far away as Malaysia.

For a computational linguist, to come here is, in a very real sense, to come home. In recent years, computational linguistics has been returning to its beginnings in some other ways also.

Much of the driving force in our field comes from the desire to make a translating machine, not just because this was the first problem that we attacked, but also because it is a problem that encompasses all others. It is very hard to imagine any achievement that would count as a contribution to computational linguistics without contributing to machine translation.

But, while it lost none of its motivating force in the intervening years, translation received somewhat less attention because the perception has been that the need for translation was less than had originally been thought. Now, the need is thought to be greater again, and growing. So, once again, machine translation, machine-aided translation, and machine aids for translators are coming to claim more attention, especially outside the United States.

In the early days of computational linguistics, one of the great opportunities that computers seemed to offer was that of performing massive statistical analyses of running text from which it was hoped that much of the hidden structure of language would emerge. The idea fell into the background because it became clear that, if such a program could indeed be carried through, the amount of data that would have to be considered was still beyond the reach of the machines and techniques that were then available.

The machines are now bigger and faster; orders of magnitude more data is readily available in machine treatable form; and much sharper tools have been developed. Someone entering the field of computational linguistics today will no longer be able to ignore statistics and corpus-based techniques.

But, our return to France, MT, and statistics, does not mean that, to quote Yogi Bear, it is just "déjà vu all over again". The old problems remain unsolved, but the relative naiveté of the fifties and sixties has been replaced by a notion of appropriate technology – of the impact that can be made on practical matters without having solved all the problems necessary for complete automation.

The TAUM-METEO project in Montreal demonstrated clearly and cleanly that we could do useful things with sublanguages that we could not do with unrestricted languages. Machine translation systems all over the world have shown that, when used appropriately, there is value in initial translations of altogether lower quality than would once have been thought interesting.

Interactive methods have shown us how to profit from the complementary skills of people and machines, allowing each to supply the deficiencies of the other. In short, we have learnt to approach practical problems with greater humility and greater realism.

These are some of the reasons that make me happy to welcome you all to France, to Nantes, and a week of excitement at the 15th International Conference on Computational Linguistics.

36

Unification

Introduction

This paper stands in marked contrast to many of the others in this volume in that it is intended to be entirely tutorial in nature, presupposing little on the part of the reader but a user's knowledge of English, a modicum of good will, and the desire to learn something about the notion of unification as it has come to be used in theoretical and computational linguistics. Most of the ideas I shall be talking about were first introduced to the study of ordinary language by computational linguists and their adoption by a notable, if by no means representative, subset of theoretical linguists represents an important milestone in our field, for it is the first occasion on which the computationalists have had an important impact on linguistic theory. Before going further, there may be some value in pursuing briefly why this rapprochement between these two branches has taken so long to come about. After all, the flow of information in the other direction – from theoretician to computationalist – has continued steadily from the start.

36.1 Productivity

The aspects of ordinary language that have proved most fascinating to its students all have something to do with its productivity, that is, with the fact that there appears to be no limit to the different utterances that can be made and understood in any of the languages of the world. Certainly, speakers can make and understand utterances that they have never made or understood before, and it is presumably largely in this fact that the immense power and flexibility of human language resides. If language is indeed a productive system in this sense, then it follows that what the speakers of a language must know in order to use it is a system of rules, relations, or abstractions of some sort and not simply an inventory of utterances. Further investigation suggests that these rules, relations, or abstractions have some interesting properties, important among which are the following:

· They differ remarkably little from one language to another.
· They are not easily accessible to introspection on the part of a language speaker.
· Their exact nature is greatly underdetermined by the facts of language use.

None of these properties is entirely uncontroversial. The last of them, however, has had the effect of diverting the main stream of linguistics, but notably not computational linguistics, into a particular course.

Following Chomsky, American – and many other – linguists took these three properties of language as a basis for an argument that goes somewhat as follows: if the linguistic system is complex and yet underdetermined by facts of usage, then language users presumably do not learn it by simply observing usage in themselves and others. They are presumably born with much of the system already intact, and this is supported by the observation that the particular language that a person learns seems to have little to do with the basic underlying system. I take it that this line of argument is familiar to most readers because, to the wholly uninitiated, the notion that the logical principles that organize the linguistic knowledge of, say, an Englishman and a Chinese are fundamentally the same would require more argument than we have time for here. For the moment, I simply want to draw attention to the fact that theoretical linguists have been led by considerations like these to concentrate a large part of their attention on the question of what it is about language that a baby knows at birth, what he or she acquires later and, in general, how the material is organized so as to make it possible for children to acquire it as effortlessly and as quickly as they apparently do.

The facts about language productivity pose other problems which are in some ways more immediate than that of accounting for the acquisition of the system. Foremost among these is the question of how the system works, and in particular, how it is that a person can compose utterances that have never been composed before – actually or essentially – so as to encapsulate a message that another person can then extract. We know something of how this is done in some very simple productive symbol systems such as the language of integers written in decimal notation, or the languages used for writing computer programs. For the most part, computational linguists have been motivated more by this question than by the acquisition problem. The reason, I believe, is not far to seek. It is the business of the computational linguist – as opposed to the linguistic technologist – to build working models of human linguistic activities in the hope that some of them will prove revealing about how people do what they do. In principle, such a program could presumably be directed as well towards the acquisition as towards the communication problem. The result of the acquisition process is itself a working model of the understanding process, so that, before any understanding model has been built, we do not even have a good idea what kind of result an acquisition model should produce. In short, from the point of view of a model builder, production and understanding are logically prior to acquisition.

There is, of course, a more radical view according to which the only way in which a production and understanding model could be constructed is by acquiring it in the way humans acquire it. According to this view, whether or not any macro-structure is discernible in language, there are no components that correspond to its parts and that are responsible for maintaining it. The brain is indeed as it initially seems to be – an essentially undifferentiated mass of neurons, and whatever the system learns suffuses and pervades it. Like an ant colony, it has only an emergent macro-structure. This view has gained a considerable amount of ground in recent years, but it has had little effect on the thinking of most linguists, computational or not. I shall have no more to say about it.

For the most part then, computational linguists have been captivated by the notion of language as a tool rather than language as a body of knowledge. They take as primary the fact that natural language works and have set themselves to discover something of how. There is another way in which this sets them apart from the great fraternity of linguists, at least in America, for many of whom language has become something that does not work in any essential sense. What a baby acquires when learning a language is not how to communicate needs, curiosities and observations using words and sentences, nor how to unpack words and sentences so as to learn about the mental states of others. Instead a baby learns how to distinguish the sentences of his or her language from other strings of words that are not sentences, how to put sentences into equivalence classes according to their logical properties, how to give a quantifier its proper scope, and the like. It is, after all, not necessarily the case that language has taken on its present form as the result of evolutionary processes that have fitted it to the needs of human communication any more than that it is necessarily the case that the survival value of flight played any role in the evolution of a bird's wings.

According to my rational reconstruction of the history of our field, then, one reason that computational linguists have concentrated on adult language as a medium of communication is that this has seemed to them to be logically prior to the acquisition problem. But there is a second reason that surely cannot be denied, namely that just about every computational linguist lives a double life as a linguistic technologist, that is, as at least an aspiring architect of well-crafted, elegant, and efficient devices that will do useful things for people with language. This, after all, is the interest that has put them in the way of a little support from time to time from the government and industry. This, of course, has served only to reinforce their disposition to view language as a tool.

36.2 Phrase structure

One of the most robust conceptions that came from the realization that languages are indefinitely productive is what has come to be known as phrase structure. As I remarked earlier, it follows from the fact of productivity that utterances are generally not remembered; they are constructed. There must be some process by which they are assembled out of parts which must often be assembled themselves, and so on. The construction must be made both by the speaker and the listener. And, if it is really true that the productivity of language knows no bounds, then the process must be a recursive one. We can get an idea of what this means in the following way. The whole point of introducing the notion of a procedure is that it will be statable in a finite space whereas the utterances it is used to characterize will not. Notice that this means that, in principle at least, there could be utterances many times the length of the procedure that it would nevertheless be able to treat. It follows from this that there must be parts of the procedure that are being used several times. This is the heart of what it means for a procedure to be recursive and this is why it is important here. If there is no limit to the number of sentences that a language allows, even though the language only contains a finite set of words, then there can be no limit on the length of a sentence. A procedure for constructing sentences must therefore be recursive, however long it is.

The particular solution to the problem of providing a procedure to characterize an infinite set of sentences was motivated by an idea that has played a central role in both linguistics and computer science, namely that the strings that make up a language – call them utterances, sentences, programs, or whatever – are made up of interchangeable parts. Each part belongs to one or more equivalence classes. A class can, and in interesting cases does, contain infinitely many members, but the number of classes is finite. A simple declarative sentence consists of two main parts, a subject and a predicate. The subject can be any one of the infinite class of noun phrases and the predicate any member of the infinite class of verb phrases. Noun phrases, like sentences, can be constituted in a variety of ways. For example, a member of the class of articles followed by a member of the class of nouns constitutes a noun phrase. The first component of the idea, then, is the common notion of a part of speech. The equivalence classes are the parts of speech and the members of a class are equivalent in that the substitution of one member for another in a string leaves its grammatical status unchanged.

This, then, is the second part of the idea – the notion of interchangeability. If a sentence is analysed into its parts, and the parts into their parts, and so on, then any one of those parts can be replaced by any other part belonging to the same class – a noun phrase by a noun phrase, a noun by a noun, and so on. Now, it is important to note that this can only be done when the sentence has been analysed completely. Consider the sentences

(1)   *John plays*

(2)   *John wins*

(3)   *Mary writes plays*

(4)   *Mary writes novels*

They each consist of a noun phrase followed by a verb phrase, and by interchanging members of these classes we get other sentences, such as

(5)   *Mary plays*

(6)   *Mary wins*

(7)   *John writes plays*

(8)   *John writes novels*

But *plays* is both a noun and an intransitive verb, so that one might expect the principle of interchangeability to give us also

(9)   ** Mary novels*

(10) ** John novels*

Examples (9) and (10) illustrate the linguistic usage of placing an asterisk before an unacceptable, or ungrammatical, string. All we have done is to start with sentence (1) and to replace its second word, which sentence (3) assures us is a noun, by another noun, namely *novels*. The point is really an obvious one. The word *plays* in (1) can be replaced only by another verb because the word figures in this sentence by virtue of being a verb. This is why we must have a complete analysis of a sentence before starting to make substitutions.

The idea of breaking strings into substrings, these into further substrings, and so on, according to some specified procedure or set of principles, gives us the key notion of phrase structure. The complete analysis, from the sentence down to the basic words, gives the structure of the sentence and of the phrases that make it up, in terms of other phrases. This is its phrase structure. The notion of interchangeability gives us a refinement, namely the notion of context-free phrase structure, or context-free phrase structure grammar, or simply context-free grammar. The term *context-free* is not intended to suggest that we are not involved with context for, clearly, the object of the enterprise we are engaged in is precisely that of determining the allowable contexts for words and strings of words in a language. What it refers to is the fact that the interchangeability of the members of an equivalence class is not constrained in any way by the context in which the member occurs. It is enough to know that a string occupies its place in a sentence by virtue of its membership in the class of noun phrases, to be able to replace it by another noun phrase without compromising the sentencehood of the string as a whole.

The word *grammar* in the phrase *context-free grammar* refers to a set of statements or rules which say how the members of the various classes may be made up in terms of members of other classes. For example, rule (11)

(11) $S \rightarrow NP\ VP$

says that when a member of the class of noun phrases (*NP*) is followed by a member of the class of verb phrases (*VP*) the result is a sentence (*S*).

We started from the notion that the set of strings that constituted a fully productive, infinite language could be specified only by means of a recursive procedure, and proceeded from there to the notions of phrase structure and context-free grammars, which are not procedures. However, these notions also clearly presuppose the existence of procedures to verify that a particular string belongs to the set specified by the grammar. To verify that a string is a sentence, for example, the strategy is to consider all the rules like (11) above that have the symbol *S* to the left of the arrow. For each of these, we attempt to show that the string can be broken down in the manner specified to the right of the arrow, in this case into a noun phrase and a verb phrase. One way to do this would be to consider all the places at which the string could be broken into two and to apply this same recursive procedure to the two parts, taking NP as the goal for the first part, and VP for the second. There are in fact many different strategies all of which can be shown to produce the same result and our present purposes do not call for us to give their details or to choose among them. For our purposes, two points are worthy of note. First, a set of phrase classes and a set of rules, taken together with a sound strategy for their application, constitute the procedure we require. Second, the articulation of the information into a grammar and the procedure proper that applies it corresponds, in large measure, to the distinction between what we expect to differ as we move from one language to another, namely the grammar, and what we expect to remain constant, namely the procedure.

For the practical business of communication that I have claimed has provided computational linguists with their main source of motivation, the question of just where the dividing line lies between the sentences and the nonsentences is not the centre of interest. The point is to know how a given string of words is to be interpreted. The same line of argument that led us from the notion of productive languages to that of a recursive procedure for characterizing them leads to a recursive procedure for assigning them interpretations. The simplest hypothesis is that the procedures are the same. Each phrase has an interpretation and the rules that state how phrases can be assembled from other phrases are enriched so as to say how the interpretation of the phrase is related to those of the smaller phrases that make it up. This hypothesis is as natural as it is simple. What it suggests, of course, is that the strings of words that belong to the language will be precisely those that have interpretations. This is in fact a matter about which it is possible to argue at length; we shall give it only a passing glance.

Chomsky (1957) claimed that the string (12) is clearly a sentence but is, just as clearly, meaningless.

(12) *Colorless green ideas sleep furiously.*

The argument that it is meaningless is easy to make. Nothing can be both colourless and green, so that the phrase *colorless green ideas*, though undoubtedly a noun phrase, has no meaning. This is enough to make the point. But, of course, the argument can be continued. It makes no sense to speak of ideas sleeping, or of anything sleeping furiously.

Notice how this same argument could be used to claim that these phrases do have meaning. We do indeed know what properties a thing would have to have to be colourless and green. Independently, we believe that these sets of properties are contradictory so that we expect the set of objects in the world that have them to be empty. In other words, the meaning is unexceptionable; the terms simply fail to refer. Likewise for *sleep* and *furiously*.

The string in (13) (also from Chomsky 1957) is not a sentence. It is also meaningless, but the kind of argument that we made for the meaninglessness of (12) cannot be made for it because it simply does not contain phrases, like *green ideas* and *sleep furiously*, whose absurdity we can point to.

(13) *Furiously sleep ideas green colorless*

36.3 Multiple structures

The notions of phrase structure and of context-free grammar have continued to play a key role in linguistics despite the discovery of evidence suggesting that the original ideas need to be replaced, embellished, or at least argued for more carefully. Even those who would replace them, however, continue to derive some inspiration from the original idea.

Consider the following sentences:

(14) *the dog runs*

(15) *the dogs run*

The point they make is simply that noun phrases do not in fact constitute an equivalence class, and neither do the verb phrases. Otherwise (16) and (17) would be sentences, which they clearly are not.

(16) **the dog run*

(17) **the dogs runs*

The problem seems about as easy to remedy as it is to recognize. Instead of a class of noun phrases, we need to recognize a class of singular, and a class of plural, noun phrases and likewise for verb phrases. This move will propagate through the complete system of phrases, requiring classes of singular and plural nouns, articles, verbs, and so forth, to be acknowledged.

Parallel examples in other languages would lead the number of classes that must be recognized, and the number of rules in a corresponding context-free grammar, to be multiplied by a much larger factor. Consider, for example, the Latin sentences (18) and (19):

(18) *Puer puellam amat (the boy loves the girl)*

(19) *Puerum puella amat (the girl loves the boy)*

Puer (boy) can take the place it has in (18) only by virtue of being singular and in the nominative case. Though the number of *puellam (girl)* is not important for objects in Latin any more than it is in modern European languages, it fits into this sentence only because it is in the accusative case. Replacing *puer* by *puerum* in (19) requires *puellam* to be replaced by *puella* in order to maintain sentencehood, and also meaningfulness.

Sentence (19) has an additional problem in that it does not contain a sequence of words that constitute a verb phrase. The verb phrase in this sentence is *puerum ... amat*. So perhaps the notion of verb phrase will have to be abandoned, in Latin at least, in favour of a description of sentences in terms of subjects, verbs and objects.

Parallel problems to the one posed by sentence (19) are also to be found in English. Consider (20) – (22):

(20) *Write everything down that she tells you.*

(21) *The students all surprised me that gave papers.*

(22) *Greater love hath no man than this.*

In (20), what you are presumably being exhorted to *write down* is *everything she tells you* but, in the string we actually have in (20), these phrases are intermixed with one another. We have a similar situation in (21). What surprised me was *all the students that gave papers*. And again in (22), what *no man hath* is *greater love than this*. This seems to be a greater challenge for context-free grammar than the agreement of subjects with verbs, or the use of cases in Latin.

The real problem that examples like these pose – and there are many more troublesome than these – is not that they make context-free grammar completely unworkable, as was commonly claimed when Chomsky's theories were just taking hold, as that they eat away at the original simple intuition that there are certain phrases that can be the subjects of sentences and certain that can be predicates. Some phrases are relative clauses and can be placed after nouns which they modify, and so on. As soon as we say that there are singular noun phrases and plural noun phrases which are related only through a partial overlap in their names, we are denying something that our intuition tells us is true. In most scientific enterprises, this would surely be no cause for concern. But, if linguists try to educate their intuitions it is because they are often the only things they have to go on. Furthermore, more is at stake than the linguist's intuitions. Once we agree to recognize singular noun phrases as distinct from plural noun phrases, we must write distinct sets of rules to say that singular articles can form singular noun phrases when they occur before singular nouns. A similar rule, not systematically related, says something parallel about plural noun phrases, and so on for many other pairs of rules. But the parallelism of singular and plural noun phrases surely does not arise by chance and we therefore almost certainly fail to capture something important when we are forced to write separate rules for the two cases. So, yes, we are able to make the system work, but only by ignoring much of its real structure and by introducing a great amount of redundancy into it. To increase redundancy is to reduce perspicuity.

Linguists have addressed these problems in two ways, both preserving the initial phrase-structure intuition. The first approach is that of transformational grammar. In its simplest form, which is the only one we shall consider, this keeps the original conception of context-free grammar entirely intact, but reduces its responsibility to that of characterizing only a particularly well behaved subset of the sentences in the language. The sentencehood of each of the remainder is assured by a set of transformational rules that permit the given sentence to be derived from one of the core set. We can, for example, imagine a rule that allows a relative clause in a core sentence to be moved to the end in suitable circumstances. In particular, it would allow *that she tells you* in (23) to be moved to the end, giving (24).

(23) *Write everything that she tells you down.*

(24) *Write everything down that she tells you.*

The same rule would derive (26) from (25).

(25) *The students that gave papers all surprised me.*

(26) *The students all surprised me that gave papers.*

However, while this shows how the relative clause is related to the noun it modifies, it still leaves the word *all* in a position that we should not expect it to occupy in a core sentence. However, the transformational scheme provides for a sentence to be derived from a core sentence, directly or indirectly. So we assume that there is another transformational rule that enables us to get (25) from (27).

(27) *All the students that gave papers surprised me.*

In like manner, we take it that there is a rule that moves the *than* phrase associated with a comparative adjective to the end of a sentence like (22).

(22) *Greater love hath no man than this.*

36.4 Descriptions

The other way in which phrase-structure grammar has been adapted to the more particular properties of natural language is more in keeping with the original phrase-structure ideas. In particular, the distinction made between core sentences and the rest is not required – all sentences are accounted for by the same set of rules. The linguistic facts suggest (1) that the number of equivalence classes of strings is very large, but that (2) various subsets of the classes need to be distinguished only for some purposes; for others they can be treated as a single larger class. This suggests a solution according to which the equivalence classes are named not by simple unanalyzable terms like *S, NP* and *VP,* but by expressions that make explicit the salient features of the members of the class. Various notations have been used for writing these expressions. The one we shall use is exemplified in (28).

(28) $\begin{bmatrix} \text{CAT} & = \text{NOUN} \\ \text{NUMBER} & = \text{SING} \end{bmatrix}$

It is easier to think of this as a *description* of a class of objects than as the name of a class as we have been doing up to now. The word *description* not only suggests the idea of a list of properties, but also something of the way in which we intend to operate on them. Before pursuing the idea of grammatical descriptions, we may find it useful to consider how the term description is used in more general contexts.

If we speak on the telephone and agree to meet somewhere, and if you do not know me, I will doubtless supply you with a description. I may say that I am about 5 feet 10 inches tall and have a beard. If we do not expect our meeting place to be very crowded, that may be sufficient. Otherwise I may add more detail, saying that I weigh about 170 pounds and will be wearing a blue striped suit. The more details I give you, the larger the crowd in which you can hope to distinguish me, because the larger a description is, the smaller the set of objects is that meet it.

My description can be written in the notation we are proposing to use for linguistic objects as in (29).

$$(29) \quad \begin{bmatrix} \text{HEIGHT} & = \text{5FT.10INS.} \\ \text{BEARD} & = \text{YES} \\ \text{SUIT} & = \begin{bmatrix} \text{COLOUR} & = \text{BLUE} \\ \text{STRIPES} & = \text{YES} \end{bmatrix} \end{bmatrix}$$

Each individual piece of information is given of an *attribute*, written to the left of an $'='$ sign, and a *value* written to the right. Notice that values can be of two forms. Either they are simple names or numbers, or they are descriptions in their own right. This makes sense in the current example. One way to describe me is to describe the suit that I will be wearing. This description is therefore embedded in my description as the value of the attribute SUIT.

A requirement that we place on descriptions is that they give at most one value for any attribute. So, if we include SUIT as an attribute, its value describes something that we can appropriately refer to as '*the* suit' in the description. This is not to say that a description could not contain two different attributes, each with a description for its value, and such that both of these embedded descriptions has its own *suit* description. This restriction makes of the description what mathematicians refer to as a *partial function*. Suppose we designate the description of me given above as F, and let $F(beard)$ be the value of the function F when applied to beard. Clearly $F(beard) = yes$. Since we allow attributes to have not more than one value, the value of $F(x)$, for any x, is never ambiguous. This is a property of all functions. However, for some – indeed, most – choices of x, $F(x)$ is not defined at all. This is what makes the function partial.

Now suppose that, when we go to our appointment, you arrive a little late and are concerned that I might have come and gone away again. You ask a bystander if they have seen anyone waiting there, and they say "yes"; there was someone with the description (30).

$$(30) \quad \begin{bmatrix} \text{AGE} & = 45 \\ \text{BEARD} & = \text{YES} \\ \text{SUIT} & = \begin{bmatrix} \text{FABRIC} & = \text{TWEED} \end{bmatrix} \end{bmatrix}$$

This is not very helpful. There is nothing about this that contradicts the description I gave, and there is one piece of evidence suggesting that the person was me, because they both describe their subject as having a beard. If you later discover that the person the bystander saw was indeed me, you will know that you missed the appointment, but you will also have learnt some things about me that you did not know previously, namely that, on that occasion, I fit the description (31).

$$(31) \quad \begin{bmatrix} \text{HEIGHT} & = 5\text{FT.10INS.} \\ \text{BEARD} & = \text{YES} \\ \\ \text{SUIT} & = \begin{bmatrix} \text{COLOUR} & = \text{BLUE} \\ \text{STRIPES} & = \text{YES} \\ \text{FABRIC} & = \text{TWEED} \end{bmatrix} \\ \\ \text{AGE} & = 45 \end{bmatrix}$$

This description is arrived at in the obvious way, namely by combining the sets of attribute-value pairs in the original descriptions, eliminating repetitions. This is the operation we refer to as *unification*.

Combining sets of attribute-value pairs does not always yield a result that meets our definition of a description. Suppose, for example, that the bystander had claimed to have seen somebody meeting the description (32).

$$(32) \quad \begin{bmatrix} \text{AGE} & = 45 \\ \text{HEIGHT} & = 6\text{FT.2INS.} \end{bmatrix}$$

Combining the sets would give two instances of the attribute HEIGHT which, however, do not count as duplicates one of which can be eliminated, because they have different values. Keeping both of them, on the other hand, would violate the requirement that the description be a partial function – that it contain at most one instance of a given attribute. When this happens, the unification operation is said to *fail*, and we conclude that the two descriptions could not be of the same person or thing.

The kind of description we have been considering corresponds to the everyday notion of a description in several ways:

- Descriptions are always essentially *partial* because new detail (attribute-value pairs) can always be added to them.
- Descriptions are related through a notion of *compatibility*. Incompatible descriptions cannot be of the same thing.
- Compatible descriptions can be combined (unified) to yield a generally more complete (less partial) one than either of the originals.

36.5 Grammar rules

We are now ready to consider how descriptions affect the business of writing grammar rules. In (33), we give an example of a grammar rule using the new notation for descriptions instead of symbols designating parts of speech.

$$(33) \quad \begin{bmatrix} \text{CAT} = \text{S} \end{bmatrix} \rightarrow \begin{bmatrix} \text{CAT} & = \text{NP} \\ \text{NUMBER} & = n \\ \text{PERSON} & = p \end{bmatrix} \begin{bmatrix} \text{CAT} & = \text{VP} \\ \text{NUMBER} & = n \\ \text{PERSON} & = p \end{bmatrix}$$

The italicized letters in the description are variables, and they may take on any value. Each instance of a variable name refers to the same variable so that the effect of writing the same variable name in more than one place is to require the same values (if any) to occupy all those positions. So what rule (33) says is that a sentence – a phrase whose category is 's' – can consist of a noun phrase followed by a verb phrase, provided that the noun and verb phrases have the same number and person.

To be completely clear about how a rule of this sort would apply, consider once again sentences (14) and (15).

(14) *the dog runs*

(15) *the dogs run*

Let us assume that, by virtue of some other rule, *the dog* and *runs* are analyzable as (34a) and (34b), respectively.

$$
(34) \quad
\begin{bmatrix}
\text{CAT} & = \text{NOUN} \\
\text{NUM} & = \text{SING} \\
\text{PERS} & = 3 \\
\text{DET} & = \text{DEF} \\
\text{HEAD} & = \text{DOG}
\end{bmatrix}
\quad
\begin{bmatrix}
\text{CAT} & = \text{VERB} \\
\text{NUM} & = \text{SING} \\
\text{PERS} & = 3 \\
\text{TENSE} & = \text{PRES} \\
\text{HEAD} & = \text{RUN}
\end{bmatrix}
$$

(a) (b)

These can be unified with the two descriptions that make up the right-hand side of rule (33) giving (34a) and (34b) as the results. In the course of the unification, the variables n and p in the rule are instantiated to 'sing' and '3', respectively. The rule therefore applies and allows a sentence to be created with these two parts. The descriptions of *the dogs* and *run* are presumably (35a) and (35b).

$$
(35) \quad
\begin{bmatrix}
\text{CAT} & = \text{NOUN} \\
\text{NUM} & = \text{PLUR} \\
\text{PERS} & = 3 \\
\text{DET} & = \text{DEF} \\
\text{HEAD} & = \text{DOG}
\end{bmatrix}
\quad
\begin{bmatrix}
\text{CAT} & = \text{VERB} \\
\text{NUM} & = \text{PLUR} \\
\text{PERS} & = 3 \\
\text{TENSE} & = \text{PRES} \\
\text{HEAD} & = \text{RUN}
\end{bmatrix}
$$

(a) (b)

These also unify with the two descriptions in the rule but, this time, n is instantiated to 'plur'. The reason the strings (16) and (17) are not accepted as sentences by the rule is that they would require inconsistent assignments to the variable n in the rule.

(16) * *the dog run*

(17) * *the dogs runs*

For the computational linguist, rules like (33) clearly introduce some additional complexity. However, there are certain tasks which they actually make simpler, notably that of relating the application of rules to the association that they establish between a sentence and its structure. In fact this responsibility can be turned over to the rules themselves, and with more far-reaching consequences than may at first be apparent.

Consider the variant of rule (33) given as (36).

$$
(36) \quad
\begin{bmatrix}
\text{CAT} & = \text{S} \\
\text{SUBJ} & = subj \\
\text{PRED} & = pred
\end{bmatrix}
\rightarrow
\begin{bmatrix}
\text{CAT} & = \text{NP} \\
\text{NUMBER} & = n \\
\text{PERSON} & = p
\end{bmatrix}_{subj}
\begin{bmatrix}
\text{CAT} & = \text{VP} \\
\text{NUMBER} & = n \\
\text{PERSON} & = p
\end{bmatrix}_{pred}
$$

We have made one minor addition to the formalism which allows us to subscript an attribute-value list with the name of a variable, and we assume that that variable takes on as its value the description to which it is subscripted. When the rule is applied, the descriptions on the right-hand side of the rule are unified with the descriptions of actual phrases, and the result of these unification procedures is also reflected in the values of the variables *subj* and *pred*. As a result, these descriptions come to be embedded in the description that is constructed for the sentence as a whole as the value of the attributes SUBJ and PRED, respectively. Applied to sentence (14), for example, they give the result in (37).

$$
(37) \quad
\begin{bmatrix}
\text{CAT} & = \text{S} \\[4pt]
\text{SUBJ} & =
\begin{bmatrix}
\text{CAT} & = \text{NOUN} \\
\text{NUM} & = \text{SING} \\
\text{PERS} & = 3 \\
\text{DET} & = \text{DEF} \\
\text{HEAD} & = \text{DOG}
\end{bmatrix} \\[30pt]
\text{PRED} & =
\begin{bmatrix}
\text{CAT} & = \text{VERB} \\
\text{NUM} & = \text{SING} \\
\text{PERS} & = 3 \\
\text{TENSE} & = \text{PRES} \\
\text{HEAD} & = \text{RUN}
\end{bmatrix}
\end{bmatrix}
$$

A point about unification that is not immediately obvious, but that deserves to be stressed, is that the use of variables is not simply a shorthand that could be dispensed with in principle. Variables, or some equivalent special device, are essential to the workings of a system that relies on unification in a non-trivial way. It would, for example, be a grave mistake to take (38) as being equivalent to (36).

$$
(38) \quad
\begin{bmatrix}
\text{CAT} & = \text{S} \\[4pt]
\text{SUBJ} & =
\begin{bmatrix}
\text{CAT} & = \text{NP} \\
\text{NUM} & = n \\
\text{PERS} & = p
\end{bmatrix} \\[20pt]
\text{PRED} & =
\begin{bmatrix}
\text{CAT} & = \text{VP} \\
\text{NUM} & = n \\
\text{PERS} & = p
\end{bmatrix}
\end{bmatrix}
\rightarrow
\begin{bmatrix}
\text{CAT} & = \text{NP} \\
\text{NUMBER} & = n \\
\text{PERSON} & = p
\end{bmatrix}
\begin{bmatrix}
\text{CAT} & = \text{VP} \\
\text{NUMBER} & = n \\
\text{PERSON} & = p
\end{bmatrix}
$$

Notice, in particular, that unifying the two descriptions that make up the right-hand side of rule (38) with some more complete descriptions, produces larger descriptions as we saw in (37). But there is no reason to suppose that the size of the descriptions that are embedded in the description on the left-hand side of the rule in (38) will be in any way affected by this, since no new attributes have been unified with them. In (36), however, one and the same description occurs as the first item on the right-hand side of the rule and as the value of the SUBJ attribute in the sentence description on the left. In our notation, we are always careful to give the details of a particular description in only one place in a larger expression and to refer to this by means of a variable if it also occurs in other places.

36.6   Augmented Transition Networks

The term *unification* arose independently in linguistics and in the field of logic programming. Indeed, even the name was chosen independently, and it was only discovered considerably later that the operations were the same in all essentials. In linguistics, the original impulse to design something like the system we have begun to sketch came from people working with Augmented Transition Networks (ATNs). They noted, with some dismay, that the ATNs that were used to analyse even very simple sets of sentences to yield a structure for them, could not be used to derive the sentences from the structures. In other words, the ATN specified the translation in only one direction. A simple example will make this clear.

Consider the ATN whose transition diagram is sketched in Figure 1. An ATN is an abstract machine which, for present purposes, can be thought of as very similar to a standard finite-state automaton (FSA). The difference is that the transitions – the arcs in the diagram – are labeled with instructions rather than simple symbols. At any given moment, the machine is in one of a given set of *states*, represented by the circles in the diagram. The machine makes discrete moves from one state to another, the possible moves being just those given by the transition arcs in the diagram. In the course of moving from the current state to a new one, the instructions associated with the corresponding transition are carried out. At the outset, the machine is in a particular designated *start* state – in the case of Figure 1, state 1 on the left of the diagram. It can cease operation only when it is in a *final* state, that is, one shown with thick lines in the diagram.

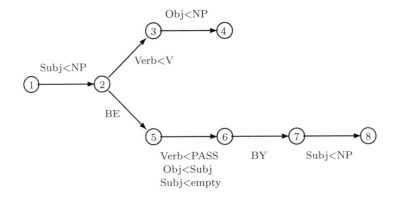

FIGURE 1 An Augmented Transition Network

The instructions on the transitions in Figure 1 are shown somewhat impressionistically. The basic idea is that, as the machine moves from state to state, a string of words or phrases is also being examined, one word or phrase with each transition. The symbols in the instruction set on the transitions that are written all in uppercase letters give the properties that these words and phrases must have. So, a string consisting of a noun phrase (NP) followed by a verb (V), followed by another noun phrase, will allow that machine to move from state 1, through states 2 and 3, to state 4. An instruction of the form $\alpha < \beta$ causes whatever β refers to to be 'put in the α register'. So, when the machine reaches state 4, the first noun phrase will have been put in the *Subj* register, the verb in the *Verb* register, and the second noun phrase in the *Obj* register. The idea of the registers is the obvious one. By examining their contents when the machine stops, we can identify the parts of a sentence that has just been examined.

The ATN in Figure 1 will also accept a sentence like *the cat was chased*, or *the cat was chased by the dog*, following the route in the lower part of the diagram. There must be a noun phrase, followed by a finite form of the verb *to be* (BE), followed by the past participle of a transitive verb (PASS). Such a sequence carries the machine into state 6. However, it may also continue to state 8 over the preposition *by* (BY) and another noun phrase. Now, one of the advantages claimed for ATNs over previous parsing schemes was that much of the work required to parse different structures could be shared. In particular, the *surface subject* – the initial noun phrase that agrees with the verb – can be recognized before any commitment is made to the voice of the sentence. Nevertheless, the constituent that the parser declares to be the subject of the sentence will be the *deep subject*, so that the distinction between an active sentence and its passive counterpart can be eliminated. The way it works is this: as the transition is taken from state 1 to state 2 (see Figure 1), the noun phrase is stored in the *Subj* register on the hypothesis that it will turn out to be the *deep* subject of an active sentence. However, if a part of the verb *to be* is encountered next, followed by the past participle of a transitive verb, the active hypothesis is changed. It is now assumed that the first noun phrase was not a subject after all, but the *deep* object of a passive verb. Accordingly, the contents of the *Subj* register are removed and placed in the *Obj* register.

The advantage of this scheme is not difficult to appreciate. The main point is that the initial noun phrase is analysed only once, and examined by the network in Figure 1 only once. The disadvantage is that the scheme cannot be operated in reverse, so as to make it generate the same sentences it is able to analyse. Suppose it were supplied with an initial set of register contents as follows:

(39)

Register	Contents
Subj	John
Verb	expected
Obj	Mary

The active sentence can be produced without difficulty, following the upper route through the diagram as before. However, the attempt to produce the corresponding passive sentence, following the lower route, can only proceed as suggested in the following table:

(40)

Transition	Word
1–2	John
2–5	was
5–6	expected
6–7	by
7–8	???

The subject is put in the first position in the sentence. This is what the first transition calls for, and there is no obvious way to predict that the 5–6 transition changes the contents of the *Subj* register, effectively invalidating this move. The final transition (7–8) calls for the subject a second time, but the register has since been emptied so no word is available to place in the last position.

The property that makes ATNs irreversible is that they allow moves in which the contents of the register are replaced by new contents, effectively destroying some part of the history in the process. When history is destroyed, it cannot be retraced. It became clear, then, that the key to reversibility was to ensure that, once a register had been set, it could never be reset.[1] This seems to imply the abandonment of some techniques that tend to enhance efficiency, in particular that of using one transition to recognize the subject of both transitive and intransitive sentences. But consider the transition diagram in Figure 2.

We call this a *restricted* ATN because it does not change register values. The idea is simply that the first noun phrase is placed in the temporary register *SSubj* (for *surface subject*), from whence it is copied either to the *Subj* or the *Obj* register after the voice of the sentence has been determined. This device performs the recognition task just as well as the original. Under an appropriate interpretation, it can also be made to perform the generation task. When the 1–2 transition is made, the *SSubj* register has no contents, so that no word can be immediately assigned to the first position in the sentence. However, the name of the register can be associated with the first position, and its contents will occupy that position when they become known.

---

[1]In general, ATNs are nondeterministic and the restriction is only intended to refer to the current nondeterministic path through the control structure.

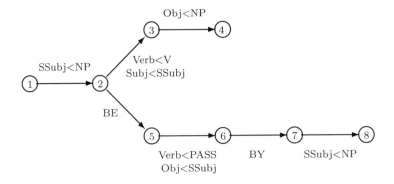

FIGURE 2 A restricted Augmented Transition Network

In general, we cannot know if a given empty register will acquire contents but, at least, once it does they will not change, so that there will be no ambiguity about what should occupy the slot. Contents are indeed assigned to the *SSubj* register along both paths through the diagram, on the upper path from the *Subj*, and on the lower from the *Obj* register.

36.7 Logical variables

What we have done in moving from Figure 1 to Figure 2 is to make the registers of the ATN less like *program variables*, and more like *logical variables*. Programmers are used to using the term *variable* to refer to a storage location in a computer that can contain, now one value, and now another. In logic, and generally in mathematics, on the other hand, the term *variable* refers to a specific quantity, which may or may not be known at certain of the times when it is used, but which does not change its value as the discussion proceeds. To put it another way, what we have done is to make the registers of the ATN for all the world like the attributes of our earlier structures.

One of the effects of observing the restriction that makes logical variables of program variables is to shift the emphasis in the design of a system from *process* and *temporal sequence* to *relations* and *constraints*. It is extremely striking that computational linguists, like computer scientists, whose subject matter *par excellence* is abstract processes and changes of state through time, seek to eliminate time dependencies wherever they are inessential. As the jargon has it, they seek *declarative* rather than *procedural* formulations of problems.

Theoretical linguists have tended to prefer procedural formalisms to declarative ones and, indeed, much of the discussion among linguists has concerned the fine adjustment of temporal sequences. In transformational grammar, for example, that we referred to earlier, the particular order in which transformational rules are applied has an important effect on the outcome and much has been made of this. As a consequence, however, transformational grammar is a system that has no known algorithm for analyzing sentences.

There is a fairly direct relationship between unification and the notion of a logical variable. It is natural to think of the descriptions we discussed earlier as conjunctions of logical variables, one for each of the attributes of the object described. The variables corresponding to attributes that have values are instantiated to those values and the remainder will be uninstantiated. In the notation for attribute-value unification introduced earlier, we did not mention variables. This is not because there is no role for them in that scheme, but because it shows up relatively rarely. As we have remarked, variables that correspond to attributes without values are not generally mentioned explicitly. We did not have any cause to introduce variables into these expressions because we had no instances of descriptions that had undergone unification. However, consider the following examples:

$$
(41) \quad
\begin{bmatrix}
\text{CAT} & = \text{S} \\
\text{SUBJ} & = \alpha \\
\text{OBJ} & = \alpha
\end{bmatrix}
\qquad
\begin{bmatrix}
\text{CAT} & = \text{S} \\
\text{SUBJ} & = \alpha = \begin{bmatrix} \text{CAT} & = np \\ \ldots & = \ldots \end{bmatrix} \\
\text{OBJ} & = \alpha
\end{bmatrix}
$$

$\qquad\qquad$ (a) $\qquad\qquad\qquad\qquad$ (b)

These are both descriptions of passive sentences. In (41a), we know that the sentence is passive, and that its (deep) subject and object are therefore the same. However, the description says nothing about what the subject is like. In (41b), the subject and object are also the same, and we also have some details on the kind of constituent it is.

There are in fact alternatives to the explicit use of variable names that are frequently used in the attribute-value notation. The most often used convention is to choose one place in the description at which the variable would appear, and use a reference to this position in all the other places. The reference usually takes the form of a so-called path, that is, a list of attributes that can be followed from the outermost level of the description to the distinguished location. Using this convention, (41a) looks like (42a) or equivalently (42b).

$$
(42) \quad
\begin{bmatrix}
\text{CAT} & = \text{S} \\
\text{OBJ} & = \text{SUBJ}
\end{bmatrix}
\qquad
\begin{bmatrix}
\text{CAT} & = \text{S} \\
\text{SUBJ} & = \text{OBJ}
\end{bmatrix}
$$

$\qquad\qquad$ (a) $\qquad\qquad\qquad$ (b)

36.8 Clausal form and term unification

A notation for descriptions that makes variables explicit is the one on which the languages of logic programming in general, and Prolog in particular, are based. In these languages, what we have been calling descriptions are expressed in so-called *clausal* form. Each description corresponds to a *term* and, in general, a term is a word, or *functor*, followed by a parenthesized list of arguments, each of which is either a variable or a term. The list of arguments can be empty, in which case the parentheses are not written. Following the Prolog convention for distinguishing variables from constants, we capitalize the names of the former, and begin the latter with lower-case letters. The following are examples:

(a) `john`
(b) `np(Pers, sing)`
(c) `np(3, number)`
(d) `np(3, sing)`
(e) `np(3, sing, Case)`

A functor that takes n arguments is said to be of *arity* n. In example (a), 'john' is an *atom*, that is, a functor of arity O. In (b), (c) and (d), 'np' is a functor of arity 2, and in (e), 'np' is a functor of arity 3.

Functors with different arities are not systematically related to one another except perhaps mnemonically. But terms with the same names and arities are related in the sense that they are candidates for unification with one another. In fact, in the above examples, (d) is the expression that results from unifying (b) and (c). The rules for unification of these expressions are straightforward and, for the most part, obvious. If a and b are the expressions to be unified, then the result is given by the first of the following rules that applies:

- If a is a variable, it acquires the value b and the result of the unification is b.
- If b is a variable, it acquires the value a and the result of the unification is a.
- If a and b are of the forms $f(a_1, \ldots, a_n)$ and $f(b_1, \ldots, b_n)$ respectively, that is, they have the same functor and arity, the unification is $f(c_1, \ldots, c_n)$ where c_i is the result of unifying a_i with b_i for $0 < i \leq n$.
- If a and b are atoms, and $a = b$, the result is a.

Clausal form does away with explicit attribute names in favour of a place-valued scheme for identifying attributes. The two schemes are equivalent in many respects. However, one obvious and important difference is that clausal form provides only for those attributes to which positions have been assigned. Within this system there is therefore a notion of a *complete* description which is lacking when attributes are named explicitly. A term which contains no variables at any level in its structure can never be made more explicit by unification with other terms and is therefore complete. In this respect, the attribute-value notation comes closer to representing the everyday notion of a description.

Clausal form is used by a large community of computational linguists who work with logic programming systems. The fact that their systems work with a closed set of attributes is not a serious impediment for them because the set of attributes that are mentioned in a grammar is also closed. A simple grammar written in this notation is the following:

(43)
s	$\rightarrow$ np(X), vp(X)
np(X)	$\rightarrow$ det(X), n(X)
vp(X)	$\rightarrow$ v(X), np(_)
det(f(3, _))	$\rightarrow$ the
det(f(3, sing))	$\rightarrow$ a
n(f(3, sing))	$\rightarrow$ cat
n(f(3, plur))	$\rightarrow$ cats
n(f(3, sing))	$\rightarrow$ dog
n(f(3, plur))	$\rightarrow$ dogs
n(f(3, _))	$\rightarrow$ sheep
v(f(3, sing))	$\rightarrow$ chases
v(f(3, _))	$\rightarrow$ chased

Following once again the standard conventions of Prolog, we have used the underline symbol ('_') to represent the so-called *anonymous* variable. In the above examples, it behaves just like an ordinary variable. However, it is standard practice to use it where the variable is needed in only one place in an expression. If an expression contains more than one instance of the anonymous variable, each is treated as unrelated to the remainder – it is as though they had each been called by a unique, and different name.

The above example illustrates the use of logical variables and of term unification to control the agreement of subjects and predicates, and also of determiners (articles) with their nouns. The determiner 'a', for example, is a determiner that can be used only with singular nouns, and nouns, incidentally, are all third person. Accordingly, the argument to det is given as f(3,sing). The determiner 'the', on the other hand, can be used with both singular and plural nouns and is therefore annotated with the term f(3, _), where the position of number is taken by the anonymous variable. Nouns are treated similarly. The nouns 'cat' and 'cats' are marked singular and plural respectively, but 'sheep' is the same in the singular as in the plural, and the position of its number is therefore taken by the anonymous variable. The functor f has no particular significance. It serves only to collect the indicators of person and number into a single expression which will unify with the variable X in the rules at the beginning of the grammar.

Consider now what happens when some simple noun phrases are analysed. The following table shows four sentences with, written above the words, the result of applying rules to the individual words in them. Above this is the result of applying the second rule in the above grammar to these expressions. This involves unification of the arguments of the terms in the line below.

```
(44)  (a)  np(f(3, sing))
                 det(f(3, sing))   n(f(3, sing))
                 a                 cat

      (b)  np(f(3, sing))
                 det(f(3, _))      n(f(3, sing))
                 the               cat

      (c)  np(f(3, sing))
                 det(f(3, sing))   n(f(3, _))
                 a                 sheep

      (d)  np(f(3, _))
                 det(f(3, _))      n(f(3, _))
                 the               sheep
```

The result of applying the np rule in (a) is a description of a third person, singular noun phrase because the determiner and the noun agree on these attributes. When unification is applied to two identical copies of the expression np(f(3, sing)) it succeeds, producing that identical expression as the result. After all, the expression contains no variables that could be instantiated.

In (b), the two expressions that are unified are not identical. To make them so, the unification procedure must instantiate the anonymous variable in the expression corresponding to 'the', giving it the value 'sing'. Essentially the same thing happens in (c), except that the variable that must be instantiated is in the expression corresponding to the noun 'sheep'. Finally, in (d), the expressions are identical again, and no variables need to be instantiated to make them so.

The rules we have been considering have a strong family resemblance to the context-free rules familiar to linguists for decades. But the addition of arguments which may, in general, involve variables increases what can be done with them in many ways, extending far beyond verifying agreements of articles and nouns, or subjects and predicates. We will give one other example which has to do with the kinds of structure delivered by a program that conducts the syntactic analysis of a sentence. Generally speaking, such a program, which is referred to in the trade as a *parser*, must not only apply the rules of the grammar to the string, but must keep records of the structure that comes from applying them because this is the result that it must eventually return to its client. Now, it turns out that this second responsibility can be taken over by the grammar itself and, perhaps somewhat more surprisingly, there can be distinct advantages in doing this.

Consider the following variant of grammar (43):

```
(45)  s(s(NP, VP))              → np(NP, X), vp(VP, X)
      np(np(D, N), X)           → det(D, X), n(N, X)
      vp(vp(V, NP), X)          → v(V, X), np(NP, _)
      det(det(the), f(3, _))    → the
      det(det(a), f(3, sing))   → a
      n(n(cat), f(3, sing))     → cat
      n(n(cat), f(3,plur))      → cats
      n(n(dog), f(3,sing))      → dog
      n(n(dog), f(3,plur))      → dogs
      n(n(sheep), f(3, _))      → sheep
      v(v(chase), f(3,sing))    → chases
      v(v(chase), f(3, _))      → chased
```

Now let us consider what the descriptions of the noun phrases (44a)–(44d) would be like when constructed according to the rules of this grammar.

```
(46)  (a)  np(np(det(a), n(cat)), f(3, sing))
               det(det(a), f(3, sing))        n(n(cat), f(3, sing))
               a                              cat

      (b)  np(np(det(the), n(cat)), f(3, sing))
               det(det(the), f(3, _))         n(n(cat), f(3, sing))
               the                            cat

      (c)  np(np(det(a), n(sheep)), f(3, sing))
               det(det(a), f(3, sing))        n(n(sheep), f(3, _))
               a                              sheep

      (d)  np(np(det(the), n(sheep)), f(3, _))
               det(det(the), f(3, _))         n(n(sheep), f(3, _))
               the                            sheep
```

Each of the rules in the latter part of the grammar effectively assigns a part of speech to a single word. In a real system, this function would be assigned to a different module than the main part of the grammar – one concerned only with the lexicon. Here, we simplify things by throwing the lexicon together with the grammar. Most of the terms in the grammar now have two arguments. The second performs the role of the single argument in the earlier grammar – that of monitoring agreement in number and person between articles and nouns and between subjects and predicates. The first argument contains an expression with a part of speech as functor and the word assigned to that part of speech as the only argument.

Now, consider the first three rules in the grammar. These are the rules that would indeed be part of the grammar in a more realistic system. The first argument of the term on the right-hand side of these rules also has a part of speech as its functor. Now, however, there are two arguments, because there are two terms making up the right-hand side of the rule. Each of these two arguments is a variable the value of which is obtained, by unification, from whatever a corresponding item of the right-hand side of the rule matches.

So, now consider (a) once again. The variables NP and VP in the expression s(NP,VP) on the left-hand side of the rule unify with det(a) and n(cat) respectively, giving the result np(det(a), n(cat)). This is simply a representation in the form of a term of the structure of the noun phrase.

We made the point at the beginning of this paper that the need for grammars arises from the fact that ordinary language admits an unlimited number of sentences. If the structures of these sentences are to be represented by single terms as we are now suggesting, then there can be no limit on the size and complexity of the terms. This is, of course, provided for in an entirely natural manner, because the language of terms has exactly the same recursive structures that natural languages presumably also have. A functor can have any number of arguments, and each of these can be a functor with arguments, and so on indefinitely.

36.9   Path equations

Any atomic value in an attribute-value matrix or in a term can be located by an expression known as a *path*, which is simply an ordered set of attribute names. To locate the value in question, we first locate the value of the first attribute in the path. If this is also the last member of the path, then we have the result. Otherwise, that value should itself be an attribute-value matrix or a term in which we now locate the second attribute in the path, and so on until either an attribute is called for in a structure for which it is not defined, or we reach the end of the path and retrieve the value. The ability to uniquely locate any value in this way comes, of course, from the functional property that these structures are required to have. Using it, we can specify any arbitrary attribute-value structure by means of a set of *path equations*, that is, pairs consisting of a path and the associated value. A plausible structure for the sentence *The dog chased the cat* might be the one given by the following equations:

(47) (cat)   = s
      (subj, cat)   = np
      (subj, num)   = sing
      (subj, pers)   = 3
      (subj, lex)   = dog
      (verb, lex)   = chase
      (verb, tense)   = past
      (obj, cat)   = np
      (obj, num)   = sing
      (obj, pers)   = 3
      (obj, lex)   = dog

Unification of a pair of equation sets consists in taking the union of the two sets and rejecting the result just in case it contains two instances of the same path with different values. Path equations have come to be the standard notation for specifying attribute-value structures in grammatical formalisms, such as Lexical Functional Grammar (Kaplan and Bresnan 1982) and PATR II (Shieber 1986).

36.10   Long-distance dependency

There are a great many problems in syntax that can be treated by unification and for which more complex mechanisms were previously thought necessary. This is an important fact because unification makes for much more straightforward computational processes. Take the example of so-called *long-distance dependency*. This is a phenomenon that is demonstrated in examples like the following:

- *This is the car I expected you to be able to persuade them to buy ◇.*
- *Everyone does not even claim ◇ to like garlic.*
- *This is the violin the sonatas are easy to play ◇ on ◇.*

Each of these sentences contains a sentence fragment from which, however, something seems to have been deleted. Here are the fragments in question, with the missing parts replaced, as above, by a diamond (◇):

- *to buy* ◇
- ◇ *to like garlic*
- *to play* ◇ *on* ◇

There is an intuitive sense in which, to understand these fragments, we need to copy into the marked places some material from the enclosing context. If we do this, we get the following:

- *to buy the car*
- *everyone to like garlic*
- *to play the sonatas on the violin*

As the first two examples illustrate, there can be any number of intermediate-sized sentences (or sentence fragments) intervening between the outer one, from which the inserted material is taken, and the innermost one where it is needed for proper interpretation. Hence the term *long-distance dependency*. Now consider the following grammar rule schemata:

(48)
$$\begin{aligned}
\texttt{np( )} &\rightarrow \texttt{X, s(...X, [ ], ...)} \quad :- \texttt{X = np( )} \\
\texttt{s(...X, Y ...)} &\rightarrow \texttt{np( ), vp(...X, Y ...)} \\
\texttt{vp(...X, Y ...)} &\rightarrow \texttt{v( ), np(...X, Y ...)} \\
\texttt{vp(...X, Y ...)} &\rightarrow \texttt{vp(...X, Z ...), pp(...Z, Y ...)} \\
\texttt{np(...X, [ ], ...)} &\quad :- \texttt{X = np( )}
\end{aligned}$$

The first says that a noun phrase can be made up of something that we designate with the variable X and constrain to be a noun phrase, followed by a sentence which has as one of its arguments that same noun phrase. It also has another argument which is constrained to be an empty list.

The second and third rules show how the values of these arguments are passed down through the structure, from sentence to verb phrase, from verb phrase to noun phrase, and so on. The fourth rule, which allows a verb phrase to consist of a verb phrase and a prepositional phrase, associates the first argument of the larger verb phrase with the first argument of the smaller one, and the second of the relevant arguments of the prepositional phrase with the second argument of the larger verb phrase, and it unifies the second argument of the embedded verb phrase with the first argument of the prepositional phrase. If we think of these arguments as channels through which information can be passed, and of the first of the two distinguished variables as an *input*, and the second as an *output* channel, then this rule can be seen as passing input to the first phrase, taking the output from there and passing it to the second phrase, and then returning the output it receives from there.

The last rule is unusual in having no right-hand side. What this rule means is that, at a place where a noun phrase would normally be required, it can be omitted, provided that the first of the two variables is bound to a noun phrase, and the second to an empty list.

The overall effect of this scheme is that the noun phrase that is bound to the *input* channel variable by the first rule is passed from phrase to phrase, and from input to output, until a rule like the fifth one above is encountered. Now, for the first time, the output is different. Now it is an empty list, and it is this that continues to be passed from phrase to phrase until it emerges as the output in the first rule. Only if a rule like the fifth one above is found at some point will the output variable unify with the value required of it in the first rule. And the only way that the input in the first rule can be a noun phrase, and the output an empty list, is by using a rule like the fifth one at some point. For reasons that will be clear by now, this particular way of accounting for long-distance dependencies is known as *gap-threading*.

Conclusion

In this chapter I have tried to show how the cause of linguistic computing can be carried forward by what at first appears to be an unpromising approach, namely that of removing from the statement of linguistic facts all mention of process, of events and of time sequences. It turns out to be possible to do this by replacing these powerful things with one operation which is, itself, of quite unexpected power, namely unification. The reason for removing procedural statements from the statement of linguistic facts is so that they can be reintroduced in the ways, and in the places, that are dictated by good computational practice. Although this approach has caught on only in small enclaves of the linguistic community, it is more in line with the declared principles of the majority of linguists, at least in America, than what they themselves do. Processes and the ordering of events are clearly matters of performance. Competence, which is the domain of the theoretical linguist, is concerned with relations and constraints.

Publications referenced

Chomsky 1957; Kaplan and Bresnan 1982; Shieber 1986.

## 37

Foreword to
"An Introduction to Machine Translation"

Machine translation was a matter of serious speculation long before there were computers to apply to it; it was one of the first major problems to which digital computers were turned; and it has been a subject of lively, sometimes acrimonious, debate every since. Machine translation has claimed attention from some of the keenest minds in linguistics, philosophy, computer science, and mathematics. At the same time it has always attracted the lunatic fringe, and continues to do so today.

The fascination with machine translation doubtless has many sources. No one who reads the King James Bible, or FitzGerald's *Rubaiyat of Omar Khayyam* or any of the dozen or so translations that are made every month of *Scientific American* or *Geo* magazine, or the facing pages of the magazines airlines give their clients, can retain any doubt that translation is one of the highest accomplishments of human art. It is comparable in many ways to the creation of an original literary work. To capture it in a machine would therefore be to capture some essential part of the human spirit, thereby coming to understand its mysteries. But just because there is so much of the human spirit in translation, many reject out of hand any possibility that it could ever be done by a machine. There is nothing that a person could know, or feel, or dream, that could not be crucial for getting a good translation of some text or other. To be a translator, therefore, one cannot just have some parts of humanity; one must be a complete human being.

Many scientists believe that there is insight to be gained from studying machine translation even when it is applied to very pedestrian kinds of text with the expectation of producing results of a quite pedestrian kind. This is because translation is a task that obviously exercises every kind of linguistic ability, except those involved with the production and perception of speech, without requiring any other contact with the world. For example, a scientist interested in how people collect words to make up sentences, and sentences to make up texts, might seek to test his theories in a computer program that produced sentences and texts. Such a scientist would face the problem of how to provide his program with something that it wanted to say. Programs do not generally have needs or desires that they might expect to fulfill by talking, or perceptions of the world that might strike them as worthy of comment. The investigator would therefore be faced with the logically prior problem of how to provide his machine with an urge to talk. One way to do this that avoids the problems of perception, and most of the problems of motivation, is to have the program simply say what it is told to say. This proposal clearly runs the risk of trivializing the problem. The solution is to provide the stimulus in a different language from the one in which the response must be given.

Much of the motivation for studying machine translation has been very different, coming from the perceived need to produce more translations, to produce them faster, and to produce than at lower cost. More and more of the world's commerce is conducted across national, and therefore linguistic, boundaries so that letters, agreements, contracts, manuals, and so forth, must be produced in several languages. Modern technology develops and changes faster than ever before, and the accompanying texts must therefore be replaced correspondingly sooner. Furthermore, advanced technology, such as cars, computers, and household appliances, is no longer available only to people with advanced education, so that the texts that are needed to operate and maintain these products can no longer be produced only in English. In the countries of the European Communities, in Canada, in many developing countries, and doubtless soon in the Soviet Union, translations are required for legal or nationalistic reasons even when a single version might fill the primary need.

In recent years, this perceived need for more translations than human translators can produce has led to a great increase in activity in the field, especially in Europe and Japan. To be sure, the aims of this work do not encompass anything comparable to the King James Bible or the *Rubaiyat of Omar Khayyam*. They do not even include the *Scientific American* or even advertising copy. In the near term, practical machine translation is intended to be applied to two kinds of material. The first is material that covers such a narrow subject matter, and in such a routine fashion, as to require little on the part of the translator that could really count as understanding. The second is material that will be read by people seeking only a rough idea of what is being said, so that an extremely rough translation will be adequate. Maintenance manuals for machines belong in the first category and the second finds its customers in companies with major competitors abroad and in government agencies with unlisted addresses.

Only under very special circumstances are the readers of translated texts allowed to see what emerges from the translation machine and, if they did they would surely be surprised at how different it is from what they actually get. This is because it has almost invariably undergone a process called "post-editing" by a human translator. This, the defenders of the machine are quick to point out, is no different from what happens when translations are made in the traditional manner; an initial translation is checked by a "reviser", who often changes the first version quite extensively. But critics of machine translation, of whom there are many, are more inclined to credit the translation to the post-editor, and only some occasional hints to the machine. Certainly, even when applied to texts on very limited subjects by authors with no literary pretentions, machine translation still generally produces results that would not be acceptable from a human translator under any circumstances. Just what would improve the quality of the result, and even whether any substantial improvement is possible, are open questions. Indeed, it is an open question whether the great investment that has been made in the enterprise since the first systems were put to use in the 1960s has resulted in any real improvement.

As an observer of machine translation, John Hutchins has, in several other publications, provided many readers with their first introduction to the subject. Harold Somers has stimulated the interest of generations of students in it at the University of Manchester Institute of Science and Technology which, largely as a result of his endeavours, has also become one of the world's foremost centres for research in machine translation. They clearly both have opinions on the open questions of machine translation, but they are not the subject of this book. The reader who seeks insight into the open questions, however, will do well to begin here. This is a technical book, in the sense of explaining the parts of machine translation systems, the principles behind the parts, and such relevant theory as is available from linguistics and computer science. It is a non-technical book in that it assumes no prior knowledge of these matters on the part of its readers. The first part of the book gives all the background necessary for the remarkable detailed and insightful descriptions of several representative systems that make up the second part. These must be few people, even among those who are professionally engaged in this work, who would not find information in this second part that was new and surprising to them.

38

Text-Translation Alignment

WITH MARTIN RÖSCHEISEN

Abstract

We present an algorithm for aligning texts with their translations that is based only on internal evidence. The relaxation process rests on a notion of which word in one text corresponds to which word in the other text that is essentially based on the similarity of their distributions. It exploits a partial alignment of the word level to induce a maximum likelihood alignment of the sentence level, which is in turn used, in the next iteration, to refine the word level. The algorithm appears to converge to the correct sentence alignment in only a few iterations.

38.1   The Problem

To align a text with a translation of it in another language is, in the terminology of this paper, to show which of its parts are translated by what parts of the second text. The result takes the form of a list of pairs of items – words, sentences, paragraphs, or whatever – from the two texts. A pair $\langle a,b \rangle$ is on the list if a is translated, in whole or in part, by b. If $\langle a,b \rangle$ and $\langle a,c \rangle$ are on the list, it is because a is translated partly by b and partly by c. We say that the alignment is partial if only some of the items of the chosen kind from one or other of the texts are represented in the pairs. Otherwise, it is complete.

It is notoriously difficult to align good translations on the basis of words, because it is often difficult to decide just which words in an original are responsible for a given one in a translation and, in any case, some words apparently translate morphological or syntactic phenomena rather than other words. However, it is relatively easy to establish correspondences between such words as proper nouns and technical terms, so that partial alignment on the word level is often possible. On the other hand, it is also easy to align texts and translations on the sentence or paragraph levels, for there is rarely much doubt as to which sentences in a translation contain the material contributed by a given one in the original.

The growing interest in the possibility of automatically aligning large texts is attested to by independent work that has been done on it since the first description of our methods was made available (Kay and Röscheisen 1988). In recent years it has been possible for the first time to obtain machine-readable versions of large corpora of text with accompanying translations. The most striking example is the Canadian "Hansard," the transcript of the proceedings of the Canadian parliament. Such bilingual corpora make it possible to undertake statistical, and other kinds of empirical, studies of translation on a scale that was previously unthinkable.

Alignment makes possible approaches to partially, or completely, automatic translation based on a large corpus of previous translations that have been deemed acceptable. Perhaps the best-known example of this approach is to be found in Sato and Nagao (1990). The method proposed there requires a database to be maintained of the syntactic structures of sentences together with the structures of the corresponding translations. This database is searched in the course of making a new translation for examples of previous sentences that are like the current one in ways that are relevant for the method. Another example is the completely automatic, statistical approach to translation taken by the research group at IBM (Brown et al. 1990), which takes a large corpus of text with aligned translations as its point of departure.

It is widely recognized that one of the most important sources of information to which a translator can have access is a large body of previous translations. No dictionary or terminology bank can provide information of comparable value on topical matters of possibly intense though only transitory interest, or on recently coined terms in the target language, or on matters relating to house style. But such a body of data is useful only if, once a relevant example has been found in the source language, the corresponding passage can be quickly located in the translation. This is simple only if the texts have been previously aligned. Clearly, what is true of the translator is equally true of others for whom translations are a source of primary data, such as students of translation, the designers of translation systems, and lexicographers. Alignment would also facilitate the job of checking for consistency in technical and legal texts where consistency constitutes a large part of accuracy.

In this paper, we provide a method for aligning texts and translations based only on internal evidence. In other words, the method depends on no information about the languages involved beyond what can be derived from the texts themselves. Furthermore, the computations on which it is based are straightforward and robust. The plan rests on a relationship between word and sentence alignments arising from the observation that a pair of sentences containing an aligned pair of words must themselves be aligned. It follows that a partial alignment on the word level could induce a much more complete alignment on the sentence level.

A solution to the alignment problem consists of a subset of the Cartesian product of the sets of source and target sentences. The process starts from an initial subset excluding pairs whose relative positions in their respective texts is so different that the chance of their being aligned is extremely low. This potentially alignable set of sentences forms the basis for a relaxation process that proceeds as follows. An initial set of candidate word alignments is produced by choosing pairs of words that tend to occur in possibly aligned sentences. The idea is to propose a pair of words for alignment if they have similar distributions in their respective texts. The distributions of a pair of words are similar if most of the sentences in which the first word occurs are alignable with sentences in which the second occurs, and vice versa. The most apparently reliable of these word alignments are then used to induce a set of sentence alignments that will be a subset of the eventual result. A new estimate is now made of what sentences are alignable based on the fact that we are now committed to aligning certain pairs. Because sentence pairs are never removed from the set of alignments, the process converges to the point when no new ones can be found; then it stops.

In the next section, we describe the algorithm. In Section 3 we describe additions to the basic technique required to provide for morphology, that is, relatively superficial variations in the forms of words. In Section 4 we show the results of applying a program that embodies these techniques to an article from *Scientific American* and its German translation in *Spektrum der Wissenschaft*. In Section 5 we discuss other approaches to the alignment problem that were subsequently undertaken by other researchers (Gale and Church 1991; Brown, Lai, and Mercer 1991). Finally, in Section 6 we consider ways in which our present methods might be extended and improved.

38.2 The Alignment Algorithm

38.2.1 Data Structures

The principal data structures used in the algorithm are the following:

Word-Sentence Index (WSI) One of these is prepared for each of the texts. It is a table with an entry for each different word in the text showing the sentences in which that word occurs. For the moment, we may take a word as being simply a distinct sequence of letters. If a word occurs more than once in a sentence, that sentence occurs on the list once for each occurrence.

Alignable Sentence Table (AST) This is a table of pairs of sentences, one from each text. A pair is included in the table at the beginning of a pass if that pair is a candidate for association by the algorithm in that pass.

Word Alignment Table (WAT) This is a list of pairs of words, together with similarities and frequencies in their respective texts, that have been aligned by comparing their distributions in the texts.

Sentence Alignment Table (SAT) This is a table that records for each pair of sentences how many times the two sentences were set in correspondence by the algorithm.

Some additional data structures were used to improve performance in our implementation of the algorithm, but they are not essential to an understanding of the method as a whole.

38.2.2 Outline of the Algorithm

At the beginning of each cycle, an AST is produced that is expected to contain the eventual set of alignments, generally amongst others. It pairs the first and last sentences of the two texts with a small number of sentences from the beginning and end of the other text. Generally speaking, the closer a sentence is to the middle of the text, the larger the set of sentences in the other text that are possible correspondents for it.

The next step is to hypothesize a set of pairs of words that are assumed to correspond based on similarities between their distributions in the two texts. For this purpose, a word in the first text is deemed to occur at a position corresponding to a word in the second text if they occur in a pair of sentences that is a member of the AST. Similarity of distribution is a function of the number of corresponding sentences in which they occur and the total number of occurrences of each. Pairs of words are entered in the WAT if the association between them is so close that it is not likely to be the result of a random event. In our algorithm, the closeness of the association is estimated on the basis of the similarity of their distributions and the total number of occurrences.

The next step is to construct the SAT, which, in the last pass, will essentially become the output of the program as a whole. The idea here is to associate sentences that contain words paired in the WAT, giving preference to those word pairs that appear to be more reliable. Multiple associations are recorded.

If there are to be further passes of the main body of the algorithm, a new AST is then constructed in light of the associations in the SAT. Associations that are supported some minimum number of times are treated just as the first and last sentences of the texts were initially; that is, as places at which there is known to be a correspondence. Possible correspondences are provided for the intervening sentences by the same interpolation method initially used for all sentences in the middle of the texts.

In preparation for the next pass, a new set of corresponding words is now hypothesized using distributions based on the new AST, and the cycle repeats.

38.2.3 The Algorithm

The main algorithm is a relaxation process that leaves at the end of each pass a new WAT and SAT, each presumably more refined than the one left at the end of the preceding pass. The input to the whole process consists only of the WSIs of the two texts. Before the first pass of the relaxation process, an initial AST is computed simply from the lengths of the two texts:

Construct Initial AST

If the texts contain m and n sentences respectively, then the table can be thought of as an $m \times n$ array of ones and zeros. The average number of sentences in the second text corresponding to a given one in the first text is n/m, and the average position of the sentence in the second text corresponding to the ith sentence in the first text is therefore $i \cdot n/m$. In other words, the expectation is that the true correspondences will lie close to the diagonal. Empirically, sentences typically correspond one for one; correspondences of one sentence to two are much rarer, and correspondences of one to three or more, though they doubtless occur, are very rare and were unattested in our data. The maximum deviation can be stochastically modelled as $O(\sqrt{n})$, the factor by which the standard deviation of a sum of n independent and identically distributed random variables multiplies.[1]

We construct the initial AST using a function that pairs single sentences near the middle of the text with as many as $O(\sqrt{n})$ sentences in the other text; it is generously designed to admit all but the most improbable associations. Experience shows that because of this policy the results are highly insensitive to the particular function used to build this initial table.[2]

The main body of the relaxation process consists of the following steps:

Build the WAT

For all sentences s^A in the first text, each word in s^A is compared with each word in those sentences s^B of the second text that are considered as candidates for correspondence, i.e., for which $\langle s^A, s^B \rangle \in$ AST. A pair of words is entered into the WAT if the distributions of the two words in their texts are sufficiently similar and if the total number of occurrences indicates that this pair is unlikely to be the result of a spurious match. Note that the number of comparisons of the words in two sentences is quadratic only in the number of words in a sentence, which can be assumed to be not a function of the length of the text. Because of the constraint on the maximum deviation from the diagonal as outlined above, the computational complexity of the algorithm is bound by $O(n\sqrt{n})$ in each pass.

Our definition of the similarity between a pair of words is complicated by the fact that the two texts have unequal lengths and that the AST allows more than one correspondence, which means that we cannot simply take the inner product of the vector representations of the word's occurrences. Instead, we use as a measure of similarity[3]:

$$\frac{2c}{N_A(v) + N_B(w)}$$

---

[1] In such a model, each random variable would correspond to a translator's choice to move away from the diagonal in the AST by a certain distance (which is assumed to be zero mean, Gaussian distributed). However, the specific assumptions about the maximum deviation are not crucial in that the algorithm was observed to be insensitive to such modifications.

[2] The final results showed that no sentence alignment is at a distance greater than ten from the diagonal in texts of 255 and 300 sentences. Clearly, any such prior knowledge could be used for a significant speed-up of the algorithm, but it was our goal to adopt as few prior assumptions as possible.

[3] Throughout this paper, we use the word *similarity* to denote this similarity measure, which does not necessarily have to be an indicator of what one would intuitively describe as "similar" words. In particular, we will later see that similarity alone, without consideration of the total frequency, is not a good indicator for "similarity."

where c is the number of corresponding positions, and $N_T(x)$ is the number of occurrences of the word x in the text T. This is essentially Dice's coefficient (Rijsbergen 1979). Technically, the value of c is the cardinality of the largest set of pairs $\langle i,j \rangle$ such that

1. $\langle s_i^A(v), s_j^B(w) \rangle \in \text{AST}$, where $s_z^T(x)$ is the sentence in text T that contains the zth occurrence of word x.

2. Pairs are *non-overlapping* in the sense that, if $\langle a,b \rangle$ and $\langle c,d \rangle$ are distinct members of the set then they are distinct in both components, that is, $a \neq c$ and $b \neq d$.

Suppose that the word occurs in sentences 50, 52, 75, and 200 of the English text, and in sentences 40 and 180 of the German, and that the AST contains the pairs $\langle 50,40 \rangle$, $\langle 52,40 \rangle$, and $\langle 200,180 \rangle$, among others, but not $\langle 75,40 \rangle$. There are two sets that meet the requirements, namely $\{\langle 1,1 \rangle, \langle 4,2 \rangle\}$ and $\{\langle 2,1 \rangle, \langle 4,2 \rangle\}$. The set $\{\langle 1,1 \rangle, \langle 2,1 \rangle, \langle 4,2 \rangle\}$ is excluded on the grounds that $\langle 1,1 \rangle$ and $\langle 2,1 \rangle$ overlap in the above sense – the first occurrence of "Hund" is represented twice. In the example, the similarity would be computed as $\frac{2}{4+2-2} = \frac{1}{2}$ regardless of the ambiguity between $\langle 1,1 \rangle$ and $\langle 2,1 \rangle$.

The result of the comparisons of the words in all of the sentences of one text with those in the other text is that the word pairs with the highest similarity are located. Comparing the words in a sentence of one text with those in a sentence of the other text carries with it an amortized cost of constant computational complexity,[4] if the usual memory-processing tradeoff on serial machines is exploited by maintaining redundant data structures such as multiple hash tables and ordered indexed trees.[5]

The next task is to determine for each word pair, whether it will actually be entered into the WAT: the WAT is a sorted table where the more reliable pairs are put before less reliable ones. For this purpose, each entry contains, as well as the pair of words themselves, the frequencies of those words in their respective texts and the similarity between them. The closeness of the association between two words, and thus their rank in the WAT, is evaluated with respect to their similarity and the total number of their occurrences. To understand why similarity cannot be used alone, note that there are far more one-frequency words than words of higher frequency. Thus, a pair of words with a similarity of 1, each of them occurring only once, may well be the result of a random event. If such a pair was proposed for entry into the WAT, it should only be added with a low priority.

The exact stochastic relation is depicted in Figure 1, where the probability is shown that a word of a frequency k that was aligned with a word in the other text with a certain similarity s is just the result of a random process.[6] Note that, for a high-frequency word that has a

---

[4] The basic idea is this: more processing has to be done to compute the similarity of a high-frequency word to another frequent word, but there are also more places at which this comparison can later be saved. Recall also that we assume sentence length to be independent of text length.

[5] For very large corpora, this might not be feasible. However, large texts can almost invariably be broken into smaller pieces at natural and reliable places, such as chapter and section headings.

[6] The basis for this graph is an analytic derivation of the probability that a word with a certain frequency in a 300-sentence text matches some random pattern with a particular similarity. The analytic formula relies on word-frequency data derived from a large corpus instead of on a stochastic model for word frequency distribution (such as Zipf's law, which states that the frequency with which words occur in a text is indirectly proportional to the number of words with this frequency; for a recent discussion of more accurate models, see also Baayen (1991)). Clearly, the figure is dependent on the state of the AST (e.g. lower similarities become more acceptable as the AST becomes more and more narrow), but the thresholds relevant to our algorithm can be precomputed at compile-time. The figure shown would be appropriate to pass 3 in our experiment. In the formula used, there are a few reasonable simplifications concerning the nature of the AST; however, a Monte-Carlo simulation that is exactly in accordance with our algorithm confirmed the depicted figure in every essential detail.

high similarity with some other word (right front corner), it is very unlikely (negligible plateau height) that this association has to be attributed to chance. On the other hand, low similarities (back) can easily be attained by just associating arbitrary words. Low-frequency words – because there are so many of them in a text – can also achieve a high similarity with some other words without having to be related in an interesting way. This can be intuitively explained by the fact that the similarity of a high-frequency word is based on a pattern made up of a large number of instances. It is therefore a pattern that is unlikely to be replicated by chance. Furthermore, since there are relatively few high-frequency words, and they can only contract high similarities with other high-frequency words, the number of possible correspondents for them is lower, and the chance of spurious associations is therefore less on these grounds also. Note that low-frequency words with low similarity (back left corner) have also a low probability of being spuriously associated to some other word. This is because low-frequency words can achieve a low similarity only with words of a high frequency, which in turn are rare in a text, and are therefore unlikely to be associated spuriously.[7]

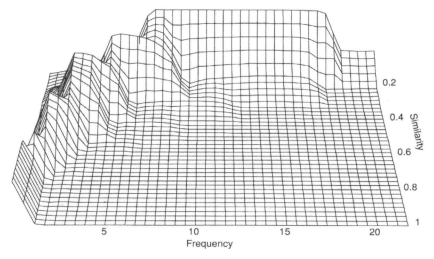

FIGURE 1 Likelihood that a word pair is a spurious match as a function of a word's frequency and its similarity with a word in the other text (maximum 0.94)

Our algorithm does not use all the detail in Figure 1, but only a simple discrete heuristic: a word pair whose similarity exceeds some threshold is assigned to one of two or three segments of the WAT, depending on the word frequency. A segment with words of higher frequency is preferred to lower-frequency segments. Within each segment, the entries are sorted in order of decreasing similarity and, in case of equal similarities, in order of decreasing frequency. In terms of Figure 1, we take a rectangle from the right front. We place the left boundary as far to the left as possible, because this is where most of the words are.

Build the SAT

In this step, the correspondences in the WAT are used to establish a mapping between sentences of the two texts. In general, these new associations are added to the ones inherited from the preceding pass. It is an obvious requirement of the mapping that lines of association should

---

[7]This discussion could also be cast in an information theoretic framework using the notion of "mutual information" (Fano 1961), estimating the variance of the degree of match in order to find a frequency-threshold (see Church and Hanks 1990).

not cross. At the beginning of the relaxation process, the SAT is initialized such that the first sentences of the two texts, and the last sentences, are set in correspondence with one another, regardless of any words they may contain. The process that adds the remaining associations scans the WAT in order and applies a three-part process to each pair $\langle v, w \rangle$.

1. Construct the *correspondence set* for $\langle v, w \rangle$ using essentially the same procedure as in the calculation of the denominator, c, of word similarities above. Now, however, we are concerned to avoid ambiguous pairs as characterized above. The set contains a sentence pair $\langle s_i^A(v), s_j^B(w) \rangle$ if (1) $\langle s_i^A(v), s_j^B(w) \rangle \in$ AST, and (2) v occurs in no other sentence h (resp. w in no g) such that $\langle s_i^A(v), h \rangle$ (resp., $\langle g, s_j^B(w) \rangle$) is also in the AST.

2. If any sentence pair in the correspondence set crosses any of the associations that have already been added to the SAT, the word pair is rejected as a whole. In other words, if a given pair of sentences correspond, then sentences preceding the first of them can be associated only with sentences preceding the second.

3. Add each sentence pair in the correspondence set of the word pair $\langle v, w \rangle$ to the SAT. A count is recorded of the number of times a particular association is supported. These counts are later thresholded when a new AST is computed or the process terminates.

Build a New AST

If there is to be another pass of the relaxation algorithm, a new AST must be constructed as input to it. This is based on the current SAT and is derived from it by supplying associations for sentences for which it provides none. The idea is to fill gaps between associated pairs of sentences in the same manner that the gap between the first and the last sentence was filled before the first pass. However, only sentence associations that are represented more than some minimum number of times in the SAT are transferred to the AST. In what follows, we will refer to these sentence pairs as anchors.

As before, it is convenient to think of the AST as a rectangular array, even though it is represented more economically in the program. Consider a maximal sequence of empty AST entries, that is, a sequence of sentences in one text for which there are no associated sentences in the other, but which is bounded above and below by an anchor. The new associations that are added lie on and adjacent to the diagonal joining the two anchors. The distance from the diagonal is a function of the distance of the current candidate sentence pair and the nearest anchor. The function is the same one used in the construction of the initial AST.

Repeat

Build a new WAT and continue.

38.3 Morphology

As we said earlier, the basic alignment algorithm treats words as atoms; that is, it treats strings as instances of the same word if they consist of identical sequences of letters, and otherwise as totally different. The effect of this is that morphological variants of a word are not seen as related to one another. This might not be seen as a disadvantage in all circumstances. For example, nouns and verbs in one text might be expected to map onto nouns with the same number and verbs with the same tense much of the time. But this is not always the case and, more importantly, some languages make morphological distinctions that are absent in the other. German, for example, makes a number of case distinctions, especially in adjectives, that are not reflected in the morphology of English. For these reasons, it seems desirable to allow words to contract associations with other words both in the form in which they actually occur, and in a more normalized form that will throw them together with morphologically related other words in the text.

38.3.1 The Basic Idea

The strategy we adopted was to make entries in the WSI, not only for maximal strings of alphabetic characters occurring in the texts, but also for other strings that could usefully be regarded as normalized forms of these.

Clearly, one way to obtain normalized forms of words is to employ a fully fledged morphological analyzer for each of the languages. However, we were concerned that our methods should be as independent as possible of any specific facts about the languages being treated, since this would make them more readily usable. Furthermore, since our methods attend only to very gross features of the texts, it seemed unreasonable that their success should turn on a very fine analysis at any level. We argue that, by adding a guess as to how a word should be normalized to the WSI, we remove no associations that could have been formed on the basis of the original word, but only introduce the possibility of some additional associations. Also, it is unlikely that an incorrect normalization will contract any associations at all, especially in view of the fact that these forms, because they normalize several original forms, tend to occur more often. They will therefore rarely be misleading.

For us, a normalized form of a word is always an initial or a final substring of that word – no attention is paid to morphographemic or word-internal changes. A word is broken into two parts, one of which becomes the normalized form, if there is evidence that the resulting prefix and suffix belong to a paradigm. In particular, both must occur as prefixes and suffixes of other forms.

38.3.2 The Algorithm

The algorithm proceeds in two stages. First a data structure, called the *trie* , is constructed in which information about the occurrences of potential prefixes and suffixes in the text is stored. Second, words are split, where the trie provides evidence for doing so, and one of the resulting parts is chosen as the normalization.

1. A trie (Knuth 1973; pp. 481–490) is a data structure for associating information with strings of characters. It is particularly economical in situations where many of the strings of interest are substrings of others in the set. A trie is in fact a tree, with a branch at the root node for every character that begins a string in the set. To look up a string, one starts at the root, and follows the branch corresponding to its first character to another node. From there, the branch for the second character is followed to a third node, and so on, until either the whole string has been matched, or it has been discovered not to be in the set. If it is in the set, then the node reached after matching its last character contains whatever information the structure contains for it. The economy of the scheme lies in the fact that a node containing information about a string also serves as a point on the way to longer strings of which the given one is a prefix. In this application, two items of information are stored with a string, namely the number of textual words in which it occurs as a prefix and as a suffix.

2. Consider the possibility of breaking an n-letter word before the ith character of the word $(1 < i \leq n)$. The conditions for a break are: The number of other words starting with characters $1...i-1$ of the current word must be greater than the number of words starting with characters $1...i$ because, if the characters $1...i-1$ constitute a useful prefix, then this prefix must be followed, in different words, by other suffixes than characters $i...n$. So, consider the word "wanting," and suppose that we are considering the possibility of breaking it before the 5th character, "i". For this to be desirable, there must be other words in the text, such as "wants" and "wanted", that share the first $i-1 = 4$ characters. Conversely, there must be more words ending with characters $i...n$ of the word than with

$i - 1...n$. So, there must be more words with the suffix "ing" than with the suffix "ting"; for example "seeing" and "believing".

There is a function from potential break points in words to numbers whose value is maximized to choose the best point at which to break. If p and s are the potential prefix and suffix, respectively, and $P(p)$ and $S(s)$ are the number of words in the text in which they occur as such, the value of the function is $kP(p)S(s)$. The quantity k is introduced to enable us to prefer certain kinds of breaks over others. For the English and German texts used in our experiments, $k = length(p)$ so as to favor long prefixes on the grounds that both languages are primarily suffixing. If the function has the same value for more than one potential break point, the one farthest to the right is preferred, also for the reason that we prefer to maximize the lengths of prefixes.

Once it has been decided to divide a word, and at what place, one of the two parts is selected as the putative canonical form of the word, namely, whichever is longer, and the prefix if both are of equal length. Finally, any other words in the same text that share the chosen prefix (suffix) are split at the corresponding place, and so assigned to the same canonical form.

The morphological algorithm treats words that appear hyphenated in the text specially. The hyphenated word is treated as a unit, just as it appears, and so are the strings that result from breaking the word at the hyphens. In addition, the analysis procedure described above is applied to these components, and any putative normal forms found are also used. It is worth pointing out that we received more help from hyphens than one might normally expect in our analysis of the German texts because of a tendency on the part of the *Spektrum der Wissenschaft* translators, following standard practice for technical writing, of hyphenating compounds.

38.4 Experimental Results

In this section, we show some of the results of our experiments with these algorithms, and also data produced at some intermediate stages. We applied the methods described here to two pairs of articles from *Scientific American* and their German translations in *Spektrum der Wissenschaft* (see references). The English and German articles about human-powered flight had 214 and 162 sentences, respectively; the ones about cosmic rays contained 255 and 300 sentences. The first pair was primarily used to develop the algorithm and determine the various parameters of the program. The performance of the algorithm was finally tested on the latter pair of articles. We chose these journals because of a general impression that the translations were of very high quality and were sufficiently "free" to be a substantial challenge for the algorithm. Furthermore, we expected technical translators to adhere to a narrow view of semantic accuracy in their work, and to rate the importance of this above stylistic considerations. Later we also give results for another application of our algorithm to a larger text of 1257 sentences put together from two days from the French-English Hansard corpus.

Table 1 shows the first 50 entries of the WAT after pass 1 of the algorithm. It shows part of the first section of the WAT (lines 1-23) and the beginning of the second (lines 24-50). The first segment contains words or normalized forms with more than 7 occurrences and a similarity not less than 0.8. Strings shown with a following hyphen are prefixes arising from the morphological procedure; strings with an initial hyphen are suffixes. Naturally, some of the word divisions are made in places that do not accurately reflect linguistic facts. For example, English "proto-" (1) comes from "proton" and "protons"; German "-eilchen" (17) is the normalization for words ending in "-teilchen" and, in the same way, "-eistung" (47) comes from "-leistung".

Of these 50 word pairs, 42 have essentially the same meanings. We take it that "erg" and

"Joule", in line 4, mean the same, *modulo* a change in units. Also, it is not unreasonable to associate pairs like "primary"/"sekundären" (26) and "electric"/"Feld" (43), on the grounds that they tend to be used together. The pair "rapid-"/"Pulsare-" (49) is made because a pulsar is a rapidly spinning neutron star and some such phrase occurs with it five out of six times. Notice, however, that the association "pulsar-"/"Pulsar-" is also in table (6). Furthermore, the German strings "Pulsar" and "Pulsar-" are both given correct associations in the next pass (lines 17 and 20 of Table 2).

TABLE 1 The WAT after pass 1

	English	German	Eng.Freq.	Similarity
1	proto-	Proto-	14	1
2	proton-	Proton-	13	1
3	interstellar	interstellare-	12	1
4	ergs	Joule	10	1
5	electric-	electrisch-	9	1
6	pulsar-	Pulsar-	17	16/17
7	photo-	Photo-	14	14/15
8	and	und	69	11/12
9	per	pro	12	11/12
10	relativ-	relativ-	11	10/11
11	atmospher-	Atmosphäre-	10	10/11
12	Cygnus	Cygnus	63	59/65
13	cosmic-	kosmische-	82	39/43
14	volts	Elektronvolt	19	19/21
15	telescope-	Teleskop-	9	8/9
16	univers-	Univers-	8	7/8
17	particle-	-eilchen	53	51/59
18	shower-	Luftschauer-	20	19/22
19	X-ray-	Röetgen	19	19/22
20	electrons	Elektronen	12	11/13
21	source-	Quelle-	40	37/45
22	magnetic	Magnetfeld	11	9/11
23	ray-	Strahlung-	141	135/167
24	Observatory	diesem	6	1
25	shower	Gammaquant	6	1
26	primary	sekundären	6	1
27	percent	Prozent	6	1
28	galaxies	Galaxien	5	1
29	Crimean	Krim	5	1
30	ultrahigh-	ultraho-	5	1
31	density	Dichte	5	1
32	synchrotron	Synchrotronstrahlung	5	1
33	activ-	aktiv-	5	1
34	supernova	Supernova-Explosion-	5	1
35	composition	Zusammensetzung	55	1
36	detectors	primäre	5	1
37	data	Daten-	7	7/8
38	University	Universit-	7	6/7
39	element-	-usammensetzung	7	6/7
40	neutron	Neutronenstern	7	6/7
41	Cerenkov	Cerenkov-Licht-	7	6/7
42	spinning	rotier-	6	6/7
43	electric	Feld	6	5/6
44	lines	-inien	6	5/6
45	medium	Medium	6	5/6
46	estimate-	abschätz	6	5/6
47	output	-eistung	6	5/6
48	bright-	Astronom-	5	5/6
49	rapid-	Pulsare-	5	5/6
50	proposed	vorgeschlagen	6	5/6

The table shows two interesting effects of the morphological analysis procedure. The word

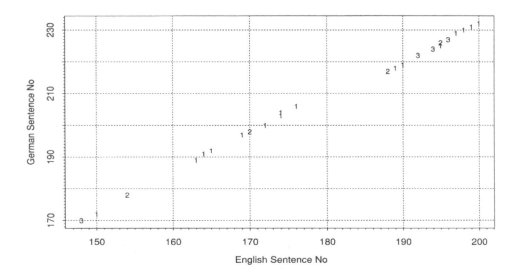

FIGURE 2 The SAT after pass 1

is wrongly associated with the word "Gammaquant" (25) with a frequency of 6, but the prefix is correctly associated with "Luftschauer-" (18) with a frequency of 20. On the other hand, the incorrect association of "element" with "-usammensetzung" (39) is on the basis of a normalized form (for words ending in "Zusammensetzung"), whereas "Zusammensetzung", unnormalized, is correctly associated with "composition" (35). Totally unrelated words are associated in a few instances, as in "Observatory"/"diesem" (24), "detectors"/"primäre-" (36), and "bright-"/"Astronom-" (48). Of these only the second remains at the end of the third pass. The English "Observatory" is then properly associated with the German word "Observatorium-". At that stage, "bright-" has no association.

Figure 2 shows part of the SAT at the end of pass 1 of the relaxation cycle. Sentences in the English text and in the German text are identified by numbers on the abscissa and the ordinate respectively. Entries in the array indicate that the sentences are considered to correspond. The numbers show how often a particular association is supported, which is essentially equivalent to how many word pairs in the WAT support such an association. If there are no such numbers, then no associations have been found for it at this stage. For example, the association of English sentence 148 with German sentence 170 is supported by three different word pairs. It is already very striking how strongly occupied entries in this table constrain the possible entries in the unoccupied slots.

Figure 3 shows part of the AST before pass 2. This is derived directly from the material illustrated in Figure 2. The abscissa gives the English sentence number and in direction of the ordinate the associated German sentences are shown (bullet). Those sentence pairs in Figure 2 supported by at least three word pairs, namely those shown on lines 148, 192, 194, and 196, are assumed to be reliable, and they are the only associations shown for these sentences in Figure 3. Candidate associations have been provided for the intervening sentences by the interpolation method described above. Notice that the greatest number of candidates are shown against sentences occurring midway between a pair assumed to have been reliably connected (English sentence numbers 169 to 171).

TABLE 2 The WAT after pass 3

	English	German	Eng.Freq.	Similarity
1	interstellar	interstellare-	12	1
2	ergs	Joule	10	1
3	per	pro	12	11/12
4	univers-	Univers-	8	7/8
5	proto-	Proto-	14	13/15
6	X-ray-	Röntgen	19	19/22
7	proton-	Proton-	13	6/7
8	volts	Elektronvolt	19	19/11
9	photo-	Photo-	14	13/16
10	light-	Licht-	23	21/26
11	earth	Erde	9	4/5
12	accelerate-	beschleunigt	9	7/9
13	object	Objekt	9	7/9
14	Cygnus	Cygnus	63	27/35
15	accelerat-	beschleunig-	18	16/21
16	model-	Modell-	17	16/21
17	pulsars-	Pulsare-	8	3/4
18	cosmic-	kosmische-	81	35/47
19	galaxy	Milchstraße	19	17/23
20	pulsar-	Pulsar-	17	14/19
21	electrons	Elektronen	12	5/7
22	magnetic	Magnetfeld	11	5/7
23	shower-	Luftschauer-	20	17/24
24	telescope-	Teleskop-	9	7/10
25	source-	Quelle-	40	33/49
26	Second-	Sekund-	20	2/3
27	low-	nied-	9	2/3
28	part-	Teil-	59	49/76
29	and	und	69	9/14
30	electric-	electrisch-	9	7/11
31	gamma-	Gammastrahl-	61	27/43
32	gas-	Gas-	16	5/8
33	relativ-	relativ-	11	8/13
34	atmospher-	Atmosphäre-	10	8/13
35	direction	-ichtung	10	3/5
36	years	Jahre-	11	10/17
37	object	Objekt	14	10/17
38	period-	Stunden-	11	7/12
39	electro-	elektr-	83	63/109
40	only	Nur	18	15/26
41	source	-uelle	26	4/7
42	photon-	Photon-	10	4/7
43	high-energy	hochenerg-	13	9/16
44	directions	-ichtungen	8	5/9
45	thousand-	Tausend-	8	5/9
46	stars	Sterne-	11	6/11
47	number	Anzahl	8	6/11
48	interact-	wechselwirk-	9	6/11
49	signal	Signal-	12	7/13
50	the	die-	496	313/582
51	energy	Energie	28	22/41
52	wave-	Wellen-	13	8/15
53	star-	Stern-	29	9/17
54	sources	Quellen	14	11/21
55	nucle-	Atom-	19	12/23
56	of	ein-	304	1/2
57	not	nicht	30	1/2
58	ray	Gammaquant-	14	1/2
59	arrival	Ankunfts-	9	1/2

Table 2 (continued) The WAT after pass 3.

	English	German	Eng.Freq.	Similarity
60	percent	Prozent	6	1
61	ultrahigh-	ultraho-	5	1
62	galaxies	Galaxien	5	1
63	composition	Zusammensetzung	5	1
64	Crimean	Krim	5	1
65	supernova	Supernova-Explosion-	5	1
66	activ-	aktiv-	5	1
67	synchrotron	Synchrotronstrahlung	5	1
68	detectors	primäre-	5	1
69	muons	Myonen	4	1
70	massive	Masse-	4	1
71	meteorite-	Meteorit-	4	1
72	Low-energy	niederenergetische-	4	1
73	Fermi	Fermi-	4	1
74	decay-	Zerfall-	4	1
75	discovery	Entdeckung	4	1
76	limit	Grenze	4	1
77	ground	Erdboden	4	1
78	day-	Tag-	3	1
79	Robert	Robert	3	1
80	mirrors	Spiegel-	3	1
81	absorption	Absorptionslinie-	3	1
82	David	David	3	1
83	average	Mittel-	3	1
84	light-years	Lichtjahre	3	1
85	Neutrons	Neutronen	3	1
86	Gregory-	Gregory-	3	1
87	explosions	Supernova-Explosionen	3	1
88	electrically	elektrisch	3	1
89	electromagnetic	elektromagnetische-	3	1
90	candidates	Kandidaten	3	1
91	data	Daten-	7	7/8
92	University	Universit-	7	6/7
93	spinning	rotier-	6	6/7
94	neutron	Neutronenstern	7	6/7
95	proposed	vorgeschlagen	6	5/6
96	lines	-inien	6	5/6
97	colleague-	Kollegen	4	4/5
98	interactions	Wechselwirkungen	5	4/5
99	Physic-	Physik-	5	4/5
100	models	Modelle-	4	4/5

Table 2 shows the first 100 entries of the WAT after pass 3 where the threshold for the similarity was lowered to 0.5. As we pointed out earlier, most of the incorrect associations in Table 1 have been eliminated. German "Milchstraße" (19) is not a translation of the English "galaxy", but the Milky Way is indeed a galaxy and "the galaxy" is sometimes used in place of "Milky Way" where the reference is clear. The association between "period-" and "Stunden-" (38) is of a similar kind. The words are strongly associated because of recurring phrases of the form "in a 4.8-hour period."

Figure 4 gives the SAT after pass 3. It is immediately apparent, first, that the majority of the sentences have been associated with probable translations and, second, that many of these associations are very strongly supported. For example, note that the correspondence between English sentence 190 and German sentence 219 is supported 21 times. Using this table, it is in fact possible to locate the translation of a given English sentence to within two or three sentences in the German text, and usually more closely than that. However, some ambiguities remain. Some of the apparent anomalies come from stylistic differences in the way the texts were presented in the two journals. The practice of *Scientific American* is to collect sequences

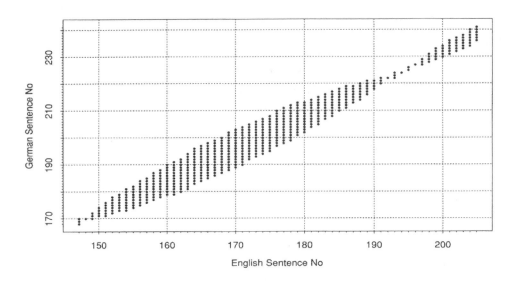

German Sentence No
English Sentence No

FIGURE 3 The AST before pass 2

of paragraphs into a logical unit by beginning the first of them with an oversized letter. This is not done in *Spektrum der Wissenschaft*, which instead provides a subheading at these points. This therefore appears as an insertion in the translation. Two such are sentences number 179 and 233, but our procedure has not created incorrect associations for them.

Recall that the alignment problem derives its interest from the fact that single sentences are sometimes translated as sequences of sentences and conversely. These cases generally stand out strongly in the output that our method delivers. For example, the English sentence pair (5, 6):

> Yet whereas many of the most exciting advances in astronomy have come from the detailed analysis of X-ray and radio sources, until recently the source of cosmic rays was largely a matter of speculation. They seem to come from everywhere, raining down on the earth from all directions at a uniform rate.

is rendered in German by the single sentence (5):

> Dennoch blieben die Quellen der kosmischen Strahlung, die aus allen Richtungen gleichmäßig auf die Erde zu treffen scheint, bis vor kurzem reine Spekulation, während einige der aufregendsten Fortschritte in der Astronomie aus dem detaillierten Studium von Röntgen- und Radiowellen herrührten.

The second English sentence becomes a relative clause in the German.

More complex associations also show up clearly in the results. For example, English sentences 218 and 219 are translated by German sentences 253, 254, and 255, where 254 is a translation of the latter part of 218 and the early part of 219:

> When a proton strikes a gas nucleus, it produces three kinds of pion, of which one kind decays into two gamma rays. The gamma rays travel close to the original trajectory of the proton, and the model predicts they will be beamed toward the earth at just two points on the pulsars orbit around the companion star.

> Trifft ein Proton auf einen Atomkern in dieser Gashülle, werden drei Arten von Pionen erzeugt. Die neutralen Pionen zerfallen in jeweils zwei Gammaquanten, die sich beinahe in dieselbe Richtung wie das ursprüngliche Proton bewegen. Nach der Modellvorstellung gibt es gerade zwei

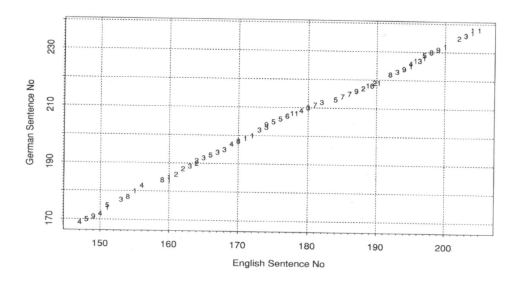

FIGURE 4 The SAT after pass 3

Positionen im Umlauf des Pulsars um seinen Begleitstern, bei denen die Strahlung in Richtung zum Beobachter auf der Erde ausgesandt wird.

Another example is provided by English sentences 19 and 20, which appear in German as sentences 21 and 22. However the latter part of English sentence 19 is in fact transferred to sentence 22 in the German. This is also unmistakable in the final results. Notice also, in this example, that the definition of "photon" has become a parenthetical expression at the beginning of the second German sentence, a fact which is not reflected.

> The other end of the cosmic-ray energy spectrum is defined somewhat arbitrarily: any quantum greater than 108 electron volts arriving from space is considered a cosmic ray. The definition encompasses not only particles but also gamma-ray photons, which are quanta of electromagnetic radiation.

> Das untere Ende des Spektrums der kosmischen Strahlen ist verhältnismäßig unscharf definiert. Jedes Photon (Quant der elektromagnetischen Strahlung) oder Teilchen mit einer Energie von mehr als 10^8 Elektronenvolt, aus dem Weltraum eintrifft, bezeichnet man als kosmischen Strahl.

It frequently occurred in our data that sentences that were separated by colons or semicolons in the original appeared as completely distinct sentences in the German translation. Indeed, the common usage in the two languages would probably have been better represented if we had treated colons and semicolons as sentence separators, along with periods, question marks, and the like. There are, of course, situations in English in which these punctuation marks are used in other ways, but they are considerably less frequent and, in any case, it seems that our program would almost always make the right associations. An example involving the colon is to be found in sentence 142 of the original, translated as sentences 163 and 164:

> The absorption lines established a lower limit on the distance of Cygnus X-3: it must be more distant than the farthest hydrogen cloud, which is believed to lie about 37,000 light-years away, near the edge of the galaxy.

> Aus dieser Absorptionslinie kann man eine untere Grenze der Entfernung von Cygnus X bestimmen. Die Quelle muß jenseits der am weitesten entfernten Wasserstoff-Wolke sein, also weiter als ungefähr 37000 Lichtjahre entfernt, am Rande der Milchstraße.

English sentence 197, containing a semicolon, is translated by German sentences 228 and 229:

> The estimate is conservative; because it is based on the gamma rays observed arriving at the earth, it does not take into account the likelihood that Cygnus X emits cosmic rays in all directions.

> Dies ist eine vorsichtige Abschätzung. Sie ist nur aus den Gammastrahlen-Daten abgeleitet, die auf der Erde gemessen werden; daß Cygnus X-3 wahrscheinlich kosmische Strahlung in alle Richtungen aussendet, ist dabei noch nicht berücksichtigt.

Table 3 summarizes the accuracy of the algorithm as a function of the number of passes. The (thresholded) SAT is evaluated by two criteria: the number of correct alignments divided by the total number of alignments, and – since the SAT does not necessarily give an alignment for every sentence – the coverage, i.e., the number of sentences with at least one entry relative to the total number of sentences.

TABLE 3 Correctness of sentence alignment in the various passes of the algorithm

Pass	Correctness in SAT	Coverage of SAT	Constraint by AST
1	100%	12%	4%
2	100%	47%	17%
3	100%	89%	38%
4	99.7%	96%	41%

An alignment is said to be correct if the SAT contains exactly the numbers of the sentences that are complete or partial translations of the original sentence. The coverage of 96% of the SAT in pass 4 is as much as one would expect, since the remaining nonaligned sentences are one-zero alignments, most of them due to the German subheadings that are not part of the English version. The table also shows that the AST always provides a significant number of candidates for alignment with each sentence before a pass: the fourth column gives the number of true sentence alignments relative to the total number of candidates in the AST. Recall that the final alignment is always a subset of the hypotheses in the AST in every preceding pass.

Figure 5 shows the true sentence alignment for the first 50 sentences (dots), and how the algorithm discovered them: in the first pass, only a few sentences are set into correspondence (circles); after the second pass (crosses) already almost half of the correspondences are found. Note that there are no wrong alignments in the first two passes. In the third pass, almost all of the remaining alignments are found (for the first 50 sentences in the figure: all), and a final pass usually completes the alignment.

Our algorithm produces very favorable results when allowed to converge gradually. Processing time in the original LISP implementation was high, typically several hours for each pass. By trading CPU time for memory massively, the time needed by a C++ implementation on a Sun 4/75 was reduced to 1.7 min for the first pass, 0.8 min for the second, and 0.5 min for the third pass in an application to this pair of articles. (Initialization, i.e., reading the files and building up the data structures, takes another 0.6 min in the beginning.) It should be noted that a naive implementation of the algorithm without using the appropriate data structures can easily lead to times that are a factor of 30 higher and do not scale up to larger texts.

The application of our method to a text that we put together from the Hansard corpus had essentially no problem in identifying the correct sentence alignment in a process of five passes. The alignments for the first 1000 sentences of the English text were checked by hand, and seven errors were found; five of them occurred in sentences where sentence boundaries were not correctly identified by the program because of periods that did not mark a sentence boundary and were not identified as such by a very simple preprocessing program. The other

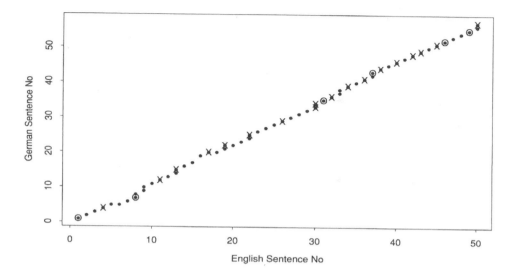

FIGURE 5 Sentence alignment of the first 50 sentences of the test texts: true alignment (dots) and hypothesis of the SAT after the first pass (circles) and after the second pass (crosses)

two errors involved two short sentences for which the SAT did not give an alignment. Processing time increased essentially linearly (per pass): the first pass took 8.3 min, the second 3.2 min, and it further decreased until the last pass, which took 2.1 min. (Initialization took 4.2 min.) Note that the error rate depends crucially on the kind of "annealing schedule" used: if the thresholds that allow a word pair in the WAT to influence the SAT are lowered too fast, only a few passes are needed, but accuracy deteriorates. For example, in an application where the process terminated after only three passes, the accuracy was only in the eighties (estimated on the basis of the first 120 sentences of the English Hansard text checked by hand). Since processing time after the first pass is usually already considerably lower, we have found that a high accuracy can safely be attained when more passes are allowed than are actually necessary.

In order to evaluate the sensitivity of the algorithm to the lengths of the texts that are to be aligned, we applied it to text samples that ranged in length from 10 to 1000 sentences, and examined the accuracy of the WAT after the first pass; that is, more precisely, the number of word pairs in the WAT that are valid translations relative to the total number of word pairs with a similarity of not less than 0.7 (the measurements are cross-validated over different texts). The result is that this accuracy increases asymptotically to 1 with the text length, and is already higher than 80% for a text length of 100 sentences (which is sufficient to reach an almost perfect alignment in the end). Roughly speaking, the accuracy is almost 1 for texts longer than 150 sentences, and around 0.5 for text length in the lower range from 20 to 60. In other words, texts of a length of more than 150 sentences are suitable to be processed in this way; text fragments shorter than 80 sentences do not have a high proportion of correct word pairs in the first WAT, but further experiments showed that the final alignment for texts of this length is, on average, again almost perfect: the drawback of a less accurate initial WAT is apparently largely compensated for by the fact that the AST is also narrower for these texts; however, the variance in the alignment accuracies is significantly higher.

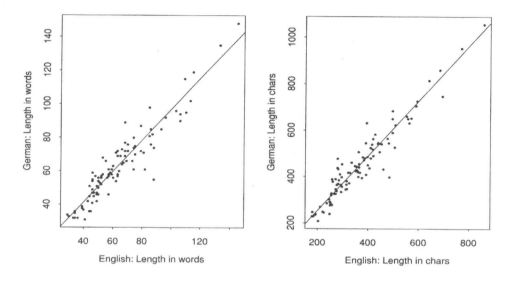

FIGURE 6 Lengths of aligned paragraphs are correlated: Robust regression between lengths of aligned paragraphs. Left: length measured in words. Right: length measured in characters.

38.5 Related Work

Since we addressed the text translation alignment problem in 1988, a number of researchers, among them Gale and Church (1991) and Brown, Lai, and Mercer (1991), have worked on the problem. Both methods are based on the observation that the length of text unit is highly correlated to the length of the translation of this unit, no matter whether length is measured in number of words or in number of characters (see Figure 6). Consequently, they are both easier to implement than ours, though not necessarily more efficient. The method of Brown, Lai, and Mercer (1991) is based on a hidden Markov model for the generation of aligned pairs of corpora, whose parameters are estimated from a large text. For an application of this method to the Canadian Hansard, good results are reported. However, the problem was also considerably facilitated by the way the implementation made use of Hansard-specific comments and annotations: these are used in a preprocessing step to find anchors for sentence alignment such that, on average, there are only ten sentences in between. Moreover, this particular corpus is well known for the near literalness of its translations, and it is therefore unclear to what extent the good results are due to the relative ease of the problem. This would be an important consideration when comparing various algorithms; when the algorithms are actually applied, it is clearly very desirable to incorporate as much prior knowledge (say, on potential anchors) as possible. Moreover, long texts can almost always be expected to contain natural anchors, such as chapter and section headings, at which to make an a priori segmentation.

Gale and Church (1991) note that their method performed considerably better when lengths of sentences were measured in number of characters instead of in number of words. Their method is based on a probabilistic model of the distance between two sentences, and a dynamic programming algorithm is used to minimize the total distance between aligned units. Their implementation assumes that each character in one language gives rise to, on average, one character in the other language.[8] In our texts, one character in English on average gives rise

---

[8]Recall that, in a similar way, we assumed in our implementation that one sentence in one language

to somewhat more than 1.2 characters in German, and the correlation between the lengths (in characters) of aligned paragraphs in the two languages was with 0.952 lower than the 0.991 that are mentioned in Gale and Church (1991), which supports our impression that the *Scientific American* texts we used are hard texts to align, but it is not clear to what extent this would deteriorate the results. In applications to economic reports from the Union Bank of Switzerland, the method performs very well on simple alignments (one-to-one, one-to-two), but has at the moment problems with complex matches. The method has the advantage of associating a score with pairs of sentences so that it is easy to extract a subset for which there is a high likelihood that the alignments are correct.

Given the simplicity of the methods proposed by Brown, Lai, and Mercer and Gale and Church, either of them could be used as a heuristic in the construction of the initial AST in our algorithm. In the current version, the number of candidate sentence pairs that are considered in the first pass near the middle of a text contributes disproportionally to the cost of the computation. In fact, as we remarked earlier, the complexity of this step is $O(n\sqrt{n})$. The proposed modification would effectively make it linear.

38.6   Future Work

For most practical purposes, the alignment algorithm we have described produces very satisfactory results, even when applied to relatively free translations. There are doubtless many places in which the algorithm itself could be improved. For example, it is clear that the present method of building the SAT favors associations between long sentences, and this is not surprising, because there is more information in long sentences. But we have not investigated the extent of this bias and we do not therefore know it as appropriate.

The present algorithm rests on being able to identify one-to-one associations between certain words, notably technical terms and proper names. It is clear from a brief inspection of Table 2 that very few correspondences are noticed among everyday words and, when they are, it is usually because those words also have precise technical uses. The very few exceptions include "only"/"nur" and "the"/"die-". The pair "per"/"pro" might also qualify, but if the languages afford any example of a scientific preposition, this is surely it. The most interesting further developments would be in the direction of loosening up this dependence on one-to-one associations both because this would present a very significant challenge and also because we are convinced that our present method identifies essentially all the significant one-to-one associations.

There are two obvious kinds of looser associations that could be investigated. One would consist of connections between a single vocabulary item in one language and two or more in the other, or even between several items in one language and several in the other. The other would involve connections – one-one, one-many, or many-many – between phrases or recurring sequences.

We have investigated the first of these enough to satisfy ourselves that there is latent information on one-to-many associations in the text, and that it can be revealed by suitable extensions of our methods. However, it is clear that the combinatorial problems associated with this approach are severe, and pursuing it would require much fine tuning of the program and designing much more effective ways of indexing the most important data structures. The key to reducing the combinatorial explosion probably lies in using tables of similarities such as those the present algorithm uses to suggest combinations of items that would be worth considering. If such an approach could be made efficient enough, it is even possible that it would

---

gives rise to, on average, n/m sentences in the other language (see first footnote in Section 2.30).

provide a superior way of solving the problem for which our heuristic methods of morphological analysis were introduced. Its superiority would come from the fact that it would not depend on words being formed by concatenation, but would also accommodate such phenomena as umlaut, ablaut, vowel harmony, and the nonconcatenative process of Semitic morphology.

The problems of treating recurring sequences are less severe. Data structures, such as the Patricia tree (Knuth 1973; pp. 490–493) provide efficient means of identifying all such sequences and, once identified, the data they provide could be added to the WAT much as we now add the results of morphological analysis. Needless to say, this would only allow for uninterrupted sequences. Any attempt to deal with discontinuous sequences would doubtless also involve great combinatorial problems.

These avenues for further development are intriguing and would surely lead to interesting results. But it is unlikely that they would lead to much better sets of associations among sentences than are to be found in the SATs that our present program produces, and it was mainly these results that we were interested in from the outset. The other avenues we have mentioned concern improvements in the WAT which, for us, was always a secondary interest.

Publications referenced

Baayen 1991; Brown et al. 1991; Brown et al. 1990; Church and Hanks 1990; Drela and Langford 1985; Drela and Langford 1986; Fano 1961; Gale and Church 1991; Kay and Röscheisen 1988; Knuth 1973; MacKeown and Weekes 1985; MacKeown and Weekes 1986; van Rijsbergen 1979; Sato and Nagao 1990.

39

Regular Models of Phonological Rule Systems

with Ronald M. Kaplan

This paper presents a set of mathematical and computational tools for manipulating and reasoning about regular languages and regular relations and argues that they provide a solid basis for computational phonology. It shows in detail how this framework applies to ordered sets of context-sensitive rewriting rules and also to grammars in Koskenniemi's two-level formalism. This analysis provides a common representation of phonological constraints that supports efficient generation and recognition by a single simple interpreter.

39.1 Introduction

Ordered sets of context-sensitive rewriting rules have traditionally been used to describe the pronunciation changes that occur when sounds appear in different phonological and morphological contexts. Intuitively, these phenomena ought to be cognitively and computationally simpler than the variations and correspondences that appear in natural language syntax and semantics, yet the formal structure of such rules seems to require a complicated interpreter and an extraordinarily large number of processing steps. In this paper, we show that any such rule defines a regular relation on strings if its non-contextual part is not allowed to apply to its own output, and thus it can be modeled by a symmetric finite-state transducer. Furthermore, since regular relations are closed under serial composition, a finite set of rules applying to each other's output in an ordered sequence also defines a regular relation. A single finite-state transducer whose behavior simulates the whole set can therefore be constructed by composing the transducers corresponding to the individual rules. This transducer can be incorporated into efficient computational procedures that are far more economical in both recognition and production than any strategies using ordered rules directly. Since orthographic rules have similar formal properties to phonological rules, our results generalize to problems of word recognition in written text.

The mathematical techniques we develop to analyze rewriting rule systems are not limited just to that particular collection of formal devices. They can also be applied to other recently proposed phonological or morphological rule systems. For example, we can show that Koskenniemi's (1983) two-level parallel rule systems also denote regular relations. Section 2 below provides an intuitive grounding for the rest of our discussion by illustrating the correspondence between simple rewriting rules and transducers. Section 3 summarizes the mathematical tools that we use to analyze both rewriting and two-level systems. Section 4 describes the properties of the rewriting rule formalisms we are concerned with, and their mathematical characterization is presented in Sections 5 and 6. A similar characterization of two-level rule systems is provided in Section 7.

By way of introduction, we consider some of the computational issues presented by simple morphophonemic rewriting rules such as these:

Rule 1

$N \to m \;/\; \underline{} [+\text{labial}]$

Rule 2

$N \to n$

According to these rules an underspecified, abstract nasal phoneme N appearing in the lexical forms *iNpractical* and *iNtractable* will be realized as the *m* in *impractical* and as the *n* in *intractable*. To ensure that these and only these results are obtained, the rules must be treated as obligatory and taken in the order given. As obligatory rules, they must be applied to every substring meeting their conditions. Otherwise, the abstract string *iNpractical* would be realized as *inpractical* and *iNpractical* as well as *impractical*, and the abstract N would not necessarily be removed from *iNtractable*. Ordering the rules means that the output of the first is taken as the input to the second. This prevents *iNpractical* from being converted to *inpractical* by Rule 2 without first considering Rule 1.

These obligatory rules always produce exactly one result from a given input. This is not the case when they are made to operate in the reverse direction. For example, if Rule 2 is inverted on the string *intractable*, there will be two results, *intractable* and *iNtractable*. This is because *intractable* is derivable by that rule from both of these strings. Of course, only the segments in *iNtractable* will eventually match against the lexicon, but in general both the N and *n* results of this inversion can figure in valid interpretations. Compare the words *undecipherable* and *indecipherable*. The *n* in the prefix *un-*, unlike the one in *in-*, does not derive from the abstract N, since it remains unchanged before labials (c.f. *unperturbable*). Thus the results of inverting this rule must include *undecipherable* for *undecipherable* but *iNdecipherable* for *indecipherable* so that each of them can match properly against the lexicon.

While inverting a rule may sometimes produce alternative outputs, there are also situations in which no output is produced. This happens when an obligatory rule is inverted on a string that it could not have generated. For example, *iNput* cannot be generated by Rule 1 because the N precedes a labial and therefore would obligatorily be converted to *m*. There is therefore no output when Rule 1 is inverted on *iNput*. However, when Rule 2 is inverted on *input*, it does produce *iNput* as one of its results. The effect of then inverting Rule 1 is to remove the ambiguity produced by inverting Rule 2, leaving only the unchanged *input* to be matched against the lexicon. More generally, if recognition is carried out by taking the rules of a grammar in reverse order and inverting each of them in turn, later rules in the new sequence act as filters on ambiguities produced by earlier ones.

The existence of a large class of ambiguities that are introduced at one point in the recognition process and eliminated at another has been a major source of difficulty in efficiently reversing the action of linguistically motivated phonological grammars. In a large grammar, the effect of these spurious ambiguities is multiplicative, since the information needed to cut off unproductive paths often does not become available until after they have been pursued for some considerable distance. Indeed, speech understanding systems that use phonological rules do not typically invert them on strings but rather apply them to the lexicon to generate a list of all possible word forms (e.g. Woods et al. 1976; Klatt 1980). Recognition is then accomplished by standard table lookup procedures, usually augmented with special devices to handle phonological changes that operate across word boundaries. Another approach to solving this computational problem would be to use the reversed cascade of rules during recognition, but to somehow make the filtering information of particular rules available earlier in the process. However, no general and effective techniques have been proposed for doing this.

The more radical approach that we explore in this paper is to eliminate the cascade altogether, representing the information in the grammar as a whole in a single more unified device, namely, a finite-state transducer. This device is constructed in two phases. The first is to create for each rule in the grammar a transducer that exactly models its behavior. The second is to compose these individual rule transducers into a single machine that models the grammar as a whole.

Johnson (1972) was the first to notice that the noncyclic components of standard phonological formalisms, and particularly the formalism of *The Sound Pattern of English* (Chomsky and Halle 1968), were equivalent in power to finite-state devices despite a superficial resemblance to general rewriting systems. Phonologists in the SPE tradition, as well as the structuralists that preceded them, had apparently honored an injunction against rules that rewrite their own output but still allowed the output of a rule to serve as context for a reapplication of that same rule. Johnson realized that this was the key to limiting the power of systems of phonological rules. He also realized that basic rewriting rules were subject to many alternative modes of application offering different expressive possibilities to the linguist. He showed that phonological grammars under most reasonable modes of application remain within the finite-state paradigm.

We observed independently the basic connections between rewriting-rule grammars and finite-state transducers in the late 1970s and reported them at the 1981 meeting of the Linguistic Society of America (Kaplan and Kay 1981). The mathematical analysis in terms of regular relations emerged somewhat later. Aspects of that analysis and its extension to two-level systems were presented at conferences by Kaplan (1984, 1985, 1988), in courses at the 1987 and 1991 Linguistics Institutes, and at colloquia at Stanford University, Brown University, the University of Rochester, and the University of Helsinki.

Our approach differs from Johnson's in two important ways. First, we abstract away from the many details of both notation and machine description that are crucial to Johnson's method of argumentation. Instead, we rely strongly on closure properties in the underlying algebra of regular relations to establish the major result that phonological rewriting systems denote such sets of string-pairs. We then use the correspondence between regular relations and finite-state transducers to develop a constructive relationship between rewriting rules and transducers. This is accomplished by means of a small set of simple operations, each of which implements a simple mathematical fact about regular languages, regular relations, or both. Second, our more abstract perspective provides a general framework within which to treat other phonological formalisms, existing or yet to be devised. For example, two-level morphology (Koskenniemi 1983), which evolved from our early considerations of rewriting rules, relies for its analysis and implementation on the same algebraic techniques. We are also encouraged by initial successes in adapting these techniques to the autosegmental formalism described by Kay (1987).

39.2 Rewriting Rules and Transducers

Supposing for the moment that Rule 2 ($N \rightarrow n$) is optional, Figure 1 shows the transition diagram of a finite-state transducer that models it. A finite-state transducer has two tapes. A transition can be taken if the two symbols separated by the colon in its label are found at the current position on the corresponding tapes, and the current position advances across those tape symbols. A pair of tapes is accepted if a sequence of transitions can be taken starting at the start-state (conventionally labeled 0) and at the beginning of the tapes and leading to a final state (indicated by double circles) at the end of both tapes. In the machine in Figure 1, there is a transition from state 0 to state 0 that translates every phoneme into itself, reflecting the fact that any phoneme can remain unchanged by the optional rule. These are shown schematically in the diagram. This machine will accept a pair of tapes just in case they stand in a certain relation: they must be identical except for possible replacements of N on the first tape with n on the second. In other words, the second tape must be one that could have resulted from applying the optional rule to the string on the first tape.

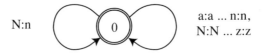

FIGURE 1 Rule 2 as optional

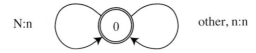

FIGURE 2 Rule 2 as obligatory

But the rule is in fact obligatory, and this means that there must be no occurrences of N on the second tape. This condition is imposed by the transducer in Figure 2. In this diagram, the transition label "other" abbreviates the set of labels $a{:}a$, $b{:}b$, ... $z{:}z$, the identity pairs formed from all symbols that belong to the alphabet but are not mentioned explicitly in this particular rule. This diagram shows no transition over the pair $N{:}N$ and the transducer therefore blocks if it sees N on both tapes. This is another abbreviatory convention that is typically used in implementations to reduce transducer storage requirements, and we use it here to simplify the state diagrams we draw. In formal treatments such as the one we present below, the transition function is total and provides for transitions from every state over every pair of symbols. Any transition we do not show in these diagrams in fact terminates at a single nonfinal state, the "failure" state, which we also do not show.

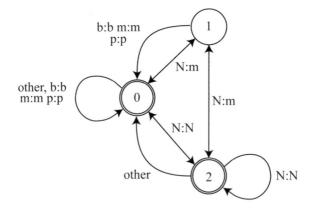

FIGURE 3 Rule 1 as obligatory

Figure 3 is the more complicated transducer that models the obligatory behavior of Rule 1 ($N \to m/\ +[labial]$). This machine blocks in state 1 if it sees the pair $N{:}m$ not followed by one

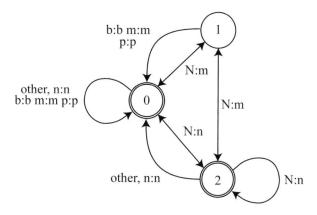

FIGURE 4 Composition of obligatory Rules 1 and 2

of the labials *p, b, m*. It blocks in state 2 if it encounters the pair *N:N* followed by a labial on both tapes, thus providing for the situation in which the rule is not applied even though its conditions are satisfied. If it does not block and both tapes are eventually exhausted, it accepts them just in case it is then in one of the final states, 0 or 2, shown as double circles. It rejects the tapes if it ends up in the nonfinal state 1, indicating that the second tape is not a valid translation of the first one.

We have described transducers as acceptors of pairs of tapes that stand in a certain relation. But they can also be interpreted asymmetrically, as functions either from more abstract to less abstract strings or the other way around. Either of the tapes can contain an input string, in which case the output will be written on the other. In each transition the machine matches the symbol specified for the input tape and writes the one for the output. When the first tape contains the input, the machine models the generative application of the rule; when the second tape contains the input, it models the inversion of the rule. Thus, compared with the rewriting rules from which they are derived, finite-state transducers have the obvious advantage of formal and computational simplicity. Whereas the exact procedure for inverting rules themselves is not obvious, it is clearly different from the procedure required for generating. The corresponding transducers, on the other hand, have the same straightforward interpretation in both directions.

While finite-state transducers are attractive for their formal simplicity, they have a much more important advantage for our purposes. A pair of transducers connected through a common tape models the composition of the relations that those transducers represent. The pair can be regarded as performing a transduction between the outer tapes, and it turns out that a single finite-state transducer can be constructed that performs exactly this transduction without incorporating any analog of the intermediate tape. In short, the relations accepted by finite-state transducers are closed under serial composition. Figure 4 shows the composition of the *m*-machine in Figure 3 and the *n*-machine in Figure 2. This transducer models the cascade in which the output of Rule 1 is the input to Rule 2.

This machine is constructed so that it encodes all the possible ways in which the *m*-machine and *n*-machine could interact through a common tape. The only interesting interactions involve *N*, and these are summarized in the following table:

input	*m*-machine	output			
			input	*n*-machine	output
N	*labial follows*	m	m		m
N	*nonlabial follows*	N	N		n

An N in the input to the m-machine is converted to m before a labial and this m remains unchanged by the n-machine. The only instances of N that reach the n-machine must therefore be followed by nonlabials and these must be converted to n. Accordingly, after converting N to m, the composed machine is in state 1, which it can leave only by a transition over labials. After converting N to n, it enters state 2, from which there is no labial transition. Otherwise, state 2 is equivalent to the initial state.

Figure 5 illustrates the behavior of this machine as a generator applied to the abstract string *iNtractable*. Starting in state 0, the first transition over the "other" arc produces i on the output tape and returns to state 0. Two different transitions are then possible for the N on the input tape. These carry the machine into states 1 and 2 and output the symbols m and n respectively. The next symbol on the input tape is t. Since this is not a labial, no transition is possible from state 1, and that branch of the process therefore blocks. On the other branch, the t matches the "other" transition back to state 0 and the machine stays in state 0 for the remainder of the string. Since state 0 is a final state, this is a valid derivation of the string *intractable*. Figure 6 is a similar representation for the generation of *impractical*.

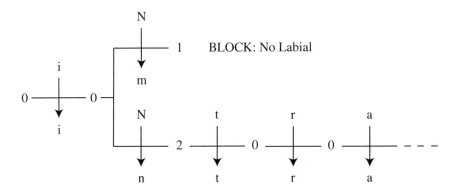

FIGURE 5 Generation of *intractable*

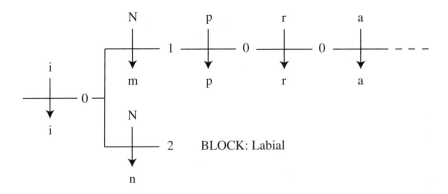

FIGURE 6 Generation of *impractical*

Figures 7 and 8 illustrate this machine operating as a recognizer. As we pointed out earlier, there are two results when the cascade of rules that this machine represents is inverted on the string *intractable*. As Figure 7 shows, the *n* can be mapped into *n* by the *n:n* transition at state 0 or into *N* by the transition to state 2. The latter transition is acceptable because the following *t* is not a labial and thus matches against the "other" transition to state 0. When the following symbol is a labial, as in Figure 8, the process blocks. Notice that the string *iNput* that would have been written on the intermediate tape before the machines were composed is blocked after the second symbol by constraints coming from the *m*-machine.

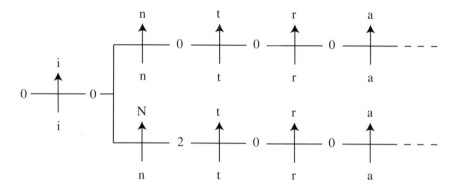

FIGURE 7 Recognition of *intractable*

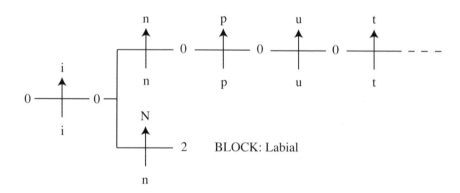

FIGURE 8 Recognition of *input*

Repeated composition reduces the machines corresponding to the rules of a complete phonological grammar to a single transducer that works with only two tapes, one containing the abstract phonological string and the other containing its phonetic realization. General methods for constructing transducers such as these rely on fundamental mathematical notions that we develop in the next section.

39.3   Mathematical Concepts and Tools

Formal languages are sets of strings, mathematical objects constructed from a finite alphabet Σ by the associative operation of concatenation. Formal language theory has classified string sets, the subsets of Σ^*, in various ways and has developed correspondences between languages, grammatical notations for describing their member strings, and automata for recognizing them.

A similar conceptual framework can be established for *string relations* . These are the collections of ordered tuples of strings, the subsets of $\Sigma^* \times ... \times \Sigma^*$.

We begin by defining an n-way concatenation operation in terms of the familiar concatenation of simple strings. If $X = \langle x_1, x_2, ...x_n \rangle$ and $Y = \langle y_1, y_2, ...y_n \rangle$ are n-tuples of strings, then the concatenation of X and Y, written $X \cdot Y$ or simply XY, is defined by

$$X \cdot Y =_{df} \langle x_1 y_1, x_2 y_2, ...x_n y_n \rangle$$

That is, the n-way concatenation of two string-tuples is the tuple of strings formed by string concatenation of corresponding elements. The length of a string-tuple $|X|$ can be defined in terms of the lengths of its component strings:

$$|X| =_{df} \sum_i |x_i|$$

This has the expected property that $|X \cdot Y| = |X| + |Y|$, even if the elements of X or of Y are of different lengths. Just as the empty string ϵ is the identity for simple string concatenation, the n-tuple all of whose elements are ϵ is the identity for n-way concatenation, and the length of such a tuple is zero.

39.3.1 Regular Relations and Finite-State Transducers

With these definitions in hand, it is immediately possible to construct families of string relations that parallel the usual classes of formal languages. Recall, for example, the usual recursive definition of a regular language over an alphabet Σ (superscript i denotes concatenation repeated i times, according to the usual convention, and we let Σ^ϵ denote $\Sigma \cup \{\epsilon\}$):

1. The empty set and a for all a in Σ^ϵ are regular languages.
2. If L_1, L_2, and L are regular languages, then so are

   $L_1 \cdot L_2 = \{xy | x \in L_1, y \in L_2\}$ (concatenation)

   $L_1 \cup L_2$ (union)

   $L^* = \bigcup_{i=0}^{\infty} L^i$ (Kleene closure)

3. There are no other regular languages.

We can use exactly the same scheme to define regular n-relations in terms of n-way concatenation:

1. The empty set and a for all a in $\Sigma^\epsilon \times ... \times \Sigma^\epsilon$ are regular n-relations.
2. If R_1, R_2, and R are regular n-relations, then so are

   $R_1 \cdot R_2 = \{xy | x \in R_1, y \in R_2\}$ (n-way concatenation)

   $R_1 \cup R_2$ (union)

   $R^* = \bigcup_{i=0}^{\infty} R^i$ (n-way Kleene closure)

3. There are no other regular n-relations.

Other families of relations can also be defined by analogy to the formal language case. For example, a system of context-free rewriting rules can be used to define a context-free n-relation simply by introducing n-tuples as the terminal symbols of the grammar. The standard context-free derivation procedure will produce tree structures with n-tuple leaves, and the relational yield of such a grammar is taken to be the set of n-way concatenations of these leaves. Our analysis of phonological rule systems does not depend on expressive power beyond the capacity of the regular relations, however, and we therefore confine our attention to the mathematical and computational properties of these more limited systems. The relations we refer to as "regular," to emphasize the connection to formal language theory, are often known as "rational relations" in the algebraic literature, where they have been extensively studied (e.g. Eilenberg 1974).

The descriptive notations and accepting automata for regular languages can also be generalized to the n-dimensional case. An n-way regular expression is simply a regular expression whose terms are n-tuples of alphabetic symbols or ϵ. For ease of writing we separate the elements of an n-tuple by colons. Thus the expression $a : b \ \epsilon : c$ describes the two-relation containing the single pair $\langle a, bc \rangle$, and $a : b : c^* \ q : r : s$ describes the three-relation $\{\langle a^n q, b^n r, c^n s \rangle | n \geq 0\}$. The regular-expression notation provides for concatenation, union, and Kleene-closure of these terms. The accepting automata for regular n-relations are the n-way finite-state transducers. As illustrated by the two-dimensional examples given in Section 2, these are an obvious extension of the standard one-tape finite-state machines.

The defining properties of the regular languages, regular expressions, and finite-state machines are the basis for proving the well-known Kleene correspondence theorems showing the equivalence of these three string-set characterizations. These essential properties carry over in the n-way generalizations, and therefore the correspondence theorems also generalize. In particular, simple analogs of the standard inductive proofs show that

> Every n-way regular expression describes a regular n-relation;
> Every regular n-relation is described by an n-way regular expression;
> Every n-tape finite-state transducer accepts a regular n-relation; and
> Every regular n-relation is accepted by an n-tape finite-state transducer.

The strength of our analysis method comes from the equivalence of these different characterizations. While we reason about the regular relations in algebraic and set-theoretic terms, we conveniently describe the sets under discussion by means of regular expressions, and we prove essential properties by constructive operations on the corresponding finite-state transducers. In the end, of course, it is the transducers that satisfy our practical, computational goals.

A nondeterministic (one-tape) finite-state machine is a quintuple $(\Sigma, Q, q, F, \delta)$ where Σ is a finite alphabet, Q is a finite set of states, $q \in Q$ is the initial state, and $F \subseteq Q$ is the set of final states. The transition function δ is a total function that maps $Q \times \Sigma^\epsilon$ to 2^Q, the set of all subsets of Q, and every state s in Q is vacuously a member of $\delta(s, \epsilon)$. We extend the function δ to sets of states, so that for any $P \subseteq Q$ and $a \in \Sigma^\epsilon$, $\delta(P, a) = \cup_{p \in P} \delta(p, a)$. We also define the usual extension of δ to a transition function δ^* on Σ^* as follows: for all r in Q, $\delta^*(r, \epsilon) = \delta(r, \epsilon)$, and for all $u \in \Sigma^*$ and $a \in \Sigma^\epsilon$, $\delta^*(r, ua) = \delta(\delta^*(r, u), a)$. Thus, the machine accepts a string x just in case $\delta^*(q, x) \cap F$ is nonempty; that is, if there is a sequence of transitions over x beginning at the initial state and ending at a set of states at least one of which is final. We know, of course, that every regular language is also accepted by a deterministic, ϵ-free finite-state machine, but assuming vacuous ϵ transitions at every state reduces the number of special cases that have to be considered in some of the arguments below.

A nondeterministic n-way finite-state transducer (fst) is defined by a quintuple similar to that of an fsm except for the transition function δ, a total function that maps $Q \times \Sigma^\epsilon \times ... \times \Sigma^\epsilon$ to 2^Q. Partly to simplify the mathematical presentation and partly because only the binary relations are needed in the analysis of rewriting rules and Koskenniemi's two-level systems, from here on we frame the discussion in terms of binary relations and two-tape transducers. However, the obvious extensions of these properties do hold for the general case, and they may be useful in developing a formal understanding of autosegmental phonological and morphological theories (for an illustration, see Kay 1987).

The transition function δ of a transducer also extends to a function δ^* that carries a state and a pair of strings onto a set of states. Transitions in fsts are labeled with pairs of symbols and we continue to write them with a colon separator. Thus, $u{:}v$ labels a transition over a u on the first tape and a v on the second. A finite-state transducer T defines the regular relation $R(T)$, the set of pairs $\langle x, y \rangle$ such that $\delta^*(q, x, y)$ contains a final state. The pair $\epsilon : \epsilon$ plays the same role as a label of transducer transitions that the singleton ϵ plays in one-tape machines, and the ϵ-removal algorithm for one-tape machines can be generalized to show that every regular relation is accepted by an ϵ-free transducer. However, it will also be convenient for some arguments below to assume the existence of vacuous $\epsilon : \epsilon$ transitions.

We write xRy if the pair $\langle x, y \rangle$ belongs to the relation R. The image of a string x under a relation R, which we write x/R, is the set of strings y such that $\langle x, y \rangle$ is in R. Similarly, R/y is the set of strings that R carries onto y. We extend this notation to sets of strings in the obvious way: $X/R = \cup_{x \in X} x/R$. This relational notation gives us a succinct way of describing the use of a corresponding transducer as either a generator or a recognizer. For example, if R is the regular relation recognized by the transducer in Figure 4, then $R/intractable$ is the set of strings that R maps to $intractable$, namely $\{intractable, iNtractable\}$, as illustrated in Figure 7. Similarly, $iNtractable/R$ is the set of strings $\{intractable\}$ that R maps from $iNtractable$ (Figure 5).

We rely on the equivalence between regular languages and relations and their corresponding finite-state automata, and we frequently do not distinguish between them. When the correspondence between a language L and its equivalent machine must be made explicit, we let $M(L)$ denote a finite-state machine that accepts L. Similarly, we let $T(R)$ denote a transducer that accepts the relation R, as provided by the correspondence theorem. We also rely on several of the closure properties of regular languages (Hopcroft and Ullman 1979): for regular languages L_1 and L_2, $L_1 L_2$ is the regular language containing all strings $x_1 x_2$ such that $x_l \in L_1$ and $x_2 \in L_2$. We use superscripts for repeated concatenation: L^n contains the concatenation of n members of L, and L^* contains strings with arbitrary repetitions of strings in L, including zero. The operator Opt is used for optionality, so that $Opt(L)$ is $L \cup \{\epsilon\}$. We write $\overline{L}$ for the complement of L, the regular language containing all strings not in L, namely, $\Sigma^* - L$. Finally, $Rev(L)$ denotes the regular language consisting of the reversal of all the strings in L.

39.3.2 Properties of Regular Relations

There are a number of basic connections between regular relations and regular languages. The strings that can occur in the domain and range of a regular relation R $(Dom(R)= R/\Sigma^*$ and $Range(R) = \Sigma^*/R)$ are the regular languages accepted by the finite-state machines derived from $T(R)$ by changing all transition labels $a{:}b$ to a and b respectively, for all a and b in Σ^ϵ. Given a regular language L, the identity relation $Id(L)$ that carries every member of L into itself is regular; it is characterized by the fst obtained from an fsm $M(L)$ by changing all transition labels a to $a{:}a$. Clearly, for all languages L, $L = Dom(Id(L)) = Range(Id(L))$. The inverse R^{-1} of a regular relation R is regular, since it is accepted by a transducer formed from $T(R)$ by changing all labels $a{:}b$ to $b{:}a$. The reversal $Rev(R)$, consisting of pairs containing the reversal of strings in R's pairs, is also regular; its accepting transducer is derived from $T(R)$ by generalizing the standard one-tape fsm construction for regular language reversal.

Given a pair of regular languages L_1 and L_2 whose alphabets can, without loss of generality, be assumed equal, the relation $L_1 \times L_2$ containing their Cartesian product is regular. To prove this proposition, we let $M_1 = (\Sigma, Q_1, q_1, F_1, \delta_1)$ and $M_2 = (\Sigma, Q_2, q_2, F_2, \delta_2)$ be fsms accepting L_1 and L_2 respectively and define the fst

$$T = (\Sigma, Q_1 \times Q_2, \langle q_1, q_2 \rangle, F_1 \times F_2, \delta)$$

where for any $s_1 \in Q_1, s_2 \in Q_2$ and $a, b \in \Sigma^\epsilon$

$$\delta(\langle s_1, s_2 \rangle, a, b) = \delta_1(s_1, a) \times \delta_2(s_2, b)$$

We can show by induction on the number of transitions that for any strings x and y,

$$\delta^*(\langle q_1, q_2 \rangle, x, y) = \delta_1^*(q_1, x) \times \delta_2^*(q_2, y)$$

This result holds trivially when x and y are both ϵ by the general definition of δ^*. If a and b are in Σ^ϵ and u and v are in Σ^*, then, using the definition of δ^* and the definition just given for δ of the Cartesian product machine, we have

$$
\begin{aligned}
\delta^*(\langle q_1, q_2 \rangle, ua, vb) &= \delta(\delta^*(\langle q_1, q_2 \rangle, u, v), a, b) \\
&= \delta(\delta_1^*(q_1, u) \times \delta_2^*(q_2, v), a, b) \qquad \text{by induction} \\
&= \delta_1(\delta_1^*(q_1, u), a) \times \delta_2(\delta_2^*(q_2, v), b) \\
&= \delta_1^*(q_1, ua) \times \delta_2^*(q_2, vb)
\end{aligned}
$$

Thus, $\delta^*(\langle q_1, q_2 \rangle, x, y)$ contains a final state if and only if both $\delta_1^*(q_1, x)$ and $\delta_2^*(q_2, y)$ contain final states, so T accepts exactly the strings in $L_1 \times L_2$. $\qquad\square$

Note that $L \times L$ is not the same as $Id(L)$, because only the former can map one member of L onto a different one. If L contains the single-character strings a and b, then $Id(L)$ only contains the pairs $\langle a, a \rangle$ and $\langle b, b \rangle$ while $L \times L$ also contains $\langle a, b \rangle$ and $\langle b, a \rangle$.

A similar construction is used to prove that regular relations are closed under the composition operator discussed in Section 2. A pair of strings $\langle x, y \rangle$ belongs to the relation $R_1 \circ R_2$ if and only if for some intermediate string z, $\langle x, z \rangle \in R_1$ and $\langle z, y \rangle \in R_2$. If $T(R_1) = (\Sigma, Q_1, a_1, F_1, \delta_1)$ and $T(R_2) = (\Sigma, Q_2, a_2, F_2, \delta_2)$ the composition $R_1 \circ R_2$ is accepted by the composite fst

$$(\Sigma, Q_1 \times Q_2, \langle q_1, q_2 \rangle, F_1 \times F_2, \delta)$$

where

$$\delta(\langle s_1, s_2 \rangle, a, b) = \{\langle t_1, t_2 \rangle | \text{ for some } c \in \Sigma^\epsilon, t_1 \in \delta(s_1, a, c) \text{ and } t_2 \in \delta(s_2, c, b)\}$$

In essence, the δ for the composite machine is formed by canceling out the intermediate tape symbols from corresponding transitions in the component machines. By an induction on the number of transitions patterned after the one above, it follows that for any strings x and y,

$$\delta^*(\langle q_1, q_2 \rangle, x, y) = \{\langle t_1, t_2 \rangle | \text{ for some } z \in \Sigma^*, t_1 \in \delta_1^*(q_1, x, z) \text{ and } t_2 \in \delta_2^*(q_2, z, y)\}$$

The composite transducer enters a final state just in case both component machines do for some intermediate z. This establishes that the composite transducer does represent the composition of the relations R_1 and R_2, and that the composition of two regular relations is therefore regular. Composition of regular relations, like composition of relations in general, is associative: $(R_1 \circ R_2) \circ R_3 = R_1 \circ (R_2 \circ R_3) = R_1 \circ R_2 \circ R_3$. For relations in general we also know that $Range(R_1 \circ R_2) = Range(R_1)/R_2$.

We can use this fact about the range of a composition to prove that the image of a regular language under a regular relation is a regular language. (It is well known that the images under a regular relation of languages in other classes, for example the context-free languages, also remain within those classes (e.g. Harrison 1978), but these other results do not concern us here.) That is, if L is a regular language and R is an arbitrary regular relation, then the languages L/R and R/L are both regular. If L is a regular language, we know there exists a regular relation $Id(L)$ that takes all and only members of L into themselves. Since $L = Range(Id(L))$ it follows that

$$
\begin{aligned}
L/R &= (Range(Id(L)))/R \\
&= Range(Id(L) \circ R)
\end{aligned}
$$

$Id(L) \circ R$ is regular and we have already observed that the range of any regular relation is a regular language. By symmetry of argument we know that R/L is also regular.

Just like the class of regular languages, the class of regular relations is by definition closed under the operations of union, concatenation, and repeated concatenation. Also, the Pumping Lemma for regular languages immediately generalizes to regular relations, given the definitions of string-tuple length and n-way concatenation and the correspondence to finite-state transducers. The regular relations differ from the regular languages, however, in that they are not closed under intersection and complementation. Suppose that R_1 is the relation $\{\langle a^n, b^n c^* \rangle | n \geq 0\}$ and R_2 is the relation $\{\langle a^n, b^* c^n \rangle | n \geq 0\}$. These relations are regular, since they are defined by the regular expressions $a : b^* \epsilon : c^*$ and $\epsilon : b^* a : c$ respectively. The intersection $R_1 \cap R_2$ is $\{\langle a^n, b^n c^n \rangle | n \geq 0\}$. The range of this relation is the context-free language $b^n c^n$, which we have seen is not possible if the intersection is regular. The class of regular relations is therefore not closed under intersection, and it immediately follows that it is also not closed under complementation: by De Morgan's law, closure under complementation and union would imply closure under intersection. Nonclosure under complementation further implies that some regular relations are accepted by only nondeterministic transducers. If for every regular relation there is a deterministic acceptor, then the standard technique (Hopcroft and Ullman 1979) of interchanging its final and nonfinal states could be used to produce an fst accepting the complement relation, which would therefore be regular.

39.3.3 Same-Length Regular Relations

Closure under intersection and relative difference, however, are crucial for our treatment of two-level rule systems in Section 7. But these properties are required only for the same-length regular relations, and it turns out that this subclass is closed in the necessary ways. The same-length relations contain only string-pairs $\langle x, y \rangle$ such that the length of x is the same as the length of y. It may seem obvious that the relevant closure properties do hold for this subclass, but for the sake of completeness we sketch the technical details of the constructions by which they can be established.

We make use of some auxiliary definitions regarding the *path-language* of a transducer. A path-string for any finite-state transducer T is a (possibly empty) sequence of symbol-pairs $u_1 : v_1 \ u_2 : v_2 ... u_n : v_n$ that label the transitions of an accepting path in T. The path-language of T, notated as $Paths(T)$, is simply the set of all path-strings for T. $Paths(T)$ is obviously regular, since it is accepted by the finite-state machine constructed simply by interpreting the transition labels of T as elements of an alphabet of unanalyzable pair-symbols. Also, if P is a finite-state machine that accepts a pair-symbol language, we define the path-relation $Rel(P)$ to be the relation accepted by the fst constructed from P by reinterpreting every one of its pair-symbol labels as the corresponding symbol pair of a transducer label. It is clear for all fsts T that $Rel(M(Paths(T))) = R(T)$, the relation accepted by T.

Now suppose that R_1 and R_2 are regular relations accepted by the transducers T_1 and T_2, respectively, and note that $Paths(T_1) \cap Paths(T_2)$ is in fact a regular language of pair-symbols accepted by some fsm P. Thus $Rel(P)$ exists as a regular relation. Moreover, it is easy to see that $Rel(P) \subseteq R_1 \cap R_2$. This is because every string-pair belonging to the path-relation is accepted by a transducer with a path-string that belongs to the path-languages of both T_1 and T_2. Thus that pair also belongs to both R_1 and R_2.

The opposite containment does not hold of arbitrary regular relations. Suppose a pair $\langle x, y \rangle$ belongs to both R_1 and R_2 but that none of its accepting paths in T_1 has the same sequence of transition labels as an accepting path in T_2. Then there is no path in $Paths(T_1) \cap Paths(T_2)$ corresponding to this pair and it is therefore not contained in $Rel(P)$. This situation can arise when the individual transducers have transitions with ϵ-containing labels. One transducer may then accept a particular string pair through a sequence of transitions that does not literally match the transition sequence taken by the other on that same pair of strings. For example, the first fst might accept the pair $\langle ab, e \rangle$ by the transition sequence $a : \epsilon b : c$, while the other accepts that same pair with the sequence $a : cb : \epsilon$. This string-pair belongs to the intersection of the relations, but unless there is some other accepting path common to both machines, it will not belong to $Rel(P)$. Indeed, when we apply this construction to fsts accepting the relations we used to derive the context-free language above, we find that $Rel(P)$ is the empty relation (with no string-pairs at all) instead of the set-theoretic intersection $R_1 \cap R_2$.

However, if R_1 and R_2 are accepted by transducers none of whose accepting paths have ϵ-containing labels, then a string-pair belonging to both relations will be accepted by identically labeled paths in both transducers. The language $Paths(T_1) \cap Paths(T_2)$ will contain a path-string corresponding to that pair, that pair will belong to $Rel(P)$, and $Rel(P)$ will be exactly $R_1 \cap R_2$. Thus, we complete the proof that the same-length relations are closed under intersection by establishing the following proposition:

Lemma

R is a same-length regular relation if and only if it is accepted by an ϵ-free finite-state transducer.

Proof

The transitions of an ϵ-free transducer T set the symbols of the string-pairs it accepts in one-to-one correspondence, so trivially, $R(T)$ is same-length. The proof in the other direction is more tedious. Suppose R is a same-length regular relation accepted by some transducer T which has transitions of the form $u : \epsilon$ or $\epsilon : v$ (with u and v not ϵ; we know all $\epsilon : \epsilon$ transitions can be eliminated by the obvious generalization of the one-tape ϵ-removal algorithm). We systematically remove all ϵ-containing transitions in a finite sequence of steps each of which preserves the accepted relation. A path from the start-state to a given nonfinal state will contain some number of $u : \epsilon$ transitions and some number of $\epsilon : v$ transitions, and those two numbers will not necessarily be identical. However, for all paths to that state the difference between those numbers will be the same, since the discrepancy must be reversed by each path that leads from that state to a final state. Let us define the imbalance characterizing a state to be the difference in the number of $u : \epsilon$ and $\epsilon : v$ transitions on paths leading to that state. Since an acyclic path cannot produce an imbalance that differs from zero by more than the number of states in the machine, the absolute value of the imbalance is bounded by the machine size. On each iteration our procedure has the effect of removing all states with the maximum imbalance. First, we note that transitions of the form $u : v$ always connect a pair of states with the same imbalance. Such transitions can be eliminated in favor of an equivalent sequence of transitions $\epsilon : v$ and $u : \epsilon$ through a new state whose imbalance is one less than the imbalance of the original two states. Now suppose that $k > 0$ is the maximum imbalance for the machine and that all $u : v$ transitions between states of imbalance k have been eliminated. If q is a k-imbalance state, it will be entered only by $u : \epsilon$ transitions from k-1 states and left only by $\epsilon : v$ transitions also to k-1 states. For all transitions $u : \epsilon$ from a state p to q and all transitions $\epsilon : v$ from q to r, we construct a new transition $u : v$ from p to r. Then we remove state q from the machine along with all transitions entering or leaving it. These manipulations do not change the accepted relation but do reduce by one the number of k-imbalance states. We repeat this procedure for all k states and then move on to the k-1 states, continuing until no states remain with a positive imbalance. A symmetric procedure is then used to eliminate all the states whose imbalance is negative. In the end, T will have been transformed to an ϵ-free transducer that still accepts R. $\square$

The same-length regular relations are obviously closed under union, concatenation, composition, inverse, and reverse, in addition to intersection, since all of these operations preserve both regularity and string length. An additional path-language argument shows that they are also closed under relative difference. Let T_1 and T_2 be ϵ-free acceptors for R_1 and R_2 and construct an fsm P that accepts the regular pair-symbol language $Paths(T_1) - Paths(T_2)$. A string-pair belongs to the regular relation $Rel(P)$ if and only if it has an accepting path in T_1 but not in T_2. Thus $Rel(P)$ is $R_1\text{--}R_2$. Being a subset of R_1, it is also same-length.

39.3.4 Summary of Mathematical Tools

Let us summarize the results to this point. If L_1, L_2, and L are regular languages and R_1, R_2, and R are regular relations, then we know that the following relations are regular:

$$R_1 \cup R_2 \quad R_1 \cdot R_2 \quad R^* \quad R^{-1} \quad R_1 \circ R_2 \quad IdL \quad L_1 \times L_2 \quad Rev(R)$$

We know also that the following languages are regular (x is a string):

$$Dom(R) \quad Range(R) \quad L/R \quad R/L \quad x/R \quad R/x$$

Furthermore, if R_1, R_2, and R are in the same-length subclass, then the following also belong to that restricted subclass:

$$R_1 \cup R_2 \quad R_1 \cdot R_2 \quad R^* \quad R^{-1} \quad R_1 \circ R_2 \quad RevR \quad R_1 \cap R_2 \quad R_1 - R_2$$

$Id(L)$ is also same-length for all L. Intersections and relative differences of arbitrary regular relations are not necessarily regular, however. We emphasize that all these set-theoretic, algebraic operations are also constructive and computational in nature: fsms or fsts that accept the languages and relations that these operations specify can be constructed directly from machines that accept their operands.

Our rule translation procedures makes use of regular relations and languages created with five special operators. The first operator produces a relation that freely introduces symbols from a designated set S. This relation, $Intro(S)$, is defined by the expression $[Id(\Sigma) \cup [\{e\} \times S]]^*$. If the characters a and b are in Σ and S is $\{\$\}$, for example, then $Intro(S)$ contains an infinite set of string pairs including $\langle a, a \rangle$, $\langle a, \$a \rangle$, $\langle a, a\$\$ \rangle$, $\langle ab, \$\$a\$b\$\$ \rangle$, and so on. Note that $Intro(S)^{-1}$ removes all elements of S from a string if S is disjoint from Σ.

The second is the *Ignore* operator. Given a regular language L and a set of symbols S, it produces a regular language notated as L_S and read as "L ignoring S." The strings of L_S differ from those of L in that occurrences of symbols in S may be freely interspersed. This language is defined by the expression $L_S = Range(Id(L) \circ Intro(S))$. It includes only strings that would be in L if some occurrences of symbols in S were ignored.

The third and fourth operators enable us to express if-then and if-and-only-if conditions on regular languages. These are the operators *If-P-then-S* ("if prefix then suffix") and *If-S-then-P* ("if suffix then prefix"). Suppose L_1 and L_2 are regular languages and consider the set of strings

$$\textit{If-P-then-S}(L_1, L_2) = \{x|\ \text{for every partition } x_1x_2 \text{ of } x, \text{ if } x_1 \in L_1, \text{ then } x_1 \in L_2\}$$

A string is in this set if each of its prefixes in L_1 is followed by a suffix in L_2. This set is also a regular language: it excludes exactly those strings that have a prefix in L_1 followed by a suffix not in L_2 and can therefore be defined by

$$\textit{If-P-then-S}(L_1, L_2) = \overline{L_1 \overline{L_2}}$$

This operator, the regular-language analog of the logical equivalence between $P \rightarrow Q$ and $\neg(P \wedge \neg Q)$, involves only concatenation and complementation, operations under which regular languages (though not relations) are closed. We can also express the symmetric requirement that a prefix be in L_1 if its suffix is in L_2 by the expression

$$\textit{If-S-then-P}(L_1, L_2) = \overline{\overline{L_1} L_2}$$

Finally, we can combine these two expressions to impose the requirement that a prefix be in L_1 if and only if its suffix is in L_2:

$$P\text{-}iff\text{-}S(L_1, L_2) = If\text{-}P\text{-}then\text{-}S(L_1, L_2) \cap If\text{-}S\text{-}then\text{-}P(L_1, L_2)$$

These five special operators, being constructive combinations of more primitive ones, can also serve as components of practical computation.

The double complementation in the definitions of these conditional operators, and also in several other expressions to be introduced later, constitutes an idiom for expressing universal quantification. While a regular expression $\alpha\beta\gamma$ expresses the proposition that an instance of β occurs between *some* instance of α and *some* instance of γ, the expression $\overline{\alpha\overline{\beta}\gamma}$ claims that an instance of β intervenes between *every* instance of α and a following instance of γ.

39.4 Rewriting Rule Formalisms

Phonological rewriting rules have four parts. Their general form is

$$\phi \rightarrow \psi / \lambda \,\_\_\_\, \rho$$

This says that the string ϕ is to be replaced by (rewritten as) the string ψ whenever it is preceded by λ and followed by ρ. If either λ or ρ is empty, it is omitted and, if both are empty, the rule is reduced to

$$\phi \rightarrow \psi$$

The *contexts*, or *environments*, λ and ρ are usually allowed to be regular expressions over a basic alphabet of *segments*. This makes it easy to write, say, a vowel-harmony rule that replaces a vowel that is not specified for backness as a back or front vowel according as the vowel in the immediately preceding syllable is back or front. This is because the Kleene closure operator can be used to state that any number of consonants can separate the two vowels. The rule might be formulated as follows:

$$V_i \rightarrow B_i / B_j C * \,\_\_\_$$

where B_i is the back counterpart of the vowel V_i, and B_j is another (possibly different) back vowel. There is less agreement on the restrictions that should apply to ϕ and ψ, the portions that we refer to as the *center* of the rule. They are usually simple strings and some theorists would restrict them to single segments. However, these restrictions are without interesting mathematical consequences and we shall be open to all versions of the theory if we continue to take it that these can also denote arbitrary regular languages.

It will be important to provide for multiple applications of a given rule, and indeed, this will turn out to be the major source of difficulty in reexpressing rewriting rules in terms of regular relations and finite-state transducers. We have already remarked that our methods work only if the part of the string that is actually rewritten by a rule is excluded from further rewriting by that same rule. The following optional rule shows that this restriction is necessary to guarantee regularity:

$$\epsilon \rightarrow ab / a \,\_\_\_\, b$$

If this rule is allowed to rewrite material that it introduced on a previous application, it would map the regular language ab into the context-free language $\{a^n b^n | 1 \leq n\}$, which we have already seen is beyond the power of regular relations.

However, we do not forbid material produced in one application of a rule from serving as *context* for a subsequent application of that rule, as would routinely be the case for a vowel-harmony rule, for example. It is this restriction on interactions between different applications of a given rule that motivates the notation

$$\phi \rightarrow \psi / \lambda \_\_\_ \rho$$

rather than

$$\lambda \phi \rho \rightarrow \lambda \psi \rho$$

The context refers to a part of the string that the current application of the rule does not change but which, since it may have been changed in a previous application, allows for an interaction between successive applications.

The important outstanding question concerning interactions between applications of one and the same rule at different positions in a string has to do with the relative order in which they take place. Consider the obligatory rule

$$a \rightarrow b / ab \_\_\_ ba$$

as applied to the string

$$ababababab a$$

At least three different outcomes are possible, namely:

(1) *abbbabbbaba*

(2) *ababbbabbba*

(3) *abbbbbbbbba*

Result (1) is obtained if the first application is at the leftmost eligible position in the string; each successive application applies to the output of any preceding one, and further to the right in the string. We call this the *left-to-right* strategy. The corresponding *right-to-left* strategy gives rise to (2). Result (3) comes from identifying all possible rule applications in the original string and carrying them out *simultaneously*. All three strategies have been advocated by phonologists. We shall assume that each rule is marked individually to show which strategy is to be employed for it. We shall concentrate on these three strategies, but other less obvious ones can also be treated by simple rearrangements of our techniques.

Optional rules and most obligatory rules will produce at least one output string, perhaps just a copy of the input if the conditions for application are nowhere satisfied. But certain obligatory rules are anomalous in that they may produce no output at all. The following left-to-right rule is a case in point:

$$\epsilon \rightarrow b / b \_\_\_$$

If a string containing the symbol b is input to this rule, another b will be inserted immediately after it, and that one will serve to trigger the rule again. This process will never terminate, and no finite-length output is ever produced. Strange as they may seem, rules like this are useful as filters to eliminate undesired paths of derivation.

In contrast to obligatory rules, optional rules typically produce many outputs. For example, if the rule above ($a \rightarrow b / ab \_\_\_ ba$) is marked as optional and left-to-right and is also applied to the string *ababababab*, the following, in addition to (1), would be among its outputs:

(4) *abbbabababa*

(5) *ababbbababa*

The string (4) is similar to (1) except that only the leftmost application of the rule has been carried out. For (5) the application in the middle would not have been possible for the obligatory rule and is possible here only because the necessary context was not destroyed by an application further to the left.

Kenstowicz and Kisseberth (1979), who discuss a number of rule application strategies in great detail, cite a case in which one rule seems to be required in the grammars of two languages. However, it must be applied left to right in one, but right to left in the other. In the Australian language Gidabal, the long vowel of certain suffixes becomes short if the vowel of the preceding syllable is long. We find, for example, $yag\bar{a} + ya$ 'should fix' where we would otherwise expect $yag\bar{a} + y\bar{a}$. (We use $+$ to mark the point at which the suffix begins and a bar over a vowel to show that it is long.) The interesting question concerns what happens when several of these suffixes are added to the same stem. Some examples are:

Underlying	Surface
$barbar + y\bar{a} + d\bar{a}ng$	$barbar + \bar{a} + dang$
	'straight above'
$djalum + b\bar{a} + d\bar{a}ng + b\bar{e}$	$djalum + b\bar{a} + dang + b\bar{e}$
	'is certainly right on the fish'
$gun\bar{u}m + b\bar{a} + d\bar{a}ang + b\bar{e}$	$gun\bar{u}m + ba + d\bar{a}ng + be$
	'is certainly right on the stump'

The rule that Kenstowicz and Kisseberth propose is essentially the following:

$$\bar{V} \rightarrow V/\bar{V}C^* \_\_\_$$

This produces the desired result only if applied left to right and only if obligatory. The alternation of long and short vowels results from the fact that each application shortens a long vowel that would otherwise serve as part of the context for a subsequent application.

The same rule appears as the *rhythmic law* in Slovak – all suffix vowels are shortened following a long vowel, as in the following examples:

$vol + \bar{a} + me$ 'we call' $\qquad$ $chit + a + me$ 'we read'

$vol + \bar{a}v + a + me$ 'we call often' $\qquad$ $ch\bar{i}t + av + a + me$ 'we read often'

This time the rule must be applied either simultaneously or from right to left.

It might seem that a transducer mimicking the operation of a right-to-left rule would have to examine its tapes in the opposite order from one that implemented a left-to-right rule, and it is difficult to see how two transducers operating in different directions could then be composed. However, we shall see that directionality in rewriting rules is not mirrored by directionality in the transducers. Instead, directionality determines which of the two tapes the left and right contexts must appear on. In a left-to-right rule, the left context of the rule is to be verified against the portion of the string that results from previous applications of that rule, whereas the right context is to be verified against the portion of the string that has not yet been changed but may eventually be modified by applications further to the right. In a right-to-left rule, the situation is reversed.

Consider again the left-to-right rule schema

$$\bar{V} \rightarrow V/\bar{V}C^* \_\_\_$$

which applies to the string $\bar{a}b\bar{e}c\bar{i}d\bar{o}$ to give $\bar{a}becido$. The portions of the tapes that support the two applications of the rule are boxed in the diagram on the left below. The diagram on the right shows how it comes about that there are three applications when the rule is taken as moving from right to left.

It is often convenient in phonological rules to introduce a special symbol to mark the beginning and end of the string. This allows edge-conditioned string transformations to be encoded in rewriting rules. For example, Kenstowicz and Kisseberth give the following rule to describe the devoicing of final obstruents in German and Russian:

$$[+obstruent] \rightarrow [-voiced]/ \_\_\_ \#$$

We will consider the feature notation exemplified here shortly. For the moment, it can be taken as equivalent to a set of rules whose effect is to replace any segment that is classified as an obstruent by its unvoiced equivalent before the boundary symbol that marks the end of a word. It accounts for the phonological realization of the Russian form *xleb* 'bread' as *xlep*. The boundary symbol $\#$ is special in the rule formalism in that it can only appear in the context parts of a rule, never in the input or output patterns, and it never matches an element that appears explicitly in the string. Although boundary-context rules require distinctive mathematical treatment, we show below that they also denote only regular string relations.

As we have said, we take it that each rule in a grammar will be annotated to show which strategy is to be used in applying it. We also assume that rules are annotated to show whether they are to be taken as obligatory or optional. We have considered only obligatory rules up to now, but optional rules are also commonly used to account for cases of free variation. The mathematical treatment of optional rules will turn out to be a simpler case of what must be done for obligatory rules and, therefore, a natural step in the general development.

As well as providing for various strategies for reapplying a single rule, we also consider the possibility of what we call a *batch* rule. This is a set of rules that the application strategies treat as one entity, the individual rules being otherwise unordered relative to one another. This mode of rule application will turn out to be interesting even if it is not an explicit part of any particular phonological formalism because, as we shall see, it constitutes an essential step in the interpretation of rules that use features to refer to underspecified segments. A good example of this is the vowel-harmony rule referred to earlier, namely

$$V_i \rightarrow B_i/B_j C^*$$

In feature notation, this could be written

$$\begin{bmatrix} +\text{syllabic} \\ -\text{consonantal} \end{bmatrix} \rightarrow [+back] / \begin{bmatrix} +\text{back} \\ +\text{syllabic} \\ -\text{consonantal} \end{bmatrix} [+consonantal]^* \_\_\_$$

meaning that a segment that is specified as a vowel comes also to be specified as back when the most recent preceding vowel is back; all other features remain unchanged. The grammar will presumably contain another rule that will apply in circumstances when this one does not, namely

$$V_i \rightarrow F_i/F_j C^*$$

or

$$\begin{bmatrix} +\text{syllabic} \\ -\text{consonantal} \end{bmatrix} \rightarrow [-back] / \begin{bmatrix} -\text{back} \\ +\text{syllabic} \\ -\text{consonantal} \end{bmatrix} [+consonantal]^* \_\_\_$$

except, of course, that the context can be omitted from whichever of the two is placed second in an ordered list of rules. But this is precisely the question: What is the proper order of this pair of rules?

Consider an actual case, namely, vowel harmony in Turkish. Let A represent an abstract vowel with e and a as its front and back realizations, and I another abstract vowel with i

and dotless ı as its front and back counterparts. The first of these occurs, for example, in the abstract plural suffix *lAr*, and the second occurs in the possessive suffix *Im*, meaning 'my.' Both suffixes can be used together, and the harmony is illustrated by the different realizations of the abstract vowels in the forms *apartmanlArIm* and *adreslArIm*. These appear as *apartmanlarım* 'my apartments' and *adreslerim* 'my addresses.' Using only the simple non-feature notation we started out with, we can describe this variation with the following four rules:

$$A \quad \rightarrow \quad e/eC^* \text{ ___}$$
$$A \quad \rightarrow \quad a$$
$$I \quad \rightarrow \quad i/eC^* \text{ ___}$$
$$I \quad \rightarrow \quad ı$$

The proper surface forms for these words are produced if these rules are ordered as we have given them – inserting front vowels first – and if each of them is applied from left to right. However, applying the rules in this way gives the wrong result when we create the dative possessive form of *adres* instead of the possessive plural. The dative suffix is spelled simply as the abstract vowel *A* and the abstract *adresImA* should be realized as *adresime* if harmony is respected. But the rules as given will map *adresImA* to *adresima* instead. This is because the earlier rules apply to the final *A* at a time before the context required for that vowel has been established. Reordering the rules to fix this problem will cause the previous correct analyses to fail. The proper results in all cases come only if we describe Turkish vowel harmony with rules that proceed left to right through the string as a group, applying at each position whichever one matches. This is the mode of application for a set of rules collected together as a batch.

The notion of a batch rule apparently has not arisen as a distinctive formal concept in phonological theories. The reason is doubtless that batch rules are unnecessarily prolix and, in particular, they fail to capture generalizations that can almost always be made about the individual rules that make up a batch. Phonologists prefer rules that are based on feature matrices. These rules allow segments to be referred to by specifying which members of a finite set of properties they do or do not have. A feature matrix can specify a segment completely, in which case it is equivalent to the unanalyzable segment names we have been using, or it can leave it underspecified. Feature matrices therefore constitute an abbreviatory convention with the advantage that what is easy to abbreviate will be motivated to just the extent that the features themselves are motivated. An underspecified segment corresponds to a set of fully specified segments, and a rule that contains underspecified segments corresponds to a set of rules that are to be applied in batch mode.

Feature matrices based on a well-motivated set of features allow the phonologist to capture significant generalizations and thus effectively to reduce the components of our batch rules to a single rule in most cases. A significant addition that has been made to the basic machinery of feature-based rules consists of variables written with lowercase Greek letters α, β, γ, etc. and ranging over the values + and −. We can use them, for example, to collapse our vowel-harmony rules into a single one as follows:

$$\begin{bmatrix} +\text{syllabic} \\ -\text{consonantal} \end{bmatrix} \rightarrow [\alpha back] \; / \begin{bmatrix} \alpha \text{back} \\ +\text{syllabic} \\ -\text{consonantal} \end{bmatrix} [+consonantal]^* \text{ ___}$$

Both occurrences of the variable α must be instantiated to the same value, either + or −, at each application of the rule. What the rule now says is that a vowel takes its backness from the vowel in the preceding syllable; that is, the most recent preceding vowel that is separated from it by zero or more consonants.

While the explicit use of variables is an important addition to the notation, it was in fact foreshadowed by a property of the initial feature system, namely that features not explicitly mentioned in the center of a rule were assumed to be carried over from the input to the output. Without this convention, an explicit variable would have been required for each of these. Explicit feature variables do indeed increase the abbreviatory power of the notation, but, as we show below, they can be translated systematically into batch rules over unanalyzable segments.

We pay special attention to batch rules, feature matrices, and feature variables because they require some nonobvious extensions to the treatment we provide for ordinary rules with unanalyzable symbols. On the other hand, we have nothing to say about the many other notational devices that phonologists have proposed for collapsing rules. These abbreviatory conventions are either already subsumed by the general regular languages we allow as rule components or can be translated in obvious ways to simply ordered rules or batch rules.

39.5   Rewriting Rules as Regular Relations

We now come to the central problem of proving that an arbitrary rule in our formalism denotes a regular string relation and is thus accepted by an equivalent finite-state transducer. A rule has the general form

$$\phi \to \psi / \lambda \ \_\_\_ \ \rho$$

where ϕ, ψ, λ, and ρ are arbitrary regular expressions. The mode of application of the rule is governed by additional parametric specifications, including for example whether the rule applies from left to right or right to left, and whether it is obligatory or optional.

The replacement that such a rule performs is modeled by a relation *Replace* initially defined as follows:

$$Replace= [Id(\Sigma^*)Opt(\phi \times \psi)]^*$$

The final asterisk allows for repetitions of the basic $\phi \times \psi$ mapping, and $Id(\Sigma^*)$ allows identical corresponding substrings to come between successive applications of the rule. The $\phi \times \psi$ replacement is optional to allow for the possibilities that the rule itself may be optional or that there may be no eligible instances of ϕ in the input string. *Replace* is the set of pairs of strings that are identical except for possible replacements of substrings belonging to ϕ by substrings belonging to ψ. This set clearly contains all the pairs that satisfy the rule, though perhaps other pairs as well. The problem now is to impose restrictions on this mapping so that it occurs in the proper contexts and in accordance with the parameters specified for the rule. We do this in a series of approximations.

39.5.1   Context Requirements

As a first step, we might be tempted simply to add the context restrictions as necessary conditions of the $\phi \times \psi$ replacement:

$$Replace= [Id(\Sigma^*)Opt(Id(\lambda)\phi \times \psi Id(\rho))]^*$$

This relation includes strings where the $\phi \times \psi$ replacement occurs only when immediately preceded and followed by identical substrings satisfying λ and ρ, respectively. But this formulation does not allow for the fact, noted above, that the context strings of one application may overlap either the contexts or the center strings of another. For example, consider the following optional rule, which allows an abstract B to be rewritten as b intervocalically:

$$B \to b / V \ \_\_\_ \ V$$

With the definition of *Replace* just given, the string pair on the left below would be accepted but the pair on the right would not:

V	B	V	B	V		V	B	V	B	V
V	b	V	B	V		V	b	V	b	V

But the second pair also represents a valid application of the rule, one in which the center vowel is serving as the right context of one application and the left context of the other.

The problem is that a given string symbol can simultaneously serve several different roles in the application of a rule, and all possible interactions must be accounted for. As a next approximation, we avoid this confusion by carefully distinguishing and keeping track of these various roles. We first consider how to apply a rule to strings that have been preprocessed so that every instance of the left context λ is followed by the auxiliary symbol $<$ and every instance of the right context ρ is preceded by the symbol $>$, where $<$ and $>$ are not in Σ. This means that the replacement operator can be defined solely in terms of these distinct context-marking brackets, without regard to what λ and ρ actually specify and what they might have in common with each other or with ϕ and ψ. In essence, we assume that the replacement relation for the above rule applies to the upper strings shown below, and that all three string pairs are acceptable because each of the corresponding B-b pairs is bracketed by $<$ and $>$.

$$>V<B>V<B>V< \qquad >V<B>V<B>V< \qquad >V<B>V<B>V<$$
$$>V<b>V<b>V< \qquad >V<b>V<B>V< \qquad >V<B>V<b>V<$$

To take a somewhat more realistic example, when the rule at the beginning of the paper

$$N \to m/ \ \_\_\_ \ [+labial]$$

is applied to the string *iNprobable*, the preprocessed input string would contain the sequence

$$< i < N <> p < r < o <> b < a <> b < l < e <$$

The left context of the rule is empty, so there is a left-context marker $<$ after every character from the original string. Every labial is an instance of the right context, and accordingly there is a $>$ immediately preceding p's and b's. The rule properly applies to rewrite the N because it is bracketed by $<$ and $>$. On the other hand, the $>$ is missing and the rule does not apply to the N in the preprocessed version of *iNtractable*, namely

$$< i < N < t < r < a < c < t < a <> b < l < e <$$

The definition of the *Replace* operator must be modified in two ways in order to operate on such preprocessed strings. First it must allow the $\phi \times \psi$ mapping only between the appropriate context markers. Second, some occurrences of the left and right context strings do not result in rule applications, either because the rule is optional or because the other conditions of the rule are not satisfied. Thus, the relation must disregard the markers corresponding to those occurrences inside the identity substrings between rule applications. Relations with this behavior can be obtained through the use of the ignoring operator defined in Section 3, which is notated by subscripting. Let m (for marker) be $\{<,>\}$, the set of both markers. Then our next approximation to the replacement relation is defined as follows:

$$Replace = [Id(\Sigma_m^*)Opt(Id(<)\phi_m \times \psi_m Id(>))]^*$$

This allows arbitrary strings of matching symbols drawn from $\Sigma \cup \{<,>\}$ between rule applications and requires $<:<$ and $>:>$ to key off a $\phi - \psi$ replacement. The subscript m's also indicate that $<$ and $>$ can be ignored in the middle of the replacement, since the appearance of left- or right-context strings is irrelevant in the middle of a given rule application. Figure 9 shows the general form of the state-transition diagram for a transducer that accepts a replacement relation. As before, the start-state is labeled 0 and only transitions are shown from which the final-state is reachable.

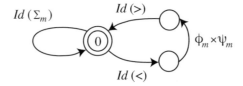

FIGURE 9 The *Replace* transducer

We must now define relations that guarantee that context-markers do in fact appear on the strings that *Replace* applies to, and only when sanctioned by instances of λ and ρ. We do this in two stages. First, we use simple relations to construct a *Prologue* operator that freely introduces the context markers in *m*:

$$Prologue = Intro(m)$$

An output string of *Prologue* is just like the corresponding input except that brackets appear in arbitrary positions. The relation $Prologue^{-1}$ removes all brackets that appear on its input.

Second, we define more complex identity relations that pair a string with itself if and only if those markers appear in the appropriate contexts. The *P-iff-S* operator is the key component of these context-identifying predicates. The condition we must impose for the left context is that the left-context bracket $<$ appears if and only if it is immediately preceded by an instance of λ. This basic requirement is satisfied by strings in the regular language *P-iff-S*$(\Sigma^*\lambda, < \Sigma^*)$. The situation is slightly more complicated, however, because of two special circumstances.

An instance of λ may have prefixes that are also λ instances. If λ is the expression ab^*, then $a < b <$ is an acceptable marking but $ab <$ and $a < b$ are not because the two λ-instances are not both followed by $<$. The brackets that necessarily follow such prefixes must not prevent the longer instances from also being identified and marked, and right-context brackets also must not interfere with left-context identification. The ignore operators in the expression *P-iff-S*$(\Sigma^*_< \lambda_<, < \Sigma^*_<)_>$ allow for these possibilities. This disregards slightly too many brackets, however: since an instance of $\lambda_<$ followed by an $<$ is also an instance of $\lambda_<$, it must be followed by another bracket, and so on. The only (finite) strings that belong to this language are those that contain no instances of λ at all! To correctly identify and mark left-contexts, the bracket following a instance must not be ignored. Thus, the requisite set of strings is the regular language *Leftcontext*$(\lambda, <, >)$, where the *Leftcontext* operator is defined as follows:

$$Leftcontext(\lambda, l, r) = P\text{-}iff\text{-}S(\Sigma^*_l \lambda_l - \Sigma^*_l l, l\Sigma^*_l)_r$$

We parameterize this operator for the left-context pattern and the actual brackets so that it can be used in other definitions below.

The other complication arises in rules intended to insert or delete material in the string, so that either ϕ or ψ includes the empty string ϵ. Consider the left-to-right rule

$$a \to \epsilon/b$$

Iterated applications of this rule can delete an arbitrary sequence of *a*'s, converting strings of the form *baaaa ... a* into simply *b*. The single *b* at the beginning serves as left-context for applications of the rule to each of the subsequent *a*'s. This presents a problem for the constructions we have developed so far: The *Replace* relation requires a distinct $<$ marker for each application of the rule. The $<$ that sanctions the deletion of the leftmost *a* in the string is therefore not available to delete the next one. However, the *Leftcontext* operator as defined disallows two left-context brackets in a row. Our solution is to insert an explicit character 0 to represent the deleted material. If *Leftcontext* ignores this character in λ, 0 will always be followed by another left bracket and thus another rule application is possible.

The auxiliary symbol 0 is not in Σ or in the set of context brackets. It will substitute for the empty strings that might appear in the center of rules (in ϕ or ψ), but it is a genuine symbol in an expanded alphabet which, unlike the normal ϵ, actually appears as a distinct element in character strings. The *Prologue* relation is extended to freely introduce 0 as well as the brackets in m:

$$Prologue = Intro(m \cup \{0\})$$

We then construct alternative versions of ϕ and ψ in which this special symbol replaces the true empty strings. We define

$$\phi^0 = \left\{ \begin{array}{ll} \phi & \text{if } \epsilon \notin \phi \\ [\phi - \epsilon] \cup 0 & \text{otherwise} \end{array} \right.$$

which contains exactly the same strings as ϕ except that the singleton string 0 is included instead of the empty string that otherwise might be in the language. ψ^0 is defined similarly, and then the replacement operator is expressed in terms of these new regular languages:

$$Replace = [Id(\Sigma^*_{m0})Opt(Id(<)\phi^0_m \times \psi^0_m Id(>))]^*$$

Now we can complete our definition of the left-context identifier:

$$Leftcontext(\lambda, l, r) = \text{P-iff-S}(\Sigma^*_{l0}\lambda_{l0} - \Sigma^*_{l0}l, l\Sigma^*_{l0})_r$$

As desired, the regular language denoted by this operator includes strings if and only if every substring belonging to λ (ignoring l, r, and 0) is immediately followed by a bracket l. This effect is illustrated by the state-transition diagrams in Figure 10. The machine on the left is a minimal-state acceptor for the empty-context language $Leftcontext(\epsilon, <, >)$. It accepts strings that have at least one $<$, and every 0 or symbol must be followed by a $<$. The $>$-labeled transitions represent the fact that $>$ is being ignored. The machine on the right accepts the language $Leftcontext(a, <, >)$; it requires $<$ to appear after every a or after any 0 that follows an a. This particular machine is nondeterministic so that its organization is easier to understand.

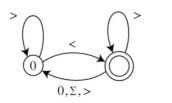
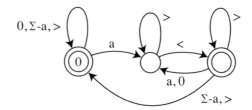

FIGURE 10 Left-context identifiers.

An operator for identifying and marking right-context strings can be defined symmetrically:

$$Rightcontext(\rho, l, r) = \text{P-iff-S}(\Sigma^*_{r0}r, \rho_{r0}\Sigma^*_{r0} - r\Sigma^*_{r0})_l$$

Thus $Rightcontext(\rho, <, >)$ includes strings if and only if every substring belonging to ρ (with appropriate ignoring) is immediately *preceded* by a right-context bracket $>$. Alternatively, taking advantage of the fact that the reversal of a regular language is also a regular language, we can define *Rightcontext* in terms of *Leftcontext*:

$$Rightcontext(\rho, l, r) = Rev(Leftcontext(Rev(\rho), r, l))$$

These context identifiers denote appropriate string-sets even for rules with unspecified contexts, if the vacuous contexts are interpreted as if the empty string had been specified. The empty string indicates that adjacent symbols have no influence on the rule application. If an omitted λ is interpreted as ϵ, for example, every *Leftcontext* string will have one and only one left-context bracket at its beginning, its end, and between any two Σ symbols, thus permitting a rule application at every position.

39.5.2 Directional and Simultaneous Application

We now have components for freely introducing and removing context brackets, for rejecting strings with mislocated brackets, and for representing the rewrite action of a rule between appropriate context markers. The regular relation that models the optional application of a rule is formed by composition of these pieces. The order of composition depends on whether the rule is specified as applying iteratively from left to right or from right to left.

As noted in Section 4, the difference is that for left-to-right rules, the left-context expression λ can match against the output of a previous (that is, leftward) application of the same rule, but the right-context expression ρ must match against the as yet unchanged input string. These observations are directly modeled by the order in which the various rule components are combined. For a left-to-right rule, the right context is checked on the input (ϕ) side of the replacement, while the left context is checked on the output (ψ) side. The regular relation and corresponding transducer for a left-to-right optional rule is therefore defined by the following sequence of compositions:

$$
\begin{aligned}
&Prologue \circ \\
&Id(Rightcontext(\rho, <, >)) \circ \\
&Replace \circ \\
&Id(Leftcontext(\lambda, <, >)) \circ \\
&Prologue^{-1}
\end{aligned}
$$

Both left- and right-context brackets are freely introduced on input strings, strings in which the right-context bracket is mislocated are rejected, and the replacement takes place only between the now-constrained right-context brackets and the still free left-context markers. This imposes the restriction on left-context markers that they at least appear before replacements, although they mayor may not freely appear elsewhere. The left-context checker ensures that left-context markers do in fact appear only in the proper locations on the output. Finally, all brackets are eliminated, yielding strings in the output language.

The context-checking situation is exactly reversed for right-to-left rules: the left-context matches against the unchanged input string while the right-context matches against the output. Right-to-left optional application can therefore be modeled simply by interchanging the context-checking relations in the cascade above, to yield

$$
\begin{aligned}
&Prologue \circ \\
&Id(Leftcontext(\lambda, <, >)) \circ \\
&Replace \circ \\
&Id(Rightcontext(\rho, <, >)) \circ \\
&Prologue^{-1}
\end{aligned}
$$

The transducer corresponding to this regular relation, somewhat paradoxically, models a right-to-left rule application while moving from left to right across its tapes.

Simultaneous optional rule application, in which the sites of all potential string modifications are located before any rewriting takes place, is modeled by a cascade that identifies both left and right contexts on the input side of the replacement:

$$Prologue \circ$$
$$Id(Leftcontext(\lambda, <, >) \cap Rightcontext(\rho, <, >)) \circ$$
$$Replace \circ$$
$$Prologue^{-1}$$

39.5.3 Obligatory Application

These compositions model the optional application of a rule. Although all potential application sites are located and marked by the context checkers, these compositions do not force a $\phi - \psi$ replacement to take place for every instance of ϕ appearing in the proper contexts. To model obligatory rules, we require an additional constraint that rejects string pairs containing sites where the conditions of application are met but the replacement is not carried out. That is, we must restrict the relation so that, disregarding for the moment the effect of overlapping applications, every substring of the form $\lambda\phi\rho$ in the first element of a pair corresponds to a $\lambda\psi\rho$ in the second element of that pair. We can refine this restriction by framing it in terms of our context-marking brackets: the *Replace* relation must not contain a pair with the substring $< \phi >$ in one element corresponding to something distinct from $< \psi >$ in the other.

We might try to formulate this requirement by taking the complement of a relation that includes the undesired correspondences, as suggested by the expression

$$\overline{Id(\Sigma_{m0}^*)Id(<)\phi_m^0 \times \psi_m^0 Id(>)Id(\Sigma_{m0}^*)}$$

This expression might be taken as the starting point for various augmentations that would correctly account for overlapping applications. However, pursuing this line of attack will not permit us to establish the fact that obligatory rules also define regular mappings. First, it involves the complement of a regular relation, and we observed above that the complement of a regular relation (as opposed to the complement of a regular language) is not necessarily regular. Second, even if the resulting relation itself turned out to be regular, the obvious way of entering it into our rule composition is to intersect it with the replacement relation, and we also know that intersection of relations leads to possibly nonregular results.

Proving that obligatory rules do indeed define regular mappings requires an even more careful analysis of the roles that context-brackets can play on the various intermediate strings involved in the rule composition. A given left-context bracket can serve in the *Replace* relation in one of three ways. First, it can be the start of a rule *application*, provided it appears in front of an appropriate configuration of ϕ, ψ, and right-context brackets. Second, it can be ignored during the identity portions of the strings, the regions between the changes sanctioned by the replacement relation. Third, it can be ignored because it comes in the middle or *center* of another rule application that started to the left of the bracket in question and extends further to the right. Suppose we encode these three different roles in three distinct left-bracket symbols $<_a, <_i$, and $<_c$ and also provide for a similar set of distinct right-context brackets $>_a, >_i$, and $>_c$. Wherever a rule is properly applied, the input side of the replacement relation will contain a substring of the form

$$<_a \phi_{<_c>_c}^0 >_a$$

The crucial difference in the case where an obligatory left-to-right rule incorrectly fails to apply is that the left-context preceding the ϕ^0 is marked with $<_i$ instead of $<_a$, since it is part of an identity sequence. This situation is undesirable no matter what types of brackets are ignored in the ϕ^0 pattern or mark the right-context of this potential application. Whether those brackets are in the center or at the boundary of replacements that are carried out further to the right of the offending situation, the leftward application marked by the $<_i$ should have taken precedence.

The symbols $<$ and $>$ were previously used as auxiliary characters appearing in intermediate strings. With a slight abuse of notation, we now let them act as cover symbols standing for the sets of left and right brackets $\{<_i, <_a, <_c\}$ and $\{>_i, >_a, >_c\}$ respectively, and we let m be the combined set $< \cup >$. A substring on the input side of the replacement is then a missed left-to-right application if it matches the simple pattern $< \phi_m^0 >$. Thus, we can force obligatory application of a left-to-right rule by requiring that the strings on the input side of its replacement contain no such substrings, or, to put it in formal terms, that the input strings belong to the regular language $Obligatory(\phi, <_i, >)$, where $Obligatory$ is defined by the following operator:

$$Obligatory(\phi, l, r) = \overline{\Sigma_{m0}^* l \phi_m^0 r \Sigma_{m0}^*}$$

By symmetry, a missed application of a right-to-left rule matches the pattern $< \phi_m^0 >_i$ and $Obligatory(\phi, <, >_i)$ is the appropriate input filter to disallow all such substrings. Note that the obligatory operator involves only regular languages and not relations so that the result is still regular despite the complementation operation.

We must now arrange for the different types of brackets to appear on the input to $Replace$ only in the appropriate circumstances. As before, the context identifiers must ensure that none of the brackets can appear unless preceded (or followed) by the appropriate context, and that every occurrence of a context is marked by a bracket freely chosen from the appropriate set of three. The $Leftcontext$ and $Rightcontext$ operators given above will have exactly this effect when they are applied with the new meanings given to $<$, $>$, and m. The $Replace$ operator must again be modified, however, because it alone distinguishes the different roles of the context brackets. The following final definition chooses the correct brackets for all parameters of rule application:

$$Replace = [Id(\Sigma_{<_i>_i0}^*)Opt(Id(<_a)\phi_{<_c>_c}^0 \times \psi_{<_c>_c}^0 Id(>_a))]^*$$

The behavior of obligatory rules is modeled by inserting the appropriate filter in the sequence of compositions. Left-to-right obligatory rules are modeled by the cascade

$$\begin{array}{c} Prologue \circ \\ Id(Obligatory(\phi, <_i, >)) \circ \\ Id(Rightcontext(\rho, <, >)) \circ \\ Replace \circ \\ Id(Leftcontext(\lambda, <, >)) \circ \\ Prologue^{-1} \end{array}$$

and right-to-left obligatory rules are modeled by:

$$\begin{array}{c} Prologue \circ \\ Id(Obligatory(\phi, <, >_i)) \circ \\ Id(Leftcontext(\lambda, <, >)) \circ \\ Replace \circ \\ Id(Rightcontext(\rho, <, >)) \circ \\ Prologue^{-1} \end{array}$$

We remark that even obligatory rules do not necessarily provide a singleton output string. If the language ψ contains more than one string, then outputs will be produced for each of these at each application site. Moreover, if ϕ contains strings that are suffixes or prefixes (depending on the direction of application) of other strings in ϕ then alternatives will be produced for each length of match. A particular formalism may specify how such ambiguities are to be resolved, and these stipulations would be modeled by additional restrictions in our formulation. For example, the requirement that only shortest ϕ matches are rewritten could be imposed by ignoring only one of $<_c$ or $>_c$ in the mapping part of *Replace*, depending on the direction of application.

There are different formulations for the obligatory application of simultaneous rules, also depending on how competition between overlapping application sites is to be resolved. Intersecting the two obligatory filters, as in the following cascade, models the case where the longest substring matching ϕ is preferred over shorter overlapping matches:

$$Prologue \circ$$
$$Id(Obligatory(\phi, <_i, >) \cap Obligatory(\phi, <, >_i)) \circ$$
$$Id(Rightcontext(\rho, <, >) \cap Leftcontext(\lambda, <, >)) \circ$$
$$Replace \circ$$
$$Prologue^{-1}$$

The operators can be redefined and combined in different ways to model other regimes for overlap resolution.

39.5.4 Boundary Contexts

A rule contains the special boundary marker # when the rewriting it describes is conditioned by the beginning or end of the string. The boundary marker only makes sense when it appears in the context parts of the rule; specifically, when it occurs at the left end of a left-context string or the right end of a right-context string. No special treatment for the boundary marker would be required if # appeared as the first and last character of every input and output string and nowhere else. If this were the case, the compositional cascades above would model exactly the intended interpretation wherein the application of the rule is edge-sensitive. Ordinary input and output strings do not have this characteristic, but a simple modification of the *Prologue* relation can simulate this situation. We defined *Prologue* above as $Intro(m \cup \{0\})$. We now augment that definition:

$$Prologue = Intro(m \cup \{0\}) \circ [\epsilon : \# Id(\overline{\Sigma_{m0}^* \# \Sigma_{m0}^*})\epsilon : \#]$$

We have composed an additional relation that introduces the boundary marker at the beginning and end of the already freely bracketed string, and also rejects strings containing the boundary marker somewhere in the middle. The net effect is that strings in the cascade below the *Prologue* are boundary-marked; bracketed images of the original input strings and the context identifiers can thus properly detect the edges of those strings. The inverse *Prologue* at the bottom of the cascade removes the boundary marker along with the other auxiliary symbols.

39.5.5 Batch Rules

It remains to model the application of a set of rules collected together in a single batch. Recall that for each position in the input string each rule in a batch set is considered for application independently. As we have seen several times before, there is a straightforward approach that approximates this behavior. Let $\{R_1, ..., R_n\}$ be the set of regular relations for rules that are to be applied as a batch and construct the relation $[\cup_k R_k]^*$. Because of closure under union, this relation is regular and includes all pairs of strings that are identical except for substrings that differ according to the rewriting specified by at least one of the rules. But also as we have seen several times before, this relation does not completely simulate the batch application of the rules. In particular, it does not allow for overlap between the material that satisfies the application requirements of one rule in the set with the elements that sanction a previous application of another rule. As usual, we account for this new array of overlapping dependencies by introducing a larger set of special marking symbols and carefully managing their occurrences and interactions.

A batch rule is a set of subrules $\{\phi^1 \to \psi^1/\lambda^1 \ \_\_\_ \ \rho^1, ..., \phi^1 \to \psi^n/\lambda^n \ \_\_\_ \ \rho^n\}$ together with a specification of the standard parameters of application (left-to-right, obligatory, etc.). We use superscripts to distinguish the components of the different subrules to avoid (as much as possible) confusion with our other notational conventions. A crucial part of our treatment of an ordinary rule is to introduce special bracket symbols to mark the appearance of its left and right contexts so that its replacements are carried out only in the proper (possibly overlapping) environments. We do the same thing for each of the subrules of a batch, but we use a different set of brackets for each of them. These brackets permit us to code in a single string the context occurrences for all the different subrules with each subrule's contexts distinctively marked.

Let $<^k$ be the set $\{<_i^k, <_a^k, <_c^k\}$ of left-context brackets for the kth subrule $\phi^k \to \psi^k/\lambda^k \ \_\_\_ \ \rho^k$ of the batch, let $>^k$ be the corresponding set of right-context brackets, and let m^k be the set $<^k \cup >^k$. We also redefine the generic cover symbols $<, >$, and m to stand for the respective collections of all brackets: $< = \cup_k <^k, > = \cup_k >^k, m = < \cup >$. Note that with this redefinition of m, the *Prologue* relation as defined above will now freely introduce all the brackets for all of the subrules. It will also be helpful to notate the set of brackets *not* containing those for the kth subrule: $m^{-k} = m - m^k$.

Now consider the regular language $Leftcontext(\lambda^k, <^k, >^k)_m^{-k}$. This contains strings in which all instances of the kth subrule's left-context expression are followed by one of the kth left-context brackets, and those brackets appear only after instances of λ^k. The kth right-context brackets are freely distributed, as are all brackets for all the other subrules. Occurrences of all other left-context brackets are restricted in similarly defined regular languages. Putting all these bracket-restrictions together, the language

$$\cap_k Leftcontext(\lambda^k, <^k, >^k)_{m^{-k}}$$

has each subrule's left-context duly marked by one of that subrule's left-context brackets. This leaves all right-context brackets unconstrained; they are restricted to their proper positions by the corresponding right-context language

$$\cap_k Rightcontext(\rho^k, <^k, >^k)_{m^{-k}}$$

These intersection languages, which are both regular, will take the place of the simple context identifiers when we form the composition cascades to model batch-rule application. These generalized context identifiers are also appropriate for ordinary rules if we regard each of them as a batch containing only one subrule.

A replacement operator for batch rules must also be constructed. This must map between input and output strings with context-brackets properly located, ensuring that any of the subrule rewrites are possible at each properly marked position but that the rewrite of the kth subrule occurs only between $<_a^k$ and $>_a^k$ of possible rewrites is encoded in the relation

$$\cup_k [Id(<_a^k)\phi_{<_c>_c}^{0k} \times \psi_{<_c>_c}^{0k} Id(>_a^k)]$$

where the generic symbol $<_c$ now stands for $\{<_c^1 ... <_c^k\}$, the set of all left-center brackets, and the generic $>_c$ is assigned a corresponding meaning. We incorporate this relation as the rewrite part of a new definition of the *Replace* operator, with the generic $<_i$ and $>_i$ now representing the sets of all left and right identity brackets:

$$Replace = [Id(\Sigma_{<_i>_i0}^*)Opt(\cup_k[Id(<_a^k)\phi_{<_c>_c}^{0k} \times \psi_{<_c>_c}^{0k} Id(>_a^k)])]^*$$

This relation allows for any of the appropriate replacements separated by identity substrings. It is regular because of the union-closure property; this would not be the case, of course, if intersection or complementation had been required for its construction.

A model of the left-to-right application optional application of a batch rule is obtained by substituting the new, more complex definitions in the composition cascade for ordinary rules with these application parameters:

$$Prologue \circ$$
$$Id(\cap_k Rightcontext(\rho^k, <^k, >^k)_{m-k}) \circ$$
$$Replace \circ$$
$$Id(\cap_k Leftcontext(\lambda^k, <^k, >^k)_{m-k}) \circ$$
$$Prologue^{-1}$$

Optional right-to-left and simultaneous batch rules are modeled by similar substitutions in the corresponding ordinary-rule cascades. Obligatory applications are handled by combining instances of the *Obligatory* operator constructed independently for each subrule. $Obligatory(\phi^k, <^k, >^k)$ excludes all strings in which the kth subrule failed to apply, moving from left to right, when its conditions of application were satisfied. The intersection of the obligatory filters for all subrules in the batch ensures that at least one subrule is applied at each position where application is allowed. Thus the behavior of a left-to-right obligatory batch rule is represented by the composition

$$Prologue \circ$$
$$Id(\cap_k Obligatory(\phi^k, <^k, >^k)) \circ$$
$$Id(\cap_k Rightcontext(\rho^k, <^k, >^k)_{m-k}) \circ$$
$$Replace \circ$$
$$Id(\cap_k Leftcontext(\lambda^k, <^k, >^k)_{m-k}) \circ$$
$$Prologue^{-1}$$

Again, similar substitutions in the cascades for ordinary obligatory rules will model the behavior of right-to-left and simultaneous application.

39.5.6 Feature Matrices and Finite Feature Variables

Using only operations that preserve the regularity of string sets and relations, we have modeled the properties of rewriting rules whose components are regular languages over an alphabet of unanalyzable symbols. We have thus established that every such rule denotes a regular relation. We now extend our analysis to rules involving regular expressions with feature matrices and finite feature variables, as in the Turkish vowel harmony rule discussed in Section 4:

$$\begin{bmatrix} +\text{syllabic} \\ -\text{consonantal} \end{bmatrix} \rightarrow [\alpha back] \ / \ \begin{bmatrix} \alpha back \\ +\text{syllabic} \\ -\text{consonantal} \end{bmatrix} [+consonantal]^* \ \_\_\_$$

We first translate this compact feature notation, well suited for expressing linguistic generalizations, into an equivalent but verbose notation that is mathematically more tractable. The first step is to represent explicitly the convention that features not mentioned in the input or output matrices are left unchanged in the segment the rule applies to. We expand the input and output matrices with as many variables and features as necessary so the value of every output feature is fully specified in the rule. The center-expanded version of this example is

$$\begin{bmatrix} +\text{syllabic} \\ -\text{consonantal} \\ \beta back \\ \beta_1 round \\ \beta_2 high \\ ... \\ \beta_n f_n \end{bmatrix} \rightarrow \begin{bmatrix} +\text{syllabic} \\ -\text{consonantal} \\ \alpha back \\ \beta_1 round \\ \beta_2 high \\ ... \\ \beta_n f_n \end{bmatrix} \begin{bmatrix} \alpha back \\ +\text{syllabic} \\ -\text{consonantal} \end{bmatrix} [+consonantal]^* \ \_\_\_$$

The input and output feature matrices are now fully specified, and in the contexts the value of any unmentioned feature can be freely chosen.

A feature matrix in a regular expression is quite simple to interpret when it does not contain any feature variables. Such a matrix merely abbreviates the union of all segment symbols that share the specified features, and the matrix can be replaced by that set of unanalyzable symbols without changing the meaning of the rule. Thus, the matrix $[+consonantal]$ can be translated to the regular language $\{p, t, k, b, d...\}$ and treated with standard techniques. Of course, if the features are incompatible, the feature matrix will be replaced by the empty set of segments.

A simple translation is also available for feature variables all of whose occurrences are located in just one part of the rule, as in the following fictitious left context:

$$[\alpha high][+consonantal]^*[-\alpha round]$$

If α takes on the value $+$, then the first matrix is instantiated to $[+high]$ and denotes the set of unanalyzable symbols, say $\{e, i, ...\}$, that satisfy that description. The last matrix reduces to $[-round]$ and denotes another set of unanalyzable symbols (e.g. $\{a, e, i, ...\}$). The whole expression is then equivalent to

$$\{e, i,...\} \{p, t, k, b, d ...\}^* \{a, e, i, ...\}$$

On the other hand, if α takes on the value $-$, then the first matrix is instantiated to $[-high]$ and denotes a different set of symbols, say $\{a, o...\}$, and the last one reduces to $[+ round]$. The whole expression on this instantiation of α is equivalent to

$$\{a, o,...\} \{p, t, k, b, d ... \}^* \{o, u, ...\}$$

On the conventional interpretation, the original expression matches strings that belong to either of these instantiated regular languages. In effect, the variable is used to encode a correlation between choices from different sets of unanalyzable symbols.

We can formalize this interpretation in the following way. Suppose θ is a regular expression over feature matrices containing a single variable α for a feature whose values are drawn from a finite set V, commonly the set $\{+, -\}$. Let $\theta[\alpha \to v]$ be the result of substituting $v \in V$ for α wherever it occurs in θ, and then replacing each variable-free feature matrix in that result by the set of unanalyzable symbols that satisfy its feature description. Then the interpretation of θ is given by the formula

$$\cup_{v \in V} \theta[\alpha \to v]$$

This translation produces a regular expression that properly models the choice-correlation defined by α in the original expression. Rule expressions containing several locally occurring variables can be handled by an obvious generalization of this substitution scheme. If $\alpha_1...\alpha_n$ are the local variables in θ whose values come from the finite sets $V_i...V_n$, the set of n-tuples

$$I = \{< \alpha_1 \to v_1, ..., \alpha_n \to v_n > | v_1 \in V_1...v_n \in V_n\}$$

represents the collection of all possible value instantiations of those variables. If we let $\theta[i]$ be the result of carrying out the substitutions indicated for all variables by some i in I, the interpretation of the entire expression is given by the formula

$$\cup_{i \in I} \theta[i]$$

When all local variables are translated, the resulting expression may still contain feature matrices with nonlocal variables, those that also occur in other parts of the rule. Indeed, the input and output expressions will almost always have variables in common, because of the feature variables introduced in the initial center-expansion step.

Variables that appear in more than one rule part clearly cannot be eliminated from each part independently, because the correlation between feature instantiations would be lost. A feature-matrix rule is to be interpreted as scanning in the appropriate direction along the input string until a configuration of symbols is encountered that satisfies the application conditions of the rule instantiated to one selection of values for all of its variables. The segments matching the input are then replaced by the output segments determined by that same selection, and scanning resumes until another configuration is located that matches under possibly a different selection of variables values. This behavior is modeled as the batch-mode application of a set of rules each of which corresponds to one variable instantiation of the original rule.

Consider a center-expanded rule of the general form $\phi \rightarrow \psi/\lambda$ ___ ρ, and let I be the set of possible value instantiations for the feature-variables it contains. Then the collection of instantiated rules is simply

$$\{\phi[i] \rightarrow \psi[i]/\lambda[i] \text{ ___ } \rho[i] | i \in I\}$$

The components of the rules in this set are regular languages over unanalyzable segment symbols, all feature matrices and variables having been resolved. Since each instantiated rule is formed by applying the same substitution to each of the original rule components, the cross-component correlation of symbol choices is properly represented. The behavior of the original rule is thus modeled by the relation that corresponds to the batch application of rules in this set, and we have already shown that such a relation is regular.

39.5.7   Summary

This completes our examination of individual context-sensitive rewriting rules. We have modeled the input-output behavior of these rules according to a variety of different application parameters. We have expressed the conditions and actions specified by a rule in terms of carefully constructed formal languages and string relations. Our constructions make judicious use of distinguished auxiliary symbols so that crucial informational dependencies can be string-encoded in unambiguous ways. We have also shown how these languages and relations can be combined by set-theoretic operations to produce a single string relation that simulates the rule's overall effect. Since our constructions and operations are all regularity-preserving, we have established the following theorem:

Theorem
For all the application parameters we have considered, every rewriting rule whose components describe regular languages denotes a regular string relation.

This theorem has an immediate corollary:

Corollary
The input-output string pairs of every such rewriting rule are accepted by some finite-state transducer.

This theoretical result has important practical consequences. The mathematical analysis that establishes the theorem and its corollary is constructive in nature. Not only do we know that an appropriate relation and its corresponding transducer exist, we also know all the operations to perform to construct such a transducer from a particular rule. Thus, given a careful implementation of the calculus of regular languages and regular relations, our analysis provides a general method for compiling complicated rule conditions and actions into very simple computational devices.

39.6 Grammars of Rewriting Rules

The individual rules of a grammar are meant to capture independent phonological generalizations. The grammar formalism also specifies how the effects of the different rules are to be combined together to account for any interactions between the generalizations. The simplest method of combination for rewriting rule grammars is for the rules to be arranged in an ordered sequence with the interpretation that the first rule applies to the input lexical string, the second rule applies to the output of the first rule, and so on. As we observed earlier, the typical practice is to place specialized rules with more elaborate context requirements earlier in the sequence so that they will override more general rules appearing later.

The combined effect of having one rule operate on the output of another can be modeled by composing the string relations corresponding to each rule. If the string relations for two rules are regular, we know that their composition is also regular. The following result is then established by induction on the number of rules in the grammar:

Theorem
If $G = \langle R_1, ..., R_n \rangle$ is a grammar defined as a finite ordered sequence of rewriting rules each of which denotes a regular relation, then the set of input-output string-pairs for the grammar as a whole is the regular relation given by $R_1 \circ ... \circ R_n$.

This theorem also has an immediate corollary:

Corollary
The input-output string pairs of every such rewriting grammar are accepted by a single finite-state transducer.

Again, given an implementation of the regular calculus, a grammar transducer can be constructed algorithmically from its rules.

We can also show that certain more complex methods of combination also denote regular relations. Suppose a grammar is specified as a finite sequence of rules but with a further specification that rules in some subsequences are to be treated as a block of mutually exclusive alternatives. That is, only one rule in each such subsequence can be applied in any derivation, but the choice of which one varies freely between derivations. The alternative choices among the rules in a block can be modeled as the union of the regular relations they denote individually, and regular relations are closed under this operation. Thus this kind of grammar also reduces to a finite composition of regular relations.

In a more intricate arrangement, the grammar might specify a block of alternatives made up of rules that are not adjacent in the ordering sequence. For example, suppose the grammar consists of the sequence $\langle R_l, R_2, R_3, R_4, R_5 \rangle$, where R_2 and R_4 constitute a block of exclusive alternatives. This cannot be handled by simple union of the block rules, because that would not incorporate the effect of the intervening rule R_3. However, this grammar can be interpreted as abbreviating a choice between two different sequences, $\langle R_l, R_2, R_3, R_5 \rangle$ and $\langle R_l, R_3, R_4, R_5 \rangle$, and thus denotes the regular relation

$$R_1 \circ [(R_2 \circ R_3) \cup (R_3 \circ R_4)] \circ R_5$$

The union and composition operators can be interleaved in different ways to show that a wide variety of rule combination regimes are encompassed by the regular relations. There may be grammars specifying even more complex rule interactions, and, depending on the formal details, it may be possible to establish their regularity by other techniques; for example, by carefully managing a set of distinguished auxiliary symbols that code inter-rule constraints.

We know, of course, that certain methods for combining regular rules give rise to nonregular mappings. This is true, for example, of unrestricted cyclic application of the rules in a finite ordered sequence. According to a cyclic grammar specification, a given input string is mapped through all the rules in the sequence to produce an output string, and that output string then becomes a new input for a reapplication of all the rules, and the process can be repeated without bound. We can demonstrate that such a grammar is nonregular by considering again the simple optional rule

$$\epsilon \rightarrow ab/a \ \_\_\_ \ b$$

We showed before that this rule does not denote a regular relation if it is allowed to rewrite material that was introduced on a previous application. Under those circumstances it would map the regular language $\{ab\}$ into the context-free language $\{a^n b^n | 1 \leq n\}$. But we would get exactly the same result from an unrestricted cyclic grammar whose ordered sequence consists only of this single rule. In effect, cyclic reapplication of the rule also permits it to operate arbitrarily, often on its own output. In the worst case, in fact, we know that the computations of an arbitrary Turing machine can be simulated by a rewriting grammar with unrestricted rule reapplication.

These results seem to create a dilemma for our regularity analysis. Many phonological formalisms based on ordered sets of rewriting rules provide for cyclic rule applications. The underlying notion is that words have a bracketed structure reflecting their morphological composition. For example, *unenforceable* has the structure $[un[[en[force]]able]]$. The idea of the cycle is that the ordered sequence of rules is applied to the innermost bracketed portion of a word first. Then the innermost set of brackets is removed and the procedure is repeated. The cycle continues in this way until no brackets remain.

The cycle has been a major source of controversy ever since it was first proposed by Chomsky and Halle (1968), and many of the phenomena that motivated it can also be given noncyclic descriptions. Even for cases where a nonrecursive, iterative account has not yet emerged, there may be restrictions on the mode of reapplication that limit the formal power of the grammar without reducing its empirical or explanatory coverage. For example, the bracket erasure convention means that new string material becomes accessible to the rules on each cycle. If, either implicitly or explicitly, there is also a finite bound on the amount of old material to which rules in the new cycle can be sensitive, it may be possible to transform the recursive specification to an equivalent iterative one. This is analogous to the contrast between center-embedding context-free grammars and grammars with only right-or left-linear rules; the latter are known to generate only regular languages. Unfortunately, phonological theories are usually not presented in enough formal detail for us to carry out such a mathematical analysis. The regularity of cyclic phonological formalisms will have to be examined on a case-by-case basis, taking their more precise specifications into account.

We have shown that every noncyclical rewriting grammar does denote a regular relation. We now consider the opposite question: Is every regular relation denoted by some noncyclic rewriting grammar? We can answer this question in the affirmative:

Theorem

Every regular relation is the set of input/output strings of some noncyclic rewriting grammar with boundary-context rules.

Proof

Let R be an arbitrary regular relation and let $T = (\Sigma, Q, q_0, F, \delta)$ be a finite-state transducer that accepts it. Without loss of generality we assume that Σ and Q are disjoint. We construct a rewriting grammar that simulates the operation of T, deriving a string y from a string x if and only if the pair $\langle x, y \rangle$ is accepted by T. There will be four rules in the grammar that together implement the provisions that T starts in state q_0, makes transitions from state to state only as allowed by δ, and accepts a string only if the state it reaches at the end of the string is in F. Let $\Sigma \cup Q \cup \{\#, \$\}$ be the alphabet of the grammar, where $\#$ is a boundary symbol not in either Σ or Q and $\$$ is another distinct symbol that will be used in representing the finality of a state. Our rules will introduce states into the string between ordinary tape symbols and remove them to simulate the state-to-state advance of the transducer. The first rule in the grammar sequence is the simple start rule:

$$\epsilon \rightarrow q_0/\# \text{ ---- (obligatory, left-to-right)}$$

The effect of this rule is to introduce the start-state as a symbol only at the beginning of the input string, as specified in the rule by the boundary symbol $\#$. The string abc is thus rewritten by this rule to q_0abc. The following sets of rules are defined to represent the state-to-state transitions and the final states of the transducer:

$$Transitions = \{u \rightarrow vq_j/q_i \text{ ---- } |q_i, q_j \in Q; u, v \in \Sigma^\epsilon; \text{ and } q_j \in \delta(q_i, u, v)\}$$
$$Final = \{\epsilon \rightarrow \$/q_i \text{ ---- } \#|q_i \in F\}$$

The second rule of the grammar is an obligatory, left-to-right batch rule consisting of all the rules in $Transitions \cup Final$. If the transition function carries the transducer from q_i to q_j over the pair $\langle u, v \rangle$, there will be a rule in $Transitions$ that applies to the string $...q_iu...$ at the position just after the substring beginning with q_i and produces $...q_ivq_j...$ as its output. Because δ is a total function on $Q \times \Sigma^\epsilon \times \Sigma^\epsilon$, some subrule will apply at every string position in the left-to-right batch scan. The state-context for the left-most application of this rule is the start-state q_o, and subrules corresponding to start-state transitions are selected. This introduces a state-symbol that makes available at the next position only subrules corresponding to transitions at one of the start-state's successors. The batch rule eventually writes a state at the very end of the string. If that state is in F, the corresponding $Final$ subrule will apply to insert $\$$ at the end of the string. If the last state is not in F, $\$$ will not be inserted and the state will remain as the last symbol in the string. Thus, after the batch rule has completed its application, an input string x will have been translated to an output string consisting of intermixed symbols from Q and Σ. We can prove by a simple induction that the string of states obtained by ignoring symbols in $\Sigma \cup \{\#, \$\}$ corresponds to a sequence of state-to-state moves that the transducer can make on the pair $\langle x, y \rangle$, where y comes from ignoring $\$$ and all state-symbols in the output string.

Two tasks remain: we must filter the output to eliminate any strings whose derivation does not include a $Final$ subrule application, and we must remove all state-symbols and $\$$ to obtain the ultimate output string. If a $Final$ rule did not apply, then the last element in the batch output string is a state, not the special character $\$$. We must formulate a rule that will "bleed" the derivation, producing no output at all if its input ends in a state-symbol instead of $\$$. We can achieve this with an anomalous obligatory rule whose output would be infinitely long if its input ever satisfies the conditions for its application. The following rule behaves in this way:

$$\epsilon \rightarrow \$/Q \text{ ---- } \# \text{ (obligatory, left-to-right)}$$

It has the effect of filtering strings that do not represent transitions to a final state by forcing indefinitely many insertions of $\$$ when no single $\$$ is present. The output of this rule will be all and only the strings that came from a previous application of a $Final$ rule. The last rule of the grammar is a trivial clean-up rule that produces the grammar's final output strings:

$$Q \cup \$ \rightarrow \epsilon \text{ (obligatory, left-to-right)}$$

This completes the proof of the theorem. We have constructed for any regular relation an ordered sequence of four rules (including a batch rule with finitely many subrules) that rewrites a string x to y just in case the pair $\langle x, y \rangle$ belongs to the relation. $\square$

We remark that there are alternative but perhaps less intuitive proofs of this theorem framed only in terms of simple nonbatch rules. But this result cannot be established without making use of boundary-context rules. Without such rules we can only simulate a proper subclass of the regular relations, those that permit identity prefixes and suffixes of unbounded length to surround any nonidentity correspondences. It is interesting to note that for much the same reason, Ritchie (1992) also made crucial use of two-level boundary-context rules to prove that the relations denoted by Koskenniemi's (1985) two-level grammars are also coextensive with the regular relations. Moreover, putting Ritchie's result together with ours gives the following:

Theorem
Ordered rewriting grammars with boundaries and two-level constraint grammars with boundaries are equivalent in their expressive power.

Although there may be aesthetic or explanatory differences between the two formal systems, empirical coverage by itself cannot be used to choose between them.

39.7 Two-Level Rule Systems

Inspired in part by our early report of the material presented in this paper (Kaplan and Kay 1981), Koskenniemi (1983) proposed an alternative system for recognizing and producing morphological and phonological word-form variants. Under his proposal, individual generalizations are expressed directly in the state-transition diagrams of finite-state transducers, and their mutual interactions emerge from the fact that every input-output string pair must be accepted simultaneously by all these transducers. Thus, he replaced the serial feeding arrangement of the independent generalizations in a rewriting grammar with a parallel method of combination. In eliminating the intermediate strings that pass from one rewriting rule to another, he also reduced to just two the number of linguistically meaningful levels of representation. In two-level parlance, these are usually referred to as the lexical and surface strings.

39.7.1 The Analysis of Parallel Automata

The lexical-surface string sets of the individual generalizations in Koskenniemi's system are clearly regular, since they are defined outright as finite-state transducers. But it is not immediately obvious that the string relation defined by a whole two-level grammar is regular. Koskenniemi gave an operational specification, not an algebraic one, of how the separate transducers are to interact. A pair of strings is generated by a two-level grammar if the pair is accepted separately by each of the transducers, and furthermore, the label on the transition taken by one fst at a particular string position is identical to the label of the transition that every other fst takes at that string position. In essence, he prescribed a transition function δ for a whole-grammar transducer that allows transitions between states in cross-product state sets just in case they are permitted by literal-matching transitions in the individual machines.

This transition function generalizes to a two-tape transducer the construction of a one-tape finite-state machine for the intersection of two regular languages. We might therefore suspect that the lexical-surface relation for a two-level grammar consisting of transducers $T_1, ... T_n$ is the relation $\cap_i R(T_i)$. However, what is actually computed under this interpretation is the relation $Rel(Paths(T_1) \cap Paths(T_2)...Paths(T_n))$ of the form discussed in Section 3. As we observed, this may be only a proper subset of the relation $\cap_i R(T_i)$ when the component relations contain string pairs of unequal length. In this case, the literal-matching transducer may not accept the intersection, a relation that in fact may not even be regular.

The individual transducers allowed in two-level specifications do permit the expansion and contraction of strings by virtue of a null symbol 0. If this were treated just like ϵ we would be able to say very little about the combined relation. However, the effect of Koskenniemi's literal-matching transition function is achieved by treating 0 as an ordinary tape symbol, so that the individual transducers are ϵ-free. The intersection of their same-length relations is therefore regular. The length-changing effect of the whole-grammar transducer is then provided by mapping 0 onto ϵ. Thus we embed the same-length intersection $\cap_i R(T_i)$ as a regular inner component of a larger regular relation that characterizes the complete lexical-to-surface mapping:

$$Intro(0) \circ [\cap_i R(T_i)] \circ Intro(0)^{-1}$$

This relation expands its lexical string by freely introducing 0 symbols. These are constrained along with all other symbols by the inner intersection, and then the surface side of the inner relation is contracted by the removal of all 0's. The entire outer relation gives an algebraic model of Koskenniemi's operational method for combining individual transducers and for interpreting the null symbol. With this analysis of the two-level system in terms of regularly-closed operations and same-length relations, we have shown that the string relations accepted by parallel two-level automata are in fact regular. We have also shown, by the way, that the two-level system is technically a four-level one, since the inner relation defines two intermediate, ϵ-containing levels of representation. Still, only the two outer levels are linguistically significant. In typical two-level implementations the *Intro* relations are implicitly encoded in the interpretation algorithms and do not appear as separate transducers.

39.7.2   Two-Level Rule Notation

Koskenniemi (1983) offered an informal grammatical notation to help explicate the intended effect of the individual transducers and make the generalizations encoded in their state-transition diagrams easier to understand and reason about. However, he proposed no method of interpreting or compiling that notation. In later work (e.g. Karttunen, Koskennienni, and Kaplan 1987; Karttunen and Beesley 1992) the mathematical techniques we presented above for the analysis of rewriting systems were used to translate this notation into the equivalent regular relations and corresponding transducers, and thus to create a compiler for a more intuitive and more tractable two-level rule notation. Ritchie (1992) summarizes aspects of this analysis as presented by Kaplan (1988). Ritchie et al. (1992) describe a program that interprets this notation by introducing and manipulating labels assigned to the states of component finite-state machines. Since these labels have no simple set-theoretic significance, such an approach does not illuminate the formal properties of the system and does not make it easy to combine two-level systems with other formal devices.

Ignoring some notational details, a grammar of two-level rules (as opposed to fsts) includes a specification of a set of "feasible pairs" of symbols that we denote by π. The pairs in π contain all the alphabet symbols and 0, but do not contain ϵ except possibly when it is paired with itself in $\epsilon : \epsilon$. The relations corresponding to all the individual rules are all subsets of π^*, and thus are all of the restricted same-length class (since π does not contain ϵ paired with an alphabetic symbol). For this class of relations, it makes sense to talk about a correspondence between a symbol in one string in a string-pair and a symbol in the other: in the pair (abc, lmn) for example, we can say that a corresponds to l, b to m, and c to n, by virtue of the positions they occupy relative to the start of their respective same-length strings. Symbol pairs that correspond in this way must be members of π. It also makes sense to talk about corresponding substrings, sequences of string pairs whose symbols correspond to each other in some larger string pair. Corresponding substrings belong to π^*.

The grammar contains a set of rules whose parts are also same-length regular-relation subsets of π^*. There are two basic kinds of rules, context restriction rules and surface coercion rules.

A simple context restriction rule is an expression of the form

$$\tau \Rightarrow \lambda \, \_\_\_ \, \rho$$

where τ, λ, and ρ denote subsets of π^*. Usually τ is just a single feasible pair, a singleton element of π but this limitation has no mathematical significance. Either of the contexts λ or ρ can be omitted, in which case it is taken to be $\epsilon : \epsilon$. Such a rule is interpreted as denoting a string relation whose members satisfy the following conditions: Every corresponding substring of a string pair that belongs to the relation τ must be immediately preceded by a corresponding substring belonging to the left-context λ and followed by one belonging to the right-context ρ. In other words, any appearance of τ outside the specified contexts is illegal. Under this interpretation, the relation denoted by the rule

$$a : b \Rightarrow c : d \, \_\_\_ \, e : f$$

would include the string pairs $\langle cae, dbf \rangle$ and $\langle cae, cge \rangle$, assuming that $a{:}g$ is in π along with the symbol pairs mentioned in the rule. The first string pair is included because the pair $a{:}b$ is properly surrounded by $c{:}d$ and $e{:}f$. The second belongs because it contains an instance of $a{:}g$ instead of $a{:}b$ and thus imposes no requirements on the surrounding context. The string pair $\langle cae, cbe \rangle$ is not included, however, because $a{:}b$ appears in a context not sanctioned by the rule.

A simple surface coercion rule is written with the arrow going in the other direction:

$$\tau \Leftarrow \lambda \, \_\_\_ \, \rho$$

For strings to satisfy a constraint of this form, they must meet a more complicated set of conditions. Suppose that a corresponding substring belonging to λ comes before a corresponding substring belonging to ρ, and that the lexical side of the paired substring that comes between them belongs to the domain of τ. Then that intervening paired substring must itself belong to τ. To illustrate, consider the surface coercion version of the context restriction example above:

$$a : b \Leftarrow c : d \, \_\_\_ \, e : f$$

The string pair $\langle cae, dbf \rangle$ satisfies this constraint because $a{:}b$ comes between the context substrings $c{:}d$ and $e{:}f$. The pair $\langle cbe, dbf \rangle$ is also acceptable, because the string intervening between $c{:}d$ and $e{:}f$ does not have a on its lexical side. However, the pair $\langle cae, dgf \rangle$ does not meet the conditions because $a{:}g$ comes between $c{:}d$ and $e{:}f$. The lexical side of this is the same as the lexical side of the τ relation $a{:}b$, but the pair $a{:}g$ itself is not in τ. Informally, this rule forces the a to be realized as a surface b when it appears between the specified contexts.

Karttunen et al. (1987) introduced a variant of a surface coercion rule called a surface prohibition. This is a rule of the form

$$\tau / \Leftarrow \lambda \, \_\_\_ \, \rho$$

and indicates that a paired substring that comes between instances of λ and ρ and whose lexical side is in the domain of τ must *not* itself belong to τ. We shall see that the mathematical properties of surface prohibitions follow as immediate corollaries of our surface coercion analysis.

The notation also permits compound rules of each type. These are rules in which multiple context pairs are specified. A compound context restriction rule is of the form

$$\tau \Rightarrow \lambda^1 \, \_\_\_ \, \rho^1; \lambda^2 \, \_\_\_ \, \rho^2; ... \lambda^n \, \_\_\_ \, \rho^n$$

and is satisfied if each instance of τ is surrounded by an instance of *some* $\lambda^k - \rho^k$ pair. A compound surface coercion rule requires the τ surface realization in *each* of the specified contexts.

For convenience, surface coercions and context restrictions can be specified in a single rule, by using $\Leftrightarrow$ as the main connective instead of $\Leftarrow$ or $\Rightarrow$. A bidirectional rule is merely an abbreviation that can be included in a grammar in place of the two subrules formed by replacing the $\Leftrightarrow$ first by $\Leftarrow$ and then $\Rightarrow$. Such rules need no further discussion.

39.7.3   Context Restriction Rules ($\Rightarrow$)

To model the conditions imposed by context restriction rules, we recall the *If-P-then-S* and *If-S-then-P* operators we defined for regular languages L_1 and L_2:

$$If\text{-}P\text{-}then\text{-}S(L_1, L_2) = \overline{L_1 \overline{L_2}} = \Sigma^* - L_1 \overline{L_2}$$

$$If\text{-}S\text{-}then\text{-}P(L_1, L_2) = \overline{\overline{L_1} L_2} = \Sigma^* - \overline{L_1} L_2$$

These operators can be extended to apply to string relations as well, and the results will be regular if the operands are in a regular subclass that is closed under complementation. For notational convenience, we let the overbar in these extensions and in the other expressions below stand for the complement relative to π^* as opposed to the more usual $\Sigma^* \times \Sigma^*$:

$$If\text{-}P\text{-}then\text{-}S(R_1, R_2) = \pi^* - R_1 \overline{R_2} = \overline{R_1 \overline{R_2}}$$

$$If\text{-}S\text{-}then\text{-}P(R_1, R_2) = \pi^* - \overline{R_1} R_2 = \overline{\overline{R_1} R_2}$$

The conditions for a simple context restriction rule are then modeled by the following relation:

$$Restrict(\tau, \lambda, \rho) = If\text{-}S\text{-}then\text{-}P(\tau^* \lambda, \tau \pi^*) \cap If\text{-}P\text{-}then\text{-}S(\pi^* \tau, \rho \pi^*)$$

The first component ensures that τ is always preceded by λ, and the second guarantees that it is always followed by ρ.

A compound contest restriction rule of the form

$$\tau \Rightarrow \lambda^1 \text{ --- } \rho^1; \lambda^2 \text{ --- } \rho^2; ...; \lambda^n \text{ --- } \rho^n$$

is satisfied if all instances of τ are surrounded by substrings meeting the conditions of at least one of the context pairs independently. A candidate model for this disjunctive interpretation is the relation

$$\cup_k Restrict(\tau, \lambda^k, \rho^k)$$

This is incorrect, however, because the scope of the union is too wide. It specifies that there must be some k such that every occurrence of τ will be surrounded by $\lambda^k - \rho^k$, whereas the desired interpretation is that each τ must be surrounded by $\lambda^k - \rho^k$, but a different k might be chosen for each occurrence. A better approximation is the relation

$$[\cup_k Restrict(\tau, \lambda^k, \rho^k)]^*$$

Because of the outer Kleene * iteration, different instances of the rule can apply at different string-pair positions. But this also has a problem, one that should be familiar from our study of rewriting rules: the iteration causes the different rule instances to match on separate, successive substrings. It does not allow for the possibility that the context substring of one application might overlap with the center and context portions of a preceding one.

This problem can be solved with the auxiliary-symbol techniques we developed for rewriting rule overlaps. We introduce left and right context brackets $<^k$ and $>^k$ for each context pair $\lambda^k - \rho^k$. These are distinct from all other symbols, and since their identity pairs are now feasible pairs, they are added to π. These pairs take the place of the actual context relations in the iterative union

$$[\cup_k Restrict(\tau, Id(<^k), Id(>^k))]^*$$

This eliminates the overlap problem. We then must ensure that these bracket pairs appear only if appropriately followed or preceded by the proper context relation. With m being the set of all bracket pairs and subscripting now indicating that identity pairs of the specified symbols are ignored, we define a two-level left-context operator

$$Leftcontext(\lambda, l) = If\text{-}S\text{-}then\text{-}P(\pi^*\lambda_m, Id(l)\pi^*)$$

so that $Leftcontext(\lambda^k, <^k)$ enforces the requirement that every $<^k$ pair be preceded by an instance of λ^k. This is simpler than the rewriting left-context operator because not every instance of λ must be marked – only the ones that precede τ, and those are picked out independently by the iterative union. That is why this uses a one-way implication instead of a biconditional. As in the rewriting case, the ignoring provides for overlapping instances of λ. The right-context operator can be defined symmetrically using $If\text{-}P\text{-}then\text{-}S$ or by reversing the left-context operator:

$$Rightcontext(\rho, \tau) = Rev(Leftcontext(Rev(\rho), r))$$

Putting the pieces together, the following relation correctly models the interpretation of a compound context restriction rule:

$$Intro(m) \circ$$
$$[\cup_k Restrict(\tau, Id(<^k), Id(>^k))]^* \cap [\cap_k [Leftcontext(\lambda^k, <^k) \cap Rightcontext(\rho^k, >^k)]]$$
$$\circ Intro(m)^{-1}$$

Auxiliary marks are freely introduced on the lexical string. Those marks are appropriately constrained so that matching brackets enclose every occurrence of τ, and each bracket marks an occurrence of the associated context relation. The marks are removed at the end. Note that there are only same-length relations in the intermediate expression, and that all brackets introduced at the top are removed at the bottom. Thus the composite relation is regular and also belongs to the same-length subclass, so that the result of intersecting it with the same-length regular relations for other rules will be regular.

39.7.4 Surface Coercion Rules ($\Leftarrow$)

A surface coercion rule of the form

$$\tau \Leftarrow \lambda \text{ --- } \rho$$

imposes a requirement on the paired substrings that come between all members of the λ and ρ relations. If the lexical side of such a paired substring belongs to the domain of τ, then the surface side must be such that the intervening pair belongs to τ.

To formalize this interpretation, we first describe the set of string pairs that fail to meet the conditions. The complement of this set is then the appropriate relation. The relation $\bar{\tau} = \tau^* - \tau$ is the set of string pairs in τ^* that are not in τ, because either their lexical string is not in the domain of τ or τ associates that lexical string with different surface strings. $Id(Dom(\tau)) \circ \bar{\tau}$ is the subset of these whose lexical strings are in the domain of τ and whose surface strings must therefore be different than τ provides for. The unacceptable string pairs thus belong to the same-length relation $\pi^*\lambda[Id(Dom(\tau)) \circ \bar{\tau}]\rho\pi^*$, and its regular complement in the *Coerce* operator

$$Coerce(\tau, \lambda, \rho) = \overline{\pi^*\lambda[Id(Dom(\tau)) \circ \bar{\tau}]\rho\pi^*}$$

contains all the string pairs that satisfy the rule.

For most surface coercions it is also the case that this contains only the pairs that satisfy the rule. But for one special class of coercions, the epenthesis rules, this relation includes more string pairs than we desire. These are rules in which the domain of τ includes strings consisting entirely of 0's, and the difficulty arises because of the dual nature of two-level 0's. They behave formally as actual string symbols in same-length relations, but they are also intended to act as the empty string. In this way they are similar to the ϵ's in the centers of rewriting rules, and they must also be modeled by special techniques. The epenthesis rule

$$0 : b \Leftarrow c : c \_\_\_ d : d$$

can be used to illustrate the important issues.

If this is the only rule in a grammar, then clearly that grammar should allow the string pair $\langle cd, cbd \rangle$ but disallow the pair $\langle cd, ced \rangle$, in which e appears instead of b between the surface c and d. It should also disallow the pair $\langle cd, cd \rangle$, in which e and d are adjacent on both sides and no epenthesis has occurred. This is consistent with the intuition that the 0 in the rule stands for the absence of explicit lexical string material, and that therefore the rule must force a surface b when lexical c and d are adjacent. In our analysis this interpretation of 0 is expressed by having the *Intro* relation freely introduce 0's between any other symbols, mimicking the fact that ϵ can be regarded as freely appearing everywhere. The pair $\langle cd, cbd \rangle$ is allowed as the composition of pairs $\langle cd, c0d \rangle$ and $\langle c0d, cbd \rangle$; the first pair belongs to the *Intro* relation and the second is sanctioned by the rule. But because 0's are introduced freely, the *Intro* relation includes the identity pair $\langle cd, cd \rangle$ as well. The *Coerce* relation as defined above also contains the pair $\langle cd, cd \rangle$ $(= \langle ced, cfd \rangle)$, since $\epsilon : \epsilon$ is not in $[0 : 0 \circ \overline{0 : b}]$. The grammar as a whole thus allows $\langle cd, cd \rangle$ as an undesired composition.

We can eliminate pairs of this type by formulating a slightly different relation for epenthesis rules such as these. We must still disallow pairs when 0's in the domain of τ are paired with strings not in the range. But we also want to disallow pairs whose lexical strings do not have the appropriate 0's to trigger the grammar's epenthesis coercions. This can be accomplished by a modified version of the *Coerce* relation that also excludes realizations of the empty string by something not in τ. We replace the $Dom(\tau)$ expression in the definition above with the relation $Dom(\tau \cup \{\epsilon : \epsilon\})$. The two-level literature is silent about whether or not an epenthesis rule should also reject strings with certain other insertion patterns. On one view, the rule only restricts the insertion of singleton strings and thus pairs such as $\langle cd, cbbd \rangle$ and $\langle cd, ceed \rangle$ would be included in the relation. This view is modeled by using the $Dom(\tau \cup \{\epsilon : \epsilon\})$ expression. On another view, the rule requires that lexically adjacent c and d must be separated by exactly one b on the surface, so that $\langle cd, cbbd \rangle$ and $\langle cd, ceed \rangle$ would be excluded in addition to $\langle cd, ced \rangle$ and $\langle cd, cd \rangle$. We can model this second interpretation by using 0^* instead of $Dom(\tau \cup \{\epsilon : \epsilon\})$. The relation then restricts the surface realization of any number of introduced 0's. It is not clear which of these interpretations leads to a more convenient formalism, but each of them can be modeled with regular devices.

Karttunen and Beesley (1992, p. 22) discuss a somewhat different peculiarity that shows up in the analysis of epenthesis rules where one context is omitted (or equivalently, one context includes the pair $\epsilon : \epsilon$). The rule

$$0 : b \Leftarrow c : c \_\_\_ d : d$$

requires that a b corresponding to nothing in the lexical string must appear in the surface string after every c:c pair. If we use either the $Dom(\tau \cup \{\epsilon : \epsilon\})$ or 0^* expressions in defining the coercion relation for this rule, the effect is not what we intend. The resulting relation does not allow strings in which a $\epsilon : \epsilon$ follows c:c, because ϵ is included in the restrictive domain expression. But $\epsilon : \epsilon$ follows and precedes every symbol pair, of course, so the result is a relation that simply prohibits all occurrences of c:c. If, however, we revert to using the domain expression without the $\{\epsilon : \epsilon\}$ union, we fall back into the difficulty we saw with two-context epenthesis rules: the resulting relation properly ensures that nothing other than b can be inserted after c:c, but it leaves open the possibility of c:c followed by no insertion at all.

A third formulation is necessary to model the intended interpretation of one-context epenthesis rules. This is given by the relation $\overline{\pi^*\lambda\overline{\tau}\pi^*}$ if only the left-context is specified, or $\overline{\pi^*\overline{\tau}\rho\pi^*}$ if only ρ appears. These exclude all strings where an instance of the relevant context is followed by paired substrings not in τ, either because the appropriate number of lexical 0's were not (freely) introduced or because those 0's correspond to unacceptable surface material. These two prescriptions can be brought together into the single formula $\overline{\pi^*\lambda\overline{\tau}\rho\pi^*}$ for all one-context rules, since whichever context is missing is treated as the identity pair $\epsilon : \epsilon$. We can bring out the similarity between this formula and the original *Coerce* relation by observing that this one is equivalent to $\overline{\pi^*\lambda[Id(Dom(\pi^*)) \circ \overline{\tau}]\rho\pi^*}$ because $Id(Dom(\pi^*)) \circ \overline{\tau}$ and $\overline{\tau}$ are the same relation.

We now give a general statement of the *Coerce* relation that models surface coercions whether they are epenthetic or non-epenthetic:

$$Coerce(\tau, \lambda, \rho) = \overline{\pi^*\lambda[Id(Dom(X)) \circ \overline{\tau}]\rho\pi^*}, \text{ where}$$

$\quad$ X = $\quad$ τ if τ has no epenthetic pairs;

$\quad$ X = $\quad$ $\tau \cup \{\epsilon : \epsilon\}$ (or perhaps $[0 : 0]^*$) if τ has only epenthetic pairs and neither λ nor ρ contains $\epsilon : \epsilon$;

$\quad$ X = $\quad$ π^* if τ has only epenthetic pairs and one of λ or ρ does contain $\epsilon : \epsilon$.

This definition assumes that τ is homogeneous in that either all its string-pairs are epenthetic or none of them are, but we must do further analysis to guarantee that this is the case. In the formalism we are considering, τ is permitted to be an arbitrary same-length relation, not just the single unit-length pair that two-level systems typically provide for. If τ contains more than one string-pair, the single rule is interpreted as imposing the constraints that would be imposed by a conjunction of rules formed by substituting for τ each of its member string-pairs in turn. Without further specification and even if τ contains infinitely many pairs, this is the interpretation modeled by the *Coerce* relation, provided that τ is homogeneous. To deal with heterogeneous τ relations, we separate the epenthetic and nonepenthetic pairs into two distinct and homogeneous subrelations. We partition an arbitrary τ into the subrelations τ^0 and $\tau^{\overline{0}}$ defined as

$$\tau^0 = Id(0^*) \circ \tau$$
$$\tau^{\overline{0}} = \tau - \tau^0$$

We then recast a rule of the form $\tau \Leftarrow \lambda \text{ ___ } \rho$ as the conjunction of the two rules

$$\tau^0 \Leftarrow \lambda \text{ ___ } \rho$$
$$\tau^{\overline{0}} \Leftarrow \lambda \text{ ___ } \rho$$

These rules taken together represent the desired interpretation of the original, and each of them is properly modeled by exactly one variant of the *Coerce* relation.

We have now dealt with the major complexities that surface coercion rules present. The compound forms of these rules are quite easy to model. A rule of the form

$$\tau \Leftarrow \lambda^1 \text{ ___ } \rho^1; \lambda^2 \text{ ___ } \rho^2; ...; \lambda^n \text{ ___ } \rho^n$$

is interpreted as coercing to the surface side of τ if any of the context conditions are met. Auxiliary symbols are not needed to model this interpretation, since there is no iteration to introduce overlap difficulties. The relation for this rule is given simply by the intersection of the individual relations:

$$\cap_k Coerce(\tau, \lambda^k, \rho^k)$$

We conclude our discussion of two-level rules with a brief mention of surface prohibitions. Recall that a prohibition rule

$$\tau/ \Leftarrow \lambda \text{ ___ } \rho$$

indicates that a paired substring must not belong to τ if it comes between instances of λ and ρ and its lexical side is in the domain of τ. We can construct a standard surface coercion rule that has exactly this interpretation by using the complement of τ restricted to τ's domain:

$$[Id(Dom(\tau)) \circ \overline{\tau}] \Leftarrow \lambda \ \_\_\_ \ \rho$$

As desired, the left side is the relation that maps each string in the domain of τ to all strings other than those to which τ maps it. Surface prohibitions are thus reduced to ordinary surface coercions.

39.7.5 Grammars of Two-Level Rules

The relation for a grammar of rules is formed just as for a grammar of parallel automata. The intersection of the relations for all the individual rules is constructed as a same-length inner relation. This is then composed with the 0 introduction and removal relations to form the outer lexical-to-surface map. Rule-based two-level grammars thus denote regular relations, just as the original transducer-based grammars do. Some grammars may make use of boundary-context rules, in which case a special symbol $\#$ can appear in contexts to mark the beginning and end of the strings. These can be modeled with exactly the same technique we outlined for rewriting rules: we compose the additional relation $[\epsilon : \#Id(\overline{\Sigma_{m0}^* \# \Sigma_{m0}^*})\epsilon : \#]$ at the beginning of the four-level cascade and compose its inverse at the end. As we mentioned before, the two-level grammars with boundary-context rules are the ones that Ritchie (1992) showed were complete for the regular relations.

In reasoning about these systems, it is important to keep clearly in mind the distinction between the outer and inner relations. Ritchie (1992), for example, also proved that the "languages" generated by two-level grammars with regular contexts are closed under intersection, but this result does not hold if a grammar's language is taken to be its outer relation. Suppose that G_1 has the set $\{a : b, 0 : c\}$ as its feasible pairs and the vacuous $a : b \Rightarrow \ \_\_\_$ as its only rule, and that G_2 has the pairs $\{a : c, 0 : b\}$ and rule $a : c \Rightarrow \ \_\_\_$. The domain of both outer (0-free) relations is a^*. A string $a"$ is mapped by G_1 into strings containing n b's with c's freely intermixed and by G_2 into strings containing n c's with b's freely intermixed. The range of the intersection of the outer relations for G_1 and G_2 thus contains strings with the same number of b's and c's but occurring in any order. This set is not regular, since intersecting it with the regular language b^*c^* produces the context-free language $b^n c^n$. The intersection of the two outer relations is therefore also not regular and so cannot be the outer relation of any regular two-level grammar.

We have shown how our regular analysis techniques can be applied to two-level systems as well as rewriting grammars, and that grammars in both frameworks denote only regular relations. These results open up many new ways of partitioning the account of linguistic phenomena in order to achieve descriptions that are intuitively more satisfying but without introducing new formal power or computational machinery. Karttunen, Kaplan, and Zaenen (1992), for example, argued that certain French morphological patterns can be better described as the composition of two separate two-level grammars rather than as a single one. As another option, an entire two-level grammar can be embedded in place of a single rule in an ordered rewriting system. As long as care is taken to avoid inappropriate complementations and intersections, all such arrangements will denote regular relations and can be implemented by a uniform finite-state transducer mechanism.

Conclusion

Our aim in this paper has been to provide the core of a mathematical framework for phonology. We used systems of rewriting rules, particularly as formulated in SPE, to give concreteness to our work and to the paper. However, we continually sought solutions in terms of algebraic abstractions of sufficiently high level to free them from any necessary attachment to that or any other specific theory. If our approach proves useful, it will only be because it is broad enough to encompass new theories and new variations on old ones. If we have chosen our abstractions well, our techniques will extend smoothly and incrementally to new formal systems. Our discussion of two-level rule systems illustrates how we expect such extensions to unfold. These techniques may even extend to phonological systems that make use of matched pairs of brackets. Clearly, context-free mechanisms are sufficient to enforce dependencies between corresponding brackets, but further research may show that accurate phonological description does not exploit the power needed to maintain the balance between particular pairs, and thus that only regular devices are required for the analysis and interpretation of such systems.

An important goal for us was to establish a solid basis for computation in the domain of phonological and orthographic systems. With that in mind, we developed a well-engineered computer implementation of the calculus of regular languages and relations, and this has made possible the construction of practical language processing systems. The common data structures that our programs manipulate are clearly states, transitions, labels, and label pairs – the building blocks of finite automata and transducers. But many of our initial mistakes and failures arose from attempting also to think in terms of these objects. The automata required to implement even the simplest examples are large and involve considerable subtlety for their construction. To view them from the perspective of states and transitions is much like predicting weather patterns by studying the movements of atoms and molecules or inverting a matrix with a Turing machine. The only hope of success in this domain lies in developing an appropriate set of high-level algebraic operators for reasoning about languages and relations and for justifying a corresponding set of operators and automata for computation.

From a practical point of view, the result of the work reported here has been a set of powerful and sometimes quite complex tools for compiling phonological grammars in a variety of formalisms into a single representation, namely a finite-state transducer. This representation has a number of remarkable advantages: (1) The program required to interpret this representation is simple almost to the point of triviality, no matter how intricate the original grammars might have been. (2) That same program can be used to generate surface or textual forms from underlying lexical representations or to analyze text into a lexical string; the only difference is in which of the two symbols on a transition is regarded as the input and which the output. (3) The interpreter is constant even under radical changes in the theory and the formalism that informed the compiler. (4) The compiler consists almost entirely of an implementation of the basic calculus. Given the operators and data types that this makes available, only a very few lines of code make up the compiler for a particular theory.

Reflecting on the way the relation for a rewriting rule is constructed from simpler relations, and on how these are composed to create a single relation for a complete grammar, we come naturally to a consideration of how that relation should comport with the other parts of a larger language-processing system. We can show, for example, that the result of combining together a list of items that have exceptional phonological behavior with a grammar-derived relation for general patterns is still a regular relation with an associated transducer. If E is a relation for a finite list of exceptional input-output pairs and P is the general phonological relation, then the combination is given by

$$E \cup [Id(\overline{Dom(E)}) \circ P]$$

This relation is regular because E is regular (as is any finite list of pairs); it suppresses the general mapping provided by P for the exceptional items, allowing outputs for them to come from E only. As another example, the finite list of formatives in a lexicon L can be combined with a regular phonology (perhaps with exceptions already folded in) by means of the composition $Id(L) \circ P$. This relation enshrines not only the phonological regularities of the language but its lexical inventory as well, and its corresponding transducer would perform phonological recognition and lexical lookup in a single sequence of transitions. This is the sort of arrangement that Karttunen et al. (1992) discuss. Finally, we know that many language classes are closed under finite-state transductions or composition with regular relations – the images of context-free languages, for example, are context-free. It might therefore prove advantageous to seek ways of composing phonology and syntax to produce a new system with the same formal properties as syntax alone.

Acknowledgements

We are particularly indebted to Danny Bobrow for helpful discussions in the early stages of the research on rewriting systems. Our understanding and analysis of two-level systems is based on very productive discussions with Lauri Karttunen and Kimmo Koskenniemi. We would like to thank John Maxwell, Mary Dalrymple, Andy Daniels, Chris Manning, and especially Kenneth Beesley for detailed comments on earlier versions of this paper. Finally, we are also indebted to the anonymous referees for identifying a number of technical and rhetorical weaknesses. We, of course, are responsible for any remaining errors.

Publications referenced

Chomsky and Halle 1968; Eilenberg 1974; Harrison 1978; Hopcroft and Ullman 1979; Johnson 1972; Kaplan 1984; Kaplan 1985; Kaplan 1988; Kaplan and Kay 1981; Karttunen and Beesley 1992; Karttunen et al. 1992; Karttunen et al. 1987; Kay 1987; Kenstowicz and Kisseberth 1979; Klatt 1980; Koskenniemi 1983; Koskenniemi 1985; Ritchie 1992; Ritchie et al. 1992; Woods et al. 1976.

40

Parsing and Empty Nodes

WITH MARK JOHNSON

This paper describes a method for ensuring the termination of parsers using grammars that freely posit empty nodes. The basic idea is that each empty node must be associated with a lexical item appearing in the input string, called its sponsor. A lexical item, as well as labeling the node for the corresponding word, provides labels for a fixed number, possibly zero, of empty nodes. The number of nodes appearing in the parse tree is thus bounded before parsing begins. Termination follows trivially. The technique is applicable to any standard parsing algorithm.

One way of guaranteeing that a parsing algorithm will terminate is to ensure that each step consumes some finite amount of the input. There are two main situations in which this does not automatically occur, both arising from properties of the grammar. The first comes from nonbranching dominance chains of unbounded length. The second comes from empty nodes. Most modern grammars do not admit unbounded nonbranching chains, so that the problem of handling the phenomenon in parsing does not arise in practice. It is widely believed that these grammars also do not admit unbounded numbers of empty nodes. However, these generally constitute a problem in the design of parsing algorithms because the parser's domain of locality does not coincide with that of the constraints that govern their appearance.

This paper presents a proposal for constraining the appearance of empty nodes that is applicable to a wide variety of parsing strategies and linguistic theories, including many of those within the GB framework. Ideas like the ones to be presented here have been a part of other parsing systems, e.g., Fong (1991a, 1991b) and Millies (1991), and our notion of *sponsorship* , which we introduce below, can be viewed as a weak version of *lexicalization* in TAGs that is specifically focused on determining the distribution of empty nodes. The novelty of our approach lies principally in the identification of a single simple constraint as sufficient to ensure termination of the process. While its motivation is computational, its justification is primarily linguistic. The next section presents the problem that empty nodes pose for standard parsing techniques. Section 2 introduces the notion of *sponsorship*, and Section 3 discusses linguistic examples that demonstrate the role we see it playing. Section 4 shows how this proposal might be integrated into general parsing strategies. The conclusion summarizes what has been achieved, suggests avenues for further development, and draws parallels with some different approaches.

40.1 The Problem with Empty Nodes

The empty-node problem arises for the following reason. Given a parsing scheme with a standard notion of locality, there is no limit on the number of empty nodes that it might be necessary to posit before a configuration emerges in which the constraints governing the appearance of any of them can be verified.

We claim that most standard parsing algorithms will face difficulties in constraining the appearance of empty nodes in structures like the one in Figure 1.

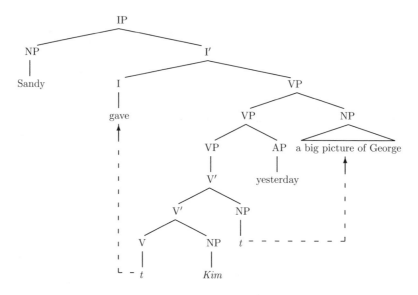

FIGURE 1 Extraposition and verb movement

A bottom-up parser would have to consider the possibility that every V′ should be combined with a following empty NP, like the upper V′ in Figure 1, to form another V′, which could then be treated in like manner. If the subcategorization frame of the V head were available, it could be used to bound the number of V′ nodes posited. But, in a structure involving verb movement, the head of the V chain is only integrated onto the structure after all of the V′ nodes have been constructed, so its subcategorization frame is not available when the V′ nodes are constructed. Similarly, the head of the NP chain is integrated too late to constrain the positing of V′ nodes.

A top-down parser would fare no better because the example is a classic case of left recursion. It might be argued that a top-down parser would have encountered the I head of the V chain before beginning to construct the V′ nodes and could therefore use its subcategorization frame to determine how many to construct. However, this would require an analysis of the grammar that is beyond the scope of standard parsing procedures. Notice that the V trace from which the subcategorization frame is projected is incorporated into the structure only after all of the V′ nodes have been constructed. Finally, the number of VP nodes is not determined by the subcategorization frame. No amount of grammar analysis will allow a top-down parser to predict the number of adjuncts attached to VP.

A head-first parser (Kay 1989; van Noord 1993) seems best adapted to the treatment of empty nodes. This mixed parsing strategy in effect predicts a head top-down and builds its complements and specifiers bottom-up. The trace of the verb would be identified immediately after the I *gave* had been recognized, since that trace is the head of the complement of the I. But it is not clear how such a strategy would cope with empty nodes that do not stand in a head-to-head relationship, such as the trace associated with the adjoined NP. The construction of the NP *a big picture of George* would take place only after that of all of the V′ nodes to its left.

In summary, all of these parsing strategies suffer from the problem that they can posit too many – in some cases infinitely many – empty nodes. They do this because there is no limit on the number of empty nodes that can be posited before the constraints governing their appearance are verified.

Sometimes relatively simple strategies suffice to constrain the appearance of empty nodes and ensure parser termination. For example, given a grammatical constraint that all empty nodes be siblings of appropriate lexical heads, then simply delaying the introduction of an empty node until the node that dominates it is constructed suffices to constrain the number of empty nodes that a bottom-up parser posits. Similarly, for some theories of filler-gap dependencies, notably those based on 'slash features' (Gazdar, Klein, Pullum, and Sag 1985; Pereira 1981), it is possible to use a kind of prediction to constrain the possible occurrences of empty nodes in a wide variety of parsing strategies. However, with more complex theories of grammar, such as those within the GB framework, it is no longer so clear how, or even if, these sorts of techniques can be applied.

40.2   Sponsoring

Our solution to this problem is a device inspired by the notion of licensing in GB (Abney 1986). According to this conception, the presence and location of each empty node is justified by the specific structural relations it stands in with other nodes. For example, every noun phrase might be required to receive Case and a θ-role, and it may be that the phrase would have to appear at different places in the structure for both of these assignments to be made. However, it may also be that the phrase can be represented in one, or both, positions by a related empty category, a *trace* of the phrase, which is licensed by its fulfillment of this specific role.

To guarantee that only a finite number of empty nodes is posited in any analysis, we propose that, whatever parsing strategy is used, there be a global constraint on the number of empty nodes that can be posited in any single search path. We require that every empty node be *sponsored* by some lexical or morphological item that appears in the input. By sponsoring we mean that every empty node is associated with some nonempty lexical item, which we call its *sponsor,* and that the number of empty nodes that a single lexical token can sponsor is fixed by the lexicon, so that the set of all empty nodes to appear in the parse can be determined directly by a simple inspection of the lexical items in the input string.

Sponsorship is closely related to lexicalization in TAGs and CFGs (Schabes 1990, 1992; Schabes, Abeillé, and Joshi 1988; Schabes and Waters 1993; Vijay-Shanker and Schabes 1992).

In a lexicalized grammar every node in the parse tree originates from some lexical entry, so parsing becomes a jigsaw puzzle-like problem of finding a consistent way of assembling the pieces of trees associated with each lexical item. Sponsoring is a weaker notion, in that only some of the constituent structure, namely the lexical items and empty nodes, are specified in lexical entries. This seems plausible in a framework in which general principles of grammar (e.g., X' theory, Case theory, etc.) determine the overall structure of the parse tree. In addition, finding an appropriate association of constituent structure nodes with lexical items can be a difficult task. Because the sponsoring approach is only concerned with empty nodes, it should be easier to apply it to a wider variety of grammatical theories than a lexicalization approach, which requires that every node (empty or not) be associated with a lexical item (but see the remarks in the conclusion below).

We now discuss one way to formulate a sponsoring approach. A lexical item and the set of empty categories that it sponsors constitute an *extended lexical item* (ELI) as sketched in Figure 2. In simple systems, such as the parser described in the next section, each lexical and morphological entry explicitly specifies the traces that it sponsors, but in more sophisticated

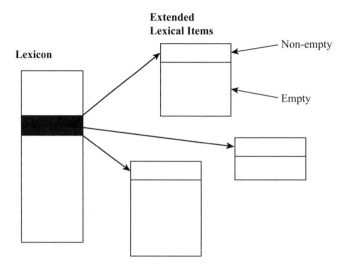

FIGURE 2 The structure of the lexicon and ELIs

implementations this could be determined automatically from principles of the grammar and properties of the lexical entry. It is not intended that sponsoring be used to change grammar, but only to impose relatively weak global constraints on the appearance of empty categories.

There are several variants of the basic idea. For example, one could require that all the empty nodes supplied by the lexicon be used in the analysis. On the one hand, this could lead to a proliferation of lexical entries. On the other, it could prune the search space more effectively if the role of each empty node were made as specific as possible.

As we remarked, previous proposals have made the number of empty nodes posited a function of the length of the input string. The novelty of our proposal is twofold. First, it provides a finer way of estimating the number of empty nodes that will occur. In fact, in the simplest version of the theory, the number of empty and nonempty terminals in a sentence is simply the sum of the sizes of the ELIs of the words in it. The number of empty categories is therefore this number minus the number of words. The fact that the number of empty nodes is bounded before parsing begins is the most important part of our proposal.

Our second proposal is that each of the items in an ELI is marked to show the specific role it must fill. Only one member, for example, will be capable of receiving a θ-role, and this member will not be capable of filling any position in which a θ-role is not assigned.

40.3   Linguistic Aspects of Sponsoring

The goal of this section is to demonstrate that the constraints that sponsoring imposes are plausible with respect to current linguistic assumptions. To the extent that they are, an important step will have been taken in establishing the decidability of these theories.

Consider once again the example in Figure 1. Because there is a government relationship between the V trace and the NP trace, and a movement relationship between the *gave* node under I and the V trace, it seems reasonable to include both of these traces in the ELI that permits *gave* to appear under I. The alternative clearly exists of allowing every N to sponsor an NP trace to allow, for example, for heavy NP shift of its maximal projection. It does not matter that this would lead to the provision of empty NP nodes in cases where no movement could occur, because the structures produced by the parser must independently satisfy all the

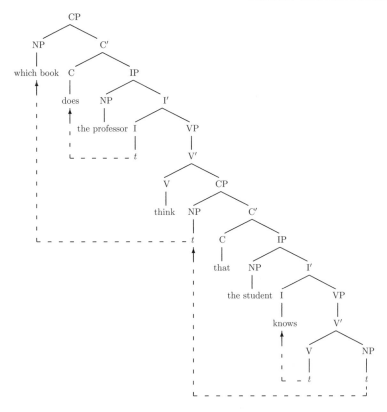

FIGURE 3 Cyclic WH-movement in English

requirements of the grammar.

Now consider an example involving cyclic WH-movement, as depicted in Figure 3. For English, WH-items such as *which* could sponsor the NP trace at the base of the chain (in Figure 3 the NP trace in embedded object position). However, we have already motivated a trace for the subcategorized complement, which should also serve as the foot of the WH-chain. Sponsors must also be found for the intermediate traces. Because the number of intermediate traces that can appear in WH-constructions is not bounded, these intermediate traces cannot be sponsored by either the WH-item or the embedded verb. However, they can be sponsored by the bridge verbs that govern their CP parents. For example, the intermediate NP trace in Figure 3 is sponsored by the verb *think*.

Another possibility, inspired by Grimshaw (1990) and Speas and Fukui (1986) on extended projections, is that inflection sponsors a complete set of empty functional nodes (and their specifiers) that can appear in the clause. Here, the intermediate trace would be sponsored by the inflection -*s* on *knows*. While the first approach is perhaps more elegant, the second also covers relative clauses, as discussed below. Either way, each potential location of an intermediate trace has a sponsor; it is the independent constraints on WH-movement that are responsible for ensuring that, if a trace appears, it will be properly incorporated into a WH-chain.

The verb movement in Figure 3 can be treated as before. Presumably the ELI for *does* that permits it to appear under C also sponsors the corresponding trace in and the ELI for *knows* (or perhaps for the inflectional ending -*s*) that permits the verb to appear under I also sponsors the trace in V.

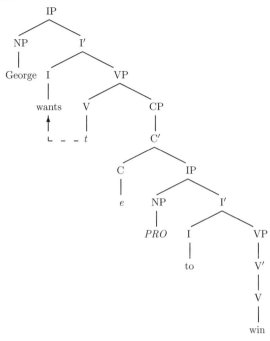

FIGURE 4 Empty C and PRO in English

Next, consider the example in Figure 4. As well as the by now familiar V to I movement, it also exhibits two examples of empty categories that are not members of chains, so their sponsors cannot be determined on this basis. Responsibility for sponsorship of the empty C as well as the PRO could be ascribed to the verb *wants* that governs the CP in which they appear. This is a control verb and is in any case responsible for identifying *George* as the antecedent of the PRO. According to this view the inflected verb *wants* (i.e., the lexical stem and the inflection) sponsors a total of three empty categories. Alternatively, one could allow the infinitive marker *to* to sponsor PRO and the empty complementizer. This approach is consistent with the view that inflection sponsors all of the empty functional nodes of the clause in which it appears.

English relative clauses are a major challenge for the sponsoring approach. Even though relative clauses share many of the structural properties of WH-question constructions such as cyclic movement, they can appear in a greater diversity of forms. All we attempt here is a survey of the problems encountered in developing the sponsoring account of empty nodes in relative clause constructions and their possible solutions.

Consider the case of a relative clause introduced by an empty operator *Op* (rather than an overt relative pronoun), such as the example in Figure 5.

The analyses discussed above provide sponsors for every empty node except the empty relative operator *Op* in the specifier position of CP. Because the number of relative clauses introduced by empty operators is not bounded (examples such as Example 1 seem to be indefinitely iterable) we are effectively forced to the conclusion that inflection, or some other lexical element present inside each relative clause, sponsors the empty operator *Op* in examples such as Example 1 and Figure 5.

EXAMPLE 1

A man [Op_1 Kim likes t_1], [Op_2 Sandy hates t_2] ... and [Op_3 Ivan ignores t_3] ...

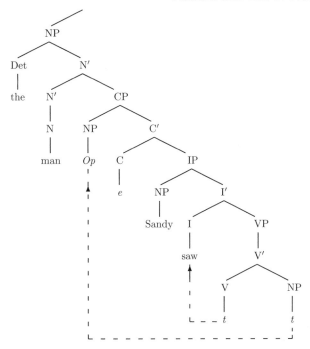

FIGURE 5 Empty operators in relative clauses

Even though the structure of reduced relative clauses such as Example 2 is not as well under-stood as ordinary relatives, they presumably involve empty operators as well. Assuming that we analyze the passive morphology on the participle as inflection (this seems linguistically motivated if we assume that movement to subject position is A-movement), the empty operator and all of its traces would be appropriately licensed.

EXAMPLE 2

A horse $[_{CP}Op[_{IP}t[_{VP}$ ridden $t]$ past the barn]] fell.

Finally, relative clauses can extrapose quite freely, as in Figure 6. (This diagram assumes that extraposed relative clauses adjoin to IP, but nothing rests on this assumption.

The sponsoring mechanisms discussed above account for all of the empty nodes except for the trace of the extraposed relative clause (adjoined to N′ in Figure 6). As an anonymous *Computational Linguistics* reviewer points out, an apparently unbounded number of relative clauses can be extraposed from a single NP.

EXAMPLE 3

A $[N'[N'[N'$ photo $t_1]t_2]t_3]$ appeared in today's paper $[_{CP_3}$ taken by Mapplethorpe] $[_{CP_2}$ showing him smiling] ... $[_{CP_1}$ that I think you would like].

Just as in the case of empty operator relative clauses, this iterability suggests that the extraposition traces must be sponsored by lexical items that appear inside the extraposed relative clauses. The inflection element in the relative clause seems to be the most appropriate lexical item to sponsor these traces.

To summarize, it seems that it is possible to identify sponsors for the empty nodes for a variety of linguistic constructions. Of course, the above examples do not demonstrate that it will always be possible to identify appropriate sponsors. In any given theory a detailed analysis

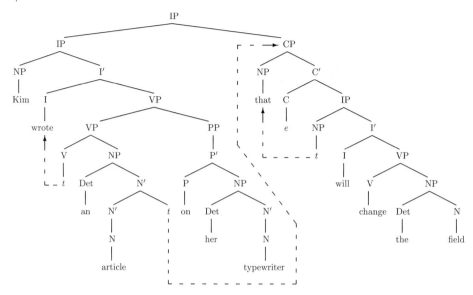

FIGURE 6 Relative clause extraposition

of each construction is required to determine the appropriate sponsors.

40.4 Implementation

The diagram in Figure 7 shows the structure of a possible implementation of a parsing system that exploits the notion of sponsoring. Square cornered boxes are used for data, and round corners for processes. Lexical access is applied to the input string to produce (nondeterministically) the extended lexical item (ELI) of each word. Its output is split into a sequence of lexical items and a bag of empty nodes.

The parser can be based on any standard algorithm. It is special only in that all the terminal items in the phrases it constructs come either from the string of lexical items or from the bag of empty nodes, so it is impossible for any empty node to appear more than once in an analysis.

An obvious defect of the architecture in this simple form is that, in the absence of some form of prediction, the parser will consider at all points in the string all the structures that can be built entirely from empty nodes. A simple solution to this problem is to compute all trees consisting solely of empty nodes sponsored by lexical items appearing in the utterance to be parsed before beginning the main parsing process. This will make it possible to use a parser that does not deal with empty nodes explicitly. The idea is to modify the interface between the parser and the grammar. The fact that sponsoring can be implemented entirely within the "rule-maker" interface shows it can be used with any parsing algorithm. We take it that the main job of this interface will be to manufacture "rules" that enshrine the local well-formedness constraints on individual nodes. The modification consists in adding rules to this set.

A rule $a \to b_1...b_n$ will be passed in its original form to the parser, which can use it to build a phrase from n nonempty daughters. In addition, the rule maker supplies the parser with rules derived from this one by replacing $k < n$ of the b_i with empty trees, yielding a rule with $n - k$ items on the right-hand side. The parser treats all these rules on equal footing. Apart from the sponsoring relationship, there is no requirement that any of the k empty trees be related to the $n - k$ nonempty trees that the parser proper gets to see.

There are certain bookkeeping tasks that can best be undertaken by the rule maker. The most important of these have to do with ensuring that no empty terminal appears more than once in any structure. Concomitantly, it makes it possible to verify, at the end of the parse, that all empty terminals appear in the structure, if this is a requirement. The rule maker can also be used to percolate constraints up or down the tree, possibly discharging some of them in the process.

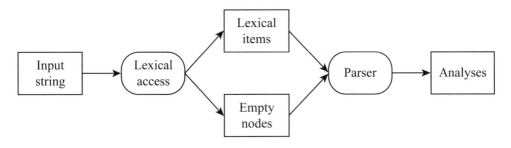

FIGURE 7 A simple architecture

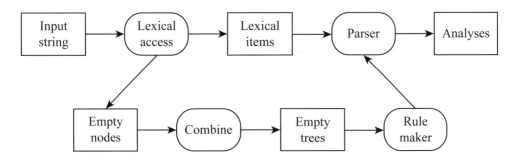

FIGURE 8 The modified architecture

One remaining problem is to arrange for the parser to include the empty trees in the structures that it builds. We assume that this information accompanies the rule, perhaps in the form of features on the parent category, as in many unification grammars.

Conclusions

It has not been our purpose here to solve the problem of parsing for GB, but only to provide a mechanism for ensuring that empty nodes do not cause nontermination of parsing in an important class of cases. We have made only very general remarks on the architecture of a parsing system that would incorporate these ideas, largely because we believe that the details of such a design would depend heavily on the mechanism that was chosen for managing constraints. Efficient implementation would depend on a good resolution of a number of interacting trade-offs, and there are several of these within our scheme that need to be explored. In particular, the components of an ELI could be more or less narrowly specified for the roles they are to fill.

If the nodes are highly specialized, there will be greater ambiguity in the lexicon and consequently greater nondeterminism in the parser. On the other hand, many of these search paths will presumably be curtailed earlier than they would have been with less specialized nodes.

A major determinant of system performance will clearly be the manner in which constraints are enforced. It is possible to distinguish a class of constraints that arise in the course of parsing but which cannot, in general, be discharged there, and should therefore be treated as part of the result that the parser delivers. Notable among these are contraindexing constraints from the Binding theory.

Ensuring that each node in an ELI fills the role for which it was intended could be resolved through the general constraint mechanism. However, more specialized mechanisms could sometimes be useful. Suppose, for example, that the lexical entry for a noun contained a node specifically intended to receive Case. If these were the only nodes whose Case attribute was unspecified, all others having an explicit zero value, the required mechanism could consist simply in having all rules assign a value to this feature, that value being zero except for rules that assign a substantive Case.

A somewhat different problem consists of verifying that nodes from a given ELI appear in a certain structural configuration. Assigning each node a unique identifier allows this problem to be solved straightforwardly by the general constraint mechanism.

It might be advantageous for the ELI to encode very specific information about a lexical item and the empty nodes that it sponsors. For example, the ELI for a WH item might specify that the traces it sponsors are coindexed with the WH item itself. Assuming that indices are just unbound variables (thus coindexing is unification and contraindexing is an inequality constraint), an interesting technical problem arises if the basic parsing engine uses a chart (Kay 1967, 1980). Because it is fundamental to such devices that the label on an edge is copied before it is used as a component of a larger phrase, the variables representing indices will be copied or renamed and the indices on the WH item and its sponsored trace will no longer be identicaL However, it is important that the sharing of variables among the components of an ELI be respected when they come together in a phrase. One way of overcoming this problem is to associate a vector of variables with each edge, in which each variable that is shared between two or more edges is assigned a unique position. Whenever edges are combined their associated vectors are unified, thus ensuring that the corresponding variables in each edge are identified.

Finally, our linguistic examples suggest to us that a more focused notion of sponsoring might be formulated. We observe that, modulo adjunction, empty nodes tend to stand in fixed structural relations to their sponsors. If this is indeed generally true, then these strong locality constraints should clearly be exploited in the parsing process. This amounts to adopting the framework of Tree Adjoining Grammars (Frank 1990; Joshi, Levy, and Takahashi 1975; Kroch and Joshi 1985; Schabes 1990). The emphasis would then fall on deriving the initial and auxiliary trees from the general principles of grammar.

Acknowledgements

This research was supported by the Institut fur maschinelle Sprachverarbeitung at the University of Stuttgart. We would like to thank Prof. Christian Rohrer and members of the Institut for providing us with this opportunity. We are also indebted to Lauri Karttunen and two anonymous *Computational Linguistics* reviewers for helpful comments during preparation of this paper.

Publications referenced

Abney 1986; Fong 1991; Fong 1991; Frank 1990; Gazdar et al. 1985; Grimshaw 1990; Joshi et al. 1975; Kay 1967; Kay 1980; Kay 1989; Kroch and Joshi 1985; Millies 1991; Pereira 1981; Schabes 1990; Schabes 1992; Schabes et al. 1988; Schabes and Waters 1993; Speas and Fukui 1986; van Noord 1993; Vijay-Shanker and Schabes 1992.

## 41

Machine Translation: The Disappointing Past and Present

The field of machine translation has changed remarkably little since its earliest days in the fifties. The issues that divided researchers then remain the principal bones of contention today. The first of these concerns the distinction between that so-called interlingual and the transfer approach to the problem. The second concerns the relative importance of linguistic matters as opposed to common sense and general knowledge. The only major new lines of investigation that have emerged in recent years have involved the use of existing translations as a prime source of information for the production of new ones. One form that this takes is that of example-based machine translation (Furuse and Iida 1992; Iida and Iida 1991; Nagao 1992; Sato 1992)   in which a system of otherwise fairly conventional design is able to refer to a collection of existing translations. A much more radical approach, championed by IBM (Brown, Cocke et al. 1990),

is the one in which virtually the entire body of knowledge that the system uses is acquired automatically from statistical properties of a very large body of existing translation.

In recent years, work on machine translation has been most vigorously pursued in Japan and it is also there that the greatest diversity of approaches is to be found. By and large, the Japanese share the general perception that the transfer approach offers the best chance for early success.

Two principal advantages have always been claimed for the interlingual approach. First, the method is taken as a move towards robustness and overall economy in that translation between all pairs of a set of languages in principle requires only translation to and from the interlingua for each member of the set. If there are n languages, n components are therefore required to be translated into the interlingua and n to translate from it, for a total of $2n$. To provide the same facilities, the transfer approach, according to which a major part of the translation system for a given pair of languages is specific to that pair, requires a separate device to translate in each direction for every pair of languages for a total of $n(n\text{-}1)$. The PIVOT system of NEC (Okumura, Muraki et al. 1991; Muraki 1989) and ATLAS II of Fujitsu (Uchida 1989) are commercial systems among a number of research systems based on the two-step method according to which texts are translated from the source language to an artificial interlingual representation and then into the target language. The Rosetta system at Philips (Landsbergen 1987), and the DLT system at BSO (Witkam 1988; Schubert 1988) in the Netherlands also adopt this approach. In the latter, the interlingua is not a language especially designed for this purpose, but Esperanto .

According to the majority transfer view of machine translation, a certain amount of analysis of the source text is done in the context of the source language alone and a certain amount of work on the translated text is done in the context of the target language, but the bulk of the work relies on comparative information about the specific pair of languages. This is argued for on the basis of the sheer difficulty of designing a single interlingua that can be all things for all languages and on the view that translation is, by its very nature, an exercise in comparative linguistics. The massive EUROTRA system (Schutz, Thurmair, et al. 1991; Arnold and des Tombe 1987; King and Perschke 1987; Perschke 1989), in which groups from all the countries of the European Union participated, was a transfer system, as is the current Verbmobil system sponsored by the German Federal Ministry for Research and Technology (BMFT).

A transfer system in which the analysis and generation components are large relative to the transfer component and where transfer is therefore conducted in terms of quite abstract entities takes on much of the flavor of an interlingual system while not making the commitment to linguistic universality that many see as the hallmark of the interlingual approach. Such semantic transfer systems are attracting quite a lot of attention. Fujitsu's ATLAS I (Uchida 1986) was an example, and Sharp's DUET system is another. The approach taken by SRI (Cambridge) with the Core Language Engine (Alshawi, Carter, et al. 1991) also falls in this category.

Just as these systems constitute something of an intermediate position between interlingua and transfer, they can also be seen to some extent as a compromise between the mainly linguistically based approaches we have been considering up to now and the so-called knowledge-based systems pursued most notably at Carnegie Mellon University (Nirenburg, Raskin, et al. 1986; Carbonell and Tomita 1987), and at the Center for Research in Language at New Mexico State University (Farwell and Wilks 1990). The view that informs these efforts, whose most forceful champion was Roger Shank, is that translation relies heavily on information and abilities that are not specifically linguistic. If it is their linguistic knowledge that we often think of as characterizing human translators, it is only because we take their common sense and knowledge of the everyday world for granted in a way we clearly cannot do for machines.

Few informed people still see the original ideal of fully automatic high-quality translation of arbitrary texts as a realistic goal for the foreseeable future. Many systems require texts to be pre-edited to put them in a form suitable for treatment by the system, and post-editing of the machine's output is generally taken for granted. The most successful systems have been those that have relied on their input being in a sublanguage (Kittredge 1987), either naturally occurring, as in that case of weather reports, or deliberately controlled. The spectacular success of the METEO system (Chevalier, Dansereau, et al. 1978) working on Canadian weather reports encouraged the view that sublanguages might be designed for a number of different applications, but the principles on which such languages should be designed have failed to emerge and progress has been very limited.

Future Directions

Research in machine translation has developed traditional patterns which will clearly have to be broken if any real progress is to be made. The traditional view that the problem is principally a linguistic one is clearly not tenable but the alternative that requires a translation system to have a substantial part of the general knowledge and common sense that humans have seems also to be unworkable. Compromises must presumably be found where knowledge of restricted domains can facilitate the translation of texts in those domains. The most obvious gains will come from giving up, at least for the time being, the idea of machine translation as a fully automatic batch process in favor of one in which the task is apportioned between people and machines. The proposal made in Kay (1980), according to which the translation machine would consult with a human speaker of the source language with detailed knowledge of the subject matter, has attracted more attention in recent times. A major objection to this approach, namely that the cost of operating such a system would come close to that of doing the whole job in the traditional way, will probably not hold up in the special, but widespread situation in which a single document has to be translated into a large number of languages.

Publications referenced

Alshawi et al. 1991; Arnold and des Tombe. 1987; Brown et al. 1990; Carbonell 1987; Chevalier 1978; Farwell et al 1990; Furuse and Iida 1992; Iida and Iida 1991; Kay 1980; King and Perschke 1987; Kittredge 1987; Landsbergen 1987; Muraki 1989; Nagao 1992; Nirenburg 1986; Okumura et al. 1991; Perschke 1989; Sato 1992; Schubert 1988; Schutz et al. 1991; Uchida 1986; Uchida 1989; Witkam 1988.

42

Chart Generation

Abstract

Charts constitute a natural uniform architecture for parsing and generation provided string position is replaced by a notion more appropriate to logical forms and that measures are taken to curtail generation paths containing semantically incomplete phrases.

42.1 Charts

Shieber (1988) showed that parsing charts can be also used in generation and raised the question, which we take up again here, of whether they constitute a natural uniform architecture for parsing and generation. In particular, we will be interested in the extent to which they bring to the generation process advantages comparable to those that make them attractive in parsing.

Chart parsing is not a well defined notion. The usual conception of it involves at least four related ideas:

Inactive edges. In context-free grammar, all phrases of a given category that cover a given part of the string are equivalent for the purposes of constructing larger phrases. Efficiency comes from collecting equivalent sets of phrases into (inactive) *edges* and constructing edges from edges rather than phrases from phrases.

Active edges. New phrases of whatever size can be built by considering existing edges pairwise if provision is made for partial phrases. Partial phrases are collected into edges that are said to be *active* because they can be thought of as actively seeking material to complete them.

The algorithm schema. Newly created edges are placed on an agenda. Edges are moved from the agenda to the *chart* one by one until none remains to be moved. When an edge is moved, all interactions between it and edges already in the chart are considered and any new edges that they give rise to are added to the agenda.

Indexing. The positions in the string at which phrases begin and end can be used to index edges so that the algorithm schema need consider interactions only between adjacent pairs.

Chart parsing is attractive for the analysis of natural languages, as opposed to programming languages, for the way in which it treats ambiguity. Regardless of the number of alternative structures for a particular string that a given phrase participates in, it will be constructed once and only once. Although the number of structures of a string can grow exponentially with the length of the string, the number of edges that needs to be constructed grows only with the square of the string length and the whole parsing process can be accomplished in cubic time.

Innumerable variants of the basic chart parsing scheme are possible. For example, if there were languages with truly free word order, we might attempt to characterize them by rules like those of context-free grammar, but with a somewhat different interpretation. Instead of replacing nonterminal symbols in a derivation with strings from the right-hand side of corresponding rules, we would remove the nonterminal symbol and insert the symbols from the right-hand side of the rule at arbitrary places in the string.

A chart parser for languages with free word order would be a minor variant of the standard one. An edge would take the form X_v where v is a vector with a bit for every word in the string and showing which of those words the edge covers. There is no longer any notion of adjacency so that there would be no indexing by string position. Interesting interactions occur between pairs of edges whose bit vectors have empty intersections, indicating that they cover disjoint sets of words. There can now be as many edges as bit-vectors and, not surprisingly, the computational complexity of the parsing process increases accordingly.

42.2   Generation

A parser is a transducer from strings to structures or logical forms. A generator, for our purposes, is the inverse. One way to think of it, therefore, is as a parser of structures or logical forms that delivers analyses in the form of strings. This view has the apparent disadvantage of putting insignificant differences in the syntax of a logical forms, such as the relative order of the arguments to symmetric operators, on the same footing as more significant facts about them. We know that it will not generally be possible to reduce logical expressions to a canonical form but this does not mean that we should expect our generator to be compromised, or even greatly delayed, by trivial distinctions. Considerations of this kind were, in part, responsible for the recent resurgence of interest in "flat" representations of logical form (Copestake *et al.*, 1996) and for the representations used for transfer in Shake-and-Bake translation (Whitelock, 1992). They have made semantic formalisms like those now usually associated with Davidson (Davidson, 1980, Parsons, 1990) attractive in artificial intelligence for many years (Hobbs 1985, Kay, 1970). Operationally, the attraction is that the notations can be analyzed largely as free word-order languages in the manner outlined above. Consider the expression (1)

(1)   r: run(r), past(r), fast(r), arg1(r,j), name(j,John)

which we will take as a representation of the logical form of the sentences *John ran fast* and *John ran quickly*. It consists of a distinguished index *(r)* and a list of predicates whose relative order is immaterial. The distinguished index identifies this as a sentence that makes a claim about a running event. "John" is the name of the entity that stands in the 'arg1' relation to the running which took place in the past and which was fast. Nothing turns on these details which will differ with differing ontologies, logics, and views of semantic structure. What concerns us here is a procedure for generating a sentence from a structure of this general kind.

Assume that the lexicon contains entries like those in (2) in which the italicized arguments to the semantic predicates are variables.

(2)

Words	Cat	Semantics
John	np(x)	x:name(x,John)
ran	vp(x,y)	x:run(x), arg1(x,y), past(x)
fast	adv(x)	x:fast(x)
quickly	adv(x)	x:fast(x)

A *prima facie* argument for the utility of these particular words for expressing (1) can be made simply by noting that, *modulo* appropriate instantiation of the variables, the semantics of each of these words subsumes (1).

42.3 The Algorithm Schema

The entries in (2), with their variables suitably instantiated, become the initial entries of an agenda and we begin to move them to the chart in accordance with the algorithm schema, say in the order given.

The variables in the 'Cat' and 'Semantics' columns of (2) provide the essential link between syntax and semantics. The predicates that represent the semantics of a phrase will simply be the union of those representing the constituents. The rules that sanction a phrase (e.g. (3) below) show which variables from the two parts are to be identified.

When the entry for *John* is moved, no interactions are possible because the chart is empty. When *run* is moved, the sequence *John ran* is considered as a possible phrase on the basis of rule (3).

(3) $s(x) \to \text{np}(y), \text{vp}(x,y)$.

With appropriate replacements for variables, this maps onto the subset (4) of the original semantic specification in (1).

(4) r: run(r), past(r), arg1(r,j), name(j,John)

Furthermore it is a complete sentence. However, it does not count as an output to the generation process as a whole because it subsumes some but not all of (1). It therefore simply becomes a new edge on the agenda.

The string *ran fast* constitutes a verb phrase by virtue of rule (5) giving the semantics (6), and the phrase *ran quickly* with the same semantics is put on the agenda when the *quickly* edge is moved to the chart.

(5) $vp(x) \to \text{vp}(x), \text{adv}(x)$.

(6) r: run(r), past(r), fast(r), arg1(r,y)

The agenda now contains the entries in (7).

(7)

Words	Cat	Semantics
John ran	s(r)	r: run(r), past(r), arg1(r,j), name(j,John)
ran fast	vp(r,j)	r: run(r), past(r), fast(r), arg1(r,y)
ran quickly	vp(r,j)	r: run(r), past(r), fast(r), arg1(r,y)

Assuming that adverbs modify verb phrases and not sentences, there will be no interactions when the *John ran* edge is moved to the chart.

When the edge for *ran fast* is moved, the possibility arises of creating the phrase *ran fast quickly* as well as *ran fast fast*. Both are rejected, however, on the grounds that they would involve using a predicate from the original semantic specification more than once. This would be similar to allowing a given word to be covered by overlapping phrases in free word-order parsing. We proposed eliminating this by means of a bit vector and the same technique applies here. The fruitful interactions that occur here are between *ran fast* and *ran quickly* on the one hand, and *John* on the other. Both give sentences whose semantics subsumes the entire input. Several things are noteworthy about the process just outlined.

1. Nothing turns on the fact that it uses a primitive version of event semantics. A scheme in which the indices were handles referring to subexpressions in any variety of flat semantics could have been treated in the same way. Indeed, more conventional formalisms with richly recursive syntax could be converted to this form on the fly.

2. Because all our rules are binary, we make no use of active edges.

3. While it fits the conception of chart parsing given at the beginning of this paper, our generator does not involve string positions centrally in the chart representation. In this

respect, it differs from the proposal of Shieber (1988) which starts with all word edges leaving and entering a single vertex. But there is essentially no information in such a representation. Neither the chart nor any other special data structure is required to capture the fact that a new phrase may be constructible out of any given pair, and in either order, if they meet certain syntactic and semantic criteria.

4. Interactions must be considered explicitly between new edges and all edges currently in the chart, because no indexing is used to identify the existing edges that could interact with a given new one.

5. The process is exponential in the worst case because, if a sentence contains a word with k modifiers, then a version of it will be generated with each of the 2^k subsets of those modifiers, all but one of them being rejected when it is finally discovered that their semantics does not subsume the entire input. If the relative orders of the modifiers are unconstrained, matters only get worse.

Points 4 and 5 are serious flaws in our scheme for which we shall describe remedies. Point 2 will have some importance for us because it will turn out that the indexing scheme we propose will require the use of distinct active and inactive edges, even when the rules are all binary. We take up the complexity issue first, and then turn to how the efficiency of the generation chart might be enhanced through indexing.

42.4 Internal and External Indices

The exponential factor in the computational complexity of our generation algorithm is apparent in an example like (8).

(8) Newspaper reports said the tall young Polish athlete ran fast

The same set of predicates that generate this sentence clearly also generate the same sentence with deletion of all subsets of the words *tall, young,* and *Polish* for a total of 8 strings. Each is generated in its entirety, though finally rejected because it fails to account for all of the semantic material. The words *newspaper* and *fast* can also be deleted independently giving a grand total of 32 strings.

We concentrate on the phrase *tall young Polish athlete* which we assumed would be combined with the verb phrase *ran fast* by the rule (3). The distinguished index of the noun phrase, call it p, is identified with the variable y in the rule, but this variable is not associated with the syntactic category, s, on the left-hand side of the rule. The grammar has access to indices only through the variables that annotate grammatical categories in its rules, so that rules that incorporate this sentence into larger phrases can have no further access to the index p. We therefore say that p is *internal* to the sentence *the tall young Polish athlete ran fast*.

The index p would, of course, also be internal to the sentences *the young Polish athlete ran fast, the tall Polish athlete ran fast,* etc. However, in these cases, the semantic material remaining to be expressed contains predicates that refer to this internal index, say 'tall(p)', and 'young(p)'. While the lexicon may have words to express these predicates, the grammar has no way of associating their referents with the above noun phrases because the variables corresponding to those referents are internal. We conclude that, as a matter of principle, no edge should be constructed if the result of doing so would be to make internal an index occurring in part of the input semantics that the new phrase does not subsume. In other words, the semantics of a phrase must contain all predicates from the input specification that refer to any indices internal to it. This strategy does not prevent the generation of an exponential number of variants of phrases containing modifiers. It limits proliferation of the ill effects, however, by allowing only the maximal one to be incorporated in larger phrases. In other words, if the final result has phrases with m and n modifiers respectively, then 2^n versions of the first and 2^m of the second will be created, but only one of each set will be incorporated into larger phrases and no factor of $2^{(n+m)}$ will be introduced into the cost of the process.

42.5 Indexing

String positions provide a natural way to index the strings input to the parsing process for the simple reason that there are as many of them as there are words but, for there to be any possibility of interaction between a pair of edges, they must come together at just one index. These are the natural points of articulation in the domain of strings. They cannot fill this role in generation because they are not natural properties of the semantic expressions that are the input to the process. The corresponding natural points of articulation in flat semantic structures are the entities that we have already been referring to as *indices*.

In the modified version of the procedure, whenever a new inactive edge is created with label $\mathbf{B}(b \; ...)$, then for all rules of the form in (9), an active edge is also created with label $\mathbf{A}(...)/\mathbf{C}(c \; ...)$.

(9) $\mathbf{A}(...) \rightarrow \mathbf{B}(b \; ...) \; \mathbf{C}(c \; ...)$

This represents a phrase of category $\mathbf{A}$ that requires a phrase of category $\mathbf{C}$ on the right for its completion. In these labels, b and c are (variables representing) the first, or *distinguished* indices associated with $\mathbf{B}$ and $\mathbf{C}$. By analogy with parsing charts, an inactive edge labeled $\mathbf{B}(b \; ...)$ can be thought of as *incident* from vertex b, which means simply that it is efficiently accessible through the index b. An active edge $\mathbf{A}(...)/\mathbf{C}(c \; ...)$ should be thought of as incident from, or accessible through, the index c. The key property of this scheme is that active and inactive edges interact by virtue of indices that they share and, by letting vertices correspond to indices, we collect together sets of edges that could interact. We illustrate the modified procedure with the sentence (10) whose semantics we will take to be (11), the grammar rules (12)–(14), and the lexical entries in (15).

(10) The dog saw the cat.

(11) dog(d), def(d), saw(s), past(s), cat(c), def(c), arg1(s,d), arg2(s,c).

(12) $s(x) \rightarrow np(y), vp(x,y)$.

(13) $vp(x,y) \rightarrow v(x,y,z), np(z)$.

(14) $np(x) \rightarrow det(x), n(x)$.

(15)

Words	Cat	Semantics
cat	$n(x)$	x: $cat(x)$
saw	$v(x,y,z)$	x: $see(x)$, $past(x)$, $arg1(x,y)$, $arg2(x,z)$
dog	$n(x)$	x: $dog(x)$
the	$det(x)$	x: $def(x)$

The procedure will be reminiscent of left-corner parsing. Arguments have been made in favor of a head-driven strategy which would, however, have been marginally more complex (e.g. in Kay 1989, Shieber, *et al.* 1989)   and the differences are, in any case, not germane to our current concerns.

The initial agenda, including active edges, and collecting edges by the vertices that they are incident from, is given in (16).

The grammar is consulted only for the purpose of creating active edges and all interactions in the chart are between active and inactive pairs of edges incident from the same vertex.

(16)

Vert	Words	Cat	Semantics
d	the	det(d)	d: def(d)
	the	np(d)/n(d)	d: def(d)
	dog	n(d)	d: dog(d)
s	saw	v(s,d,c)	s: see(s), past(s), arg1(s,d), arg2(s,c)
c	saw	vp(s,d)/np(c)	r: see(s), past(s), arg1(r,j)
	the	det(c)	c: def(c)
	the	np(c)/n(c)	c: def(c)
	cat	n(c)	c: cat(c)

(17)

Vert	Words	Cat	Semantics
d	the dog	np(d)	d: dog(d), def(d)
	saw the cat	vp(s,d)/np(d)	s: see(s), past(s), arg1(s,d), arg2(s,c), cat(c), def(c)
c	the cat	np(c)	c: cat(c), def(c)
s	saw the cat	vp(s,d)	s: see(s), past(s), arg1(s,d), arg2(s,c), cat(c), def(c)

Among the edges in (16), there are two interactions, one at vertices c and d. They cause the first and third edges in (17) to be added to the agenda. The first interacts with the active edge originally introduced by the verb "saw" producing the fourth entry in (17). The label on this edge matches the first item on the right-hand side of rule (12) and the active edge that we show in the second entry is also introduced. The final interaction is between the first and second edges in (17) which give rise to the edge in (18).

This procedure confirms perfectly to the standard algorithm schema for chart parsing, especially in the version that makes predictions immediately following the recognition of the first constituent of a phrase, that is, in the version that is essentially a caching left-corner parser.

(18)

Vert	Words	Cat	Semantics
s	The dog saw the cat	s(s)	dog(d), def(d), see(s), past(s), arg1(s,d), arg2(s,c), cat(c), def(c)

Acknowledgements

Whatever there may be of value in this paper owes much to the interest, encouragement, and tolerance of my colleagues Marc Dymetman, Ronald Kaplan, John Maxwell, and Hadar Shem Tov. I am also indebted to the anonymous reviewers of this paper.

Publications referenced

Copestake et al. 1996; Davidson 1980; Hobbs 1985; Kay 1970; Kay 1989; Parsons 1990; Shieber 1988; Shieber et al. 1989; Whitelock 1992.

43

It's Still the Proper Place

In the sixteen years that have elapsed since this paper was written, little has happened to change the overall assessment we should make of the proper place of humans and machines in language translation. The EUROTRA project began shortly after that writing as a massive attempt to build a practical fully automatic translation system incorporating the best linguistic technology of the day. It ended lamely attempting to justify the expenditure of close to a hundred million ECU on the grounds that researchers even in the poorest European nations had learnt something of computational linguistics. As always, translation was treated as an entirely linguistic problem, and the parts of the project read like the chapters of an elementary linguistics textbook. In 1992, the German Federal Ministry for Research and Technology, presumably encouraged by recent achievements in translation and speech recognition, initiated the Verbmobil project, a program of research that would depend on major advances in both of these fields. The first of the two phases planned for this project, involving some 130 researchers from Germany and abroad, is just coming to an end and the second phase, involving only 100 researchers, is about to begin. At a cost of some 60 million marks, the project has reached the point where it can interpret a small number of short sentences chosen from a predetermined corpus. The design of the project is essentially identical to that of its predecessors and it would be truly remarkable if it produced interestingly different results. Government and bureaucracy do indeed appear to be imbued with a sad fatalism that forces upon them a future that repeats the follies of the past.

Verbmobil is especially disheartening for the great opportunities that it offers but that are not being pursued. The aim is to provide interpretation services for the participants in a face-to-face conversation so that the originators of the material it must translate can be assumed to be available to help clarify their intentions. However, only a vanishingly small proportion of the enormous resources of the project are devoted to designing ways in which this might be achieved.

While the differences between past and present translation projects are minuscule relative to what would be required to affect substantially the value of the resulting system, it is of course by no means the case that they all start on an even footing. Computers are faster; the art of programming advances; storage is cheaper; large corpora of text are more readily available; new algorithms are constantly being devised; and, above all, our understanding of language and linguistics is improving steadily. Soundly designed translation systems, if there were any, would clearly improve as understanding of the workings of language improved. However, systems that are made up entirely of linguistic components actually degrade as the linguistics on which they are based improves. This should not be surprising. It is the job of the linguist to describe and account for the meaning potential of words, phrases, sentences, texts and dialogues. It is not the job of the linguist to say what part of this meaning potential is being exercised in any given circumstance. Simply put, the better the linguistics, the greater the number and the subtlety of the ambiguities that will be unearthed and the greater the resulting strain on the nonlinguistic components of the system whose job it is to resolve them. Previous systems had little or nothing in the way of non-linguistic components and essentially none are proposed for those being built today. It is for this reason that Systran remains the best MT system available, and that Verbmobil will, with sickening surety, fail to produce anything of the slightest interest.

While researchers and sponsors remain obdurate in their refusal to take seriously the problems of resolution that are crucial to all language processing, the range of practical approaches that one might take to these problems is clearly much larger than was envisaged in my original paper. The following, for example, is a fact from which it should be possible to profit: The likelihood that a document picked up at random in a government or corporate office will ever be translated into another language is very small. But, given that it has been, or is destined to be, translated into one other language, then the chance of its being translated into additional languages becomes very much higher. In the offices of a major international corporation or the European Union, translation into one language might well predict translation into eight, ten, or more others. Any part of the understanding of the document that was achieved in the course of making the initial translation would presumably be of potential value in making subsequent translations. The effort involved in capturing some part of this understanding is more completely amortized as the number of target languages increases. Furthermore, each translation will generally add to the richness of the information available on the document.

How might information relevant to the translation of a document be collected and reused? One suggestion was made in the original paper, namely to put questions to a human consultant who knew the source language and the subject matter of the document. Another would make use of information coming from the human revisors of earlier translations. The following is but one of the approaches that might be taken. Suppose that the translation system produced large numbers of candidate translations for ambiguous words and phrases, even though it presented only its best guess to the revisor. The revisor would then be encouraged, perhaps through the editing software used for the revisions, to use alternatives already countenanced by the system wherever possible. The choice of a particular alternative is presumably tantamount to answering in a certain way questions that could have been raised in the course of the translation process. When the same questions are raised in the course of later translations into other languages, many of them will be answerable in a more informed way.

Suppose that *Il y aura encore une conférence et il la fera demain* has been accepted as the translation of *There will be one more lecture and he will give it tomorrow* and that the machine is now faced with translating it into German. The question of whether *lecture* should be translated as *Vorlesung*, suggesting that it is part of a pedagogical series, or as *Vortrag* will have to be investigated and the information perhaps used later when translating into a fourth language. The fact that the corresponding French word is *conférence* provides no information on the matter. But on the matter of the remarkably versatile English word *give*, we have not only the presence in the same sentence of the word *lecture*, but the much stronger information that *give* has been translated by the equally versatile *faire*. The pair *give/faire* is altogether less versatile, however, than either in isolation and serves to point to *halten* as a suitable German translation. The English pronoun *it* must refer to something inanimate. The French *la* must refer to something feminine. Jointly, they narrow the range of possible referents more than either would in isolation.

In the first phase of Verbmobil, a very small investment was made in studying translation and interpretation as it is done by people. For one reason or another, essentially none of this work was reflected in the system that was finally put together and the conclusion was drawn that it was therefore without value. It was also argued that there was no reason to suppose that MT could succeed only by emulating humans. Airplanes, we were reminded, do not flap their wings. But, the parallel is a bad one.

The aim of the early pioneers of flight was to build a machine that could fly and the fact that there were animals that could fly, while surely worthy of consideration, was not necessarily related to the enterprise. With translation, the matter is quite different. The aim of the translator is to convey in another language what an original text conveys to a person. It is possible that one must be a person to do this, but it is surely barely coherent to propose achieving a human understanding of a text by means that are not closely related to the ones that a human uses.

This is a procedural issue having to do with the methods and techniques that a translating machine would use. But there is a more fundamental issue that requires empirical study of human translation having to do with the nature of translation itself. Workers in this field usually take it as self-evident what constitutes a translation, especially within the relatively limited domains in which automatic methods might be applied. In particular, it is assumed that the sequence of sentences that make up the translation should preserve the intended meanings of the corresponding sentences in the original. An old example from MT folklore can easily be adapted to show that this cannot be the case. Suppose that you see me at a restaurant with a woman whom you take to be my cousin and that, the following morning, in the office, you say to me *"Est-ce que tu étais avec ta cousine hier soir?"* and I reply *"Non, je n'ai pas de cousine."* Translating into English in such a way as to maintain the meaning as faithfully as possible, we get "Were you with your female cousin yesterday evening," and "No, I have no female cousin." The word female makes things awkward and, given that we both remember the happenings of the previous night, it adds nothing of importance. But to leave it out would be to depart from the meaning of the original and, in any case, it is not easy to see on what grounds the machine could decide on the omission. But matters are worse. "No, I have no female cousin" is the wrong translation of the second sentence because, unlike the French original, it implies that I do, in fact, have one or more male cousins. There will, of course, be those that say that the meanings of *cousine* and *female cousin* are shown to be different by this very fact, but the burden of showing what other notion of meaning would be more appropriate then falls on them.

In summary, I find MT from today's vantage point considerably more depressing than I did in 1980. The challenges and opportunities that it offers are even more varied and exciting today than they were then, but the determination of those working in the field doggedly to pursue old questions with old methods is apparently without bounds.

44

Chart Translation

Abstract

For efficiency reasons, machine translation systems are generally designed to eliminate ambiguities as early as possible even if delaying the decision would make a more informed choice possible. This paper takes the contrary view, arguing that essentially all choices should be deferred so that large numbers of competing translations will be produced in typical cases. Representing all the data structures in a suitable packed form, much as alternative structures are represented in a chart parser, makes this practicable.

44.1 Translation and Knowledge

Judging by the great increase in activity in machine translation in the last few years, an outside observer might easily conclude that researchers in the field had finally reached the goal of truly practical translation systems towards which they have been striving for some forty years. Maybe some breakthrough has occurred, or maybe all the little incremental efforts have finally proved just enough to push us over an important invisible line. Insiders know differently. If we somehow seem to be winning the game that has been going against us for so long, it is not because we have learnt to play better; it is because the goal posts have been moved. Simply stated, the market for low-quality machine translation has grown from nothing to one clearly worthy of commercial interest in a matter of two or three years.

Whatever the reasons may be for this change in the translation market, the Worldwide Web surely played an important part. Browsers now routinely offer happy explorers the opportunity to have the results of their quests translated into their own language at the click of a mouse. Their expectations of this process are, however, no greater than they were of the initial search. Web usage is essentially casual, even when a lot could turn on the outcome. If our search comes up with nothing, at least little time will have been lost. If we find something useful, it will be frosting on the cake – something we knew we had no real right to expect. So it is with a translation that is offered. If by reading it fast with little attention to detail, we seem to perceive something in it that touches on the subject of our quest, at best we may gain some useful information; at worst we will be amused.

There will continue to be a market for this kind of translation until substantially better results can be produced with little or no increase in the price. But there is also a great and growing need for high-quality translation and, as I have argued repeatedly (Kay *et al.* 1994, Kay 1997), computers will do little to help fill this need until very large strides have been made towards building programs that could pass the Turing test – programs that could, in other words, successfully masquerade as human beings on the other end of a telephone or computer-mediated connection. My claim is that substantial proportion of the linguistic problems that need to be solved in order to achieve high quality translation are already fairly well in hand but that linguistics is a relatively minor part of what is required for translation. The remaining problems are not confined to any particular field of endeavor. Anything that a person might know, or believe, or suspect, or impute to the knowledge, belief or suspicions of another, could be crucial for translating the next sentence in some text. Furthermore, the sentences for which a good translation is possible only in the light of such nonlinguistic, unsystematic, knowledge are the rule rather than the exception. In short, translation is what is sometimes called an *AI-complete* problem.

My conclusion from this has been, and continues to be. not that computers are out of place in high-quality translation, but simply that they cannot be expected to do the job alone. The human contribution to the enterprise is indispensable. However, it absolutely need not take the form of actually making the translation and, indeed, substantial increases in the quality of current fully automatic systems may be possible with contributions by humans that know only a single language. A person that knew the source language and the subject matter of the material to be translated, might be called upon to answer questions about the meanings of particular words and phrases or the referents of pronouns and definite noun phrases. If the questions are chosen with care, and the answers interpreted at a sufficiently high level of abstraction, then they may contribute to translations into several different target languages. This is important in view of the observation that, while most documents are not translated at all, those that are, are usually translated into several different languages.

Once beyond the narrow realm of meteorological reports, humans are always involved in translation whenever any importance attaches to the comprehensibility, not to mention the naturalness and fluidity, of the result. These people are called *post-editors* in MT jargon, *revisors* more traditionally. Their work could also be a source of input to a semi-automatic system for, if there are nonlinguistic problems that must be solved in the course of translating a document from English into French, then many of them can be expected to crop up again when the document is translated into German and, certainly, when it is translated into Italian. If the answers to even some of these problems could be inferred from the changes that the revisor makes, then the cost of the next translation might be substantially reduced.

In the balance of this paper, I will sketch a framework for the design of translation systems that would allow for these, and a variety of other approaches to the problem of nonlinguistic knowledge in translation, to be experimented with and exploited in a broad and robust manner.

44.2 History

I begin with some history. A reasonable candidate for the year of birth of computational linguistics is 1960, the year in which John Cocke devised, without publishing, what later came to be known as the Cocke-Kasami-Younger (CKY) algorithm, the precursor of chart parsing. This is important for several reasons including the following:

1. It was the first algorithm designed to solve a major class of linguistic problems;
2. It separated program from data and grammaticality from considerations of contextual appropriateness;
3. It showed that an exponential number of objects could be computed and represented in polynomial time and space so it was no longer necessary to curtail search paths prematurely.

Actually, the last of these was only partially understood at the time, when matters of computational complexity were generally much less well understood than they are today. More specifically, the finding was this: a representation of all the structures that an arbitrary context-free grammar assigns to a given n-word sentence can be constructed using time and space proportional to n^3, even though the number of such structures grows in proportion to a series known as the *Catalan numbers*, which grows exponentially. As the following graph clearly shows, while the Catalan numbers initially grow more slowly than n^3, the ninth member of the series is 1430, almost twice $9^3 = 729$.

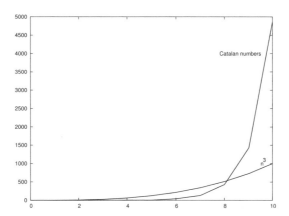

This is a surprising result because, on the face of it, there is no way of doing anything whatsoever to a number, say k, of objects, and of recording the results for each of them, at a cost in time and space that grows more slowly than k. Lest any mystery remain as to how this comes about, consider the sentence (1) consisting of a noun phrase and a verb phrase, each of which contains an ambiguity resulting from a present participle.

(1) *Visiting relatives would beat entertaining children*

However, the ambiguities play no part in determining the well-formedness of the sentence as a whole and a single rule application is in fact sufficient to construct a representation of the four different structures that the sentence has. In other words, the chart parser constructs phrases, not out of other phrases, but out of equivalence classes of phrases belonging to a given grammatical category and covering a given part of the string. The structures that are built up in this way are referred to as *packed* structures.

The polynomial cost of chart parsing can be very high for long sentences, but the exponential cost of simple backtracking schemes places them entirely beyond practicality. Before the advent of chart parsing, it was therefore taken for granted that a syntactic analyzer could not be expected to deliver all the structures that a grammar assigned to a sentence but that it must attempt to find one, or perhaps a small number of, probably correct structures early and to abandon the search for any others. This reflects on my second reason for the historical importance of the CKY algorithm, namely that it allowed for a strong separation of program and data, grammar and algorithm. Such a separation is theoretically possible with backtracking algorithms, but impractical because such procedures had always to incorporate heuristics based on nongrammatical information to prune the search space early.

44.3   The Translation Relation

The proposal I want to make here is simply that the move that was made in parsing with the CKY algorithm in 1960 is the same move that needs to be made in translation. The ideas are based in large measure on ideas worked out in some detail in Shemtov (1997). The results will be similar and the benefits even more dramatic. In particular:

1. This will provide the first complete implementation of the linguistic component of the translation process;
2. It will separate the translation relation from considerations of contextual appropriateness;
3. It will show that a very large number of candidate translations can be computed and represented at reasonable cost in time and space so that it will no longer be necessary to curtail search paths prematurely.

There is, of course, a potential problem with the parallel I am trying to draw between parsing and translation. Parsing has to do with grammaticality and grammatical structure. In other words, it is based on the notion of grammar as a set of rules that define a function from strings to sets of structures independently of external considerations such as the context in which the strings occur. The image of this in the translation domain will presumably be a set of rules associating strings in a pair of languages, possibly with structural information relating parts of one string with parts of the other, but independently of contextual considerations. The notion of grammar that parsers presuppose is an idealization that does not work for marginal cases and this will surely also be true of translation but, up until now, no one has seriously contemplated a context-free notion of translation, and it remains to be shown that such a notion is coherent.

In this paper, there is space to little more than acknowledge the problem which, in its full generality is certainly difficult, subtle and multidimensional. Let us glance in passing at the well known problem of strings that can be translated into some other languages only by adding some information that is not explicit, at least locally, in the source text. Thus, we must supply pronouns with gender when translating from English into many other European languages, aspect when translating verbs into Russian, tenses when translating from Chinese, and so on. We must decide whether an English *chair* is a French *chaise* or a *fauteuil,* whether a *window* is a *fenêtre,* a *vitrine,* or a *guichet,* and whether a *book* is a *livre,* a *cahier,* or a *carnet.* In some cases, the choice is from a very large, possibly an open, set. Consider the French question *Où voulez-vous que je me mette?* which can be translated into English as *Where do you want me to X?,* where X can be replaced by any number of things, including *stand, sit, park, tie up (my boat), sign (my name),* and *leave my coat.*

For the moment, I will retreat to the position that cases like these are problems for the approach I am advocating to just the extent that they are problems for any competing approach. Any translation system is capable of rendering certain words and phrases in several alternative ways among which it chooses, sooner or later, based on more or less good grounds. At its weakest, the proposal I am making can be understood as nothing more than a recommendation that these alternatives all be left to be resolved by some other module at a time still to be specified.

44.4 Charts and Contexted Sets

Consider the sentence (2).

(2) *Her face seemed to have become thinner*

Suppose, contrary to fact. that its only possible French translations are the following:

Sa figure paraissait être devenue plus maigre
Sa figure paraissait être devenue plus petite
Sa figure semblait être devenue plus maigre
Sa figure semblait être devenue plus petite
Son visage paraissait être devenu plus maigre
Son visage paraissait être devenu plus petit

Son visage semblait être devenu plus maigre
Son visage semblait être devenu plus petit

A chart can readily be built that comes tantalizingly close to representing this set, namely the following:

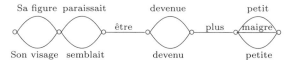

This chart could not, of course, have arisen as the result of parsing an input string because it has different word sequences covering one and the same stretch of the string. But the set of 24 strings that can be read out of it in the obvious way contain the 8 translations of the English sentence that we are interested in. The incorrect strings arise because there are dependencies among the edges that the chart mechanism itself is not sufficient to represent. In particular, the choice between *Sa figure* and *Son visage* determines the choice between *devenue* and *devenu* and between *petite* and *petit*. We can take care of this quite straightforwardly as follows:

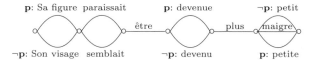

All we have done is to annotate some of the edges with expressions from the propositional calculus – in this case, trivially simple ones. We now require that, when a string is read out of the chart, the conjunction of the expressions on the edges visited be satisfiable. This makes, for example

Sa figure paraissait être devenu plus maigre

impossible because *Sa figure* can be part of the string only if **p**, and *devenu* only if ¬**p**.

It is a short step from charts with logical annotations to the more general notion of *contexted sets*. A contexted set is a set of sets of arbitrary kinds of individuals represented in a particular way. Instead of representing it as a list of lists of individuals, we represent it as a single list on which an individual that belongs to any of the sets appears just once with an annotation in the form of a Boolean expression. Each different set of individuals corresponds to a different assignment of the values **true** or **false** to the logical variables. This scheme is sufficiently general to accommodate representations for just about any imaginable abstract structure. Furthermore, under certain circumstances which occur routinely in linguistic structures, it has clear advantages over listing the members of each set separately. Intuitively stated, the circumstances are those in which the constraints on the sets to which a given individual belongs are independent of those governing most other individuals. This was not the case for the French translations of (2). but we do not expect interactions like these to involve more than small subsets of the words in a long sentence.

Consider the sentence in (3).

(3) *Teachers like the English book.*

I take it this has two different syntactic structures corresponding to the paraphrases in (4-5):

(4) *The English book pleases teachers.*
(5) *Teachers like the English ones make reservations.*

The following table contains deliberately simplified versions of its two structures in the form of a contexted set. Since we are representing structural information, we need the members of the set to be able to refer to one another and, for this, we use the number in the first column. The second column gives a part of speech and either a word or a sequence of numbers identifying other set members that are the constituents of the phrase. The last column gives the Boolean expression that determines which sets the individual belongs to. The logical variables are all of the form $\mathbf{p}_i$, where i is an integer.

	Phrase	Context		Phrase	Context
1	N: Teachers		11	NP: $< 4, 10 >$	$\mathbf{p}_2 \wedge \neg\mathbf{p}_3$
2	Prep: like	$\mathbf{p}_1$	12	VP: $< 3, 11 >$	$\mathbf{p}_1 \wedge \mathbf{p}_2 \wedge \neg\mathbf{p}_3$
3	Vt: like	$\neg\mathbf{p}_1$	13	S: $< 9, 12 >$	$\mathbf{p}_1 \wedge \mathbf{p}_2 \wedge \neg\mathbf{p}_3$
4	Det: the		14	NP: $< 4, 6 >$	$\neg\mathbf{p}_2$
5	Adj: English	$\mathbf{p}_2$	15	PP: $< 2, 14 >$	$\mathbf{p}_1 \wedge \neg\mathbf{p}_2$
6	N: English	$\neg\mathbf{p}_2$	16	N: $< 1, 15 >$	$\mathbf{p}_1 \wedge \neg\mathbf{p}_2$
7	Vi: book	$\mathbf{p}_3$	17	NP: $< 16, >$	$\mathbf{p}_1 \wedge \neg\mathbf{p}_2$
8	N: book	$\neg\mathbf{p}_3$	18	VP: $< 7 >$	$\mathbf{p}_3$
9	NP: $< 1 >$		19	S: $< 17, 18 >$	$\mathbf{p}_1 \wedge \neg\mathbf{p}_2 \wedge \mathbf{p}_3$
10	N: $< 5, 8 >$	$\mathbf{p}_2 \wedge \neg\mathbf{p}_3$			

The sets for which $\mathbf{p}_1$ is true contain *like* as a preposition. The complement of this set of sets contains *like* as a verb. The sets for which $\mathbf{p}_2$ is true contain *English* as an adjective. No set for which $\mathbf{p}_1$ and $\mathbf{p}_2$ are both true contains a sentence because, if *like* is taken to be a preposition and *English* is taken to be an adjective, then the string does not contain a sentence.

Let us now add just enough information to the table to suggest how alternative translations might be produced while continuing to profit from the compact representation. We will write French words in italics to keep them apart from the English ones.

	Phrase	Context		Phrase	Context
20	Det: *les*	$\mathbf{q}_1$	31	Vi: *réservent*	$\mathbf{p}_3$
21	Det: *des*	$\neg\mathbf{q}_1$	32	N: *livre*	$\neg\mathbf{p}_3$
22	N: *professeurs*		33	N: $< 29, 32 >$	$\mathbf{p}_2 \wedge \neg\mathbf{p}_3$
23	NP: $< 20, 22 >$	$\mathbf{q}_1$	34	NP: $< 27, 33 >$	$\mathbf{p}_2 \wedge \neg\mathbf{p}_3$
24	NP: $< 21, 22 >$	$\neg\mathbf{q}_1$	35	VP: $< 25, 34 >$	$\neg\mathbf{p}_1 \wedge \mathbf{q}_2 \wedge \mathbf{p}_2 \wedge \neg\mathbf{p}_3$
25	Vt: *aiment*	$\neg\mathbf{p}_1 \wedge \mathbf{q}_2$	36	Prep: *à*	$\neg\mathbf{p}_1 \wedge \neg\mathbf{q}_2$
26	Vt: *plaît*	$\neg\mathbf{p}_1 \wedge \neg\mathbf{q}_2$	37	PP: $< 36, 23 >$	$\neg\mathbf{p}_1 \wedge \neg\mathbf{q}_2 \wedge \mathbf{q}_1$
27	Det: *le*	$\neg\mathbf{p}_3$	38	PP: $< 36, 24 >$	$\neg\mathbf{p}_1 \wedge \neg\mathbf{q}_2 \wedge \neg\mathbf{q}_1$
28	Det: *les*	$\neg\mathbf{p}_2$	39	VP: $< 26, 37 >$	$\neg\mathbf{p}_1 \wedge \neg\mathbf{q}_2 \wedge \mathbf{q}_1$
29	Adj: *anglais*	$\mathbf{p}_2$	40	VP: $< 26, 38 >$	$\neg\mathbf{p}_1 \wedge \neg\mathbf{q}_2 \wedge \neg\mathbf{q}_1$
30	N: *anglais*	$\neg\mathbf{p}_2$			

We are assuming the English bare plural 'teachers' can be translated into French either as the definite *les professeurs* or the indefinite *des professeurs*. A new context variable, $\mathbf{q}_1$, is introduced to keep these apart. Each will be derived and represented only once, and then used repeatedly in translations like

> *Le livre anglais plaît aux professeurs*
> *Le livre anglais plaît à des professeurs*

Les professeurs aiment le livre anglais
Des professeurs aiment le livre anglais
Les professeurs comme les anglais réservent
Des professeurs comme les anglais réservent

The first two of these are the only ones we develop in the table. Needless to say, we gloss over the mechanisms required to reduce *à les* to *aux,* which clearly belong to a component of the system that we are not concerned with. The two noun phrases are items 23 and 24 and these contribute to a pair of prepositional phrases in 37 and 38. Together with the verb in 26, these give rise to the verb phrases in 39 and 40. The fact that these phrases differ only in the determiner in the object of the prepositional phrase is reflected in the fact that the corresponding Boolean expressions differ only in that one has $\mathbf{q}_1$ where the other has $\neg\mathbf{q}_1$. Both have $\neg\mathbf{q}_2$ showing that the verb will be *plaît* rather than *aiment,* and $\mathbf{p}_1$ because the original English is construed as containing the verb *like* rather than the preposition.

This sketch has, of course, been very superficial. This is partly because of the obvious constraints of time and space, but it is also because I do not wish to give the impression that the approach to machine translation I am trying to advocate turns on using one particular set of algorithms or representing grammatical structures in a particular way, or adopting a particular approach to transfer. A more particular instantiation of at least some of the ideas is described in some detail in Frank (1999).

44.5   Choosing the Best Translation

Our initial motivation for adopting something like contexted sets as the basic framework for a machine translation system had two components. On the one hand, we pointed out that it can introduce to a translation system the same kinds of efficiency gains, both in time and space, that charts make possible for parsing. If one wishes to pursue all paths through the search space, and if the chart constructed by the parser must be converted to disjunctive normal form before the next component can work on its output, then the claim that the parser operated in polynomial time will be of little interest. It is only if the advantages of the packed representation can be maintained throughout the entire system that the real advantages will be realized. Generalizing from charts to contexted sets makes this a quite reasonable goal.

The second advantage that we claimed for this approach comes from the sharp division that it makes between the fully automatic linguistic system that explores a large space of potential translations and a possibly only partially automatic component that chooses a single translation for each input. There are several reasons for claiming this as a advantage. The first is that of simplicity. Every machine translation system generates alternatives and chooses among them though few of them reflect the great difference between these two operations or the kinds of information that each of them calls for. Nothing but clarity can come from disengaging linguistic from nonlinguistic considerations in the way we are advocating.

Perhaps more important is the fact that the more traditional approach calls for choices to be made early, presumably on the grounds that this makes for efficiency. However, it also means that choices tend to be made among alternatives before they are completely specified so that the information on which the choice is made is partial at best. Idioms and technical phrases provide the simplest of examples. Suppose it is determined that the words *power amplifier* should be recognized as a set phrase on the grounds that its meaning is not a simple function of the meanings of the individual words and it is translated as a whole into some other languages. There is nothing wrong with this so long as the possibility of its actually being two words on some occasions is not foreclosed. One such occasion would be the sentence *Amplifiers with higher power supply the main array of loudspeakers.*

The advantages of separating the generation of translation alternatives from the process of choosing among them go further. To simplify the discussion, let us assume that the set of alternative translations for a given string is so large that it typically contains at least one member – let us simplify again and say exactly one member – that would in fact be acceptable. That is to say that, after the generation of alternatives is complete, selection among existing alternatives is all that is required to complete the job. Within the framework we have outlined, selecting an alternative is tantamount to assigning truth values to logical variables so that the system of Boolean expressions in the contexted sets constitute a universal interface between the generation and the selection components. If a post-editor selects a particular string as the preferred translation into French. and the time comes to produce a translation of the same original into German, then those variables that occur in both the French and the German contexted sets will have the same values so that the choice that the German post-editor has to make will be among a smaller set of alternatives.

Suppose the sentence to be translated is *There are three windows in the room* and the post-editor chooses (7) rather than (6), then the choice in German between (8) and (9) is presumably determined to be (9).

(6) *Il y a trois fenêtres dans la salle*
(7) *Il y a trois guichets dans la salle*
(8) *Es gibt drei Fenster in dem Zimmer*
(9) *Es gibt drei Schalter in dem Zimmer*

Whether this would in fact happen, given the system as we have described it, turns on a technicality. If the word *window* is regarded as unambiguous, then the choice between *fenêtre* and *guichet* on the one hand, and *Fenster* and *Schalter* on the other, will presumably be made independently and there will be nothing to suggest the French choice correlates in any way with the German choice. But, if in the course of the English analysis that is common to the French and German systems, the English *window* is separated into $window_1$ (as in the window of a house) and $window_2$ (as in a ticket window) each of which is then translated unambiguously into each of the other languages, then the same logical variable will be associated with the choice and the postediting of one will be reflected in the other.

Publications referenced
Frank 1999; Kay et al. 1994; Kay 1997; Maxwell and Kaplan 1991; Shemtov 1997.

## 45

David G. Hays

There is nothing trite in characterizing David Glen Hays (1928-1995) as the father of his field. He invented the very name computational linguistics, was the main force behind the foundation of the Association for Computational Linguistics – originally the Association for Machine Translation and Computational Linguistics – and established and set his seal on the International Committee on Computational Linguistics and the series of conferences that it organizes. He built one of the first machine-translation systems, championed dependency theory in American linguistics, conducted some of the earliest exercises in corpus linguistics, and provided training, encouragement and support for the generation that would succeed him.

David Hays went to Harvard as an undergraduate and immediately set his sights on becoming an announcer with the University's radio station because this would demonstrate to others and to himself that he had eradicated all trace of his North Carolina accent. He succeeded in this as in just about all the goals he set himself. He received his doctorate in social relations from Harvard in 1956 but had already taken up an invitation to spend a year at the Center for Advanced Studies in the Behavioral Sciences at Stanford in 1954. By 1955, he had arrived at the RAND Corporation as part of its Systems Development Division. It turned out, however, that his division was about to separate itself from RAND to become the System Development Corporation. Hays had the option of remaining at RAND provided he could find a new project with which to associate himself or a new line of research for which funding would be available. He learnt that the problem of keeping abreast of Soviet developments in science and technology had sparked an interest in machine translation, a project to which he devoted most of the remaining twelve years that he spent with the corporation.

By 1960, Hays had assembled a team of six or eight researchers at RAND, computer programmers and Russian language specialists, who built one of the earliest fully functional machine translation systems. While it did no more than any of the other systems of its time, or indeed later times, to show the practicability of automatic methods for opening Russian technical literature to American readers, it did a lot to demonstrate how the results of linguistic research could be transformed into processing power and perspicuity. There were separate modules in the RAND system for analysis and generation and these were further divided into submodules responsible for morphology, syntax and some minimal semantics. Hays seems to have been the first to grasp the notion that the criteria for assembling words or phrases into larger phrases or constructions come not only from the words and phrases directly involved but from the utility of the phrase for building larger structures. Syntactic analysis should therefore be seen as a search of the entire space of sentence structures for one that fit the given string and not simply as one of associating words with one another on the basis of local criteria. In 1960, this was a new insight whose importance was not widely appreciated until the latter part of the decade.

The syntactic component of the RAND translation system was based on Tesnière's theory of dependency grammar, which was dominant in Russia and Eastern Europe, and for which Hays became the principal advocate in America (Hays 1960, 1961b). In 1964, he published *Dependency theory: a formalism and some observations*, which became the defining document for this theory in the West (Hays 1964).

If language processing was to be based on independently motivated theories of language, then it would clearly require two other dimensions. On the one had, there would have to be descriptions of particular languages constructed in accordance with the theories and, on the other, there would have to be ways of applying these general descriptions to particular examples, sentences, or pieces of text. In today's terms, language processing should consist of applying grammars conforming to specific theoretical formalisms to be applied to text by general algorithms.

The first general algorithm to enter the field that would one day be called computational linguistics came into being when David Hays was entertaining at his home in California his old friend John Cocke – a man who retained his North Carolina accent quite undiminished. Cocke later developed the RISC (reduced instruction set computing) chip but, on this visit, he accompanied Hays to a conference on machine translation at which various more or less ad hoc approaches to linguistic analysis were described. At a certain point, Cocke said something like "Dave, is what these people are trying to do something like the following?", whereupon he described the formalism of context-free grammar with binary rules. Hays thought it probably was and Cocke wrote the half page of FORTRAN code that I saw less than a year later. It consisted essentially of five loops, three of which depended on the length of the sentence, demonstrating that the asymptotic time complexity of the algorithm was cubic in sentence length, and two that iterated through the grammatical categories assigned to the words or phrases covering a given stretch of the string, illustrating that the algorithm was quadratic in the number of these categories. However, the importance of these complexity facts was not appreciated at the time. The important things seemed to be, first that this was a real algorithm, dissociated from the linguistic data to which it would be applied, and second, that it revealed all the structures that a grammar assigned to a sentence while never constructing a phrase more than once. The algorithm was later independently discovered by Kasami (1965) and Younger (1967). The first description of Cocke's version is in section 2 of Chapter 6 of Hays (1967), the first textbook in computational linguistics.

During the sixties, RAND engaged in a good deal of what is now referred to as corpus linguistics and produced what I believe to have been the first tree bank. The machine translation system was directed towards articles from Soviet physics journals. As part of the project, they assembled a corpus of about a million words of such text and produced, for each article, a file containing the dependency structure of every sentence in it. Each sentence was annotated independently by two Russian language specialists and these were recorded on punched cards. To facilitate this operation, each machine in the corporation's keypunch shop had a specially designed Russian keyboard in addition to the standard one and each operator that worked in that shop was expected to learn the Cyrillic alphabet and to work with these keyboards when required. The tapes that were made from these cards were made freely available to other researchers and considerable value was later obtained from them by, for example, the machine translation project directed by Professor Bernard Vauquois at the University of Grenoble.

In 1965, the Automatic Language Processing Advisory Committee of the National Academy of Sciences delivered its report. The slim black volume that was the ALPAC report was not actually published until 1966. What it said, in essence, was that machine translation could only be constructed on a much solider theoretical foundation than the science of the day could provide. Resources should therefore be withdrawn from machine translation as a practical engineering enterprise and directed instead to linguistics and especially to the scientific study of language processing.

Hays knew what was in the report long before it appeared and was astute enough to realize that it would be used repeatedly as an excuse for withdrawing funding and only occasionally to support new scientific enquiry. The least he could do to insure what he firmly believed to be a genuine and important field of enquiry that gave an honest livelihood to many of his closest friends was to provide it with a name. Hays proposed *computational linguistics* , and it soon gained general support. He went on to propose the establishment of a professional society to be called the *Association for Machine Translation and Computational Linguistics.* He became its second president in 1963 and prevailed upon Victor Yngve to change the name of the only journal in the field from *Mechanical Translation* to *Mechanical Translation and Computational Linguistics* (in 1965).

Soon afterwards, he assembled a small group of computational linguists from around the world to form the International Committee on Computational Linguistics, which undertook to arrange that there should be an international conference on the subject every two years (the COLING conferences). The first took place in New York in 1965, but no proceedings were published. There was a three year break after the Pisa meeting in 1973, but since the Ottawa meeting in 1976, the biennial rhythm has remained unbroken.

Throughout the sixties, the RAND linguistics project conducted a weekly seminar that served as an intellectual focus for the various groups that were working in computational linguistics in the Los Angeles area. Victoria Fromkin credits her early interest in the field to these seminars which were also regularly attended by faculty members from the Linguistics and Slavic departments at UCLA, by Robert Simmons and his colleagues from the Systems Development Corporation, by Paul Garvin and his co-workers at Bunker Ramo and innumerable other computational and non-computational linguists from the greater Los Angeles area.

The seminar was just one manifestation of the concern that Hays always had for education. Another was the program of fellowships that he established at RAND with the sponsorship of the National Science Foundation, and the internships that he was able to offer to graduate students. Many prominent computational linguists began their careers in this way. Names that come to mind are Ronald Kaplan, Frances and Lauri Karttunen, and Stuart Shapiro.

The most spectacular project that Hays engaged in at the RAND Corporation proved too ambitious to attract the governmental funding it would have required to go forward. However, it got as far as President L. B. Johnson's desk, who supposedly considered it at some length before deciding that it was an idea that he would not have. The original stimulus for the idea came from the development by the National Cash Register Corporation, of a technology like microfiche but with far greater reduction and therefore far greater density of information on a single card. NCR attempted to popularize the technology by exhibiting a single card containing the whole of the King James Bible. Hays calculated that a library of a million books recorded in this way could be stored in the space required for one or two standard filing cabinets. His proposal was that the United States government should establish a standard, core, university library of a million books on ultra-microfiche, as they were called, and distribute a thousand copies throughout the developing countries of the world.

At the end of the sixties, it seemed the funding for computational linguistics was in decline and, in any case, Hays was finding it increasingly difficult to resist the attraction of academia. He was therefore quick to accept the opportunity of starting a new department of linguistics at the State University of New York at Buffalo. He threw himself into the administration of his new department with all his accustomed vigor and enthusiasm, but at the expense of his interest in computational linguistics, which was never rekindled. When he finally retired, he moved to New York City where he died of lung cancer in 1995.

Biographical details of the author

Martin Kay (born 13th July 1935, London), went to Daunstey's School near Devizes, and got a B.A., then a M.A., in Modern and Mediaeval Languages at Cambridge University. He worked under Margaret Masterman at the Cambridge Language Research Unit from 1958 until going to California in 1961. He went initially to the RAND Corporation in Santa Monica on the linguistics and translation project, with a two year absence in 1962-63 when he was on the MT project directed by Sydney M. Lamb in Berkeley. In 1969 he took over from David Hays as head of the RAND project. In 1972 he went to the University of California, Irvine, as chair of Computer Science, and then in 1974 moved to Xerox PARC, becoming a Xerox Research Fellow. In 1985 he received an honorary doctorate from the University of Gothenburg. and in the same year became a professor of linguistics at Stanford, while retaining his position at Xerox. In 1969 he was President of the Association for Computational Linguistics, in the year when he also became a member of the International Committee on Computational Linguistics (ICCL), organizers of the biennial COLING conferences; since 1980 he has been chair of the ICCL. Martin Kay is widely acknowledged for his influential contributions: the invention of chart parsing, the introduction of unification to linguistics, the development of finite-state methods in several areas of linguistics (with Ron Kaplan), and trenchant criticisms of the state and condition of machine translation. Current address (at time of publication): Xerox Palo Alto Research Center, 3333 Coyote Hill Road, Palo Alto, CA 94304, U.S.A.

References

Select list of publications by David G. Hays (in date order):

Hays, David G. 1958. "Order of subject and object in scientific Russian when other differentia are lacking." *Mechanical Translation* 5:3, 111–113.

Hays, David G. 1960. *Grouping and dependency theories*. RAND Corporation. (RAND Report P-19 10). Santa Monica, Calif.

Hays, David G. 196la. "Linguistic research at the RAND Corporation." H. P. Edmundson, ed., *Proceedings of the National Symposium on Machine Translation*, 13–25. Prentice-Hall. Englewood Cliffs, NJ.

Hays, David G. 1961b. "On the value of dependency connection". *Proceedings of the International Conference on Machine Translation and Applzed Language Anahsis*, 579–590. H.M.S.O. London.

Hays, David G. 1962. "An introduction to computational procedures in linguistic research." A. Ghizzetti, ed., *Automatic Translation of Languages*, 139–165. Pergamon Press. Oxford.

Hays, David G. 1963. "Research procedures in machine translation." P. L. Garvin, ed., *Natural language and the computer*, 183–214. McGraw-Hill. New York.

Hays, David G. 1964a. "Dependency theory: a formalism and some observations." *Language* 40:4, 511–25.

Hays, David G. 1964b. "Coimectibility calculations, syntactic functions, and Russian syntax." *Mechanical Translation* 8:1, 32–51. Repr. in Hays (1966), 107–125.

Hays, David G., ed. 1966. *Readings in automatic language processing*. American Elsevier. New York.

Hays, David G. 1967a. *Introduction to computational linguistics*. Elsevier. New York.

Hays, David G. 1967. "Computational linguistics: research in progress at the RAND Corporation." *T.A.Informations* 1, 15–20.

Hays, David G. 1974. "Information handling." , T. A. Sebeok, ed., *Current trends in linguistics* 12:4, 2719–2740. Mouton. The Hague.

Hays, David G. 1976. "Machine (aided) translation: generalities and guides to action." *American Journal of Computational Linguistics*, microfiche 46, 84–88.

Hays, David G. 1977. "Machine translation and abstract terminology." , P. J. Hopper et al., eds., *Studies in descriptive and historical linguistics: Festschrift for Winfred P.Lehmann*, 95–108. John Benjamins. Amsterdam. (*Amsterdam Studies in the Theory and History of Linguistic Science*, Series IV: *Current Issues in Linguistic Theory* 4.)

Hays, David G. 1979. "Communication and control in man and machine." *International Forum on Information and Documentation* 5:2, 6–8.

Other publications referenced

ALPAC 1966; Kasami 1965; Tesnière 1959; Younger 1967.

## 46

Preface to
"Parallel Text Processing"

In 1987, Martin Röscheisen and I set out to show that the sentences of a text and its translation in another language could be put into correspondence with one another without appealing to specific information about either language. We took the problem because, while it presented an interesting challenge, clearly nothing of importance turned on the outcome. As this book abundantly attests, we were quite wrong in this latter judgement. In fact, it turned out that the problem was already in the air, for Gale and Church were working on an alternative approach in parallel with us.

The value of what Ahrenberg *et al.* in the present volume call a "knowledge-lite approach" to sentence alignment has become apparent in the intervening time for two main reasons. First, the world of global commerce and pervasive multinational entities that we now inhabit cannot operate on English alone; it is, and will doubtless long remain, a world in which multilingual capabilities are an essential ingredient of commercial success. The problem is not limited to that of discerning the gist of a memorandum coming from a far-off place, or conducting a conversation when there is no language in which all the participants are comfortable. It is also a matter of publishing manuals, distributing advertising material, drawing up contracts, and making presentations in large numbers of unrelated languages representing a great variety of cultures. In short, the importance of translation is increasing steadily and the need to understand it better is pressing.

The second reason has to do with the direction that our discipline has been taking. Natural Language Processing, the engineering wing of Computational Linguistics, has attracted a considerable amount of well deserved attention for the solutions it has found for a small but crucially important set of problems in shallow linguistic analysis. The word *shallow* is often used in this connection with the interpretation being left, for the most part justifiably, to the reader. For me, the principal characteristic of shallow linguistic analysis is that it avoids all problems of semantic ambiguity resolution that could only be solved definitively by going beyond the language to objects, and facts, and culture – in short, to the world. It does this either by confining itself to matters that are essentially purely linguistic, or by redefining nonlinguistic problems in linguistic terms.

As an example of the latter, consider a part-of-speech tagger, the job of which is to decide which of the parts of speech that the dictionary allows for each word in a text is in fact in play at each of the places where the word appears. In general, we know that the problem is unsolvable on purely linguistic criteria because there are sentences with ambiguities that are simply not resolvable on the basis of internal evidence. Consider, for example, the sentence

The subjects had all heard that smoking can cause cancer, in which we presumably expect *that* to be tagged as a complementizer, *smoking* as a mass noun, and *can* as an auxiliary verb. But they could be a demonstrative, an adjective, and a noun, and the sentence as a whole could be parallel to *The subjects had all seen that smoking fire generate heat.*

The role of the world in making these determinations is taken over in shallow linguistics by statistical models involving individual words and their close textual neighbors. Remarkably, the picture of the world that is still discernible through this murky lens still has enough light and shade to support precision and recall scores for many tasks in the mid to high nineties, as a percentage of running words. In information retrieval, these figures are usually sufficient for practical purposes. For all its short-comings, information retrieval based on Boolean combinations of key words is often remarkably effective.

There are indications now that syntactic analysis will facilitate a finer match between questions and segments of text that answer them. Here again, there have been remarkable advances in recent years with the development of parsers, like that of Michael Collins, that deliver only the most probable structure in accordance with a statistical model. The statistical model chooses the structure for a sentence that human subjects choose with high accuracy, thanks to the immensely detailed observations that it contains on the occurrences of particular words in particular grammatical relations to other words. Here, as before, purported facts about the language are in fact standing in for facts about the world and it is remarkable that they are able to do so as effectively as they do.

For other tasks, and most notably translation, the range of texts that can be usefully treated automatically and the quality of the results achieved have remained steady since shortly after the initial attacks on these problems were made. More substantial successes in these enterprises will require a sharper image of the world than any that can be made out simply from the statistics of language use. Translation is the reexpression of meaning, and meaning is not an emergent property of text in a single language nor in several laid side by side. The question of just how large bilingual corpora, fast computers and sophisticated statistics can focus the picture of the world needed for high-quality translation remains open, but there is little to support great optimism.

Translation alignment, however, does not need machine translation to justify it. The unparalleled richness of aligned texts for a great number of purposes is clear for anyone to see; the more so if the granularity of the alignment can be brought closer to the phrase, and the word level. As a source of data for terminology banks and bilingual dictionaries, large bilingual corpora are clearly without parallel in history. The process of using such information as the foundation for tools to help human translators in such a way as to boost the productivity dramatically has hardly begun.

The question of the granularity of translation alignment brings up some fundamental issues that are currently at the center of translation theory but which receive little attention from computationalists. The theoretical question concerns the extent of the translator's responsibility to particular words and phrases on one hand, and to the overall function of the text on the other. In the relatively early stages of acquiring a foreign language, a student comes to realize that the words in the original cannot be treated in isolation, not only because they sometimes participate in idioms and set phrases, but because to do so too often gives rise to a result which is lacking in fluency, or is at variance with the intent of the original in some other way. I take a copy of *Scientific American* from my shelves (December, 1988) and pick an article. I know from experience that I can find what I am looking for in an article chosen at random, so I open the magazine at "Snakes, blood circulation and gravity" by Harvey B. Lillywhite. The translation in *Pour la Science* (February, 1989) contains an article called "La circulation sanguine des serpents" which I take to be the translation, even though the title says nothing about gravity.

The first sentence of the English article is *Gravity is a pervasive force in the world, and both animals and plants have adapted to it in a variety of ways.* The translation goes like this: *La pesanteur s'exerce partout sur la terre, et les êtres vivants se sont adaptés de façons variées.* Rendering this back into English rather slavishly gives something like: *Gravity acts everywhere on the earth, and living things have adapted to it in various ways.* So what has happened to the phrase *pervasive force?* One answer would be that it has simply been deleted. A more interesting one is to say that it has been translated as *partout (everywhere).* The phrase *both animals and plants* appears in the French as *les êtres vivants (living things or living beings).* Less radical is the translation of *a variety of ways* by *de façons variées (in various ways).* Examples like these are much more the rule than the exception, and what they illustrate is that the very notion of alignment falls apart at finer levels of granularity. The world does not naturally fall into bite-sized pieces and the skill of the translator resides largely on being able to repackage the information in accordance with the style and genius of the target language.

The abstract of the article on snakes contains a still more striking example of this. It begins *When a snake climbs or rears up ...* which appears in *Pour la Science* as *Lorsqu'un serpent se dresse ou grimpe à un arbre ... (When a snake rears up or climbs a tree...).* The French verb *grimper* can be used intransitively just as the English word *climb* can, but such a usage feels more unnatural when the context does not give a clear indication of the kind of climbing involved. Snakes can clearly climb many kinds of things, so by what right does the translator introduce a tree into this sentence? The answer is not far to seek. There is a picture on the same page of a snake climbing a tree. More importantly, nothing of importance to the article is lost if the context of the climbing is restricted in this way. This is, after all, an article about blood circulation. If it had been about the social behavior of snakes, the translator might have judged the matter differently.

Examples like these occur in every article of the *Scientific American*, the inflight magazine of every airline and wherever, in short, the quality of the translation can be taken as reflecting on the people or institutions that disseminate it. They may occasion some temporary disquiet in that small subset of machine translation researchers that know something of translation, more broadly construed, but they can calm themselves with the thought that they are, in any case, not trying to do what human translators do, and they do not expect the output of their machines to be publicly disseminated by self-conscious individuals and institutions. People who work with aligned translations are in a different case because their translations are presumably all produced by people. A machine could presumably align its own output. The question that the *Scientific American* raises for them and that cannot be side-stepped so easily has to do with the very nature of what it means to align a text and a translation. At the very least, it seems that it will have to mean different things to people with different purposes. For a researcher interested in high-quality translation, an alignment program that paired *pervasive force*, or at least *pervasive*, with *partout (everywhere)* might stimulate important insights, but as a source of potential entries in a bilingual dictionary, it might constitute a source of frustration.

Fine-grained translation alignment, for whatever purpose, clearly requires a model of the kinds of units below the sentence level that can contract alignment relations, which amounts to saying that it requires a model of translation. But, unlike translation itself, alignment is an enterprise whose success is properly assessed by precision, recall, and F-measure, and it may therefore require a less detailed model than translation itself. In this connection, the paper entitled "Bracketing and aligning words and constituents in parallel text using stochastic inversion transduction grammars" by Dekai Wu is especially interesting. Inversion transduction grammars are a clean and simple formalization of an idea that lurks in many machine translation systems, old and new. The formal version rests on the idea that any formal system that can characterize a language can also characterize a transduction relationship between a pair of languages. All that is needed is to replace words in the single language by pairs of words, one from each language. Finite-state transducers are related to regular languages in this way, and the same move can be made with context-free languages. For the case of context-free grammars with binary rules, we enrich the formalism in the following simple way. Let the rules describe the first language, using the first member of each terminal pair. For the second language, annotate each rule to show whether the items on its right-hand side should be read in the order given, or in the reverse order, and use the second member of each terminal pair. I have referred to such a system as a mobile grammar because the structural difference between a sentence in one language and its translation in the other is like a pair of positions that could be taken up by a mobile made of sticks and string. All phrases must stay together, but their parts can change places in the course of the translation.

What is attractive about this model is its simplicity. What is unfortunate about it is that it will not account for the *Scientific American*. Nevertheless, at least in a slightly weakened form, the model probably applies to a great deal of translation. Presumably large phrases that translate one another tend to be made up of smaller phrases that are translations of one another so that we should expect to be able to apply the rules of a transduction grammar in a top-down fashion to pairs of sentences down to some level. But, as the phrases became shorter, we would be confronted with pairs like *pervasive force* and *partout*, and the system would break down. If this point can be recognized, and this of course is a major question, then the attempt to divide phrases into smaller parts can simply be abandoned. We would be left with associations between phrases and phrases which, while they would often appear anomalous, might nevertheless function in a statistically well behaved manner.

For a great variety of reasons, only a few of which I have mentioned, this is an important book which deserves to be read by people with very diverse interests in ordinary language. But, all the reasons go back to one central consideration, namely that it is a book about the empirical study of translation and this is a subject that has attracted the attention of only a handful of scholars. Perhaps the single most remarkable observation about machine translation is that it has attracted the attention of a vanishingly small number of researchers with some knowledge of traditional translation. And one of the most remarkable facts about translation as a field of enquiry is that it has very rarely been treated as an empirical enterprise. As a result, the literature on translation theory is replete with simplified versions of linguistic theories about morphology, syntax, and semantics in the apparent belief that they have something to say about translation. But what translators actually do and how they do it remains largely mysterious. If the mystery is to be dispelled, it will be by pursuing the kinds of approach suggested here.

## 47

Guides and Oracles for Linear-Time Parsing

Abstract

If chart parsing is taken to include the process of reading out solutions one by one, then it has exponential complexity. The stratagem of separating read-out from chart construction can also be applied to other kinds of parser, in particular, to left-corner parsers that use early composition. When a limit is placed on the size of the stack in such a parser, it becomes context-free equivalent. However, it is not practical to profit directly from this observation because of the large state sets that are involved in otherwise ordinary situations. It may be possible to overcome these problems by means of a *guide* constructed from a weakened version of the initial grammar.

A recognition procedure for a language is a method of determining whether a given string belongs to the language. In the context-free case, it clearly reduces to showing that the string is a phrase of a particular category, the goal category of the grammar. A string α belongs to category C if either, α consists of the single symbol C, or there is a rule $C \rightarrow c_1...c_n$ and α is the concatenation of strings that are phrases of categories $c_1...c_n$ in that order. The proof that a string is a phrase of a given category can be summarized in an ordered tree with nodes named for grammar symbols and this is what we refer to as the structure of the string according to the grammar. The root is named for the grammar's distinguished symbol and the daughters of a node labeled C are labeled, from left to right, $c_1...c_n$ given that $C \rightarrow c_1...c_n$ is a grammar rule.

Concretely, a rule $s \rightarrow np\ aux\ vp$ can be transcribed directly into Prolog as a *definite-clause grammar* (DCG) somewhat as follows:

```
wof(s, A, D) :-
  wof(np, A, B),
  wof(aux, B, C),
  wof(vp, C, D).
```

There is a word or phrase (wof) of category s stretching from point A to point D in the string if, for some points B and C between A and D, there is a phrase of category np from A to B, of category aux from B to C, and of category vp from C to D. A terminal symbol, say *dog*, is recognized as belonging to category n by virtue of the clause:

```
wof(dog, [dog | X], X).
```

This is based on the convention of using suffixes of the string as names of points in it. In particular, this clause says that a string consists of a noun followed by a string X if it consists of the word *dog* followed by X.

With these, and a few more obvious definitions, the Prolog interpreter will be able to prove the proposition

```
wof(s, [the, dog, will, chase, the, cat], [])
```

The proof will be carried out in accordance with the so-called *recursive-descent* , or *top-down backtracking* strategy suggested by our initial definitions. In order to show that a string is a word or phrase of category *s*, the procedure is to first show that it begins with a phrase of category *np*, and then to show that the remainder of the string consists of the *aux* phrase followed by a *vp*. Each of these steps consists of a recursive application of the same procedure.

To get the structure of a string, one must arrange to capture the control structure of the recognition process, and this can be done in a variety of ways. To capture all the possible structures of a string, it is necessary to behave on success just as one does on failure, by backing up to the most recent choice point with hitherto unexplored branches.

As an effective recognition or parsing algorithm, the flaws of DCG are well known. The two principal ones are (1) that the asymptotic time complexity is exponential in the length of the string, and (2) that the procedure does not terminate when a phrase of a given category can have an initial substring that must be analyzed as belonging to that same category.

The information that the recognition procedure amasses about a string can be summarized in the manner exemplified below:

```
oracle(s, [the, dog, will, chase, the, cat], []).
oracle(np, [the, dog], [will, chase, the, cat]).
oracle(det, [the], [dog, will, chase, the, cat]).
oracle(vp, [will, chase, the, cat], []).
...
```

Suppose that the clauses embodying the grammar are augmented as follows.

```
wof(s, A, D) :-
  oracle(np, A, B),
  wof(np, A, B),
  oracle(aux, B, C),
  wof(aux, B, C),
  oracle(vp, C, D),
  wof(vp, C, D).
```

With this augmented grammar and the oracle, the process of recognition is completely trivialized – in fact the first `oracle` clause is all we need for recognition. Since the oracle does not provide structures, however, the control structure of the recursive-descent analysis process must still be recorded if it is required to parse the string. Notice, however, that the existence of such an oracle would eliminate one of the problems with recursive-descent analysis, namely failure to terminate in cases of left recursion, and it alleviates the other by removing from the search space all moves that do not belong to successful paths. It is this last property that motivates the use of the term "oracle".

The interest in recasting top-down syntactic analysis in this way comes from the analogy that can be drawn to chart parsing. The oracle is essentially a chart and the `wof` grammar predicate supplies the read-out procedure. It is usual to include more information in the chart so that the read-out procedure does not have to have information from the grammar rules. In the present formulation, edges contain no information about the members of a phrase, so that polynomial complexity is achieved automatically without having to conflate edges with the same category symbol and string coverage, but different internal structures.

Computational linguists are generally comfortable with the claim that chart parsing with a context-free grammar has polynomial asymptotic time complexity. Since a context-free grammar can assign a number of structures to a string that increases as an exponential function of its length, we assume that there is a tacit agreement not to count the read-out procedure, but only the process of building the chart that will serve as an oracle for the read-out procedure. How this is justified in detail is not clear. Intuitively, however, dividing the parsing process into a first stage in which a data base of grammatical information about the string is constructed and a second stage in which individual analyses are read out has the advantage of allowing different parsing algorithms to be seen as differing in complexity on the basis of the first, and intuitively more interesting part of the process.

In the balance of this paper, we outline a parsing algorithm that is very different from chart parsing in its details, but similar in that it proceeds in two stages, one in which a data base is constructed at quite attractive cost in complexity, and one in which individual analyses are read out by a simple, oracle-driven, backtracking parser. It will turn out, however, that the approach can form the basis of a practical parser only if the influence of grammar size on the overall process can be brought under control. For this purpose, we introduce the notion of a *guide*, which is a weak form of an oracle. If an oracle is available at a particular branch in a process, it can be counted on to eliminate all choices that do not lead to a successful outcome. A guide will, in general, not eliminate all unproductive choices, but it can be counted on not to eliminate any choices that do could lead to a successful outcome. As an example of a guide, consider the weakened form of chart represented in the following clauses:

```
guide([the, dog, will, chase, the, cat], []).
guide([the, dog], [will, chase, the, cat]).
guide([the], [dog, will, chase, the, cat]).
guide([will, chase, the, cat], []).
...
```

and a read-out procedure based on clauses like the following:

```
wof(s, A, D) :-
  guide(A, B),
  wof(np, A, B),
  guide(B, C),
  wof(aux, B, C),
  guide(C, D),
  wof(vp, C, D).
```

This chart shows where there are phrases in the string, but does not give their grammatical category. It is sufficient, however, to eliminate problems arising from left-recursive grammars.

The scheme we will outline provides analyses of strings in linear time with a context-free grammar. There is good reason to believe that this is not possible if all the structures allowed by the grammar are to be recovered, and our scheme will indeed ignore certain structures. However, there is also good reason to believe that the structures that we shall ignore are also not accessible to humans and, if this is the case, then nothing but good can come from leaving them out of account.

Abney and Johnson (1989) have shown that a left-corner parser with early composition uses stack space in proportion to the amount of center embedding in the structure. Such a parser is clearly also equivalent to a finite-state automaton which can recognize a string in linear time. One problem with this is that a finite-state automaton can serve only as a recognizer, and not as a parser. However, a recognizer can serve as an oracle for a parser.[1] The idea is simply to

---

[1]This is reminiscent of the way the first member of a bimachine (Schützenberger, 1961) is used to

scan the string to be parsed from right to left, using a finite-state automaton that recognizes the reverse of the depth-limited version of the context-free language and to associate with the space between each pair of words the state of the machines. When read from left to right, this sequence of states serves as an oracle for the left-corner parser with the early composition and a finite stack.

Unfortunately, even for modest sized grammars, and an early limit on stack size, the number of states in the automaton is unmanageably large so that it cannot be represented explicitly and therefore cannot be made deterministic. But, while undoubtedly a setback, this does not entirely upset the plan. Recognition with a nondeterministic automaton is possible in linear time if an appropriate strategy is employed for caching the states reached following a given substring. This follows from the fact that the number of alternative states that the automaton can be in after a given substring is limited by properties of the automaton and not by the length of string. However, even this is not enough to bring the cost of the computation within reasonable bounds because the number of stack configurations that are possible following even a fairly short string can also be unmanageably large.

The idea of providing an oracle to control the construction of the sequence of state sets that will, in its turn, serve as an oracle in reading out the structures of the string suggests itself, but it is difficult to see how such an oracle would differ from the structure it is intended to help assemble. The intuition is that a useful oracle must contain only a part of the information in the structure whose assembly it controls. However, the possibility of a guide may be more promising. The idea will be to construct a weaker version of the context-free grammar, which assigns to any given string a superset of the structures that are signed by the original grammar, but which gives rises to an automaton with a smaller set of states. These states map in a systematic way onto those of the original automaton and, when this is applied to the string, the only states that will be considered at a given point will be those corresponding to states through which the smaller automaton has passed.

A simple way to construct a weakened version of a grammar is to construct a partition of symbols and to map each class in the partition onto a single symbol. The rules of the weakened grammar are simply the images under this mapping of the rules in the original grammar. The new grammar will be weaker to the extent that it derives from a smaller number of larger classes. Since the total number of symbols in the weakened grammar is smaller than that in the original grammar, so is the number of possible stack configurations.

The picture we now have is of a parser that proceeds in three phases. First, it scans the string from left to right using a left corner recognizer based on the weakened grammar, annotating the spaces between the words with the sets of states that the automaton is in at that point. Next, it scans the string from right to left using the left-corner recognizer based on the full grammar and allowing states to be entered only if they map onto members of the list of states associated with that point in the string in the preceding phase. The reason for the reversal of direction is simply to ensure that the states on each list that is encountered are reachable from the other end of the string, thus providing a guide for the present scan that is, to the extent possible, predictive. Following the practice in chart parsing, we declare these first two phases to constitute a parser and declare its asymptotic in complexity to be linear. The third phase reads out structures using the original context-free grammar and the left-corner parser with the early composition whose stack states must be chosen from those associated with the string in the second phase.

One apparently minor matter remains, namely how to construct a weakened version of a

---

control the operation of the second member.

particular grammar that will serve as an effective guide, in this process. Surprisingly, this proves to be the sticking point. One possibility would be simply to construct the partition of the grammar symbols in a random fashion. Another would be to eliminate the distinctions made by X-bar theory, collapsing, for example, N, N-bar, and NP onto the same symbol. Yet another would be to eliminate "minor" grammatical matters, such as agreement, from the first scan. The disturbing fact is that none of these things can be counted on to give a weakened grammar with desirable properties. Either the grammar remains essentially unchanged, or it reduces to one that accepts almost everything. Minor changes can easily cause it to move, almost chaotically, from one of these conditions to the other. I offer this as a challenge to the parsing community.

Publications referenced
Abney and Johnson 1989; Schützenberger 1961.

## 48

Introduction to *Handbook of Computational Linguistics*

Computational Linguistics is about as robust a field of intellectual endeavour as one could find, with its books, journals, conferences, professorial chairs, societies, associations and the like. But, of course, it was not always so. Computational Linguistics crept into existence shyly, almost furtively. When shall we say it all began? Perhaps in 1949, when Warren Weaver wrote his famous memorandum suggesting that translation by machine might be possible. The first conference on machine translation took place at MIT in 1952 and the first journal, *Mechanical Translation*, began in 1954. However, the phrase "Computational Linguistics" started to appear only in the mid-1960s. The journal changed its name to *Mechanical Translation and Computational Linguistics* in 1965 but the words "and Computational Linguistics" appeared in very small type. This change coincided with the adoption of the journal by the Association for Machine Translation and Computational Linguistics, which was formed in 1962.

The term "Computational Linguistics" was probably coined by David Hays during the time that he was a member of the Automatic Language Processing Advisory Committee of the National Academy of Sciences. The publication of this committee's final report, generally known as the ALPAC report, certainly constituted one of the most dramatic moments in the history of the field – proposing, as it did, that machine translation be abandoned as a short-term engineering goal in favour of more fundamental scientific research in language and language processing. Hays saw this coming and realized that, if the money that had been flowing into machine translation could be diverted into a new field of enquiry, the most pressing requirement was for the field to be given a name. The name took hold. Redirection of the funds did not.

Progression from machine translation to Computational Linguistics occurred in 1974 when *Machine Translation and Computational Linguistics* was replaced by the *American Journal of Computational Linguistics*, which appeared initially only in microfiche form. In 1980, this became *Computational Linguistics*, which is still alive and vigorous today.

By the 1980s, machine translation began to look practical again, at least to some people and for some purposes and, in 1986, the circle was completed with the publication of the first issue of *Computers and Translation*, renamed *Machine Translation* in 1988. The *International Journal of Machine Translation* followed in 1991.

Warren Weaver's vision of machine translation came from his war-time experience as a cryptographer, and he considered the problem to be one of treating textual material, by fundamentally statistical techniques. But the founders of Computational Linguistics were mostly linguists, not statisticians, and they saw the potential of the computer less in the possibility of deriving a characterization of the translation relation from emergent properties of parallel corpora, than in carrying out exactly, and with great speed, the minutely specified rules that they would write. Chomsky's *Syntactic Structures* (1957) served to solidify the notion of grammar as a deductive system which therefore seemed eminently suited to computer applications. The fact that Chomsky himself saw little value in such an enterprise, or that the particular scheme of axioms and rules that he advocated was ill suited to the automatic analysis of text, did nothing to diminish the attractiveness of the general idea.

Computational Linguistics thus came to be an exercise in creating and implementing the formal systems that were increasingly seen as constituting the core of linguistic theory. If any single event marks the birth of the field, it is surely the proposal by John Cocke in 1960 of the scheme for deriving all analyses of a string with a grammar of binary context-free rules that we now know as the Cocke-Kasami-Younger algorithm. It soon became clear that more powerful formalisms would be required to meet the specific needs of human language, and more general chart parsers, augmented transition networks, unification grammars, and many other formal and computational devices were created.

There were two principal motivations for this activity. One was theoretical and came from the growing perception that the pursuit of computational goals could give rise to important advances in linguistic theory. Requiring that a formal system be implementable helped to ensure its internal consistency and revealed its formal complexity properties. The results are to be seen most clearly in syntactic formalisms such as Generalized Phrase Structure Grammar, Lexical Functional Grammar, and Head-driven Phrase Structure Grammar as well as in application of finite-state methods to phonology and morphology.

The second motivation, which had existed from the beginning, came from the desire to create a technology, based on sound scientific principles, to support a large and expanding list of practical requirements for translation, information extraction, summarization, grammar checking, and the like. In none of these enterprises is success achievable by linguistic methods alone. To varying extents, each involves language not just as a formal system, but as a means of encoding and conveying information about something outside, something which, for want of a better term, we may loosely call "the world". Much of the robustness of language comes from the imprecision and ambiguity which allow people to use it in a casual manner. But this works only because people are able to restore missing information and resolve ambiguities on the basis of what makes sense in a larger context provided not only by the surrounding words but by the world outside. If there is any field that should be responsible for the construction of comprehensive, general models of the world, it is presumably artificial intelligence, but the task is clearly a great deal more daunting even than building comprehensive linguistic models, and success has been limited.

As a result, Computational Linguistics has gained a reputation for not measuring up to the challenges of technology, and this in turn has given rise to much frustration and misunderstanding both within and outside the community of computational linguists. There is, of course, much that still remains to be done by computational linguists, but very little of the responsibility for the apparently poor showing of the field belongs to them. As I have said, a significant reason for this is the lack of a broader technological environment in which Computational Linguistics can thrive. Lacking an artificial intelligence in which to embed their technology, linguists have been forced to seek a surrogate, however imperfect, and many think they have found it in what is generally known as "statistical natural language processing".

Roughly speaking, statistical NLP associates probabilities with the alternatives encountered in the course of analysing an utterance or a text and accepts the most probable outcome as the correct one. In "the boy saw the girl with the telescope", the phrase "with the telescope" is more likely to modify "saw" than "the girl", let us say, because "telescope" has often been observed in situations which, like this one, represent it as an instrument for seeing. This is an undeniable fact about seeing and telescopes, but it is not a fact about English. Not surprisingly, words that name phenomena that are closely related in the world, or our perception of it, frequently occur close to one another so that crisp facts about the world are reflected in somewhat fuzzier facts about texts.

There is much room for debate in this view. The more fundamentalist of its proponents claim that the only hope for constructing useful systems for processing natural language is to learn them entirely from primary data as children do. If the analogy is good, and if Chomsky is right, this implies that the systems must be strongly predisposed towards certain kinds of languages because the primary data provides no negative examples and the information that it contains occurs, in any case, in too weak dilution to support the construction of sufficiently robust models without strong initial constraints.

If, as I have suggested, text processing depends on knowledge of the world as well as knowledge of language, then the proponents of radical statistical NLP face a stronger challenge than Chomsky's language learner because they must also construct this knowledge of the world entirely on the basis of what they read about it, and in no way on the basis of direct experience. The question that remains wide open is: Just how much of the knowledge of these two kinds that is required for NLP is derivable, even in principle, from emergent properties of text? The work done over the next few years should do much to clarify the issue and thus to suggest the direction that the field will follow thereafter.

This book stands on its own in the sense that it will not only bring people working in the field up to date on what is going on in parallel specialities to their own, but also introduce outsiders to the aims, methods, and achievements of computational linguists. The chapters of Part I have the same titles that one might expect to find in an introductory text on general linguistics. With the exception of the last, they correspond to the various levels of abstraction on which linguists work, from individual sounds to structures that span whole texts or dialogues, to the interface between meaning and the objective world, and the making of dictionaries. The difference, of course, is that they concentrate on the opportunities for computational exploration that each of these domains opens up, and on the problems that must be solved in each of them before they can contribute to the creation of linguistic technology. I have suggested that requiring a formal system to be implementable led linguists to attend to the formal complexity properties of their theories. The last chapter of Part I provides an introduction to the mathematical notion of complexity and explores the crucial role that it plays in Computational Linguistics.

Part II of the book gives a chapter to each of the areas that have turned out to be the principal centres of activity in the field. For these purposes, Computational Linguistics is construed very broadly. On the one hand, it treats speech recognition and text-to-speech synthesis, the fundamentals of which are more often studied in departments of electrical engineering than linguistics and on the other, it contains a chapter entitled "Corpora", an activity in which students of language use large collections of text or recorded speech as sources of evidence in their investigations. Part III is devoted to applications – starting, as is only fitting, with a pair of chapters on machine translation followed by a discussion of some topics that are at the centre of attention in the field at the present.

It is clear from the table of contents alone that, during the half century in which the field, if not the name, of Computational Linguistics has existed, it has come to cover a very wide territory, enriching virtually every part of theoretical linguistics with a computational and a technological component. However, it has been only poorly supplied with textbooks or comprehensive reference works. This book should go a long way towards meeting the second need.

## 49

Substring Alignment Using Suffix Trees

Alignment of the sentences of an original text and a translation is much better understood than alignment of smaller units such as words and phrases. This paper makes preliminary proposals for solving the problem of aligning substrings that should be treated as basic translation units though they may not begin and end at word boundaries. The proposals make crucial use of suffix trees as a way of identifying repeated substrings of the texts that occur significantly often.

It is fitting that one should take advantage of the few occasions on which one is invited to address an important and prestigious professional meeting like this to depart from the standard practice of reporting results and instead to seek adherents to a new enterprise, even if it is one the details of which one can only partially discern. In this case, I intend to take that opportunity to propose a new direction for a line of work that I first became involved in in the early 1990's (Kay and Röscheisen 1995). It had to do with the automatic alignment of the sentences of a text with those in its translation into another language. The problem is nontrivial because translators frequently translate one sentence with two, or two with one. Sometimes the departure from the expected one-to-one alignment is even greater. We undertook this work not so much because we thought it was of great importance but because it seemed to us rather audacious to attempt to establish these alignments on the basis of no *a priori* assumptions about the languages involved or about correspondences between pairs of words.

As often happens, it turned out that what we thought of as new and audacious was already "in the air" and, while we were at work, Gale and Church (1995) published a solution to the problem that was arguably somewhat less accurate than ours, but was altogether simpler, computationally less complex, and entirely adequate for practical purposes. Whereas their approach was based on nothing more than the lengths of the sentences, in terms either of characters or words, ours made hypotheses about word alignments on the basis of which it circumscribed the space of possible sentence alignments. It then refined the initial set of word alignments, and proceeded back and forth in this manner until no further refinements were possible. Fortunately the process converged fast.

In the relatively short time since this work was done, sentence alignment has come to be seen as a central tool in work on machine translation. During this time the perception has grown that the rules that direct the operation of a machine translation system should be derived automatically from existing translations rather than being composed one by one by linguists and system designers. The first step in just about any such learning procedure is to set the sentences in correspondence with one another because sentences continue to be seen as providing the framework within which translation is done.

The natural second step is to attempt an alignment of the parts of an aligned pair of sentences as a prelude to proposing some kind of translation rule. A great many approaches to this problem have been proposed, but they fall naturally into two classes depending on whether the aligned sentence sequences that they work on are analysed in some way, perhaps by associating a syntactic structure with them, or whether the work continues to be done entirely on the basis of strings. The former approach has the drawback that disambiguation of the output of a syntactic parser is still expensive, unreliable, or both. On the other hand, it suggests a much broader set of finer tools for alignment below the sentence level than are available for working simply on strings. Suppose that it has been established beyond reasonable doubt that a pair of nouns should be aligned with one another, and that each is modified by a single adjective which may not, however, occur next to it in the string. Clearly, this constitutes stronger evidence for the alignment of the adjectives than would be possible purely on the basis of the strings. More simply put, the hypothesis that phrases translate phrases is not only a strong and appealing one, but it in fact underlies a great deal of the work that has been done on machine translation.

It goes without saying that natural languages provide innumerable examples of translation units that almost certainly could not be reliably identified without recourse to the syntactic structure of the sentences in which they occurred. Discontinuities are perhaps the most obvious example. English *take ... into consideration* presumably often constitutes a unit for translation, but only when the gap is filled with a noun phrase. Separable verbs in German and their analogues present a similar problem, as do their analogues in English, namely verbs involving particles. Some less severe problems might be made less severe by working with a string of lemmas or with tagged text. In many languages, a sequence that should be treated as a translation unit, like French *carte orange* ('subway pass'; literally 'orange card') supports changes in the middle of the string. Thus, the plural of *carte orange* is *cartes oranges*. This problem is exacerbated in other languages, such as German, where various different changes are possible, depending not only on number, but also on gender.

While phrases clearly do often translate phrases, it is equally clearly the case that substrings of a sentence that do not constitute phrases can also function as units for translation. The English preposition *as* often corresponds to *au four et à mesure* in French, but this is at best a compound preposition and no phrase. The words *one and the same* might be called a fixed phrase in everyday parlance, but they do not constitute a phrase in linguistic terms. The French word *connaître* translates into English in many ways, including *know* and *get to know*, the second of which could hardly be regarded as a phrase. The question of how to identify sequences like these quickly and easily, especially during the early phases of working on a new language, is one that is surely worthy of attention.

The question of how to identify translation units that consist of several words is one side of a coin whose other side concerns translation units that are smaller than a word or whose end points are not marked by word boundaries. The most obvious examples of these are the components of compound nouns in a language like German in which these components are not separated by spaces. In a language in which word boundaries are not routinely represented in text, the problem becomes acute.

The approach to these problems that is advocated, though only partially worked out, in this paper, is to place word boundaries on an equal footing with all other characters. In particular, it gives no special status to translation units whose boundaries correspond to word boundaries.

If translation units are not to be sought between word boundaries, the first question that arises is, what substrings are considered as candidates for this status? The possibility of giving all substrings equal status can presumably be excluded on the grounds that there are simply too many of them. A text consisting of n characters contains $n(n+1)$ substrings. If the strings are confined within sentences and a string contains m sentences of k characters each, then there are $mk(k + 1)$ substrings. This is more manageable. A 50-character sentence contains 1275 substrings, and a 200-character sentence 20,100 and a 500-character sentence 125,250. But the number of substrings that actually needs to be considered is a great deal less.

The substrings that need to be considered as candidates as translation units should surely have at least two properties. The first is that they should occur enough times in the text to make them interesting. The second is that, if some set of the substrings are distributionally indistinguishable, then they should be treated as the same.

The first of these properties is fairly straightforward and uncontroversial. The second can be made clear with some examples. Consider the substrings "uncontroversia" and "uncontroversial" of the first sentence of this paragraph. The first is clearly found wherever the second is because it is a prefix of the second. But the second will probably be found, in just about any text of English, wherever the first is, because there is, I suppose, no word of English containing the letters "uncontroversia" in which they are not followed by "l". The distributions of the two strings will therefore be the same and each will be equivalent to the other from the point of view of an investigation which, like the present one, gives no special status to word boundaries. Notice that, simply by engaging in a brief discussion of these example, we have made the present text an exception to the supposed rule. In particular, this text contains two instances of the sequence "uncontroversia" followed, not by "l", but by quotation marks. Another member of this equivalence class, at least in most texts, will likely be the string "ncontroversial" because, at least outside this sentence, it will almost always follow the letter "u". Other members of the class are "uncontroversi", and "uncontrovers", but not, of course "controversial".

A fact not immediately obvious is that the number of equivalence classes exemplified in a text of n characters, even if sentence boundaries are ignored, can be no more than $2n - 1$. This, as we shall see, is a direct consequence of the fact that there are n terminal nodes, and at most $n - 1$ branching nonterminal nodes in a *suffix tree* constructed from a string of n characters.

Suffix trees constitute a well understood, extremely elegant, but regrettably poorly appreciated data structure with potentially many applications in language processing. For a gentle introduction, see Nelson (1966). We shall have space here only for the briefest of introductions, which we begin by considering a related but somewhat simpler structure called a *suffix trie*. A *trie* (Fredkin 1960) is a well-known data structure often used for storing words so that they can be looked up easily. It is a deterministic finite-state automaton whose transition diagram has the shape of a tree and in which the symbols encountered on a path from its initial state to a final state spell out a word. A suffix trie is a trie built, not from words in the usual lexicographic sense, but from the strings that are the suffixes of some text. If the entire text consists of the word "mississippi", the corresponding suffix tree is the one depicted in Figure 1. Here, the labels on every path from the start state at the root of the tree, on the left of the diagram, to a terminal node on the right spell out some suffix of the text. Since every substring of the text is a prefix of some suffix, it follows that every substring is spelled out by the characters on the path from the root to some node, terminal or nonterminal. An extra character (\$), known not to occur otherwise in the text, is added to the end for technical reasons.

Before moving from suffix tries to suffix trees, let us pause to verify that the tries already have one of the properties of "interesting" substrings of a text. A branching nonterminal node is one out of which there is more than one transition. Any substring that ends at such a node can be continued in more than one way, that is, by at least two different characters, thus meeting one of the requirements of an "interesting" substring. It follows that there can be no more "interesting" substrings of the text than there are branching nodes in the suffix tree constructed from it. As we shall see in a moment, the corresponding constraint can be verified at the left hand end of the string just as readily.

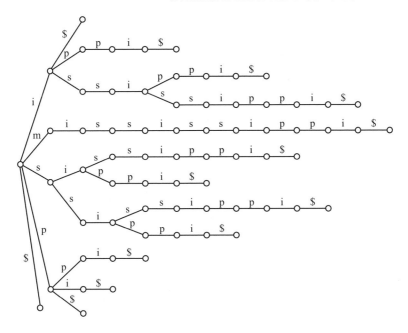

FIGURE 1 A Suffix Trie

The branching nodes in the suffix trie have a special interest for us and it is worth noting that there must be strictly less of these than there are suffixes. This follows immediately from the following pair of observations. First, when the initial suffix is placed in the tree, no branching nodes are created. Secondly, the entry into the trie of each succeeding suffix can give rise to at most one new branching node.

The trouble with suffix tries is that they are totally impractical for large texts because of their sheer size and the time it takes to build them. However, these things are suddenly brought under control in the passage from tries to trees. This is accomplished by replacing every sequence of transitions and nonbranching nodes by a single transition labelled with the corresponding sequence of characters. This sequence, however, is represented, not by the characters themselves, but by a pair of integers giving the end points of an occurrence of the string in the text. Nothing is lost by representing the tree in this way, because points represented by erased nodes can be reconstructed trivially, and pairs of integers constructed to represent the nodes in and out of them. The results of performing this operation on the trie in Figure 1 are shown in Figure 2.

The importance of this transformation cannot be overstated. The upper bound on the number of transitions in the original trie was $k(k+1)$ for a text of k characters. This has been reduced to $k-1$, and the size of the label on a transition remains constant. The size of the tree is therefore linear in the size of the text. A somewhat surprising fact that we shall not be able to go into here is that methods also exist for constructing these trees in linear time (McCreight 1976 and Ukkonen 1995).

A few words are in order on the question of how to read substrings out of the suffix tree represented in this particular way. It is generally necessary, when tracing a path from the root to a particular other node in the tree, to keep track of the length of the string traversed. This is simply a matter of adding the difference between each pair of text pointers encountered to a running count. The starting point of the string ending in a particular transition is the second

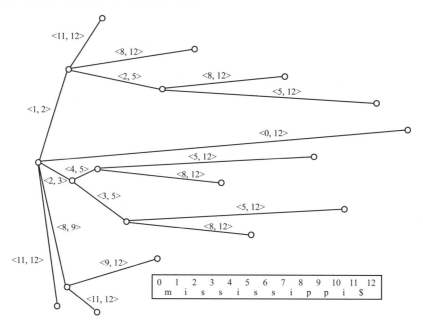

FIGURE 2 A Suffix Tree

of the numbers labelling that transition minus the current count. The various occurrences of the substring ending at a particular node, whether branching, and therefore "actual" or non-branching, and therefore "virtual", can be enumerated straightforwardly and in a time that depends on the number of them that there are in the text and not on the actual length of the text. The method of doing this depends on the following observation: Just as the beginning of the substring corresponding to a sequence of arcs starting at the root can be determined by keeping track of the lengths of the segments covered by each transition, so the end points of the various occurrences of the substring represented by a particular node can be determined by keeping track of the lengths of the segments from the node to the various terminal nodes reachable from it.

Consider the string "si" which traces out a path through the tree shown in Figure 2 over the edges <2,3> and <4,5>. The string is of length 2 and its first occurrence in the text is at position $5 - (5 - 4 + 3 - 2) = 3$. The complete set of its occurrences are found by continuing the search to all possible – in this case 2 – terminal nodes. The lengths of the suffixes of the text covered in tracing out these two paths, including the substring itself are $(3-2) + (5-4) + (12-5) = 9$ and $(3-2) + (5-4) + (12-8) = 6$. These are the lengths of the suffixes of the text that begin with the string "si" so that their locations in the text are $12 - 9 = 3$ and $12 - 6 = 6$. Now suppose that the substring of interest is "s", reachable from the root over the single transition <2,3> and with paths to terminal nodes of lengths $(3-2) + (5-4) + (5-12) = 9$, $(3-2) + (5-4) + (12-8) = 4$, $(3-2) + (5-3) + (12-5) = 10$ and $(3-2) + (5-3) + (12-8) = 7$. This shows that it has four locations in the text at positions $12 - 9 = 3$, $12 - 4 = 8$, $12 - 10 = 2$ and $12 - 7 = 5$. Notice that, if a substring occurs in k locations, finding them in this way involves visiting no more than $2k - 1$ nodes, once the first occurrence has been located.

Since it is computationally inexpensive to locate all the instances of a string in a text using a suffix tree, it is also inexpensive to determine whether these instances are all preceded by the same character, thus making them "uninteresting" for present purposes. In fact let us assume that the process of building a suffix tree for those purposes includes a step in which a bit is associated with every node to show whether the corresponding substring of the text has this property. We are now in a strong position to locate, in linear time, all substrings of an arbitrary text which, for given integers L and R,

1. consist of at least L characters,
2. are repeated at least R times,
3. are not always preceded by the same character,
4. are not always followed by the same character, and
5. do not cross a sentence boundary.

These will be our initial candidate translation units.

If we were to abandon all further concern for computational complexity at this point, the plan for completing at least the first version of the project would be fairly straightforward. It would consist in aligning the sentences of a text and its translation in another language, locating "interesting" substrings of the two text and then evaluating the similarity of pairs of "interesting" strings in terms of the overlap in the sets of aligned sentences in which they occur. Let A be the set of sentences in which one of the strings occurs, and B the set in which the other string occurs. A reasonable measure of similarity might be $|A \cap B|/|A \cup B|$ which has values v in the range $0 \leq v \leq 1$, the value 1 representing identity, and 0 representing disjointness. The only problem with the plan, at least in this simple form, lies in the fact that its time complexity is $O(mn)$, if m and n are the lengths of the two texts. Unfortunately, this represents not simply the cost of an extreme worst case. It is also a reasonable estimate of the average situation, in the absence of any *a priori* knowledge of which pairs of strings are likely to align well.

While we have no proposal reducing the worst-case complexity, there is some hope of substantially reducing the constants involved in determining the computational cost. With this in mind, we propose to increase the amount of information carried by a node in the suffix tree. We will add a new pointer from each node to its parent in the tree and a field, which we call the *count* field, capable of accommodating an integer. We will also construct an index with an entry for every (aligned) sentence, containing pointers to the terminal nodes of the suffix tree corresponding to suffixes of the text that begin in a given sentence. Using this index, and the parent pointers, we can quickly visit all the substrings of the text that occur in a given sentence. In particular, given a particular set of sentences, we can cheaply populate the counter fields of the nodes to show how many of them the corresponding string occurs in. Crucially, we can do this while visiting only nodes for strings that occur in at least one of the sentences. Notice that, if this procedure assigns a non-zero value to the count at a given node, it will also assign a non-zero value, and indeed at least as high a value, to all nodes on paths from the root to that node. Once the values have been assigned, it will therefore be possible to traverse the tree, visiting only nodes for strings that occur in the current set of sentences.

With these mechanisms in place, we are in a position to proceed as follows. Conduct traversal of the suffix tree of the first text to locate "interesting" strings and obtain for each of these, the list of the sentences in which it occurs. Using the sentence index and the parent pointers of the other tree, assign values to the count fields of the strings that occur in the corresponding sentences of the other language. We now conduct a search for "interesting" strings in the suffix tree for the second text, limiting the search to nodes whose count fields contain non-zero values. Not surprisingly, this limitation is very significant if the string in the first language is indeed "interesting". The techniques are manifestly still in need of considerable refinement.

Experiments are still in a very early stage so that it would be fruitless to give statistics. But there is some good news, both for engineers who want results, and scientists who want more problems to solve. Much of the bad news can be ascribed to the fact that the only texts that have been involved in the experiments consist of some 600 sentences from a single automobile maintenance manual and its French and German translations.

A consequence of working with too little data is that strings are allowed to qualify as "interesting" when they are in fact too long. This is because here, for example, all instances of the word *warning* are followed by *light* and there are no instances of *warn* in any but the present-participle form. But *light* remains "interesting" because it is not always preceded by *warning*. The English *warning* was set in correspondence with the German *Kontroll* in the compound *Kontrolleuchte*. Indeed there was an encouraging measure of success in properly aligning the parts of German compounds. When words are chosen as "interesting" substrings, they generally have an initial space attached. Whether they also have a final space depends on whether they have been observed at the end of a sentence, or otherwise before a punctuation mark. The word *coolant* is not "interesting" because it occurs only in *coolant in the engine* which is aligned with the French string *du liquide de refroidissment dans le moteur*. The inclusion of the initial *du* is an artifact of the very small number of contexts in which the string was found.

When the parameters were set so as to allow very short words to count as "interesting", correspondences were recognized even among function words and inflexions. The English suffixes "ic" and "ly" (with the trailing space) were aligned with French "ique" and "ment". The French sequence "les" (with spaces on both ends) was aligned with English "s" (with a trailing space). This last alignment presumably reflects the fact that French grammar requires more frequent use of the definite article than English does so that "les" more readily contracts an alignment with the plural ending of the noun. It may also have something to do with the fact that *les* occurred nowhere in this text as an object clitic.

Encouraging though these preliminary results are, they also reveal important shortcomings of the technique and challenges for the future. The most important of these will almost certainly involve additional procedures with unappealing complexity properties. As usual with ordinary language, ambiguity, or at least *relative ambiguity*, is at the heart of the severest of the problems.

A string in one language is ambiguous relative to another language if it is routinely translated differently in that other language, depending on the context. Simplifying somewhat, we can say that French *haut* translates into English as either or *high* or *tall*. If one of these adjectives were somehow replaced by the other in a English text before the alignment process began, there would be good reason to hope that a strong alignment with French *haut* would be recognized. But there appears to be no basis to make any such conflation of words, especially within a system where the very notion of a word is so carefully deemphasized. The general problem is to be able to recognize situations in which a distribution, abundantly endowed with "interesting" properties, aligns with the (disjoint) union of two or more distributions in the other language.

Another way to think about this involves abandoning the notion of similarity, which is inherently symmetrical, in favor of a notion of inclusion of one distribution in another. Continuing the above simplified example, this would allow an alignment to be established between French *haut* and English *high* on the grounds that the distribution of *haut* largely contains that of the English *high*. Suppose this were successful; it might then be possible to seek other alignments for just those instances of *haut* that did not participate in the first alignment.

Publications referenced

Fredkin 1960; Gale and Church 1995; Kay and Röscheisen 1995; Nelson 1996; McCreight 1976; Ukkonen 1995.

## 50

Translation, Meaning and Reference

President Nixon hoped to disengage the United States from the war in Vietnam by increasing training and equipment for the South Vietnamese forces and turning more and more of the responsibility for fighting the war over to them. A minor problem with the plan was that Vietnamese soldiers could not read the manuals that came with the equipment. Translating it all would be unthinkable unless a large part of the work could be automated. At the RAND Corporation, I secured a small machine translation contract to work on this and hired Ron Kaplan to help. After a short time, we were asked to work on Korean instead for reasons that remain unclear. Fortunately, for us, one language was like another. We were linguists, after all! We have worked together, on and off, ever since, on problems more or less closely related to machine translation. In this essay, I reflect, as I doubtless should have done already in Nixon's day, on just what translation is all about anyway, and why we did not always achieve as much as we had hoped.

Imagine a venerable scholar with a document in each hand. He is getting manifestly quite unhappy as he looks from one text to the other and back again. Finally, he throws both documents aside, declaring "This is rubbish! These are not translations!" The chances are that the venerable reader has allowed himself a little scholar's license in his choice of words. That is alright: he is angry and no one is listening anyway. The chances are that the documents are translations of one another, but they are such poor examples as to make him want to withhold recognition of them as such.

A poem that purports to be the translation of a poem in another language may, like Fitzgerald's "Rubaiyat of Omar Khayyam", depart in so many and in such extreme ways from the original as to cast doubt on the claim that it is a translation, rather than a new work inspired by an older one. But, in more mundane cases, it is quite difficult to imagine the quality of a translation degenerating so much as to call in question whether it should be taken to be a translation at all. Degrees of translationhood are not necessarily the same as degrees of translation quality. We rarely find ourselves faced with the problem of judging the degree of translationhood achieved by a pair of utterances or documents, but the *gedanken* experiment that involves imagining ourselves in that position may be useful for what it says about the nature of translation.

In this essay, I offer some preliminary reflections on the question of when one text should be allowed to count as a translation of another. Though logically prior to just about all other questions concerning translation, it is one that is rarely addressed. A commonly accepted criterion, namely that the texts should express the same meanings, will quickly prove to be inadequate, though the intuition remains strong that there is some property of an original text that must be preserved in any translation. If not the meaning, then the question is, what is that property? The view for which I shall attempt to argue is that what must be preserved is the sequence of mental states through which each text leads its readers. Just what a mental state is will remain somewhat elusive but, in this, it will not differ from the meanings on which the commoner view rests.

For the purposes of this discussion, it will often be convenient to refer to one of a pair of documents as the *original* and the other as the *translation*. However, we will generally be thinking of translation as a symmetrical relationship. From the point of view of the translator, which document serves as the source makes many and crucial differences, but our concern here will be mainly with static relationships that exist between the documents themselves and not with the process that brought one or the other of them into being. It is sometimes possible to tell, especially in the case of poor translations, which must be the original and, while this is interesting, it will not be at the center of our concerns.

A natural first requirement to make of a translation is that it tell the same story as the original. To make this a general requirement, we clearly must construe the word "story" very broadly. Consider, for example, the case of a document that arrives in a box along with bits and pieces intended to be assembled into some object or contraption. The story that document tells is about a sequence of events in which pieces are connected in specific ways and in a specific order. If two people were observed constructing such objects from boxes with identical contents except for the language in which the instructions were written, a *prima facie* case would surely have been made that the documents were translations of one another. The metaphor of a text as a set of instructions for assembling pieces into a complete object is perhaps more widely applicable than that of a story. After all, what a speaker or a writer is generally aiming to do is indeed to construct an object, but in the head of the hearer or reader rather than in the real world.

If texts in different languages lead to parallel sequences of events, we may be encouraged to accept them as translations, especially if other sequences could have led to the same result using the same pieces. But it may not be so. How the pieces go together might be so obvious to both constructors as to render the instructions superfluous. On the other hand one set of instructions may be altogether more detailed than the other, perhaps because it is intended for a reader with more experience in this kind of construction. It could nevertheless give rise to the same sequence of events. We will see an example of this kind shortly.

The requirements we have placed on the translation of an assembly instruction sheet might seem too narrow from a purely functional point of view. The success of the overall enterprise — that of achieving a correct final assembly — is surely paramount. The particular sequence of events plays a secondary role. Let us consider a specific example. For the sake of simplicity, both texts are in English.

You can get to the airport on the RER, line B, from the Gare du Nord. You can reach the Gare du Nord by taking the Metro from Place Monge. The Place Monge is just up the hill from the apartment.	Go up the hill from the apartment to Place Monge. Take the Metro from there to the Gare du Nord. From the Gare du Nord, take the RER line B to the airport.

They both tell the reader how to get from some, presumably contextually given, apartment to the airport. While one may seem more natural than the other in some way, they both leave the reader in possession of the same mental construct, one that connects the apartment to the airport in a particular way. They might therefore be said to tell the same story.

In both versions, the story has three episodes corresponding to the three legs of the journey. The principal difference between the two versions is that the order of the episodes in one version is the reverse of what it is in the other. As a consequence, the reader is in possession of different constructs, or partial constructs, after reading just one or two episodes, depending on the version, even though he has the same complete construct by the end of the story.

The reader's mental states, or partial constructs, are the life blood of literature. An author's skill consists, in large measure, in manipulating them in subtle ways, and a translator's skill consists in leaving them as he found them. But there is no subtle manipulation of mental states going on in our example. Indeed, if we take it that the original is on the left and the translation is on the right in the above display, we might be inclined to commend the translator for rearranging things so that the order of the mental states in the translation corresponds to the order of the physical states that would occur if the instructions were carried out. In a case like this, there might be some tension in the mind of the translator between the desire to leave the order of things under the control of the author and the desire to get the reader to the airport as reliably as possible.

As we look at larger and larger texts, the requirement to maintain the identity and the relative order of mental states dominates more and more. A redesign at this level would be seen as rewriting the story and not translation. In the translating of *belles lettres*, it is particularly important to respect the author's intended sequence of mental states as closely as possible. In these situations, the translator can be sure neither how important the sequence really is nor, indeed, exactly what the states are. So the safest policy is to translate the smallest pieces one can, consistent with maintaining the smoothness of the result, and to keep them as nearly as possible in the order that corresponds to the original. This is also the easiest thing to do. In translating more mundane texts there is rarely any cause to do otherwise except, perhaps, if one culture routinely places the ingredients in a recipe before the method, and another puts them the other way round, or something of that kind.

So we have arrived, by a somewhat circuitous route, at the notion that a translation should tell the same story as the original and, furthermore, that it should consist of as many elementary sections as possible, each being a translation of its opposite number in the other text.

Now let us examine another pseudo-translation, from English into English, that meets these requirements more nearly than our previous one:

Go out of the front door and turn left. You will pass three turnings on the right, the third being only for pedestrians. Turn right at the next possibility following this one and continue straight ahead, until you have the possibility of turning half left along a wide boulevard at the end of which you will see an impressive building with a lot of gold leaf on the roof. That is the building you are looking for.	Go west along the river and cross at the Pont du Carrouselle. Go through the Louvre and up the Avenue de l'Opéra. The opera house is at the end of that street.

This will doubtless seem a great deal less plausible as a translation than our earlier example. With a few exceptions, such as the word *go*, none of the words or phrases in the translation seems to translate a word or phrase in the original. However, both texts describe the same route from a hotel called "Les Rives de Nôtre Dame" in Paris, to the old Opera house. Since the mental states in the description correspond to the physical places mentioned, and in that same order, then these texts should surely be allowed to count as translations of one another. But maybe it is not sufficient that the observable behavior of the people following the two sets of instructions should be essentially indistinguishable. To the best of our ability, we must also look at their internal states — at the sequences of partial mental constructs that are assembled in their heads.

Both readers know that they will leave the hotel by the front door, one because the text says so, and the other because he knows that he is going to have to leave the building and, *ceteris paribus*, that is the best way to do it. But the reader of the longer text constructs a model with three turnings on the right, a half-left turn, and a wide boulevard. These will be part of the other reader's mental model only if he knows his way around Paris well enough to make the instructions largely redundant. Here, as always, the model constructed is a function both of the text and the previously constructed models that the reader has available. In this case, we can argue that similar models would be constructed only under special circumstances and the two texts should not therefore be allowed to count as translations.

Let us consider still another example taken from the magazine of the Accor hotel chain (Accor 2005).

Ci-contre: Vestiges du IIIe millénaire avant J-C, surplombés de colonnes romaines.	*Left*: Ruins dating from the third millenium BC, surrounded by Roman columns.
Ci-contre: Théâtre romain (Odéon) construit au IIIe siècle apr. J.-C.	*Right*: Roman theatre (Odeon) built in the third century AD.

The important point to note is, of course, that "Ci-contre" is translated first as "left" and then as "right". One would not wish to be forced into the position that it has both of these meanings. In fact, of course, it has neither. Taken in isolation, we might translate it as "opposite", or "on the facing page". In the situation in question, what was being referred to was not on the facing page but on the opposite side of the same page. In the first case, the text was to the right of the picture it referred to and, in the second case, on the left. The translator achieved the required mental state but using a word with opposite meanings in the two cases. The important thing — the only important thing — is to cause the reader to look at the correct picture. Whether "ci-contre" has a meaning that is in any way related to those of "left" or "right" is of secondary importance.

These examples illustrate that language is essentially *situated* in the sense of being grounded not simply in meanings such as a dictionary would supply for each of the words, but in complete situations that allow for coherent sets and sequences of mental states. To make this point, we will consider an extended example, not of a translation, but of a monolingual extract from the autobiography of the physicist Richard Feynman (1985). This passage explains how a certain kind of combination lock, a kind often used on small safes and filing cabinets, works. The lock has a single dial which is turned a certain number of times alternately in clockwise and counterclockwise directions, stopping each time when a particular number on the dial is at the top. The question is, how does the mechanism cause the lock to open in response to just one such sequence of events?

I will discuss only a few phrases from the beginning of this passage in detail, but I invite the reader — especially the reader who does not know how these locks work — to read the whole passage once or twice. I hope that this will demonstrate that the passage achieves the author's intentions for it, which is presumably that the reader should come to know how the device works.

There are three discs on a single shaft, one behind the other; each has a notch in a different place. The idea is to line up the notches so that when you turn the wheel to ten, the little friction drive will draw the bolt down into the slot generated by the notches of the three discs.

Now, to turn the disks, there's a pin sticking out from the back of the combination wheel, and a pin sticking up from the first disk at the same radius. Within one turn of the combination wheel, you've picked up the first disc.

On the back of the first disk, there's a pin at the same radius as a pin on the front of the second disc, so by the time you've spun the combination wheel around twice, you've picked up the second disc as well.

Keep turning the wheel, and a pin on the back of the second disk will catch a pin on the front of the third disc, which you now set into the proper position with the first number of the combination.

Now you have to turn the combination wheel the other way one full turn to catch the second disc from the other side, and then continue to the second number of the combination to set the second disc.

Again you reverse direction and set the first disc to its proper place. Now the notches are lined up, and by turning the wheel to ten, you open the cabinet.

This is an extremely informal piece of writing. The picture of the mechanism that is in the words is casual and impressionistic, but the one that is constructed in the mind of the attentive reader is very precise. This is because the picture is constructed from components some of which are contributed by the text while others are contributed by the reader.

Let us begin at the beginning:

There are three discs on a single shaft ...

A disk is a circular piece of material, quite thin relative to its diameter. The word "shaft" has several meanings. Among various other things, it can be (1) a long, usually vertical, space in the ground or in a building, such as an elevator or mine shaft, or (2) a solid cylinder, usually of metal, much longer than its diameter, intended to convey rotational force, as in the drive shaft of a car, or to support rotating wheels. In the interest of simplicity, let us suppose that these are the only possibilities. The first of the two meanings seems hard to involve in the workings of a lock, and maybe this is why the second immediately seems right. The difficult question is to decide in just what sense the disks are "on" the shaft. They could be screwed or welded to it so that the shaft would lie across the surface of each disk, perhaps at the diameter. Or they could be screwed or welded to the end, or ends, of the shaft. It was immediately clear to me, as to others to whom I put the question, that neither of these is intended. What we have somehow to understand is that there is a hole in the center of each disk that the shaft passes through. The disks can therefore rotate on the shaft so that they become, essentially, wheels. There is only the gentlest of invitations to this interpretation, in that the meaning we are betting on for "shaft" makes of it something intended to carry wheels and the disks are reasonable candidates for this role.

Now the disks are

...one behind the other...

If the shaft passes through a hole in the center of each disk, as I am betting they do, then are they not one beside the other or, even one on top of the other? Of course, they are one behind the other from the point of view of a person who is approaching the lock from the canonical angle, that is, from outside and in front of the safe or file cabinet. Such a person sees that disk directly in front, behind which the shaft extends away from him, carrying the disks, one behind the other. But there is no absolute or neutral position that justifies the word "behind" here, and it plays no role in understanding how the mechanism works.

Now for a real puzzle.

...each has a notch in a different place....

A notch is a small cut in the edge of something. For me, the word carries with it the suggestion that the cut has been made in a casual manner and may therefore be irregular in shape. However, I am prepared to abandon this last condition as being almost certainly inapplicable to a precisely engineered mechanism like a combination lock. The real problem comes with the phrase "in a different place". A disk with a hole in the center has only two edges in which to put a notch: the outside edge, and the one around the hole through which the shaft passes. If one disk had a notch on one of these edges and one on the other, that would be two notches in clearly different places. But, now, what of the third one? The third disk must surely have a notch in the same place as one of the others because there are simply no other alternatives. All other things being equal — and I am claiming they must be for things to make sense — the notches should be in corresponding edges of each disk.

It will turn out that the notches all have to be in the outer edge, and I had no difficulty placing them there when I first read the piece. But how, then, can they be in different places given that disks are, by definition, objects of wonderful symmetry? The problem is somewhat less perplexing if one thinks of the disks, not as they would be when first manufactured, or when removed from the lock and lined up carefully on the work bench, but as they might appear when one first opened the mechanism and looked inside. Each notch would then be in a different place, not relative to its disk, but relative to the mechanism as a whole.

Questions like these arise throughout the whole of the text. I mention a few more, without discussing them at length.

The idea is to line up the notches ...

What idea? "Line up" in what sense?

when you turn the wheel to ten

What wheel? And what does it mean to turn a wheel "to ten"?

And, please, what are we to make of the following?

the slot generated by the notches of the three discs.

In two places, the operator of the lock is assured that he will "pick up" one disk or another. What meaning of this verb is being invoked here? How can we pick up a disk that we cannot even see and whose existence we are learning about now for the first time?

Let me reiterate that I take this to be a remarkably successful piece of writing which, for me at any rate, succeeded immediately in its presumed goal of conveying how one of these combination locks works. But it does it by inviting the reader to participate in a mental journey in which the text serves only to gently suggest which way to take at each branch in the road. Each signpost makes sense only to one who has been involved from the start and who knows where we are going, and why.

The burden of this discussion was summarized by Jean Delisle in his *L'analyse du discours comme méthode de traduction*, (p. 73) where he says "Le texte d'un message ne contient pas le sens, il ne fait que pointer vers lui." [1] If everything were included that would be required so that even the most perverse reader could not misinterpret the writer's intention, it would be so heavy and complicated as to defeat that very purpose. One might be able to argue that it was strictly correct, even if it were totally incomprehensible.

Now here is the problem that this poses for the translator. The grammar and lexicon of every language requires certain kinds of information to be made explicit that can be omitted in some others. Consequently the part of the intended message that is made explicit in one language can rarely be exactly what it is in another. This means that the translator can, and often does, leave some of the information in the original implicit, allowing the momentum of the mental journey to supply it. It also means that the translator must frequently make explicit information that was left implicit in the original. Needless to say, this is only possible if the

---

[1] The text of a message does not contain the meaning, it only points to it.

translator is being carried forward by the momentum of the text in just the way intended by the author. Most of the time, this does not put an inordinate strain on the translator, though it would presumably be entirely beyond the reach of any current machine-translation system.

Vinay (1958) give many examples in which information that is required in French is optional in English, or the other way round. Consider the French question "Où voulez-vous que je me mette?" which can be glossed as "Where do you want me to put myself?". However, this is something no English speaker would ever say. Better translations are available, but there are indefinitely many of them and the choice among them depends on where we stand in the mental journey. Some possibilities are:

Where do you want me to sit

> stand
>
> park
>
> tie up my horse
>
> sign my name
>
> draw up my regiment
>
> hang my pictures
>
> . . .

Finding a good translation in a case like this requires the momentum of the mental journey to carry one forward to the next state where the words themselves are inadequate to do it. There is often no alternative to this. In this particular case, a cunning translator who was not carried forward strongly by the momentum might write "Where do you want me?", but such a possibility may not be available in every case.

As another example, the French noun "promenade" describes movements through space that a person undertakes for recreational purposes. By default, one would probably translate it as "go for a walk", or "take a walk". But it could also be "go for a ride" if the context made it clear that a horse or bicycle was involved, or "go sailing" in situations where walking would require superhuman powers, and so on.

As a final example, a chair in French must be specified as either "chaise" (straight chair) or "fauteuil" (easy chair). Leaving other alternatives aside, let us ponder what considerations would be involved in the following examples of the word in use:

I found this change purse on a chair in the kitchen.	J'ai trouvé ce porte-monnaie sur une chaise dans la cuisine.	(6)
I found this change purse in a chair in the living room.	J'ai trouvé ce porte-monnaie dans un fauteuil dans le salon.	(7)
Let's put Mary in the chair at the other end of the table.	Mettons Marie dans la chaise à l'autre bout de la table.	(8)
There is plenty to eat. That is not the problem. The problem is that we don't have enough chairs.	Il y a assez à manger. Ça, ce n'est pas le problème. Le problème, c'est que nous n'avons pas assez de chaises.	(9)
There are plenty of barbers. That is not the problem. The problem is that we don't have enough chairs.	Il y a assez de coiffeurs. Ça, ce n'est pas le problème. Le problème, c'est que nous n'avons pas assez de fauteuils.	(10)

In each case, a larger context could change our judgment about which word to use for "chair", but given only what is here, the following considerations, at least, seem relevant. We might expect to find more straight chairs in the kitchen and more easy chairs in the living room, but the key distinction between (6) and (7) lies in the preposition. The arms of an easy chair give it more the aspect of a container, so that you would find things *in* it, whereas you find things *on* the surface of a straight chair. Likewise for *dans* and *sur* in French. This is the kind of clue that a statistical machine translation system might easily learn to pick up because the preposition is only one word removed from the word "chair". But, then, it would probably get (8) wrong. Presumably what is happening here is that decisions are being made about where to seat people around a table. This is a situation in which the preposition *in* is generally used in English, regardless of the kind of chair involved. This is *chair* as a position round a table, rather than *chair* as an article of furniture.

In both (9) and (10), there are three sentences. And the second one can be thought of as standing for an arbitrary amount of intervening material, just so long as it does not upset the connection between the first sentence and the third. In both cases, there is a problem in that we do not have enough chairs of some kind. In (9), the momentum carries the reader naturally to the idea that the food of which we have sufficient quantities will be consumed by people who will be seated, presumably around one or more tables. They will be sitting on straight chairs because those are the kinds of chairs one sits on while seated around a table eating. In (10) we are presumably envisaging some number of barbers, presumably attending in some appropriate way to the hair of their clients. It is usual for a barber to do this while the client is seated in a chair and that chair is called a *fauteuil* in French, however comfortable or uncomfortable it may be.

I have argued for the view that a text and its translation must consist of sequences of corresponding segments each of which should be as short as possible while honoring grammatical and stylistic constraints. Such corresponding segments should add similar pieces to the mental structure that is under construction in each reader's mind. Any requirement to preserve meaning must be subservient to these. But, if this effect is to be achieved, there must presumably be some properties of segments that are preserved. The most important one is not far to seek. It is the referential properties of the segment, where we construe the term "referential" very broadly. The reference, of course, is to objects in the mental model that is under construction rather than to objects in the world.

When we come upon the words "There are three disks on a single shaft", we are already committed to a collaboration with the author in which we will do our best to make a replica in our minds of a picture that he has in his. The references will not be to anything in the real world — it is a generic lock we are talking about and not any particular instantiation — and we will give everything we hear the interpretation that seems best fitted to advancing that enterprise. We know quite a lot even before the first word arrives because the explanation we are being given is of a device that we are already familiar with from the outside and our understanding of the first words comes partly from their meanings and grammatical relationships and partly from that prior knowledge. Suppose the text had contained the following sequence:

> The Ministry keeps its archives in a tunnel about thirty feet underground, and reachable by two special elevators, one in each of its office buildings. There are three disks on a single shaft.

We have no context beyond what the words themselves provide. The first sentence invites us to imagine a ministry — perhaps part of a government — that occupies a pair of buildings from each of which it is possible to take an elevator to a subterranean tunnel in which the ministry stores its archives. We need to bring only some very general knowledge of the world to the task of constructing the image from the words. But the next sentence is more puzzling because we need to interpret it as a blueprint for an addition to the existing structure and, indeed, it does seem to refer to some parts of that structure where the new material might be added, namely at the shafts through which the elevators presumably move. But now we must somehow install three disks on one of these shafts. We can only hope that the immediately following text will provide some assistance in doing this because I, for one, am entirely at a loss. If we were translating the text into a language that had different words for elevator shafts and the mechanical engineer's shafts, we might lean towards the former, but presumably without complete confidence. We desperately need to have a mental model for the disks, and of the situation in which several of them are on an elevator shaft.

"Ci-contre" must achieve the same reference as "left" in one context, and the same as "right" in another. The problem is not hard because the reference is to the real world in this case; indeed it is to the very paper on which the words appear. In the case of "Où voulez-vous que je me mette?", we need a replacement for x in "Where do you want me to x" that achieves the same reference as the French. But if x refers to anything here it must surely be an action that has not been performed yet and is therefore not available in the real world to be referred to. But it is available in the mental model that we are constructing as we read the text. This is why we need to construe the notion of reference very broadly. In particular, we must construe it against the background of a very promiscuous ontology (Hobbs 1985). In "Où voulez-vous que je me mette?", the actions that the last three words are most likely to refer to are narrowly constrained by the surroundings in the real world, or as established by the foregoing text. If we are contemplating a table around which people are being seated in preparation for a meal, it is natural to take it as referring to an act of sitting down, or taking one's place, and we can achieve the same reference in English by saying "Where do you want me to sit?", but if I am addressing the official at a polling station before casting my vote, a better rendering would be "Where do you want me to sign?". I can even change the meaning and say something like "Where do I sign?" or "I have to sign somewhere here, don't I?" so long as I can be reasonably sure that the effect on the reader's mental model will be the same.

It goes without saying that there can be quite a lot of guesswork in translating. An author may be unconscious of potential ambiguities in his text, or may abstain from clarification that would be cumbersome or that might seem to reflect adversely on the intelligence or good sense of the reader.

Consider the following sentences:

I just got back from Dallas/Prague. I had forgotten how good beer tastes.	Ich komme eben von Dallas/Prague (11) zurück. Ich hatte vergessen, wie gutes Bier schmeckt.
I just got back from Provo/Riyadh. I had forgotten how good beer tastes.	Ich komme eben von Provo/Riyadh (12) zurück. Ich hatte vergessen, wie gut Bier schmeckt.

The second sentence in each English pair can be paraphrased either as "I had forgotten how good it is that beer tastes" and "I had forgotten the taste of good beer". In the syntax underlying the first, but not the second interpretation, "good" is an attributive adjective modifying "beer". The corresponding German requires agreement between the adjective and the noun, and hence the form "gutes". In the other interpretation, "good" is predicative and therefore has the uninflected form "gut".

In these examples, I take it that, all other things being equal, the first interpretation will seem more natural for Utah and Riyadh, and the second for Texas and Prague based on common stereotypes according to which beer is hard, if not impossible, to obtain in Utah and Saudi Arabia whereas in Texas and the Czech republic, it is not only readily available, but it is especially good.[2] The point is simply that an infusion of information, based on fact or

---

[2] Ivan Sag, to whom I owe this set of examples, points out that the stereotypes, particularly concerning Utah, are inaccurate.

fancy, stereotype or surmise, is indispensable for determining the morphology of the German adjective. Moreover, any connection between these inferences and the meanings of the words is mediated through the mental model that the hearer constructs, and not directly through the meanings of the words.

It has been my intension to cast some doubt on the rarely questioned claim that a translation is successful to the extent that it preserves the meaning of the source text, *modulo* requirements on fluency, register, and the like. I have suggested replacing meaning in this role with a notion of a sequence of mental states. A mental journey is a sequence of mental states, and a mental state is a partially constructed mental model. A mental model is inhabited by objects, properties, beliefs and so forth, which may or may not have correspondents in some real or imaginary world. From a purely logical point of view, we do not need to ascribe any properties to these objects beyond that of distinguishability. As with the *atoms* of some programming languages, like Lisp, we need to be able to say of a pair of variables that have atoms as their values if they are the same or different.

It has been proposed, notably by Johnson-Laird (1983), that models of inference based on mental models constitute a superior theory of the way humans solve logical tasks. Clearly, translation involves solving many and diverse logical tasks, but it also serves to underline how little of the information required for the construction of the mental model is typically furnished by the text itself, and how much must be supplied from the hearer's preexisting stock of models and partial models. This is where the designers of machine translation systems need to concentrate their efforts because, without some means of storing such models, and constructing new ones as text is processed, high quality machine translation will remain an illusion.

Publications referenced

"À livre ouvert" 2005; Feynman 1985; Vinay and Darbelnet 1958; Hobbs 1985; Johnson-Laird 1983.

## 51

Antonio Zampolli

Every second Saturday through the summer of 1956, I left Victoria station in London charged with escorting some three hundred holiday makers who had never left their homeland before to a variety of sunny places between Genoa and Rome. On the intervening Saturdays, I left Roma Termini to collect those that had been delivered two weeks before by somebody else, and took them back to London. On arriving in Rome, I took a long hot shower in the place that large Italian stations provided for that purpose and headed for the Piazza Navona to feast my eyes on its three Bernini fountains, to watch cheerful children who play and laugh and never cry, and to consume a cool half bottle of Orvieto. I loved the Piazza Navona and could regain my physical and mental strength there better than anywhere else.

Some forty years later, the telephone rang in the middle of the night at an hour when good news rarely arrives. It was Antonio saying that he had kept his part of our bargain, and found me an apartment on the top floor, overlooking the fountains. It remained for me to keep my part and find him a house on the steep and winding section of Lombard Street in San Francisco.

Antonio was very fond of San Francisco, and my wife and I generally made a point of taking him there for dinner when he was in the Bay Area. Naturally, we did not seek out Italian restaurants, but he had a sense that told him when there had been an Italian hand in the preparation of the meal, and he marched off into the kitchen, emerging some minutes later with a Sicilian or a couple of Tuscans and a bottle of Brunello di Montalcino. On one occasion, he found an Italian chef with a German assistant and kept everyone in the car in hysterics, including himself, all the way back to Palo Alto by declaiming loudly in Italian with a heavy German accent various things that the assistant might have said. "Kvanti ziamo a kvesto tavólo?"

Antonio was the little magician who could turn a fantasy into reality and reality into a source of marvelous merriment. But beneath the surface, there was deep and genuine concern for his friends and colleagues, for the field of endeavor he had done so much to bring into being, for Pisa, for Italy, for Europe and the world. Oh, yes, and for the Dolomites. Lombard Street was fantasy, but Cortina d'Ampezo was the center of the world, and Antonio had a house in the mountains nearby in which I believe he was able to feel a peace that he could not find in any other place. That was his Piazza Navona. My wife and I visited him there once and he took us walking among the towering chimneys and along the ledges that make that place unique in the world. When we reached a break in the path that Iris thought she might not be able to cross, Antonio said he would carry her. He was not joking. In this place, he was sure footed and knew exactly what he could do. When the ledge became so narrow that I no longer had the courage to continue, there was no macho urging forward, because he knew that you could not be safe if you did not feel safe. He was a man of the mountains: careful, and professional, and competent.

In 1978, Professor Antonio Zampolli founded what I believe to have been the second department of computational linguistics in the world (after Gothenberg the year before), though he
had been leader of the linguistic division of CNUCE since 1968. But his reputation as the father
of European computational linguistics goes back to the early seventies when he organized a
truly remarkable series of summer schools in Pisa to which many of today's foremost research
centers owe their origins. He scoured the world for anyone with experience in this fledgling field
and brought them to pass on what they had learned. Before our very eyes, he turned what
had been a hobby or a passing fantasy for a few people into a discipline and a profession. The
hotels and parks and bars and restaurants of Pisa were awash in algorithms, and lexica, and
morphemes, and parsing, and semantics. We were born too late to have been with Sartre and
Hemingway in Paris, but we were with Zampolli in Pisa when the history of what matters to
us was in the making. If the leaning tower has been closed to the public since those days, it
is probably because the people who should have been working on keeping it from falling were
seduced away from engineering and geology to language and computing.

Antonio was not simply a member of just about every organization that connected computing with the humanities or ordinary language; he was a vigorous member and, in many cases,
a founding member. The International Committee on Computational Linguistics had frequent
cause to be grateful for his innumerable contributions to their work and, most especially, for
his bringing the fifth International Conference on Computational Linguistics to Pisa in 1973.
This vintage year of the period of the great Pisa summer schools was also the one in which
the Association for Literary and Linguistic Computing came into being with Antonio as one
of its founding members. In 1983, he became president of that organization, a position that he
retained for the rest of his life.

I vividly remember an occasion on which Antonio had been assigned by the organizers of a
workshop that we both attended to respond to my contribution. To my shame, I allowed his
restless activity during my presentation to strengthen the conviction that my efforts were about
to receive less than the treatment they deserved. They got what they deserved, and more. With
charm and humor and even deference, the weaknesses I had thought might go unnoticed were
revealed one by one, and remedies were suggested for errors I had not even suspected. I was
put, gently but firmly, where I belonged. From the experience, I learned a lot about myself
that I should have learned earlier. But I learned a respect for Antonio Zampolli, which was
to grow continually deeper over the years. He gave so much of his life to making good things
possible for other people that one was always in danger of forgetting that he was a man of
great intellectual power and creativity.

I am able to appreciate, probably better than most, one particularly arcane activity in which
Antonio's creativity was manifested, namely that of causing the punched-card machinery that
were the precursors of modern computers do things beyond the imagination of their designers.
I have this privileged perspective because, at about the same time in the early history of our
field, Antonio was working with Padre Busa in Milan, I was working with Margaret Masterman
in Cambridge. He was trying to derive a phonemic representation from Italian written texts
and I was trying to parse sentences with a formalism now mercifully forgotten. We were both
trying to do these things by finding ingenious new ways of wiring the plug boards of various
punched-card machines designed to meet the needs of accountants. He succeeded.

I have said that Antonio devoted most of his time and energy to making good things possible for others. In the latter years, he spent much of his time in Brussels and Luxemburg
and Washington, not only securing the support of his institute but also tending to health of
his discipline and bringing people together in whose potential interactions he saw benefits for

a wider community. He was justifiably proud of his achievements as a match-maker, forging collaborations and even life-long friendships among the most unlikely partners. At every Coling conference, he organized a panel on the funding of research in computational linguistics throughout the world, mainly so that young people in our field should be exposed to as many opportunities as possible.

I have tried to limit the flow of anecdotes that flood the mind when one thinks of Antonio because, like no one else that I have known, he enriched the lives of everyone that he touched with unforgettable little personal things. I will end with just one more. After a noisy dinner with much wine and laughter during one of the summer schools, a number of us emerged from a restaurant long after its accustomed closing time into the relative cool of the outside air. Everything was illuminated by the eerie green light of a full moon. Antonio stopped as he came out of the building and suddenly fell quiet and serious. "Everybody follow me," he said, and set off towards the grassy close that surrounds the cathedral, the baptistery and the tower. Everyone followed in silence. When we arrived, he said, "This place is called Piazza dei Miracoli – The Square of Miracles. I will show you why." And slowly he walked through the square, following a particular path that he knew well, pointing silently now at a carving on a building, now at a formation of stones in the wall, now at a silhouette on the other side of the square. Nothing was said, but we all understood the reason for the name. One more miracle had occurred there by the little miracle maker of Pisa.

## 52

A Life of Language:
ACL Lifetime Achievement Award

This is a truly overwhelming experience. Since I am not a cat, I expect to have one lifetime in which to achieve anything, and one award for it at the most. So this is it, and I am honored and humbled and, of course, delighted. It is wonderful to be among so many of the friends who have enriched my life in so many ways. Thank you for permitting me to feel, for some short moments, that one or two of the things I have done may be allowed to count as accomplishments.

There is only one thing that gave me pause for a moment when I heard about the award, and that was its title. But my concern was soon put to rest when I checked up on the previous three recipients and found that, as far as I could tell, they were doing quite well.

If you will forgive me, I will tell you a little about this lifetime, such as it has been. After all, as I have said, one has but one chance for such gross indulgence.

The ambiguities that are a linguist's constant companion were with me from the start for, if I say I was born in London, then do I mean that the place where I was born was part of London at the time of my birth, or that it is part of London now? In fact, only the second proposition is true. I was born in 1935 in Edgeware, which was in the county of Middlesex then, but was later absorbed by London for reasons that I believe to be unrelated.

The first event that lodged in my memory was the declaration of war in 1939. I had no idea what it meant, but everyone took it so seriously that it made some kind of impression on me even at the age of four. London was bombed a lot, and Edgeware a little. My mother was afraid of the bombing, but I found it fun. My father was never afraid of anything. He was an inspector of schools and was charged with evacuating children from London. I was sent to a variety of places but invariably returned to London after a few weeks because my mother could not stand to be away from the excitement of the capital for more than a few weeks, even if it did mean being bombed. We went to Dorchester, and Devizes, in the west country, and I encountered new kinds of vowels and discovered that syllables could end in an "r". I started mimicking people and learning to associate the way people talked with where they came from. We went to Leeds, in the north country, and I learned how diphthongs could become monophthongs and how to tell whether a person came from Leeds or Bradford, despite the fact that these cities are barely fifteen miles apart. People told me I was destined to become a linguist. I did not know what a linguist was, and it turns out, in retrospect, neither did they.

One of the places I was sent to avoid the bombs was Llambadarn, a small village in southern Wales where only Welsh was spoken. The idea that there could be a place where people did not speak English had not occurred to me before, and it fascinated me. One of the things I still regret about the experience is that my mother could not stand it for more than three weeks.

Had she been able to, I might have learned Welsh.

Why I was called "Martin," I do not know. The plan for my life that was beginning to take shape seems to have attracted people called "Henry" in the past. For example, there was Henry Lee Smith, who had a radio show in the United States. After hearing somebody talk for 30 seconds, he told them where they came from, where they went to school, where they had moved to after that, and so forth. He would give a history of the person based on how they spoke. Something like that had already become my "party piece" when I was six or seven. Then there was Henry Sweet, who did similar kinds of things in Britain, and another well-known character called Henry Higgins, who was actually based on Henry Sweet, and so should not, I suppose, really count.

In 1947, I was sent to one of those rather exclusive places the British like to call "public schools" to get an education. Soon after, since I wanted to learn languages, I went to Tours to learn French and Baden-Baden to learn German. Then I went into the army to defend Britain. And, against the kinds of things that I am equipped to defend a country against, I defended it magnificently.

After that, I went to Cambridge to get more education and, as they say in Britain, to read modern and medieval languages. Reading a subject in Cambridge is approximately like majoring in it in America, except that there is nothing but the major. You spend all your time on what you are reading; there is nothing else. Modern and medieval languages constituted about the closest thing I could find to what I was looking for, but somewhere in the back of my mind, I knew that what I wanted to do was linguistics, even though all I knew about it was what adults had said to me when I was a child. It turns out that it did exist. In fact, it existed in Michael Halliday's department, within walking distance of where I lived in London. Whether it would have been better to go there, or whether the experience of going to Cambridge was worth it in its own right, I do not know. But, instead of doing what Henry Sweet and all those other Henry's did, I wound up reading *Le Rouge et le Noir, La Divina Comedia, Faust*, the *Chanson de Roland, Parzifal* (with a "z") and other literary monuments. But I found myself saying all the time, "What about language? Doesn't all this come from ordinary language somehow? Isn't the language that ordinary people speak a wonderful thing that deserves to be studied in its own right?"

I remember asking my French supervisor this question once, and I have to admit that the answer he gave me, wrong though it was, has remained in my memory ever since because I simply could not find any refutation for it at the time. What he said was, "If you want to study French, don't you want to study it as used by those who use it best?" In other words, would I not want to study the French of the literary giants who created great works of art in that language?

Lord Adrian, the master of my college, and also vice chancellor of the university, asked me to act as his interpreter when giving an honorary degree to Signor Gronchi, president of Italy. The president had a cold and insisted on wearing his doctoral gown over his raincoat. But he took me for a beer at the Blue Boar afterwards, and I forgave him everything.

When I was at Cambridge, it turned out that the undergraduate engineering society ordered a film from London, and the people at the film library put the wrong film in the envelope. Instead of something on steam turbines, or whatever, they got Kurasawa's Roshomon. I had for many years wanted to see this film. I don't know what it was that excited me about it. Maybe it had something to do with language, again. Maybe the idea of four people telling essentially the same story, and it coming out differently as different words were woven around it – maybe that was what fascinated me. As you probably know, it is the story of a murder, told by four witnesses one after the other. One of the accounts is that of the murdered man himself, told through a medium.

In order to see this movie, which had always eluded me up until that point, I had to join the undergraduate engineering society. The literature that I received in the mail after joining told me, among many other things, that it offered a prize of 25 pounds every year for the best paper delivered by an undergraduate. I could not avoid asking myself what a medieval linguist would have to do to secure such a prize. A serious paper would obviously stand no chance. What I had to do was find a subject that would cause people to laugh, because there was no intersection in the serious world between anything I knew and what were serious matters to them.

I decided I would offer a paper on a translating machine, an idea which, surely, nobody could take seriously. I gave the paper and stimulated some laughter. However, sitting in the audience were Margaret Masterman and Frederick Parker Rhodes. Margaret Masterman was the director of the Cambridge Language Research Unit, and Frederick Parker Rhodes was a senior researcher there. They had American money to work on machine translation. Margaret Masterman's many outstanding properties did not include a robust sense of humor. She found my paper impertinent and insisted that I visit the language unit to learn the truth about machine translation. To cut a long story short, the following year, I became a very junior member of the Cambridge Language Research Unit, having foresworn my evil ways and shown that I could speak Italian and use a soldering iron.

I worked for several years with Margaret Masterman. She was the wife of Richard Brathwaite, the Knightsbridge Professor of Ethics whose major work, however, was on the philosophy of science. Margaret Masterman was a student of Wittgenstein, a fact that she never let you forget, because it gave authority to even the most outrageous things she might choose to say. She did pioneering work on semantic nets with R. H. Richens and had a theory of translation based on thesauruses and whose principal formal tool was lattice theory. She was a member of a shadowy society called the "Epiphany Philosophers," who took it as their goal to show that Christianity and science were not only compatible but that they supported one another. My father confused the Epiphany Philosophers with the Apostles, a secret society founded in the early nineteenth century and intended to have as its members the 12 brightest undergraduates in the university. My father did not know this part of the history. What he did know was that it was based in my college – Trinity – and that its recent members had included the infamous Cambridge Four – Kim Philby, Donald Maclean, Guy Burgess, Anthony Blunt – all engaged in spying for the Soviet Union. A patriot who was concerned for my welfare, as parents are wont to be, my father occasionally expressed the hope that I was devoting my linguistic skills to worthy pursuits and that MI6 would not be coming to visit.

Margaret Masterman was one of the cofounders of Lucy Cavendish College, a most unusual institution that admits as undergraduates women who have been away as mothers and who want to come back into mainstream academic life. It is a remarkable place, and she was a remarkable woman.

The Cambridge Language Research Unit was small, but it had a number of illustrious alumni. Michael Halliday had spent some time there, mainly as an expert on Chinese. The late Roger Needham started his career there, as did his wife, Karen Sparck Jones, the previous recipient of this award. Yorick Wilks, surely well known to this audience, also started his career there.

After two years at the Cambridge Language Research Unit, I seized upon an opportunity that came up to visit the RAND Corporation in California for six months. This was a trip to the United States that I have been extending ever since. There, I worked for another remarkable person, David G. Hays, to whom we owe, among other things, the Association for

Computational Linguistics, the International Conferences on Computational Linguistics, and the very name "Computational Linguistics". At the time, the RAND Corporation was working on Russian machine translation and was ahead of its time in that it had constructed a million-word dependency tree bank of Russian already in 1962 when such things were somewhat less fashionable than they are today.

While I was at RAND, I took over from Hays the organization of a set of seminars to which people interested in computers and language came every week. Several of those people told me later that the meetings had played an important role in determining the later course of their lives. Also, about the same time, I started teaching computational linguistics at UCLA.

At RAND, I had the great privilege of rubbing shoulders with a wonderfully rich variety of people who either worked there or who came on extended visits. Some names that come immediately to mind are those of George Danzig, inventor of the Simplex Method for Linear Programming; Norman Dalkey, one of the originators of the Delphi method; Newell, Simon, and Shaw, who could be said to have invented Artificial Intelligence; Albert Wohlsetter, who once called the Secretary of State from my house to clarify a question that arose over dinner; Keith Uncapher, founder of the Information Sciences Institute at the University of California; Richard Bellman, who created dynamic programming; Daniel Ellsberg of Pentagon Papers fame; Paul Baran, who first proposed packet switching for computer networks; and Herman Kahn, who founded the Institute for the Future and who played war games where the score was kept in megadeaths. I would have it known that I had been gone from RAND for 10 years when Donald Rumsfeld became its chairman in 1981 and 20 years before Condoleezza Rice joined its board of trustees.

For some years, the linguistics project at RAND had an internship program that included a number of people who are still prominent in our field, and for very good reason. They include my old friends and long-time collaborators, Ron Kaplan and Lauri Karttunen.

In 1962, the Association for Machine Translation and Computational Linguistics (AMTCL) came into being. A couple of years later, the first International Conference on Computational Linguistics was held in New York. These conferences have now come to be called "Coling," so named by a Swede, who therefore pronounced it "Cooling," which is also how a Swede pronounces "Koling," the name of Albert Engström's much-loved cartoon character, a vagabond who made sage remarks about the world between swigs at a bottle of wine. This name was associated with the conferences organized every other year by the International Committee on Computational Linguistics (ICCL) by the late Hans Karlgren. I became chair of the ICCL in 1984 and have been there ever since.

The establishment of the AMTCL and ICCL foreshadowed an extremely momentous event that came about because the people involved also had to do with a document known as the ALPAC Report. This was one of the most well known, if least read, documents ever produced concerning our field. Its full title was "Languages and Machines: computers in translation and linguistics." It was called the ALPAC Report after its authors, the "Automatic Language Processing Advisory Committee," established by the U.S. National Academy of Sciences. It was a mere quarter of an inch thick, with a black cover altogether appropriate to its contents. The remit of the committee was much narrower than most people usually appreciate. The committee was supposed to tell the government how successful, how useful, how worthwhile the research that was being devoted to machine translation with government money was going to be. They were to concern themselves with the potential benefits for the government, not for anybody else. But, since the money for the work came from the government, a negative report could have dire consequences for everybody, and it did.

ALPAC discussed a number of interesting questions, but the essential conclusion consisted of two points. First, the government did not really need machine translation and second, even if it did, the lines of research that were being pursued had little chance of giving it to them. So the work should stop, and stop it did. A second recommendation of the committee almost got lost. It was that there should be a new focus of attention on the scientific questions that might provide a solid foundation for later engineering enterprises like machine translation. It was with the clear aim of responding to this recommendation that this association and these conferences came into being.

Now anybody who competes for research grants knows that while substance and competence play a significant role, the most important thing to have is a name, and we did not have one for the exciting new scientific enterprise we were about to engage upon. To be sure, the association and the committee antedated that report, but we had inside information, and we were ready. I use the word "we" loosely. I was precocious, but very junior, so that my role was no more than that of a fly on the wall. However, I was indeed present at a meeting in the office of David Hays at RAND when the name "computational linguistics" was settled upon. I remember who was there, but in the interest of avoiding embarrassment, I will abstain from mentioning their names. As I recall, four proposals were put forward, namely:

1. Computational Linguistics
2. Mechanolinguistics
3. Automatic Language Data Processing
4. Natural Language Processing

Strong arguments were put forward against the latter two because it was felt that they did not sufficiently stress the scientific nature of the proposed enterprise. The term "Natural Language Processing" is now very popular, and if you look at the proceedings of this conference, you may well wonder whether the question of what we call ourselves and our association should not be revisited. But I would argue against this. Indeed, let me briefly do so.

Computational linguistics is not natural language processing. Computational linguistics is trying to do what linguists do in a computational manner, not trying to process texts, by whatever methods, for practical purposes. Natural language processing, on the other hand, is motivated by engineering concerns. I suspect that nobody would care about building probabilistic models of language unless it was thought that they would serve some practical end. There is nothing unworthy in such an enterprise. But ALPAC's conclusions are as true today as they were in the 1960s – good engineering requires good science. If one's view of language is that it is a probability distribution over strings of letter or sounds, one turns one's back on the scientific achievements of the ages and foreswears the opportunity that computers offer to carry that enterprise forward.

Statistical approaches to the processing of unannotated text bring up the thorny philosophical question of whether the necessary properties of language are, in fact, emergent properties of text. Could it be that at least some of the facts that one needs to know about a text are not anywhere in it? There is one sense in which the answer has to be "no" for, if they are not in the text, then they are not facts about the particular text, but about texts in general, or about some class of texts to which the given one belongs. But an extreme case that might dispose one rather to answer "yes" would be one in which the "text" simply consisted of the library call number of another text that contained the real information. Someone who knows enough to be able to find what the call number leads to can find what the text is really about, but it is not spelled out in the original document. When people say that language is situated, they mean that examples of language use always have some of this latter quality. They depend for their understanding on outside references that their receivers must be in a position to resolve.

I will give a concrete example in a moment.

Part of the problem we are confronting comes from what the famous Swiss linguist Ferdinand de Saussure called *l'arbitraire du signe* – the arbitrariness of signs. The relationship between a word, a text, or any linguistic item, and its meaning is entirely arbitrary. It therefore does not matter how long you look at a text; you will never discover what it means unless you have some kind of inside information. It may very well be that the relationship between a sentence and its structure is also arbitrary, though here the situation is less clear.

This is hardly surprising. All it amounts to is that you cannot understand a text unless you know the language. You can, however, learn a lot about the translation relation from a text and its translation. If that were not the case, Jean Franois Chapolion would not have been able to decipher the Egyptian hieroglyphs on the basis of a stone that contained a translation of hieroglyphic Egyptian into Greek. It seems to follow, therefore, that meaning has little that is essentially to do with translation. Since you cannot get the meaning from the string, but you can find out about translation from two strings, then presumably the meaning is not directly involved. Let me argue against this position by giving a counterexample. There is nothing unusual about this counterexample. Examples of this kind are not unusual. At least one can be found in almost any paragraph-sized example of everyday language.

I was sitting in a train in Montpelier, and an old lady got in and said, "Does this train go to Perpignon?" The person she was addressing said, "No, it stops in Béziers." What could be simpler than that? Let's try and translate it into German. "Fährt dieser Zug nach Perpignon?" No trouble with that as far as I can see! "No, it stops in Béziers' – "Nein, er endet in Béziers." So, you should imagine a railway line that runs from Montpelier to Perpignon by way of Béziers. If a train were to end its journey in Béziers, it would never reach Perpignon.

But suppose the situation on the ground were different. Suppose that, after leaving Montpelier, there were a fork in the line, with one branch going to Perpignon and the other to a place called Findeligne by way of Béziers. Suppose, furthermore, that it is well known that all trains end their journey in either Findeligne or Perpignon. The interaction with the lady fits the new situation just as well as the old one. Since the train stops in Béziers, it must be a Findeligne train, and Perpignon is on the other branch. The German translation, however, must now be different. We can no longer translate "No, it stops in Béziers" as "Nein, er endet in Béziers" because "endet" means "stop" only in the sense of completing the journey. We now need to translate "stop" in the sense of "come to a brief stop to allow passengers to get on and off," and for this, the appropriate word is hält. It therefore seems that, in order to be able to translate this passage correctly, one needs intimate knowledge of the geography of Provence and the schedules of the trains that run there.

Another problem with attempting to learn language from text is Zipf's Law. Zipf's Law says that a small number of phenomena – letters, words, rules, whatever – occur with very great frequency, whereas a very large number occur very rarely. Zipf's Law provides encouragement to people just starting to work on language because it means that almost anything you try to do with language works wonderfully at first. You do something on 100 common words with 20 rules designed for unremarkable situations and it works wonderfully. The trouble is that new phenomena that you had not thought of continue to appear indefinitely, but with steadily decreasing frequency. It is true that a textual example does not have to exemplify a new phenomenon in order to be interesting, because, as well as new phenomena, we are often interested in the frequencies of occurrence of old ones. But as a method of learning about different kinds of phenomena, it is subject to a crippling law of diminishing returns. Fortunately, there is an alternative, which is to talk to people who speak the language and who know what the phenomena are. This is what linguists do.

Another question is: Do the models that we build actually respect the fact that language is in accordance with Zipf's Law? If a probability distribution is established over a set of characters, and random text is generated in accordance with that distribution, the expected lengths of "words" will be determined by the probability of the space character, and the distribution of words will be approximately in accordance with Zipf's Law. If, instead of characters, we work with covert features of some sort, but still including one that determines when we move to the next word, we presumably get a similar distribution. But the models we actually work with rarely, if ever, predict that language will have this striking and invariable statistical property.

Time to return to serious things. For me, the event that most clearly marked the birth of computational linguistics was the invention by John Cocke in 1960 of what I always took to be the first context-free parsing algorithm that allowed for ambiguity. If it indeed was the first – and that turns out not to be beyond doubt – then this was the first algorithm designed expressly to meet needs that arose in our field. This happened at RAND just before I got there, and it became a source of great excitement for me.

The algorithm works only with binary rules, that is, rules with two symbols on the right-hand side. In its simplest form, the algorithm is based on a triangular matrix, which we can call a chart, with a box for each substring of the string being parsed. The idea is to fill the boxes one by one in such an order that the boxes containing potential constituents of the phrases in the current box will already have been filled. We assume that the boxes corresponding to single words are filled in an initial dictionary look-up phase. The remaining boxes are filled in order of increasing length of the corresponding substring, thus maintaining the required invariant. Several other regimes would have the same effect.

The original algorithm was embodied in a FORTRAN program with five loops, as follows:

1. for *Length* from 2 to *string.length*
2. for *Position* from 0 to *string.length* − *Length* + 1
3. for *FirstLength* from 1 to *Length* − 1
4. for *FirstConstituent* in *Chart*[*Position, FirstLength* − 1]
5. for *SecondConstituent* in *Chart*[*Position* + *FirstLength, Length* − *FirstLength* − 1]

The maximum number of iterations of the first three loops is determined by the length of the sentence, and this corresponds nicely with the observation, made later, that the time complexity of chart parsing with context-free grammar is $\mathbf{O}(n^3)$ where n is the string length. The number of iterations of the last two loops, on the other hand, is controlled by the number of items that there could be in a single box in the chart which, in the original algorithm, could grow exponentially with string length.

Ron Kaplan and I recognized that, with only very minor adjustments, this algorithm can be turned into one with the $\mathbf{O}(n^3)$ time complexity I just mentioned. One way to do this would be to give the chart an additional dimension so that, for each substring of the input, there comes to be a separate box for each grammatical symbol. The boxes contain the various structures that the given substring has, and whose top node is labeled with the corresponding symbol. The parser never needs to rehearse these different structures because, for the purposes of building larger structures, they are all equivalent. This means that loops 4 and 5 are no longer controlled by the length of the string, but only by the number of nonterminal symbols in the grammar. What could be more inspiring than this elegant algorithm to a young person trying to see a little bit of rationality in an otherwise apparently random field?

Another change that we made to the original algorithm involved the introduction of partial phrases, sometimes known as *active edges* because they could be thought of as on the lookout for complete edges that they could absorb, thus creating either a new complete edge or a partial edge that was nearer to completion. Since one can obviously construct a phrase of arbitrary size by assimilating words one by one to partial phrases, any algorithm that works only with binary context-free rules can easily be turned into one that operates with arbitrary rules. More importantly, partial phrases enabled us to break loose from the rigid regime of loops embedded in a particular way, effectively replacing the algorithm with what I came to refer to as an *algorithm schema* (Kay 1982). The basic idea was this: At any given moment, a phrase, or partial phrase that had been recognized, was stored in just one of two data structures, which we referred to as the *agenda* and the *chart*. If it was on the agenda, then the possibility that it might be extended by absorbing other edges had not been explored. But if it was in the chart, all such interactions with other phrases already in the chart had been systematically explored. The parsing algorithm consisted in moving phrases and partial phrases from the agenda to the chart in such a way as to maintain this invariant. In other words, repeat the following cycle until the agenda is empty:

1. Remove an arbitrary partial or complete phrase from the agenda.
2. Locate all current items in the chart that it could either absorb or that could be absorbed by it, putting all resulting new phrases and partial phrases on the agenda.

In 1974, Ron Kaplan and I joined Xerox PARC, and before long, I had an Alto computer in my office with 64K of memory just for me. This was one of the machines that Steve Jobs saw during a legendary visit. My intellectual history, if I may use such a pompous term, is studded with programming languages, and one that I encountered soon after arriving at PARC was Prolog. Yes, I encountered Smalltalk, but Prolog made a more lasting impression, and I still use it today. Prolog is a way of extracting generalizations from algorithmic problems which, if they are just the right problems, cannot be done as effectively in any other way. Here, for example, is a top-down parser.

```
parse([], String, String).
parse([Goal | Goals], [Goal | String0], String) :-
  parse(Goals, String0, String).
parse([Goal | Goals], String0, String) :-
  rule(Goal, Rhs),
  parse(Rhs, String0, String1),
  parse(Goals, String1, String).
```

It defines a single predicate, called `parse`, which is true of a sequence of goals and a pair of lists of words or phrases if the first list of words and phrases has a prefix that can be broken into sublists that match the goals in the given order, and the remaining suffix is identical with the second string. Notice that, if there is a single goal, namely, *Sentence*, and if the third argument is the empty list, then the second argument must be a sentence. Given particular arguments, there are three ways in which we can attempt to show the predicate to be true of them; hence the three clauses that make up the program. Here is what the three cases do:

1. If the list of goals is empty, then they can be met only by the empty string and the second and the third arguments are identical.
2. If the first goal is met trivially, by matching the first item in the list that is the second argument, then if the remainder of that argument is identical to the third argument, the clause succeeds.
3. If the grammar contains a rule that would replace the first goal by a sequence of other goals, and if parsing some prefix of the second argument meets these goals, and if, furthermore, it can be shown that the remaining part of the string meets the remainder of the initial goals, then the clause will have succeeded.

This is a Prolog implementation of the classical recursive-descent parser, or top-down left-to-right parser, celebrated for its inability to handle grammars with left-recursive rules. The Prolog implementation reveals in a unique way the similarity between this parser and the following bottom-up left-corner parser:

```
parse([], String, String).
parse([Goal | Goals], [Goal | String], String) :-
  parse(Goals, String0, String).
parse([Goal | Goals], [First | String0], String) :-
  rule(Lhs, [First | Rhs]),
  parse(Rhs, String0, String1),
  parse([Goal | Goals], [Lhs | String1], String).
```

There are only minor changes, and they are all in the third clause. Instead of looking for a grammar rule that expands the next goal, we look for one with a righthand side whose first item matches the first item in the second argument. If such a rule can be found, we treat the remaining items as goals that we try to find in what remains of the second argument. If this can be done, we can replace the matching sequence with the single symbol that constitutes the left-hand side of the rule, and we attempt to meet the original set of goals with a string modified in this way.[1]

The parallelism exemplified is surely elegant almost to the point of being beautiful and, in the design of algorithms, as Richard O'Keefe said, elegance is not optional (O'Keefe 1999).

Ron Kaplan had spent a lot of time working on augmented transitions networks (ATNs) before coming to PARC and, when we got together again, I became interested in them also. They seemed to me to have the power one needed for syntactic analysis, but they lacked a property that I thought crucial, namely reversibility. An ATN that did a good job in analysis was of no use when it came to generation. An ATN, as you doubtless know, is different from a standard finite-state automaton in two key ways. First, the condition for making a transition in a given network can be that the symbols starting at the current state in the string are acceptable to some other network named in the transition. In other words, they are recursive. The second difference is that networks produce output by making assignments to variables, or *registers*. The collection of these registers at the end of the network traversal constitutes the output.

Consider a greatly simplified example. Suppose the *Sentence* network is applied to the string *The book was accepted by the publisher*. We can assume that one of the transitions from the initial state calls the *Noun Phrase* network, which recognizes the first two words. The transition in the *Sentence* network puts the phrase in the *subject* register and moves to the next state, where one of the transitions allows a part of the verb *to be*, which is put in the *verb* register. At the next state, one of the possibilities is the past participle of a transitive verb. The system now abandons the search for an active sentence and proceeds on the assumption that it is passive. However, the work that has been done is not abandoned. The noun phrase in the *subject* register is simply moved to the *object* register because, if the sentence is passive, it will presumably fill the role of deep object. The *subject* register is cleared at this point. The *Sentence* automaton will presumably now be in a final state because the sentence could end here. But, if the word *by* follows, and then another noun phrase, this latter goes into the *subject* register.

Notice that, given the contents of the registers as they would be at the end of this process, it would not be possible to follow the same path through the network and generate the original

---

[1] No award acceptance speech would be complete without a homework problem. So the question is: Why is it important to write [Goal — Goals] in the third clause, and not simply Goals?

string. To start with, *the publisher* would be in the *subject* register, and not *the book*.

In retrospect, it seems that the answer to this problem should have been obvious. But it is often so. Ron noticed that the key thing here is that you must never replace substantive contents of a register with a new one. If the register is still empty, you can put something in it, but once it has a value, that value must stay there. In other words, registers must be variables, in the mathematical understanding of that term, and not FORTRAN variables that can be assigned and reassigned indefinitely. And so, he proposed what he called the *same* predicate. It meant:

1. If the contents are the same as the argument to the predicate, continue.
2. If the register is empty, and the current item in the string matches the predicate's argument, put that item in the register, and
3. otherwise fail.

On the first branch, it seems that we are indeed dealing with a predicate. On the second, we have an assignment operator, and on the last, a predicate. This mixture is now quite familiar and we refer to it as *unification* .

In everyday terms, unification can be thought of like this. The CIA sends out a couple of observers to write reports on people they are watching, and given their reports, the question arises as to whether they could be watching the same person. One report says that the person's eyes are blue, and the other one does too, so they could be watching the same person. One says the subject's hair is black or brown and the other one says it is brown or red so, if we assume that it is brown, they could still be watching the same person. Furthermore, we have more specific information on the person's hair color than either observer gave us individually. One report says the person had an Italian accent. The other one does not have any idea, so we will take it that he is Italian. As long as the properties remain compatible with one another, we take the most specific version of that property that you can and add it to the output. As soon as they become incompatible, we decide that the reports cannot be about the same person and the process fails.

So much for what unification is. Now what about the name? Here is the true and unblemished story. I formulated the scheme I have just outlined and wanted a name for it. Until it fails, the process is conflating information from the two observers and is thus somewhat like the union operation on sets. But it is not exactly union, because it can fail. So I settled on a name like "union", namely, *unification* . However it was soon brought to my attention that this word already had a meaning in logic programming. So I started working on two problems in parallel. I started looking for another name and at the same time, I started trying to find out how my first choice was used in logic programming. To my great surprise, I discovered that, although some of the details were different – in particular, the logic programmers did not have the attributes that I had taken over from ATNs – we were doing essentially the same thing. So I did not have to give up the word.

Out of this, there came a whole new view of how the deep structure of a sentence might be related to its surface structure, or how its predicate-argument structure might be related to its tree structure. The dominant view – and it is still dominant today – is that you produce a deep structure, of the same data type as the surface structure, and you carry out a number of transformations. They may not be specified by transformational rules, but they are changes, perhaps in accordance with some principles, that replace one structure by a different one of the same general kind. When the sequence of transformations comes to an end, what is left is the *surface structure* . This scheme, as you know, has been complicated in a variety of different ways that need not concern us. According to this view, the relationship between the deep structure and the surface structure is an essentially procedural one. Now, a computationalist never wants to be handed a set of procedures designed by someone else and asked to implement it, because the procedures may be hard or impossible to implement, or to reverse, or even to understand in usual computational terms. The computationalist wants to be given a declarative statement about relationships and allowed to work on the procedures himself; that is his job.

What came out of these considerations is a view that there is one data structure that represents both deep and surface structures. It is a tree[2] whose nodes have complex labels, and this object as a whole more or less corresponds to the surface structure. The topmost label of the tree, however, has enough articulation to constitute the entire deep structure. So the label will not just simply say 'S'; it will say that the structure represents a sentence and, furthermore, that it has this subject and that object, that the subject is definite and singular, and so forth. So all that led to unification grammar.

Another thing we worked on at PARC was finite-state technology, something that is probably still hot enough for many of you to be quite familiar with it. We noticed that it is a fact about regular languages, which are generated and accepted by finite-state automata and which occupy a position almost at the bottom of the Chomsky hierarchy, that they are closed under the operations of set theory and concatenation. This means that, if you can write an algebraic expression that describes the language that you are interested in, then the computing of it will be straightforward and can be specified algebraically.

Regular relations, which are modeled by finite-state transducers and are very closely related to finite-state machines of the standard kind, have just the power that is needed for many linguistic operations, particularly at the low end of the hierarchy – phonology, morphology, and spelling rules. In particular, as Ron and I pointed out (Kay and Kaplan 1994), a slight adjustment to the rules of engagement, as they are called in military circles these days, moves simple string-rewriting rules right from the top of the Chomsky hierarchy to the bottom or, at least, one step from the bottom. The rules I have in mind are of the form:

$$\alpha \to \beta/\gamma\_\delta$$

meaning "replace α by β if there is γ on the left and δ on the right". If we stipulate that no rule be allowed to rewrite any part of the string that is part of the output of a previous application of that same rule, and if the rules are ordered, then the set of them can be modeled by a finite-state transducer that we can construct automatically from the rules. In this form, they are highly efficient to apply and reversible.

My professional life almost encompasses the history of computational linguistics. But I was only fourteen when Warren Weaver wrote his celebrated memorandum drawing a parallel between machine translation and code breaking. He said that, when he saw a Russian article, he imagined it to be basically in English, but encrypted in some way. To translate it, what we would have to do is break the code, and the statistical techniques that he and others had developed during the second world war would be a major step in that direction. However, neither the computer power nor large bilingual corpora were at hand, and so the suggestions were not taken up vigorously at the time. But the wheel has turned, and now statistical approaches are pursued with great confidence and disdain for what went before. In a recent meeting, I heard a well-known researcher claim that the field had finally come to realize that quantity was more important than quality.

The young Turks blame their predecessors, the advocates of so-called *symbolic* systems, for many things. Here are just four of them. First, symbolic systems are not robust in the sense

---

[2]Actually, it usually allows reentrancy and is therefore not strictly a tree, but this need not concern us here.

that there are many inputs for which they are not able to produce any output at all. Second, each new language is a new challenge and the work that is done on it can profit little, if at all, from what was done previously on other languages. Third, symbolic systems are driven by the highly idiosyncratic concerns of linguists rather than real needs of the technology. Fourth, linguists delight in uncovering ambiguities but do nothing to resolve them. This is actually a variant of the third point.

This is a bad rap, and the old-school computational linguists who have made such a resounding success of their field should not take it sitting down. Let me say a quick word about the first three points and then expand a little more on the last.

First, robustness is an engineering issue. To throw out the theory because of inadequate engineering is to throw out the baby with the bath water. There are many approaches that could, and should, be taken to this problem, some statistical, and some not. Second, one of the things that linguists know that often surprises others is that the similarities among languages are much more striking and important than their differences. They can and do profit from these insights. Third, what look like the cute examples and arbitrary infatuations of linguists often, though not always, represent a distillation of important and wide-ranging issues.

Now I come to the fourth point, which is ambiguity. This, I take it, is where statistics really come into their own. Symbolic language processing is highly nondeterministic and often delivers large numbers of alternative results because it has no means of resolving the ambiguities that characterize ordinary language. This is for the clear and obvious reason that the resolution of ambiguities is not a linguistic matter. After a responsible job has been done of linguistic analysis, what remain are questions about the world. They are questions of what would be a reasonable thing to say under the given circumstances, what it would be reasonable to believe, suspect, fear, or desire in the given situation. If these questions are in the purview of any academic discipline, it is presumably artificial intelligence. But artificial intelligence has a lot on its plate and to attempt to fill the void that it leaves open, in whatever way comes to hand, is entirely reasonable and proper. But it is important to understand what we are doing when we do this and to calibrate our expectations accordingly. What we are doing is to allow statistics over words that occur very close to one another in a string to stand in for the world construed widely, so as to include myths, and beliefs, and cultures, and truths and lies and so forth. As a stop-gap for the time being, this may be as good as we can do, but we should clearly have only the most limited expectations of it because, for the purpose it is intended to serve, it is clearly pathetically inadequate. The statistics are standing in for a vast number of things for which we have no computer model. They are therefore what I call an "ignorance model."

Finally, a very quick word about machine translation. The days of the ALPAC report are long gone, and there can no longer be any doubt that there is a need for machine translation. There are two kinds of people who need machine translation. There are people who need it because they need to disseminate documents in more than one language. The European Union needs to produce material in 20 languages, either because it has an operational need for it in 20 languages, or because the law says it must be available in 20 languages – not always the same thing. So it must be translated, and the result must be readable. Some of it has to be *very* readable because, in most cases, a document that has legal force has the property that, if you have to go to court, you can choose which one of those 20 versions you are going to base your case on. Caterpillar Corporation produces huge amounts of documentation – almost more weight of documentation than of bulldozers – in an average of 14 languages. These have to be high-quality translations. What is required in these situations is entirely different from what people need who are consumers of translation. The canonical examples of these are people who are concerned with homeland security or people at Google. They are interested in anything you can tell them about a document. If you can't tell them anything, well that is too bad. If you can tell them a little, then they will be grateful for what you can tell them. Any kind of translation is better than no translation at all.

Not surprisingly, what the very word "translation" means for these two sets of people is entirely different. And I just would like to hope that you, the computational linguists of the future, will keep in mind the needs of both of these very worthy communities.

So, just a couple of final reflections. Statistical NLP has opened the road to applications, funding, and respectability for our field. I wish it well. I think it is a great enterprise, despite what I may have seemed to say to the contrary.

Language, however, remains a valid and respectable object of study, and I earnestly hope that the ACL will continue to pursue it.

We have made little headway in computational psycholinguistics, which to me has always been the nub, the center, the thing that computational linguistics stood the greatest chance of providing to humanity. To build models of language that reflect in some interesting way on the ways in which people use language. There has been some wonderfully interesting work on such matters, but not nearly enough. I am sorry that it has not been pursued as earnestly as I think it could have been, but it is a difficult field and perhaps that is enough reason in itself. My friends, I have spent some 40 years with you in this association, and I hope to spend many more.

Publications referenced

Kay 1982; Kay and Kaplan 1994; O'Keefe 1999.

Cumulative References

Abney, S. 1986. "Licensing and parsing." *North Eastern Linguistic Society* 17, 1–15.

Abney, S. 2010. "Experimental linguistics." *Linguistic Issues in Language Technology Special Issue on Linguistics and Computatonal Linguistics.*

Abney, S. and M. Johnson. 1989. "Memory requirements and local ambiguities of parsing strategies." *Journal of Psycholinguistic Research* 18:1, 129–144.

Abramson, H. and V. Dahl. 1969. *Logic Grammars.* Springer Verlag. New York.

"À livre ouvert" (An Open Book). 2005. *Accor Magazine* 68.

ALPAC. 1966. *Languages and machines: computers in translation and linguistics.* A report by the Automatic Language Processing Advisory Committee, Division of Behavioral Sciences, National Academy of Sciences, National Research Council, Publication 14 16. Washington, DC.

Alshawi, H., D. Carter et al. 1991. "Translation by quasi-logical form transfer." In *Proceedings of the 29th Annual Meeting of the Association for Computational Linguistics*, Berkeley, California. Association for Computational Linguistics.

Arnold, D. and L. des Tombe. 1987. "Basic theory and methodology in EUROTRA." In S. Nirenburg, ed., *Machine Translation: Theoretical and Methodological Issues*, 114–135. Cambridge University Press.

Baayen, H. 1991. "A stochastic process for word frequency distributions." In *Proceedings, 29th Annual Meeting of the Association for Computational Linguistics*, Berkeley, CA.

Barwise, J. and J. Perry. 1982. *Meanings and attitudes.* Unpublished manuscript. Stanford.

Barwise, J. and J. Perry. 1983. *Situations and Attitudes.* Bradford Books/MIT Press. Cambridge, Massachusetts.

Bisbey, R. 1971. *A Tree Grapher for the Linguist.* The Rand Corporation, P-4730.

Bisbey, R. and M. Kay. 1971. *The MIND System: A Transformational Generator.* The Rand Corporation.

Bisbey, R., R. Kaplan and M. Kay. 1971. *The MIND System: A Powerful Parser.* The Rand Corporation.

Bresnan, J. 1978. "A Realistic Transformational Grammar." In M. Halle, J. Bresnan and G. A. Miller, eds., *Linguistic Theory and Psychological Reality.* MIT Press.

Bresnan, J. 1982. *The Mental Representation of Grammatical Representations.* MIT Press.

Brown, P., J. C. Lai and R. L. Mercer. 1991. "Aligning sentences in parallel corpora." In *Proceedings, 29th Annual Meeting of the Association for Computational Linguistics*, Berkeley, CA.

Brown, P., J. Cocke, S. Della Pietra, V. Della Pietra, F. Jelinek, J. Lafferty, R. Mercer and P. Roossin. 1990. "A statistical approach to machine translation." *Computational Linguistics* 16:2, 79–85.

Carbonell, J.G. and M. Tomita. 1987. "Knowledge-based machine translation, the CMU approach." In S. Nirenburg, ed., *Machine Translation: Theoretical and Methodological Issues*, 68–89. Cambridge University Press.

Chafe, W. L. 1976. "Givenness, contrastiveness, definiteness, subjects, topics, and point of view." In Charles N. Li, ed., *Subject and topic*, 25–26. Academic Press. New York.

Chevalier, M., J. Dansereau et al. 1978. *TAUM-METEO: Description du Système*. Université de Montréal.

Chomsky, N. 1957. *Syntactic Structures*. Mouton, The Hague.

Chomsky, N. and M. Halle. 1968. *The Sound Pattern of English*. Harper and Row.

Church, K. W. and P. Hanks. 1990. "Word association norms, mutual information, and lexicography." *Computational Linguistics* 16:1, 22–29.

Colmerauer, A. 1982. "An interesting subset of natural language." In K. L. Clark and S.-A. Tarnlund, eds., *Logic Programming*. Academic Press. New York.

Cooper, R. 1983. *Quantification and Syntactic Theory*, vol. 21 of *Synthese Language Library*. D. Reidel. Dordrecht.

Copestake, A., D. Flickinger, R. Malouf, S. Riehemann, and I. A. Sag. 1996. "Translation Using Minimal Recursion Semantics." *Proceedings of The Sixth International Conference on Theoretical and Methodological Issues in Machine Translation*, Leuven.

Copestake, A., D. Flickinger, C. Pollard and I. A. Sag. 2005. "Minimal Recursion Semantics: an Introduction." *Research on Language and Computation* 3:281–332.

Coppinger, L. and S. von Susich. 1961. "Grammatical Coding." *Mathematical Linguistics and Automatic Translation,* Report NSF-7.

Davidson, D. 1967. "The logical form of action sentences." In N. Rescher, ed., *The Logic of Decision and Action*. University of Pittsburgh Press. Pittsburgh. Pennsylvania.

Davidson, D. 1980. *Essays on Actions and Events*. Oxford: The Clarendon Press.

de Saussure, F. 1915. *Course in General Linguistics*. London: Peter Owen Ltd. W.Baskin (1959).

Dik, S. C. 1978. *Functional Grammar*. North Holland (North Holland Linguistic Series 37).

Drela, M. and J. S. Langford. 1985. "Human-powered flight." *Scientific American* 253:5.

Drela, M. and J. S. Langford. 1986. "Fliegen mit Muskelkraft." *Spektrum der Wissenschaft*.

Edmundson, H. P. et al. 1961. *Studies in Machine Translation: Manual for Pre-editing Russian Scientific Text*. The RAND Corporation, RM-2065-1.

Eilenberg, S. 1974. *Automata, Languages, and Machines*. Academic Press.

Fano, R. 1961. *Transmission of Information. A Statistical Theory of Communications*. MIT Press.

Farwell, D. and Y. Wilks. 1990. *Ultra: A Multi-lingual Machine Translator*. New Mexico State University.

Feigenbaum, E. A. 1961. "The Simulation of Verbal Learning Behaviour." *Proceedings of the Western Joint Computer Conference*. Los Angeles.

Fenstad, J. E. et al. 1987. *Situations, Language and Logic*. Reidel. Dordrecht.

Feynman, Richard P. 1985. *Surely You're Joking, Mr. Feynman*. W. W. Norton. New York.

Firbas, J. 1964. "On Defining the Theme in Functional Sentence Analysis." *Travaux Linguistiques de Prague* 1, 267–280.

Fong, S. 1991a. "The computational implementation of principle-based parsing." In R. C. Berwick, S. P. Abney, and C. Tenny, eds., *Principle-Based Parsing: Computation and Psycholinguistics.* Kluwer Academic Publishers.

Fong, S. 1991b. *Computational properties of principle-based grammatical theories.* Doctoral dissertation, Pennsylvania. Massachusetts Institute of Technology.

Frank, A. 1999. "From Parallel Grammar Development towards Machine Translation – A Project Overview." *Proceedings of Machine Translation Summit VII "MT in the Great Translation Era".* Singapore.

Frank, R. 1990. *Computation and linguistics theory: A government binding parser using tree adjoining grammar.* Master's dissertation, University of Pennsylvania.

Frazier, L. 1978. "On comprehending sentences: syntactic parsing strategies." Unpublished doctoral dissertation, University of Connecticut.

Frazier, L. and J. D. Fodor. 1978. "The sausage machine: a new two-stage parsing model." *Cognition* 6, pp. 291–325.

Fredkin, E. 1960. "Trie memory." Informal Memorandum. *Communications of the ACM* 3:9, 490–500.

Furuse, O. and H. Iida. 1992. "Cooperation between transfer and analysis in example-based framework." In *Proceedings of the 14th International Conference on Computational Linguistics*, Nantes, France. ACL.

Gale, W. A. and K. W. Church. 1995. "A program for aligning sentences in bilingual corpora." *Computational Linguistics* 19:1, 61–74. Also in *Proceedings, 29th Annual Meeting of the Association for Computational Linguistics*, Berkeley, CA.

Gazdar, G. 1979a. "English as a context-free language." Mimeo, University of Sussex.

Gazdar, G. 1979b. "Constituent structures." Mimeo, University of Sussex.

Gazdar, G. and G. Pullum. 1982. "Subcategorization, constituent order, and the notion of 'head'." In M. Moortgat, H. v. d. Hulst and T. Hoekstra, eds., *The scope of lexical rules*, 107–24. Foris. Dordrecht, Holland.

Gazdar, G., E. Klein, G. Pullum, and I. A. Sag. 1985. *Generalized Phrase Structure Grammar.* Blackwell.

Gazdar, G., G. Pullum and I. A. Sag. 1981. "Auxiliaries and related phenomena in a restricted theory of grammar." Indiana University Linguistics Club.

Goldsmith, J. A. 1979. *Autosegmental Phonology.* New York; Garland Publishing Inc.

Griffiths, T. V. and S. R. Petrick. 1965. "On the relative efficiencies of context-free grammar recognizers." *Communications of the ACM* 8, 289–300.

Grimshaw, J. 1990. *Argument Structure.* MIT Press.

Hakulinen, A. and F. Karlsson. 1979. *Nykysuomen lauscoppia.* Suomalaisen Kirjallisuuden Seura. Helsinki, Finland.

Hakulinen, A. and F. Karlsson. 1980. "Finnish syntax in text: Methodology of a quantitative study." *Nordic Journal of Linguistics* 3:2, 93–129.

Halliday, M. A. K. 1961. "Categories of the Theory of Grammar." *Word* 17:3.

Halliday, M. A. K. 1967-68. "Notes on Transitivity and Theme I–III." *Journal of Linguistics* 3:1, 3:2, 4:1.

Halvorsen, P.-K. 1983. "Semantics for lexical-functional grammar." *Linguistic Inquiry* 14:4, 567–615.

Harman, G. H. 1963. "Generative grammars without transformation rules: a defense of phrase structure." *Language* 39:4, 597–616.

Harper, K., D. G. Hays and D. Mohr. 1960. *Studies in Machine Translation 6: Manual for Coding Russian Grammar*. RM-2066-1. The RAND Corporation.

Harris, Z. S. 1952. "Discourse analysis". *Language* 28:1–30.

Harris, Z. S. 1957. "Co-occurrence and transformation in linguistic structure". *Language* 33:283–240.

Harrison, M. A. 1978. *Introduction to Formal Language Theory*. Addison-Wesley.

Hays, D. G. and M. Kay. 1969. "The Failure of Chomskian Theory in Linguistics." The RAND Corporation.

Heinamaki, O. 1980. "Problems of basic word order." In *Proceedings of the Fourth International Congress of Fenno-Ugrists*. University of Turku. Turku. Finland.

Hobbs, J. R. 1985. "Ontological Promiscuity." In *Proceedings of the 23rd Annual Meeting of the Association for Computational Linguistics*, 61–69. Chicago.

Hobbs, J. R. and S. M. Shieber. 1988. "An algorithm for generating quantifier scopings." In *Computational Linguistics* 13:1-2, 47–63.

Hoenigswald, H. M. 1950. "The Principal Step in Comparative Grammar." *Language* 26, 357–65.

Hopcroft, J. E. and J. D. Ullman. 1979. *Introduction to Automata Theory, Languages and Computation*. Addison-Wesley.

Hudson, R. A. 1971. *English Complex Sentences: An Introduction to Systemic Grammar*. North Holland (North Holland Linguistic Series 4).

Iida, E.S. and H. Iida. 1991. "Experiments and prospects of example-based machine translation." In *Proceedings of the 29th Annual Meeting of the Association for Computational Linguistics*, 185–192. Berkeley, California. Association for Computational Linguistics.

Ikola, O., ed. 1968. *Suomen kielen kasikirja*. Weilin and Goos. Helsinki, Finland.

Jakobson, R. 1971. *Roman Jakobson: Selected Writings, vol. II: Word and Language*. The Hague: Mouton.

Johnson, C. D. 1972. *Formal Aspects of Phonological Description*. Mouton.

Johnson-Laird, P. N. 1983. *Mental Models: Towards a Cognitive Science of Language, Inference, and Consciousness*. Cambridge University. Cambridge.

Johnson, M., and E. Klein. 1986. "Discourse, anaphora and parsing." In *Coling 88*. Bonn, West Germany.

Joshi, A. K. L. S. Levy and M. Takahashi. 1975. "Tree adjunct grammars." *Journal of Computer and System Sciences* 10:1.

Kamp, H. 1981. "A theory of truth and semantic representation." In J. A. G. Groenendijk, T. M. V. Janssen and M. B. J. Stokhof, eds., *Formal Methods in the Study of Language* 136, 277–322. Mathematical Centre Tracts. Amsterdam.

Kaplan, R. M. 1970. *The MIND System: A Grammar Rule Language*. The Rand Corporation, RM-6265/1-PR.

Kaplan, R. M. 1972. "Augmented transition networks as psychological models of sentence comprehension." *Artificial Intelligence* 3, 77–100.

Kaplan, R. M. 1973. "A General Syntactic Processor." In R. Rustin, ed., *Natural Language Processing*. Algorithmics Press. New York.

Kaplan, R. M. 1978. "Computational resources and linguistic theory." *TINLAP* 2.

Kaplan, R. M. 1984. "Finite-state models of phonological rule systems." Paper presented to the First Mathematics of Language Conference. University of Michigan.

Kaplan, R. M. 1985. "Finite-state models of phonological rule systems." Paper presented to the Workshop on Finite State Morphology. Center for the Study of Language and Information, Stanford University.

Kaplan, R. M. and J. Bresnan. 1982. "Lexical-functional grammar: A formal system for grammatical representation." In Joan Bresnan, ed., *The mental representation of grammatical relations*, 173–281. MIT Press. Cambridge, Mass.

Kaplan, R. M. and M. Kay. 1981. "Phonological rules and finite-state transducers." Paper presented to the Winter Meeting of the Linguistic Society of America. New York.

Kaplan, R. M. and M. Kay. 1994. "Regular models of phonological rule systems". *Computational Linguistics* 20:331–378.

Karttunen, L. 1976. "Discourse referents." In J. McCawley, ed., *Syntax and Semantics* 7, 363–385. Academic Press. New York.

Karttunen, L. and K. Beesley. 1992. "Two-level rule compiler." Technical report, Xerox Palo Alto Research Center, Palo Alto, California.

Karttunen, L., K. Koskenniemi and R. M. Kaplan. 1987. "A compiler for two-level phonological rules." In Report No. CSLI-87-108. Center for the Study of Language and Information, Stanford University.

Karttunen, L., R. M. Kaplan and A. Zaenen. 1992. "Two-level morphology with composition." *COLING-02*, 141–148. Nantes.

Karttunen, L., R. Root and H. Uszkoreit. 1981. "Morphological analysis of Finnish by computer." Paper presented at the 1981 Winter Meeting of the Linguistic Society of America.

Kasami, T, 1965. *An efficient recognition and syntax algorithm for context-free languages.* Technical Report AF-CRL-65-758), Air Force Cambridge Research Laboratory. Bedford, MA.

Kay, M. 1967. "Experiments with a powerful parser." In *2ème Conference Internationale sur le Traitement Automatique des Langues*, Grenoble. Also as Report RM-5452-PR, The Rand Corporation, Santa Monica, California. Also as *2ème Conference International sur le traitment automatique des languages*. Grenoble, France.

Kay, M. 1970. "From Semantics to Syntax." in Manfred Bierwisch and K. E. Heidolf (eds.), *Progress in Linguistics*, 114–126. The Hague, Mouton. Also as Report P-3746, The Rand Corporation. Santa Monica, California.

Kay, M. 1973. "The MIND system." In R. Rustin, ed., *Natural language processing.* Algorithmics Press. New York.

Kay, M. 1977. "Morphological and syntactic analysis". In A. Zampolli, ed., *Syntactic Structures Processing.* North-Holland. Amsterdam.

Kay, M. 1979. "Functional Grammaer." *Proceedings of the Fifth Annual Meeting of the Berkeley Linguistic Society.*

Kay, M. 1980. "The Proper Place of Men and Machines." In *Language Translation.* Xerox Palo Alto Research Center, Palo Alto, California.

Kay, M. 1986. "Algorithm schemata and data structures in syntactic processing." In Barbara J. Grosz, Karen Sparek Jones, and Bonnie Lynn Weber, eds., *Readings in Natural Language Processing*, 35–70. Morgan Kaufmann. Also in Sture Allen, editor, *Text Processing: Proceedings of Nobel Symposium 51.* Almqvist and Wiksell International, Stockholm. Also as Report CSL-80-12, Xerox PARC. Palo Alto, California.

Kay, M. 1987. "Nonconcatenative finite-state morphology." In *Proceedings, Third European Conference of the Association for Computational Linguistics*, 2–10. Copenhagen.

Kay, M. 1989. "Head-driven parsing." in *Proceedings, 1st International Workshop on Parsing Technologies*, 52–62. Pittsburgh, PA.

Kay, M. 1997. "The Proper Place of Men and Machines in Language Translation." *Machine Translation*.

Kay, M. and G. Martins. 1970. *The* MIND *System: The Morphological-Analysis Program*. The Rand Corporation, RM-6265/2-PR.

Kay, M. and M. Röscheisen. 1995. "Text-Translation Alignment." *Computational Linguistics* 19:1.

Kay, M. and R. M. Kaplan. 1981. "Phonological Rules and Finite-State Transducers." Presented at the Fifty-sixth Meeting of the Linguistic Society of America.

Kay, M. and R. M. Kaplan. 1994. "Regular models of phonological rule systems." *Computational Linguistics* 20:3, 331–378.

Kay, M. and S. Su. 1970. *The* MIND *System: The Structure of the Semantic File*. The Rand Corporation, RM-6265/3-PR.

Kay, M., J. M. Gawron and P. Norvig. 1994. *Verbmobil: A Translation System for Face-to-Face Dialog*. CSLI.

Kenstowicz, M. and C. Kisseberth. 1979. *Generative Phonology: Description and Theory*. Academic Press.

Kimball, J. 1973. "Seven principles of surface structure parsing in natural language." *Cognition* 2, 15–47.

King, M. and S. Perschke. 1987. *Machine Translation Today: The State of the Art*. Edinburgh University Press. EUROTRA.

Kittredge, R. 1987. "The significance of sublanguage for automatic translation." In S. Nirenburg, ed., *Machine Translation: Theoretical and Methodological Issues*, 59–67. Cambridge University Press.

Klatt, D. H. 1980. "Scriber and Lafs: Two new approaches to speech analysis." In Wayne Lea, ed., *Trends in Speech Recognition*, 529–555. Prentice-Hall.

Knuth, D. E. 1973. *The Art of Computer Programming, Vol. 3, Sorting and Searching*. Addison-Wesley.

Koskenniemi, K. 1983. *Two-Level Morphology: A General Computational Model for Word-Form Recognition and Production*. Doctoral Dissertation, University of Helsinki.

Koskenniemi, K. 1985. "Compilation of automata from morphological two-level rules." In *Papers from the Fifth Scandinavian Conference of Computational Linguistics*, 143–149. Helsinki, Finland.

Kroch, A., and A. K. Joshi. 1985. *Linguistic relevance of tree adjoining grammars*. Technical Report MS-CIS-85-18, Department of Computer and Information Science, University of Pennyslvania.

Kuno, S. 1965. "The predictive analyzer and a path elimination technique." *CACM* 8, 453–462.

Kuno, S. and A. Oettinger. 1962. "A multiple path syntactic analyzer." *Information Processing* 62. North Holland.

Landsbergen, J. 1987. "Isomorphic grammars and their use in the ROSETTA translation system." In *Machine Translation Today: The State of the Art*. Edinburgh University Press, Edinburgh.

Leben, W. 1973. *Suprasegmental Phonology*. Doctoral Dissertation, MIT. Cambridge, Massachussetts.

Lopez, A. 2008. *Machine Translation by Pattern Matching*. Ph.D. thesis, University of Maryland.

Lyons, J. 1963. *Structural Semantics. An Analysis of Part of the Vocabular y of Plato*. Blackwell. Oxford.

MacKeown, P. K. and T. C. Weekes. 1985. "Cosmic rays from Cygnus X-3." *Scientific American* 253:5.

MacKeown, P. K. and T. C. Weekes. 1986. "Kosmische Strahlen von Cygnus X-3." *Spektrum der Wissenschaft*.

Marcus, M. P. 1978. "A theory of syntactic recognition for natural language." Unpublished doctoral dissertation, MIT.

Mathesius, V. 1929. "Zur Satzperspective in modernen English." *Archiv für das Studium der neueren Sprachen und Literaturen* 155, 202–210.

Maxwell, J. T. and R. M. Kaplan. 1991. "A Method for Disjunctive Constraint-Satisfaction." In Masaru Tomita, *Current Issues in Parsing Technology*. Kluwer.

McCarthy, J. J. 1979. *Formal problems in Semitic Phonology and Morphology*. Doctoral Dissertation, MIT. Cambridge, Massachussetts.

McCarthy, J. J. 1981. "A Prosodic Tehory of Nonconcatenative Morphology." *Linguistic Inquiry* 12:3.

McCord, M. C. 1986. "Focalizers, the scoping problem, and semantic interpretation rules in logic grammars." In *Logic Programming and Its Applications*. Ablex. New Jersey.

McCreight, E. M. 1976. "A space-economical suffix tree construction algorithm." *Journal of the ACM* 23, 262–272.

Millies, S. 1991. *Modularity parallelism and licensing in a principle-based parser for German*. CLAUS Report Nr. 17, Computerlinguistik, Universität des Saarlandes.

Muraki, K. 1989. "PIVOT: Two-phase machine translation system." In *Proceedings of the Second Machine Translation Summit*. Tokyo. Ohmsha Ltd.

Nagao, M. 1992. "Some rationales and methodologies for example-based approach." *Fifth Generation Natural Language Processing*. Publisher unknown.

Nelson, M. 1996. "Fast String Searching With Suffix Trees." *Dr. Dobb's Journal*, August.

Nirenburg, S., V. Raskin et al. 1986. "On knowledge-based machine translation." In *Proceedings of the 11th International Conference on Computational Linguistics*. Bonn. ACL.

O'Keefe, R. 1999. *The Craft of Prolog*. MIT Press Cambridge, MA.

Okumura, A., K. Muraki and S. Akamine. 1991. "Multi-lingual sentence generation from the PIVOT interlingua." In *Proceedings of the Third Machine Translation Summit*. Carnegie Mellon University.

Parker-Rhodes, A., R. McKinnon Wood, M. Kay and P. Bratley. 1960. *The Cambridge Language Research Unit Computer Programme for Syntactic Analysis*, M.L. 136. Cambridge Language Research Unit.

Parsons, T. 1990. *Events in the Semantics of English*. Cambridge, Mass. MIT Press.

Pereira, F. C. N. 1981. "Extraposition grammars." *Computational Linguistics* 7:4, 243–256.

Pereira, F. C. N. and S. M. Shieber. 1987. *Prolog and Natural Language Analysis*, vol. 10 of *CSLI Lecture Notes Series*. Chicago University Press. Chicago.

Perschke, S. 1989. "EUROTRA project." In *Proceedings of the Second Machine Translation Summit*. Tokyo. Ohmsha Ltd.

Petrick, S. R. 1965. *A Recognition Procedure for Transformational Grammars*. M.I.T. Press. Cambridge, Mass.

Prince, E. 1981. "Topicalization, focus-movement, and Yiddish-movement: A pragmatic differentiation." *BLS 7. Proceedings of the Seventh Annual Meeting of the Berkeley Linguistics Society*. Berkeley, Calif.

Ritchie, G. D. 1992. "Languages generated by two-level morphological rules." *Computational Linguistics* 18:1, 41–59.

Ritchie, G. D., G. J. Russell, A. W. Black and S. G. Pulman. 1992. *Computational Morphology*. MIT Press.

Sato, S. 1992. "CTM: An example-based translation aid system using the character-based best match retrieval method." In *Proceedings of the 14th International Conference on Computational Linguistics*. Nantes, France. ACL.

Sato, S. and M. Nagao. 1990. "Toward memory-based translation." In *Proceedings, 15th International Conference on Computational Linguistics (COLING-90)*. Helsinki, Finland.

Schabes, Y. 1990. *Mathematical and computational aspects of lexicalized grammars*. Doctoral dissertation, University of Pennsylvania.

Schabes, Y. 1992. "Stochastic lexicalized tree-adjoining grammars." In *Proceedings, Fifteenth International Conference on Computational Linguistics (COLlNG-92)*, 426–432. Nantes, France,

Schabes, Y., A. Abeille and A. K. Joshi. 1988. "Parsing strategies with 'lexicalized' grammars: application to tree adjoining grammars." In *Proceedings, 12th International Conference on Computational Linguistics*. Budapest, Hungary.

Schabes, Y. and R. C. Waters. 1993. "Lexicalized context-free grammars." In *Proceedings, 31st Annual Meeting of the Association for Computational Linguistics*, 121–129. Columbus, Ohio.

Schubert, K. 1988. "The architecture of DLT – interlingual or double direct." In *New Directions in Machine Translation*. Foris Publications, Dordrecht, Holland.

Schützenberger, M. P. 1961. "A remark on finite transducers." *Information and Control* 4, 185–187.

Schutz, J., G. Thurmair et al. 1991. "An architecture sketch of Eurotra-II." In *Proceedings of the Third Machine Translation Summit*. Carnegie Mellon University.

Shapiro, S. 1971. *The MIND System: The Data Structure for Semantic Information Processing*. The Rand Corporation, R-837-PR.

Shemtov, H. 1997. *Ambiguity Management in Natural Language Generation*. Ph.D. Dissertation, Stanford University.

Shieber, S. 1986. *An Introduction to Unification-Based Approaches to Grammar*. Number 4 in CSLI Lecture Notes. CSLI, Stanford.

Shieber, S. 1988. "A Uniform Architecture for Parsing and Generation." *COLING-88*. Budapest, John von Neumann Society for Computing Sciences.

Shieber, S. *et al.* 1989. "A Semantic-Head-Driven Generation Algorithm for Unification Based Formalisms." *27th Annual Meeting of the Association for Computational Linguistics*. Vancouver. B.C.

Speas, M. and N. Fukui. 1986. "Specifiers and projections." In *MIT Working Papers in Linguistics 8*, Department of Linguistics and Philosophy, MIT, Cambridge, MA.

Tesnière, L. 1959. *Elèments de syntaxe structurale*. Klincksieck. Paris.

Thomason, R. 1974. *Formal Philosophy. Selected Papers of Richard Montague*. Yale University Press. New Haven, Connecticut.

Uchida, H. 1986. "Fujitsu machine translation system: ATLAS." In *Future Generations Computer Systems 2*, 95–100. Publisher unknown.

Uchida, H. 1989. "ATLAS-II: A machine translation system using conceptual structure as an interlingua." In *Proceedings of the Second Machine Translation Summit*. Tokyo. Publisher unknown.

Ukkonen, E. 1995. "On-line construction of suffix trees." *Algorithmica* 14:3, 249–260.

van Noord, G. 1993. *Reversibility in natural language processing*. Doctoral dissertation, University of Utrecht.

van Rijsbergen, C. J. 1979. *Information Retrieval*. Butterworths.

Vijay-Shanker, K. and Y. Schabes. 1992. "Structure sharing in lexicalized tree-adjoining grammars." In *Proceedings, 15th International Conference on Computational Linguistics (COLING-92)*, 205–211. Nantes, France.

Vinay, J.-P. and J. Darbelnet. 1958. *Stylistique comparée du français et de l'anglais*. Harrap.

Wanner, E. and M. Maratsos. 1978. "An ATN approach to comprehension." In M. Halle, J. Bresnan and G. A. Miller, eds., *Linguistic Theory and Psychological Reality*. MIT Press.

Wanner, E., R. Kaplan and S. Shiner. 1975. "Garden paths in relative clauses." Unpublished paper. Harvard University.

Whitelock, P. 1992. "Shake and-Bake Translation." *COLING-92*. Nantes.

Witkam, T. 1988. "DLT – an industrial R&D project for multilingual machine translation." In *Proceedings of the 12th International Conference on Computational Linguistics*. Budapest.

Woods, W. A. 1970. "Transition Network Grammars for Natural Language Analysis." *Communications of the ACM* 13, 591–602.

Woods, W. A. and R. M. Kaplan. 1971. *The Lunar Sciences Natural Language Information System*, Report No. 2265. Bolt, Beranek and Newman. Cambridge, Mass.

Woods, W. A., M. Bates, G. Brown, B. C. Bruce, C. C. Gook, J. W. Klovstad, J. Makhoul, B. Nash-Webber, R. Schwartz, J. Wolf and V. Zue. 1976. "Speech understanding systems: Final report." Report No. 3438, Bolt Beranek and Newman, Inc. Cambridge, Mass.

Younger, D.H. 1967. "Recognition and parsing of context-free languages in time." In *Formation and Control* lO:2, 189–208.

Complete List of Publications to Date

Kay, Martin. 1959. "Marcode." Cambridge Language Research Unit, M.L. 81. Cambridge. [no copy available]

Kay, Martin. 1959. "The Relevance of Linguistics to Machine Translation." Cambridge Language Research Unit, M.L. 88. Also in Margaret Masterman, A. F. Parker-Rhodes, Karen Sparck Jones, Martin Kay, E. B. May, Roger M. Needham, E. W. Bastin, C. Wordley, F.H. Ellis, R. Mckinnon Wood, eds., *Essays on and in Machine Translation by the Cambridge Language Research Unit*. M.L. 84, not published. [no copy available]

Masterman, Margaret and Martin Kay. 1959. *Mechanical pidgin translation*. Cambridge Language Research Unit, M.L. 133. Distributed at the US ONR Colloquium on Machine Translation in Princeton, July 1960. Condensed version later published under the same title as single-author article by Margaret Masterman in Sergei Nirenburg, Harold Somers, and Yorick Wilks, eds., *Readings in Machine Translation*. MIT Press, 2003. Masterman article also reprinted in Yorick Wilks, ed., *Language, Cohesion and Form*, Cambridge University Press, 161–186, 2005. [no copy available]

Parker-Rhodes, A. F., R. McKinnon Wood, M. Kay, and P. Bradley. 1960. *The Cambridge Language Research Unit Computer Programme for Syntactic Analysis*. Cambridge Language Research Unit, M.L. 136. [no copy available]

Kay, Martin and R. McKinnon Wood. 1960. *A Flexible Punched-Card Procedure for Word Decomposition*. Cambridge Language Research Unit, M.L. 119. Referenced by Masterman in "Mechanical pidgin translation," described as "word chunking by 'exhaustive extraction' ...invented by Roger Needham". [no copy available]

Kay, Martin. 1962. "A Parsing Procedure." In *Symposium on Modern Techniques of Language Translation*, 328–329. [this volume]

Kay, Martin. 1963. "Rules of Interpretation — An Approach to the Problem of Computation in the Semantics of Natural Language." In Cicely M. Popplewell, ed. *Proceedings of IFIP Congress* 62, 318–321. Munich, Germany. Amsterdam, The Netherlands: North-Holland Publishing Company. [this volume]

Kay, Martin. 1964. A General Procedure for Rewriting Strings. In: The annual meeting of the Association for Machine Translation and Computational Linguistics in Bloomington, Indiana. [online]

Kay, Martin. 1964. "The Logic of Cognate Recognition in Historical Linguistics." The RAND Corporation, Report RM-4224-PR. [this volume]

Kay, Martin. 1964. "A Parsing Program for Categorial Grammars." The RAND Corporation, Report RM-4283-PR. [online]

Kay, Martin. 1965. "Large Files in Linguistic Computing." The RAND Corporation, Report P-3136. [online]

Kay, Martin and Theodore Ziehe. 1965. "Natural Language in Computer Form." The RAND Corporation, Report RM-4390-PR. [this volume]

Ziehe, T. W. and Martin Kay. 1965. "The Catalog: A Flexible Data Structure for Magnetic Tape." The RAND Corporation, Report RM-4645-PR. [online]

Kay, Martin. 1966. "The Tabular Parser: A Parsing Program for Phrase Structure and Dependency." The RAND Corporation, Report RM-4933-PR. [this volume]

Graves, P. A., D. G. Hays, T. W. Ziehe, and Martin Kay. 1966. "Computer Routines to Read Natural Text with Complex Formats." The RAND Corporation, Report RM-4920-PR. [pdf]

Kay, Martin, Frederick Valadez and Theodore Ziehe. 1966. "The Catalog Input/Output System." The RAND Corporation, Report RM-4540-PR. [pdf]

Kay, Martin. 1967. "A File of Russian Text on Magnetic Tape." The RAND Corporation, Report RM-5509-RADC. [online]

Kay, Martin. 1967. "Experiments with a Powerful Parser." In *Proceedings of the Second International Congress sur le Traitement Automatique des Langues ('Automatic Language Processing')*, 1–20. Grenoble, France. Reprinted in *American Journal of Computational Linguistics* 2, 1976. [this volume]

Kay, Martin. 1967. "Standards for Encoding Linguistic Data." In *Computers and the Humanities* 1:5, 170–177. [online]

Kay, Martin and Terril D. Taft. 1967. "Collect: A Program for the Retrieval of Grammatical Information from Annotated Text." The RAND Corporation, Report RM-5243-RADC. [online]

Kay, Martin. 1968. "From Semantics to Syntax." In Manfred Bierwisch and Karl Erich Heidolf, eds., *Progress in Linguistics*, 114–126. The Hague: Mouton. [this volume]

Kay, Martin. 1969. "Computational Linguistics at RAND." The RAND Corporation, Report P-4023. Presentation to RAND Board of Trustees. [this volume]

Kay, Martin. 1969. "A Computer System to Aid the Linguistic Field Worker." The RAND Corporation, Report P-4095. [this volume]

Kay, Martin. 1969. "Computational Competence and Linguistic Performance." The RAND Corporation, Report P-4093. The May 1969 presidential address to the Association for Computational Linguistics. [this volume]

Kay, Martin. 1970. "Performance Grammars." The RAND Corporation, Report P-4391. [this volume]

Kay, Martin and Gary R. Martins. 1970. "The MIND System: The Morphological Analysis Program." The RAND Corporation, Report RM-6265/2-PR. [online]

Kay Martin and Stanley Y. W. Su. 1970. "The MIND System: The Structure of the Semantic File." The RAND Corporation, Report RM-6265/3-PR. [pdf]

Sparck Jones, Karen and Martin Kay. 1971. "Automated Language Processing." In Carlos Cuadra, ed., *Annual Review of Information Science and Technology 6, Encyclopedia Britanica*, 141–166. [online]

Bisbey, Richard and Martin Kay. 1972. "The MIND Translation System: A Study in Man-Machine Collaboration." The RAND Corporation, Report P-4786. [this volume]

Kay, Martin. 1973. "The MIND System." In Randall Rustin, ed., *Natural Language Processing*, 155–188. New York: Algorithmics Press. [this volume]

Kay, Martin. 1973. "Automatic Translation of Natural Languages." In *Daedalus, Journal of the American Academy of Arts and Sciences* 102:3, 217–230. [this volume]

Kay, Martin. 1973. "Morphological analysis." In *Proceedings of the 5th Conference on Computational Linguistics*, 205–223. Pisa, Italy. [this volume]

Jones, Karen Sparck and Martin Kay. 1973. *Linguistics and Information Science*. Academic Press. [monograph]

Balzer, Robert, Norton Greenfeld, Martin Kay, William Mann, Walter Ryder, David Wilczynski, Albert L. Zobrist. 1974. "Domain-Independent Automatic Programming." In Jack Rosenfeld, ed., *Information Processing 74, Proceedings of IFIP Congress*, 326–330. Stockholm, Sweden. [online]

Sparck-Jones, Karen and Martin Kay. 1974. *Linguistic and Information Science*. Orlando: Academic Press. [monograph]

Kay, Martin. 1975. "Syntactic Processing and the Functional Sentence Perspective." In *Theoretical Issues in Natural Language Processing (TINLAP-1)*, 12–15. Cambridge, Massachusetts. [this volume]

Kay, Martin. 1977. "Morphological and Syntactic Analysis." In A. Zampolli, ed., *Linguistic Structures Processing*, 131–234. Amsterdam: North-Holland Publishing Company. [pdf]

Kay, Martin. 1977. "Reversible grammar: Summary of the formalism." Technical report, Xerox Palo Alto Research Center, Palo Alto, California. [no copy available]

Bobrow, D. G., R. M. Kaplan, M. Kay, D. A. Norman, H. Thompson, and T. Winograd. 1977. "GUS: A Frame-Driven Dialog System." *Artificial Intelligence* 8:2, 155–73. [online]

Sparck Jones, Karen and Martin Kay. 1977. "Linguistics and Information Science: A Postscript." In Donald Walker, Hans Karlgren, and Martin Kay, eds., *Natural Language in Information Science*, 183–192. Stockholm: Skriptor. [online]

Kay, Martin. 1978. "Overview of Computer Aids in Translation." In *Proceedings of FBIS Seminar on Computer Support to Translation*, 23–29. Washington D.C.: Foreign Broadcast Information Service. [this volume]

Kay, Martin. 1978. "The Proper Place of Men and Machines in Translation." In *The Foreign Broadcast Information Service Seminar on Machine Translation*. Washington D.C. Reprinted in *Machine Translation* 12:1-2 3–23, 1997. Reprinted again in Sergei Nirenburg, Harold Somers, and Yorick Wilks, eds., *Readings in machine translation*, MIT Press, 2003. [this volume]

Kay, Martin. 1979. "Functional Grammar." In Christina Chiarello et al., eds., *The Fifth Annual Meeting of the Berkeley Linguistics Society*, 142–158. Berkeley, California: Berkeley Linguistics Society. [this volume]

Kay, Martin. 1979. "Syntactic Processing." In *Proceedings of the Association for Computational Linguistics*, 1–2. [online]

Kay, Martin. 1980. "Algorithm Schemata and Data Structures in Syntactic Processing." Xerox CSL 80-12. Reprinted in Sture Allen, ed., *Text Processing, Proceedings of Nobel Symposium 51*, pp 327–58. Stockholm: Almqvist and Wiksell International, 1982. Reprinted again in Barbara J. Grosz, Karen Sparck Jones and Bonnie Lynn Webber, eds., *Readings in Natural Language Processing*, 35–70. Los Altos, California: Morgan Kaufman, 1986. [this volume]

Kay, Martin. 1980. "An Algorithm for Compiling Parse Tables from a Grammar." Technical Report, Xerox Palo Alto Research Center. Also in *Proceedings of a Symposiom on Modeling Human Parsing Strategies*, Center for Cognitive Science, University of Texas, Austin, 1981. [pdf]

Kay, Martin. 1981. "Unification Grammars". Technical report, Xerox Palo Alto Research Center. [no copy available]

Kaplan, Ronald and Martin Kay. 1981. "Phonological rules and finite-state transducers." *Fifty-sixth Linguistic Society of America Meeting Handbook.* [pdf, abstract only]

Kay, Martin. 1982. "The Dictionary of the Future and the Future of the Dictionary." In *Proceedings of the Association for Computational Linguistics*, Houston, Texas. [online]

Kay, Martin. 1982. "Machine Translation." *American Journal of Computational Linguistics* 8:2, 74–78. [online]

Kay, Martin. 1983. "When Meta-rules are not Meta-rules." In Karen Sparck Jones and Yorick Wilks, eds., *Automatic Natural Language Parsing,* 94–116. Chichester/New York: Ellis Horwood/Wiley. [this volume]

Kay, Martin. 1984. "Functional Unification Grammar: A Formalism for Machine Translation." In *International Conference on Computational Linguistics (COLING 84),* 75–78. Stanford, California: Association for Computational Linguistics. [this volume]

Kay, Martin. 1984. "The dictionary server." In *Proceedings of COLING-84,* 461–461. [online]

Kay, Martin. 1984. "Computational Linguistics = Generalized Unification + Applied Graph Theory." In *Proceedings of the Fifth Biennial Conference of the Canadian Society for Computational Studies of Intelligence,* 1–5. [pdf]

Kay, Martin. 1985. "Parsing in Functional Unification Grammar." In David R. Dowty, Lauri Karttunen, and Arnold M. Zwicky, eds., *Natural Language Parsing,* 251–278. Cambridge, UK: Cambridge University Press. Reprinted in Barbara J. Grosz, Karen Sparck Jones and Bonnie Lynn Webber, eds., *Readings in Natural Language Processing,* Morgan Kaufman, 1986. [this volume]

Karttunen, Lauri and Martin Kay. 1985. "Parsing in Free Word Order Languages." In David R. Dowty, Lauri Karttunen, and Arnold M. Zwicky, eds., *Natural Language Parsing,* 279–306. Cambridge, UK: Cambridge University Press. [this volume]

Karttunen, Lauri and Martin Kay. 1985. "Structure Sharing with Binary Trees." In *Proceedings of the 23rd Annual Meeting of the Association for Computational Linguistics,* 133–136. Chicago, Illinois. Also appeared as a chapter in CSLI Report CSLI-86-48, Stanford, included from a previously published SRI Technical Note 527 called "Notes from the Unification Underground: A Second Compilation of Papers on Unification-based Grammar Formalisms." [this volume]

Kay, Martin. 1985. "Unification in Grammar." In Veronica Dahl and Patrick Saint-Dizier, eds., *Natural Language Understanding and Logic Programming,* 233-240. Amsterdam: North Holland. [this volume]

Kay, Martin. 1986. "Machine Translation will not work." In *ACL Proceedings, 24th Annual Meeting,* 268–268. [this volume]

Kay, Martin. 1986. "Monotonicity in Linguistics." In *Proceedings of ESCOL 86.* Univ. of Pittsburgh and CMU. [pdf]

Kay, Martin. 1986. "Two-Level Morphology with Tiers." Technical report, Xerox Palo Alto Research Center, from talk given at the Workshop on Finite State Morphology at CSLI, Stanford on July 30, 1985. [no copy available]

Sag, Ivan A., Ronald M. Kaplan, Lauri Karttunen, Martin Kay, Carl Pollard, Stuart Shieber, and Annie Zaenen. 1986. "Unification and grammatical theory." In *Proceedings of the Fifth West Coast Conference on Formal Linguistics,* 228–254. Stanford, CA: Stanford Linguistics Association. [pdf]

Kay, Martin, 1987. "The Linguistic Connection." In *Proceedings of the 1987 Workshop on Theoretical Issues in Natural Language Processing*, 51–57. Las Cruces, New Mexico. [this volume]

Kay, Martin. 1987. "Nonconcatenative Finite-State Morphology." *Proceedings of the Third Conference of the European Chapter of the Association for Computational Linguistics*, 2–10. Copenhagen, Denmark. [this volume]

Kay, Martin, Roger Needham, Karen Sparck Jones, and Yorick Wilks. 1987. "Margaret Masterman." In *The Finite String Newsletter* 13:1-2, 79–80. [online]

Kay, Martin. 1989. "Concluding Remarks 2." In Makoto Nagao, ed., *Machine Translation Summit*, 192–6. Tokyo: Ohmsha. [online]

Kay, Martin. 1989. "The concrete lexicon and the abstract dictionary." In *Proceedings of the Fifth Annual Conference of the University of Waterloo Centre for the New Oxford English Dictionary*, 35–41. Waterloo, Canada. [online]

Kay, Martin. 1989. "Head-Driven Parsing." In *International Parsing Workshop*, 52–62. Pittsburgh. [this volume]

Kay, Martin. 1989. "Machines and People in Translation." In Makoto Nagao, ed., *Machine Translation Summit*, 26–27. Tokyo: Ohmsha. [this volume]

Johnson, Mark and Martin Kay. 1990. "Semantic Abstraction and Anaphora." In H. Karlgren, ed., *Proceedings of the 13th International Conference on Computational Linguistics*, 17–27. Helsinki, Finland. [this volume]

Kay, Martin. 1990. "Computational Linguistics." In Allen Kent and James G. Williams, eds., *The Encyclopedia of Computer Science and Technology*, volume 21, supplement 6. [this volume]

Kay, Martin. 1992. "Ongoing directions in Computational Linguistics." *Proceedings of COLING*. [this volume]

Kay, Martin. 1992. "Unification." In Michael Rosner and Roderick Johnson, eds., *Computational Linguistics and Formal Semantics*, 1–29. Cambridge University Press. [this volume]

Kay, Martin. 1992. "Foreword." In W. J. Hutchins and H. L. Somers, eds., *An introduction to machine translation*. [this volume]

Röscheisen, Martin and Martin Kay. 1993. "Text-Translation Alignment." In *Computational Linguistics (Special issue on using large corpora)* 19:1, 121–142. [this volume]

Kaplan, Ronald M. and Martin Kay. 1994. "Regular Models of Phonological Rule Systems." In *Computational Linguistics (Special Issue on Computational Phonology)* 20:3. [this volume]

Johnson, Mark and Martin Kay. 1994. "Parsing and Empty Nodes." In *Computational Linguistics* 20:2, 289–300. [this volume]

Kay, Martin. 1994. "Machine Translation. The Disappointing Past and Present." In Ronald A. Cole, Joseph Mariani, Hans Uszkoreit, Annie Zaenen, and Victor Zue, eds., *Survey of the State of the Art in Human Language Technology*, 232–234. [this volume]

Kay, Martin, Peter Norvig and Mark Gawron. 1994. *Verbmobil: A Translation System for Face-to-Face Dialog*. Chicago: University of Chicago Press. [monograph]

Kay, Martin. 1996. "Chart Generation." *Proceedings of the ACL*, 200–204. [this volume]

Kay, Martin. 1996. "Limited parsing in linear time." Technical report, Xerox Palo Alto Research Center. [no copy available]

Kay, Martin. 1997. "It's Still the Proper Place." In *Machine Translation*, 12:1-2, 35–38. [this volume]

Kay, Martin. 1997. "Multilinguality: Overview." In *Survey of the state of the art in human language technology*, 245–248. [online*]

Kay, Martin. 1999. "Chart Translation." In *Proceedings of Machine Translation Summit VII "MT in the Great Translation Era"*, 9–14. Singapore. [this volume]

Kay, Martin. 2000. "David G. Hays." In W. John Hutchins, ed., *Early Years in Machine Translation: Memoirs and Biographies of Pioneers*, 165–170. Amsterdam/Philadelphia: John Benjamins Publishing Company. [this volume]

Kay, Martin. 2000. "Preface." In Jean Vronis, ed., *Parallel text processing: alignment and use of translation corpora*, xv-xx. Dordrecht: Kluwer. [this volume]

Kay, Martin. 2000. "Guides and oracles for linear-time parsing." In *Proceedings of the 6th International Workshop on Parsing Technologies (IWPT 03)*, 6–9. [this volume]

Kay, Martin. 2002. "Ambiguity and Efficiency in Unification Grammar." Unpublished manuscript, Stanford University. [no copy available]

Kay, Martin. 2003. "Introduction." In Ruslan Mitkov, ed., *Handbook of Computational Linguistics*, xvii-xx. Oxford, UK: Oxford University Press. [this volume]

Kay, Martin 2004. "Arabic script-based languages deserve to be studied linguistically." In *Proceedings of the Workshop on Computational Approaches to Arabic Script-based Languages*, 42–42. Geneva.

Kay, Martin. 2004. "Substring Alignment Using Suffix Trees." *Proceedings of CICLing*, 275–282. [this volume]

Kay, Martin. 2004. "Antonio Zampolli." In *Proceedings of Fourth International Conference on Language Resources and Evaluation*, xli-xliii. Lisbon, Portugal. [this volume]

Kay, Martin. 2005. "A Life of Language." In *Computational Linguistics* 31:4, 425–438. [this volume]

Kay, Martin. 2006. "Translation, Meaning, and Reference." In Miriam Butt, Mary Dalrymple, and Tracy Holloway King, eds., *Intelligent Linguistic Architectures. Variations on Themes by Ronald M. Kaplan.* Stanford: CSLI Publications. [this volume]

Chen, Yu, Martin Kay and Andreas Eisele 2009. "Intersecting multilingual data for faster and better statistical translations." In *Proceedings of Human Language Technologies: The 2009 Annual Conference of the North American Chapter of the Association for Computational Linguistics.* [online*]

Name Index

Subject Index